# Life Span Development

# Bases for Preventive and Interventive Helping

# MARTIN BLOOM

VIRGINIA COMMONWEALTH UNIVERSITY

# LIFE SPAN

# SPAN

# Development

MACMILLAN PUBLISHING CO., INC.

*New York*

COLLIER MACMILLAN PUBLISHERS

*London*

Macmillan Publishing Co., Inc.
866 Third Avenue, New York, New York 10022

Collier Macmillan Canada, Ltd.

Library of Congress Cataloging in Publication Data

Main entry under title:
Life span development.
  Bibliography: p.
  Includes indexes.
  1. Developmental psychology.   I. Bloom, Martin (date)
BF713.L55            155            79-718
  ISBN 0-02-311020-1

Printing:      3  4  5  6  7  8         Year:    1  2  3  4  5  6

JAN 2 7 1984

# Preface

M UCH OF THE LITERATURE on human growth and development has, in
effect, described how an individual white, middle-class male goes
through the various stages of life. For example, let us consider that quintes-
sential representative of American child-rearing texts, the early editions of
Dr. Spock's *Baby and Child Care,* which described the baby in terms of "he"
does this, "he" does that, whereas his "mother" did all the rest. When feminists sharply called Dr. Spock's attention to the subtle sexist, racist, if not
class-oriented, semantic biases he had been expressing, he duly incorporated
baby daughters and fathers and minority persons into the pictures and text of
his justifiably famous book. Although Dr. Spock proved himself capable of
adapting to the new consciousness of society, the same cannot be said about
the traditional literature read by even recent generations of students in the
helping professions, in spite of the obvious need for them to be aware of, and
sensitive to, a much broader range of human behavior than the white middle-
class male. *This present book takes as one of its explicit goals the providing
of a broad range of readings about the young, the middle-aged, and the old;
about males and females; about blacks and whites as well as ethnic and cultural groups; and about the various classes making up our society.*

Another characteristic of the literature on human growth and development
is that it is often presented as if one person moves through the life span in
splendid isolation, like a spot light following the star of the show across a
stage, while the supporting cast dash in and fade out, as if fully subordinate
to the star. This is, of course, only a convenient fiction to enable writers to
deal clearly with one portion of a very complex whole. However, it still gives
the readers the impression that each stage has its star, whereas each of us in
our personal lives knows full well what a totally complex social affair it is to
do even the simplest of things, like getting a child off to school or getting a
teenager ready for a date or getting packed for a short family vacation. *This
book attempts to convey a more realistic impression of life development as
involving multiple generations of persons and tandem events.* As the young
infant enters the toddler stage, his or her parents likewise enter a new phase
of their family life-style—more energy is expended in monitoring the child's
movements and whereabouts, more control is exercised as the child under-
takes a wider range of activities, and more of the parents' time is required
that cannot be spent in other ways. Each change in one person's life affects,
in small or large ways, the lives of persons closely involved with him or her.
Each change in the physical environment, in the neighborhood, the community, the state and region, as well as nationally and internationally, likewise

has its impact on the others who share this spaceship, Earth. It is difficult to grasp the specific effects of individual events; it is necessary to attempt to understand the major trends of events if we are to control our lives and to provide services for those in need.

Yet another characteristic of the literature on human development is that it is often treated only as reporting basic scientific information, whereas the majority of readers of this literature—and definitely the audience to whom this present book is directed—are students of the helping professions, such as social work, community psychology, counseling, education, public health, and psychiatry, among others. *This book takes the position that helping professionals need not only empirical and theoretical information, but also models for translating this knowledge base into strategies of action and tests of the effectiveness of that action.* Therefore, in addition to reports of empirical research and conceptual analysis, readers will also find many articles that describe action programs.

Moreover, when practice articles have been included in human development anthologies, it has usually been the case that the helping involved "treatment." There is no problem with this so far as it goes, but there has been a massive omission of *preventive* materials accessible to all levels of students in the helping professions (except public health), and especially materials that have multidisciplinary orientations. It is not so much that prevention has been ill-treated as ignored, in spite of these words by President John F. Kennedy:

> 'An ounce of prevention is worth more than a pound of cure.' For prevention is far more desirable for all concerned. It is far more economical and it is far more likely to be successful. [February 5, 1963. Message from the President of the United States Relative to Mental Illness and Mental Retardation.]

Prevention—working with persons who are currently functioning adequately, so as to promote their desired goals and to obviate the untoward events predicted to affect the population of which they are a part—suffers from too few conceptual, empirical, and programmatic examples available to students in the helping professions. *This book provides numerous illustrations of* preventive *thinking, action, and evaluation in order to stimulate interest and recognition that preventive work is a fully legitimate dimension of helping practice.* This is not to say that interventive examples are slighted. Indeed, it is often the case that helping situations provide opportunities for intervening in existing problems while engaging in preventive work for problems that appear to be on the horizon. An interesting example of this is the paper in this book by Klein, Alexander, and Parsons (1977), which describes a program involving efforts at tertiary prevention (rehabilitation) aimed at the interaction patterns of families of delinquents after treatment, secondary prevention (treatment) working with identified delinquents to reduce recidivism, and primary prevention focusing on the nondelinquent siblings in trying to prevent their coming into contact with the courts.

Science is a self-correcting enterprise, and earlier work is often superseded by later research that it stimulated. *This book seeks to present the best available current information, even where it challenges the myths that were the reified hypotheses of not so many years ago.* For example, Sameroff's (1975) article on early influences in human development and the impact of intervention in these early years explodes a number of widely held beliefs by providing a summary of the empirical facts as we presently know them. However, today's facts will be tomorrow's fancies if we hang on too tightly. Students of the helping professions should challenge current "facts" and be capable of incorporating new validated information as it comes along. Thus, the articles in this collection should not be looked upon as Truth but rather as the basis for strategies of practice, which, in turn, are to be tested for their effectiveness.

Anthologies are smorgasbords, an array of delicacies that tempt the intellectual palates of some, while giving others a case of academic indigestion. In order to prevent the latter form of "mental illness," I have added a section of this book that provides statistical perspective for the other sections of readings. Part I contains an overview summary of physical, psychological, and social factors involved in human growth and development. Part II includes readings on developmental stages, their critical tasks and challenges, and some examples of helping responses to the problems and potentials of the human life-span. These readings are divided into conventional stages of the life-span—from infancy to later adulthood. Part III deals with preventive or interventive actions for special populations of persons—women, minorities, migrant workers, among others—to emphasize the fact that human service workers need to be well acquainted with the variations in human development. Part IV contains selected statistical tables related to life development, the collective picture about birth, education, marriage, work, and death.

This array of facts and ideas and questions is presented not only for the information or stimulation it offers but also to illustrate the vital point that every practitioner is, in part, a working theorist who reconstructs for him or herself the bits and pieces of the knowledge base on human behavior in order to create a map to guide helping practice. The great theorists of the past were in exactly the same position. They sorted through these pieces of knowledge and speculation in order to come up with a systematic network of ideas and strategies for action. This is an identical task that all students face when they try to reduce the multitude of facts and readings to some manageable size. We benefit by careful study of how others have performed this task, so as to construct our own models of practice. And this is, after all, the aim of advanced education—to enable the student to become the practitioner and the teacher.

It is impossible to identify, let alone acknowledge, the many persons who have shaped this book. But as a brief biographical note, I would like to express appreciation to my own family of origin and particularly to my family of mutual creation, Lynn, and Bard and Laird; to the many students and colleagues who shared experiences in that course of many names, Human Be-

viii

havior and the Social Environment—I must mention particularly Enola Proctor, Larry Davis, Carel B. Germain, William Sze; to the deans who have graciously supported my writing projects—Shanti Khinduka of the George Warren Brown School of Social Work, Washington University, and Elaine Rothenberg of the School of Social Work, Virginia Commonwealth University; to my editor at Macmillan, Kenneth Scott, who always had the right word of encouragement; and to the many authors whose works appear on these pages, a scientific treasure and a wealth for social action.

M. B.

# Contents

## PART I
## DEVELOPMENTAL PERSPECTIVES

## PART II
## READINGS IN HUMAN GROWTH AND DEVELOPMENT

ix

# PART III
# SPECIAL POPULATIONS AND ISSUES IN HUMAN GROWTH AND DEVELOPMENT 397

# PART IV
# STATISTICAL TABLES 461

## B. Tables:

# Life Span Development

PART

# DEVELOPMENTAL
# PERSPECTIVES

# Developmental Tables: Physical, Psychological, and Sociocultural Factors—A Brief Overview

THIS SECTION of the book contains a brief developmental table, which is reconstructed from the writings in human growth and development. It is a collage, an assemblage of facts and theoretical conceptions that attempt to give an overall impression of the complexity and variety of life development as it is presented in the enormous literature on this topic. Table 1 is organized according to age groupings and to the major factors in development. It is interesting to note the uneven distribution of knowledge about life-span development: some portions of this table are crowded with information whereas others are thin. It is also very difficult to portray rapidly changing conditions, so that the beginning of one section will have the young child, for instance, starting to creep and will end with the advent of walking—great milestones in a human life. But if the reader accepts these flaws and recognizes the table as reflecting an average picture—from which all individuals will vary to a degree—then this condensed version of developmental information will serve a useful overview.

I must emphasize that this table is certainly not complete, and different readers may find one event more suitable to another part of the life-span. This table is a working tool—readers should feel free to correct and to supplement it as additional empirical information permits. It is intended as a stimulus for life-span considerations—to provide an outline of the whole picture so that the particular readings and experiences of the reader will have some frame of reference.

## SOURCES FOR TABLE

It is difficult to provide specific sources for each of the statements in Table 1. Some concepts indicated by quotation marks can be directly attributed, and other statements of fact derive from known research studies. But much of this picture emerges from the common base of knowledge, including the disagreements as to when a given developmental event is supposed to occur on the average. I have tried to present a reasonably consistent pic-

2

ture, but I caution the reader to take these brief statements as an overview, not as a complete systematic review of developmental knowledge.

The following citations represent the major resources used in constructing this table:

AUSUBEL, D. *Theories and Problems of Child Development*. New York, Grune & Stratton, 1958.

BERELSON, B., and G. STEINER. *Human Behavior: An Inventory of Scientific Findings*. New York: Harcourt, Brace, World, 1964.

BROMLEY, D. B. *The Psychology of Human Aging*. Baltimore: Penguin, 1966.

CRAIG, G. J. *Human Development*. Englewood Cliffs, New Jersey: Prentice-Hall, 1976.

ERIKSON, E. H. *Childhood and Society*. 2d ed. New York: Norton, 1963.

GESELL, A. *The First Five Years of Life: The Preschool Years*. New York: Harper, 1940.

GESELL, A., and F. L. ILG. *The Child from Five to Ten*. New York: Harper, 1946.

GESELL, A.; F. L. ILG.; and L. B. AMES. *Youth: The Years from Ten to Sixteen*. New York: Harper, 1956.

GOSLIN, D. A., ed. *Handbook of Socialization Theory and Research*. Chicago: Rand-McNally, 1969.

GOLDBERG, S. R., and F. DEUTSCH. *Life-span Individual and Family Development*. Monterey, California: Brooks/Cole, 1977.

HAVIGHURST, R. J. *Developmental Tasks and Education*. 2d ed. New York: David McKay, 1952.

KALUGER, G., and M. F. KALUGER. *Human Development: The Span of Life*. St. Louis: Mosby, 1974.

KENISTON, K. "Youth: A 'New' Stage of Life." *The American Scholar*, 39 (1970):631–654.

LEVINSON, D. J., and colleagues. *The Seasons of a Man's Life*. New York: Knopf, 1978.

LOWREY, G. H. *Growth and Development of Children*. 6th ed. Chicago: Year Book Medical Publisher, 1973.

MEDINNUS, G. R., and R. C. JOHNSON. *Child and Adolescent Psychology*. 2d ed. New York: Wiley, 1976.

NEUGARTEN, B. L., ed. *Middle Age and Aging: A Reader in Social Psychology*. Chicago: University of Chicago Press, 1968.

PECK, R. C. "Psychological Developments in the Second Half of Life." In *Middle Age and Aging: A Reader In Social Psychology*. Ed. B. L. Neugarten. Chicago: University of Chicago Press, 1968.

RILEY, M. W., and A. FONER. *Aging in Society*. Vol. I. *An Inventory of Research Findings*. New York: Russell Sage Foundation, 1968.

SPOCK, B. *Baby and Child Care*. 3d ed. New York: Pocket Book, 1976.

STOTT, L. H. *The Psychology of Human Development*. New York: Holt, Rinehart and Winston, 1974.

TAVRIS, C., and C. OFFIR. *The Longest War: Sex Differences in Perspective*. New York: Harcourt Brace Jovanovich, 1977.

Table 1.
*Life-span Developments Viewed as Normative Stages*

| Age | Physical changes | Motor developments | Affective developments |
|---|---|---|---|
| 1st Year (birth to 12 months) | Feeding: from 5–8 times a day to 3 regular meals plus snacks; teeth begin to erupt. Sleeping: From 20 hours a day to about 12 hours, plus naps. Sensory: From learning to use oral and visual modes of exploration to greater differentiation and control of these modes. Height and weight—see Part IV, Table 11. | Development of control over various portions of the body; turning head, lifting head, turning body, purposive grasping, apposition of thumb and forefingers, sitting up, crawling, climbing up low furniture, cruising (walking with support). | Development from a general excitation at birth to increasingly differentiated emotional states: distress and delight at 3 months; fear, disgust, anger by 6 months; elation and affection by 12 months. |
| 2nd Year (12 months to 24 months) | Feeding: able to grasp objects (finger-thumb opposition) to feed self. Sleeping: About 13 hours at night, 1 long daytime nap. Sensory: More hand-eye coordination, as in drawing on paper. | High level of activity: walks; creeps upstairs and down; jumps, both feet; seats self in chair; turns pages, several at a time; runs; other gross motor skills in play. Basic control of body is complete: bladder control—dry during day; capable of bowel control. Feeds self. | Development of specific fears; upset when separated from parents. Resentment of new baby; jealousy. |
| 3rd Year (25 months to 36 months) | Sleeping: about 12 hours at night, some short naps. | Continued high level activity: jumps; is able to ride a tricycle. Helps to dress him/herself. | Development of imaginary fears (e.g., of the dark). |
| 4th Year (37 to 48 months) | No significant differences in height and weight between the sexes (see Part IV, Table 11. | Dresses him- or herself. Increasing large muscle control and some small muscle control. Eye-hand coordination developing. Brushes teeth. | Affectionate but also quarrelsome and argumentative. Learning how to control own anger. Fears separation from parents and injury to self. Strong "mine" feelings. |

4

| Age | Physical Growth | Motor Development | Emotional / Social |
|---|---|---|---|
| 5th Year (49 to 60 months) | Muscles growing more rapidly than rest of body. Appetite is usually good. | Mature motor control, with increasing developments in small muscle movements. | Strong affection for home, and persons and objects associated with it. Fears of unreal events diminished, but fear of loss of mother high. |
| 6th Year (61 to 72 months) | Eruption of first permanent teeth. General growth continues. Appetite good. | Very active physically, but still clumsy; apt to have accidents. Works hard in sports but tires easily. | Extremes in mood—loving and hating things. Temper tantrums. Rudeness may be common. Favorite activities and programs followed religiously. Basic emotions established but continue to develop subtlety in how, when, and where to express them. |
| 7th to the 11th Year | Beginnings of physical differences of the sexes: Onset of prepubescence (accelerating growth) in girls (about 10 yrs) with boys starting later (around 12). Wide variations in developments within and between the sexes. Ages 9–12 often the healthiest because lymphoid masses (which fight infection) have reached their maximum (about twice adult amount), vigorous activities, eating, etc. | More integrated and coordinated motor activity. High expenditure of energy and experimentation with new skills. Shows poise. | Has definite likes and dislikes, but less vehement in expressing them. Has worries (of school work, being liked, etc.) but often in good mood. There is increasing sensitivity about sex and nudity. |
| 12 to the 15th Year | Pubescence (maximum growth and abrupt deceleration) in girls (age 12) and boys (age 14) on the average. Most children have permanent teeth (except wisdom teeth) by 13 or 14. Changes occurring in height and weight gain, and broadening of shoulders (boys) and hips (girls), along with developments in primary sex organs. First menstrual period at peak of pubescence (between 12 and 13). Facial acne common. | Owing to uneven development (e.g., hands, feet reach mature size before arms, legs), there is some awkwardness in prepubescence until physical changes and control functions are coordinated. High performance in puberty, but with lack of experiential judgment and discretion. | Variable swings of emotion reflecting concerns over appearance, new skills and achievements, or pace of physical growth. Hero worship may be present. Affection and respect for parents and other role models, without dependence on them. Affection for peers, especially "chums" but also opposite-sex friends. Increased concern about one's body. |

| Age | Physical changes | Motor developments | Affective developments |
| --- | --- | --- | --- |
| 16th to the 18th Year | Postpubescence shows a slowing down of growth in height and weight, but with continued muscle growth and the maturing of sex organs and secondary sexual characteristics. Skeletal structure reaches maturity by the end of this period—girls by 18, boys around 19. | Continues high level of motor performance, with practice adding to the experiential judgment (as in driving a car). | Strong feelings of affection and anger (especially over issues of independence). Favorable attitude about one's body and performance. |
| 19th to the 21st Year | Highpoint in physical fitness and vigor. Adult proportions reached between 18 and 22. | Continues high level of motor performance, but overconfidence may become a problem (as in auto accidents, especially for males of this age). | Favorable attitude about one's body and high level of its performance. Emergence of adult levels and focuses of affection. |
| 22nd to the 30th Year | Beginnings of physical changes making the person vulnerable, from the visible (e.g., increased proportion of body fat) to the invisible (minute decreases in height owing to hardening of bones; Muscle tone peaks and begins to lose elasticity. | Continue high level of motor performance with increased judgment. | Emergence of psychological and social maturity. Also, social stresses in occupational area, family, and social life. |
| 31st to the 40th Year | Continued physical changes, such as accumulation of subcutaneous fat, beginnings of sensory defects—vision, hearing. | Motor performance does not necessarily decrease even with physical changes, if one exercises routinely. | Favorable attitude toward one's body, even with changes in agility, etc. Some culturally bound negative feelings about being "over 30." |
| 41st to the 50th Year | Continued physical changes: Menopause in women (from about 45 to 55 years); in men, the climacteric occurs more slowly and lasts longer. Sensory changes continuing—bifocals may be used to adapt. | | Fears of aging may emerge (especially with death of parents). Concerns: regarding discrepancy between career aspirations and realities; changes in one's body are becoming noticeable. |

| Age | Physical development | Intellectual and language developments; creativity | Psychosocial; sexual; moral developments | "Personality" development (theoretical conceptions) |
|---|---|---|---|---|
| 51st to the 60th Year | Increased signs of physical aging: skin: wrinkled; skeletal: more brittle, arthritic pains; hair: gray, stiffer; sensory: defects in vision (more farsighted) and hearing (loss of hearing of high tones, especially in men); energy level: may be decreased; locomotion slower; circulatory system: possible problems with high blood pressure, etc. | | | Grief concerning widowhood. Depending on personality and social environment, some are satisfied with retirement's disengagements; others are frustrated by inactivity forced on them. |
| 61st to the 70th Year | Continued physical changes. Average life expectancy completed for men in this decade. | Performance may be at same levels as earlier, but experience rather than agility helps to attain goals. | | |
| 71st to the 80th Year | Average life expectancy completed for women in this decade. | | | |
| 81st Year to the end of life | Biologically superior persons in supportive environments. However, physical defects impose limits on activity. | | | |
| 1st Year (birth to 12 months) | | Intellectual: "Sensory-motor phase" (Piaget)—information gained by visual exploration and grasping. Testing behavior by dropping and throwing objects. Language: Makes noises such as fussing, crying, cooing; then responding to adults; by end of first year, says a few words—"Mama" and responds to simple commands—"no, no." | Psychosocial: Basically helpless, yet the child's instinctive responses (e.g., sucking) set off physiological changes in mother and subsequent social bonding. Begins to react differentially to family caretakers and strangers. Plays simple games, e.g., "Peek-a-boo." Sexual: bodily sensations provide pleasure; explorations of own body. | Basic learning conditions: Erikson's first psychosocial stage of Trust vs. Mistrust (paralleling Freud's psychosexual stage of orality): the degree to which an infant comes to trust the world, other people, and him- or herself in order to be helped to grow in a dependable environment. Chess, Birch and Thomas argue that infants have inborn (innate) temperamental differences that produce "easy," "difficult," and "slow-to-warm-up" children. |

| Age | Intellectual and language developments; creativity | Psychosocial; sexual; moral developments | "Personality" development (thoretical conceptions) |
|---|---|---|---|
| 2nd Year (13 months to 24 months) | Intellectual: Exploring behavior, testing simple causes and effects; leads from practical understandings to the beginnings of abstract ideas; imaginative play. Language: One-word sentences and social routine words ("Bye-bye"); relational words ("more"); beginning of "why?" questions. By end of second year, vocabulary of about 300 words, with some two-word sentences. | Psychosocial: Dependency on parents; becomes upset when separated; conscious of adult approval. Negativism emerges and gets (temporarily) resolved; some sibling hostility; beginnings of sense of possessiveness. Can be helpful in small ways; beginnings of humor. Development of independence but still demanding. | Beginnings of self-awareness. Erikson's second psychosocial stage: Autonomy vs. Doubt (2nd and 3rd years) (paralleling Freud's anal stage): accomplishing mental and motor acts him- or herself, in order to have self-confidence in being able to do so. |
| 3rd Year (25 months to 36 months) | Intellectual: Piaget's Preoperational period, 2–7 years: classifies by single salient feature. Language: Short sentences combining relational words and object words, e.g., "more cookie." Vocabulary over 900 words. Creativity: The first creations in drawing, constructions, etc. | Psychosocial: Negativism reappears (about 2½ yrs) with resistance to parental requests, possessiveness, yet with dependency. Models parents' behavior. Parallel play with peers. Dependency and insistence on routine. | Self-oriented; use of "I" talk. Beginnings of intellectual aspect of personality controlling the impulsive emotional side. |
| 4th Year (37 to 48 Months) | Intellectual: Piaget's subphase of the Preoperational period: the intuitive (intuiting meanings in terms of class, relationship, etc.) Language: Engages in word games, silly humor. Asks many questions. Uses long sentences. Vocabulary—about 1,500 words. Able to learn a foreign language easily without accent, an ability that declines with age. | Beginning to incorporate social attitudes and prejudices. | Erikson's stage of Initiative vs. Guilt (ages 4 to 5) (Parallels Freud's phallic stage): Taking the initiative to act on one's own, rather than to react to another or to imitate. |

8

|  | | | |
|---|---|---|---|
| 5th Year (49 to 60 Months) | Language: The child has mastered the basic grammar of his/her culture. Vocabulary is about 2,000 words. | The child of this age is cooperative but dependent on adult support and supervision. Makes a good adjustment to school and enjoys the routine of planned activities. Tends to be literal and serious; often shy in first contacts. Play often involves "playing house" for both sexes. For interpretation of sexuality of this age, see Oedipal Complex hypothesis. | Proud of own appearance. Freud's Oedipal Stage (ages 4 to 5 years)—the parent of the opposite sex is seen as source of sensual satisfaction, and same sex parent is viewed as rival—this constellation of events hypothesized to characterize the personality dynamics of the five-year-old. |
| 6th Year | Vocabulary expanding rapidly. | Entrance to school; new adult authority (teacher) and new peers with whom to establish relationships, as well as structured learning tasks. Is self-centered; peer relations fragile, rapidly changing. "Premoral" moral development (Kohlberg) occurs—concern for outward acts and consequences, not intentions, etc. (years 6 to 9) | Erikson's stage of Industry vs. Inferiority—ages 6 to 11 (parallel to Freud's latency stage)—a concern for how things work and how to make things. Parsons and Bales note the impact of the social system (school) on personality development. |
| 7th to the 11th Year | Piaget's period of concrete operations (7 to 11 years) where the person is able to use some logical operations like true classification, ordering, etc. Curiosity about all things. Vocabulary expanding. | Increased sensitivity to others; has stronger and longer lasting friendships with same-sex peers. Segregation by sexes usual. Emergence of memberships in clubs (e.g., scouts). "Conventional" moral development (Kohlberg) occurs—conforms to avoid disapproval (years 9 to 12) | |

| Age | Intellectual and language developments; creativity | Psychosocial; sexual; moral developments | "Personality" development (theoretical conceptions) |
|---|---|---|---|
| 12th to the 15th Year | Piaget's period of formal operations (11 to 15 years) where the person is developing abstract thinking and hypothesis testing. Performance on standardized tests peaks during adolescence. Beginning explorations with abstract social ideas—religion, philosophy, utopias. Over 7,000 words in spoken vocabulary; 50,000 in reading vocabulary by 12. | Emergence of peers as powerful influence on specific and immediate events; parents influential on long-range values. Change possible from egocentrism to a concern for welfare of others or ideals. "Principled" moral development *may* occur—from social contract philosophy to universal ethical principles (later adolescence, if ever). Minor conflicts over dress, personal appearance between parents and teenager. Incidence of delinquency rises in early teens, but only 5 per cent of all teenagers ever involved. Sexual experimentation begins; masturbation for some, intercourse for others. | Erikson's stage of Identity vs. Role Confusion—ages 12 to 18 (parallel to Freud's genital stage)—integrating various aspects of one's self into a sense of who one has been and who one may become. |
| 16th to the 18th Year | Peak of biologically based intellectual potential, which then decreases as the experientially based intelligence begins to increase. About 80 per cent of teenagers complete high school, but dropouts not due only to intellectual problems. About 25 per cent go on to college. | Rates of delinquency rising sharply during these years, until about 19th year. Drugs (including alcohol) may be introduced around 16 or 17; hard narcotics around age 20. Sexual experiences include sexual intercourse for a majority of 16- to 19-year olds. | Social roles—worker, continuing student, military—have strong impact on self-image. Unemployment, other social failures, have harmful effects on self-image. |

|  | | | |
|---|---|---|---|
| 19th to the 21st Year | The "College Years" for a sizable and growing proportion of persons. Trade and technical schools also draw from this age group. | Becoming accepted as "adult" socially and legally (but differentially for given behaviors—voting, drinking, armed services, etc.). Major adult decisions: career, marriage, homemaker. Role change may begin from single to attached (by marriage or otherwise). Leave family of orientation to form family of procreation. Delinquency rates continue, but more gradual rise. | Erikson's stage of Intimacy vs. Isolation —from young adulthood to middle age—dealing with the ability to share with and care about another person without the fear of losing one's identity in the process. Keniston uses the term *youth* to refer to prolonged or settled adolescence. Levinson's period of early adult (male) transition (from 17 to 30) deals with modifying existing relationships and exploring possibilities in the adult world. |
| 22nd to the 30th Year | The period of major creative contributions for persons in some fields—mathematics, physics. | Role changes continue: from spouse to parent. Family life cycle with its tasks unfolds as children grow, enter school, become involved—and involve parents thereby. Persons in this decade expand their social world to civic and social tasks. They develop a style and standard of living. Time "passes" rapidly owing to may involvements. Delinquency (criminal activity) reaches peak at age 25. | Levinson's first adult (male) life structure (from about 22 to 28) focuses on linking one's valued self and the adult society by exploring options and creating a stable life structure. |
| 31st to the 40th Year | Creativity reaches its highest output on the average; different occupations, such as law, manifest major contributions at later ages. | Becoming established and "establishment"; occupational achievements emerging. Women who have been homemakers may return to work after children are in school. Social contribution becoming important. Sexuality enjoyed, even if routinized within life cycle. | Levinson hypothesizes another adult (male) transition period from about 28 to 33, a stressful period with a peaking of marital problems and divorce. Then, a second adult life structure phase, from about 32 to 40, with its investments in work, family, friends, leisure, and/or community involvements. This is called Early Adulthood. |

| Age | Intellectual and language developments; creativity | Psychosocial; sexual; moral developments | "Personality" development (theoretical conceptions) |
|---|---|---|---|
| 41st to the 50th Year | Vocabulary and information peak around forties. Comprehension skills declining slightly, and arithmetic and other subtests of Wechsler-Bellevue Scale show steeper decline during middle age. | Consolidation of career with beginning thoughts to retirement. Crises of the "empty nest" (last child leaves home); achievement in career goals; the task of caring for aged parents emerges; sexual activity and interest remains high during middle-age period. | Roughly, Erikson's stage of Generativity vs. Self-absorption—a social concern (as Adler suggested) beyond oneself and family to others and to future generations. Blenkner refers to filial maturity—being able to accept mature helping relationship with parents. Peck distinguishes other phases of this period: Valuing Wisdom vs. Valuing Physical Powers; Socializing (companionship with both men and women) vs. Sexualizing; Emotional and Mental Flexibility vs. Rigidity. Levinson posits a mid-life transition (from about 40 to 45)—the termination of early adulthood and initiation of middle adulthood, with the experiencing of one's mortality and waning of functioning to a slight but noticeable degree. |

|  | | | |
|---|---|---|---|
| 51st to the 60th Year | The declines mentioned above continue, but vocabulary and information maintain their high levels. | This is the period of peak earnings (about 53- to 58-year-old period). | Levinson's middle adulthood (from 45 to 60) is the period of the dominant generation, governing every sector of society. |
| 61st to the 70th Year | | The period of retirement from gainful employment, reduction of income, loss of work and colleagues, and changes of social status. Increases in numerous leisure/consumer roles (often viewed as "roleless roles"). Release from some social control mechanisms after retirement; some focusing on inner needs and functions. Continued sexuality, though decrease in frequency (not related to physical capacity). The period of widowhood, especially for women; also loss of friends and family. | Roughly, Erikson's stage of Integrity vs. Despair—the ability to look back with satisfaction and ahead to serenity at one's whole life, through a "life review" process (Butler). Peck adds additional phases: Ego Differentiation (finding meaning in one's own life rather than in Work-Role Preoccupation); Body Transcendence, not being preoccupied with aches and pains of illness, which is Body Preoccupation; and Ego Transcendence, not being preoccupied with thoughts of death, which is Ego Preoccupation). Levinson's late adulthood (ages 65 to 85) may be demarcated by illness or retirement in the late adult transition (from about 60 to 65). There is the experience and the reality of physical decline and loss of some middle adult powers. The focus returns to the self, one's achievements, and the integrity of one's whole life—even if it involves flaws and failures as an inevitable part of living. |
| 71st to the 80th Year | Vocabulary and information begin to decline, as other cognitive functions have done earlier. But the decline in overall "verbal" intelligence is very gradual. | | |
| 81st to end of life | | | |

PART II

# READINGS
# IN HUMAN
# GROWTH AND
# DEVELOPMENT

# A. Theoretical Perspectives on the Life-span: Preventive or Interventive Responses to Problems and Potentials of Human Growth and Development: Introduction

ARTICLES IN THIS SECTION represent some of the major theoretical perspectives on human development. One set of papers presents perspectives of normative development for individuals (Erikson) or families (Rhodes). Another set of papers indicates how minority persons or persons with different cultural backgrounds make their way through the life-span in an environment dominated by an often hostile cultural majority (Chestang; Sotomayor). These papers represent the point and counterpoint of life-span development—the stages and tasks through which we all may pass, but by ways and means that differ as we ourselves differ by sex, race, social class, cultural backgrounds, and the thousand ways we experience life as unique individuals.

There are many other theoretical perspectives on the life-span. In presenting the next set of readings (A. Freud, Wolpe, Kohlberg, and Ellis), I have shifted perspectives from conceptual views of the life-span to ways in which helping professionals react to these developments, either in an interventive sense (Freud and Wolpe) or in a preventive orientation (Kohlberg and Ellis). Implicit in their papers are views of human growth and development, but more important are the presentations of views of nonnormative development, how problems or pathology develops (Freud; Wolpe) and how higher levels of moral decision making or effective interpersonal actions might be attained (Kohlberg; Ellis).

The last paper in this section provides a different type of overview, an historical perspective on American parent-child relationships over the past 200 years (L. Z. Bloom). It includes the dominant philosophies of child rearing, which reflect, in broad strokes, the major theories of

16

human behavior current today—the psychodynamic, the behavioral, and the humanistic.

The papers in this section are presented in order to stimulate readers to form some perspectives in which the many other theoretical, research, or practice articles they encounter during their professional careers will fit together. Integration of knowledge does not come easily; we must prepare the ground so that new ideas will grow in orderly fashion, so that pieces of information may be connected fruitfully, so that we may continually draw on our accumulated but growing knowledge base. To aid in the understanding of how these many perspectives and the numerous theoretical, empirical, and applied papers that follow fit together, I would like to introduce a metaphor that will connect the various readings throughout the book—the metaphor of the social atom.

One part of atomic theory concerns the structure and dynamics of the atom, involving a central nucleus (itself composed of subatomic elements, the proton and the neutron) and surrounded by a system of electrons in one or more rings or shells around the nucleus. The relationship between the electrons and the nucleus is maintained by attracting and repelling charges of energy. One hypothesis about the rings or shells surrounding the nucleus is that each shell has a given number of places or positions where electrons may go. Atoms differ in being more or less stable in having (or lacking) their full component of electrons. Combinations of atoms emerge when the electrons of one atom fill in missing places in the shell of another atom. This combination between atoms forms larger chemical entities (molecules). In some cases, the combination of atoms forms a wholly unique entity—for example, common table salt is the combination of a deadly gas (chlorine) and an unstable metal (sodium). The basic properties of atoms and elements are such as to permit lawful description and prediction.

Now consider life-span development as a metaphorical formation and dissolution of a social atom within the field of other social entities. First, let's consider the structure of this social atom. The nucleus of a given social atom is composed of the genetic contributions of the two sexes. The "shells" orbiting this nucleus are the various characteristics of a person—from the physical characteristics to psychological and social. The genetic makeup sets absolute limits on human growth and development; it is as if the number of positions open to the influence of experience is determined biologically, whereas an enriched (or deprived) environment either does (or does not) fulfill the potentials of these positions. The closer to the biological center of the person, the more the positions influenceable by experience are closed. For example, physical characteristics are heavily influenced by genetic factors even though enriched nutrition may make some important modifications. The outer shell of social factors is heavily influenced by experience, yet biological energy level may have much to do with how an individual interacts with others.

To continue the metaphor, when the outer shell or orbital of two atoms overlaps such that there is an open position on the one and a corresponding filled position on the other, then a bonding occurs, the formation of a new entity, the social molecule, which involves the exchange of energy. In the case of the social atom, the open position may be like a "need" (such as that of an infant for food) whereas the filled position of the other person may be like a resource (such as a mother who is nursing). (The need may also be a learned one, "to be a 'good' mother," whereas the resource comes from the infant whose hunger agitation subsides as he or she is nursed, a gratifying event for the mother.)

For any given person, there are large numbers of other individuals and groups or collectivities with whom he or she may potentially interact. The metaphor of the social atom underscores that the nature of this interactive experience is limited by the biological potentials of all parties involved. For example, a colicky baby and a parent with a low threshold for being upset by prolonged noise are a dangerous combination unless there are some other caretakers who are able to cope with the child while the parent calms down. These caretakers may be relatives or friends or, in special cases, strangers holding institutionalized roles of child care workers. But having a paid job as babysitter does not guarantee a high threshold of tolerance for noise: helping professionals must analyze situations both for the dimensions of the social systems and roles involved as well as by the characteristics of the individuals.

Unlike the physical atom, under special conditions the social atom undergoes changes in its basic structure that are equivalent to forming new outer shells that allow new experiences to be added to the structure of personality, as during the time of puberty. Likewise, social conditions may reduce or constrict an individual, as when a person is forceably retired or discriminated against for cultural reasons. In general, there is a tendency to maintain a relatively stable state at any given moment, but stability for a living organism is based on continually resolving internal and external challenges, and even on creating challenges for itself and others. Depending on the perspective of the viewer, a person may be quietly at rest or furiously digesting some food or thoughts.

The import of this metaphor for students of human growth and development is not simply to put the nature/nurture discussion into context but also to stress the intrinsic relationships between a biological organism and the social, economic, political, and cultural events that coexist with it. We may look at an individual's behavior apart from the whole system, but it is like analyzing the characteristics of the proton and the neutron apart from the larger field within which they exist. And we may analyze the general characteristics of the social, economic, and political systems apart from the individuals who are their constituent members; but as helping professionals we must know the unique attributes of the persons and situations that we seek to change. We should look for lawful relationships of individual growth and development as part of the social and physical contexts of which they are a part. In studying the basic themes of human behavior and development, we should also be attentive to the variations on these themes produced by the social, economic, political, and other forces acting on given individuals, including us. We can read a given article for what information it presents—and scientists have to focus their efforts on specific groups of variables—but as helping professionals we are obliged to integrate this information with other bodies of knowledge.

Therefore, I suggest that each article be read as if it had points or places missing that require other articles to fill in a body of knowledge. The reader will note that articles selected here have overlapping threads—on purpose—to aid in integrating these papers. The conceptual and the empirical structures they describe, life-span development of individuals in groups, will also become a growing body of knowledge with the challenge of "missing points" being a stimulus to seek further information.

---

# Life Cycle*
## *Erik H. Erikson*

THE OBSERVER of life is always immersed in it and thus unable to transcend the limited perspectives of his stage and condition. Religious world views usually evolve pervasive configurations of the course of life: one religion may envisage it as a continuous spiral of rebirths, another as a crossroads to damnation or salvation. Various "ways of life" harbor more or less explicit images of life's course: a leisurely one may see it as ascending and descending

* Reprinted with permission of the publisher from *The International Encyclopedia of the Social Sciences*, David L. Sills, Editor. Volume 9, 286–292. Copyright © 1968 by Crowell, Collier and Macmillan, Inc.

steps with a comfortable platform of maturity in between; a competitive one may envision it as a race for spectacular success—and sudden oblivion. The scientist, on the other hand, looks at the organism as it moves from birth to death and, in the larger sense, at the individual in a genetic chain; or he looks at the cultural design of life's course as marked by rites of transition at selected turning points.

The very choice of the configuration "cycle of life," then, necessitates a statement of the writer's conceptual ancestry—clinical psychoanalysis. The clinical worker cannot escape combining knowledge, experience, and conviction in a conception of the course of life and of the sequence of generations—for how, otherwise, could he offer interpretation and guidance? The very existence of a variety of psychiatric "schools" is probably due to the fact that clinical practice and theory are called upon to provide a total orientation beyond possible verification.

Freud confessed only to a scientific world view, but he could not avoid the attitudes (often in contradiction to his personal values) that were part of his times. The original data of psychoanalysis, for example, were minute reconstructions of "pathogenic" events in early childhood. They supported an orientation which—in analogy to teleology— could be called *originology*, i.e., a systematic attempt to derive complex meanings from vague beginnings and obscure causes. The result was often an implicit fatalism, although counteracted by strenuously "positive" orientations. Any theory embracing both life history and case history, however, must find a balance between the "backward" view of the genetic reconstruction and the "forward" formulation of progressive differentiation in growth and development; between the "downward" view into the depth of the unconscious and the "upward" awareness of compelling social experience; and between the "inward" exploration of inner reality and the "outward" attention to historical actuality.

This article will attempt to make explicit those psychosocial insights that often remain implicit in clinical practice and theory. These concern the individual, who in principle develops according to predetermined steps of readiness that enable him to participate in ever more differentiated ways along a widening social radius, and the social organization, which in principle tends to invite such developmental potentialities and to support the proper rate and the proper sequence of their unfolding.

"Cycle" is intended to convey the double tendency of individual life to "round itself out" as a coherent experience and at the same time to form a link in the chain of generations from which it receives and to which it contributes both strength and weakness.

Strategic in this interplay are developmental crises—"crisis" here connoting not a threat of catastrophe but a turning point, a crucial period of increased vulnerability and heightened potential, and, therefore, the ontogenetic source of generational strength and maladjustment.

# The Eight Stages of Life

Man's protracted childhood must be provided with the psychosocial protection and stimulation which, like a second womb, permits the child to develop in distinct steps as he unifies his separate capacities. In each stage, we assume a new drive-and-need constellation, an expanded radius of potential social interaction, and social institutions created to receive the growing individual within traditional patterns. To provide an evolutionary rationale for this (for prolonged childhood and social institutions must have evolved together), two basic differences between animal and man must be considered.

We are, in Ernst Mayr's terms (1964), the "generalist" animal, prepared to adapt to and to develop cultures in the most varied environments. A long childhood must prepare the newborn of the species to become specialized as a member of a pseudo species (Erikson 1965), i.e., in tribes, cultures, castes, etc., each of which behaves as if it were the only genuine realization of man as the heavens planned and created him. Furthermore, man's drives are characterized by instinctual energies, which are, in contrast to other animals, much less bound to instinctive patterns (or inborn release mechanisms). A maximum of free instinctual energy thus remains ready to be invested in basic psychosocial encounters which tend to fix developing energies into cultural patterns of mutuality, reliability, and competence. Freud has shown the extent to which maladaptive anxiety and rage accompany man's instinctuality, while postulating the strength of the ego in its defensive and in its adaptive aspects (see Freud, 1936; Hartmann, 1939). We can attempt to show a systematic relationship between man's maladjustments and those basic strengths which must emerge in each life cycle and re-emerge from generation to generation (Erikson, 1964). . . .

[Erikson presents a model of psychosocial development (growth in trust, autonomy, initiative, and so on) in which eight crises in human relationships (beginning with mistrust, shame, guilt) are related to eight stages of the life span (infancy, early childhood, play age, through old age) such that each basic psychosocial trend meets a crisis during the corresponding stage (for example, basic trust versus basic mistrust in infancy, and the like). All of these aspects of development are in principle present all the time, but as the person develops, he or she becomes ready to experience and to manage the critical conflicts within specific cultural contexts and to incorporate the resolution of these normal crises into his or her personality. It is this theme, one stage growing out of the events of the previous stages, that Erikson terms the epigenetic principle.]

The epigenetic pattern will have to be kept in mind as we now state for each stage: (*a*) the psychosocial crisis evoked by social interaction, which is in turn facilitated and necessitated by newly developing drives and capacities, and the specific psychosocial strength emanating from the solution of this crisis; (*b*) the specific sense of estrangement awakened at each stage and its connection with some major form of psychopathology; (*c*) the special relationship between all of these factors and certain basic social institutions (Erikson 1950).

**Infancy (Basic Trust Versus Mistrust—Hope).**   The resolution of the first psychosocial crisis is performed primarily by maternal care. The newborn infant's more or less coordinated readiness to incorporate by mouth and through the senses meets the mother's and the society's more or less coordinated readiness to feed him and to stimulate his awareness. The mother must represent to the child an almost somatic conviction that she (his first "world") is trustworthy enough to satisfy and to regulate his needs. But the infant's demeanor also inspires hope in adults and makes them wish to give hope; it awakens in them a strength which they, in turn, are ready and needful to have confirmed in the experience of care. This is the ontogenetic basis of hope, that first and basic strength which gives man a semblance of instinctive certainty in his social ecology.

Unavoidable pain and delay of satisfaction, however, and inexorable weaning make this stage also prototypical for a sense of abandonment and helpless rage. This is the first of the human estrangements against which hope must maintain itself throughout life.

In psychopathology, a defect in basic trust can be evident in early malignant disturbances or can become apparent later in severe addiction or in habitual or sudden withdrawal into psychotic states.

Biological motherhood needs at least three links with social experience—the mother's past experience of being mothered, a method of care in trustworthy surroundings, and some convincing image of providence. The infant's hope, in turn, is one cornerstone of the adult's faith, which throughout history has sought an institutional safeguard in organized religion. However, where religious institutions fail to give ritual actuality to their formulas they may become irrelevant to psychosocial strength.

Hope, then, is the first psychosocial strength. It is the enduring belief in the attainability of primal wishes in spite of the anarchic urges and rages of dependency.

**Early Childhood (Autonomy Versus Shame, Doubt—Will Power).**   Early childhood sets the stage for psychosocial autonomy by rapid gains in muscular maturation, locomotion, verbalization, and discrimination. All of these, however, create limits in the form of spatial restrictions and of categorical divisions between "yes and no," "good and bad," "right and wrong," and "yours and mine." Muscular maturation sets the stage for an ambivalent set of social modalities—holding on and letting go. To hold on can become a destructive retaining or restraining, or a pattern of care—to have and to hold. To let go, too, can turn into an inimical letting loose, or a relaxed "letting pass" and "letting be." Freud calls this the anal stage of libido development because of the pleasure experienced in and the conflict over excretory retention and elimination.

This stage, therefore, becomes decisive for the ratio of good will and willfulness. A sense of self-control without loss of self-esteem is the ontogenetic source of confidence in free will; a sense of overcontrol and loss of self-control can give rise to a lasting propensity for doubt and shame. The matter is complicated by the different needs and capacities of siblings of different ages—and by their rivalry.

Shame is the estrangement of being exposed and conscious of being looked at disapprovingly, of wishing to "bury one's face" or "sink into the ground." This potentiality is exploited in the "shaming" used throughout life by some cultures and causing, on occasion, suicide. While shame is related to the consciousness of being upright and exposed, doubt has much to do with the consciousness of having a front and a back (and of the vulnerability of being seen and influenced from behind). It is the estrangement of being unsure of one's will and of those who would dominate it.

From this stage emerges the propensity for compulsive overcompliance or impulsive defiance. If denied a gradual increase in autonomy of choice the individual may become obsessed by repetitiveness and develop an overly cruel conscience. Early self-doubt and doubt of others may later find their most malignant expression in compulsion neuroses or in paranoiac apprehension of hidden critics and secret persecutors threatening from behind.

We have related basic trust to the institutions of religion. The enduring need of the individual to have an area of free choice reaffirmed and delineated by formulated privileges and limitations, obligations and rights, has an institutional safeguard in the principles of law and order and of justice. Where this is impaired, however, the law itself is in danger of becoming arbitrary or formalistic, i.e., "impulsive" or "compulsive" itself.

Will power is the unbroken determination to exercise free choice as well as self-restraint in spite of the unavoidable experience of shame, doubt, and a certain rage over being controlled by others. Good will is rooted in the judiciousness of parents guided by their respect for the spirit of the law.

**Play Age (Initiative Versus Guilt—Purpose).** Able to move independently and vigorously, the child, now in his third or fourth year, begins to comprehend his expected role in the adult world and to play out roles worth imitating. He develops a sense of initiative. He associates with age-mates and older children as he watches and enters into games in the barnyard, on the street corner, or in the nursery. His learning now is intrusive; it leads him into ever new facts and activities, and he becomes acutely aware of differences between the sexes. But if it seems that the child spends on his play a purposefulness out of proportion to "real" purposes, we must recognize the human necessity to simultaneously bind together infantile wish and limited skill, symbol and fact, inner and outer world, a selectively remembered past and a vaguely anticipated future—all before adult "reality" takes over in sanctioned roles and adjusted purposes.

The fate of infantile genitality remains determined by the sex roles cultivated and integrated in the family. In the boy, the sexual orientation is dominated by phallic-intrusive initiative; in the girl, by inclusive modes of attractiveness and "motherliness."

Conscience, however, forever divides the child within himself by establishing an inner voice of self-observation, self-guidance, and self-punishment. The estrangement of this stage, therefore, is a sense of guilt over goals contemplated and acts done, initiated or merely fantasied. For initiative includes competition with those of superior equipment. In a final contest for a favored position with the mother, "oedipal" feelings are aroused in the boy, and there appears to be an intensified fear of finding the genitals harmed as punishment for the fantasies attached to their excitability.

Infantile guilt leads to the conflict between unbounded initiative and repression or inhibition. In adult pathology this residual conflict is expressed in hysterical denial, general inhibition, and sexual impotence, or in overcompensatory exhibitionism and psychopathic acting-out.

The word "initiative" has for many a specifically American, or "entrepreneur," connotation. Yet man needs this sense of initiative for whatever he learns and does, from fruit gathering to commercial enterprise—or the study of books.

The play age relies on the existence of some form of basic family, which also teaches the child by patient example where play ends and irreversible purpose begins. Only thus are guilt feelings integrated in a strong (not severe) conscience; only thus is language verified as a shared actuality. The "oedipal" stage thus not only results in a moral sense restricting the horizon of the permissible, but it also directs the way to the possible and the tangible, which attract infantile dreams to the goals of technology and culture. Social institutions, in turn, offer an ethos of action, in the form of ideal adults fascinating enough to replace the heroes of the picture book and fairy tale.

That the adult begins as a playing child means that there is a residue of play acting and role playing even in what he considers his highest purposes. These he projects on a larger and more perfect historical future; these he dramatizes in the ceremonial present with uniformed players in ritual arrangements; thus men sanction aggressive initiative, even as they assuage guilt by submission to a higher authority.

Purpose, then, is the courage to envisage and pursue valued and tangible goals guided by conscience but not paralyzed by guilt and by the fear of punishment.

**School Age (Industry Versus Inferiority—Competence).** Before the child, psychologically a rudimentary parent, can become a biological parent, he must begin to be a worker and potential provider. Genital maturation is postponed (the period of latency). The child develops a sense of industriousness, i.e., he begins to comprehend the tool world of his culture, and he can become an eager and absorbed member of that productive situation called "school," which gradually supersedes the whims of play. In all cultures, at this stage, children receive systematic instruction of some kind and learn eagerly from older children.

The danger of this stage lies in the development of a sense of inadequacy. If the child despairs of his skill or his status among his tool partners, he may be discouraged from further learning. He may regress to the hopeless rivalry of the oedipal situation. It is at this point that the larger society becomes significant to the child by admitting him to roles preparatory to the actuality of technology and economy. Where he finds, however, that the color of his skin or the background of his parents rather than his wish and his will to learn will decide his worth as an apprentice, the human propensity for feeling unworthy (inferior) may be fatefully aggravated as a determinant of character development.

But there is another danger: If the overly conforming child accepts work as the only criterion of worthwhileness, sacrificing too readily his imagination and playfulness, he may become ready to submit to what Marx called a "craft-idiocy," i.e., become a slave of his technology and of its established role typology.

This is socially a most decisive stage, preparing the child for a hierarchy of learning experiences which he will undergo with the help of cooperative peers and instructive adults. Since industriousness involves doing things beside and with others, a first sense of the division of labor and of differential opportunity—that is, a sense of the technological ethos of a culture—develops at this time. Therefore, the configurations of cultural thought and the manipulations basic to the prevailing technology must reach meaningfully into school life.

Competence, then, is the free exercise (unimpaired by an infantile sense of inferiority) of dexterity and intelligence in the completion of serious tasks. It is the basis for cooperative participation in some segment of the culture.

### Adolescence (Identity Versus Identity Confusion—Fidelity).

With a good initial relationship to skills and tools, and with the advent of puberty, childhood proper comes to an end. The rapidly growing youths, faced with the inner revolution of puberty and with as yet intangible adult tasks, are now primarily concerned with their psychosocial identity and with fitting their rudimentary gifts and skills to the occupational prototypes of the culture.

The integration of an identity is more than the sum of childhood identifications. It is the accrued confidence that the inner sameness and continuity gathered over the past years of development are matched by the sameness and continuity in one's meaning for others, as evidenced in the tangible promise of careers and life styles.

The adolescent's regressive and yet powerful impulsiveness alternating with compulsive restraint is well known. In all of this, however, an ideological seeking after an inner coherence and a durable set of values can be detected. The particular strength sought is fidelity—that is, the opportunity to fulfill personal potentialities (including erotic vitality or its sublimation) in a context which permits the young person to be true to himself and true to significant others. "Falling in love" also can be an attempt to arrive at a self-definition by seeing oneself reflected anew in an idealized as well as eroticized other.

From this stage on, acute maladjustments due to social anomie may lead to psychopathological regressions. Where role confusion joins a hopelessness of long standing, borderline psychotic episodes are not uncommon.

Adolescents, on the other hand, help one another temporarily through much regressive insecurity by forming cliques and by stereotyping themselves, their ideals, and their "enemies." In this they can be clannish and cruel in their exclusion of all those who are "different." Where they turn this repudiation totally against the society, delinquency may be a temporary or lasting result.

As social systems enter into the fiber of each succeeding generation, they also absorb into their lifeblood the rejuvenative power of youth. Adolescence is thus a vital regenerator in the process of social evolution, for youth can offer its loyalties and energies to the conservation of that which it feels is valid as well as to the revolutionary correction of that which has lost its regenerative significance.

Adolescence is least "stormy" among those youths who are gifted and well trained in the pursuit of productive technological trends. In times of unrest, the adolescent mind becomes an ideological mind in search of an inspiring unification of ideas. Youth needs to be affirmed by peers and confirmed by teachings, creeds, and ideologies which express the promise that the best people will come to rule and that rule will develop the best in people. A society's ideological weakness, in turn, expresses itself in weak utopianism and in widespread identity confusion.

Fidelity, then, is the ability to sustain loyalties freely pledged in spite of the inevitable contradictions of value systems. It is the cornerstone of identity and receives inspiration from confirming ideologies and "ways of life."

**Young Adulthood (Intimacy Versus Isolation—Love).** Consolidated identity permits the self-abandonment demanded by intimate affiliations, by passionate sexual unions, or by inspiring encounters. The young adult is ready for intimacy and solidarity—that is, he can commit himself to affiliations and partnerships even though they may call for significant sacrifices and compromises. Ethical strength emerges as a further differentiation of ideological conviction (adolescence) and a sense of moral obligation (childhood).

True genital maturity is first reached at this stage; much of the individual's previous sex life is of the identity-confirming kind. Freud, when asked for the criteria of a mature person, is reported to have answered: *"Lieben und Arbeiten"* ("love and work"). All three words deserve equal emphasis.

It is only at this stage that the biological differences between the sexes result in a full polarization within a joint life style. Previously established strengths have helped the two sexes to converge in capacities and values which enhance communication and cooperation, while divergence is now of the essence in love life and in procreation. Thus the sexes first become similar in consciousness, language, and ethics in order then to be maturely different. But this, by necessity, causes ambivalences.

The danger of this stage is possible psychosocial isolation—that is, the avoidance of contacts which commit to intimacy. In psychopathology isolation can lead to severe character problems of the kind which interfere with "love and work," and this often on the basis of infantile fixations and lasting immaturities.

Man, in addition to erotic attraction, has developed a selectivity of mutual love that serves the need for a new and shared identity in the procession of generations. Love is the guardian of that elusive and yet all-pervasive power of cultural and personal style which binds into a "way of life" the affiliations of competition and cooperation, procreation and production. The problem is one of transferring the experience of being cared for in a parental setting to an adult affiliation actively chosen and cultivated as a mutual concern within a new generation.

The counterpart of such intimacy, and the danger, is man's readiness to fortify his territory of intimacy and solidarity by exaggerating small differences and prejudging or excluding foreign influences and people. Insularity thus aggravated can lead to that irrational fear which is easily exploited by demagogic leaders seeking aggrandizement in war and in political conflict.

Love, then, is a mutuality of devotion greater than the antagonisms inherent in divided function.

**Maturity (Generativity Versus Stagnation—care).** Evolution has made man the teaching and instituting as well as the learning animal. For dependency and maturity are reciprocal: mature man needs to be needed, and maturity is guided by the nature of that which must be cared for.

Generativity, then, is primarily the concern with establishing and guiding the next generation. In addition to procreativity, it includes productivity and creativity; thus it is psychosocial in nature. From the crisis of generativity emerges the strength of care.

Where such enrichment fails, a sense of stagnation and boredom ensues, the pathological symptoms of which depend on variations in mental epidemiology: certainly where the hypocrisy of the frigid mother was once regarded as a most significant malignant influence, today, when sexual "adjustment" is in order, an obsessive pseudo intimacy and adult self-indulgence are nonetheless damaging to the generational process. The very nature of generativity suggests that the most circumscribed symptoms of its weakness are to be found in the next generation in the form of those aggravated estrangements which we have listed for childhood and youth.

Generativity is itself a driving power in human organization. For the intermeshing stages of childhood and adulthood are in themselves a system of generation and regeneration given continuity by institutions such as extended households and divided labor.

Thus, in combination, the basic strengths enumerated here and the structure of an organized human community provide a set of proven methods and a fund of traditional reassurance with which each generation meets the needs of the next. Various traditions transcend divisive personal differences and confusing conditions. But they also contribute to a danger to the species as a whole, namely, the defensive territoriality of the pseudo species, which on seemingly ethical grounds must discredit and destroy threateningly alien systems and may itself be destroyed in the process.

Care is the broadening concern for what has been generated by love, necessity, or accident—a concern which must consistently overcome the ambivalence adhering to irreversible obligation and the narrowness of self-concern.

**Old Age (Integrity Versus Despair—Wisdom).**   Strength in the aging and sometimes in the old takes the form of wisdom in its many connotations—ripened "wits," accumulated knowledge, inclusive understanding, and mature judgment. Wisdom maintains and conveys the integrity of experience, in spite of the decline of bodily and mental functions. Responding to the oncoming generation's need for an integrated heritage, the wisdom of old age remains aware of the relativity of all knowledge acquired in one lifetime in one historical period. Integrity, therefore, implies an emotional integration faithful to the image bearers of the past and ready to take (and eventually to renounce) leadership in the present.

The lack or loss of this accrued integration is signified by a hidden fear of death: fate is not accepted as the frame of life, death not as its finite boundary. Despair indicates that time is too short for alternate roads to integrity: this is why the old try to "doctor" their memories. Bitterness and disgust mask such despair, which in severe psychopathology aggravates senile depression, hypochondria, and paranoiac hate.

A meaningful old age (preceding terminal invalidism) provides that integrated heritage which gives indispensable perspective to those growing up, "adolescing," and aging. But the end of the cycle also evokes "ultimate concerns," the paradoxes of which we must leave to philosophical and religious interpreters. Whatever chance man has to transcend the limitations of his self seems to depend on his full (if often tragic) engagement in the one and only life cycle permitted him in the sequence of generations. Great philosophical and religious systems dealing with ultimate individuation seem to have remained (even in their monastic establishments) responsibly related to the cultures and civilizations of their times. Seeking transcendence by renunciation, they remain ethically concerned with the maintenance of the world. By the same token, a civilization can be measured by the meaning which it gives to the full cycle of life, for such meaning (or the lack of it) cannot fail to reach into the beginnings of the next generation and thus enhance the potentiality that others may meet ultimate questions with some clarity and strength.

Wisdom, then, is a detached and yet active concern with life in the face of death.

## Conclusion

From the cycle of life such dispositions as faith, will power, purposefulness, efficiency, devotion, affection, responsibility, and sagacity (all of which are also criteria of ego strength) flow into the life of institutions. Without them, institutions wilt; but without the spirit of institutions pervading the patterns of care and love, instruction and training, no enduring strength could emerge from the sequence of generations.

We have attempted, in a psychosocial frame, to account for the ontogenesis not of lofty ideals but of an inescapable and intrinsic order of strivings, which, by weakening or strengthening man, dictates the minimum goals of informed and responsible participation.

Psychosocial strength, we conclude, depends on a total process which regulates individual life cycles, the sequence of generations, and the structure of society simultaneously, for all three have evolved together.

Each person must translate this order into his own terms so as to make it amenable to whatever kind of trait inventory, normative scale, measurement, or educational goal is his main concern. Science and technology are, no doubt, changing essential aspects of the course of life, wherefore some increased awareness of the functional wholeness of the cycle may be mandatory. Interdisciplinary work will define in practical and applicable terms what evolved order is common to all men and what true equality of opportunity must mean in planning for future generations.

The study of the human life cycle has immediate applications in a number of fields. Paramount is the science of human development within social institutions. In psychiatry (and in its applications to law), the diagnostic and prognostic assessment of disturbances common to life stages should help to outweigh fatalistic diagnoses. Whatever will prove tangibly lawful about the cycle of life will also be an important focus for anthropology insofar as it assesses universal functions in the variety of institutional forms. Finally, as the study of the life history emerges from that of case histories, it will throw new light on biography and thus on history itself. . . .

## BIBLIOGRAPHY

BÜHLER, CHARLOTTE (1933) 1959 *Der menschliche Lebenslauf als psychologisches Problem.* 2d ed., rev. Leipzig: Hirzel.

BÜHLER, CHARLOTTE 1962 *Values in Psychotherapy.* New York: Free Press.

ERIKSON, ERIK H. (1950) 1964 *Childhood and Society.* 2d ed., rev. & enl. New York: Norton.

ERIKSON, ERIK H. 1958 *Young Man Luther.* New York: Norton.

ERIKSON, ERIK H. 1964 *Insight and Responsibility.* New York: Norton.

ERIKSON, ERIK H. 1965 The Ontogeny of Ritualisation in Man. Unpublished manuscript.

FREUD, ANNA (1936) 1957 *The Ego and the Mechanisms of Defense.* New York: International Universities Press. → First published as *Das Ich und die Abwehrmechanismen.*

FREUD, ANNA 1965 *Normality and Pathology in Childhood: Assessment of Development.* New York: International Universities Press.

HARTMANN, HEINZ (1939) 1958 *Ego Psychology and the Problem of Adaptation.* Translated by David Rapaport. New York: International Universities Press. → First published as *Ich-Psychologie und Anpassungs-problem.*

MAYR, ERNST 1964 The Evolution of Living Systems. National Academy of Sciences, *Proceedings* 51:934–941.

WERNER, HEINZ (1926) 1965 *Comparative Psychology of Mental Development.* Rev. ed. New York: International Universities Press → First published as *Einführung in die Entwicklungs-psychologie.*

# A Developmental Approach to the Life Cycle of the Family*

*Sonya L. Rhodes*

. . . IT IS THE PURPOSE of this article to identify stages in the life cycle of the family in the tradition of Erik Erikson's life cycle of the individual.[1] Erikson's theory postulates a cogwheeling of life cycles: the intermeshing of phase-specific needs at different stages of the life cycle. The successful achievement of one person's task is dependent on and contributory to the successful achievement by others in the family of their appropriate tasks. A developmental approach to the family is a natural outgrowth of the central concept of cogwheeling. It is the objective of this article to translate the interdependent life tasks relevant to members of a family into developmental tasks. . . .

* Reprinted by permission of the publisher, Family Service Association of America, from *Social Casework:* 58:5, (May 1977), 301–311.

[1] Erik H. Erikson, Identity and Life Cycle, *Psychological Issues,* vol. 1, no. 1, monograph 4 (New York: International Universities Press, 1959).

# Characteristics of the Developmental Model of the Family Life Cycle

Each stage in the life cycle of the family is characterized by an average expectable family crisis brought about by the convergence of bio-psycho-social processes which create phase-specific family tasks to be confronted, undertaken, and completed. These family tasks reflect the assumption that developmental tasks of individual family members have an overriding influence or effect on the nature of family life at a given time and represent family themes that apply to family members as individuals as well as a group.

The conceptual unit under scrutiny is the family as a whole. The developmental approach to the study of the family relies primarily on general systems concepts[2] to give it a coherent systematic set of basic assumptions. To summarize, the family constitutes a social system because it has the following characteristics:

1. Its members occupy various family positions which are in a state of interdependency. A change in the position, status, behavior, or role of one member leads to change in the behavior of other members.
2. The family is a boundary-maintaining unit with varying degrees of rigidity and permeability in defining the family and nonfamily world. Family composition (who comprises the family) differs from culture to culture; moreover, shifts in family composition can be identified at different points in the life cycle.
3. The family is an adaptive and equilibrium-seeking unit with patterns of interaction repeating themselves over time. Complementarity in the marital pair is paralleled in other dyadic and triadic constellations within the family.
4. The family is a task-performing unit that meets both the requirements of external agencies representing society and also the internal needs and demands of its members. This reciprocity between individual and social needs is known as the socialization of family members.

Implicit in a synthesis of developmental and systems thinking about the family is the assumption that the family is an adaptive unit with the resources for the growth and maturation of its members. Transitional crises are conceived as predictable and necessary, in response both to the changing needs of family members and to pressures exerted from external systems. The family copes with maturational and social demands through task management involving shifts in internal organization as well as in transaction with outside social and cultural structures. The phase-specific family tasks have a cumulative effect; adequate task handling at early stages strengthens the family's ability to handle subsequent stages effectively.

---

[2] Norbert Wiener, *Cybernetics* (New York: John Wiley & Sons, 1949); Marshall McLuhan. *Understanding Media* (New York: McGraw Hill Book Co., 1964); and Ludwig von Bertalanffy. *Problems of Life* (New York: Harper & Brothers, 1960).

The developmental perspective which is grounded in general systems theory has some distinctive advantages.

> The strengths of this [developmental] framework include the consideration of the internal functioning of the family systems without ignoring the external or environmental transactions of the family as a social unit. This framework is particularly helpful in viewing the process of family change. It approaches change as a facet related to the interaction of the individual member within and without the family system, as well as the structural implications of position and role derived both from society and from the internal aspects of family size, age, and sex of its members.[3]

Applying systems concepts to the family as a developmental unit which changes over time provides a frame of reference to the family as a system in transaction with other social systems as well as to the interactional impact of individuals at different stages in the life cycle and their reciprocal effect on one another over time.

The author, having presented key concepts which anchor the developmental approach to other theoretical conceptions, describes below the seven stages of the family. "The family" as it is conceived in this article is the two-parent nuclear family of varied socioeconomic status. The model may prove to be adaptive to other family forms (single parent, extended, newly formed "second", and communal families) with some modifications. The model begins arbitrarily, at the time at which two people join in a coupling process, and ends with the death of one of the founding members. In reality, however, there is no beginning or end; the stages, artificially numbered for the purposes of explication, are in reality sequential and cyclical, and involve multigenerational processes.

## Intimacy Versus Idealization or Disillusionment

This stage applies to the first phase of forming a dyadic relationship and precedes the advent of offspring. The issues can be confronted with or without institutional validation—in traditional courtship, in nonmarital unions—the essential criterion of this stage is that the couple is making an investment in the relationship.

The major struggle in forming a relationship viable and durable enough to withstand the stresses of later stages concerns the efforts to achieve intimacy based on a realistic perception of the partner as a whole person, as opposed to the idealization of one's partner as a romantic image, or disillusionment with one's partner as unresponsive. It corresponds on an interactional level

---

[3] Diane I. Levande, Family Theory as a Necessary Component of Family Therapy, *Social Casework*, 57:291–95 (May 1976), p. 294.

to what Erikson describes as the essential task of the individual in young adulthood to achieve intimacy in love and friendship as an alternative to isolation. It is an implicit assumption that each partner's capacity to achieve intimacy as opposed to idealization is reflective of the extent to which he or she has completed the tasks relevant to his or her own nuclear family. Thus, the multigenerational perspective which resonates throughout the model surfaces meaningfully in this first stage.

As the fundamental aspect of building a relationship this task involves assuming responsibility for oneself in the relationship, negotiating differences and conflict with one another, resolving unrealistic expectations of one's partner, and finding mutually satisfying ways to nurture and support one another. Because of the critical nature of the tasks, this stage is a period of extensive upheaval and conflict.

Courtship patterns and expectations, the nature of early interactional pacts (usually implicit), the vying for power positions, and the assignment of roles and responsibilities and early indicators of the couple's mutual capacity for intimacy, of their progress in working toward intimacy, and of potentially dysfunctional patterns in the achievement of intimacy. . . .

How does the shift from idealization to intimacy come about? The idealized notions and expectations that provided the initial momentum for the relationship give way to a period of some disillusionment and disapppointment. In experiencing these emotions, a couple confronts a major juncture in the relationship. Three attempts at resolution may be sought. First, one or both members of the couple can withdraw from or terminate the relationship, unwilling or unable to make an investment in the struggle to open issues up between them. Second, disillusionment can provide the motivation to collusively seek a retreat from the major difficulties, but stay together in pseudoharmony or open rigidified conflict. Third, a shared awareness of mutually felt dissatisfactions and frustrations can be the foundation for greater openness and appreciation of differences. Locating areas of conflict, differing expectations, and self-identified needs prepares the way for negotiation which recognizes the individuals as separate people. Confronting each other as real people, as opposed to ideal images, counters fantasies and stereotypes and liberates self-disclosures which create meaningful opportunities for contact, closeness, and support. This sharing can lead to the identification of struggles within and some awareness that these struggles get displaced in the relationship.

It should be emphasized, however, that the goal of true intimacy based on mutual efforts to achieve a workable complementarity is relative. If idealization without disillusionment prevents intimacy, then intimacy without idealization obliterates romance. The ability to achieve a realistic appreciation of one's partner as a person needs to be balanced by the retention of some illusions. Thus, the relinquishment of the idealized person which responds to one's inner fantasy and secret longings of romantic union need not be total, and, in fact, may be an important component of enduring and satisfying relationships.

## Replenishment Versus Turning Inward

This stage[4] applies to the childbearing years and begins with the birth of the first child and ends when the last child enters school. The major struggle entails the development of nurturing patterns among all family members so that food, in an emotional sense, is available to adult suppliers as well as to their helpless offspring. Parenting results in the depletion of one's ability to give, and ultimately in self-absorption if replenishment is not available. The ability to succor, to be available and responsive to the needs of young children depends on the presence of both inner resources and a responsive, caring environment which provides opportunity for refueling[5] the adults.

An impending crisis in the life of the family is created by the birth of the first and successive offspring. The birth of the first offspring probably presents the most complex adaptations.[6] The couple who have achieved intimacy are in a position to make the necessary adaptations to a new family member who is both helpless and demanding. Regardless of how the caretaking functions are divided or assumed by mother and father, substantial shifts will be required in the giving and taking patterns of the parents. The dyad has become a triad with all the attendant complications of triadic relations. Two members of the triad can form a close alliance which excludes the third. In our culture, the intense mother-child bond which emphasizes the mother as nurturer can be exemplarily achieved at the expense of the husband-father. Or, the mother may become the source of supplies of all family members at the expense of her own needs. . . .

## Individuation of Family Members Versus Pseudomutual Organization[7]

This stage applies to those families who have passed through the bearing and rearing of preschool children years. In response to the progressive indepen-

---

[4] I am indebted to my friend and colleague, Joanna Strauss, for her contribution to this section derived from casual discussion together on being parents.

[5] The concept of "refueling" is borrowed and extracted from Margaret Mahler, Fred Pine, and Ann Bergman, *The Psychological Birth of the Human Infant* (New York: Basic Books, 1975), p. 69.

[6] E. E. LeMasters, Parenthood in Crisis, in *Crisis Intervention*, ed. Parad, pp. 111–17.

[7] This term was developed by the following authors to conceptualize a family pattern in families with schizophrenics. The author is taking liberty with this concept in her approach to nonclinical "normal" families. The text is self-explanatory in developing her application of the term. Lyman C. Wynne, Irving M. Ryckoff, Julian Day, and Stanley I. Hirsch, Pseudo-Mutuality in the Family Relations of Schizophrenics, *Psychiatry*, 21:205–20 (May 1958).

dence and freedom of family members, these families must shift the foci of their energies from family concerns to individual interests. The major struggle for the parents released from the early dependence of children as well as for latency-age children is to prepare for an identity which is not defined by one's roles and responsibilities within the family. It is a period of major crisis for many women who find their predominant role as caretakers of children diminished by their last child's progressive independence.

Perhaps this task is easiest for the children whose increasing self-sufficiency and competence propels them out into the world of the community and neighborhood. Analogously, this task may be hardest for women who experience a deflation of self-esteem, as their competencies are no longer needed or valued. For many women faced with this task, there are many obstacles to overcome, including the realistic ones of lack of availability of training opportunities, educational programs, and jobs, as well as the emotional conflicts engendered by being a female in a male-dominated society. Men at this time experience a life crisis similarly related to questions of identity, as issues of expectation, success, lifestyle, and death emerge.[8] . . .

The individuation which takes place as a result of one's expansion of self into other spheres of activity is not available to people belonging to families which collusively seek to fend off the nonfamily world. It is to Lyman Wynne[9] that we are indebted for the concept of the pseudomutual family: one that preserves harmony and denies differences; one that confuses "closeness" with fusion; one that confers acceptance to those who accommodate themselves to the family dogma. Pseudomutual families are characterized not only by a shared fear that individuation heralds irreconcilable tensions, but also by a conviction that the nonfamily world is populated by unprecedented and unmentionable dangers which one can survive only by a suffocating attachment to one another at the expense of autonomy. The only security one has is to belong, even if belonging jeopardizes one's integrity of self. These families often shield a troubled child from confronting a difficulty by blaming problems on external factors (such as "bad friends"), thereby conveying the family theme that associations outside the family are hazardous. The ability of the family to support and nurture individuation for all family members at this juncture may be the single most important feature of a healthy family.

## Companionship Versus Isolation

This stage applies to those families with teenage children. Once again the impetus to shifts within the family arises from the developmental currents in the lives of individual family members. The burgeoning sexuality of children and

---

[8] Robert Gould, The Phases of Adult Life: A Study in Developmental Psychology, *American Journal of Psychiatry,* 129:5 (November 1972).

[9] Wynne, Pseudo-Mutuality in the Family Relations, pp. 205–20.

the surfacing of separation themes arouse intense feelings for all family members. These are the precursors of later developments involving major alteration in parent-child relationships, parent-parent relationships, and ultimately in family composition. The major crisis for family members rests on their ability to develop companionship outside and inside the family.

For teen-agers this task is most naturally accomplished throughout the social network of the peer group which often exists in antagonism to the parents, and functions as an opportunity for experimentation with sex roles, modeling, interpersonal skills, and independence from parents. For parents the task is more complex. First, companionship can be sought by revitalizing or renewing the marital relationship. Companionship aspects of a relationship are often pushed aside in favor of parenting responsibilities. A shift from family activities to those shared and enjoyed by the couple often reignites pleasurable experiences from courtship days. Reinvesting in the marital relationship can offset longings and regrets stimulated by the children's budding sexuality as well as fill a place vacated by the children's refuge in the peer group. Sexually interested and active teen-agers expose the sexual vitality of the marriage.

Companionship also refers to the shift in parenting role from arbitrary authority to the negotiation of differences through mutual accommodation. It is incumbent upon the parents to support the separation-individuation process of their children by handling conflict and decision making in areas which involve parental authority in a way which provides structure in the form of discussion. Limit setting, an important aspect of parental functioning, is accomplished through rule setting for the latency-age child, thus corresponding to the child's psychological development which relies on an alliance between conscience and reality. For a family with adolescents, however, the spheres of authority are not so clearly delineated between parent and children and "the children" have cognitive capacities to deal with issues, ideas, and decisions in a way which respects their intellectual abilities.[10] Companionship does not suggest that parents and adolescent children become pals or buddies. What is being suggested, however, is that new kinds of parent-child relationships be established based on a recognition of the child's growing independence.

The alternative to finding friendship with peers and in one's marriage is to suffer from painful isolation. The parents of adolescents who have not renewed an attachment to each other as a "couple" (as well as "parents") are people who, fearing the impending desolation in the course ahead of them, invade their children's lives and unwittingly impeded the natural process of disengagement.

---

[10] Jean Piaget and Barbel Inhelder. *The Psychology of the Child* (New York: Basic Books, 1969).

# Regrouping Versus Binding or Expulsion

This stage applies to those families whose children are leaving home to establish their own lives apart from the parents. A major crisis is encountered by the family in coping with the advancing independence of offspring and the bio-psycho-social pressure for separation. The essential task is to allow for the departure of the children as a natural outgrowth of their growth and maturity. The accomplishment of the task rests primarily on the viability of the marital relationship apart from the parenting function, and secondarily on the resources within the sibling and peer relationships to support separation efforts. In the normal process of disengagement from the family, a strengthening and shifting of alliances in the sibling subsystem as well as in the marital dyad is often observed.

Because the process of separation is so intense and conflictual for all family members, and because the disengagement of the children from the family of origin results in major, and sometimes sudden, modifications in the composition of the family, this phase of family life is usually experienced as particularly difficult. As with all the previous stages, the ability to resolve the tasks specific to the phase depends on the degree of success of preceding developments. The ability to regroup along generational lines and to tolerate the distancing and schisms that accompany separation reflects on the family members' previous struggles to achieve differentiation without sacrificing intimacy. It relates specifically to the family's ability to foster and support individuation (versus pseudomutuality) as well as to the coupling process (intimacy versus idealization) which is influenced by separation experiences in the families of orientation. . . .

As one can see from the preceding discussion, there are several criteria by which to distinguish or assess the normal process of disengagement from that which is a harbinger of family dysfunction. First and foremost, is the quality of the marital relationship. It is a phase in which the viability of the marriage without the primary gratification of children is at issue. If the children are needed to sustain the marital relationship, disengagement will obviously be in jeopardy. Second, an assessment of the vitality and effectiveness of the sibling system is revealing. Sibling support can aid differentiation and individuation. . . .[11]

# Rediscovery Versus Despair

This stage is the first of two post-parental phases. The significance of the tasks is felt when you consider that about 50 percent of a couple's married

---

[11] Stephen Bank and Michael D. Kahn, Sisterhood-Brotherhood Is Powerful: Sibling Subsystems and Family Therapy, *Family Process*, 14:311–37 (September 1975).

life cycle is represented by these last two phases.[12] On the other hand, marital dysfunction is so unsettling that there is a high percentage of divorces which terminate the life cycle of the family during these stages.[13] These statistics suggest that, although a period of disequilibrium of traditional coping patterns in the marriage may follow the departure of the last child, the durability of the marriage depends on the adaptations sought to reestablish a satisfactory marital balance. The adaptations upon which the survival of the integrity of the marriage depend are captured in the notion of rediscovery. Without a revival of interest in one's partner, and a mutual attempt by parents and child to reconnect, the "empty nest" can be corroded with despair. The task of rediscovery, however, refers to intergenerational connectedness as well, with parents and children reinvesting in one another and renegotiating their relationship.

A related task is devoted to the renegotiation of the parent-child interactions to that of adult-adult. This task involves all affected participants, and is an often overlooked and misunderstood aspect of the separation process. Sometimes, in the enthusiasm for autonomy, independence and individuality, distance (physical and psychological) is erroneously equated with separation. True separation of parents and children means that closeness can be achieved without fear of engulfment, and on the same continuum, without the contamination of one's identity. In post-departure phases for children as well as for parents, some self-protective distance may be temporarily necessary in order to insure the investment one makes in being one's own person. Completion of the separation process, however, may entail a rapprochement[14] signifying an attempt to reaffiliate, with one's parents and siblings in a way which corresponds to one's adult status. That this task is impeded by prior role assignments and familiar patterns can be attested to by experience and validated by knowledge of resistance to change in any system. Because the present focus is on health, not pathology, however, resiliency and not rigidity must be located in those families with whom helping professionals come into contact. For all involved, resiliency in the form of returning to former relationships as potent sources of vitality and continuity serves to combat despair. The family that has restabilized through the processes of rediscovery is one that does not feel amputated by the disengagement of children; the rejoining of children and parents in new ways, the addition of daughters- and sons-in-law, and grandchildren contribute to a sense of continuity and wholeness.

[12] This percentage is an estimate based on the developmental scheme of Rodgers and Hill, The Developmental Approach, in *Handbook of Marriage*, ed. Christensen.

[13] These data were extrapolated from *Statistical Abstract of the U.S. 1975*. U.S. Bureau of the Census, 1975, table #47, Marital Status of the Population by Sex and Age, 1974, p. 38.

[14] The concept of rapprochement is borrowed and extracted from Mahler, Pine, and Bergman, *The Psychological Birth*, pp. 90–108.

# Mutual Aid Versus Uselessness

This stage is the second of the postparental phases and the last stage in the life cycle of the family. In the traditional nuclear family the author is describing the period from the parents' retirement to their death. Starting with the couple, she has traced the life of the family to include offspring and now must address the likelihood that the two generation family has become one spanning three generations. The couple, once parents, are now grandparents and the children are now parents. . . .

As this author sees it, the major task is to develop a mutual aid system which would combat generational disconnectedness and feelings of uselessness. The concept of mutual aid between generations also transcends the pitfalls of role reversal which breeds feelings of helplessness and resentment. Diseased mutual aid systems exist in the form of role patterns based on obligations and exploitation. Mutual aid can be achieved without the loss of dignity; roles may be initially redefined based on the exchange of services, and thus provide a structure of respect and cooperation. Subsequent negotiation proceeds to locate the overlap between self-reliance and reliance upon each other. Spheres of competency, acceptance of real and psychological needs, and the willingness to give and to get are dimensions of the negotiation process. . . .

# Implications

An attempt has been made to outline average expectable crises in the life cycle of the family which are characterized by phase-specific tasks. Developmental tasks are oriented to the family as an ecological system. The stages of the family span courtship, childbearing and rearing, and postparental phases. A basic assumption is that while qualitatively different adaptations are required at successive stages, momentum for task management is accrued from crisis to crisis.

Because the emphasis is on normal development, the developmental approach is clearly applicable to programs aimed at primary prevention. The organization and content of family life education programs geared to non-clinical populations and located for direct access at critical points flow from this theoretical conception. Furthermore, criteria for planned short-term treatment can be identified by developmental crises.[15]

Family therapy as a treatment modality targeting change in the total system relies on conceptions which capture the essence of interlocking tasks for all

---

[15] Blanca Rosenberg, Planned Short Term Treatment in Developmental Crisis, SOCIAL CASEWORK, 56:195–204 (April 1975).

family members. In the author's clinical experience, the timing and nature of client requests support an approach which is developmentally based, in that the model specifies therapeutic interventions that take advantage of the progressive forces for health and growth in the family, are task oriented, and work toward achievable client-identified goals. . . .

# Character Development in a Hostile Environment*
## *Leon W. Chestang*

IN RECENT YEARS, social work practice in its efforts to effect changes in individuals or in social systems has been confounded by charges of "irrelevance" and "insensitivity." These charges, made largely by black people in high and low places, stem from the persistent awareness of the failure of traditional concepts about black people to provide a basis for confronting their personal and social problems effectively. Laden with notions that assign to the victims responsibility for their condition, traditional concepts tend to skirt the peculiar nature of the black experience and its impact on character development and transracial interaction. When these notions instruct social work practice, interracial communication is checked, giving rise to rhetoric about racism, on the one hand, and retorts about irrationality, on the other.

If we are to move beyond this stalemate, social work must devise and be guided by concepts that comprehend the nature, structure, and dynamics of the black experience as a social syndrome that develops out of the values, norms, and beliefs projected and acted upon by the larger society and dealt with and integrated by members of the black community.

This paper seeks to outline an operational articulation of the black experience, not only to describe that experience but to define it and to analyze, in greater detail, the characterological response that results from it. A tentative framework, to be elaborated in a later paper, will be presented as a model for understanding the interplay between the black individual and his environment and the adaptation he makes to it.

The term "black experience," which has edged its way into the American vocabulary, serves the language as a multipurpose phrase that encompasses

* © Leon W. Chestang, 1972. Reprinted also by permission of the author. Parts of this article have appeared previously in Leon Chestang, "The Dilemma of Biracial Adoption," *Social Work* 17, no. 3 (May 1972): 100–105, and are reprinted here by permission of the publisher.

events and processes and makes for difficulty in communication and analysis. It connotes "dreams deferred" and frustrated aspirations of a people oppressed by society; it expresses what Lerone Bennett has called "a certain dark joy" celebrating the triumph of a man over a social order that would degrade him; it may also convey the ideas of culture, styles, and social patterns developed in order to cope with the social situation to which the larger society consigns him.

These varied connotations reflect isolated aspects of the black experience; they fail, however, to synthesize and specify the process of this encounter of person and environment. Without such synthesis and specificity, we are unable to communicate about the notion with sufficient conceptual substance and clarity to make it operationally useful.

The concept of the black experience finds its origin in the minority status of black people and the prevailing social attitudes toward them. These attitudes—negative and pervasive—have potent implications for the character development of the black individual.[1]

What is the nature of the black condition? What are its psychological ramifications? Consideration of these questions must become the basis for our analysis of the characterological response of blacks to their circumstances.

# The Black Experience:
# Injustice, Inconsistency, Impotence

Three conditions, socially determined and institutionally supported, characterize the black experience: social injustice, societal inconsistency, and personal impotence. To function in the face of any one of them does cruel and unusual violence to the personality. To function in the face of all three subjects the personality to severe crippling or even destruction. These three crucial conditions, however, confront the black person throughout his life, and they determine his character development.

The failure of many majority-group Americans to appreciate the psychic impact of these conditions can be attributed to the absence of what Professor Roland Warren of Brandeis University calls an "institutionalized thought structure" supporting any but an individual-deficit model for understanding racial problems.[2] Moreover, the failure to perceive the distinction between the natures of injustice and inconsistency, the ambiguity surrounding the role of each of the three elements in shaping the character of black persons, and the absence of substantive concepts related to the elements add further to the

[1] See Kenneth Clark's *Dark Ghetto* (New York: Harper & Row, 1965), p. xxiii, for a discussion of the uniqueness of the black experience.

[2] Roland L. Warren, "The Sociology of Knowledge and the Problems of the Inner Cities," mimeographed (Research Report no. K-3-MH-21,869, Florence Heller Graduate School for Advanced Studies in Social Welfare, Brandeis University, Waltham, Mass., 1970).

problem of operationally articulating the black experience. There is a need for a view that takes environmental effects into account.

Social injustice is the denial of legal rights. Since laws represent group consensus, injustice is a violation of social agreements. When one group acts against another, the consequences reach the individual through the intermediary of his group; hence, the effects are diffuse rather than direct. Social injustice, then, is a group phenomenon resulting in violence to character development of members of groups that are treated differently. Were it not for the import of social injustice on human lives, it would be trite to repeat even briefly the frequently cataloged list of social wrongs against black people. It is sufficient to say that schools remain segregated, courts remain largely unjust, and officers of the law treat blacks unlawfully.

Social inconsistency, on the other hand, is the institutionalized disparity between word and deed. It is social immorality perpetrated on the oppressed group by the manners, morals, and traditions of the majority group. In a person-to-person transaction, it is the individual expression of group rejection, a personalized injustice that attacks the individual without his group supports and that is experienced subjectively by him.

The characterological violence of inconsistency is related to the personal experience of frustration, confusion, bewilderment, and hurt. Each single act of this institutionalized behavior deprives the black person of what feeling of self-worth and esteem he has derived from his attempts to achieve acceptance of self through adhering to the values, norms, and beliefs prescribed by society. Since it expresses the informal and unofficial rejection of blacks, societal inconsistency leaves the individual without recourse to regulatory agencies and courts of law. There are no laws, for example, that say that black skin is unattractive; black art, unaesthetic; black culture, uncivilized; black persons, unworthy of respect. These are expressions of manners, morals, and traditions, the correction of which is beyond the courts.

No discussion of the black experience, however abbreviated, can avoid reference to the impotence felt by blacks as they try to effect changes in their lives. The pervasiveness of this feeling has been recounted by numerous writers of both races over many years.[3] An effect of social inconsistency and injustice, impotence is the feeling of powerlessness to influence the environment. On a personal level, it is the feeling of the father unable to secure employment and therefore unable to support his family. It is experienced by the black man consigned to prison because he is unable to secure justice in the courts and depicted by the black politician who recites platitudes issued from "the man," whereas his father bowed, grinned, and scraped.

Impotence is undergirded by the institutions of society. A recent study con-

---

[3] See, e.g., Alexis de Tocqueville, *Democracy in America*, vol. 1 (New York: Vantage Books, 1954); Clark, "Introduction"; Eldredge Cleaver, *Soul on Ice* (New York: Delta Books, 1968); E. Franklin Frazier, *Black Bourgeoisie* (New York: Collier Books, 1962); and Gunnar Myrdal, *An American Dilemma* (New York: Harper & Bros., 1944).

ducted by the Chicago Urban League found that blacks, who comprise 40 per cent of that city's total population, held less than 3 per cent of the decision-making positions in major institutions, including business, social welfare, and education.[4] Similar testimony to the impotence of blacks can be found in every city, town, and village in the nation.

## Consequences for the Personality

What are the personality consequences of injustice, inconsistency, and impotence when they are intrinsic to the environment in which the personality develops? What is the ransom posted by blacks to assure their survival? What is the thought structure of blacks as it pertains to themselves and their relations with whites?

### Injustice

Erikson has spoken of the importance of a sense of justice in building feelings of confidence in one's self and in one's world.[5] The rampant injustice to which blacks are exposed poses both blatant and insidious threats to their feelings of confidence and personal security. The consequences of injustice and inconsistency, however, are to be distinguished.

Since injustice damages the person through the intermediary of the group, its consequences are diffuse and not direct, affecting the individual but not shaping him. Hence, its effect on character development is not intimate but casual. Put another way, injustice affects the black person's attitude by determining his behavioral inclination, which shifts with the demand of the moment as he seeks to cope with the assault of injustice from his environment. He may develop vital strengths and capacities in the face of injustice; he can seek redress, fight, and hope for change. The popularity of the civil rights movement and the struggle for community control attest to this.

We are accustomed to thinking about the effects of racial injustice on blacks as a group. Historically, we have created movements (abolition, civil rights) in our efforts to deal with this problem. It was the now-famous 1954 Supreme Court decision (*Brown* vs. *Board of Education*) which gave attention to and brought broad public recognition of the personal, individual consequences of racial injustice. This decision came too late to inhibit the development of cynicism among blacks. That the goals of this decision remain unrealized is proof to many black persons that their cynicism is warranted. Injustice and unfairness, whether they characterize a society's or an individual's relations, give rise to relativistic morals and situational ethics. The dis-

---

[4] "Negroes in Policy-making Positions in Chicago: A Study in Black Powerlessness," mimeographed (Chicago: Chicago Urban League, 1968), p. 5.

[5] Erik H. Erikson, *Childhood and Society* (New York: W. W. Norton & Co., 1963), p. 250.

parity between the black superego and that of the culture in general is not synonymous with the concept of superego lacunae. Rather, there is an alternative conscience, one which serves as a buffer against the immoral and conflicting expectation that blacks will be just and fair in the face of injustice and unfairness.

## Inconsistency

Societal inconsistency, with its more subtle implications, is more erosive and destructive to the individual and the national character. It is related to the personal experience of frustration, confusion, and bewilderment. Since societal inconsistency occurs in a transaction between two persons, its assaults are direct: there is no intermediary, no shield between the individuals. Therefore, the declaration or implication of depreciation, worthlessness, and degradation is profoundly painful. Again, inconsistency is personalized injustice attacking the individual without his group supports. The individual alone must experience the peculiar effects of a single act of societal inconsistency, which pierce to the core, affecting feelings and attitudes and tainting self-image and self-esteem.

Because of the uncertainty about his status, the black's expectations vacillate. Dealing with societal inconsistency necessitates the expenditure of an inordinate amount of energy to demonstrate one's equality, competence, and humanity. This leads to a certain superficiality and artificiality in black-white transactions, to a basic dishonesty that dilutes the authenticity of the relationship and perpetuates the distrust and suspicion so commonly observed. Moreover, the emotional contortions required to adapt to this generalized societal inconsistency generate frustration and anger.

In sum, societal inconsistency gives rise to ego-syntonic feelings of distrust, suspicion, and anger. On an individual level, they are internalized with the potential for becoming adaptive modes of protection (against pervasive inconsistency) and enhancing personality integration or maladaptive defenses, leading to rigidity of personality and eventual disintegration.

Our distinction between injustice and inconsistency is pertinent: it should be recalled that such a distinction is precisely what members of minority groups refer to as racism, with their preference for the more direct discrimination in the South to the more hypocritical stance of the North, to their greater comfort, if not ease, in dealing with the bigot than with the liberal.

## Impotence

The fruits of impotence are a loss of autonomy, a diminished sense of self-worth, and low self-esteem. The feelings impotence generates are fear, inadequacy, and insecurity, which transcend all classes of blacks. The familiar helplessness, hopelessness, and despair which Harrington observed among the poor were spawned by the real and ever-present impotence that undermines each black person's life. These feelings, while more behaviorally apparent among poor blacks, are no less real to blacks of middle and upper income levels. This is true if only because our society assigns all black people to a single category, regardless of attainments, income, or any criterion by which it extends recognition. A black person's potential for ego enhancement is always reduced by the need to question whether recognition represents an acknowledgment of his contribution or the expediency of adhering to guidelines and meeting quotas.

Before E. Franklin Frazier wrote *Black Bourgeoisie,* it was generally assumed that among the lives of the few blacks who had achieved middle incomes and who had adopted middle-class attitudes and values, significant progress was being made in alleviating the debilitating effects of impotence. Frazier's myth-shattering treatise destroyed this illusion and earned him the criticism of the white community, which had elected to deny the reality of the black condition. Those blacks who disavowed Frazier's work were, for their part, reacting to the explosion of a valued but fragile defense against a reality that at every turn attested to their basic inability to influence their destinies. Frazier's most telling penetration of this defense comes in his analysis of the role of the Negro press:

> The Negro press reveals the inferiority complex of the black bourgeoisie and provides a documentation of the attempts of this class to seek compensations for its hurt self-esteem and exclusion from American life. Its exaggerations concerning the economic well-being and cultural achievements of Negroes, its emphasis upon Negro "society" all tend to create a world of make-believe into which the black bourgeoisie can escape from its inferiority and inconsequence in American society.[6]

## Tasks of Socialization

Coping under the circumstances imposed by the society has required the development of ego-syntonic modes that are often at variance with personality trends considered normal by the majority group.[7] The familiar process of socialization is the means by which the skills needed for effective functioning in both the black and the white culture are developed. These skills include competence in a behavioral style designed to ward off the negative consequences of social inconsistency, social injustice, and personal impotence. The style is characterized by a duality of response, which has both conscious and

---

[6] Frazier, p. 146.

[7] William H. Grier and Price M. Cobbs, *Black Rage* (New York: Harper & Row, 1968); Horace R. Cayton, "The Psychology of the Negro under Discrimination," in *Being Black,* ed. Robert G. Guthrie (San Francisco: Canfield Press, 1970), pp. 57–61; Leon W. Chestang, "The Issue of Race in Casework Practice," *Social Welfare Forum, 1970,* pp. 121–24.

unconscious aspects and which is internalized as a central aspect of the personality. The black man is not a marginal man but a bicultural man. He does not live on the fringes of the larger society; he lives in both the larger society and the black society. The experience of functioning in two cultures results in dual responses. We emphasize response because we are not suggesting duality of personality, but two ways of coping with the tasks, expectations, and behaviors required by his condition. They converge in the adequately functioning black individual as an integrated whole.

The experience and condition of being black in American society have resulted in the development of two parallel and opposing thought structures—each based on values, norms, and beliefs and supported by attitudes, feelings, and behaviors—that imply feelings of depreciation on the one hand and a push for transcendence on the other.[8] Effective social functioning and environmental reality require that black individuals incorporate both these trends into their personalities—the one to assure competence in dealing with reality, the other as an impetus for transcending reality.

## *The Depreciated Character*

The personality trend manifesting a sense of worthlessness, inadequacy, and impotence may be called the depreciated character. It is suggestive of the stereotypes attributed to blacks—laziness, incompetence, dirtiness, childishness, etc.—and commonly associated with "nigger imagery." The term "depreciated" connotes not intrinsic worthlessness but an extrinsically imposed devaluation. The depreciated character acts in both offensive and defensive modes. As the protagonist, it knows no shame. Its goal must be attained at any cost, save destruction, for it is a compromiser, and the force that impels it, survival, is powerful indeed. Erikson has commented on the consequences of excessive shaming:

> There is a limit to a child's and an adult's endurance in the face of demands to consider himself, his body, and his wishes as evil and dirty, and to his belief in the infallibility of those who pass judgment. He may be apt to turn things around, and to consider as evil only the fact that they exist: his chance will come when they are gone or when he will go from them.[9]

Erikson was talking about pathology, but we are talking about adaptation.

As the antagonist, the depreciated character "stoops to conquer" and

---

[8] Professor Warren uses the term "institutionalized thought structure" to represent an "interlocking, mutually supporting cognitive ordering of the 'poverty problem' which is reflected not only in a knowledge and belief system but in the social structure to address the problem" (p. 1). I have borrowed the phrase "thought structure" and transformed it to refer to the psychological organization of black individuals, i.e., the characterological patterns developed in response to the definitions, expectations, constraints, and affects projected in their interactions with the larger society.

[9] Erikson, p. 235.

thereby aggresses passively. It sacrifices pride in victory for victory is its pride. The colloquialisms "makin' it" and "gettin' over" capture the attitudes that accompany its pursuits. "Makin' it," not simply in the carnal sense, but also in the sense of travail and the struggle to endure—if not, in Faulkner's phrase, to prevail—in the face of societal assault or the "slings and arrows of outrageous fortune," reflects a quality of desperation in its pursuit of ends.

In the carnal sense, "makin' it" implies, in its stronger forms, the "rape" of society. Its objective is to "know" (in the sense of having been intimate with) the environment against its will and later to mock it defensively for its inadequacies—that is, its failure to be aware that it was "being had"—and, hence, for the ridiculousness and pettiness of its pretenses and its constraints against blacks. In a less intense form, "makin' it" suggests seduction of the environment by redefining the relationship between the environment and the self. Examples of this mode are seen in acceptance of negative attributions and impotence by some blacks in order to gain an advantage or to reach a goal. The pertinent and poignant comments of Ralph Ellison's invisible man deserve lengthy quotation here.:

> I was simply a material, a natural resource to be used. . . .
> So I'd accept it, I'd explore it, rine and heart, I'd plunge into it with both feet and they'd gag. . . . I didn't know what my grandfather had meant, but I was ready to test his advice. I'd overcome them with yesses, undermine them with grins, I'd agree them to death and destruction. Yes, and I'd let them swallow me until they vomited or burst wide open. Let them gag on what they refused to see. Let them choke on it. . . . That was a risk they had never dreamt of in their philosophy. Nor did they know that they could discipline themselves to destruction, that saying "yes" could destroy them. Oh, I'd yes them, but wouldn't I yes them! I'd yes them till they puked and rolled in it. All they wanted of me was one belch of affirmation and I'd bellow it out loud. Yes! Yes! Yes! That was all anyone wanted of us, that we should be heard and not seen, and then heard only in one big optimistic chorus of yassuh, yassuh, yassuh! All right, I'd yea, yea and oui, oui, and si, si and see, see them too; and I'd walk around in their guts with hobnailed boots. . . . They wanted a machine? Very well, I'd become a supersensitive confirmer of their misconceptions, and just to hold their confidence I'd try to be right part of the time. Oh, I'd serve them well and I'd make invisibility felt if not seen, and they'd learn that it could be as polluting as a decaying body, or a piece of bad meat in a stew. And if I got hurt? Very well again. Besides, didn't they believe in sacrifice? They were the subtle thinkers—would this be treachery? Did the word apply to an invisible man? Could they recognize choice in that which wasn't seen . . . ?[10]

Similarly, "gettin' over" suggests conquering steep environmental mountains and broad social rivers, both potentially destructive to the individual. Again, the motif is sexual, suggesting qualities of intrusion and deceit.

To "make it" or to "get over," then, is to succeed, but since it requires that

[10] Ralph Ellison, *Invisible Man* (New York: Signet Books, 1953), pp. 439–40.

men relate to each other as things, victory is diminished, bitter-sweet, inauthentic.

## The Transcendent Character

For all its opportunism, the depreciated character trend serves the vital functioning of nurturing, protecting, and sustaining the "transcendent character." Functionally, the depreciated character serves to heighten awareness of the society's projections by exploiting and manipulating the environment when such strategy is prudent. Pragmatism is its axis, survival its goal. In the absolute state of being it is amoral; only in the relative is it corrupt.

The transcendent force, acting from faith, hope, and optimism undergirded by patience, impels men to be. The transcendent character's hopes, based on the assurances promised by the order observed in the universe, stem not from illusion, but from trusting with expectation. In the absence of pejorative evidence, the transcendent character elects to believe in its own and man's essential humanity. Its patience suggests not idle waiting but forbearance; it reflects the strength of character in the qualities of fortitude and self-control under provocation.

The transcendent character stands in opposition to the depreciated character, but in the sense that male and female, positive and negative are opposed: they are opposites seeking unity. It is suggestive of all the aspirations, qualities, and inalienable rights universally possessed by human beings. Idealism is its axis. Being, in the existential sense, is its goal. It is moral and uncorruptible.

The transcendent, like the depreciated, is subject to assaults from the environment, but if the two are united, an awareness emanating from the depreciated shields it, repelling the environment's projections, rejecting them as alien to its goal. Thus the transcendent character is able to approach its objective sustained by the depreciated character's memories of degradation and soothed by its own unfaltering trust.

The basis for unity is established when the depreciated character, having performed the vital functions of reconnoitering reality and assuring survival, vindicates itself. For its part, the transcendent character acknowledges the validity of those functions, and by merging with the depreciated, it is prepared for more efficient pursuit of its goal. Thus constituted, the transcendent differentiates itself from the depreciated by this central trait: the depreciated will sell its soul to survive; the transcendent will give its life to be.

It is beyond the scope of this paper to discuss in detail problems that occur in functioning when fragmentation—with either character motif in isolation—persists. However, a brief statement is relevant here.

Problems that occur for the individuals when the depreciated character is dominant and in isolation from the transcendent are easily recognized. Such individuals, having experienced excessive and repeated environmental assault without relief or support, yield to the environment. Their psychological attitude is characterized by hopelessness and helplessness. Societal inconsistency has produced distortions in their perceptions, its injustice has rendered them cynical, and experiences in impotence have forced them to retreat from battle. Their behavior, when viewed benevolently from the perspective of the larger society, is thought to be "simply the way they are"; when viewed contemptuously, it is thought to be "all you can expect from those people." They sustain the stereotypes. Blacks whose deficiency resides in a loss of contact with the depreciated, having themselves identified with the aggressor environment, see them as "typical niggers, what we are trying to get away from."

Individuals whose transcendent character is fragmented from the depreciated are commonly referred to by their transcendent-deficient counterparts as "white-niggers" or, in today's vernacular, "oreos." Their problem lies in their failure to maintain contact with their past. They seek being, but it is a quasi-being. Their fallacy was the belief that transcendence could be achieved by casting off a part of themselves. Their failure is assured when they identify completely with the environment at the expense of psychological unity.

Encounters between blacks and whites attest to the existence of the duality described here and to its centrality to blacks as a barometer of the level of understanding possessed by numbers of other groups. The situation will also remind some blacks of encounters with members of their own race who are deficient in one or the other character trend:

> Two friends, one black and the other white, are discussing the racial problem. The white person, attempting honest communication with his friend, will demonstrate his familiarity with and understanding of the depreciated character of the black experience. The black person will resent his friend's assertions. The white person is then perplexed; he was trying to show his understanding of the evils that society perpetrates upon blacks, as well as his awareness of the deficiencies in experience and the effects upon the black person of these events and attitudes. The black person, in turn, feels degraded and misunderstood. When his white friend, aware of his past "error," attempts later to relate his awareness of the black person's drive to be, of his essential equality and humanity, he is even more confused to find his friend rejecting these approaches and recounting how difficult it is to bear the evils of society. The black person now feels patronized and misunderstood. In both instances, the failure in communication resulted from the white person's failure to relate to the totality of his black friend's experience, to the totality of his depreciated and his transcendent characters.

# Conclusion

This paper has attempted to outline briefly a conceptual model for understanding black character structure as it develops in response to society's assaults. Admittedly hypothetical, it leaves some significant questions unanswered and still others, of equal importance, unexplored. A more exhaustive treatment is in preparation.

Although this discussion has been focused on the black experience, the commonality of human experience precludes an interpretation pertaining exclusively to blacks. The concepts presented may be applicable to other groups that must negotiate a hostile environment. The author has limited his attention to blacks, however, for reasons of experiential knowledge and research focus. Further exploration and refinements of these ideas should provide additional understanding of the dimensions that may be appropriate for generalization to other groups. This statement should be considered a rough chart by which we may find our way into the unexplored territory of black character development.

# Language, Culture, and Ethnicity in Developing Self-concept*
*Marta Sotomayor*

. . . THIS ARTICLE traces some philosophical and theoretical underpinnings of language, culture, and ethnicity in an effort to highlight the role these three elements play in human behavior. The role of language and culture in the mental processes, which determine the perception and definition of reality, is particularly emphasized. The intrapsychic and intrapersonal aspects of language presented here were selected on the basis of their applicability to the understanding of the colonized experience, specifically in terms of the majority-minority of color groups relationship in this country.

It has become customary to define the colonized experience in terms of the concrete conditions faced by these groups such as poor housing, poor nutrition and health, high unemployment rates, and school drop-out rates; economic and political forces external to the colonized group are seen as the causes for such conditions. A more popular approach, although not more accurate, utilized to describe the colonized experience, ascribes the problems encountered by the colonized to the innate, or internal, characteristics of the group in question, such as asserting that the maintenance of different cultural and linguistic factors create the major barriers to entry into the mainstream of American life. Rather than dichotomize by following the above mentioned

* Reprinted by permission of the author and the publisher, Family Service Association of America, from *Social Casework*, 58:4 (April 1977), 195–203.

schema, this article assumes that the external and internal factors play a significant part in the development and selection of coping patterns of colonizerd groups.[1]

# The Self-concept

The self-concept consists of sets of images organized and internalized according to group norms, communicated and reinforced over time through a variety of daily experiences and symbolic interactions. The individual discovers who he is as the self-image becomes affected by relationships, expectations, failures and successes in experiences with others. It is generally agreed upon that a positive self-perception is crucial to functioning adequately and comfortable in one's surroundings. Self-worth and self-identity in the context of the environment become inseparable. Ortega y Gasset, the Spanish writer and scholar, succinctly describes the relationship between the self and the transactional field when he states, *"Soy yo y mis circunstancias"* ("I am I and my circumstances.)[2]

Psychologically, the self-concept is the most vulnerable component in the transactions between minorities of color and majority populations. Negative stereotypes, for example, aim at the perpetuation of the depreciation and undermining of the self-worth. The self-concept can suffer irreparable damage if the socialization process prevents significant and familiar symbols to be present and reinforced at various levels of experience. The sense of belonging, crucial in the development of the self-concept, becomes blurred if one's language, cultural patterns, and ethnic experiences are not reflected and supported, but rather given a negative connotation in the environment.

# Language

. . . Language assumes a series of unique functions, among which providing the medium of expression for a particular society and becoming a reproducing instrument for ideas are the most readily understood, and its function in defining reality, the most complex one. The "real world" is reflected and recorded in linguistic symbols, or inventories of experiences, that eventually form the language habits of a group. The parameters, grammars, and repertoire vocabularies of such linguistic systems assume a crucial role in the

---

[1] See Robert Blauner, Internal Colonialism and Ghetto Revolt. *Social Problems*, 16:393–402 (Spring 1960). Blauner expands the notion of colonialism to internal colonialism whereby the following elements appear: (1) forced, involuntary entry, (2) the "Colonizing power carries out a policy which constrains, transforms, or destroys indigenous values, orientations, and ways of life," (3) "an experience of being managed and manipulated by outsiders," and (4) racism.

[2] Ortega y Gasset, *Esquema dela Crisis* (Madrid: Revista de Occidente, 1942), p. 8.

definition of reality, for they not only determine what we observe, but also analyze, evaluate, and synthesize external experiences and by doing so, language becomes a guide to social reality. It is quite possible for two linguistic groups to arrive at two different perceptions and a different organization of reality as the implicit expectations of our own language, with its self-contained system of meanings, are projected into the field of experience as a conceptual system that foresees all possible experience. Thus, "Meanings are not so much discovered in experience as imposed upon it, because the tyrannical hold that linguistic form has upon our orientation, of the world." [3] Furthermore, "the phenomena of a language are to its own speakers largely of a background character and so are outside the critical consciousness and control of the speaker." [4]

The Whorf-Sapir hypothesis also supports the culture-forming role of language, in that it postulates that the language with which a given community speaks, thinks, and organizes a set of experiences, shapes the immediate world and influences the way a community grasps reality. [5] Language, socially conditioned, is a symbolic system of experiences in the actual context of behavior, therefore never divorced from action. . . .

## Social Functions of Language

The functions of language in the process of socialization are comprehensive. These processes, among others, include language as a communication vehicle between the members of the group, language usage in the establishment of a relationship and solidarity, language as a declaration of the place and psychological distance held by its various members, and language use in the coordination of the activities of the group. Uriel Weinreich suggests that "language shifts," typical of the bilingual individual, can be understood in "terms of the functions of the language in contact situations as well as in the domain of the language in use since a mother tongue (speaker) may switch to a new language in certain circumstances and functions, but not in others." [6] . . .

"Language was ever the fellow of empire and accompanied it everywhere so that together they waxed strong and flourished and together they later fell." [7] The role of language imposition, which followed conquest, was to

[3] Edward Sapir, Conceptual Categories in Primitive Languages, *Science* 71 (1930), p. 578.

[4] Benjamin L. Whorf, *Collected Papers on Metalinguistics* (Washington, D.C.: U.S., Department of State, Foreign Service Institute, 1952), p. 4.

[5] Edward Sapir, *Culture, Language and Personality* (Berkeley: University of California Press, 1964), p. 141.

[6] Uriel Weinreich, *Languages in Contact* (The Hague: Mouton, 1953), p. 107.

[7] Nebrija, an early Spanish grammarian quoted in Carmelo Delgado Cintron, Colonial Language Status Achievement; Mexico, Peru and the U.S., unpublished manuscript, 1973.

exclude from access to power those who had not had sufficient contact with the conquerors. Additionally, language discrimination was oftentimes related to religious conflict, because the religion of an individual could often be identified by the language he spoke.

Certain governmental actions with respect to language are attributed to the function of control of language. For example, it was significant that the Treaty of Guadalupe Hidalgo guaranteed the Mexican residents of the Southwest the preservation of their mother tongue, but it was equally significant that this guarantee was quickly removed from the books and the English language was established as an official designation. This official designation was, and continues to be, applied through the courts, the legislature, the school system, and the various economic groups. The end result is exclusion of certain linguistic groups, that is Spanish-speaking, from the normal processes of a free society.

For the bilinguals of color, such as Chicanos, language has played a most significant social and survival function; for example, language has had a definite role in providing the group feeling of solidarity to deal with the oppressive majority culture. It is a common language that often coordinates the activities of the in-group, by making individuals conscious of the relationships between members and outsiders, thus promoting a sense of belonging. Language, in exercising one of its primary functions, has enabled this group to retain its distinctive characteristics over many generations, despite the rejection and hostility experienced from the majority community, permitting a sense of symbolic continuity and thus survival.[8]

The domains of a language can be a useful conception to understand the bilingual experience. For many bilingual populations, such as Chicanos, Spanish has been the language of the family, but the forbidden language of schools. The psychological effects and the implications of language acceptance or rejection, in the high drop-out rate of Chicanos from schools, are yet to be recognized by the schools and other human service delivery systems. . . .

## Culture

The definitions of culture that are more popular among human service providers are time-bound and value-laden, and reflect the majority-minority rela-

---

[8] Nearly two-thirds of the Chicano population report that they spoke Spanish in their home when they were children. The majority continue to speak Spanish in the home. The percentages still using Spanish in the home is highest among older persons (55 years and over) and teenagers, particularly at the critical ages of 14–19. By and large, children and teenagers still speak Spanish with their peers and parents, although the majority were born in this country. U.S. Bureau of the Census. 1970 *Census of Population, Subject Reports: National Origin and Language*, PC(2)-IV, p. 58.

tionship which often undermines the self-worth of the ethnic minority in consideration. For example, the cultural deterministic, and by extension of culture of poverty approach, is entrenched in the position that perceives the individual and the group in a pathological position, and at best, at a disadvantaged position that values the "blaming the victim" strategy. The cultural relativist perspective assumes a monolithic, traditional culture (for example the Mexican traditional culture) that often utilizes a continuum of degrees of acculturation into the majority culture;[9] the linear direction inevitably leads to assimilation and loss of culture specificity and language. The marginal man paradigm places the subject in a precarious position of marginality, belonging neither to one group nor another, resulting in a state of anomie, alienation, and confusion.[10] The narrow parameters of these various conceptualizations negate the self-realization of the ethnic group in question, but serve the purpose of the inherent demeaning processes typical of oppression, conquest, and colonization. People in a constant state of vulnerability and potential conflict with a dominant group develop appropriate coping mechanisms and behaviors for survival and do achieve a degree of cultural, linguistic, and psychological equilibrium. . . . Fernando Peñalosa has defined Chicano culture to include the "sum total of techniques a people has in coping with and adapting to its physical and social environment that have been developed as a special cultural response to its minority status."[11]

# Ethnicity

Ethnicity can be defined in terms of cultural and linguistic uniqueness that allows for membership in a particular group. There is, however, a more fundamental attribute that allows ethnicity to play a crucial role in the aspects of the identity of the self and the group. Ethnicity refers to the character, the spirit of a culture, or more succinctly, to the cultural ethos. Specifically, ethnicity is related to the underlying sentiment among individuals based on a sense of commonality of origin, beliefs, values, customs, or practices of a specific group of peoples. While it is primarily based on ancestry, there is also a sense of having been an independent group sometime in the past from which the present population is descended. What is important is the mythic meaning

[9] For illustrations of this point see Miles V. Zintz, *Education Across Cultures,* 2d ed. (Dubuque, Iowa: Kendall/Hunt Publishing Co., 1960); Lyle Saunders, *Cultural Differences and Medical Care: The Case of the Spanish Speaking People of the Southwest* (New York: Russell Sage Foundation, 1954); and Nick C. Vaca, The Mexican American in the Social Science, 1912–1970, pt. 1, *El Grito,* 3:3–24, (Summer 1970).

[10] See primarily the works of Robert E. Parks on the marginal man theory.

[11] Fernando Peñalosa, Toward an Operational Definition of the Mexican American, *Aztlan: Chicano Journal of the Social Sciences and the Arts,* 1:6 (Spring 1970).

of the unit of descent that can provide a sense of historical continuity for the development of the self-concept and social identity. Although ethnicity is relevant to behavior it is not deterministic of behavior per se. . . .

For example, the historical sense of separateness and isolation from the majority ethnic community, experienced by Chicanos, has precipitated and perpetuated constant struggle and conflict. The permeability of group boundaries, typical of cultural pluralism that allows for mutual cultural borrowing, cultural interpenetration, accommodation, and social mobility is lost in this type of relationship, but in turn, futher solidifies respective group boundaries thus increasing and perpetuating the sense of separateness and isolation.

On the other hand, for Chicanos, ethnic, cultural, and linguistic identification and affirmation have acted to ease internal stress felt as a result of outside political, economic, and social degradation. The rebirth of ethnic pride, with emphasis on *Indiginismo* (Indian ancestry) that has evoked old images and cultural symbols is an example of strategies used to allow renewed pride, and a sense of self-acceptance, so crucial to the sense of self-worth.

For a bilingual minority of color groups such as Chicanos, a separate language has constituted the most important single characteristic of a separate ethnic identity. Language has gained importance more as a symbol that provides cohesion and unity to the group rather than to its actual use or proficiency of all members of the group. A subjective symbolic use of different aspects of various cultural roots have added to the differentiation from other ethnic groups but as well has provided a sense of belonging. The participation in nationalistic movements such as the Chicano and black movements, popular since the 1960s, is an attempt to link with the past in order to feel a sense of continuity of belonging so essential in the process of reordering statuses.

While culture deals with symbolic generalities and universals, ethnicity deals with the individual's mode and depth of identification as well as providing a sense of belonging to a reference group. In American society the institutionalization of ethnics of color separateness (expressed in many concrete realities such as poor housing, lack of social mobility, and lack of access to necessary resources) has become the main vehicle for social stratification practices that create tension and conflict, typical of a system of racism.

In any interpersonal contact, but more so in any therapeutic relationship, it is most important to understand and acknowledge the intrapsychic meanings of ethnic sense of belonging and identification, the meaning and utilization of cultural symbols and the understanding of the various functions of language for the individual and the group. The consideration of these three components become crucial in the amelioration of the effects of racism on the individual and group but also in the process of dealing with social stratification whereby the three components of culture, language, and ethnicity are utilized to attack the self-worth of individuals and groups.

# Psychopathology Seen Against the Background of Normal Development*

*Anna Freud*

W HEN CHOOSING a title for this lecture, I hesitated between two possible ones, the one above which I selected finally and another, termed 'Links between Adult Psychiatry and Child Psychiatry'. Although in wording they seem different enough from each other, I hope to show in what follows where the two subject-matters meet.

## The First Object of Psychoanalytic Investigation

To begin with, a look at the history of psychoanalysis.

The first object of psychoanalytic study was the neuroses. This was not due to any predilection of the originator of the new discipline but to the exigencies of his private practice. Nevertheless, the nature of the matter under investigation proved decisive for many characteristics of the evolving theory. Since the neurotic manifestations emanate from the depth, psychoanalysis embarked on the study of the unconscious. Since they are due to conflict between internal forces, it became a dynamic psychology. Since conflicts are solved according to the relative strength of these forces, the economic viewpoint was developed. Since the roots of every neurosis reach back to the early years of the individual's life, the genetic aspects of the theory played a paramount part. Incidentally, this last mentioned point represented also the first opportunity for bringing infantile psychopathology within the orbit of the therapist of adults.

## The Widening Scope of Psychoanalysis

All this, of course, was only the beginning of the story. It did not take long for psychoanalytic exploration to widen its scope, with therapeutic efforts always in its wake. Its path went from the neuroses to the psychoses; from sexual inhibitions to the perversions; from character disorders to the delin-

* Delivered as the 1975 Maudsley Lecture to the Royal College of Psychiatrists. Published in *The British Journal of Psychiatry*, 29 (1976): 401–406. Reprinted by permission of the author and publisher. © Copyright 1976 Royal College of Psychiatrists.

quencies; from adult psychopathology to adolescence; from adolescence to childhood. As early as 1925, Freud can be read to say: 'Children have become the main subject of psychoanalytic research and have thus replaced in importance the neurotic on whom its studies began.'* Although at the date when it was written this statement may have been prophetic rather than factual, child analysts today will be glad to claim it as the motivation and justification governing their work. In fact, it is less the increasing dissection of the adult's personality and more the analysis of children and the analytic observation of young children that are responsible for two important results: first, for a chart of normal personality development, and second, for pointing out the relevance of its details for the assessment of adult psychopathology.

## Reconstruction Versus the Direct View

As regards the developmental chart, it would be unjustified, of course, for child analysts to claim major credit for its setting up. It was reconstruction from the analyses of adults, and not the direct analytic study of the child, which established the fact of an infantile sex life, with its sequence of libidinal phases; the existence of the Oedipus and castration complexes; the developmental line of anxiety from separation anxiety, fear of object loss, fear of loss of love and castration anxiety to guilt; the division of the personality into id, ego and superego, each inner agency pursuing its own purposes; the advance from primary process to secondary process functioning; the gradual building up of a defence organization; and so forth. What was left to the child analysts was to make amendments wherever the direct contact with infantile functioning did not seem to confirm what had been glimpsed from the distance. There was the point, for instance, that in reconstruction no early developmental stage appears ever in its true colours, since it is invariably overlaid by characteristics which belong to later phases, even where regression in the transference has taken place; or that what appears in later analysis as a one time traumatic event may in reality have been a series of such happenings, telescoped into one in the individual's memory. But besides and beyond these minor corrections there emerged one major assumption, namely that reconstruction from adult analysis is inevitably weighted towards pathology, to the neglect of normal developmental happenings; that it is always the conflictual and unsolved which does not come to rest in the individual's mind, welcomes the opportunity to reestablish itself in the transference situation, and thus captures and monopolizes the analyst's attention. In contrast, the satisfied impulses, the successful adaptive conflict solutions disappear from view by entering the fabric of the personality. They are outgrown, with little incentive left for revival at a later date.

---

* In the Foreword to August Aichhorn's *Wayward Youth*.

Thus, while the analysts of adults become expert in tracing psychopathology back to its early roots, only the child analysts appear to hold the key to the description of the course taken by normal infantile development.

# The Child Analyst's Picture of Normal Development

**The "Abnormal" Aspects of the Norm.**    It may be necessary to stress that normal growth and development, as seen by the child analyst, does not appear as a smooth, unbroken line leading from early infancy via the latency period, preadolescence and adolescence to a healthy adulthood. On the contrary, every single developmental phase, as well as every single forward move, can be shown to contain disturbing concomitants which are characteristic for them.

To take the first year of the child as an example. Belonging to this period of life are the diffuse distress states to which all infants are subject. We regard them as the normal forerunners of later anxiety and as such inevitable. Nevertheless, unlike the affect of anxiety, which is psychologically caused and felt, they can be aroused and experienced on the physical as well as on the mental side, and they demand from the mothering person the utmost in care, comfort and attention to the infant's body and mind. They are thus an instructive illustration of the double regime which governs functioning at this early date when the individual's body and mind interact freely: physical excitation such as pain, discomfort, etc., can be discharged via mental upset, while mental excitation such as frustration, impatience or longing can find its outlet via the body, in disturbances of sleep, food intake or elimination. This double source and experience of distress is disturbing to infant and environment alike. But nothing can prevent it from existing until developmental growth itself alters the situation by creating new mental pathways for the discharge of mental stimuli via the maturing ego (thought, speech, etc.).

On the other hand, these new developments, beneficial as they are in one respect, contain their own hazards in another. Evidence for this is found in the sleeping disorders which appear frequently at the border between the first and second year and cause distress to both infant and mother, usually in the form of inability to fall asleep. As analytic observers we ascribe these upsets to the child's reluctance to renounce recently acquired functions such as his emotional hold on the object world and his ego interest in his surroundings. Both militate against the body's need for rest and interfere with the return to narcissistic withdrawal and to renunciation of ego interests, which are the preconditions for sleep.

There are other examples of difficulties which arise from developmental progress. Motor skills advance in leaps and bounds at the toddler stage but are not equaled on the ego side by similar advances in motor control and or appreciation of danger from heights, water, fire, traffic and so on. Consequently the young child becomes accident-prone, a developmental occurrence which makes formidable demands on environmental protection. Simultaneously the increasing complexities in the infant-mother relationship affect food intake. Since food and mother are still equated for the child, every hostile or ambivalent feeling towards her leads to food refusal, and further to the endless and developmentally harmful battles at meal times. Other 'normal' developmental manifestations are the upsetting temper tantrums which before the acquisition of speech are the growing toddler's typical mode of discharge for anger, frustration, rage, etc., with major involvement of the motor apparatus. There is also the excessive and distressing clinging which accompanies the fading out of the biological unity between child and mother, i.e., the upsets within the individuation separation phase as described by Margaret Mahler.

The upsetting upheavals of the next phases are even more familiar in their characteristics. Obviously, the child in the anal-sadistic stage cannot be expected to deal with his instinctual tendencies on the one hand and environmental demands on the other without experiencing conflict, extreme distress and emotional turmoil, resulting in occasional regression with accompanying loss of acquired functions or with sullenness, rebelliousness, obstinacy; or else with phase-bound obsessional characteristics such as insistence on sameness and routine and anxiety outbreaks whenever the self-imposed order and regularity are infringed by the environment.

As regards the phallic/oedipal development, we do not expect the child to cope with the accompanying emotional complications and anxiety increases without pathological byproducts. Long before the advent of child analysis it was one of the accepted psychoanalytic tenets that this is the time when the whole turmoil of anxieties, affects and conflicts is organized into the clinical picture of one of the infantile neuroses. Whatever the fate of the latter, whether transitory or permanent in its impact on the developmental progress, it represents the individual child's crowning achievement in his struggle for simultaneous adaptation to the inner and outer world.

**Relevance of This Developmental Chart for Adult Psychopathology.** There are several items in this chart of normal growth which therapists in the adult field may find relevant for their assessments of symptomatology.

The psychosomatic illnesses in adult life, for instance, may be easier to understand when seen as the survival of the psychosomatic regime which is legitimate in infancy. Although the communicating doors between body and mind are never completely closed for anybody, as evidenced for example by headaches after mental upset, or by the physical accompaniments of anxiety, they are more open in some individuals than in others, and this becomes responsible for the mental contributions to such severe afflictions as migraine, asthma, high blood pressure, gastric ulcers, etc.

Also, the pattern of some sleep disorders in adult life has something in common with those described for early childhood. Even though the sleepless adult's depressed or agitated state of mind differs in its content from the child's, what is identical in both instances is the painful struggle between a tired body longing for relaxation and a restless mind unable to rid itself of excitation.

There are some other characteristics of normal child development which serve as patterns for later pathology. One is the forerunner of object-love proper, i.e., the infant's tie to the mother which is based on the satisfactions received from her. Certain disturbances of adult love-life, such as shallowness, promiscuity, etc., are better understood when seen as residues of this early stage of which too large a proportion has remained.

Similarly, the anxiety attacks of hysterical patients can be likened to the panic states of young children before the ego has acquired the mental mechanisms which defend against anxiety and reduce debilitating panic to the adaptive form of signal anxiety.

# The Prerequisites of Normal Development

When describing the chain of events leading from the infant's complete immaturity to the comparative maturity of the mental apparatus at latency age, the fact was stressed that progress—even if normal—is interspersed with conflicts, emotional upsets and distress states; that it is also interrupted by regressive setbacks and halted by temporary arrests; in short that it is neither smooth, nor unimpeded, nor effortless, nor painless. What has not been emphasized sufficiently so far is the experience that even this chequered advance is extremely vulnerable and open to a variety of threats. We see the developmental process as dependent on the interaction of three factors: endowment; environment; rate of structuralization and maturation within the personality. Provided that all three are within the expectable norm the child will arrive at every crucial developmental phase with the right inner equipment and meet the right environmental response, i.e., have a chance of normal growth. If, however, any of the three deviates too far from the average, the developmental result will become distorted in one direction or another.

Examples of Normal Developmental Advance. That developmental achievements are not due to single factors but are multiple-based is illustrated by certain instances in the child analytic literature. René Spitz, in *The First Year of Life,* traced in detail the origins of the infant's first tie to the mother and pinpointed three prerequisites for it: an adequate advance in the infant's libidinal capacity; normal maturation of the perceptive apparatus which enables interest to be turned from the infant's own body to the environment; the mother's sufficient libidinal involvement with the child, expressed in comforting and satisfying handling. Provided that in the life of a normally born infant these various influences are at work and interact, the first step on the ladder towards mature object love will be taken.

Similarly, Margaret Mahler, when exploring the complexities of the separation/individuation phase in the second year of life, makes us realize how many elements are needed for its successful negotiation: sufficient maturation of motility to enable the child to run away from the mother as well as toward her; in the ego, the unfolding of inquisitiveness and curiosity; on the libidinal side some advance towards object constancy and 'basic trust' to allow for temporary separation without distress; on the mother's side, her readiness to release the child from the close union with her own person, to accept and even enjoy his status as a separate person.

Similar combinations of forces can be seen at work behind any further developmental advance, whether from one of the major libidinal stages to the next, or from one small step to the next on one of the long 'developmental lines'* leading towards mature object love; to companionship with peers; to independent body management; to the ability to work; etc.. Even to achieve reliable sphincter control, beyond mere reflex action, depends on a multiplicity of intact factors, such as: maturation of the muscular apparatus; adequately timed and exerted maternal intervention; the child's compliance due to his object tie; the process of identification with the environmental demand leading finally to the individual's own, so-called sphincter morality.

**Examples of Developmental Deviations.** None of these positive developmental results can be expected if either endowment, or environmental conditions or the rate of personality structuration depart too far from the average.

As regards *endowment* first, our child-analytic studies of the blind, deaf and mentally deficient show that any single defect in the individual's inborn equipment suffices to throw the entire developmental course into disarray, far beyond the sphere where the damage itself is located. With the blind, attachment to the object world is delayed; once formed, it remains longer on primitive levels; motility matures later than normal and remains restricted; prolonged dependence interferes with the unfolding of aggression; verbalization suffers from a gap between words and their meaning; superego formation bears the mark of the initial differences in object relationship. With the deaf, the absence of acoustic elements affects the thought processes and the important step from primary to secondary process functioning. The mentally deficient miss out, not only as regards understanding of the environment, i.e., in-

---

* Anna Freud: 'The concept of developmental lines', *Psychoanalytic Study of the Child.* Vol XVIII, 1963.

tellectually, but vitally as regards the ego's defence organization, i.e., impulse and anxiety control.

Concerning, secondly, abnormal *environmental conditions,* their harmful impact on development was always recognized, even without the added evidence from child analyses. What needs emphasis, though, is the fact that there is no one-to-one, invariable relationship between the fact of parents being absent, neglecting, indifferent, punitive, cruel, seductive, overprotective, delinquent, psychotic, etc., and the resultant distortions in the personality picture of the child. Cruel treatment can produce either an aggressive, violent or a timid, crushed passive being; parental seduction can result either in complete ability to control sexual impulses ever after or in severe inhibition and abhorrence of any form of sexuality. In short, the developmental outcome is determined, not by the environmental interference *per se,* but by its interaction with the inborn and acquired resources of the child.

The third important influence on personality building, namely the *rate of internal structuralization,* has received comparatively little attention so far. The facts are that individual children differ considerably with regard to the timing when their ego emerges from the undifferentiated ego/id matrix, or when their superego emerges from the ego; when they advance from the primary process to secondary process functioning; when the borders between unconscious and conscious are set up; when signal anxiety replaces panic attacks; when defences change from the primitive to the sophisticated. Normally, this sequence of achievements matches the sequence of internal instinctual and external parental pressures and enables the child to find more or less adaptive solutions for the arising conflicts. However, when ripening of the mental apparatus is either delayed or accelerated, there is no such match between conflict situations and the appropriate means for coping with them.

Child analytic studies yield various examples of the developmental confusion which ensues.

For instance, during the boy's phallic stage, there occurs an age-adequate conflict between active and passive strivings. This is dealt with by repression of passivity, compensating masculine phantasies, heroic daydreams and so forth, provided that the mental structure is up to date. But in cases where the latter is delayed in its unfolding no such sophisticated mechanisms are available, and their place is taken by muscular action (as in the infantile tantrums) resulting in aggressive outbursts, self-injury, and atypical or borderline manifestations.

In the girl's age-adequate emotional move towards the oedipal father there occurs the need to free herself by whatever means from her ties to the mother. This healthy advance is interfered with where the superego preconsciously upholds moral demands which forbid rivalry, hostility, death wishes, etc.

Precocious understanding of the difference between the sexes may involve a little girl in the throes of penis envy before there are adequate means at her disposal for defence against massive unpleasure.

## Relevance for Adult Psychopathology

Knowledge of these developmental complications is relevant for the psycho-therapist of adults so far as they affect the therapeutic possibilities.

Analytic and analytically oriented therapy is directed toward the patient's ego and attempts to widen its controlling powers. It is a radical therapy so far as it deals with damage which the ego has inflicted on itself by excessive repression which limits its sphere of influence; by unsuitable other defence mechanisms which distort it; by regressions which lower its functioning; by arrests which prevent further unfolding. However, with regard to harm inflicted on the ego by endowment, environment and vagaries of internal maturation, i.e., by influences beyond its control, it is no more than an alleviating therapy, dealing not with causes but with their aftereffects and working towards better integration of the latter. A distinction of this kind may help to explain some of the therapeutic limitations which patients as well as analysts deplore.

## Summary

It has been the object of this paper to pursue some links between mental health and illness, immaturity and maturity. It was its further aim to convince psychiatrists of adults that there is much to be learned from child psychiatry and to convince child psychiatrists that infantile psychopathology should be assessed against the background knowledge of normal development.

# Basic Principles and Practices of Behavior Therapy of Neuroses*

*Joseph Wolpe*

BEHAVIOR THERAPY or conditioning therapy was formally introduced to American psychiatry 14 years ago (21). The term *behavior therapy* was first used by Skinner and Lindsley (16) and subsequently popularized by Eysenck (3, 4, 5). It denotes the use of experimentally established principles of learning for the purpose of changing unadaptive behavior. Behavior ther-

---

* From *American Journal of Psychiatry*, vol. 125, pp. 1242–1247, 1969. © Copyright 1969, The American Psychiatric Association. Reprinted by permission.

apy is thus an applied science, in every way parallel to other modern technologies and in particular to the technologies constituting medical therapeutics. Therapeutic possibilities emerge when we know the lawful relations of organismic processes. In the psychotherapeutic field the lawful relations that are most often relevant are those established by experimental psychology.

Persistent maladaptive (unadaptive) *anxiety* responses are the nucleus of most cases that are labeled "neurotic," and therefore much of the effort of behavior therapists has been directed toward overcoming them. "Anxiety" is defined as a particular organism's characteristic pattern of autonomic responses to noxious stimulation (22). Anxiety is conditionable; conditioned anxiety responses are in fact far more common than unconditioned ones. Anxiety responses are called maladaptive when they have been conditioned to stimulus situations that do not pose any objective threat. It is implicit in this formulation that neurotic responses are not ways of avoiding stress; they *are* stress responses.

Behavior therapy of human neuroses had its origin in observations of animal neuroses (20, 22). An animal placed in a confined environment and subjected to either strong ambivalent stimulation or noxious stimulation acquires a persistent habit of responding with marked anxiety to the environment concerned, and with weaker anxiety to other environments according to their similarity to the original one.

The most effective way of procuring unlearning is to feed the animal repeatedly while it is in an environment which evokes *weak* anxiety. The effect of this is to diminish progressively—ultimately to zero—the strength of the anxiety response to the particular stimulus. Increasingly "strong" stimulus situations are successively dealt with in the same way, so that finally the animal shows no anxiety to any of the situations to which anxiety has been conditioned. The basis of this gradual elimination of the anxiety response habit is considered to be an example(22), at a more complex level, of the phenomenon of *reciprocal inhibition* described by Sherrington (15). Each time the animal eats, the anxiety response is to some extent inhibited, and each occasion of inhibition diminishes the anxiety habit. Apparently the evocation of a response that inhibits anxiety weakens the bond between the anxiety-evoking stimulus and the anxiety response.

Human neuroses resemble those of the animal in all basic respects (26). Even though not all human neuroses present themselves as anxiety states, anxiety underlies most of them. For example, the patient with a stutter is not as a rule aware of the stimuli that produce the anxiety that is usually a necessary condition for stuttering. Indeed, he may not realize that he has any special anxiety in the situations in which he stutters, even though he can contrast them with other situations in which his speech is normal. Investigation generally shows that there is an emotional undercurrent, the intensity of which determines the degree of stutter.

The same is true of a host of other conditions in which the main presenting complaint is not anxiety—obsessions and compulsions, psychosomatic states, character neuroses, impotence, frigidity, homosexuality, and many others. The key to recovery is generally the deconditioning of anxiety. This is why a detailed behavioral analysis is an essential prerequisite to effective behavior therapy. The behavior therapist makes a practice of obtaining a detailed life history and a full account of the present life situation and administers various questionnaires designed to reveal stimulus situations conditioned to neurotic anxiety responses (27).

# Methods of Behavior Therapy

Many of the methods of behavior therapy derive from the therapeutic experiments with animals described above. They exemplify reciprocal inhibition (counterconditioning). Other methods derive from positive reinforcement, experimental extinction, and various other experimental paradigms (27).

## *Counterconditioning by the Emotions of Life Situations*

Where neurotic responses are conditioned to situations involving direct interpersonal relations, the essence of reciprocal inhibition therapy has been to inhibit anxiety by the instigation of patterns of motor behavior that express anger (or whatever other feelings may be relevant). The repeated exercise of these patterns in the proper context weakens the anxiety response habit.

For example, a patient may need to be taught how to stand up for his rights when somebody gets in front of him in a line. The teaching will be either by direct instruction and exhortation or by actual rehearsal of the desired new behavior in the consulting room. A recent patient had become so intent on acceding to his wife's requirements that his own needs were completely subordinated. He repeatedly went into states of depression that he attempted to relieve by heavy drinking. He was shown how to assert himself appropriately—for example, by refusing to allow whatever he might be doing, such as reading the newspaper, to be interrupted by his wife's demands for conversation. By dint of a program along these lines he achieved reasonable control of this interpersonal situation and stopped having depressions.

Sexual responses are used to overcome anxiety responses to sexual situations that are the basis of impotence or premature ejaculation. The essence of treatment is to control sexual approaches so that anxiety is never permitted to be strong. Inhibition of anxiety can then be obtained by the parasympathetic dominated sexual arousal and the anxiety response habit can consequently be weakened.

Tactics vary from case to case but always involve the cooperation of the spouse. The therapist must determine at what point in the patient's sexual approach there are the first indications of anxiety. He then instructs the patient to take love-making no farther than this point, having obtained the acquiescence of the spouse. In the course of a few amorous sessions, anxiety usually ceases to be felt at the permitted point, and then the patient is permitted to go on to the next stage. Usually several preliminary stages need to be passed before coitus is attempted; and it, too, requires a succession of graded steps.

## Systematic Desensitization Based on Relaxation

Neurotic anxiety responses conditioned to stimuli other than those arising from direct interpersonal relations (e.g., phobic responses) do not lend themselves to behavioral treatment in the life situation of the patient. In such cases, reciprocal inhibition of anxiety must be obtained by methods that do not involve motor activity on the part of the patient toward the fearful object. In the earliest deliberate example of therapy on this basis, the anxiety of phobic children was inhibited by eating (8), very much as in the case of the experimental neuroses described above.

Deep muscle relaxation (7) has had the widest use in this way, mainly in a method known as *systematic desensitization* (21, 22, 27). In brief, desensitization consists of repeatedly presenting to the imagination of the deeply relaxed patient the feeblest item in a list of anxiety-evoking stimuli until no more anxiety is evoked either as reported by the patient or as psychophysiologically recorded. The next higher item in the list is then presented—again until the anxiety response to it is extinct. The procedure is continued until eventually even the strongest of the anxiety-evoking stimuli fails to evoke any stir of anxiety in the patient. It is almost always found in those subjects in whom imagined scenes have initially evoked anxiety that a situation that no longer evokes it in imagination also ceases to evoke it when encountered in reality.

## Variants of Systematic Desensitization

Other inhibitors of anxiety may also be employed therapeutically in a systematic way. In some patients the therapeutic situation itself evokes anxiety-inhibiting emotions. These are very likely the usual basis of whatever therapeutic changes result from therapies other than behavior therapy. They must also account for part of the success of behavior therapy (22). But they can in addition be deliberately used in behavior therapy—usually in what is called desensitization in vivo, in which real stimuli take the place of imaginary ones, and the anxiety may be inhibited by these emotions.

For example, a patient who has a fear of humiliation at making mistakes is made to perform minor errors and then progressively more serious ones in the presence of the therapist—in each instance until all feelings of anxiety disappear. To the extent that this succeeds it is probably due to the anxiety being inhibited by competing interpersonal emotions. Tests of this assumption are now being planned.

Use has also been made of the observation that anxiety can be inhibited by cutaneous stimulation by nonaversive electric shocks. The therapist arranges for these to break in on the anxiety evoked by images from hierarchies by getting the patient to signal when the image is clear, and then delivering two or three shocks in quick succession. This apparently weakens anxiety on the basis of *external inhibition* (13).

Another method of procuring inhibition of anxiety depends on presenting a neutral stimulus just before the cessation of a strong continuous current to the forearm. The effect of this is to condition cessation (inhibition) of anxiety to the neutral stimulus (21, 22, 27). The conditioned stimulus can then be systematically used to inhibit neurotic anxieties in the life situation.

## Avoidance Conditioning

Avoidance (aversive) conditioning is an application of the reciprocal inhibition principle to overcoming responses other than anxiety. A noxious stimulus—usually a strongly unpleasant electric shock—is administered to the patient in an appropriate time relation to the stimulus to which avoidance conditioning is desired. It has been effectively used to overcome obsessional thinking, compulsive acts, fetishes, and homosexuality. It is, however, not always successful for reasons that are often quite clear.

Homosexuality, for example, is often based on neurotic interpersonal anxiety, which should be treated by deconditioning the anxiety (17). But when aversion is used for homosexuality, the most promising technique consists of administering a very unpleasant shock as long as a homosexual figure is projected onto a screen and terminating the shock at the appearance of an attractive female (6). Further details and other applications have been discussed in my book, *The Practice of Behavior Therapy* (27).

## Experimental Extinction

Experimental extinction is the breaking of a habit through repeated performance of the relevant response without reinforcement (reward). The therapeutic use of extinction was formally introduced by Dunlap (2) under the name "negative practice."

The method did not then achieve much popularity, but recently there has been renewed interest in it, mainly in the context of the treatment of tics. The patient is instructed to perform deliberately the undesired movement very many times, and in the course of some weeks it may be found that spontaneous evocations of the tic have decreased, perhaps markedly (14, 18, 28). Kondas (10) has reported that many resistent tics can be cured if the negative practice is accompanied by a strong aversive stimulus that is terminated each time the practice stops (cf. anxiety-relief conditioning described above).

## Positive Reinforcement

The deconditioning of unadaptive autonomic response habits is the central approach to behavior therapy of neuroses, but it is often also necessary to condition new motor habits. This often occurs as a result of the same measures that break down the anxiety habit. For example, in assertive training (see above), simultaneously with the counterconditioning of anxiety, motor (operant) habits of assertion are conditioned. They are reinforced by the rewarding consequences of the assertive act, such as gaining control of a situation.

But operant conditioning can also be effected on its own. Anorexia nervosa has been successfully treated by arranging for eating to be followed by social rewards such as the use of a radio or company and withholding the rewards when the patient does not eat (1). The same principles have been effective in a variety of cases. For example, Williams (19) has described how tantrum behavior is completely under the control of the adult attention it elicits.

# Results of Behavior Therapy

The distinctive feature of behavior therapy is that the therapist selects his targets and plans his strategy in respect to each of them. He can sometimes—for example, in desensitization of classical phobias—even calculate the quantitative relations between number of therapeutic operations and amount of change (24).

## Statistical Data

R. P. Knight's (9) five criteria—symptomatic improvement, increased productiveness, improved adjustment and pleasure in sex, improved interpersonal relationships, and ability to handle ordinary pschological conflicts and reasonable reality stresses—have been generally adopted by behavior therapists. By these criteria, the results of behavior therapy of neurosis have been quite notably good. For example, in several series of neurotic patients totaling 618 cases, about 87 per cent either apparently recovered or were much improved (27). In the last published series of my own (22), the median number of sessions for 88 cases was 23. Follow-up studies in this as in other series have shown neither the spontaneous relapses nor the symptom substitutions that psychoanalytically oriented colleagues have prognosticated.

Compare these results with the 60 per cent "cured" or "greatly improved" among the *completely analyzed* patients in the study of the Central Fact-Finding Committee of the American Psychoanalytic Association. While the psychoanalyzed patients were treated an average of four times a week for three to four years, i.e., about 700 sessions, and the average course of behavior therapy covered about 30 sessions (22), it is fair to point out that the comparison is not a controlled one.

A controlled comparative study is currently under way in the department of psychiatry at Temple University. Meanwhile, laboratory controlled studies have been distinctly favorable to behavior therapy. Paul (12) found that "dynamically" trained therapists did significantly better with systematic desensitization than with their own insight-giving techniques in treating fears of public speaking. Moore (11) reported a controlled study of cases of asthma in a London clinic. One schedule she employed was relaxation training; the second was support and suggestion under relaxation; and the third was systematic desensitization. In terms of both immediate and delayed effects, desensitization was clearly superior to the other two methods. In terms of maximum peak flow of respired air the difference was significant at .001.

One popular fallacy about behavior therapy is that it is useful in its place— for simple cases but not for complex ones. In 1964 I made a reexamination (25) of some previously published results dividing 86 cases into simple and complex. A neurosis was regarded as complex if it had one or more of the following features: (a) a wide range of stimuli conditioned to neurotic responses (not just one), (b) reactions to which the conditioned stimuli are obscure and determined with difficulty, (c) reactions that include unadaptiveness in important areas of general behavior (character neuroses), (d) obsessional neuroses, and (e) reactions that include pervasive anxiety.

Of the 86 cases reviewed, 65 were complex in one or more of the senses defined. Fifty-eight of these (89 per cent) were judged either apparently cured or much improved. This percentage was exactly the same as that obtained for the whole group. However, the median number of sessions for the complex group was 29 and the mean 54.8 in contrast to a median for the noncomplex remainder of 11.5 and a mean of 14.9. Thus, while complex cases responded to behavior therapy as often as simple ones did, therapy took longer.

# How Fundamental Are the Effects of Behavior Therapy?

It is sometimes contended that behavior therapy is superficial and possibly even dangerous because it does not attempt to deal with the "basic dynamic conflict" that is alleged to underlie neuroses. In particular, it is prognosticated that recovery will be followed by relapse or symptom substitution sooner or later. A survey (23) of the results of follow-up studies on neuroses successfully treated by a variety of methods not concerned with the dynamic conflict revealed only a 1.6 per cent incidence of relapse or symptom substitution. Skilled behavior therapists hardly ever encounter relapse or symptom substitution.

The weight of the evidence is thus that neuroses are indeed nothing but habits—the results of conditioning—often very complex conditioning. The implication is that a therapy based on principles of conditioning is fundamental therapy.

## REFERENCE NOTES

1. Bachrach, A. J., Erwin, W. J., and Mohr, J. P.: "The Control of Eating Behavior in an Anorexia by Operant Conditioning Techniques," in Ullman, L., and Krasner, L., eds.: Case Studies in Behavior Modification. New York: Holt, Rinehart and Winston, 1965.
2. Dunlap, K.: Habits, Their Making and Unmaking. New York: Liveright Publishing, 1932.
3. Eysenck, H. J.: Learning Theory and Behaviour Therapy, J. Ment. Sci. 105:61–75, 1959.
4. Eysenck, H. J.: Behavior Therapy and the Neuroses. New York: Pergamon Press, 1960.
5. Eysenck, H. J.: Experiments in Behavior Therapy. Oxford: Pergamon Press, 1965.
6. Feldman, M. P., and MacColloch, M. J.: The Application of Anticipatory Avoidance Learning to the Treatment of Homosexuality. I. Theory, Technique, and Preliminary Results, Behav. Res. Ther. 2:165–183, 1965.
7. Jacobson, E.: Progressive Relaxation. Chicago, Ill.; University of Chicago Press, 1938.
8. Jones, M. D.: A Laboratory Study of Fear. The Case of Peter, J. Genet. Psychol. 31:308–315, 1924.
9. Knight, R. P.: Evaluation of the Results of Psychoanalytic Therapy, Amer. J. Psychiat. 98:434–446, 1941.
10. Kondas, O.: The Possibilities of Applying Experimentally Created Procedures when Eliminating Tics, Studia Psychol. 7:221–229, 1965.
11. Moore, N.: Behaviour Therapy in Bronchial Asthma: A Controlled Study, J. Psychosom. Res. 9:257–276, 1965.
12. Paul, G. L.: Insight vs. Desensitization in Psychotherapy; An Experiment in Anxiety Reduction. Stanford, Calif.: Stanford University Press, 1966.
13. Pavlov, I. V.: Conditioned Reflexes, trans. by G. V. Anrep. New York: Liveright Publishing, 1927.
14. Rafi, A. A.: Learning Theory and the Treatment of Tics, J. Psychosom. Res. 6:71–76, 1962.
15. Sherrington, C. S.: Integration Action of the Nervous System. New Haven, Conn.: Yale University Press, 1906.
16. Skinner, B. F., and Lindsley, O.: Studies in Behavior Therapy, Status Reports II and III. Naval Research Contract N5 ori-7662, 1954.
17. Stevenson, I., and Wolpe, J.: Recovery from Sexual Deviations Through Overcoming Nonsexual Neurotic Responses, Amer. J. Psychiat. 116:737–742, 1960.
18. Walton, D.: Experimental Psychology and the Treatment of a Tiquer, J. Child Psychol. Psychiat. 2:148–155, 1961.
19. Williams, C. D.: The Elimination of Tantrum Behavior by Extinction Procedures, J. Abnorm. Soc. Psychol. 59:269, 1959.
20. Wolpe, J.: Experimental Neuroses as Learned Behavior, Brit. J. Psychol. 43:243–268, 1952.
21. Wolpe, J.: Reciprocal Inhibition as the Main Basis of Psychotherapeutic Effects, Arch. Neurol. Psychiat. 72:205–226, 1954.

22. Wolpe, J.: Psychotherapy by Reciprocal Inhibition. Stanford, Calif.: Stanford University Press, 1958.

23. Wolpe, J.: The Prognosis in Unpsychoanalyzed Recovery from Neurosis, Amer. J. Psychiat. 118:35–39, 1961.

24. Wolpe, J.: Quantitative Relationships in the Systematic Desensitization of Phobias, Amer. J. Psychiat. 119:1062–1068, 1963.

25. Wolpe, J.: Behavior Therapy in Complex Neurotic States, Brit. J. Psychiat. 110:28–34, 1964.

26. Wolpe, J.: "Parallels Between Animal and Human Neuroses," in Hoch, P., and Zubin, J., eds.: Comparative Psychopathology. New York: Grune & Stratton, 1967.

27. Wolpe, J.: The Practice of Behavior Therapy. New York: Pergamon Press, 1968.

28. Yates, A. J.: The Application of Learning Theory to the Treatment of Tics, J. Abnorm. Soc. Psychol. 56:175–182, 1958.

# Counseling and Counselor Education: A Developmental Approach*

*Lawrence Kohlberg*

COUNSELING AS PRACTICE and counselor education training programs are now at a cross-roads in the search for an effective educational model. The overall goal of counseling—the promotion of human growth and development—as well as the overall goal of counselor education programs is well recognized but still difficult to achieve. The model for counseling practice and counselor education training is often unclear, usually because of ambiguous or contradictory assumptions concerning the nature of its developmental objectives. Without a relatively systematic developmental framework, counseling and counselor education programs may become a potpourri of approaches, a set of eclectic activities mostly oriented toward secondary prevention. In this article I am advocating another model for counseling and counselor education oriented toward the newer findings of developmental psychology. In this model the role of counseling as educational intervention is the stimulation of cognitive and emotional development in all children through a variety of didactic and experiential learning activities. The role of counselor education is then developed through training experiences to prepare counselors for such new activities.

* From *Counselor Education and Supervision*, 1975, 250–256. © 1975 by American Personnel and Guidance Association. Reprinted with permission of the publisher and the author.

The teaching, which involves discussion, readings, and experiences, demands that special expertise be used by counselors and counselor education programs (i.e., skill in areas such as the development of values and cognition, interpersonal relationships, and understanding human behavior; affecting the stimulation of natural trends of ego development of the child, the teen, and the young adult). This article discusses moral and psychological education, two areas in which counseling and counselor education programs can help schools and colleges contribute to the development of all children rather than those who come labeled as problems.

The secondary prevention model of psychological services in schools and colleges for offering diagnosis and treatment of disturbed or problem children is inadequate for our purposes, partly because it is impossible in terms of time and costs but more basically because it is unsound from a research standpoint. In recent reviews of longitudinal studies of the adult outcome of childhood disturbances, Kohlberg, La Crosse, and Ricks (1971, p. 1271) concluded as follows:

> The continuity hypothesis, that emotionally disturbed children will become mentally ill adults, has received only mild research support. The extent to which a childhood predisposition to mental illness influences appearance of problems in adult life is not a clearly predictive factor. There are exceptions, some forms of schizophrenia are predictable in terms of a biological disposition detectable in childhood caused by a compound of hereditary and perinatal brain-damage factors, and criminality and poor moral character (sociopathy and character disorders) are predictable from a compound of family environment factors and from overt antisocial behavior in childhood. On emotional disturbance grounds alone, however, prediction is currently impossible. Childhood emotional disturbance symptoms are not now useful predictors. Neither is adult emotional disturbance or neurosis currently predictable from childhood symptoms. Put bluntly, there is no research evidence available indicating that clinical analysis of the child's emotional status or dynamics leads to any more effective prognosis of adult mental health or illness than could be achieved by the man on the street who believes psychosis is hereditary and that criminality is the result of bad homes and neighborhoods in the common sense meaning of that concept.

The evidence favoring the effectiveness of counseling and psychotherapy for adolescence and young adults is also problematic. Bergin's (1972, p. 228) reanalysis of the Eysenck conclusion yielded a carefully couched suggestion that counseling and psychotherapy with such populations, "has modestly positive effects." Thus there is only weak evidence supporting the individual counseling/psychotherapy approach. Certainly the most sophisticated test of the effectiveness of counseling at the college level yielded unmistakably negative results (Volsky et al. 1965).

Furthermore, current diagnosis is unsuccessful if it is seen as a means for selecting into publicly supported therapy or special classes just those students most likely to have adult mental health problems if left untreated. A heavy concentration of secondary prevention services on a few pupils through procedures of diagnosis and treatment rests on currently unjustified assumptions.

Clearly, a more community mental health or "re-ed" approach to mental health services should be adopted. Such approaches would be oriented toward creating an environment in which the coping and ego development of all children and teenagers are facilitated, rather than segregating pupils into a special therapeutic environment radically different from that in which most of their coping efforts are directed. Although children and teenagers with problems receive more attention than those without manifest problems and children with severe problems may receive more than those with less severe problems, the actual distinctions are fluid since diagnostic decisions about long-term placement in segregated treatment groups are not required. In such an approach, improvement of a person's mental health in a school or college setting involves maturation of the ego as it relates to school learning, the formation of social values, and relationships to other children and the teacher.

# Ego Development

In another article (Kohlberg 1972), I have elaborated the meaning of ego development as a focus of psychoeducational intervention. Viewing the concepts of developmental psychology as the central guide to education, I summarize various schemata for defining ego stages, including my own and those of Peck and Havighurst (1960), Loevinger (1970), and Harvey, Hunt, and Schroeder (1961). Overlapping ego and moral stages are defined as follows:

Stage 0. Presocial, amoral, and egocentric.
Stage 1. Impulsive, fearful, absolutistically oriented to obedience and punishment-avoidance.
Stage 2. Expedient, opportunistic, instrumentally oriented to hedonistic rewards and exchange.
Stage 3. Conformist; oriented to interpersonal relations and approval for its own sake.
Stage 4. Conscientious; duty, rules, and authority-oriented.
Stage 5. Autonomous; rationally oriented to social contract and social welfare.
Stage 6. Integrated or principled; oriented to universal human ethical principles.

Regardless of differences in the conceptions of ego stages, a good correlation can be found between measures of ego maturity based on the different schemes. As Loevinger (1970) has pointed out, all measures of ego development will correlate, regardless of theory. Furthermore, all stages of ego development correlate with stages of moral development, because all ego development schemes are based on certain large regularities in the age development of self and social attitudes, regardless of the theoretically proposed causes of these developments.

Not only is *ego development* acquiring an empirically sound common meaning, but aspects of ego maturity, such as moral development, have a long-range predictive relationship to life-outcome in which pathology measures fail. These predictive relationships are implied by theories of ego development which assume that humans move through a series of stages and developmental tasks or crises and that retardation or conflict at one stage colors task solutions at later stages.

With regard to the school years, the longitudinal findings suggest four "critical period" focuses of mental health intervention. The first is a concern for cognitive orientation, interest, style, and attention in the years 6 to 9. The second is a special concern for peer relations (and relations to adults) in the years 9 to 12, when conventional moral character development appears to become crystallized. The third is in later adolescence with all the discovery of the self, the inner life, and abstract values. A fourth area of developmental concern occurs during late adolescence as the actual transition to adulthood takes place. In all these areas, there is a continuum between the efforts of humane education to stimulate ego development and more therapeutic efforts to achieve the same end. Ego development represents a common focus of three divergent approaches: the psychoanalytic approach, the human potential or humanistic psychology approach, and the cognitive-developmental approach. Recent interventive innovations for ego development have stemmed mainly from the last two approaches.

# The Cognitive-Developmental Approach

John Dewey is the originator of the cognitive-developmental approach in education, and Jean Piaget is its most distinguished living representative. Like the human potential approach, the focus of the cognitive-developmental approach to education is on personal development and experience. Differences between the two approaches are suggested by the fact that the humanistic sometimes goes under the name of "affective education" and sometimes assumes not only that emotional aspects of education are important components of the educational process but that spontaneous emotional experience and expression are educational goods or aims in themselves. A more complete rationale for suggesting a cognitive-developmental objective for education can be found in Kohlberg and Mayer (1972).

The cognitive-developmental approach stresses the cognitive reorganization of experience through successively higher levels, including emotional experience, as the basic aim of education. It thus focuses on stimulating discussions of psychological and moral issues, which, although open and nondidactic, still emphasize reasoning and personally accepted standards of rationality. In like manner, the emphasis of humanistic psychology on the here and now and the uniquely individual in defining educational aims contrasts the cognitive-developmental view, which emphasizes the unique and immediate as elements or processes in the universal progressions of human development. This has led cognitive-developmental interventionists to address their interventions by "hard" criteria of change in stage, as measured for exactness by Loevinger's (1970) ego measure and by our own moral stage measure (Kohlberg & Turiel 1971) which is based on reasoning about a set of hypothetical moral dilemmas.

Two complementary interventions based on this point of view are the programs of deliberate psychological education reported on in this issue by Aubrey at the elementary level; by Sprinthall, Mosher, Erickson, and Rustad and Rogers, at the secondary school level; and by Parker, Widick, and Knefelkamp at the college level. Our own programs of moral education represent a second approach. The rationale, objectives, and methods of a psychologically oriented approach to moral education are presented elsewhere by Kohlberg and Turiel (1971).

# Moral Education

Moral education has a forbidding sound to school and college counselors, although teachers do constantly act as moral educators. They must tell pupils what to do, make evaluations of pupil behavior, and direct interpersonal relationships in the classroom. Teachers have literally oriented their moralizing to what we have called the bag of virtues—honesty, altruism, self-control, responsibility, and respect for authority. Typically, psychologists involved in sensitivity, affective, or psychological education are also oriented to a bag of virtues that involves moral assumptions and include such things as spontaneity, creativity, openness, and trust. The inadequacy of such humanistic virtues for counseling practice and counselor education programmatic constructs has been elaborated on by Sprinthall (1972).

The cognitive-developmental approach to moral education does not teach virtues but rather, by open discussions of moral dilemmas, stimulates movement to the next stage of reasoning. Its basic principles involve the use of open or difficult moral conflicts and dialogues with students at adjacent stages. Our experiments have indicated that students understand not more than one stage above their own, and they reject reasoning at all stages below their own. Accordingly, a stage 3 student may induce movement in a stage 2 student by dialogue, whereas the reverse does not occur. Classroom discussions based on these principles have been conducted with junior and senior high school middle- and lower-class blacks and whites (Blatt & Kohlberg in press). Most students moved up from one-third to one-half a stage in moral judgment and retained their favored position one year later, compared to controls.

This approach has also been tried with imprisoned youthful offenders yielding similar results (Hickey in press). In such cases, moral discussions often become discussions of personal problems, and moral education and psychological counseling tend to merge. Furthermore, moral education becomes a part of institutional change, the effort to create a more just moral atmosphere in the school or institution.

## Psychological Education

If moral education sounds forbidding so does psychological education as a basis for educational programs in schools and colleges. Schools and colleges themselves are de facto psychological educators. Mosher and Sprinthall (1970, p. 914) have noted the negative psychological impact of the so-called hidden agenda or implicit curriculum of schooling:

> The school, at minimum, reinforces the child in the psychological advantages or disadvantages with which he enters it, and may often confirm negative expectations for large groups of children (especially poor black and white children). In short, teachers are, whether they realize it or not, psychological educators . . . they often teach children that adults have power, that children are impotent, irresponsible, and should be intellectually and personally dependent. A value for achievement, competitiveness . . . and a belief that self-worth is tied to academic achievement are further examples. This is a harsh critique of schooling, but our evidence suggests that this hidden curriculum is typically more inimical and psychologically crippling than it is positive and developmental. That these effects of schooling are largely unrecognized (and presumably unintended) is hardly an extenuating factor.

In conjunction with the programs of psychological education discussed in this issue the developmental approach suggests a new role for the counselor. Instead of waiting for referrals for diagnosis and diluted therapy, the school counselor and the college counselor will work to revise the narrow curriculum and modify the negative learning atmosphere in class. The focus of intervention is the classroom group, and the vehicle of development, the relationships of students to one another.

Changing the role of the counselor to that of a psychological and moral educator carries obvious implications for counselor education programs. The democratic educator must be guided by a set of psychological and ethical principles which he or she openly presents to the students, inviting criticism as well as understanding. The concept of education for development is based on the idea of stimulating natural human growth. Dewey's view on the importance of this objective is supported by Piagetian psychological findings, which indicate that all children, not only well-born college students, are philosophers intent on organizing their lives into universal patterns of meaning. Thus our educational system in general and counselor education programs specifically face a choice of whether to capitalize on the educational opportunity that each child and teenager presents to us. If counselor education training programs can incorporate a cognitive-developmental conception as a basis for planned intervention, then knowledgeable practitioners and programs may flow into the mainstream of schools and colleges.

## REFERENCES

AUBREY, R. F. Issues and Criteria in Developing Psychological Education Programs for Elementary Schools. *Counselor Education and Supervision,* 1975, 14:4, 268–276.

BERGIN, A. E. The evaluation of therapeutic outcomes. In A. E. Bergin and S. L. Garfield (Eds.), *Handbook of psychotherapy and behavior change.* New York: Wiley, 1971.

BLATT, M., & KOHLBERG, L. The effects of classroom discussion on the development of moral judgment. In L. Kohlberg and E. Turiel (Eds.), *Recent research in moral development.* New York: Holt, Rinehart & Winston, in press.

ERICKSON, V. L. Deliberate Psychological Education for Women: From Iphigenia to Antigone. *Counselor Education and Supervision,* 1975, 14:4, 297–309.

HARVEY, O. J.; HUNT, D.; & Schroeder, D. *Conceptual systems.* New York: Wiley, 1961.

HICKEY, J. Stimulation of moral reasoning in delinquents. In L. Kohlberg and E. Turiel (Eds.), *Recent research in moral development.* New York: Holt, Rinehart & Winston, in press.

KOHLBERG, L. A concept of developmental psychology as the central guide to education: Examples from cognitive, moral, and psychological education. In M. C. Reynolds (Ed.), *Psychology and the Process of Schooling in the next decade: Alternative conceptions.* Washington, D.C.: U.S. Office of Education, 1972. Pp. 1–56.

KOHLBERG, L.; LACROSSE, R.; & RICKS, D. The predictability of adult mental health from childhood behavior. In B. Wolman (Ed.), *Handbook of child psychopathology.* New York: McGraw-Hill, 1972. Pp. 1217–1284.

KOHLBERG, L., & MAYER. R. Development as the aim of education. *Harvard Educational Review,* 1972, 42(4), 449–496.

KOHLBERG, L., & TURIEL, E. Moral development and moral education. In G. Lesser (Ed.), *Psychology and educational practice.* Chicago: Scott Foresman, 1971. Pp. 410–465.

LOEVINGER, J. *Measuring ego development.* San Francisco: Jossey-Bass, 1970.

MOSHER, R. L. and SPRINTHALL, N. A. Deliberate Psychological Education. *Counseling Psychologist,* 1971, 2(4), 3–82.

MOSHER, R. L., & SPRINTHALL, N. A. Psychological education in secondary schools. *American Psychologist,* 1970, 25(10), 911–924.

PECK, R. F., & HAVIGHURST, R. J. *The psychology of character development.* New York: Wiley, 1960.

RUSTAD, K. and ROGERS, C. Promoting Psychological Growth in a High School Class. *Counselor Education and Supervision,* 1975, 14:4, 277–285.

SPRINTHALL, N. A. Fantasy and Reality in Research: How to Move Beyond the Unpopular Paradox. *Counselor Education and Supervision,* 1975, 310–322.

SPRINTHALL, N. A. Humanism: A new bag of virtues for guidance? *Personnel and Guidance Journal,* 1972, 50(5), 349–356.

VOLSKY, T.; MAGOON, T. M.; NORMAN, W. T.; & HOYT, D. P. *The outcomes of counseling and psychotherapy.* Minneapolis, Minn.: University of Minnesota Press, 1965.

WIDICK, C.; KNEFELKAMP, l. l.; and PARKER, C. A. The Counselor as Developmental Instructor. *Counselor Education and Supervision,* 1975, 14:4, 286–296.

# Rational-Emotive Therapy and Its Application to Emotional Education*

*Albert Ellis*

RATIONAL-EMOTIVE THERAPY (RET) is a form of psychotherapy which I originated in the 1950's, after practicing classical psychoanalysis, psychoanalytically-oriented psychotherapy, and various other methods. Although I did as well with these techniques as any of the other practitioners in the field, I began to see with greater clarity that they all were largely ineffective. For no matter how much insight I was able to help my clients achieve, and how emotionally they abreacted and were utterly sure that they now understood themselves deeply and were no longer going to continue their maladaptive behavior, they largely kept making New Years' resolutions to change rather than significantly modifying their actions and actually giving up their phobias, obsessions, compulsions, shirking, psychosomatic reactions, depressions, hostilities, and other complaints. Not that they didn't usually improve to some degree; for they did. But I could see, and they usually could see too, that their improvements were moderate rather than profound, and that they still had a long way to go, after the completion of "successful" therapy, to overcome their basic self-defeating patterns.

I consequently kept trying new techniques and finally realized that unless they included a great deal of activity, both on my part and that of the client, they were not likely to be very effective. For the average client is terribly anxious about doing some act poorly—such as failing in his social, sexual, academic, or vocational affairs—and to quell his anxiety he inhibits himself and stays away from the "dangers" that he has largely created by *defining* these activities as perilous. And no matter how much he tries to convince himself that it is not really too risky or too "awful" to fail, he underlyingly continues to believe that it *is* horrible until he has actually forced himself to do the so-called dangerous act many, many times. Thus, no matter how often he tells himself that seeing black cats is *not* unlucky, he will still tend to superstitiously believe that it is until and unless he forces himself to approach black cats and pats a sufficient number of them on the head.

As I learned this therapeutic truth, I gave up more and more of my psychoanalytic passivity, began to actively disabuse my clients of the irrational beliefs, values, and philosophies that underlay and caused their emotionally disordered behavior, and gave them concrete activity-oriented homework as-

* Reprinted by permission of the author.

signments that would help them contradict in practice what I was helping them disbelieve in theory. The better this new therapeutic method worked, the more I thought about *why* it was working and constructed a theory of rational-emotive therapy to back up my procedure.

According to this theory, when an individual becomes emotionally disturbed or suffers from neurotic or psychotic symptoms, which are referred to as point C (emotional Consequences), these are not caused by the Activating events (point A) which occur in his life. These point A events, whether they occur in his infancy or his later years, may cause him all kinds of annoyances, frustrations, and rejections which may *contribute* to his point C Consequences (such as feelings of anxiety, depression, and hostility); but A does not really *cause* C. Instead, the individual has, at point B, a Belief System which more directly and concretely causes his point C dysfunctional Consequences or reactions.

The person's Belief System consists, first, of a set of empirically-based, rational Beliefs (rB's). Thus, when he fails at a job or is rejected by a love partner, at point A, he rationally tells himself, "How unfortunate it is for me to fail! I would much rather succeed or be accepted." If he sticks rigorously to these rational Beliefs, he feels appropriately sorry, regretful, frustrated, and irritated, at point C; but he does *not* feel emotionally upset or destroyed. In order to make himself feel inappropriately or neurotically, he adds the non-empirically-based, irrational Beliefs: "How *awful* it is that I failed! I *must* succeed. I am a *thoroughly worthless person* for failing or for being rejected." *Then* he feels anxious, depressed, or worthless.

In the course of rational-emotive therapy I and my associates show the individual how to vigorously challenge, question, and Dispute (at point D) his irrational Beliefs. Thus, he is shown how to ask himself: "*Why* is it awful that I failed? Who says I *must* succeed? Where is the evidence that I am a worthless person if I fail or get rejected?" and if he persistently and forcefully Disputes his insane ideas, he begins to acquire a new cognitive Effect (at point E): namely, the beliefs that (1) "It is not awful but only quite inconvenient if I fail." (2) "I don't *have* to succeed; though there are several good reasons why I'd *like* to do so." (3) "I am never a worthless person for failing or being rejected; I am merely a person who has done poorly, for the present, in these particular areas, but who probably can do better later, or can succeed at other things, or can enjoy myself in some ways even if I never succeed at anything very important."

While I am teaching the individual, cognitively and didactically, to see clearly that he *creates* his emotional Consequences by his own values, philosophies, and Beliefs, and that he can understand exactly what these Beliefs are and logically parse them and insist that, to be valid, they'd better be backed by empirical data, I also use powerful evocative-emotive and behaviorist-activity methods of getting him to Dispute his irrational, magic-based attitudes. Thus, on the emotive side, I dramatically confront him, engage in role-playing and behavioral rehearsal exercises, get him to encounter me and members of his therapy or marathon group, present my own authentic feelings to him, show him that I have unconditional positive regard for him no matter how crummy his behavior may be, and otherwise try to stir him up. Behavioristically, I get him to assume roles that contradict and undermine his irrational Beliefs, give him activity homework assignments that force him to counterattack them in practice, give him practice in assertion training, teach him self reinforcement principles, and otherwise use behavior therapy methods with him. All told, I employ a concerted and comprehensive cognitive-behavior-emotive attack on his self-sabotaging value system, and help him change it to a more enjoying, self-actualizing set of values (Ellis, 1962, 1969a, 1971a, 1971b; Ellis and Harper, 1970, 1971).

Although I designed and have kept modifying rational-emotive procedures mainly for the treatment of individuals with emotional disturbances, and although there is now a good deal of experimental and clinical evidence that it works quite well in those areas (Burkhead, 1970; di Loreto, 1971; Maultsby, 1969a, 1969b; Maes and Heimann, 1970; Sharma, 1970; Trexler, 1971), it has also been found that its theory and practice are so simple and direct that they can be used with "normal" populations. Thus, it has been used effectively with organizational executives (Ellis and Blum, 1967; Ellis, 1971b); and it has been found valuable when used with children in regular classroom situations (Daly, 1971; Ellis, 1969c, 1972a, 1972b; Glicken, 1968; Lafferty, Dennerll, and Rettich, 1964; Wolfe, 1970).

How, exactly, can rational-emotive psychology be employed in regular schooling? To answer this question, The Institute for Advanced Study in Rational Psychotherapy has started a private school for normal children, The Living School, which it operates in New York City. The purpose of the school is to teach children the regular elements of academic education; but at the same time to provide them prophylactically with emotional education. And by emotional education we do not merely mean encouraging the children to enjoy themselves, to make freer choices of what they do in school, or to express themselves affectively. These are all worthy goals; but at most they are merely aids to, rather than the essence of, what we conceive of as emotional training.

For in RET we do not merely see the child as a product of his early environment; nor do we believe that he is naturally a fully healthy, self-actualizing, creative creature and that his parents and his society unduly restrict, constrict, and warp him so that he soon becomes alienated from himself and disturbed. Instead, we think that his [moderately or severely alienated relationship to the world], his ultraconventionalism, and his emotional constriction or over-impulsiveness result from his innate as well as his acquired tendencies to think crookedly, to be grandiosely demanding, and to refuse to accept hassle-filled reality (Ellis, Wolfe, and Moseley, 1966).

Children, in other words, *naturally* acquire several basic irrational ideas which they tend to perpetuate and to sabotage their lives with forever. They religiously, devoutly believe that they "absolutely *need* and utterly *must have* others' approval; that they've *got to* achieve outstandingly and thereby prove how worthwhile they are; that people who act unjustly or inconsiderately to them are bad, wicked, or villainous, and should be severely condemned and punished for their villainy; that it is awful and catastrophic when things are not the way they would like them to be; that obnoxious situations and events *make them* feel anxious, depressed, or angry; that if they endlessly worry about something they can control whether or not it happens; that it is easier for them to avoid than to face certain life difficulties and responsibilities; and that they absolutely *need* a well-ordered, certain, pretty perfect universe. These are the same kinds of crazy ideas which most human adults more or less tend to believe; but children often believe them more rigidly and profoundly.

The main reason for the Living School's existence is to teach its pupils, on innumerable occasions and in many ways, that these typically human irrational ideas do not hold water, will inevitably lead to poor results, can be radically changed, and would better be surrendered and surrendered and surrendered, until the child no longer often holds them. This teaching, moreover, is designed to be done almost exclusively by the regular school teacher, and not by psychologists, counselors, or other special personnel. The teachers are trained—along with the psychotherapists that we train at the Institute for Advanced Study in Rational Psychotherapy—to understand and use rational-emotive methods. Then they employ them with the children. Here are some of the ways in which the rational-emotive philosophy is taught:

1. Regular lessons in rational thinking are given. The children are shown how to distinguish rational ideas—such as "I would like to do well in school because it has certain specific advantages"—from irrational ones—such as "I *must* do well in school because otherwise I am a worthless individual." Discussions of emotional behavior, and how one produces appropriate and inappropriate reactions in oneself, are frequently held.

2. Emotional problems that rise during classroom situations are often dealt with immediately as they arise, and are used for purposes of general emotional education. If Jane is shy about reciting, she may be shown that her shyness really consists of extreme anxiety about what others would think of her if she did not recite perfectly well; and she is shown how to challenge and dispute the notion that she *has* to do well in this or any other respect. If Jane does not soon see what her real problem is and how to handle it, other children in the class are asked what they think she is doing to upset and constrict herself and what she could do instead of this.

3. In situations outside the classroom—as, for example, when the children are in the playground or are on a trip to a museum—destructive and disruptive behavior is called to their attention and alternative, more constructive ways of behaving are considered and suggested.

4. Stories, fables, plays, and other forms of literature are employed to put

across rational philosophies of living. Stories, such as the conventional fairy tales, are frequently read and discussed to show the children that the main point of such stories may well be an entirely irrational notion—such as the notion that Cinderella completely *needs* the love of her stepmother and step-sisters, a fairy godmother, and a fairy prince, before she accepts her existence as being potentially enjoyable and worthwhile—and that this notion can be observed, logically parsed, and rejected.

5.  Audiovisual aids—such as filmstrips, films, recordings, and video tapings—are employed to help the children understand and utilize some of the rational-emotive principles of living.

6.  Group counseling is regularly held, with the teacher (at first under psychotherapeutic supervision and later on her own) talking to six or eight of the children about their personal problems, including their home problems, and showing them (just as regular RET therapists show their group counseling adolescents and adult clients) how to handle these problems.

7.  Individual sessions are often held between the teacher and a child who is temporarily upset about something, to get at the basic sources of his upsetness and to show him exactly what he is doing to make himself disturbed and what he can do to undisturb himself.

8.  Behavior therapy principles and methods are employed, so that the children are rewarded or reinforced for some of their effective and constructive conduct and penalized for some of their ineffectual behavior. At the same time, however, that the children are penalized if they act disruptively or antisocially, a strong attempt is made to help them distinguish between penalty and punishment—to show them that *they* are never damnable or rotten, even though some of their *deeds* and *performances* are execrable and are not allowable.

9.  Instead of trying to create an atmosphere of schools without failure, as Glasser (1969) and certain other affective educators try to do, the teachers in The Living School sometimes deliberately go to the other extreme and pretend that the children have failed at some task or test when they actually have not done badly at it. Their reactions to this "failure" are then elicited and analyzed, in an attempt to show them that although it is good (for practical purposes) to succeed and unfortunate to fail, they can always unconditionally accept themselves and strive for an enjoyable life *whether or not* they fail at academic or other tasks.

10. Various means of encouraging the children to express themselves openly and authentically and to reveal their real feelings about themselves and others are employed. Through games, plays, role-playing, sports, art, writing, and other means they are stimulated to show what they truly think and feel. But just as rational-emotive group and encounter therapy does not merely *emphasize* authentic self-expression but *also* tries to show the group member that some of his feelings (such as assertion) are appropriate and healthy while other feelings (such as rage) are inappropriate and unhealthy, so do the teachers try to help the children acknowledge and understand the feelings they express, and consider the creation of alternative emotions when they are over- or under-reacting to life's stimuli. Rational-emotive psychology makes concrete use of encounter methods with adults, particularly in the marathon weekends

of rational encounter which I and my associates give in many parts of the country every year (Ellis, 1969b); and it also uses these methods of affective encountering and release with the children in The Living School. But it always places them within a cognitive-behavioral framework and does not see them as sacrosanct or highly efficient in their own right.

11. As noted above, RET is one of the main psychotherapies that has pioneered in the giving of explicit, activity-oriented homework assignments to adolescent and adult clients. Similarly, the teachers in The Living School use rational-emotive methods of working with the children's problems while they are in the classroom and also of giving them emotionally educating homework. Thus, if Robbie is shy and withdrawn in his relations with his neighborhood peers, he may be assigned the task of trying to make one new friend or acquaintance a week; and if Susan fights incessantly with her sister over which TV program they are going to watch, she may be assigned to try going along with her sister's choices for a few weeks, while convincing herself that it is not awful, horrible, and catastrophic that she is being deprived of the programs she most wants to see.

In many important ways, in sum, rational-emotive methodology is applied to emotional education. And what emerges at The Living School is a full fledged meaning of this term. For RET is intrinsically didactic, pedagogic, instructional, and *educative:* more concretely and more fully, perhaps, than any other widely used form of psychotherapy. Not every therapeutic orientation is easily adaptable to teaching. Freud's psychoanalysis has largely failed in this respect; while Adler's individual psychology has succeeded much better. I think that we shall eventually show, in our work with normal youngsters, that rational-emotive psychology is as beautifully designed for the educative process as this process is already largely designed for it. For schooling, essentially, is a concerted, long-range attempt to help the child grow up in many ways and assume adult roles and responsibilities which will presumably be creative, productive, and enjoyable. And rational-emotive schooling, as we experimentally practice it at The Living School, is a concerted, long-range attempt to help the child grow up emotionally and to become a reasonably independent-thinking, self-actualizing, minimally disturbed person.

And by person I mean *human* person. For RET is one of the most humanistic psychologies in contemporary use. It has no truck whatever with anything that smacks of the superhuman or the subhuman. It believes that people can fully accept themselves as enormously fallible, incredibly human beings, who have no magical powers, and who reside in an immense but still material and unmystical universe which doesn't really give a special damn about them and most probably never will. It holds that there are no gods nor devils; that people have no immortal souls or immutable essences; that immortality is a silly, grandiose myth; that there is no absolute truth; and that although reasoning and the logico-empirico method of validating reality have their distinct limits (because they, too, originate with and are employed by eminently fallible humans), they are the best means we have of understanding ourselves and the world and would better be fairly rigorously applied in the understanding of life processes.

Rational-emotive education, consequently, teaches children to fully accept themselves as humans, to give up all pretensions of reaching heaven or finding the Holy Grail, to stop denigrating the value of themselves or any other person, to accept their mortality, and to become unabashed long-range hedonists: that is, individuals who heartily strive to have a ball in the here-and-now *and* in their future lives without giving too much heed to what others dogmatically think that they *should, ought,* or *must* do. Is this humanistic way of life, as explicitly taught—and I mean *taught*—in the Living School going to help us raise saner, happier, and more creative people? I, naturally, think so; but we shall see!

## REFERENCES

BURKHEAD, D. E. *The reduction of negative affect in human subjects: a laboratory test of rational-emotive psychotherapy.* Doctoral dissertation, Western Michigan University, 1970.

DALY, S. Using reason with deprived pre-school chilren. *Rational Living,* 1971, 5(2), 12–19.

DILORETO, A. *Comparative psychotherapy.* Chicago: Aldine, 1971.

ELLIS, A. *Reason and emotion in psychotherapy.* New York: Lyle Stuart, 1962.

ELLIS, A. *How to live with a neurotic.* New York: Crown Publishers and Award Books, 1969a.

ELLIS, A. A weekend of rational encounter. In Burton, A. (Ed.), *Encounter.* San Francisco: Jossey-Bass, 1969b.

ELLIS, A. Teaching emotional education in the classroom. *School Health Review,* November 1969c, 10–13.

ELLIS, A. *Growth through reason.* Palo Alto: Science and Behavior Books, 1971a.

ELLIS, A. *Rational sensitivity: self-fulfillment for executives.* New York: Citadel Press, 1971b.

ELLIS, A. *Emotional education.* New York: Julian Press, 1972a.

ELLIS, A. Emotional education with groups of normal school children. In Ohlsen, M. M. (Ed.), *Counseling children in groups.* New York: Holt, Rinehart and Winston, 1972b.

ELLIS, A., and BLUM, M. L. Rational training: a new method of facilitating management and labor relations. *Psychological Reports,* 1967, 20, 1267–1284.

ELLIS, A., and HARPER, R. M. *A guide to successful marriage.* (Original title: *Creative Marriage*). New York: Lyle Stuart and Hollywood: Wilshire Books, 1970.

ELLIS, A., and HARPER, R. M. *A guide to rational living.* Englewood Cliffs, N.J.: Prentice-Hall and Hollywood: Wilshire Books, 1971.

GLASSER, W. *Schools without failure.* New York: Harper and Row, 1969.

GLICKEN, M. D. Rational counseling: a new approach to children. *Journal of Elementary Guidance and Counseling.* 1968, 2(4), 261–267.

LAFFERTY, C., DENNERLL, D., and RETTICH, P. A. A creative school mental health program. *National Elementary Principal,* 1964, 43(5), 28–35.

MAULTSBY, JR., M. C. The implications of successful rational-emotive psychotherapy for comprehensive psychosomatic disease. Manuscript, 1969a.

MAULTSBY, JR., M. C. Psychological and biochemical test change in patients who were paid to engage in psychotherapy. Manuscript, 1969b.

SHARMA, K. L. *A rational group therapy approach to counseling anxious underachievers.* Thesis, University of Alberta, 1970.

TREXLER, L. D. *Rational-emotive therapy, placebo, and no-treatment effects on public-speaking anxiety.* Ph.D. Thesis, Temple University, 1971.

# "It's All for Your Own Good:"* Parent-Child Relationships in Popular American Child Rearing Literature, 1820–1970

*Lynn Z. Bloom*

. . . THIS STUDY ANALYZES [parent-child] relationships as they are manifested in representative nineteenth and twentieth century child rearing literature, intended primarily for white, middle and upper class, intact families, often Protestant and native born.[1]

Three basic and conflicting attitudes toward children prevailed in America throughout the earlier nineteenth century. They may be labeled the views of the child as "depraved," a "tabula rasa," and "a tender bud." These formed the basis for the relations between parents and children.[2]

The most prevalent view of children was based on the Calvinist belief that infants were born " 'totally depraved,' "[3] " 'by nature sinners,' "[4] 'not too little to go to hell'."[5] Consequently, "parents must vigilantly guard children against the tendency of their depraved impulses; enforcing absolute obedience to adult demands could alone secure the child's salvation" (Sunley, p. 163). To obtain submission, the child's evil impulsive "will"—any defiance of the parent's wishes, at any age" (Sunley, p. 159) had to be "broken for his own good and for God's Glory" (Miller and Swanson, p. 8). "Breaking the will" was commonly attained by whipping (even of infants),[6] tying children to the bedpost, or shutting them up in solitude and darkness.[7] This conventional training also involved adherence to a strict daily routine and to bland, monotonous diets—all for the child's good.[8] As practiced by many other Protestants in addition to Calvinists, it "emphasized the sense of sin, fervent and constant prayer, deeply stirred feelings, strict parental care, authority and restraint" (Wishy, p. 18). One of its major aims was "infant conversion" (Sunley, p. 160). Parents were admonished to avoid "indulgence" of their child's whims and desires to keep him free from "depravity" in the religious sense, as well as to avoid "spoiling" him in the secular senses of accommodating to unreasonable demands and letting him tyrannize the family (Sunley, p. 161).

Another view, diametrically opposed to the Calvinist perspective and much less popular, derived from John Locke (1632–1704) and Jean Jacques Rousseau (1712–1778), who assumed the child's "essential innocence, or at least

* From *Journal of Popular Culture*, X: 1 (Summer 1976): 191–198. Reprinted by permission of the publisher, the Popular Press, and the author.

moral flexibility" (Wishy VII). The child's "manly virtues" has to be strengthened against the dangerous, weakening effects of civilization (Sunley, pp. 161, 163); physical ebullience was a natural tendency, to be encouraged, rather than a sign of wicked depravity. Practical activities, physical exercises, and cold baths would harden children against "the effects of animality and prevent moral flabbiness and laziness"[9]; these children would be strong, vigorous, and unspoiled, like the early American frontiersmen (Sunley, p. 161).

Lockeian theories could also be used to promote an orthodox religious morality, as the Reverend Thomas H. Gallaudet's *The Child's Book on the Soul* (Hartford, 1831) illustrates. He recommends that the mother not overtax her child's mind or " 'tender emotions' " with rote learning of concepts he can't understand.[10] Rather, she should instruct the child by example, such as teaching him to appreciate the " 'glory of the immortality of the soul' " (Wishy, p. 30) by allowing him to touch the corpse of a dead child. Thus Gallaudet anticipates John Dewey's empiricism, with a vengeance!

The third perspective, the view of the child as a "tender bud," did not become popular until after the Civil War. Parent educators and others who shared this view saw the child, "an immortal bud just commencing to unfold its leaves . . . a beautiful flower opening to the sunshine,"[11] as having certain needs and potentialities which the parents were to help fulfill and encourage into full development. Immaturity replaced wilfulness as the basis for the child's transgressions;[12] his motives, rather than the consequences of his acts, were to be the basis for determining punishments and rewards (Sunley, p. 161). Parents should be consistent and gently firm, fair and understanding, carefully cultivating the "nobler principles of the heart,"[13] and avoiding corporal punishments, which were believe to be ineffective. As the notion of infant depravity gradually disappeared, so did the pre-Civil War antagonism between the little sinner and his parents, earthly surrogates for the stern God.

In a post-Darwinian universe, parents who strongly believed in "the survival of the fittest" which Darwin's theory of evolution propounded in 1859 might have been expected to try to make their children as "fit as possible— not for God's greater glory, as in the past, but simply for their own self-preservation, and for the improvement of the race.

The Reverend Jacob Abbott, bestselling parent advisor after the Civil War, adopted the prevailing and "conventional optimistic Christian compromise: evolution toward ever better forms of life was God's beneficent plan for man" (Wishy, p. 94). His book title illustrate his major emphases: *Gentle Measures in the Management and Training of the Young: or The Principles on Which a Firm Parental Authority may be Established and Maintained, without Violence or Anger, and the Right Development of the Moral and Mental Capacities be Promoted by Methods in Harmony with the Structure and the Characteristics of the Juvenile Mind* (New York: Harper, 1871). Abbott maintains that the mother's first duty is to establish her absolute and unlimited authority over her child, and to form, on his moral tabula rasa, "the habit of immediate, implicit, and unquestioning obedience to all her commands" (p. 26). "Gentle measures . . . do not react in a violent and irritating manner upon the extremely delicate, and almost embryonic condition of the child's cerebral and nervous organization," (p. 25) and are therefore best calculated to promote unquestioning *"submission to authority"* (p. 15). Foremost among the "gentle measures" are "slight penalties" (p. 58), such as sitting in the corner, which are the "natural consequence of the offense" (p. 75), "firmly, decisively, and invariably enforced—without violence, without scolding, without any manifestation of resentment or anger . . . [or] even expressions of displeasure" (p. 58). Punishment, never retributive, is a remedial and a deterrent measure.

Yet Abbott also encourages parents to "allow their children the greatest possible freedom of action" (p. 253) in nonessential matters. Parents should notice and commend their childen's proper behavior, rather than only to reprove their wrongdoings, for "it is much easier to allure [children] to what is right than to drive them from what is wrong" (p. 107). To be effective, parental sympathy and understanding must "be real, not merely assumed" (p. 134); the parent must become one with the child. (This view is a precursor to the twentieth century concept of positive reinforcement, as developed by B. F. Skinner.)

Dr. Luther Emmett Holt's widely used child care manual, *The Care and Feeding of Children: A Catechism for the Use of Mothers and Childen's Nurses* (New York: Appleton, 1896–1929), supplemented and eventually supplanted Abbott. Though his orientation is thoroughly secular, in contrast to Abbott's nondenominational Christianity, Holt, like Abbott, recommends that parents treat their children in ways that are partly for the child's own physical good, and partly for the parent's convenience. The parent, in Holt's view, is supreme in the household, and the child tends to be regarded as a somewhat troublesome "young animal," whose habits must be molded to fit those of the adult members of the household. Thus if the infant is bowel trained by his second month, it "makes regularity in childhood much easier and also saves the nurse much trouble and labour" (p. 161). For the same reasons, rather than from Calvinistic principles, the child's will should be broken—and early, by letting the infant "cry it out" perhaps for two or three hours the first night. Holt confidently predicts that "a second struggle will seldom last more than ten or fifteen minutes, and a third will rarely be necessary" (p. 168).

Holt, like his nineteenth century predecessors, is not concerned with child psychology as such, nor the feelings or emotion of either parents or children, except to discourage displays of infant temper. "Happiness" is an irrelevancy (as it is in the earlier Calvinist books)—the subject doesn't come up. Neither does the relative dependence or independence of child or parent; nor parent-child communication; nor sibling or peer relationships.[14]

Thus to accommodate these omissions, behavioral psychologist John B. Watson, Ph.D., saw his classic *Psychological Care of Infant and Child* (New York: W.W. Norton, 1928) as complementary to the physical care recommended by Holt. Watson's aims are antithetical to those of his predecessors, who encouraged conditioned docility, unquestioning obedience and, consequently, highly conformist child behavior. Watson, instead, wants to produce *"a happy child free as air* because he has mastered the stupidly simple demands society makes upon him. *An independent child* because all during his training you have made him play and work alone a part of the time, and you have made him get out of difficulties by his own efforts. *A child that meets and play with other children* frankly, openly, untroubled by shyness and inferiority. *An original child* because his perfect adjustment to his environment gives him leisure to experiment" (p. 150).

Watson, like most other writers on child rearing, is confident of success. Like the Lockeians, he starts with the child as tabula rasa. But unlike many of his predecessors, who are generally on the parents' side, Watson detests parents: *"No one today knows enough to raise a child"* (p. 12)—except Watson, one may infer—who adds that the world would be better off if a moratorium were declared on childbirth for twenty years until behavioral psychologists straightened parents out (p. 12).

Whereas Abbott's "gentle measures" were designed, in part, to counteract parental hostility, and thereby to produce dependent, submissive children, Watson intends his behavioral conditioning to extinguish the devastating effects of parental love, which he finds loathsomely inhibiting of his aims of juvenile and adult independence: "Mothers just don't know, when they kiss their children and pick them up and rock them, caress them . . . that they are slowly building up a human being totally unable to cope with the world it must later live in" (p. 44). Instead, parents should treat children "as though they were young adults . . . Let your behavior always be objective and kindly firm. Never hug and kiss them, never let them sit in your lap. If you must, kiss them once on the forehead when they say good night. Shake hands with them in the morning" (pp. 81–82).

In Watson's regimen, spartan independence training begins early. Parents should *"let the child learn as quickly as possible to do everything for itself"*; [15] this will enhance the maturity that should come at about three years, for "at this age children should begin to dress and act like youthful men and women and should be scrupulously treated as such" (p. 111). Yet independent and self-reliant though the child may be, parents should communicate constantly and freely with him—a twentieth century innovation in child-rearing. A "talk-it-out" club of parents and children "is a safeguard to health and sanity" for it enormously minimizes "the chance that *anything can go wrong with a child* so brought up" (p. 163). Thus the Watsonian child mirrored his newly-emancipated flapper mother, though whether either was really free as the image is a matter of conjecture.

Vestiges of both remained well into the 1940s, as revealed Dr. Herman Bundesen's *The Baby Manual: A Practical Guide from Early Pregnancy through the Second Year of Life* (New York: Simon and Schuster, 1924–1944), which sold over ten million copies. But although Bundesen advocates juvenile self-reliance, he has more confidence in parents than Watson does and envisions a more mutually loving and expressive parent-child relationship than does Watson. Bundesen's parents are permitted to cuddle their children occasionally—a Watsonian heresy: "the baby will not be spoiled if he is picked up and held only every now and then when he is not crying" (p. 426).

Bundesen, on the whole, promotes *gentleness*, as Abbott does, but for the very sorts of reasons that Abbott deplores. The young child should be "taught to obey, but in doing so his spirit should not be broken by shouting at him and making him 'blindly' obey commands because of fear" (p. 273). Understanding—on the parts of parents and children—is the basis for appropriate parent-child relations. The young child should be treated as a reasonable being, and should be expected to behave reasonably, once he is given an explanation. He should be helped to understand what he is doing right and wrong and why; he should be praised for doing right, but not scolded, nagged, or bribed to produce compliance (pp. 275–276). When possible, children should be diverted and deterred from wrong doing rather than being punished after the fact (p. 275). Punishments should be suited to the misdemeanor (such as deprivation of a desired object for a short time) and should not inflict prolonged physical or mental anguish (pp. 276–571).

Bundesen is the first parent advisor to recommend that parents accommodate their children's individual differences in temperament, tastes and abilities. For instance, although parents should still begin to toilet train babies of three months (Watson would start at three weeks!), Bundesen recognizes that some infants are not as tractable as others. If a mother encounters resistance, rather than scolding, punishing, or trying to force compliance, she should simply retreat for a week or two and try again (p. 281).

In many respects the gentle, rational parent-child relationships propounded in Bundesen would appear to be similar to those in Spock's *Baby and Child Care,* the first edition of which appeared in 1946, only two years after the last edition of Bundesen's *Baby Manual.* Yet the similarities are somewhat superficial, because of the fundamentally different psychological orientation of the two authors.

Dr. Spock's views on the ideal parent-child relationships differ from those of his predecessors primarily in his Deweyan pragmatism and, most distinctively, in his emphasis on Freudian psychology. Like John Dewey, Spock "encouraged parents to relax their discipline, to understand their child's nature, to trust his drive to become mature and responsible, and to regard his needs as equally legitimate and important as those of grownups" (Bloom, p. 135). Spock learned from Dewey that "significant learning takes place by ex-

periencing, feeling, exploring, practicing rather than by rote. Children learn—
and learn well—through desire rather than coercion as, according to Freud,
they grow to be responsible adults not by being controlled by fear of punishment, but mainly by their loving ties to their parents" (Bloom, p. 135).

From a Freudian perspective, Dr. Spock continually emphasizes the principles of preventive psychiatry that he believes should govern the parents' relations with their children. In Spock's view prior to 1968 (somewhat modified
since) the child's welfare is paramount, even if it means placing the child's
psychological needs before those of the parents—a reversal of the nineteenth
century family hierarchy. In order to promote the child's sound psychological
health, Spock encourages parents to maintain a psychologically healthful
home environment—a warm, responsive, stable household guided by love
and discipline which he sees as identical, at times. Predictably, then, throughout the pre-women's lib days of the '40s, '50s, and '60s, Spock has been opposed to mothers of small children holding jobs outside the home, however
much they might wish to, so they can stay at home and provide the optimum
constancy, love, and stability.[16]

Dr. Spock often suggests that, when the psychological (or other) going gets
tough, the parent-child relations be supplemented with help from "a good
psychiatrist or social worker or a wise and tolerant minister."[17] For parents
seeking counsel and perspective, Spock substitutes helping therapists for God
at the top of the hierarchy and never suggests that parents question their advice.

On the other hand, he balances this orientation with frequent suggestions
that the parents depend on their own intuitive sense of how to rear their
children. All three editions of *Baby and Child Care* begin, "Trust yourself.
You know more than you think you do."[18] Spock assumes that the instinctive parental reaction—which good parents should follow—is to provide un-
wavering love, in large doses.

Because he consistently emphasizes love, warmth, security, flexibility, and a
relaxed home atmosphere, Dr. Spock is sometimes accused of being overly
permissive. A colleague of Spock's has observed, "Because of his strict upbringing and rigorous moral sense, when Ben says 'relax' his assumption is
that an awful lot of control is in the air. In a more casual background, 'relax'
is interpreted quite differently" (Bloom, p. 135). Perhaps for this reason
Spock's advice to parents to "relax" and to "trust yourself" has been interpreted as a cue for greater laxity than he intended, particularly by readers
of the 1946 edition, and by some politicians of the late '60s who blamed
Spockian persmissiveness for creating the youthful protestors of the Vietnam
war. In 1946 Spock claimed that punishment was "seldom required" and
generally undesirable because it might make the child "furious, defiant, and
worse behaved than before"—or it might break his heart or his spirit. The
seeming need for frequent punishment was more the parent's problem than
the child's (I, 257–258).

Because so many parents erroneously interpreted this and similar advice to mean that the child always knew best and that the parents should therefore follow the child's lead, Dr. Spock toughened up his advice on Discipline in the 1957 and 1968 editions, and recommended that the parents, as the family leaders, should insist on "reasonably good behavior" and could maintain it by physical punishment if necessary (II, 332; III, 336).

By 1968 Dr. Spock sought to modify the "child-centered psychological approach" which he had come to believe was useful but insufficient unless "backed up by a moral sense of what's right and proper" (III, 12). He broke out of the exclusively child-centered focus that he believed many parents in the 1940s and '50s had held (again, partly as a result of overreacting to some of his earlier advice) and came full-circle, in some ways, back, to the position held by the Calvinist parent advisors of the early nineteenth century, recommending that children should be reared to feel that "they are in this world not for their own satisfaction but primarily to serve others" (III, 16). Dr. Spock the moralist now objects strongly to allowing children of any age to be excessively self-indulgent, whether through jealousy, rudeness, aggressiveness, or selfishness (III, 10–20).

With the moralistic Spock of 1968 we have returned somewhat to the position from which we started this survey of parent-child relationships in popular child rearing literature of the last century and a half. As we have seen, all the parent advisors are idealistic, whether they envision a familial utopia in heaven or on earth. All except Watson are in league with the parents to promote the child's welfare; Watson's ultimate goal is the same, but he sees the conventional loving parent as an impediment in its pursuit. All operate in an hierarchical framework. Whether God or the psychiatrist is supreme, next on the hierarchy is the parent advisor, usually followed by the parent, and then by the child, though in Watson and Spock's first edition the positions of the latter two are sometimes reversed. All parent advisors are optimistic, and all assume the relatively easy accomplishment of their goals if their advice is followed. Though they often contradict one another, they all invariably proffer recommendations for the same noble purpose—the child's own good.

## REFERENCE NOTES

1. Historically, the lower and working classes have been more oriented toward tradition than toward books, and more likely to take advice from grandmother than from the "experts." See Daniel R. Miller and Guy E. Swanson, *The Changing American Parent* (New York: Wiley, 1958), pp. 6–7, and Lynn Z. Bloom, *Doctor Spock: Biography of a Conservative Radical* (New York: Bobbs-Merrill, 1972), pp. 142–145.

2. Robert Sunley, "Early Nineteenth-Century American Literature on Child Rearing," in *Childhood in Contemporary Cultures*, ed. Margaret Mead and Martha Wolfenstein (Chicago: University of Chicago Press, 1955), pp. 160–167.

3. Rev. Alvan Hyde, *Essay on the State of Infants* (New York: C. Davis, 1830), in Sunley, p. 159.

4. Hyde, in Bernard Wishy, *The Child and the Republic* (Philadelphia: University of Pennsylvania Press, 1968), p. 18.

5. James Janeway, *A Token for Children:* quoted in Sanford Fleming, *Children and Puritanism* (New Haven: Yale University Press, 1933), p. 66, in Wishy, p. 12.
6. Anonymous, *Mother's Magazine,* 1834; quoted in Sunley, p. 160.
7. Jacob Abbott, *Gentle Measures in the Management and Training of the Young* (New York: Harper, 1871), p. 17. In fairness to the Rev. Abbott, it should be noted that he did not consider these to be "gentle measures"; he was inveighing against them.
8. Dr. Luther Emmett Holt devotes nearly two-thirds of his popular manual (see pp. 193–194) to feeding, and recommends the diet typical of the century. (The quotations throughout are from the 1912 edition.) Babies under a year old should imbibe an exclusively liquid diet: milk, gruel, orange juice, and beef juice (pp. 53–54). During the next year unsugared cereal "cooked for at least three hours," unbuttered "very stale bread," egg, baked apple, and prune pulp were added (pp. 124–125). Not until the child is over ten years is he permitted the gastronomic delights of "ham, bacon, sausage, pork, liver, kidney, game . . . cod, mackerel . . . halibut" (p. 135), raw vegetables, salads, ready-to-serve cereals, hot breads, griddle cakes, pastry, nuts, candy, dried fruits, cherries, berries, bananas, pineapple, lemonade, and soda-water (p. 139). Dr. Benjamin Spock's mother was a devotee of Holt's, and Spock grew to be 6 ft. 4 in. on a childhood diet of milk, stewed fruit, oatmeal, and eggs. (See Bloom, p. 12; see also Wishy, pp. 36–38.)
9. Dr. Heman Humphrey, *Domestic Education* (Amherst: Adams, 1840), p. 63; in Wishy, p. 38.
10. Gallaudet, p. 49; in Wishy, p. 30.
11. Catherine L. Taylor, "Education," *Mother's Assistant* (1849), XV:4, 24; and Caroline A. Briggs. "Intellect of Children," *Mother's Assistant* (1849), XIV:5, 97, in Sunley, p. 161.
12. T. S. Arthur, *The Mother's Rule* (Philadelphia: Peck and Bliss, 1856), p. 298; in Wishy, p. 43.
13. Edgar W. Knight, ed. *A Documentary History of Education in the South Before 1860* (Chapel Hill: University of North Carolina Press, 1953), V, 241–242; in Wishy, p. 44.
14. In fact, except for Spock's discussion of sibling rivalry, none of the child rearing experts discussed here is much concerned with sibling or peer relationships. The human focus is almost exclusively on the parent-child relationships, with occasional references—mostly negative—in the nineteenth century literature to servants who either drug or overindulge the child or encourage him to masturbate, all with the intention of pacifying him.
15. p. 108. Watson habitually dehumanizes children by referring to them in the neuter.
16. I, 459–460; II, 570; III, 563–564. In the 1970s's Spock has modified his position somewhat, as a result of pressure from women's liberation groups, to accommodate the possibility of day care centers and communal living arrangements, but he is still firm on the need for a constant loving caretaker. See for instance, *Decent and Indecent,* revised edition (Greenwich, Conn.: Fawcett, 1971), Chapter 11. In general, by 1972 the women's lib movement had made relatively little impact on manuals of child development or child rearing. See Zelda Klapper. "The Impact of the Women's Liberation Movement on Child Development Books," in *The Women's Movement: Social Psychological Perspectives,* eds. Helen Wortis and Clara Rabinowitz, (New York: AMS Press for the American Orthopsychiatric Association, 1972), pp. 21–31.
17. I, 457; II, 567; III, 561.
18. I, 3; II, 3; III, 3.

# B. Infancy and Early Childhood: Introduction

WILL CONTINUE the metaphor of the social atom with its many physical, biological, psychological, and social contexts surrounding the nucleus of human personality. The infant, product of a union of other persons, is wholly dependent and yet is very active in influencing his or her environment. The infant's capacity to add pieces to his or her personality structure is largely determined by biological factors in the early time of life, but what is added and how much are highly influenced by the social contexts. Although we are beginning to accumulate information about normative development (that which is common to most individuals), we have a long way to go to make available to helping professionals knowledge about the variations in that development that are specific to persons of certain races, classes, or other characteristics. Knowledgeable social action comes from this knowledge of theme and variations.

The papers in this section represent an attempt to explore the important dimensions of the educational "shell" surrounding the person. Some forms of education like learning one's mother tongue, occur "naturally" (L. Bloom), almost in spite of what social contexts exist. But most education, formal or informal, is influenced by the contexts in which it occurs; from the moment of birth (Hersh and Levin); in private homes or in institutions (Collard); in the home of natural parents or substitutes (Eiduson); in the connection between home and educational institutions (Richmond, Zigler, and Stipek); in schools alone (Shure and Spivack); or in how different types of schooling affect development (Bronfenbrenner).

Ultimately, the applied social scientist, like the chemist, has to begin formulating patterns among pieces of information so as to have a viable base for taking action. One important example of this translating research into practice is the paper by Bronfenbrenner, who attempts to integrate a large literature by means of principles that he sees emerging from the separate facts. As he points out, some of the linkages in his summary about our knowledge of early intervention are strong; others are weak and subject to change. But overall, the reader may perceive a system among these ideas and facts that is a basis for action. Such interconnections are what we should seek for each stage of development.

At the conclusion of this section, readers should have some understanding of the basic tasks of the infant and the young child:

*Physical Tasks:* Developing physiological homeostasis in the postuterine environment—breathing, digestion, elimination, temperature regulation, sleeping and wakefulness, and crying as a form of communication. Learning how to use one's body: such matters as grasping with the hands; coordination and balance involving the hands, eyes, and body; lying down and sitting up; moving by crawling, walking, and climbing.

*Psychological Tasks:* Developments in one's mental experiences, including distinguishing oneself from objects in the physical world and objects (persons) in the social world; differentiating the various aspects of one's own body; learning to be aware of satisfactions and satisfiers (both persons and things); and learning to be aware of one's own actions that lead to these satisfactions.

*Social Tasks:* Learning forms of communication through physical actions and eventually through vocal actions that conform to the rules of the culture. Another task is to learn to receive messages by observing, touching, and in various ways exploring objects directly.

Another form of social task involves learning social actions and states: there are human time cycles that the young child has to adjust to, such as time for sleeping, time for eating, and so on. There are social roles that are beginning to emerge as expectations made by others on one's behavior. And there are a number of social values that take the form of demands for the very young, the "no, no" as a control mechanism, but also the various forms of stimulations that draw the child into some desired form of activity (cf. Havighurst, 1952).

---

# How Love Begins Between Parent and Child*

## Stephen P. Hersh and Karen Levin

T HE EXPECTANT MOTHER, no less than the father, often finds it hard to imagine how she is going to feel about the unborn infant. But once the child arrives the mother love that so strongly shapes the infant's future unfolds in a complex and wonderful pattern. This mysterious process begins

* Reprinted by permission of the publisher and authors from *Children Today*, 7:2 (1978): 2–6.

before birth. As our knowledge increases, all who bother to look at the process find themselves instilled with awe and respect.

The newborn, it turns out, is not the passive creature most people have assumed him to be. Recent research shows that the newborn comes well-endowed with charm and a full potential for social graces. His eyes are bright and equipped with surprisingly good vision. Shortly after birth, he likes to watch the human face. He looks at his mother and soon recognizes and prefers her. Dr. Robert Emde, of the University of Colorado Medical School, observes, "Little in life is more dramatic than the mother's moment of discovery that the baby is beaming at her with sparkling eyes." This is the time, mothers often say, when affection begins. The infant's cry alerts her and causes a biological as well as emotional reaction. Swedish studies using thermal photography have shown that the cry increases the flow of blood to her nipples, increasing milk secretion. The newborn hears the mother's or caretaker's voice and turns his head towards that person. The infant's ability to cling and cuddle communicates a pleasurable warmth to the mother. The infant's odor, too, is pleasant and uniquely his own. Although some experts say the smile is not "real" until some weeks after birth, the newborn does smile. Dr. Burton L. White of Harvard University says, "God or somebody has built into the human infant a collection of attributes that guarantee attractiveness."

Some argue about whether the child sparks the development of love, or whether a special physiological state of the mother prompts her to interact with the new infant. Each view probably offers a partial explanation. In any case, a number of researchers agree that the infant does mold or trigger adult behavior. Dr. Michael Lewis, Director of the Infant Laboratory, Educational Testing Service, Princeton, N.J., believes that "The neonate organizes the mother by crying, starting, and by eye to eye contact." When an infant opens his mouth to feed, the mother automatically opens hers, too. When the infant smiles, she smiles back.

The newborn's cry almost always causes an adult reaction. To prove his point, one researcher played a record of a newborn in his office, and secretaries from nearby rooms came running in to find out what was "wrong" with the baby.

To get a close look at what happens between mother and the new infant, Dr. T. Berry Brazelton of Harvard has studied video-tapes of their interactions. Frame-by-frame "micro-analysis" of the pictures shows that the baby moves in smooth, circular "ballet-like" patterns as he looks up at the mother. The baby concentrates his attention on her while body and limbs move in rhythm; the infant then withdraws briefly, but returns his attention averaging several cycles a minute. The mother falls in step with the baby's cycles by talking and smiling, in a kind of "dance." If the mother falls out of step and disappoints the infant by presenting a still, unresponsive face when he gazes at her, the baby becomes "concerned" and keeps trying to get her attention.

If he fails, the baby withdraws into a collapsed state of helplessness, face turned aside, and body curled up and motionless. If the mother becomes responsive again, the baby looks puzzled but returns to his cyclical motions.

Intrigued by these patterns, Dr. Louis W. Sander, professor of psychiatry at the University of Colorado Medical Center, Denver, had mothers of 7-day-old babies wear masks while they fed and cared for their infants. The babies became disturbed, and for 24 hours their rhythms of sleep and feeding were completely off schedule.

Indeed, even before birth, the infant is a responsive creature. We know that the fetus can see and hear during the third trimester. A soft red light or certain kinds of sound cause the fetus to slowly turn; a bright light or certain noises can startle the unborn child. Some fetuses seem to signal their personalities to the mother ahead of time by being active or quiet. All third trimester fetuses appear to be somnolent at some times and very alert or "hyper-vigilant" at others. Over the next five years, investigations in this area may allow for prediction (and hence possible earlier remediation) of certain vulnerabilities and difficulties now too subtle to detect.

Is it any wonder, given the above information, that the experienced and much-loved clinician, teacher and researcher, Dr. Brazelton, laments: "Why do we still embrace the passive model of the newborn, plunging him/her into a delivery room hardly safe for adults and immediately thereafter into an over-stimulating neonatal nursery?"

Curiosity about how mothers begin to love their babies grew out of observations of premature infants. Separated from their families at birth for weeks and sometimes months, "premies" often have no opportunity to interact with their mothers. The mothers find it hard to feel a close tie to these infants in the beginning. This suggests to some that one important milestone in mother-child love takes place soon after birth.

A number of pediatricians began to look for hard evidence that the mother-infant tie starts early, and how it benefits the child. Drs. Marshall H. Klaus and John H. Kennell of Case Western Reserve University School of Medicine divided 28 mothers and their firstborns into two matched groups. In one, mothers were given their nude babies to nurse and care for in bed for one hour in the first two hours after delivery, and for five extra hours on each of the next three days of life. The other group of mothers received the care that is routine in most U.S. hospitals: a glimpse of the baby at birth, brief contact for identification at six to eight hours, then visits of 20 to 30 minutes for feedings every four hours.

When the mothers and infants returned to the hospital a month later, there were marked differences in the two groups. The "early contact" mothers showed a closer tie to their infants. They were more concerned, more soothing, fondled their infants more, and were more reluctant to leave them with others than the second group. At one year, the same differences were observed between the two groups of mothers. Two years after birth, the mothers who had early and extended contact with their infants asked them more questions, and issued fewer commands, than the second group. The scientists decided that the children had made an impact on the mothers' behavior for two years. But what was the effect on the children? A recent comparison of the two groups of children at five years of age shows that the "early contact" youngsters had significantly higher I.Q.'s and a better command of language than the control group.

Studies of mothers and newborns in other cultures showed similar results. In Guatemala, Dr. Deborah Hales (of Montifiore Hospital and Medical Center, New York City) attempted to pinpoint the time when the mother-child tie was made. One group of mothers lay next to their infants for 45 minutes right after leaving the delivery room; the second spent the same amount of time with their new babies, but at 12 hours after delivery. A third group received routine hospital care. When the mothers were observed a day and a half later, the first group showed significantly more affectionate behavior than the other mothers. They spent more time talking to the infant and fondling, kissing and smiling at him or her.

Recent Swedish research also suggests the importance of early mother-child contact in the hospital. First-time mothers who held their naked infants one hour immediately after birth showed more affection to the babies when observed several days later. In another Swedish study, new mothers were given their infants for 15 to 20 minutes right after birth. Three months later, these mothers showed more affection than those routinely separated from their infants by the hospital. The babies, smiled and laughed more, and cried less.

*Early exposure to the new infant seems to have an effect on the father as well as the mother.* When he attends the birth, sees the newborn in the first hours, and holds him, the father remains more closely tied to the child, researchers report.

In America, the father is playing an increasingly important part in caring for the infant. The work of Dr. Ross D. Parke at the University of Illinois, Urbana-Champaign dispels some common myths about the father—that he is not interested in the newborn, does not nurture him, prefers leaving him to the mother, and is not so competent as she. Dr. Parke has found that when left alone with the infant, the father is very sensitive to his needs, and shows affection and considerable skill in handling him. Nine months later, infants cope better with stress (when a stranger appears) if the father has taken part early in his care. Dr. Parke concludes, "There are very few differences between mother-child and father-child interactions."

Keeping the newborn and the father as well as the mother together in the earliest hours apparently improves the child's outlook in a number of problem families. Dr. Peter Vietze of the National Institute of Child Health and Human Development, NIH, recently reported on a large study of infants born in a large city hospital to disadvantaged families. Half of the infants roomed-in with their mothers seven hours after birth and remained there throughout the hospital stay. Fathers were encouraged to visit at all hours and to handle the new child. The rooming-in infants were held more, cried less, and were more alert than those kept in the hospital nursery. When observed months later, the rooming-in infants enjoyed better general health and a closer tie with their mothers than the control children. There were also fewer cases of inadequate child care, neglect and abuse. Dr. Vietze believes that rooming-in with the mother right after birth plus the frequent visiting by the father "means that the child will have a better chance in life."

The new research has prompted doctors to identify developmental differences among newborns, and to take preventive steps early if something is wrong. Some pediatricians go beyond the usual physical examination of the newborn to check him or her for a number of personal qualities. They include alertness, cuddliness, irritability, persistence and determination. Some infants are more active or more cuddly than others, and doctors think they can help parents get a better understanding of their infant's personality in the earliest days. By identifying the infant's special characteristics, mental health professionals think they can help prevent emotional problems later on.

In June 1976, child specialists gathered in Washington, D.C., at the White House for a Conference on the Prevention of Psychosocial Disabilities in Infancy. New infant research was reviewed in that setting for the purpose of calling to the attention of the executive branch of government the hypothesis that major preventive mental health measures could be launched at relatively modest costs in the perinatal period. Research and information reviewed at that meeting included:

○ The results of a 10-year study by Dr. Elsie Broussard, professor of psychiatry, University of Pittsburgh, demonstrating that maternal attitude towards an infant *when consistent* between two and 30 days after birth is highly correlative with future adjustment difficulties in the children studied.

○ Studies by Dr. Gordon Bronson, professor of psychology, Mills College, Oakland, Calif., showing that about 20 per cent of infants appear to be temperamentally disposed to avoid or at least to have difficulty with new situations; such infants were found to respond to new stimuli by avoidance or by stopping their activity, pouting and crying.

○ Some infants seem naturally happy, lively and without fear; others seem naturally subdued and easily made uncomfortable; such differences in behavioral responses may be due to actual differences in neurological and hormonal endowments.

As a result of research documentation of the profound effects of interaction between infants and their mothers, the National Institute of Mental Health has organized, under the leadership of Drs. Stanley Greenspan, Reginald Lourie and Robert Nover, a clinical infant research program to help develop multidisciplinary approaches to prevent problems in the newborn. In addition, based on the encouragement of a distinguished panel of researchers and clinicians a private nonprofit National Center for Clinical Infant Programs has been established in Washington, D.C. The center will convene experts in the field and transmit new knowledge as it is produced to physicians, child development centers and interested others throughout the nation.

The new findings have already contributed to some major changes in the nation's maternity wards. More and more hospitals are altering their services to give parents more information and a bigger role in decision making and to provide more homelike settings. As one hospital administrator put it, "We are treating birth as a normal process rather than a disease." . . .

---

# Language Development and Language Disorders in Children*
## *Lois Bloom*

LANGUAGE IS THE INTERSECTION of linguistic forms (the sounds or signs that individuals produce) with content (meaning, or what individuals talk about) for some use in a social context. After a brief discussion about the nature of language, development and disorders of language will be described in terms of (1) the precursors of language content, form and use in infancy; (2) the intersection of content, form and use in children's language development in the second and third years of life; and (3) the disorders of language that occur when children fail to make the necessary inductions about the intersection of content, form, and use.

## Linguistic Grammars and Mental Grammars

There are a number of agreed-upon facts of language, but different explanations for the same facts. One linguistic fact is that language is patterned: there are such structural patterns as among the sentences,

1. "John swept the floor."
2. "Jane chopped the wood."

and so on (one pattern), and

3. "The floor was swept by John."
4. "The wood was chopped by Jane."

---

* Reprinted by permission of the author.

(a second pattern). In addition to such structure patterns as these, there is also an important relationship among such sentences as:

5. "John swept the floor."
6. "The floor was swept by John."
7. "What John did was sweep the floor."
8. "Did John sweep the floor?
9. "What did John do?"
10. "Who swept the floor?"

Each of these sentences (5 to 10) has a different surface structure pattern, but they are all related to one another as transforms of the same underlying or deep structure that specifies the relations among *John, sweep* and *floor*.

Different linguistic theories have attempted to account for these same facts of language in different ways. In the more traditional view in theories of structural linguistics (from L. Bloomfield in the 1920s and 1930s to C. Hockett in the 1960s and others), individuals learn basic sentence patterns from the language that they hear in everyday events. Linguistic knowledge consists of the conceptual representations of such patterns. More recently, transformational theory (for example, Harris, 1957; Chomsky, 1957, 1965) pointed out that there is a closer relationship among the sentences (5 to 10 above than among such sentences as 1 and 2 or 3 and 4. The sentences 5 to 10 and sentences 1 and 3 and 2 and 4 are related by virtue of an abstract system of rules, a grammar that is not itself directly available from the language that one hears in the environment (cf. Chomsky, 1965). Linguistic theory, especially transformational linguistic theory, has attempted to specify rules of grammar, that is, linguistic grammars, to account for what individuals know about language, or mental grammar—the abstract knowledge that individuals have of rules for sentences.

# Precursory Capacities of Infants

Research with infants in the last decade has resulted in a wealth of information about the antecedents of language behaviors in infant behaviors with respect to language form. Eimas et al. (1971) and others have demonstrated that infants as young as two to four months of age are able to perceive the category boundaries of different speech sounds (such as the differences between /p/ and /b/) but not differences within the same category (such as different productions of /p/ that vary, for example, in the extent of plosion). It has been well known that the sounds that infants babble have many of the features of the sounds of the adult model, and the intonation contours of infant vocalizations are consistent with the mature intonation of adult speech segments (Delack, 1977). With respect to language content, Piaget (1954 and elsewhere) and Werner and Kaplan (1953) have described the growing awareness of self in relation to concepts of objects in the world. The knowledge that infants acquire about the permanence of objects and about relations between objects and between self and objects provides the basis for the content of children's earliest messages when they begin to say words and then phrases. With respect to language use, there have been a number of studies of the patterns of interaction between caregivers (mothers most often) with their infants. For example, Stern, Jaffe, Beebe, and Bennett (1975) described the systematic coactional and reciprocal gaze and vocalization that take place between mothers and infants as young as two months of age. Aspects of content, form, and use, then, are represented among the capacities of very young infants and begin to come together at the end of the first year of life with the inductions that children form about the relations among linguistic and nonlinguistic aspects of experiences.

# Early Language Development

Children learn different kinds of words in the second year of life, in addition to social routine words like *Hi, Byebye,* and so on. Many words name objects; the first objects named or at least the objects named most often are those objects (and persons) who are closest and most familiar to the child. Such words as *Mommy, Daddy, Rover,* or *Kitty* as well as words for *bottle* or *blanket* are not category labels but are words for single instance concepts or unique objects much like *Queen Elizabeth* and *Kentucky Derby* are in the adult language. Children learn names for categories of objects like *cookie, dog, ball* (to stand for different cookies, dogs, and balls in different contexts) gradually in the first half of the second year, but with increasing frequency toward the end of the second year. For many children there is a small group of words that are each used far more frequently than names of objects (except for such "unique" objects as *Mommy*). These words are relational or function words like *no, more, gone, up,* and so on, that can be used in many different contexts to refer to many different objects and classes of objects. Such different words as names for particular objects, names for classes of objects, and relational words that apply across many different objects are related to different mental representations of experience (see Bloom, 1973).

The words that children learn to use in the second year help to determine the kinds of sentences that they learn to say in the third year. For many children the first phrases that they say are formed by combining relational words like *this, gone, more* with object words, for example, *this ball, this cookie* to talk about existence; *ball gone, cookie gone* to talk about disappearance (or nonexistence) and *more ball* or *more cookie* to talk about recurrence. Object words and person names also combine with action words, and children learn grammatical relations to talk about action on objects and persons doing things (for example, *Mommy read, read book* and *Mommy book*). The child's mental grammar is progressively elaborated over a long period of time, as language development extends well into the school years.

There are regularities in the sentences that children learn to say. There is a limited set of semantic relations that provide the content of early sentences: children learn to talk about the existence, nonexistence, and recurrence of objects and about actions, locations, possession and attributions of objects (Bloom, 1970; Brown, 1973). Children learn to talk about actions before they learn to talk about states, and at least some children learn to talk about simple actions before they learn to talk about locative actions (Bloom, Lightbown and Hood, 1975). In addition to such regularity in content, there is regularity in form for individual children but variation in form among children. Some children express sentence relations by combining verbs with nouns ("Make a bridge," "eat cookie," "Danny build"), but other children regularly combine verbs with pronouns to represent the same relations ("make it," "eat this one," "I build it").

Children learn to use language in contexts that include other persons, and their language can be used for both pragmatic or practical functions and mathetic or learning functions (Halliday, 1975). Children learn language in pragmatic contexts to regulate and direct the behaviors of others, and they learn language in mathetic contexts to obtain information about objects and events in the world. Once children acquire certain forms of language, to represent certain kinds of content for different purposes or functions, they need to learn how to vary language form in order to express the same content, for the same purpose, according to the demands of different situations. Learning language use involves learning to distinguish between among situations for, for example, making a statement ("I'm starved") and asking a question ("Is there any cake left?") or, as another example using a noun: "The *bus* is coming" or a pronoun: "*It*'s coming." An important part of language use is learning how to say the same thing in different ways.

Just as children's grammar is progressively elaborated throughout the school years, children continue to learn about language every time they use language. Although many of the fundamentals of language content/form/use are acquired in the preschool years, language is not considered to be fully developed until the early adolescent years and the development of formal operational thought. Even though an individual's mental grammar, with rules for sentences and discourse, is well established by early adolescence, individuals continue to add words to their mental dictionaries. Similarly, although learning the social conventions for the use of language begins in the early preschool years, learning to use language continues through the adult years, as the contexts for the use of language change throughout the life-span—from earliest childhood, through the school years, into adulthood with family and occupational contexts and eventually into old age, which may include contexts of loneliness and illness.

## Language Disorder in Children

Some children fail to learn language normally, and such failure can be due to a disruption in the sensory system (as happens with deaf children), in the conceptual system (as with brain damage and/or mental retardation), or in the child's affective and social development (as with childhood schizophrenia or autism). Children need to hear speech in order to learn the form/content interactions of language. Conceptually, they need to be able to form abstractions and make generalizations in order to learn about objects and events and about sounds, words, and sentence structures. Children also need to be able to interact with other persons in order to learn to take account of the needs of the listener in different situations and circumstances.

The behaviors of children with language disorders, then, can be described in terms of disruption in the content, form, and use of language; in the intersection of the three components with one another. Some children with language disorders develop certain ideas about the world (content) and interact in communicating with other persons (use) but are unable to learn words and structures that provide the forms of language. Other children may learn certain forms, which they use in a routinized, mechanical way in certain interactions, but they are not able to represent regularities in language content in a meaningful way. Other children may learn linguistic forms to represent certain categories of content, but be unable or unwilling to interact with other persons to learn to use such content/form interactions. Still other children may learn language in much the same way as normal children do, but more slowly, with difficulty, and with arrest at some early stage in the course of development (see Bloom and Lahey, 1978).

It is not clear what happens to such children with language disorders through the life-span. However, a language disorder is, itself, a learning disability. A child of one to four years of age who is learning language slowly or with difficulty is a child with a learning problem and is a child who, in prospect, can be expected to continue to have difficulty in learning in the school years—that is, the child with a language disorder in the preschool years will be the child with a learning disability in the school years. And the older child who is six, seven, eight years old and older, having difficulty learning reading, writing, and other skills, is a child who, in retrospect, probably had difficulty in learning language when he or she was one, two, or three years of age: he or she was and still is a child with a learning disability. Thus, school-age children with learning disabilities and preschool children with language disorders are most probably the *same* children. They are children who, for whatever reason, have had difficulty learning, in general, and difficulty learning language, in particular.

## REFERENCES

BLOOM, L. *Language Development: Form and Function in Emerging Grammars.* Cambridge, Massachusetts: The M. I.T. Press, 1970.

BLOOM, L., ed. *Readings in Language Development.* New York: John Wiley and Sons, Inc., 1978.

BLOOM, L., and LAHEY, M. *Language Development and Language Disorders.* New York: John Wiley and Sons, Inc., 1978.

BLOOM, L.; LIGHTBOWN, P.; and HOOD, L. *Structure and Variation in Child Language Monographs of the Society for Research in Child Development,* 40, no. 160, 1975.

BLOOMFIELD, L., *Language.* New York: Holt, Rinehart and Winston, 1933.

BROWN, R. *A First Language, the Early Stages.* Cambridge, Massachusetts: Harvard University Press, 1973.

CHOMSKY, N. *Aspects of the Theory of Syntax.* Cambridge: The M. I.T. Press, 1965.

———. "On the Biological Basis of Language Capacities." In *The Neuropsychology of Language.* Ed. by R. W. Rieber. New York: Plenum Press, 1976.

———. *Syntactic Structures.* The Hague: Mouton, 1957.

DELACK, J. "Aspects of Infant Speech Development in the First Year of Life." In *Readings in Language Development.* Ed. by L. Bloom. New York: John Wiley and Sons, Inc., 1978.

EIMAS, P.; SIQUELAND, E.; JUSCZYK, P.; and VIGORITO, J. "Speech Perception in Infants." *Science,* 171 (1971):303–306.

HALLIDAY, M. *Learning How to Mean—Explorations in the Development of Language.* London: Edward Arnold, 1975.

HARRIS, Z. *Structural Linguistics.* Chicago: University of Chicago Press, 1955.

HOCKETT, C. *A Course in Modern Linguistics.* New York: Macmillan Company, 1958.

———. *The State of the Art.* The Hague: Mouton, 1968.

LAHEY, M., ed. *Readings in Childhood Language Disorders.* New York: John Wiley and Sons, Inc., 1978.

PIAGET, J. *The Construction of Reality in the Child.* New York: Basic Books, 1954.

STERN, D.; JAFFE, J.; BEEBE, B.; and BENNET, S. "Vocalizing in Unison and Alternation: Two Modes of Communication Within the Mother-Infant Dyad." In *Developmental Psycholinguistics and Communication Disorders.* Ed. by D. Aronson and R. Rieber. Annals of the New York Academy of Sciences, pp. 263, 89–100, 1975.

WERNER, H., and KAPLAN, E. *Symbol Formation.* New York: John Wiley and Sons, Inc., 1963.

# Early Influences on Development: Fact or Fancy?*

*Arnold J. Sameroff*

T HE CONCERN of developmental psychology is directed toward understanding the changes which occur in behavior as the individual grows to
maturity. Scientists with a bias for either a maturational or an environ-
mentalist position generally make an implicit assumption that behaviors necessarily build on each other to produce a continuity of functioning from conception to adulthood. The continuity seen in the physical identity of each
individual is generalized to the psychological identity of each individual. Just
as an individual retains the same body throughout the lifespan, so must he
have the same mind. The pragmatic needs of educators, clinicians, and scientists reinforce these views of long-range continuities in human behavior. The
need of educators is to feel that the didactic exercises they go through are
more than merely exercises and are truly affecting the prospective outcomes
of their charges; the need of clinicians is to seek the roots of current deviancy
retrospectively in either the experiential or constitutional history of the individual; and the pragmatic need of scientists is to feel that the small piece of
the world they are studying really has a relation to the whole of life.

However, biologists have shown that physically the body does not maintain a constancy in development. At an elemental level it has long been clear
that the material constituents of each organ, tissue, and cell are in constant
transition. As a consequence, continuities must be sought in the organization
of the body rather than in its ingredients (Bertalanffy, 1968). On a larger
time scale it is also clear that the structure of the body goes through changes
which produce qualitative differences in organization during development
(Waddington, 1966). For humans there is an illusion of structural continuity
since the major changes occur during the gestational period while the individual is hidden from view. Perhaps if human physical development consisted of
the metamorphoses found in insects, a much more segmented view of biological growth would have been prevalent.

The increasing sophistication of biological theorizing combined with a
series of psychological issues left unresolved by conventional wisdom influenced developmentalists, most notably Piaget (1950) and Werner (1961), to
reconsider the continuous nature of mental development. Piaget focused on
the logic of thought and confronted psychology with a separation between

* Reprinted by permission of the publisher and the author from *Merrill-Palmer Quarterly*,
1975, 21:4, 267–294.

the seeming continuities in performance and dramatic discontinuities in competence. Piaget's stages of cognitive development are based on qualitatively different structural organizations at different points in life.

Werner (1957) offers a wider perspective in his concept of the multiformity of development. Recognizing the nonspecificity of his orthogenetic principle that development moves in the direction of more complex differentiations and integrations, Werner allowed for reaching a particular level of functioning by means of a variety of pathways. In a material vein, modern biological research has demonstrated that the same mature organs can arise from the activities of differing genes, cells, and tissues (Waddington, 1966). A psychological example of "multiformity" of functioning can be found in Goldstein's (1939) explorations of the consequences of war injuries to the brain. Not only did identical lesions in different individuals produce different effects, but similar deficits in functioning could also be compensated by a variety of mechanisms. . . .

# Origins of Deviancy

The influence of psychoanalytic thinking, together with the increased knowledge of the complexity of behavior found in young children, has raised concerns about the effects of a variety of early trauma on functioning later in life.

## Continuum of Reproductive Casualty

In recent years increasing attention has been directed toward the study and early identification of various factors which place children at a greater than average risk to later disease or disorder. Although persons of all ages are menaced by a range of life hazards, most of the available research literature has focused on a variety of trauma that are suffered early in infancy and that are expected to play a principal role in the developmental outcome of the affected individual. The seriousness of such early hazards is underscored by the fact that the death rate during the perinatal period are four times greater than those of other ages (Niswander & Gordon, 1972). Of perhaps even greater significance is a broad *continuum of reproductive casualty*, hypothesized to include congenital malformations, cerebral palsy, mental retardation, deafness, blindness, and other neurosensory defects which are thought to result from early hazards and traumas (Lilienfeld & Parkhurst, 1951; Lilienfeld, Pasamanick & Rogers, 1955). It has been estimated that approximately 10 per cent of the population in the United States has handicaps or defects that are present at or soon after birth (Niswander & Gordon, 1972).

Of the 5–10 million conceptions occurring annually in the United States, 2–3 million result in spontaneous abortions due to genetic or chromosomal defects and pathogens, and another one million are terminated legally or illegally. Of the approximately 3.5 million fetuses that reach 20 weeks of gestational age, 1.5 per cent die before delivery, 1.5 per cent die in the first postnatal month, 1.5 per cent have severe congenital malformations, and about 10 per cent will have learning disorders that range from mild to severe retardation (Babson & Benson, 1971).

The large number of general learning disorders and specific deficits in behaviors such as reading are of great concern to clinicians. The lack of either a clear genetic basis or anatomical damage in many children with sensory and behavioral disorders was puzzling to investigators who adhered closely to a traditional "medical model." If, according to this point of view, a disorder existed, there should have been some clear etiological factor, preferably biological, somewhere in the patient's history. If such a factor could not be located, it was presumably because diagnostic techniques were not yet sufficiently sophisticated to detect it. Gesell & Amatruda (1941), strong advocates of such a straightforward cause-effect model, proposed the concept of "minimal cerebral injury" as an explanation. The supposed reason for not being able to document the existence of such injury is because it is, by definition, minimal, i.e., undetectable. Current usage of terms like "minimal brain damage" or "special learning disabilities" are expressions of the continuing need for clinicians to be able to explain disorder on the basis of simple cause-effect relationships rather than complex developmental processes.

Pasamanick & Knobloch (1966) reviewed a series of retrospective studies which examined the delivery and birth complications of children with a variety of subsequent disorders. They found a number of such later disorders to be significantly associated with greater numbers of complications of pregnancy and prematurity. These included cerebral palsy, epilepsy, mental deficiency, behavior disorders, and reading disabilities.

Almost all studies in this area have proceeded on the general assumption that it is possible to specify particular characteristics of either the child or his parents that will permit long range predictions regarding the ultimate course of growth and development.

These retrospective studies have implicated a number of factors in early development, such as (1) anoxia, (2) prematurity, (3) delivery complications, and (4) social conditions, as being related to later disorder. After a lengthy review of studies exploring the later effects of perinatal factors Sameroff & Chandler (1975) were forced to conclude that "even if one continues to believe that a continuum of reproductive casualty exists, its importance pales in comparison to the massive influences of socio-economic factors on both prenatal and postnatal development." Space does not permit a lengthy survey of the evidence for this conclusion to be made here. . . . For more detail the reviews of Gottfried (1973) and Sameroff & Chandler (1975) are recommended.

## Socio-Economic Influences

A recurrent theme that has run through much of the research in this area is that social status variables seem to play an important role in modulating the effects of perinatal factors. Birch & Gussow (1970) argued that high risk to infants is associated with depressed social status and ethnicity. The highest rates of infant loss were found among populations which are both poor and black. Pasamanick, Knobloch, & Lilienfeld (1956) found that the proportion of infants having some complication increased from 5 per cent in the white upper social class stratum, to 15 per cent in the lowest white socio-economic group, to 51 per cent among all nonwhites. These data imply that the biological outcomes of pregnancy are worse for those in poorer environments.

One of the most ambitious and revealing of the longitudinal studies of the effects of early complications has recently been completed in Hawaii. Werner, Bierman & French (1971), reported on all 670 children born on the island of Kauai in 1955. Because of the multiracial nature of Hawaii and the variety of social classes sampled when the whole population was used, Werner et al. were able to provide ample controls for both variables.

Each infant was initially scored on a four-point scale for severity of perinatal complications. At twenty months and again at ten years of age, these perinatal scores were related to assessments of physical health, psychological status, and the environmental variables of socio-economic status, family stability, and the mother's intelligence.

At 20 months of age infants who had suffered severe perinatal stress were found to have lower scores on their assessments. In addition, however, there was a clear interaction between the impairing effect of perinatal complications and environmental variables, especially socio-economic status. For infants living in a high socio-economic environment, with a stable family, or with a mother of high intelligence, the IQ differences between children with and without complication scores was only 5–7 points. For infants living in a low socio-economic environment, with low family stability, or with a mother of low intelligence, the difference in mean Cattell IQs between the high and low perinatal complications groups and between infants without perinatal complications ranged from 19 to 37 points.

The results of the Kauai study seem to indicate that perinatal complications were consistently related to later physical and psychological development only when combined with and supported by persistently poor environmental circumstances. In addition, when good prenatal care is available, socio-economic differences in the initial distribution of perinatal complications were found to disappear.

The infants of the Kauai sample were again examined when they reached 10 years of age (Werner, Honzik & Smith, 1968). There was no correlation between the perinatal-stress score and the 10-year measures. Some correlation was, however, found between the 20-month and 10-year data, especially when social-economic status and parents' educational level were taken into consideration. Stability of intellectual functioning was much higher for those children who had IQs below 80 at the 10-year testing. All of these children had 20-month Cattell scores of 100 or less, with almost half below 80. The majority of these children had parents with little education and of low socio-economic status. The Kauai study seemed to suggest that risk factors operative during the perinatal period disappear during childhood as more potent familial and social factors exert their influence.

Werner and her associates (Werner et al., 1971) noted that of every 1000 live births in Kauai, by age 10 only 660 would be adequately functioning in school with no recognized physical, intellectual, or behavior problems. Of the 34 per cent who would have problems at the age of 10 only a minor proportion could be attributed to the effects of serious perinatal stress. The biologically vulnerable child represents only a small proportion of those children who will not function adequately. The authors concluded that in their study "ten times more children had problems related to the effects of poor early environment than to the effects of perinatal stress."

The data from these various longitudinal studies of prenatal and perinatal complications have yet to produce a single predictive variable more potent than the familial and socio-economic characteristics of the caretaking environment. The predictive efficiency of the variable of socio-economic class is especially pronounced for the low end of the IQ scale. Willerman, Broman & Fiedler (1970), compared Bayley developmental scores obtained at 8 months with Stanford-Binet IQs at age 4. For children with a high socio-economic status there was little relationship between their 8-month Bayley scores and their 4-year scores. For children with a low socio-economic status, however, those who did poorly at 8 months continued to do so at 4 years of age. In addition, there was a crossover effect, where the high socio-economic status children who were in the lowest quartile at the 8-month examination were performing better at 4 years than were the low socio-economic status children who scored in the highest quartile at 8 months. Willerman et al. (1970) see poverty as amplifying IQ deficits in poorly developed infants.

The preceding survey of early biological complications conceptualized in the continuum of reproductive casualty (Lilienfeld, Rogers & Pasamanick, 1955) has not found much support for direct long-range consequences. The hypothesized "continuity" in development from early trauma to later deviancy does not appear to hold. There is a serious question as to whether a child who has suffered perinatal trauma, but shows no obvious physical damage, is at any greater risk for later deviancy, either neurological, perceptual, or intellectual, than a child who has not suffered perinatal trauma. In the studies reviewed the effects of social status tended to reduce or amplify intellectual deficits. In advantaged families infants who had suffered perinatal complications generally showed minor residual effects, if any, at follow-up. Many infants from lower social class homes with identical histories of complications showed significant retardations in later functioning. Socio-economic status appears to have much stronger influence on the course of development than perinatal history.

# Continuum of Caretaking Casualty

Sameroff & Chandler (1975) were led to propose a *continuum of caretaking casualty* to incorporate the environmental risk factors leading toward poor developmental outcomes. Although reproductive casualties may play an initiating role in the production of later problems, it is the caretaking environment that will determine the ultimate outcome. At one end of the caretaking continuum, supportive, compensatory and normalizing environments appear to be able to eliminate the effects of early complications. On the other end of the continuum, caretaking by deprived, stressed, or poorly educated parents tends to exacerbate early difficulties.

Where environmental factors have generally been ignored in research efforts aimed at finding linear chains of causality between early pregnancy and delivery complications and later deviancy, they have been the central focus for investigators exploring the role of caretaking practices in producing poor developmental outcomes. Unfortunately, environmentally oriented researchers have generally been equally one-sided in the way they ignore the child's individuality as a major influence on the caretaking to which he is exposed. Despite these limitations, research into the developmental implications of early caretaking practices has identified many circumstances that contribute to risk. Breakdowns in the parent-child relationship may take a great variety of forms. The most heavily researched and carefully documented of these transactional failures relates to the inability of parents and their children to work out an interactional style which both guarantees the child a reasonable margin of safety and satisfies the child's basic biological and social needs. This is the issue of child abuse. Physical abuse is dramatic evidence of a disorder in the parent-child relationship.

## *Child Abuse*

The major focus of research on the battered child has been devoted to characterizing the personality of the abusive parent. Spinetta & Rigler (1972) in a summary of this research characterized these deviant parents as of lower intelligence and with higher levels of aggressiveness, impulsivity, immaturity, self-centeredness, tenseness and self-criticism. However, knowing this constellation of personality characteristics does not greatly improve the probability of correctly predicting that child abuse will occur. Other parents with very similar characteristics do not abuse their children, while parents who are abusive will only batter one or two of their children. It appears that certain children are selected for abuse, or rather, that certain children tend to elicit abusive behavior from their parents.

Sameroff & Chandler (1975) were able to find support for the hypothesis that characteristics of the child may predispose the parents to battering or neglect. Klein & Stern (1971), for example found an association between low birth weight and the battered-child syndrome. Whereas typically 10 per cent of births are of low birth weights, among battered children the rate runs as high as 40 per cent. Klaus & Kennell (1970) suggested that the birth of a premature child may function to overtax the limited resources of certain mothers and precipitate an acute emotional crisis. Many battered children whose birth weights were within normal limits had other significant medical illnesses which might also have served to deplete their mothers' emotional resources.

It has been suggested that these problems may be partly the result of separation in the newborn period (Klaus & Kennell, 1970). Because of prematurity or serious illness a high proportion of battered children had been separated earlier from their parents for prolonged periods. Early prolonged separation may permanently impair the affectional ties between parents and children and leave the children vulnerable to parental abuse and neglect.

Although it is not always possible to separate truth from rationalization, the parents of abused children frequently describe their offspring as difficult and unmanageable. In one study (Morse, Sahler & Friedman, 1970), for example, 15 of the 25 children studied were considered "difficult" by their parents. Other data collected tended to support the impressions of the parents that many battered children were problem children preceding the reported abuse or neglect.

## Reciprocity in Child-Caretaker Relations

Bell (1968) took a fresh view of the literature on direction of effects in the caretaking interaction. He pointed out that while viewing infants as helpless victims fits a one-sided model of parental determination of behavior, many studies have shown that the infant is more involved in determining the nature of the interpersonal relationship than was once supposed. Many parent behaviors are not spontaneously emitted in the service of educating the child, but rather are elicited by many of the child's own characteristics and behaviors.

The infant's appearance of helplessness and dependency appears to be a strong contributor to the parents' desire to provide care (Rheingold, 1966). However, the response of all caretakers is not necessarily the same. The helplessness of a child can arouse negative as well as positive parental response. To the extent that the helplessness and dependency are accompanied by aggravating factors such as, restlessness, colic, and digestive difficulties, the chance of eliciting negative caretaking responses is increased (Bell, 1968).

The frequent assumption that the newborn is too ineffectual to carry any legitimate burden of responsibility for the quality of his or her relationship with various caretakers is contradicted by much current research. Constitutional variability in children strongly affects the parents' attitudes and caretaking styles. The systematic investigation of such idiosyncrasies in the child's behavioral organization is, however, of fairly recent origin. In research at New York University, Thomas, Chess & Birch (1968) studied the changes that occur in the child's temperament as a function of the transactions with his family environment. These investigators have described a temperamental constellation which they have labelled "the difficult child." Difficult infants were found to have low thresholds for arousal, intense reactions when aroused, poor adaptability and irregularity in biological functioning. Although only 10 per cent of their sample were categorized as difficult, 25 per cent of the children who later had behavioral disturbances fell in this group. Without the benefit of longitudinal studies one could easily misinterpret these difficulties of temperament as constitutional weaknesses that predisposed the child to later emotional difficulties. Such static predictions would not, however, prove to be very accurate. In fact, when Thomas, et al. examined the relationship between behavior in the first and fifth year of life few signifcant correlations were found. What made the difference in outcome for these children appeared to be the behavior of their parents. If the parents were able to adjust to the child's difficult temperament, a good behavioral outcome was likely. If not, the difficulties were exacerbated and behavioral disturbance often resulted.

The transaction was not simply the unidirectional influence of the parents on the child, but also the reciprocal influence of the child on his parents. The impact of these difficult children was such as to disrupt the normal caretaking abilities of their parents. The New York group reported that there were no marked differences in child-rearing attitudes expressed among the various parents in the sample. Whatever differences eventually characterized the parental attitudes of the deviant children apparently arose as a consequence of experience in the parent-child interaction.

The range of findings cited in the preceding section tends to support the hypothesis that knowing *only* the temperament of the child or knowing *only* the child-rearing attitudes and practices of the parents would not allow one to predict the developmental outcome for the child. It would appear, rather, that it is the character of the *specific transactions* that occurred between a given child and his parents which determined the course of his subsequent development. If the continuum of caretaking casualty is to be useful in elucidating developmental consequences, it must be related to the individual characteristics of the child in question. Neither the constitutionally oriented "continuum of reproductive casualty" nor the environmentally oriented "continuum of caretaking casualty" is predictive when taken alone. It is the combination of these dimensions which would make an understanding of development possible. . . .

## Continuity in Intelligence and Temperament

How is one to explain the general finding of the longitudinal studies reviewed above, that effects of severe early physiological trauma disappear with age? A possible explanation is that the quality of cognitive functioning changes with age, so that early aberrations may be irrelevant to later intelligence. Bayley (1949), commenting on the data from the Berkeley Growth Study of intelligence from birth to 18 years of age, noted that individual scores on the tests were unstable and that long-range predictions based on early IQ testing were not possible.

McCall, Hogarty, & Hurlbut (1972), in a review of longitudinal studies of intelligence, examined the common finding of low correlations between assessments of "intelligence" during infancy and later "intelligence." These investigators concluded that low correlations were not a consequence of unreliabilities in the test instruments, but were rather a consequence of qualitative shifts in what is defined as "intelligence" at different ages. They argued against the belief in a "pervasive and developmentally constant intelligence" on which most longitudinal comparisons have been based. From the available data it would appear that there is no basis for assuming a simple continuity in intellectual competence. . . .

## Developmental Models

The preceding review of the search for continuities in psychological functioning was not designed primarily to argue that such continuities are nonexistent, although the evidence seems to point in that direction. Rather, the discussion was aimed toward producing a conclusion that if continuities did exist we were not effectively searching for them. In order to find a more effective strategy one must "decenter," to use Piaget's terminology. Where investigators have focused on searching for developmental stabilities in either the constitution or the environment of the child, decentering would permit placing both the child's constitution and environment into a common system. A substantial increase in the sense one can make out of the developmental process could be provided by a simultaneous integration of these two factors in development. Sameroff & Chandler (1975) outlines three models—main effect, interactional, and transactional—that have been applied with varying degrees of success to explain the data presented earlier.

## Main-effect Model

The essence of the main-effect model is found in the typical nature-nurture argument as to whether constitution and environment exert influences on development which are independent of each other. A defect in the constitution of an individual will, according to this model, produce a defective adult irrespective of environmental circumstance, while a pathogenic environment will produce a defective adult independent of his constitution. Such a model is attractive to many investigators because of its parsimony and has been given strong currency in etiological research. Genetic factors as well as constitutional defects caused by pregnancy and delivery complications have often been assumed to exert such unilateral influences on development. As seen in the above review, the general findings of retrospective investigations that individuals suffering a wide range of disorders were more likely to have experienced complicated births than individuals without the disorders have not been supported by prospective studies. Although some of the effects of early trauma can be detected during infancy, by the age of seven these effects are almost completely attenuated. . . .

Clearly, there are extremes of constitutional disorders, such as severe brain damage, the developmental consequences of which would be deviant in any environment. Similarly, there are obvious extremes of environmental disorder which may well produce deviancy in a child of any constitution. These extreme examples are not, however, representative of the vast majority of children who evidence poor developmental outcomes. A main-effects model seems to apply neither to constitutional nor environmental components in development.

## Interactional Model

The preceding discussion would suggest that, at a minimum, any prognostic equation for predicting long range developmental outcomes must include information concerning both the child's constitutional make-up and his caretaking environment. From this point of view one should be able to create a two-dimensional array of constitutions and environments (see Figure 1), with an entry describing the child's developmental outcome for any combination of these two factors. Children with constitutional problems raised in a deviant environment would have poor outcomes. Children with constitutional problems raised in supportive environments and children without problems raised in deviant environments would having middling outcomes. The best outcomes of all would be expected for children without constitutional problems raised in a supportive environment.

While this interactive model substantially increases the statistical efficiency of developmental predictions, it is insufficient to facilitate our understanding

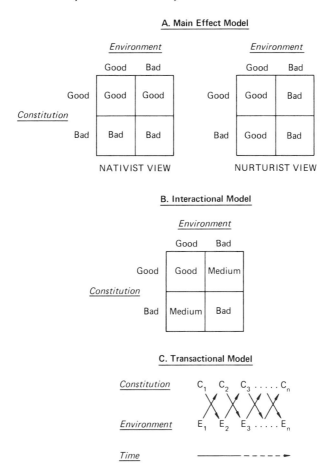

FIGURE 1. Models of development with outcomes predicted by main-effect and interactional models.

of the actual mechanisms leading to later outcomes. The major reason behind the inadequacy of this model is that neither constitution nor environment are necessarily constant over time. At each moment, month, or year the characteristics of both the child and his environment change in important ways. Moreover, these differences are interdependent and change as a function of their mutual influence on one another. The child alters his environment and in turn is altered by the changed world he has created. In order to incorporate these progressive interactions one must move from a static interactional model to a more dynamic theory of developmental *transaction* where there is a continual and progressive interplay between the organism and its environment.

## Transactional Model

Any truly transactional model must stress the plastic character of both the environment and the organism as it actively participates in its own growth. In this model the child's behavior is more than a simple reaction to his environment. Instead, he is actively engaged in attempts to organize and structure his world. The child is in a perceptual state of active re-organization and cannot properly be regarded as maintaining inborn characteristics as static qualities. In this view, the constants in development are not some set of traits but rather the *processes* by which these traits are maintained in the transactions between organism and environment.

Exceptional outcomes from this organismic or transactional point-of-view are not seen simply as a function of an inborn inability to respond appropriately, but rather as a function of some *continuous* malfunction in the organism-environment transaction across time which prevents the child from organizing his world adaptively. Forces preventing the child's normal integration with his environment act not just at one traumatic point, but must operate throughout his development.

Another major shortcoming resulting from the focus of the interactional model on product rather than process is its inability to deal with the directionality found in development. Despite the great variety and range of influences on development, there are a surprisingly small number of developmental outcomes. Evolution appears to have built into the human organism regulative mechanisms to produce normal developmental outcomes under all but the most adverse of circumstances (Waddington, 1966). Any understanding of deviancies in outcome must be interpreted in the light of this self-righting and self-organizing tendency, which appears to move children toward normality in the face of pressure toward deviation.

Two possibilities that defeat the self-righting tendencies of the organism and produce deviant development can be considered. The first possibility is that an insult to the organisms' integrative mechanisms prevents the functioning of its self-righting ability, and the second possibility is that environmental forces present throughout development prevent the normal integrations that would occur in a more modal environment. The former possibility can be seen in the pregnancy and delivery complications related to the *continuum of reproductive casualty*. The latter possibility can be seen in the familial and social abnormalities related to the *continuum of caretaking casualty*. These two sources of risk appear to be closely interrelated in the production of positive or negative developmental outcomes. Where the child's vulnerability is heightened through massive or recurrent trauma only an extremely supportive environment can help to restore the normal integrative growth process. A seriously brain-damaged child requiring institutional care would be an instance of such an extreme case of reproductive casualty. On the other extreme a highly disordered caretaking setting might convert the most sturdy and integrated of children into a caretaking casualty. . . .

# REFERENCES

BABSON, S. G., & BENSON, R. C. *Management of high-risk pregnancy and intensive care of the neonate.* St. Louis: Mosby, 1971.

BAYLEY, N. Consistency and variability in the growth of intelligence from birth to eighteen years. *Journal of Genetic Psychology,* 1949, Vol. 75, 165–196.

BEISER, H. R. Discrepancies in the symptomatology of parents and children. *Journal of the American Academy of Child Psychiatry,* 1964, Vol. 3, 457–468.

BELL, R. Q. A reinterpretation of the direction of effects in studies of socialization. *Psychological Review,* 1968, Vol. 75, 81–95.

BELL, R. Q., WELLER, G. M., & WALDROP, M. Newborn and preschooler: Organization of behavior and relations between periods. *Monographs of the Society for Research in Child Development,* 1971, Vol. 36, (2, Whole No. 142).

BERTALANFFY, L VON. *General system theory.* New York: Braziller, 1968.

BIRCH, H. & GUSSOW, G. D. *Disadvantaged children.* New York: Grune & Stratton, 1970.

BRAZELTON, T. B. Psychophysiologic reactions in the neonate. II. Effect of maternal medication on the neonate and his behavior. *Journal of Pediatrics,* 1961, Vol. 58, 513–518.

CAMPBELL, D. T. From description to experimentation: Interpreting trends as quasi-experiments. In C. W. Harris (Ed.), *Problems in measuring change.* Madison: University of Wisconsin Press, 1963. Pp. 212–44.

CHANDLER, M. J. Egocentrism and antisocial behavior: The assessment and training of social perspective-taking skills. *Developmental Psychology,* 1973, Vol. 9, 373–379.

CHESS, S. Genesis of behavior disorder. In J. G. Howells (Ed.), *Modern perspectives in international child psychiatry.* New York: Bruner/Mazel, 1971. Pp. 61–79.

CLARKE-STEWART, K. A. Interactions between mothers and their young children: Characteristics and consequences. *Monographs of the Society for Research in Child Development,* 1973, Vol. 38 (6–7, Whole No. 153).

COLE, M. & BRUNER, J. S. Cultural differences and inferences about psychological processes. *American Psychologist,* 1971, Vol. 26, 867–876.

COLE, M., GAY, J. GLICK, J. A., & SHARP, D. W. *The cultural context of learning and thinking: An exploration in experimental anthropology.* New York: Basic Books, 1971.

CORAH, N. L., ANTHONY, E. J., PAINTER, P., STERN, J. A., & THURSTON, D. L. Effects of perinatal anoxia after seven years. *Psychological Monographs,* 1965, Vol. 79, (3, Whole No. 596).

DENNIS, W. & NAJARIAN, P. Infant development under environmental handicap. *Psychological Monographs,* 1957, Vol. 71 (7, Whole No. 436).

ESCALONA, S. K. & HEIDER, G. M. *Prediction and outcome: A study in child development.* New York: Basic Books, 1959.

FREUD, S. *A general introduction to psychoanalysis.* New York: Washington Square Press, 1960.

FURTH, H. G. *Thinking without language: Psychological implications of deafness.* New York: Free Press, 1966.

GALDSTON, R. Dysfunction of parenting: The battered child, the neglected child, the emotional child. In J. G. Howells (Ed.), *Modern Perspectives in International Child Psychiatry.* New York: Brunner/Mazel, 1971. Pp. 571–488.

GESELL, A., & ARMATRUDA, C. *Developmental diagnosis.* New York: Hoeber, 1941.

GOLDSTEIN, K. *The organism.* New York: American Book, 1939.

GOTTFRIED, A. W. Intellectual consequences of perinatal anoxia. *Psychological Bulletin,* 1973, Vol. 80, 231–242.

GRAHAM, F. K., ERNHART, C. B., THURSTON, D., & CRAFT, M. Development three years after perinatal anoxia and other potentially damaging newborn experiences. *Psychological Monographs,* 1962, Vol. 76, (3, Whole No. 522).

GRAHAM, F. K., MATARAZZO, R. G., & CALDWELL, B. M. Behavioral differences between normal and traumatized newborns: II Standardization, reliability, and validity, *Psychological Monographs,* 1956, Vol. 70 (21, Whole No. 428).

GRAHAM, F. K., PENNOYER, M. M., CALDWELL, B. M., GREENMAN, M., & HARTMAN, A. F. Relationship between clinical status and behavior test performance in a newborn group with histories suggesting anoxia. *Journal of Pediatrics,* 1957, Vol. 50, 177–189.

HUNT, J. V. & BAYLEY, N. Explorations into patterns of mental development and prediction from the Bayley Scales of Infant Development. In J. P. Hill (Ed.), *Minnesota Symposia on Child Psychology.* Vol. 5. Minneapolis: University of Minnesota Press, 1971. Pp. 52–71.

KAGAN, J. & KLEIN, R. E. Cross-cultural perspectives on early development. *American Psychologist,* 1973, Vol. 28, 947–961.

KESSEN, W., HAITH, M. M., & SALAPATEK, P. H. Human infancy: A bibliography and guide. In P. H. Mussen (Ed.), *Carmichael's manual of child psychology.* (3d ed.) Vol. 1. New York: Wiley, 1970. Pp. 287–446.

KLAUS, M. H. & KENNELL, J. H. Mothers separated from their newborn infants. *Pediatric Clinics of North America,* 1970, Vol. 17, 1015–1037.

KLEIN, M. & STERN, L. Low birth weight and the battered child syndrome. *American Journal of Diseases of Children,* 1971, Vol. 122, 15–18.

KOHN, M. L. *Class and conformity.* Homewood, Ill.: Dorsey, 1969.

LABOV, W. The logical non-standard English. In F. Williams (Ed.), *Language and poverty.* Chicago: Markham Press, 1970. Pp. 153–89.

LEWIS, M. & McGURK, H. Evaluation of infant intelligence. *Science,* 1972, Vol. 170, 1174–1177.

LILIENFELD, A. M., & PARKHURST, E. A study of the association of factors of pregnancy and partuition with the development of cerebral palsy: A preliminary report. *American Journal of Hygiene,* 1951, Vol. 53, 262–282.

LILIENFELD, A. M., PASAMANICK, B. & ROGERS, M. Relationships between pregnancy experience and the development of certain neuropsychiatric disorders in childhood. *American Journal of Public Health,* 1955, Vol. 45, 637–643.

LOOFT, W. R. Egocentrism and social interaction across the life span. *Psychological Bulletin,* 1972, Vol. 78, 73–92.

McCALL, R. B., HOGARTY, P. S., & HURLBUT, N. Transitions in infant sensorimotor development and the prediction of childhood IQ. *American Psychologist,* 1972, Vol. 27, 728–748.

McGRADE, B. J. Newborn activity and emotional response at eight months. *Child Development,* 1968, Vol. 39, 1247–1252.

MORSE, C., SAHLER, O., & FRIEDMAN, S. A three-year follow-up study of abused and neglected children. *American Journal of Diseases of Children,* 1970, Vol. 120, 439–446.

NISWANDER, K. R. & GORDON, M. (Eds.) *The collaborative perinatal study of the national institute of neurological diseases and stroke: The women and their pregnancies.* Philadelphia: Saunders, 1972.

PARMALEE, A. H. & HABER, A. Who is the "risk infant"? In H. J. Osofsky (Ed.), *Clinical obstetrics and gynecology,* in press.

PARMALEE, A. H. & MICHAELIS, R. Neurological examination of the newborn. In J. Hellmuth (Ed.), *Exceptional infant: Studies in abnormalities,* Vol. 2. New York: Brunner/Mazel, 1971. Pp. 3–21.

PASAMANICK, B. & KNOBLOCH, H. Retrospective studies on the epidemiology of reproductive casualty: old and new. *Merrill-Palmer Quarterly,* 1966, Vol. 12, 7–26.

PASAMANICK, B., KNOBLOCH, H., & LILIENFELD, A. M. Socio-economic status and some precursors of neuropsychiatric disorders. *American Journal of Orthopsychiatry,* 1956, Vol. 26, 594–601.

PIAGET, J. *Psychology of intelligence.* New York: Harcourt, Brace & World, 1950.

RHEINGOLD, H. L. The development of social behavior in the human infant. In H. W. Stevenson (Ed.), Concept of development, *Monographs of the Society for Research in Child Development,* 1966, Vol. 31 (5, Whole No. 107).

SAMEROFF, A. J. Transactional models in early social relations. *Human Development,* 1975, 18:65–79.

SAMEROFF, A. J., & CHANDLER, M. J. Reproductive risk and the continuum of caretaking casualty. In F. D. Horowitz, M. Hetherington, S. Scarr-Salapatek, & G. Siegel (Eds.), *Review of Child Development Research.* Vol. 4. Chicago: University of Chicago, 1975. Pp. 187–244.

SAMEROFF, A. J., & ZAX, M. Schizotaxia revisited: Model issues in the etiology of schizophrenia. *American Journal of Orthopsychiatry,* 1973, Vol. 43, 744–754.

SPINETTA, J. J., & RIGLER, D. The child-abusing parent: A psychological review. *Psychological Bulletin,* 1972, Vol. 77, 296–304.

THOMAS, A., CHESS, S., & BIRCH, H. *Temperament and behavior disorders in children.* New York: New York University, 1968.

TINBERGEN, N. Ethology and stress diseases. *Science,* 1974, Vol. 185, 20–26.

WADDINGTON, C. H. *Principles of development and differentiation.* New York: Macmillan, 1966.

WERNER, E. E., BIERMAN, J. M., & FRENCH, F. E. *The children of Kauai.* Honolulu: University of Hawaii, 1971.

WERNER, E., HONZIK, M., & SMITH, R. Prediction of intelligence and achievement at ten years from twenty months pediatric and psychologic examinations. *Child Development,* 1968, Vol. 39, 1063–1075.

WERNER, H. *Comparative psychology of mental development.* New York: Science Editions, 1961.

WERNER, H. The concept of development from a comparative and organismic point of view. In D. B. Harris (Ed.), *The Concept of Development.* Minneapolis: University of Minnesota Press, 1957. Pp. 125–48.

WHITE, R. W. Motivation reconsidered: The concept of competence. *Psychological Review,* 1959, Vol. 66, 297–333.

WILLERMAN, L., BROMAN, S. H., & FIEDLER, M. Infant development, preschool IQ, and social class. *Child Development,* 1970, Vol. 41, 69–77.

WINDLE, W. F. Structural and functional changes in the brain following neonatal asphyxia. *Psychosomatic Medicine,* 1944, Vol. 6, 155–156.

WITKIN, H. A., OLTMAN, P. K., CHASE, J. B., & FRIEDMAN, F. Cognitive patterning in the blind. In J. Hellmuth (Ed.), *Cognitive Studies.* Vol. 2: *Deficits in Cognition.* New York: Brunner/Mazel, 1971. Pp. 16–46.

---

# Child Development in Emergent Family Styles*

## Bernice T. Eiduson

FOUR YEARS AGO we reported on the plan and design of our long-term study of 200 children who are growing up in a variety of family styles that illustrate the pluralistic development of the family in the United States today.[1] The families include 50 single-mother households; 50 social (rather than legal) contract couples; 50 communities or living groups, including religious and charismatic leader groups, triads and other domestic, rural and urban family communities; and a comparison group of 50 traditional, nuclear two-parent families. Now, in 1978, our study project is being viewed in its first

* Reprinted with permission of the author and publisher, from *Children Today,* March-April, 1978, 24–31.

and middle phases, covering the birth, infancy and entry into the preschool period of the study children.[2]

As we continue to scrutinize their family environments, to document childrearing practices and to seek to understand how they are shaping and influencing child growth, so the family members continue to welcome us into their homes. Once there, we conduct systematic home observations and detailed interviews. To date, every one of the 200 families is still part of our study.

The oldest child is now over four years of age, about one-third of the children are in the midst of the 3-year assessments and some of the younger children are approaching 2½ years. The length of time over which families were recruited into the study makes data collection at any specific chronological age stretch over an 18-month period. Although this slows the pace of working up our findings specific to any single age period, it is not an undesirable situation, since we realize that knowledge of the trends observed might influence the subsequent childrearing behaviors of the participants and thus affect the results of the study. Some of our participants are trained professionals, working in child-related areas, so it would not be unusual for them to read any articles we might publish on childrearing patterns. How such information and feedback would actually influence their parental behaviors is unknown; childrearing is to a much greater extent influenced by such factors as one's own experiences with one's parents, one's needs, aspirations and expectations surrounding the child and one's psychological sophistication. Yet we also know that "social desirability" or performing as expected can also be a powerful influence on parent behavior.

Our early findings are intriguing. They will ultimately comprise a very small part of our total effort, which aims to follow children from birth through entrance into the first elementary school years. Yet in only the few highlights presented here, it is obvious that the findings may challenge some of our perhaps complacent notions about how young children are being reared, and how they are faring in some very diverse families.

## Socialization Practices

The middle-class upbringing to which our 200 Caucasian parents were exposed as children comes into play when they have their own children. Concerns about the child's welfare seem to provide an important impetus in modifying the living plans of parents who are ideologically committed to living in a particular way. This is a very important development when one considers that many of these parents were originally part of the counterculture, the group of young people who thought that their own needs, values and aloofness from the mainstream culture should be the primary motivations for determining their lifestyles.

The early backgrounds of our parents made them concerned about the importance of good nutrition and prenatal medical care and of the impact of drugs on the expected child. Therefore, drug use decreased dramatically and food fads were abandoned when parenthood loomed.

Only 20 per cent of the mothers had home deliveries, although twice as many had earlier expressed an interest in them. Most of the families having home births were in the alternative groups—34 per cent of social contract mothers chose home delivery. The single mothers were like the traditional married couples in their rejection of home births.

## Home Environments

The prevalence of these middle-class prenatal practices was of particular interest, for they were occurring in residences that looked very different, and operated quite differently, from those of traditional nuclear families. There were hand-hewn houses—with stereos, pianos and pictures as well as lofts and outdoor plumbing—hidden in remote areas, accessible only if one ignored the "road ends here" signs. There were compounds of small modest units, dominated by a large central structure usually containing a kitchen, dining room and meeting areas. We found children's quarters, with separate play and sleeping areas, contiguous to adult quarters. Conventional small apartments, with contemporary accoutrements designed to lighten the housewife's burdens, were common in urban areas, while far-from-modest suburban ranch houses that showed the unmistakable hand of an interior decorator were seen occasionally. Project children were growing up in grandparents' homes and in large converted beach houses; some families had moved from California to Alaska, Hawaii or other parts of the United States. Both the pluralism of American life and the mobility of young parents—trends noted by so many observers—were apparent in the family lifestyles we were documenting, a factor that made our studies difficult but compelling.

It is easy to convey pluralism through slides and photographs. However, since our study had to assess the significance of a family's functioning, structure and membership for a child's health, cognitive growth and emotional development, we looked at the diverse home settings with some of the following questions in mind.

Was an environment stimulating enough intellectually for the child at specific age periods? If there were sufficient visual and aural stimuli, was there also some personal space, some place for the child to have privacy? We also looked at how people in the family interacted with the child. Did they reinforce babbling and smiles? How many tasks did the mother usually perform in her daily routines? How did her schedule affect the amount of time she had to attend to her child? If the mother was unavailable, were regular substitutes on hand, or were caretaking arrangements more casual?

The environmental studies designed and conducted by Thomas S. Weisner, the co-principal investigator on the project, and his staff, were planned to make possible the differentiation of areas in which the four family styles were very similar, and those in which they differed. For example, looking at the environments of 6-month-old children, there were significant differences in such characteristics as family size, number and variety of people present in the family and number and variety of people other than parents involved in child care. There were also differences in the routine tasks that mothers and fathers performed and, generally, in the nature of the supporting network available "in house" to the parent.

In all of these areas, the living group family is a much more complex unit than the two-parent, traditional married unit. With more people present, there are more available caretakers and persons with whom to share tasks and responsibilities and more involvement of the father with the child, since he is usually around more.

Mothers were present and involved in child care in nearly all of the families, except for the relatively small number of creedal living groups. In these, child caretakers supervised 24-hour nurseries, so that mothers' responsibility for child care was reduced after the first six months. The involvement of biological mothers with their own children in these settings varied with a group's philosophy and individual preference. In a few families, when mothers hovered too close child and parent were separated, a procedure instituted on the rationale that children should build trust in a number of "significant other family members." In these and in a number of living groups, the children live in special quarters. However, the most frequent child lifestyle in living groups, as well as in other alternative families, features close physical proximity between child and parent.

Given this overall high maternal involvement, then, we found that differences in caretaking patterns of the infant were mainly related to whether or not the mother had additional support at home. In 71 per cent of the conventionally married families, she was the sole primary caretaker of the infant, while 67 per cent of the living group children had significant caretakers in addition to their mothers.[3] The father was a secondary primary caretaker in 20 per cent of the traditionally married and 35 per cent of the communal families.

It is important to note that the biological mother of a baby was the primary caretaker in more than 90 per cent of the family units. This was borne out at the 6-month home observation period and again at the one-year period. Fathers are more actively involved in caretaking as the *second* caretaker in the living group than they are in conventional families. Of course, living groups or communities also have some third- and fourth-level regular caretakers, while most traditional households do not.

Single mother and social contract households fall in between these two groups in regard to some ideological and lifestyle patterns—with a few interesting differences. Of all the alternative groups, single mothers were the most upwardly mobile. In regard to values, they appeared closer to the two-parent traditional nuclear family than mothers in the other two lifestyles—more drawn to conventional achievement goals and material values, for example, and more accepting of our societal dependence on technology and science.

Studies of our single mothers showed that within this category three groups could be identified: nest builders—women who consciously chose and planned to have a baby and start a new household; post-hoc adaptors—women who had not planned to become pregnant but adjusted happily to this circumstance; and a small group of unwed mothers, women who were more like the unwed mothers of yesteryear in attitudes and circumstance.[4] The levels of education and of professional development, income status and general lifestyle were distinctive for each group, with the nest-builders being the women who were most self-sufficient and whose goals were most closely tied to those of the women's movement. Roles and responsibilities toward the child also differed among the groups, depending on the availability of economic, psychological and social supports.

Social contract families are essentially two-person households in which the fathers are active secondary caretakers. Despite the families' commitment to "distributed" parenting,[5] the fathers are never as equally involved as mothers because economic needs too frequently force them to work outside the home. As a group, these families have the greatest affiliation for espoused counter-culture values, especially in regard to sex role egalitarianism and humanistic perspectives.

# Childrearing

Once the babies were born into these diverse family units, how were they reared? Two previous observations provide clues to the socialization practices of parents. First, their prenatal practices, which reflected their middle-class backgrounds, were excellent predictors of their postnatal patterns. Secondly, the mothers were the primary caretakers of a baby in most of the families, despite their differing lifestyles.

This means that during the baby's first year, child socialization practices were generally similar among the four family groupings, although some differences did exist. At five months, 60 per cent of the children had their own room for sleeping, 30 per cent slept in their own bed in the parents' room, and eight per cent slept with parents in the parents' bed. Sleep problems were generally defined by mothers as fussiness at bedtimes and the incidence and methods of handling these did not vary a great deal across the groups; all reported that they would ignore, comfort or hold the child.

Feeding patterns were similar across lifestyles and among mothers and were determined primarily on a demand schedule. Breast feeding was undertaken by 81 per cent of all mothers: by 94 per cent in living groups, 89 per cent in social contract families, 79 per cent among single mothers and 64 per cent in the traditional married group.

A significant difference was found in the length of time the babies were breast-fed. For example, two-thirds of the living groups were still breast-feeding at six months, a time when two-thirds of the traditional marrieds had given it up. At one year, 44 per cent of living group families were breast-feeding, versus six per cent of traditional marrieds.

Forty-two per cent of the babies were already feeding themselves by the time they were five months old, and 62 per cent of the mothers reported that they could pick up a spoon successfully. By this time also, 87.5 per cent of all babies were on some daily feeding schedule.

Alternative families appear to have their babies eating with them more often than do traditional married families.

Seventy-eight per cent of the others in the latter group reported that their babies do *not* eat with them, compared to approximately half in the other lifestyle groups. Overall, the data suggest that many of the early childrearing practices we examined seemed to continue the middle-class, conventional patterns of the participants' own families.

These socialization tendencies also had counterparts in attentional, interactional and emotional aspects of the basic mother/child unit. We monitored these during the course of customary caretaking activities during a noontime feeding period. There were strong individual differences in such aspects of caretaker attentiveness as touching and holding, affective tone and expressiveness between child and caretaker and vocalization and mutuality of vocal responsiveness. In these aspects of child-parent interaction, caretakers showed the range of behaviors found in most populations.

The behaviors of babies showed strong individual differences, too: in levels of arousal during a feeding situation, in the proportions of crying and smiling in a 3-hour period and in range of affects displayed, for example. But no single family style had a premium on any of these parameters. Whether or not the mother was the sole caretaker and the family was big or small, rural or urban, close ideologically or free-wheeling—none of these or other characteristics that we have analyzed to date appear to override the individual differences within each group to any significant extent.

As we had anticipated, our alternative populations were more mobile and less stable, so far as residence is concerned, than traditional families. For example, only 31 per cent showed no moves in the first year, compared to 47 per cent of traditional families. In regard to changes in family lifestyle the same trend was true: by the end of the baby's first year, 90 per cent of traditional marrieds were in the same lifestyle as they had been during pregnancy. This was true of only 67 per cent of alternative families.

The greatest change took place in the move—by 12 participants—from living group situations to two-parent families. Living groups gained three participants who had formerly been in social contract families and four living group members changed from one family group to another. Ten single mothers married by the end of the child's first year, while seven participants (two of them traditional marries) dissolved their two-parent families. The amount of change in family status was paralleled by residential moves which often, but not invariably, accompanied lifestyle changes.

Both of these change indices attest to the experimental orientation of alternative group members, and to their active search for more satisfying lifestyles when discontented or troubled. Yet despite these indices of external instability and change, the mother/child unit remained intact. Relationships between mother and child seemed in every lifestyle to be regulated by the child's early biological and psychological needs, and by the mothers' tendencies to be responsive. Thus, often mothers reported pushing aside their personal interests and needs in favor of their child's. (The importance of this finding can be appreciated when we keep in mind that most parents initially selected their alternative lifestyle with their own needs in mind.)

## Children's Physical Status

Did any of the young children demand special kinds of physical care from birth which might predict differences in the children's development and in the families' caretaking styles? Reports of countercultural practices based on casual observation and early informal studies by other investigators had led us to anticipate multiple and serious health problems in mothers and children living in alternative lifestyles. However, the babies in our study proved to be, by and large neurologically normal at birth, and the mothers to have no more than the expected range of complications at birth.

Results of the Parmalee Obstetrical Complications Scale (OCS) showed that the mothers' scores fell generally within the normal range, with the number of below- and above-average scores normally distributed. Scores suggesting that a child might be at physical risk were usually due to a cumulative or combinatory series of adverse factors during the pregnancy or delivery, such as phlebitis or hypertension in the mother, premature rupture of membranes, Caesarean performed because of desultory labor, anasthesia given to the mother and twin births.

When babies were given a Newborn Neurological Examination, the total sample fell within normal limits. The seven babies in the total sample who were below standard deviation on both of the examinations were flagged as being "at risk." However, these children were randomly distributed among the four family styles, with the traditional parent group contributing two cases.

Of all the groups, single mothers scored lowest in our birth measures, reflecting potentially complicating birth conditions. Living group mothers obtained the highest scores, and traditional married mothers and social contract mothers fell in between. None of the babies who were born at home were at risk.

Were babies in large families ill more often? Were they prone to contagious diseases or more subject to accidents, falls and bruises—the kinds of problems that come with neglect or abuse? To obtain this information we looked at the records of more than 1,000 contacts between pediatric service providers and the study children. Our use of a pediatric payment plan as an incentive for parents to continue in the project enabled us to collect such information. Under this plan, $80 per year is paid to providers of services used by parents in exchange for data supplied by them on the reason for the child's visit and the diagnosis and disposition of the case. We realize that the ability of the payment plan might have influenced our participants' use of pediatric services, and that this has to be kept in mind in interpreting our findings.

Data on medical usage patterns showed that children were generally seen by private physicians or at well-baby clinics; almost every one had been immunized by five months, and the most common illnesses were respiratory infections, diarrhea, roseola and otitis media. The incidence of these diseases and the less frequently found anomalies were comparable to the "illness" patterns reported for children under six years of age by the National Center for Health Statistics in 1974. We found that ours was not an unusually sickly group, a fact then validated by a standardized pediatric examination documented at one year. Only a handful of babies—two with congenital heart murmers and one with anemia, for example—were identified as showing other than normal physical development. Again, identified problems tended to cross alternative/traditional family lines, although some nutritional practices, such as adherence to a vegetarian or macrobiotic diet maintained in accordance with religious belief, contributed to some nutritional deficits.

## Developmental Differences

Do ideological differences in parenting goals and diversities in family structure affect a child's growth and development? Our data show that one-year-olds can develop as healthy, normal children in what appear outwardly to be very diverse physical and social family environments.

Using standardized developmental measures, assessments of the infants established the extent to which caretaking differences in style affected developmental outcome by age one. Babies were evaluated at eight months and at one year on the Bayley Scale of Infant Development (Mental and Performance Indexes) and at one year on the Strange Situation Test (Ainsworth).

At eight months, when the infants were seen in the home, results of the Bayley Scale of Infant Development showed that they were, on the whole, normal. The children in our four groups differed somewhat in intellectual level, with infants of both two-parent family groupings (traditional marrieds and social contracts) scoring highest; however, the differences were not significant.

In performance on motor items at eight months, infants in two-parent unwed families considerably surpassed the group of babies in multiple parenting families. Infants of both single mothers and traditional married mothers were closer to the children of two-parent unwed families than to infants in multiple caretaking situations. When Bayley tests were readministered at one year, neither the mental nor motor scores highlighted differences among our four parenting styles—which suggests that developmental differences seen at eight months do not necessarily predict later growth patterns.

The Strange Situation Test provided an early opportunity to explore socioemotional development of the very young child. Two outcome scores on this test pertained to the baby's ability to recover from distress, as indicated by the amount of play behavior shown following separation from the mother and being left alone, and when a stranger entered during the mother's absence. Two other outcome scores pertained to the child's behavior when the mother returned.

Our data suggested that the attachment of most infants to their mothers was strong and similar to that reported for other populations. Of the total sample of one-year-olds, over three-quarters showed a secure attachment to the mother; less than one-fifth were calm or uninvolved, perhaps defensively so, after they had been separated from the mother; and an even smaller group were very distressed during the separation episode. However, the insecure or indifferent children were not in any single family group. Infants of single mothers seemed singularly securely attached to the mother, but the reactions of other babies were remarkably similar and, in general, indicated a secure group of babies. This finding was unexpected; however, it supported other data suggesting that certain factors—such as the number of people in the home and whether a child is a first or second child or demanded special caretaking attention—do not appear at this point in our data analysis to significantly influence the reactions of one-year-olds to a short separation from the mother.

Since there is so much variability in the composition and membership of our families *within* our four lifestyle groupings, and since this makes for differences in regard to the kind of supporting network the mother has available for helping her in many caretaking activities, we studied how the way certain aspects of her caretaking activities, especially those in which others assist her in caring for the child, affected child development. Baby books and interviews collected at close intervals throughout the babies' first years provided detailed data on numerous specific features of both childrearing and parent activities. From first-year data we selected over 50 items telling us the number and kind of caretakers occasionally used by a mother when she went out or was away overnight; the frequency and length of time the child was left with others; the mother's non-child related involvements, such as work, school and community activities; and the proportion of time that the mother was child-occupied during our home observations. Together, these items give a rather detailed picture of certain facets of the child's experience, as well as of the parent's caretaking practices.

When the data were analyzed, they reaffirmed that some environmental and caretaking factors are important indicators of environmental conditions which influence growth, but that they do not tell the whole story, and in fact account for a small per cent of the differences in developmental scores at one year. Our data suggested that the larger the family, the higher the Bayley scores; the extent to which a mother was occupied with activities other than the child reduced scores; and the extent to which other caretakers were involved with the baby lowered scores. However, these data must be interpreted with caution: while they appear to support our thinking in child development that mothers play salient roles as social facilitators for development during the first year, and that the stimulation provided by the more varied social nexus of the child may encourage development when it does not dilute the mother's involvement; these environmental factors do not seem to influence scores in a very substantial way. We are continuing to search for other meaningful influence on development.

# What Does the Future Hold?

We have found in year one, then, that our families—despite their different value systems and diverse housing, family environments, routines and life-styles—socialize infants in similar, growth-facilitating ways, and that their childen, by and large, look physically and psychologically healthy. Will this continue to be the case? We anticipate (from looking at data collected since the one-year period) that child behaviors and parental attitudes and practices will become much more diverse as children grow older. Preschoolers participate more extensively in the lives of family members, for one thing, and they are also more subject to influence outside of the home. Furthermore, the older child's mobility and growing self-reliance permits parents to regenerate their prepregnancy plans and activities and to gravitate toward earlier interests and involvements.

The issue of whether the parent's needs or the child's have priority at any given time has periodically emerged. We anticipate that as parents and children move beyond some of the constraints and satisfactions of their early interactions and relationships, the desire of both groups to express their own needs will increasingly determine both children's and parents' activities. It will be interesting to see how families resolve these sometimes conflicting needs.

What can our research contribute to the much-debated question of whether or not the nuclear unit we have always identified as the American family is here to stay? The pluralistic family forms that we are studying certainly indicate that the American family is no longer limited to the traditional parent nuclear structure that has become so stereotyped as the middle-class model. Our families are middle-class in their backgrounds and in many practices involving their very young children. The parent/child unit remains—as it does in many societies—the core element in widely varying family forms. In those behaviors that reflect this unit—its stability, composition and interaction—our families have much in common, and there is little data to suggest that major changes in the parent/child unit take place during the first year.

Such differences in family forms as the number of kin versus non-kin present, family size, kinds of support networks and family routines and organization—all ecological features of the family unit—may influence other behaviors which will emerge as the child grows older, and it is for this reason that we expect to find increasingly greater diversity in developmental outcomes as a function of family form.

As we study children and families, we cannot help but be cognizant of the major changes in the alternative scene that have taken place since our project was initated. Some of our families are reflecting these changes, for in some ways their family units and lifestyles are assuming a more traditional cast—some have moved from alternative into traditional married relationships, and many who once "dropped out" are returning to school or to work in the community. As this tendency becomes more apparent, we also observe that conventional society is becoming more accepting of alternative practices and attitudes and is thus facilitating the alternative family's assumption of roles in the dominant society. However, we continue to wonder, as do others, whether these changes are more apparent than real. As one alternative group member explained:

> I am angered by the continual pronouncement of the death of the alternative movement. It is not dead; it has changed. A generation grew up in the 60s, and thousands of us have made the principles of the movement a part of our lives. If we are now professionals, and parents, rather than students, working rather than demonstrating, our dedication is no less. We staff the free clinics, work within unions and community organzations, and incorporate political education into our dealings with people. If our style seems to have changed, our goals have not.[6]

How will this attitude affect childrearing perspectives and practices? This is one of the important questions we seek to answer. Our "alternative" parents continue to report that they want their children to become independent at an early age, to make decisions for themselves, to be able to choose among multiple identificatory models, to be able to adapt flexibility to a rapidly changing world and to find relationships with others the most satisfying and powerful parts of their lives. Can one quarrel with such aspirations for any child, whether he or she is being reared in an alternative or traditional lifestyle?

How are children being prepared to achieve these goals and what degree of success will be attained? We expect that the answers to these significant questions will be found in our longitudinal study.

## REFERENCE NOTES

1. See "Looking at Children in Emergent Family Styles" by Bernice T. Eiduson, *Children Today,* July-August 1974.
2. This work is supported in part by the National Institute of Mental Health, the U.S. Public Health Service and the Carnegie Corporation of New York.
3. Thomas S. Weisner and Joan C. Martin, Learning Environments for Children in Conventionally-Married Families and Communes in California," paper presented at the meeting of the American Anthropological Association, November 1976.
4. Madeleine Kornfein, Thomas S. Weisner and Joan C. Martin, "Women into Mothers: Experimental Family Life Styles," in Chapman and Gates (eds.), *Women into Wives: The Legal and Economic Impact of Marriage,* Beverly Hills, California, Sage Publications, 1977.
5. Bernice T. Eiduson, Jerome Cohen and Jannette W. Alexander, "Alternatives in Child Rearing in the 1970's," *American Journal of Orthopsychiatry,* 1973, 43. (Also in J. Cohen (Chair), *Child Development in Alternative Family Settings,* symposium presented at the meeting of the American Orthopsychiatric Association, New York, June 1973 and reprinted in J. Clarke (ed.), *Intimacy, Marriage and the Family,* New York, Allyn and Bacon, 1975 and J. T. Gibson and P. Blumberg, *Readings for Child Psychology,* New York, Addison-Wesley, 1976.
6. Excerpted from "Letters," *Time Magazine,* October 10, 1977.

# Exploratory and Play Behaviors of Infants Reared in an Institution and in Lower- and Middle-class Homes*

*Roberta R. Collard*

. . . ACCORDING TO PIAGET (1952), during the first year of life, the development of some schemas and their combinations into new patterns may be influenced by the infant's opportunities for certain experiences with objects, and the appearance of a stage of sensorimotor intelligence may be accelerated by such experiences. During the first 2 months of life, schemas such as looking at, grasping, and mouthing an object appear in isolation, but later such

* From *Child Development,* 1971, 42, 1003–1015. © 1971 by the Society for Research in Child Development, Inc. All rights reserved. Reprinted by permission of the publisher and the author.

simple schemas are combined into coordinated patterns to form more complex ones. . . .

Piaget (1952) implies that curiosity is the motive for developing new schemas in his description of "secondary circular reactions" in which infants learn to repeat acts leading to "interesting" sights or sounds which, in turn, serve as intrinsic rewards for learning new behavior patterns. After infants develop memory for the results of some of their behavior patterns, they begin to combine schemas into means-end relationships, an ability which Piaget calls the beginning of "true intelligence." Thus in Piaget's theory, exploratory behavior and the development and combination of schemas into new patterns form the bases of early intelligence.

If the number of different schemas developed by an infant depends upon his opportunities to play with a variety of objects and to learn social play with objects by playing with other persons, one would expect to observe fewer patterns of exploration and play in infants reared in most institutions than in those reared at home, and fewer patterns in infants from less privileged homes than in those from more privileged ones. Infants in most institutions are exposed to a smaller variety of objects and situations than are home infants, and the former often receive less social stimulation than do home infants (Rheingold 1960; Rubenstein 1967). Institutional babies also tend to show less exploratory behavior than do babies reared at home (Collard 1962; Rubenstein 1967). It is probably true in most instances that infants from less affluent homes are exposed to fewer material objects than are infants from more affluent ones. Lower-class mothers usually have more children and fewer labor-saving devices and thus less time to spend with their babies than middle-class mothers do, which also may lead to fewer patterns of exploration and play in their infants. Kagan (1969) observed that a group of lower-class mothers spent less time playing with their babies, and they also did not reward their children's maturational achievements as often as mothers of higher-socioeconomic status did.

The present study attempts to test the above assumptions by measuring the varieties of response and the number of exploratory and play responses made to a toy in a standard situation by a group of institutional infants, one from lower-class homes, and one from middle-class homes. The institutional environment and child-care practices were examined in detail, and the mothers of the home infants were given a questionnaire concerning their infants' opportunities for exploration and play. . . .

[Method: Dr. Collard used three groups of sixteen babies, ranging in age from 8.5 to 13 months. One group were institutional infants of Negro, Spanish-American, and Anglo-American parentage; the second group were from working-class families matched to the institutional subjects in age, sex, race, and occupational level of fathers; and the third group of infants were from upper-middle-class white American homes who were matched in age and sex to the other subjects. All infants were in good health at the time they were tested. The three groups differed

in the ratio of caretakers to babies: there was one caretaker to five institutional infants; the average number of children in the lower-class homes was four; and in
the middle-class homes, three. All of the home infants had been cared or predominantly by their mothers in intact homes; none of the mothers worked outside their
homes.

Tests were conducted at a well-baby clinic. Various types of toys were given to
the infant and his/her reactions observed. Standardized measures of the babies'
maturity of manipulation were made, using two subtests of the Gesell Developmental Schedules (Gesell & Amatruda, 1954).]

# Discussion

The results of this study indicate that opportunity for exploration and play
with a variety of objects may be one factor which increases the number of
schemas in a baby's repertoire as well as the amount of his exploratory behavior. The home-reared subjects who had been given more freedom to explore in a more complex environment not only explored more in the experimental situation than the institutional babies did but also showed
significantly more patterns of exploration and play than did the latter. The
middle-class-home infants did not explore more during the test than the
lower-class-home babies did, possibly because both had been given ample opportunity to explore, but the middle-class-home babies had developed more
varieties of schemas in relation to objects and persons than had the lower-
class subjects. This may have occurred because the middle-class-home babies
were exposed to a larger variety of objects and had been played with more by
their mothers. Middle-class-home infants showed much more social play with
the test object which they probably had learned through play with their
mothers or other family members.

The results of the Gesell subtests suggest that previous experience with objects similar to those in the tests may have increased the scores of some of the
subjects relative to others. The institutional infants, who had played with
blocks, performed as well as or better than did the lower-class-home infants,
most of whom had not played with blocks. The middle-class-home babies,
who not only had played with blocks but had someone who played with
them, performed best of all. The institutional infants performed at a lower
level on the Cup and Cubes subtest, probably because they had never had a
chance to play with containers and contained objects. They appeared to be
distracted by the novelty of the cup and to ignore the cubes. They tended to
mouth, wave, and bang the cup in much the same way as they had responded
to the novel toy. . . . Not the least of the differences among the environments in this study is the number of children cared for by one adult in the
three groups. In the institution each caretaker was responsible on the average
of five babies, the lower-class mothers for four children, and the middle-class
mothers for only three. Because the spacing of the children was wider in the

middle-class families than in the lower-class ones, the middle-class mothers had fewer young children to care for and thus would have had more time available to spend with their babies.

## REFERENCES

COLLARD, R. R. A. study of curiosity in infants. Unpublished doctoral dissertation, University of Chicago, 1962.

GESELL, A., & AMATRUDA, C. S. *Developmental diagnosis.* New York: Hoeber, 1954.

KAGAN, J. Inadequate evidence and illogical conclusions. *Harvard Educational Review,* 1969, 39, 126–129.

PIAGET, J. *Origins of intelligence in children.* New York: International Universities Press, 1952.

RHEINGOLD, H. L. The measurement of maternal care. *Child Development,* 1960, 31, 565–75.

RUBENSTEIN, J. Maternal attentiveness and subsequent exploratory behavior in the infant. *Child Development,* 1967, 38, 1089–1100.

# Head Start: The First Decade*
## *Julius Richmond, Edward Zigler and Deborah Stipek*

. . THERE CAN BE little question that Head Start is the most significant and the most comprehensive program ever mounted to serve the nation's economically disadvantaged children and their families. However, it must be acknowledged that, though Head Start has been enthusiastically received by participating families and has been praised by leaders in the child development field, the program has also been seriously criticized by some professionals. Perhaps this criticism by the professional community can be traced to a confusion over Head Start's objectives.

During Head Start's early years, there was a failure to communicate clearly the program's specific goals and the methods designed to achieve those goals. This should not be interpreted to mean that those who conceptualized or administered the program did not have a clear idea of the purpose of Head Start, as well as a firm commitment to certain procedures for accomplishing that purpose. Perhaps much of the confusion about Head Start has been the inevitable consequence of mounting a greatly expanding and continuously evolving program in a very brief period of time.

Like many important social action programs, Head Start was the result of a number of forces simultaneously at work in the nation. In 1965, a combination of forces helped create the program: (1) new ideas about the nature of

* Reprinted by permission of the authors from an unpublished paper, 1975.

the developing child,[1] (2) a new social consciousness in the country that produced the War on Poverty, and (3) the efforts of a small group of dedicated individuals, both in and outside the federal government.

In 1965, the committee that planned Project Head Start engaged in considerable discussion on the issue of the number of children that should be enrolled in the program during its first summer. One point of view was that this first Head Start program should be a small, closely monitored effort involving no more than 100,000 children. When substantial funds were committed to Head Start, it was decided to plan a program for over 500,000 children for the summer of 1965. The committee felt that Head Start would be helpful to many children and families, and there was no indication that the program would have negative consequences. Indeed, if this first summer Head Start program did little more than provide immunizations and other badly needed health services for many of these children, it seemed well worth doing.

It is important to note the optimistic outlook of many Americans in the mid-1960s, when the Head Start program was first conceived. Many leaders in government and the child development field during that period felt that the problems of poverty could be readily solved and that even modest social intervention efforts could bring about significant results in improving the lives of children from low-income families. It is clear that the optimism of professionals in the field of early childhood during the mid-1960s contrasts sharply with the more cautious, conservative viewpoint of those who plan programs for children in the mid-1970s.[2]

It is the authors' view that the nay-saying and defeatism we are currently witnessing are grave dangers to the development of a sound national policy for children and families. Any pioneering social program like Head Start is a likely target for the criticism of skeptics. This situation is exacerbated by a lack of agreement over how to determine objectively the worth of any broad-based social program. In the case of Head Start, though new measures are available for evaluating the program, agreement has not been reached on all criteria for assessing a program with such complex and comprehensive objectives.

Now that Head Start has passed its tenth anniversary, the authors believe that this is an especially appropriate time to present a progress report on the goals and achievements of the program. We hope that this report will be timely and of interest to families who have participated in the program, to citizens whose tax dollars have supported the program, and to professionals who have followed the development of Head Start since 1965.

## Goals and Components of Head Start

After the Economic Opportunity Act was passed by Congress in 1964, Sargent Shriver, director of the new Office of Economic Opportunity, appointed an interdisciplinary committee to advise him on programs for children. In 1965, the committee, chaired by Dr. Robert Cooke, then pediatrician-in-chief of Johns Hopkins Hospital, submitted recommendations for a Head Start program for disadvantaged preschool children. Within a few months, the seven pages of recommendations were transformed into a nationwide summer program serving 561,000 children.

Because of past misunderstandings about Head Start, it should be helpful to restate the program's seven goals exactly as they were set forth in the recommendations of the Advisory Committee in 1965:

1. Improving the child's physical health and physical abilities.
2. Helping the emotional and social development of the child by encouraging self-confidence, spontaneity, curiosity, and self-discipline.
3. Improving the child's mental processes and skills, with particular attention to conceptual and verbal skills.
4. Establishing patterns and expectations of success for the child that will create a climate of confidence for his or her future learning efforts.
5. Increasing the child's capacity to relate positively to family members and others, while at the same time strengthening the family's ability to relate positively to the child and his problems.
6. Developing in the child and his or her family a responsible attitude toward society and encouraging society to work with the poor in solving their problems.
7. Increasing the sense of dignity and self-worth within the child and his or her family.[3]

Perhaps the most innovative idea found in these recommendations—an idea that continues to be fundamental to Head Start—is that effective intervention in the lives of children can only be accomplished through involving parents and the community in the intervention effort. Unlike America's public school systems, Head Start has pioneered in advocating the involvement of parents in program planning and operation.

The recommendations of the Advisory Committee also emphasized the importance of flexible programs, tailored to the needs of each community. Although communities have been given considerable latitude in developing their own Head Start programs, every Head Start program is required to include six major components. These components, which together provide a comprehensive program of services for children, illustrate the broad goals of Head Start:[4]

1. *Health.* Many children entering Head Start have never seen a doctor or dentist. Head Start provides these children from low-income families with a complete medical examination, including vision and hearing tests, immunizations, identification of handicapping conditions, and a dental checkup. A medical history is prepared for each child, and follow-up treatment is provided to correct identified health problems.
2. *Nutrition.* Head Start centers give every child at least one hot meal and one snack every day. Usually, a trained nutritionist supervises the nutritional activities of each Head Start program and plans educational programs to teach parents how to select healthy foods and prepare well-balanced meals at home.

3. *Education.* Head Start's educational program is designed to meet the needs of
each child. With one teacher, one aide, and one volunteer for every fifteen
children, the program can give a child individual attention. Children participate in a variety of learning experiences and are encouraged to develop self-
confidence and the ability to get along with others. Head Start also aims to
meet the needs of ethnic groups in the community. For example, if a program
has a majority of bilingual children, at least one teacher or aide must speak
their native language.

4. *Parent Involvement.* Every Head Start program is required to involve parents
in all phases of program planning. Many parents serve as members of Policy
Councils and have a voice in management decisions. On a paid or voluntary
basis, some parents serve as aides to Head Start teachers and social workers or
as cooks, clerks, storytellers, and supervisors of play activities. Fathers often
join in the activities of the children and also paint and repair buildings, make
furniture, and turn outdoor areas into playgrounds. Through classes held at
the center, parents learn about child care, preparing meals, and educational
activities that can be carried out at home. Language classes for non-English-
speaking parents are often arranged at the centers.

5. *Social Services.* In every center, a Head Start social service coordinator maintains close relationships with community agencies that provide help for families. The coordinator meets with parents and refers them to local agencies that
can provide the family services they need.

6. *Mental Health Services.* In recent years, Head Start has stressed the importance of providing mental health and psychological services to children of low-
income families, to help foster their emotional and social development. A
mental health professional must be available to every Head Start program to
provide mental health training to staff and parents and to make them aware of
the need for early attention to the special problems of children.

When programs were monitored during Head Start's early years, a great
deal of variation was found in the extent to which individual programs included these major components. To help centers that had difficulty in meeting
the requirements, a Head Start Improvement and Innovation program was
launched in 1973. This effort also aimed to make local programs more responsive to the needs of individual children and communities. Through this
long-range continuing effort, new performance standards have been tested
and made mandatory for all Head Start programs, and local grantees have
been encouraged to develop variations in the Head Start program. For example, in some centers, children have one three-hour program each day; in
others, there are two three-hour sessions, in the morning and afternoon; and
in still others, children spend the entire day at the center while their parents
work.

# Some Misconceptions About Head Start

It might be helpful at this point to take up some of the misconceptions about
Head Start that have grown through the years. For example, many believe

that there is a single, standardized educational curriculum for every Head Start program throughout the country. This has never been true. From the beginning, local programs have been allowed a great deal of flexibility in planning educational curricula that meet the needs of their own children and communities. Since the Improvement and Innovation effort began in 1973, Head Start programs have been encouraged to become even more flexible in programming. A variety of approaches for preschool children—center-based programs, home-based programs, and local variations—have been developed by grantees across the country.

Another misconception is based on the idea that Head Start was designed primarily to develop the cognitive capabilities and improve the IQs of disadvantaged young children. Raising IQ scores has never been the major objective of Head Start. It is worth noting that only one of seven original Head Start goals, listed above, deals specifically with improving a child's educational skills. From its inception, Head Start has aimed to improve not just the cognitive abilities of children, but also their physical well-being, social skills and self-image.

Why then has IQ been used so often in assessing Head Start? Early reports of substantial gains in IQ by Head Start children certainly contributed to this use of IQ as a measure of the program's effectiveness. To some, it seemed natural to employ the standard IQ tests in evaluating Head Start, because these tests are well-developed instruments that have proved valid and reliable over the years. On the other hand, there are few measures of social-emotional variables, and those available are not well understood.

Still another misconception stems from the idea that Head Start was intended as a program solely for children of families with incomes below the poverty level. The program's Planning Committee agreed that children lose a great deal by being segregated along socioeconomic lines and that, whenever possible, Head Start should give children from different income groups an opportunity to learn from one another. Since 1965, Head Start has provided that up to 10 per cent of the children in the program can be drawn from families above the poverty income line. In 1966, the value of mixing children of varied socioeconomic groups was supported by the findings of the Coleman Report.[5] Some Head Start programs have achieved this goal of integration. However, because of the limited funds available, many Head Start programs have found it difficult to meet the needs of the poor children in their communities and at the same time to integrate these children with children of other income groups.

## Head Start's Mandate and Funding

The Economic Opportunity Act of 1964, under which Head Start was originally authorized, did not mention the program by name. This antipoverty legislation established a Community Action Program, and Head Start was considered a part of that program. The only reference at the time to a child development program was in the Senate Report on the Economic Opportunity Act:

> . . . a balanced program of educational assistance might include, although it need not be limited to, the following: creation of, and assistance to, preschool day care, or nursery centers for 3- to 5-year-olds. This will provide an opportunity for a Head Start by cancelling out deficiencies associated with poverty that are instrumental in school failure . . . Such special education programs could be open to all needy children.[6]

This quotation shows how broad the expectations of Congress were at that time for a child development program. "Cancelling out deficiencies associated with poverty that are instrumental in school failure" is not a very realistic goal for any child development program. Perhaps that is why the Senate Report did not indicate how this goal might be accomplished.

The original legislation not only failed to mention a Head Start program, but it also provided no guidelines for such a program. Moreover, as is customary, Congress did not become involved in any policy decisions related to the program. Nor did Congress directly authorize funds for Head Start during its early years. Prior to 1969, the director of the Office of Economic Opportunity allocated funds authorized for the Community Action Program to Head Start and submitted these allocations to Congress for approval. After the 1969 Amendment to the Economic Opportunity Act, Congress began to authorize specified amounts to Head Start each year. During the program's first decade, the funds actually available for Head Start were often substantially less than the amounts authorized. It should also be noted that by law, 80 per cent of Head Start's funds are to come from the federal government, and 20 per cent are required to be funds received from nonfederal sources.

. . . The Head Start, Economic Opportunity, and Community Partnership Act of 1974 (P.L. 93-644), which superseded the original Economic Opportunity Act, is the act under which Head Start now operates. It is interesting to note that the use of Head Start in the title of this act demonstrates the increased recognition of the program by Congress over the years. Though Head Start has continued to receive congressional support, other legislation in Congress proposing child development programs failed to pass. A significant setback for advocates of child development programs was the veto of the Head Start Child Development Act of 1969, which proposed a number of programs for children and families and also authorized an extension of Head Start.

. . . Federal appropriations for Head Start showed strong increases during the first few years of the program. During the following years, there were only small annual increases. However, funds for the program grew substantially in Fiscal Years 1975 and 1976. Over the past seven years, the increase in Head Start funding has been considerably less than the increase in the level of prices across the country.

Although Head Start began as a summer program, most Head Start programs today are full-year programs. There are now approximately 1,200 full-year programs and only 200 summer programs throughout the country. About 15 per cent of eligible children are currently enrolled in Head Start. Eligibility requirements are that most children in the program must be between the ages of three and five and that 90 per cent must be from families whose income is less than the poverty line set annually by the U.S. Office of Management and Budget. The decline in the number of children in summer programs . . . has been offset by the increase in the number of children in full-year programs and in a variety of innovative programs now conducted by Head Start. Thus, Head Start has increased its services to the nation's children over the years through expanding the program to a full-year program for most children and through developing new and innovative demonstration programs rather than through adding to the total number of children enrolled.

## Innovative Head Start Demonstration Programs

The original planners of Project Head Start realized that no single approach could meet the needs of every child in every community. From its inception, Head Start has developed new, flexible ways to serve children and families with varied needs.

After the program became a part of HEW's Office of Child Development in 1969, continuous evaluation of local programs showed the strengths and weaknesses of different approaches to child development. Based on these evaluations, Head Start has stepped up its development of new, innovative programs in recent years. The age range of children enrolled in Head Start has been broadened, and there has been an increased emphasis on working with the entire family. Innovative Head Start demonstration programs now involve over 11,000 children. A number of these experimental Head Start programs and Head Start-related programs are described below.

*Follow Through,* established in 1967 and administered by the U.S. Office of Education, was designed to continue and build on the cognitive and social gains made by children in full-year Head Start programs or in similar preschool programs for children from low-income families. The program provides nutritional and health care, social and psychological services, and special teaching assistance to children during their early years in elementary school.

Head Start's *Project Developmental Continuity* is another demonstration project planned to insure continuity of child development services for children making the transition from preschool to elementary school. In a number of pilot projects, Head Start staff work with school administrators and teachers to plan programs that provide Head Start children with continued health, social, and educational services through the third grade. An effort is made to maintain parent involvement during a child's first years in elementary school.

*Parent and Child Centers* (PCCs), launched in 1967, were the first Head Start experimental programs designed to serve young children from birth to age three and their families. In thirty-three urban and rural communities, these centers seek to improve services for over 4,000 children. The centers also help parents learn about the needs of their children and about supportive services available in the community. In 1973, seven selected PCCs were provided with funds to develop a child advocacy component and to promote services for all children in the community.

In 1970, three Parent and Child Centers became *Parent and Child Development Centers* (PCDCs) as part of an intensive research and demonstration program launched by the Office of Economic Opportunity and later sponsored by the Office of Child Development. The PCDC program was based on research that showed the significance of developmental processes in infants and the important role of parents in the development of children. In the three PCDC sites, different models of parent-infant interventions were developed and carefully evaluated. These models will be tested in additional sites, and the research findings may be incorporated in some PCC programs.

*Home Start,* a three-year demonstration begun in 1972, also focused on the family. The program provided Head Start health, social, and educational services to children and parents at home rather than at a center. Parents were trained to work with their children in their own home. Evaluations showed that this home-based approach was a viable alternative to providing services at a center. Some 300 Head Start programs are now using a home-based approach, and Home Start training centers have been set up to provide training and technical assistance to Head Start and other programs that may want to establish home-based programs.

*The Child and Family Resource Program* is another family-oriented Head Start project, designed to make community services available to families with children from the prenatal period through age eight. In this demonstration, the entire family is enrolled. CFRPs work closely with each family to identify their particular needs and cooperate with local community agencies to help meet those needs. Each Child and Family Resource Program acts as a base to link needed local services to children and families.

An important program now under way aims to provide *Head Start Services to Handicapped Children.* In 1972, Congress mandated that at least 10 per cent of Head Start's national enrollment consist of handicapped children. In Fiscal Year 1976, $20 million was appropriated by Congress for this program. Head Start has successfully carried out the congressional mandate, and handicapped children in Head Start now receive the full range of Head Start services, as well as services tailored to their special needs. In cooperation with the Office of Education's Bureau of Education for the Handicapped,

Head Start has funded a network of fourteen Resource Access Projects to provide training materials to Head Start teachers working with handicapped children and to give technical assistance to Head Start programs to help them improve their services for these children.

Head Start's *Bilingual-Bicultural* effort focuses on the needs of Spanish-speaking children who now comprise more than 15 per cent of all Head Start children. This program is another step in Head Start's continued effort to meet the special developmental and cultural needs of children in the program. Projects have been funded to develop curricula providing instruction in two languages for Spanish-speaking Head Start children. Other projects are under way to train Head Start staff in bilingual-bicultural education and to set up resource centers providing technical assistance to Head Start grantees with programs for Spanish-speaking children and families.

Although many teachers are trained in elementary education today, there is still a shortage of qualified staff for Head Start and other preschool programs across the country. Head Start's *Child Development Associate* program was initiated in 1972 to train workers in Head Start and day care centers and to help them achieve professional status in the child care field. CDAs receive credentials based on their demonstrated performance in working with young children rather than on academic credits. About 4,000 men and women are now receiving Child Development Associate training in pilot programs funded by OCD and in Head Start Supplementary training programs. As it is expanded, this Child Development Associate program will help meet the urgent nationwide need for more trained child care workers.

A national program called *Education for Parenthood,* jointly sponsored by the Office of Child Development and the Office of Education, now plays a significant role in Head Start programs for children and families. As part of this Education for Parenthood program, high school students learning about early childhood work with children in Head Start centers. Curricula in child development and parenthood are also being developed to help train Head Start parents.

These new and innovative demonstration programs show clearly that Head Start today is not a single, standardized program but a flexible, evolving program. While a strong effort has been made to maintain uniformly high performance standards in the more than 1,200 Head Start programs throughout the country, there are as many different approaches to child development in Head Start as there are in other preschool programs.

In the years ahead, Head Start will continue to seek new and better ways to provide services to children and their families. During the next few years, an increased effort will be made to provide continued support to Head Start children after they enter elementary school and to improve services for families by coordinating the activities of Head Start and other community programs.

It is the authors' belief that the present Head Start program may be replaced in the future by a more comprehensive Head Start child development program serving the needs of a wide variety of children and their families.

# Evaluation of Head Start

Head Start at times has been praised as a success and at other times dismissed as a failure. Before any final judgment is made, however, consideration should be given to the basis on which many evaluations of Head Start have been made. We have already discussed the error in using IQ scores to measure the program's effectiveness, especially because cognitive development is only one of a number of Head Start goals. Nor has Head Start failed in the area of cognitive gains, as some critics would have you believe. Though many evaluation studies of Head Start have been made, the most highly publicized was a nationwide study conducted in 1969 by Ohio State University, in cooperation with the Westinghouse Learning Corporation.[7] This study noted many significant and lasting gains for some groups of children within Head Start, particularly for urban black Head Start children. However, the most publicized finding of the Westinghouse-Ohio University study was that the cognitive gains made by children in Head Start were often lost after the children had been in elementary school for a few years. Although some interpreted this finding as a case against Head Start, it seems instead an indictment of the schools.

Although not all Head Start children have maintained cognitive gains after leaving the program, a number of studies show that many Head Start children have demonstrated superior cognitive ability well into the early elementary grades, when compared with non-Head Start children.[8] Unfortunately, many critics have ignored the considerable evidence provided by these studies, which indicate the ability of Head Start children to continue to make gains in elementary school. Recent longitudinal studies conducted by Yale University suggest that Head Start children often demonstrate a "sleeper effect" as they move through school. One group of Follow Through children studied, for example, showed no greater gains at the third grade level than gains shown by a control group of other children. However, these Head Start children demonstrated a significant superiority in three out of five academic measures by the end of the fifth grade.[9] A similar delayed effect resulting from a preschool intervention program was reported by Palmer in 1975.[10] Because the children in the first Head Start programs have only recently entered their teens, evidence is not yet available concerning the effect of their Head Start experience on their later education, as well as on the incidence of emotional problems and juvenile delinquency in these children.

Though some Head Start critics have focused on the need to improve the IQ scores of enrollees, Head Start parents and staff have been more concerned with improving the overall well-being of the children in the program.

In their preoccupation with IQ, critics seem to lose sight of the many benefits that Head Start brings to children of low-income families. In evaluating the program, they often overlook the enthusiastic support of the program by the many Head Start parents who believe that Head Start has helped their children significantly. Perhaps it would be worthwhile at this point to review the success Head Start has had in achieving several major goals often ignored by critics of the program.

Health care for children is an important area rarely considered in critical assessments of Head Start. In 1975, more than 85 per cent of the children enrolled in Head Start received both medical and dental examinations. Head Start children have received immunizations at a rate about 20 per cent higher than the national average for children. Through a collaboration between Head Start and the Medicaid Early and Periodic Screening, Diagnosis and Treatment Program (EPSDT), many eligible Head Start children have been assisted in enrolling in Medicaid and in receiving the health services available through the program. This cooperative effort has served as a model for local collaboration between Head Start programs, State Medicaid agencies, and community health resources in the delivery of health services to children. During the program's first decade, Head Start has been the nation's largest deliverer of health services to disadvantaged children.

In evaluating Head Start, critics often overlook the program's pioneering effort to encourage parent involvement. From its inception, Head Start has demonstrated that parents want to participate in the education of their children and that it benefits the children when they do. In 1965, during Head Start's first summer of operation, more than 150,000 people volunteered to help set up and run the new Head Start centers across the country. Many parents of Head Start children and individuals from minority and low-income groups were among these volunteers. This kind of social involvement by disadvantaged people may lead to greater participation by groups that historically have felt powerless to influence their communities and the quality of their own lives. In a perceptive paper published in 1971, Edmund Gordon intimated that building leadership potential among the poor might play an important role in the development of their children.[11] The modeling theory of socialization tells us that children feel they can influence their future lives when they interact with adult models who feel able to shape their own lives and environment. Thus, by encouraging parents to play a positive role in the education of their children, Head Start's parent involvement effort helps stimulate positive attitudes in the children as well.

In addition to involving parents in the educational programs of their children, Head Start has made it possible for many men and women who have been underemployed to develop new job opportunities as professionals or paraprofessionals in the child care field. Through a supplementary Training Program, Head Start employees are able to study child development at universities in courses leading to academic degrees or to certification in early childhood education. Some 10,000 Head Start staff members are now enrolled in this Supplementary Training Program. About half of these men and women are receiving Child Development Associate training, as described above, which will provide them with credentials to work as professionals in the child care field. Through these career development and training programs, Head Start has not only provided opportunities for job advancement to many but has also taken steps to help meet the nation's growing need for trained child care workers.

We have discussed Head Start's contribution to the lives of many thousands of children and adults of low-income families. It is important to note that Head Start has also had a significant impact on many communities by influencing local health and educational institutions to become more responsive to the needs of the poor. In 1970, a Study was made of a number of communities, some with Head Start programs and some with no Head Start programs. The survey, published as the Kirschner Report,[12] documented approximately 1,500 instances in which health and educational services for poor children were improved in the Head Start communities. Nothing approaching this record was found in the non-Head Start communities. Head Start seemed to serve as a catalyst in encouraging the improvement of services for children. With Head Start's increased emphasis on coordinating local services, the impact of the program on communities should become even more significant in the years ahead.

## Looking Back and Ahead

Though Head Start's overall record has been good, there continue to be shortcomings in some local programs. Although a greater degree of parent participation has been achieved by Head Start than by any other program sponsored by the federal government, some Head Start grantees still show signs of the kind of paternalism found in many programs designed to aid the poor. They fail to allow parents to play the decisive role in policy making that is required for all Head Start programs.

Some Head Start programs need to work for greater flexibility. Children of low-income families are not a homogeneous group, all with the same developmental characteristics and in need of the same kinds of intervention. Some of these children may require a full range of compensatory programs, and some may not. Head Start programs must improve their ability to meet the individual needs of these children.

If we look back on Head Start's first decade, it is clear that a preschool intervention program like Head Start cannot eliminate the consequences of poverty and the effects of inadequate housing, poor nutrition, and unsatisfactory health care. It is more realistic to judge Head Start on its contribution to the well-being and happiness of children and families rather than on its ability to solve society's problems. Judged on the basis of these more modest but nevertheless significant objectives, Head Start can undoubtedly be considered a success.

Unlike most educational programs, Head Start has undergone constant self-evaluation and has continued to experiment in order to increase its effectiveness as a comprehensive program for children. Head Start's innovative programs have led to new approaches to parent involvement, in-service training, career development, and meeting the needs of the nation's children of low-income families.

Although much was accomplished during Head Start's first ten years, much still remains to be done. Through the program's continued effort to help children and families live fuller, happier lives, Head Start should be able to serve the nation's children even more effectively in the decade ahead.

## REFERENCE NOTES

1. B. Caldwell. Speech delivered at the Idaho Early Childhood Education Conference, Boise State College, Boise, Idaho, April 3, 1972. J. B. Richmond, "The State of the Child: Is the Glass Half Empty or Half Full?" *American Journal of Orthopsychiatry*, vol. 44 (1974), pp. 484–490.

2. B. Caldwell. "A Decade of Early Intervention Programs: What We Have Learned, *American Journal of Orthopsychiatry*, vol. 44 (1974), pp. 491–496.

3. R. Cooke, Chairman, "Recommendations for Head Start Program," February 19, 1965 (U.S. Department of Health, Education, and Welfare, Office of Child Development, 1972).

4. Office of Economic Opportunity, "Head Start: A Community Action Program" (Washington, D.C., U.S. Government Printing Office, 1968).

5. J. Coleman, et al., "Equality of Educational Opportunity" (Washington, D.C., U.S. Government Printing Office, 1966).

6. Senate Reports, No. 23626, 1964, p. 20.

7. Westinghouse Learning Corporation, "The Impact of Head Start: An Evaluation of the Effects of Head Start on Children's Cognitive and Affective Development, Executive Summary," Ohio University Report to the Office of Economic Opportunity, Clearinghouse for Federal Scientific and Technical Information, June 1969.

8. F. Palmer, "Has Compensatory Education Failed? No, Not Yet." Unpublished manuscript (Stony Brook, New York: University of New York, 1975).

9. E. Zigler, Yale Research Group. "Summary of Findings from Longitudinal Evaluations of Intervention Programs." Mimeograph (Yale University, 1976).

10. F. Palmer, op. cit.

11. E. Gordon, "Parent and Child Centers: Their Basis in the Behavioral and Educational Sciences—an Invited Critique," *American Journal of Orthopsychiatry*, vol. 41 (1971), pp. 39–42.

12. Kirschner Associates, Inc., "A National Survey of the Impacts of Head Start Centers on Community Institutions" (Albuquerque, N. M., May 1970).

# Is Early Intervention Effective?
# Facts and Principles of Early
# Intervention: a Summary*
*Urie Bronfenbrenner*

T HE CONCLUSIONS of this analysis are presented in the form of a summary of the research findings and a set of generalizations to which they give rise.

## A. Summary of Research Results

1. *Preschool Intervention in Group Settings.* The results are based on twelve studies involving children ranging in age from one to six. Eight of these researches included comparisons between randomly constituted experimental and control groups. Conclusions regarding program effectiveness are cited only if supported by results from such comparisons.

   a) Almost without exception, children showed substantial gains in IQ and other cognitive measures during the first year of the program, attaining or even exceeding the average for their age.

   b) Cognitively structured curricula produced greater gains than play-oriented nursery programs.

   c) Neither earlier entry into the program (from age one) nor a longer period of enrollment (up to five years) resulted in greater or more enduring cognitive gains.

   d) By the first or second year after completion of the program, sometimes while it was still in operation, the children began to show a progressive decline, and by the third or fourth year of follow-up had fallen back into the problem range of the lower 90's and below. Apparent exceptions to this general trend turned out to be faulted by methodological artifacts (e.g. self-selection of families in the experimental group).

   e) The period of sharpest decline occurred after the child's entry into regular school. Preliminary data from the Follow-Through program suggest that this decline may be offset by the continuation of intervention programs, including strong parent involvement, into the early grades.

   f) The children who profited least from the program, and who showed the earliest and most rapid decline, were those who came from the most deprived social and economic backgrounds. Especially relevant in this regard were such variables as the number of children in the family, the employ-

---

* From *A Report on Longitudinal Evaluation of Preschool Programs: Vol. 2. Is Early Intervention Effective?* Washington, D.C., 1974, HEW Publication No. [OHD] 74–25.

ment status of the head of the household, the level of parents' education, and the presence of only one parent in the family.

g) Results from a number of studies pointed to factors in and around the home as critical to the child's capacity to profit from group programs both in preschool and in the elementary grades. For example, several researches revealed that the greatest loss in cognitive performance of disadvantaged children took place not while they were in school, but over the summer months. During this same period, disadvantaged children living in favorable economic circumstances not only maintained their status but showed significant gains.

2. *Home-based Tutoring Programs.* The results of the two studies in this area were similar to those for preschool programs in group settings. Children showed dramatic gains in IQ while the project was in operation but began to decline once the home visits were discontinued.

3. *Parent-Child Intervention.* A total of nine studies, involving children from the first year of life through elementary school, focused simultaneously on parent and child (almost exclusively the mother) as the targets of intervention. In seven of these researches, the principle of random assignment (either of individuals or groups) was employed in the designation of experimental and control subjects. Again conclusions regarding program effectiveness are cited only when supported by results from comparisons of randomly constituted experimental and control groups.

a) Parent-child intervention resulted in substantial gains in IQ which were still evident three to four years after termination of the program (Gordon 1972, 1973; Levenstein 1972a). In none of the follow-up studies, however, had the children yet gone beyond the first grade.

b) The effects were cumulative from year to year, both during intervention (Levenstein 1972a) and, in some instances, after the program had ended (Gordon 1973 Levenstein 1972a).

c) The magnitude of IQ gain was inversely related to the age at which the child entered the program, the greatest gains being made by children enrolled as one and two year olds (Gilmer *et al.* 1970; Gordon 1972, 1973; Karnes *et al.* 1968, 1969b, 1970; Levenstein 1972a; Radin 1969, 1972; Stanford Research Institute 1971a, 1971b).

d) Parent intervention was of benefit not only for the target child but also for his younger siblings (Gilmer *et al.* 1970; Klaus and Gray 1968; Gray and Klaus, 1970).

e) Gains from parent intervention during the preschool years were reduced to the extent that primary responsibility for the child's development was assumed by the staff member rather than left with the parent, particularly when the child was simultaneously enrolled in a group intervention program (Gilmer *et al.* 1970; Karnes *et al.* 1969c).

f) By the time the child was five years old, parent intervention appeared to have little effect so far as gains in intellectual development are concerned. *But children who were involved in an intensive program of parent intervention during, and, especially, prior to their enrollment in preschool or school, achieved greater and more enduring gains in the group program* (Gilmer *et al.* 1970; Gordon 1972, 1973; Radin 1969, 1972; Stanford

Research Institute 1971a, 1971b; Smith 1968). This effect on group programs did not appear until children were at least three years of age, but
was still strongly in evidence in the one project in which parent intervention was continued through the sixth grade (Smith 1968). Thus, from the
third year onward, parent intervention seemed to serve as a catalyst for
sustaining and enhancing the effects of group intervention.

g) Parent intervention influenced the attitudes and behavior of the mother not
only toward the child but in relation to herself as a competent person
capable of improving her own situation (Gilmer *et al.* 1970; Gordon 1973;
Karnes *et al.* 1970).

h) Families willing to become involved in parent intervention programs
tended to come from the upper levels of the disadvantaged population.
Research findings indicate that, at the most deprived levels, families are so
overburdened with the task of survival that they have neither the energy
nor the psychological resources necessary to participate in an intervention
program involving the regular visit of a stranger to the home (Klaus and
Gray 1968; Radin and Weikart 1967).

i) The complexity of findings on the effects of parent intervention prompted
a more detailed analysis of the role of parent-child interaction in fostering
the child's psychological development. An examination of the research literature (Bronfenbrenner 1968a, 1968b, 1972) indicated that, in the early
years of life, the key element was the involvement of parent and child in
verbal interaction around a cognitively challenging task. A second critical
feature was the fact that the mother not only trained the child but the child
also trained the mother. A third factor was the existence of a mutual and
enduring emotional attachment between the child and adult. It is by capitalizing on all these elements, by taking as its focus neither the child nor
the parent but the parent-child system, that parent intervention apparently
achieves its effectiveness and staying power. It is as if the child himself had
no way of internalizing the processes which foster his growth, whereas the
parent-child system does possess this capability.

j) Along with advantages, parent intervention appears to have serious limitations in terms of its applicability and effectiveness with families at the
lowest extreme of the socioeconomic distribution.

4. *Ecological Intervention.* The research results indicate that for the children
from the most deprived groups no strategy of intervention is likely to be effective that focuses attention solely on the child or on the parent-child relationship. The critical forces of destruction lie neither within the child nor
within his family but in the desperate circumstances in which the family is
forced to live. What is called for is intervention at the *ecological level,* measures that will effect radical changes in the immediate environment of the family and the child. Only three studies of this kind were found in the research literature (Heber, *et al.,* Rehabilitation of Families at Risk for Mental
Retardation 1972; Skeels 1966; Skodak and Skeels 1949). The major findings
were as follows:

a) *Severely disadvantaged children of mothers with IQ's well below average
(i.e. below 70 or 80) are not doomed to inferiority by unalterable constraints either genetic or environmental.*

    b) Substantial changes in the environment of the child and his principal caretakers can produce positive developmental changes considerably greater (gains of 25 to 28 IQ points) and more enduring than those achieved by the most effective intervention techniques when the home environment is left essentially unaltered.

    c) The processes and effects produced through ecological intervention substantiate the critical role in early development played by an enduring one-to-one relationship involving the child in verbal interaction with an adult around cognitively stimulating activities.

# B. Some Principles of Early Intervention

The principles are stated in the form of propositions specifying the elements that appear essential for early intervention programs to be effective. Although derived from results of a substantial number of studies by different researchers, these generalizations should still be regarded as tentative. Even where the supportive findings have been replicated, they are susceptible to alternative interpretations, and the crucial experiments are yet to be done.

To indicate the extent to which each of the following generalizations are supported by research results, we shall label each one by a symbol. The superscript "i" denotes that the conclusion is *inferred* from the evidence; the superscript "r" means that the generalization is supported by *replicated results* obtained in two or more well-designed studies described in the main body of this analysis, but that there is need for further research designed specifically to test and refine the proposition in question.

## *1. General Principles* [1]

    1. *Family Centered Intervention.* The evidence indicates that the family is the most effective and economical system for fostering and sustaining the development of the child.[r] The evidence indicates further that the involvement of the child's family as an active participant is critical to the success of any intervention program.[r] Without such family involvement, any effects of intervention, at least in the cognitive sphere, appear to erode fairly rapidly once the program ends.[r] In contrast, the involvement of the parents as partners in the enterprise provides an on-going system which can reinforce the effects of the program while it is in operation, and help to sustain them after the program ends.[r]

    2. *Ecological Intervention.* The first and most essential requirement is to provide those conditions which are necessary for life and for the family to function as

---

[1] The propositions are stated in terms of parent rather than mother alone in the belief that subsequent research will indicate that they apply as well to the father, or any other older member of the household who is prepared to assume a major and continuing responsibility for the care of the child.

a childrearing system.[r] These include adequate health care, nutrition, housing, employment, and opportunity and status for parenthood.[i] These are also precisely the conditions that are absent for millions of disadvantaged families in our country.[r]

To provide the conditions necessary for a family to function will require major changes in the institutions of the society and the invention of new institutional forms.[i] The results of this analysis offer no guidance on the development of new systems for providing adequate health care, nutrition, housing, or income, but they do suggest strategies for increasing opportunity and social reward for the functions of parenthood. These include extending the number and status of part-time jobs available to disadvantaged parents of young children,[i] establishing more flexible work schedules,[i] introducing parent apprentice programs in the schools to engage older children in supervised care of the young,[i] involving parents in the work of the school,[r] creating patterns of mutual assistance among disadvantaged families living in the same neighborhood,[i] meeting the basic needs of young families, (including supervised experience in child care) before they begin to raise children,[i] providing homemaker services,[i] making available insurance to meet family emergencies,[i] and using television as an adjunct to parent-child intervention.[i2]

> 3. *A Sequential Strategy of Intervention.* A long-range intervention program may be viewed in terms of five stages. Although the program may be begun with benefit to the child at any age,[r] initiating appropriate intervention at earlier stages can be expected to yield cumulative gains.[r] Ideally intervention should not be interrupted (for then the gains achieved are gradually eroded[r]) and there should be continuity from one phase to the next.[i] During every stage the first requirement is to meet the family's basic needs as outlined above.[i] Thereafter, intervention is differentiated to accommodate the developmental level of both family and child as indicated below.

# C. Stages of Intervention

## *Stage I. Preparation for Parenthood*

Ideally, intervention begins before the family is formed when the future parents are still in school. This initial phase involves providing school children of both sexes practicum experiences in the care of the young.[i] In addition, attention is given to the health requirements of the future mother in terms of nutrition and preventive medical care.[i]

---

[2] A more extended discussion of the rationale and nature of the foregoing proposals appears in Bronfenbrenner 1972b.

## Stage II. Before Children Come

The next critical point for intervention is after the family is formed but before any children are born. Here the initial emphasis is to insure adequate housing, health care, nutrition, and economic security before, during, and after pregnancy.[i] This is also the optimal period for introducing a parent intervention program with some experience with young children provided before the family's own offspring arrive on the scene.[i]

## Stage III. The First Three Years of Life

During this period the primary objective is the establishment of an enduring emotional relationship between parent and infant involving frequent reciprocal interaction[r] around activities which are challenging to the child.[r] The effect of such interaction is to strengthen the bond between parent and child,[r] enhance motivation,[r] increase the frequency and power of contingent responses,[r] produce mutual adaptation in behavior,[r] and thereby improve the parent's effectiveness as a teacher for the child,[i] further the latter's learning,[r] and, in due course, establish a stable interpersonal system capable of fostering and sustaining the child's development in the future.[r] The development of such an enduring pattern of attachment and interaction can be facilitated through a parent intervention program involving the following elements.

1. The program includes frequent home visits in which parent and child are encouraged, by example and with the aid of appropriate materials, to engage in sustained patterns of verbal interaction around tasks which gradually increase in cognitive complexity as a function of the child's development.[r]
2. The parent devotes considerable periods of time to activities with the child similar to those introduced during the home visit.[r]
3. The role of the parent as the primary agent of intervention is given priority, status, and support from the surrounding environment.[r] Intervention programs which cast the parent in a subordinate role or have the effect of discouraging or decreasing his participation in activities with the child are likely to be counter-productive.[r]
4. The effectiveness and efficiency of parent intervention can be increased by extending activities so as to involve all the members of the family.[i] In this way the effects of vertical diffusion to younger siblings can be maximized[r] while older family members, including father, relatives, and older brothers and sisters, can participate as agents of intervention.[i] Such expansion, however, should not be allowed to impair the formation and uninterrupted activity of enduring one-to-one relationships so essential to the development of the young child.[i]
5. The effectiveness and efficiency of parent intervention can be enhanced through group meetings designed to provide information, to demonstrate materials and procedures, and to create situations in which the confidence and

motivation of parents (and other family members) is reinforced through mutual support and a sense of common purpose.[r] Such meetings, however, must not be allowed to take precedence over home visits or the periods which the parent devotes to playing and working with the child.[r]

## Stage IV. Ages Four Through Six

During this period, exposure to a cognitively oriented preschool curriculum becomes a potent force for accelerating the child's cognitive development,[r] but a strong parent intervention program is necessary to enhance and sustain the effects of the group experience.[r] This combined strategy involves the following features.

1. The effectiveness of preschool experience, in a group setting is enhanced if it is *preceded* by a strong parent intervention program involving regular home visits.[r]
2. After preschool begins, the parent program must not be relegated to secondary status if it is to realize its potential in conserving and facilitating the effects of group intervention.[r] Both phases of the combined strategy should reinforce the parents' status as central in fostering the development of the child.[i] A program which places the parent in a subordinate role dependent on the expert is not likely to be effective in the long run.[r]

## Stage V. Ages Six Through Twelve

Of special importance for sustaining the child's learning in school is the involvement of parents in supporting at home the activities engaged in by the child at school and their participation in activities at school directly affecting their child.[i] The parent, however, need no longer be the child's principal teacher as at earlier stages. Rather he acts as a supporter of the child's learning both in and out of school, but continues to function, and to be identified by school personnel, as the primary figure responsible for the child's development as a person.[i]

Taken as a whole, the foregoing principles imply a major reorientation in the design of intervention programs and in the training of personnel to work in this area. In the past, such programs were primarily child-centered, age-segregated, time-bound, self-centered, and focused on the trained professional as the powerful and direct agent of intervention with the child. The results of this analysis point to approaches that are family-centered, than cut across contexts rather than being confined to a single setting, that have continuity through time, and that utilize as the primary agents of socialization the child's own parents, other family members, adults and other children from the neighborhood in which he lives, school personnel, and other persons who are part of the child's enduring environment. It is beyond the scope of this paper to attempt to spell out the implication of this reorientation for the organization of services, delivery systems, and training. Many developments in the desired direction are already taking place. It is hoped that this analysis may accelerate the process of social change in the major institutions of our nation directly affecting the lives of young children and their families.

In completing this analysis, we reemphasize the tentative nature of the conclusions and the narrowness of IQ and related measures as aspects of the total development of the child. We also wish to reaffirm a deep indebtedness to those who conducted the programs and researches on which this work is based, and a profound faith in the capacity of parents, of whatever background, to enable their children to develop into effective and happy human beings, *once our society is willing to make conditions of life viable and humane for all its families.*

## REFERENCES

AMIDON, A. and BRIM, O. G. What do children have to gain from parent education? Paper prepared for the Advisory Committee on Child Development, National Research Council, National Academy of Science, 1972.

BEE, H. L., VAN EGEREN, L. F., STREISSGUTH, A. P., NYMAN, B. A., LECKIE, M. S. Social class differences in maternal teaching strategies and speech patterns. *Developmental Psychology,* 1969, *1,* 726–734.

BELL, R. Q. A reinterpretation of the direction of effects in studies of socialization. *Psychological Review,* 1968, *75,* 81–95.

BELLER, E. K. Impact of early education on disadvantaged children. In S. Ryan (Ed.) *A Report on Longitudinal Evaluations of Preschool Programs.* Washington, D.C.: Office of Child Development, 1972.

BELLER, E. K. Personal Communications, 1973.

BEREITER, C. and ENGELMANN, S. *Teaching Disadvantaged Children in the Preschool.* Englewood Cliffs, New Jersey: Prentice-Hall, 1966.

BISSEL, J. S. *The Cognitive Effects of Preschool Programs for Disadvantaged Children.* Washington, D.C.: National Institute of Child Health and Human Development, 1970.

BISSELL, J. S. *Implementation of Planned Variation in Head Start: First Year Report.* Washington, D.C.: National Institute of Child Health and Human Development, 1971.

BLOOM, B. S. *Stability and Change in Human Characteristics.* New York: John Wiley, 1964.

BLOOM, B. S. *Compensatory Education for Cultural Deprivation.* New York: Holt, Rinehart and Winston, 1965.

BOGATZ, G. A. and BALL, S. *The second year of Sesame Street: A continuing evaluation.* Volumes 1 and 2. Princeton, New Jersey: Educational Testing Service, 1971.

BRAUN, SAMUEL J., and CALDWELL, BETTYE. Emotional adjustment of children in day care who enrolled prior to or after the age of three. *Early Child Development and Care,* 1973, *2,* 13–21.

BRONFENBRENNER, U. The changing American child: A speculative analysis. *Merrill-Palmer Quarterly,* 1961, *7,* 73–84.

BRONFENBRENNER, U. Early deprivation: A cross-species analysis. In S. Levine and G. Newton (Eds.), *Early Experience in Behavior.* Springfield, Illinois: Charles C. Thomas, 1968, 627–764(a).

BRONFENBRENNER, U. When is infant stimulation effective? In D. C. Glass (Ed.), *Environmental Influences.* New York: Rockefeller University Press, 1968b, 251–257.

BRONFENBRENNER, U. *Two Worlds of Childhood: U.S. and U.S.S.R.* New York: Russell Sage Foundation, 1970.

BRONFENBRENNER, U. Developmental research and public policy. In J. M. Romanshyn (Ed.), *Social Science and Social Welfare*. New York: Council on Social Work Education, 1972(a).

BRONFENBRENNER, U. The Roots of Alienation. In U. Bronfenbrenner (Ed.), *Influences on Human Development*. Hinsdale, Illinois: Dryden Press, 1972b, 658–677.

BRONFENBRENNER, U., and BRUNER, J. The President and the children. *New York Times*, January 31, 1972.

COLEMAN, J. S. *Equality of educational opportunity*. Washington, D.C.: U.S. Office of Education, 1966.

DEUTSCH, M. Minority group and class status as related to social and personality factors in scholastic achievement. *Society for Applied Anthropology Monograph No. 2*. Ithaca, New York: New York State School of Industrial and Labor Relations, Cornell University, 1960.

DEUTSCH, M. *et al. Regional research and resource center in early childhood: Final report*. Washington, D.C.: U.S. Office of Economic Opportunity, 1971.

DEUTSCH, M., TALEPOROS, E., and VICTOR, J. A brief synopsis of an initial enrichment program in early childhood. In S. R. Ryan (Ed.), *A Report on Longitudinal Evolutions of Preschool Programs*. Washington, D.C.: Office of Child Development, 1972.

DI LORENZO, L. T. *Pre-kindergarten programs for educationally disadvantaged children: Final report*. Washington, D.C.: U.S. Office of Education, 1969.

GARDNER, J. and GARDNER, H. A note on selective imitation by a six-week-old infant. *Child Development*, 1970, 41, 1209–1213.

GILMER, B., MILLER, J. O. and GRAY, S. W. *Intervention with mothers and young children: Study of intra-family effects*. Nashville, Tennessee: DARCEE Demonstration and Research Center for Early Education, 1970.

GORDON, I. J. *A home learning center approach to early stimulation*. Institute for Development of Human Resources, Gainsville, Florida, 1971 (Grant No. MH 16037-02).

GRAY, S. W. and KLAUS, R. A. Experimental preschool program for culturally-deprived children. *Child Development*, 1965, 36, 887–898.

GRAY, S. W. and KLAUS, R. A. The early training project: The seventh-year report. *Child Development*, 1970, 41, 909–924.

HAYES, D., and GRETHER, J. The school year and vacation: When do students learn? Paper presented at the Eastern Sociological Convention, New York, New York, 1969.

HEBB, D. O. *The Organization of Behavior*. New York: John Wiley, 1949.

HEBER, R., GARBER, H., HARRINGTON, S., and HOFFMAN, C. *Rehabilitation of Families at Risk for Mental Retardation*. Madison, Wisconsin: Rehabilitation Research and Training Center in Mental Retardation, University of Wisconsin, 1972.

HERTZIG, M. E., BIRCH, H. G., THOMAS, A. and MENDEZ, O. A. Class and ethnic differences in responsiveness of preschool children to cognitive demands. *Monograph of the Society for Research in Child Development*, 1968, 33, No. 1.

HERZOG, E., NEWCOMB, C. H. and CISIN, I. H. Double deprivation: The less they have the less they learn. In S. Ryan (Ed.), *A Report on Longitudinal Evaluations of Preschool Programs*. Washington, D.C.: Office of Child Development, 1972 (a).

HERZOG, E., NEWCOMB, C. H. and CISIN, I. H. But some are poorer than others: SES differences in a preschool program. *American Journal of Orthopsychiatry*, 1972, 42, 4–22. (b)

HESS, R. D., SHIPMAN, V. C., BROPHY, J. E. and BEAR, R. M. *The cognitive environments of urban preschool children*. Chicago: University of Chicago Graduate School of Education, 1968.

HESS, R. D., SHIPMAN, V. C., BROPHY, J. E. and BEAR, R. M. *The cognitive environments of urban preschool children: Follow-up phase*. Chicago: University of Chicago Graduate School of Education, 1969.

HODGES, W. L., McCANDLESS, B. R. and SPICKER, H. H. *The development and evaluation of a diagnostically based curriculum for preschool psychosocially deprived children*. Washington, D.C.: U.S. Office of Education, 1967.

HUNT, J. McV. *Intelligence and Experience.* New York: Ronald Press, 1961.

*Infant Education Research Project.* Washington, D.C.: U.S. Office of Education Booklet #OE-37033.

KAGAN, J. *Change and Continuity in Infancy.* New York: John Wiley, 1971.

KAGAN, J. On cultural deprivation. In D. C. Glass (Ed.), *Environmental Influence.* New York: Rockefeller University Press, 1968, 211–250.

KARNES, M. B., STUDLEY, W. M., WRIGHT, W. R. and HODGKINS, A. S. An approach to working with mothers of disadvantaged preschool children. *Merrill-Palmer Quarterly,* 1968, *14,* 174–184.

KARNES, M. B. *Research and development program on preschool disadvantaged children: Final report.* Washington, D.C.: U.S. Office of Education, 1969.

KARNES, M. B. and BADGER, E. E. Training mothers to instruct their infants at home. In M. B. Karnes, *Research and development program on preschool disadvantaged children: Final Report.* Washington, D.C.: U.S. Office of Education, 1969, 249–263. (a)

KARNES, M. B., HODGINS, A. S. and TESKA, J. A. The effects of short-term instruction at home by mothers of children not enrolled in a preschool. In M. B. Karnes, *Research and development program on preschool diadvantaged children: Final report.* Washington, D.C.: U.S. Office of Education, 1969, 197–203. (b)

KARNES, M. B., HODGINS, A. S. and TESKA, J. A. The impact of at-home instruction by mothers on performance in the ameliorative preschool. In M. B. Karnes, *Research and development program on preschool disadvantaged children: Final report.* Washington, D.C.: U.S. Office of Education, 1969, 205–212. (c)

KARNES, M. B., TESKA, J. A., HODGINS, A. S. and BADGER, E. D. Educational intervention at home by mothers of disadvantaged infants. *Child Development,* 1970, *41,* 925–935.

KARNES, M. B., ZEHRBACH, R. R. and TESKA, J. A. An ameliorative approach in the development of curriculum. In R. K. Parker (Ed.), *The Preschool in Action.* Boston: Allyn and Bacon, 1972, 353–381.

KIRK, S. A. *Early Education of the Mentally Retarded.* Urbana, Illinois: University of Illinois Press, 1958.

KIRK, S. A. The effects of early education with disadvantaged infants. In M. B. Karnes, *Research and development program on preschool disadvantaged children: Final report.* Washington, D.C.: U.S. Office of Education, 1969.

KLAUS, R. A. and GRAY, S. W. The early training project for disadvantaged children: A report after five years. *Monographs of the Society for Research in Child Development,* 1968, *33 (4, Serial #120).*

KRAFT, I., FUSHILLO, J. and HERZOG, E. Prelude to school: An evaluation of an inner-city school program. *Children's Bureau Research Report Number 3.* Washington, D.C.: Children's Bureau, 1968.

LEVENSTEIN, P. Cognitive growth in preschoolers through verbal interaction with mothers. *American Journal of Orthopsychiatry,* 1970, *40,* 426–432.

LEVENSTEIN, P. Personal communication, 1972. (a).

LEVENSTEIN, P. But does it work in homes away from home? *Theory Into Practice,* 1972, *11,* 157–162. (b)

LEVENSTEIN, P. and LEVENSTEIN, S. Fostering learning potential in preschoolers. *Social Casework,* 1971, *52,* 74–78.

LEVENSTEIN, P. and SUNLEY, R. Stimulation of verbal interaction between disadvantaged mothers and children. *American Journal of Orthopsychiatry,* 1968, *38,* 116–121.

MOSS, H. A. Sex, age, and state as determinants of mother-infant interaction. *Merrill-Palmer Quarterly,* 1967, *13,* 19–36.

RADIN, N. The impact of a kindergarten home counseling program. *Exceptional Children,* 1969, *36,* 251–256.

RADIN N. Three degrees of maternal involvement in a preschool program: Impact on mothers and children. *Child Development,* 1972 (Dec.) 43:4, 1355–1364.

RADIN, N. and WEIKART, D. A home teaching program for disadvantaged preschool children. *Journal of Special Education,* Winter 1967, *1,* 183–190.

*Rehabilitation of Families at Risk for Mental Retardation: A Progress Report.* Madison, Wisconsin: Regional Rehabilitation Research and Training Center in Mental Retardation, University of Wisconsin, October 1971.

RHEINGOLD, H. L. The social and socializing infant. In D. A. Goslin, *Handbook of Socialization Theory and Research.* Chicago: Rand McNally, 1969, 779–790.

SCHAEFER, E. S. *Progress report: Intellectual stimulation of culturally-deprived parents.* National Institute of Mental Health, 1968.

SCHAEFER, E. S. Need for early and continuing education. In V. H. Denenberg (Ed.), *Education of the Infant and Young Child.* New York: Academic Press, 1970, 61–82.

SCHAEFER, E. S. Personal communication, 1972. (a)

SCHAEFER, E. S. Parents as educators: Evidence from cross-sectional, longitudinal and intervention research. *Young Children,* 1972, *27,* 227–239. (b)

SCHAEFER, E. S. and AARONSON, M. Infant education research project: Implementation and implications of the home-tutoring program. In R. K. Parker (Ed.), *The Preschool in Action.* Boston: Allyn and Bacon, 1972, 410–436.

SCHOGGEN, M. and SCHOGGEN, P. *Environmental forces in home lives of three-year-old children in three pouplation sub-groups.* Nashville, Tennessee: George Peabody College for Teachers, DARCEE Papers and Reports, Vol. 5, No. 2, 1971.

SKEELS, H. M. Adult status of children from contrasting early life experiences. *Monographs of the Society for Research in Child Development,* 1966, *31,* Serial #105.

SKEELS, H. M. and DYE, H. B. A study of the effects of differential stimulation on mentally retarded children. *Proceedings and Addresses of the American Association on Mental Deficiency,* 1939, *44,* 114–136.

SKEELS, H. M., UPPDEGRAFF, R., WELLMAN, B. L. and WILLIAMS, H. M. A study of environmental stimulation: An orphanage preschool project. *University of Iowa Studies in Child Welfare,* 1938, *15,* #4.

SKODAK, M. and SKEELS, H. M. A final follow-up study of 100 adopted children. *Journal of Genetic Psychology,* 1949, *75,* 85–125.

SMITH, M. B. School and home: Focus on achievement. In A. H. Passow (Ed.), *Developing Programs for the Educationally Disadvantaged.* New York: Teachers College Press, 1968, 89–107.

SOAR, R. S. An integrative approach to classroom learning. NIMH Project Number 5-R11MH01096 to the University of South Carolina and 7-R11MH02045 to Temple University, 1966.

SOAR, R. S. Follow-Through classroom process measurement and pupil growth (1970–71). Gainesville, Florida: College of Education, University of Florida, 1972.

SOAR, R. S. and SOAR, R. M. Pupil subject matter growth during summer vacation. *Educational Leadership Research Supplement,* 1969, *2,* 577–587.

SPRIGLE, H. Learning to learn program. In S. Ryan (Ed.), *A Report of Longitudinal Evaluations of Preschool Programs.* Washington, D.C.: Office of Child Development, 1972.

*Stanford Research Institute. Implementation of Planned Variation in Head Start: Preliminary evaluation of planned variation in Head Start according to Follow-Through approaches (1969–70).* Washington, D.C.: Office of Child Development, U.S. Department of Health, Education, and Welfare, 1971. (a)

*Stanford Research Institute. Longitudinal evaluation of selected features of the national Follow-Through Program.* Washington, D.C.: Office of Education, U.S. Department of Health, Education and Welfare, 1971. (b)

TULKIN, S. R. and COHLER, B. J. Child rearing attitudes on mother-child interaction among middle and working class families. Paper presented at the 1971 Meeting of the Society for Research in Child Development.

TULKIN, S. R. and KAGAN, J. Mother-child interaction: Social class differences in the first year of life. *Proceedings of the 78th Annual Convention of the American Psychological Association,* 1970, 261–262.

VAN DE RIET, V. A sequential approach to early childhood and elementary education. Gainesville, Florida: Department of Clinical Psychology, University of Florida, 1972.

WEIKART, D. P. *Preschool intervention: A preliminary report of the Perry Preschool Project.* Ann Arbor, Michigan: Campus Publishers, 1967.

WEIKART, D. P. *A comparative study of three preschool curricula.* A paper presented at the Bi-annual meeting of the Society for Research in Child Development, Santa Monica, California, March 1969.

WEIKART, D. P., *et al. Longitudinal results of the Ypsilanti Perry Preschool Project.* Ypsilanti, Michigan: High/ Scope Educational Research Foundation, 1970.

WEIKART, D. P., KAMII, C. K. and RADIN, N. *Perry Preschool Progress Report.* Ypsilanti, Michigan: Ypsilanti Public Schools, 1964.

# A Preventive Mental Health Program for Young "Inner City" Children: The Second (Kindergarten) Year*

*Myrna B. Shure and George Spivack*

I S IT POSSIBLE to improve the classroom behavior of overly impulsive and inhibited children by teaching them how to think? Three years of working with children as young as four years of age have shown that such is possible and have given us a new approach in dealing with and handling behavioral difficulties (Shure and Spivack, 1973; Spivack and Shure, 1974). . . .

Youngsters beginning the training as impulsive became more able to wait for what they wanted and less nagging and demanding. They became better able to share and take turns and less easily upset in the face of frustration. Youngsters who started out inhibited, timid, fearful, or shy became more socially outgoing, better liked by their peers, and more aware of others. And most importantly, youngsters who improved most in the trained thinking skills also improved most in classroom behavioral adjustment, supporting Spivack's theoretical position that change in the mediating interpersonal cognitive problem-solving skills *generated* change in behavioral adjustment (Spivack, 1973). Moreover, the cognitive and behavioral effects of training were independent of both initial and change IQ, indicating that children within a wide IQ range (70–120+) were able to benefit.

* From a paper presented at the American Psychological Association, 1975. Reprinted by permission of the authors.

The training program is based on research findings indicating consistently from preschool through adulthood that individuals deficient in interpersonal cognitive problem-solving (ICPS) skills are significantly more poorly adjusted than those more efficient in such skills (Spivack and Shure, 1974). In children four and five years of age these skills specifically centered on alternative and consequential thinking as described earlier. The results of training four-year-olds revealed that it is possible to improve classroom behavior and adjustment not by direct modification of behavior itself but by altering the child's interpersonal problem-solving thinking style.

The purpose now is to present results of the second year, as the children moved from preschool into kindergarten. Half the nursery-trained youngsters were retrained in kindergarten (N = 39), the remaining half serving as kindergarten controls (N = 30). Half the nursery controls were first trained in kindergarten (N = 35), the remainder having never received training (N = 27). Questions asked concerned the effects of amount and timing of training as well as whether benefits would last over time.

First, we will describe the highlights of the program as used with kindergarten youngsters, then the research results and implications.

## The Training Program

The underlying approach is to teach children *how* to think, not what to think. The aim established early was to help the child develop a problem solving thinking "style" that would guide him or her in coping with typical everyday interpersonal problems.

[The authors describe the types of activities through which young children are taught to think about alternatives and consequences of their behavior. For example, there are word games that stimulate children to think about different ideas and different things that "might happen if . . ."; about how people feel and how feelings change; and some problem-solving situations such as the girl who wants her brother to let her push the grocery cart—what are all the things the girl could do or say to get her wish? For each response, the teacher would help the children to identify the consequences of their suggestions.

## Results and Discussion

**Holding Power.** The first question asked was whether effects of training in the nursery year would last throughout kindergarten without further reinforcement.

As measured by the Preschool Interpersonal Problem Solving (PIPS) Test (Shure and Spivack, 1974b), youngsters trained in nursery (but not kindergarten) conceptualized a significantly greater number of solutions to interpersonal problems than controls immediately following training (postnursery) and showed no significant loss over time. At the end of the kindergarten year (a full year later) nursery-trained youngsters remained significantly higher than those who never received training. . . .

Most importantly, the improved behavior of impulsive and inhibited youngsters, behaviors most crucial to this study, also maintained holding power as measured a full year following training. With no difference in the percentage of youngsters in each group starting nursery in the adjusted category (about 40 per cent), 83 per cent of the nursery-trained youngsters were rated by their teachers as adjusted at a point immediately following nursery training (as measured by the Hahnemann Preschool Behavior Rating Scale [Spivack and Shure], 1974). Seventy-seven per cent were still rated adjusted at the end of the kindergarten year. Of those never trained, only 41 per cent were rated adjusted at the end of nursery (no increase) and 30 per cent at the end of kindergarten (a slight decrease). Despite the changes in time, raters, and setting, the positive result of training persisted.

Another very exciting finding emerged regarding behavior. Among all youngsters judged behaviorally adjusted throughout the nursery year, significantly fewer who were trained were likely to be judged impulsive or inhibited in kindergarten than those not trained. This finding suggests the program not only helps youngsters already displaying impulsivity or inhibition, but it also helps to prevent the emergence of such behavior as measured at a later time.

**Effect of Kindergarten Training.**    I will now talk about the effect of training on youngsters exposed for the first time in kindergarten.

If one were to institute the present training program into kindergarten classes without prior nursery training, the results indicate that clear benefits could be gained. As in the nursery year, kindergarten-trained youngsters improved significantly beyond controls in their ability to conceptualize alternative solutions to interpersonal problems. . . . These findings were also true for potential consequences to an interpersonal act and in the percentage of aberrant (impulsive or inhibited) youngsters rated adjusted following training. Fourteen of twenty (70 per cent) of those beginning kindergarten training as aberrant ended up adjusted following training as compared to only one of sixteen controls (a difference significant at the .01 level). As in the nursery year, youngsters beginning as aberrant and ending adjusted improved in alternative and consequential thinking (ICPS) skills significantly more than did aberrant youngsters who remained so, again suggesting a direct link between change in the trained thinking skills and in behavioral adjustment.

Given that the present training program was effective either year, it is now important to examine effects of differential amount of training and whether at the end of the kindergarten year differences existed between youngsters trained in kindergarten and those trained a year earlier in nursery.

**Amount and Timing of Training.**   With appropriate pretest controls, analyses of variance revealed significant postkindergarten differences among the four groups on solution (p<.001) and consequence (p<.001) scores. On both measures, Newman-Keuls indicated youngsters trained two years . . . superior to all other groups (p<.01), never-trained significantly more deficient than all other groups (p<.01) and no difference between nursery-only and kindergarten-only training groups. The percentages of initially impulsive and inhibited youngsters (at Time 1) judged adjusted at postkindergarten (Time 4) was similar in all three training groups (70 per cent to 88 per cent) while only 19 per cent of never-trained youngsters beginning impulsive or inhibited were judged adjusted at the end of kindergarten (the latter group significantly different from all groups at .01).

Because two years of training had a greater impact on the measure ICPS skills and all training groups showed equal behavioral gains, differential behavioral adjustment in the first grade as a function of length of training became of interest. The N became quite small however, making interpretation only suggestive. If a child was rated aberrant at the beginning of nursery, he or she was more likely to remain so consistently throughout the first grade if he or she never received training (7 of 12; 58 per cent). Of nine nursery-trained youngsters initially rated aberrant, only two remained so throughout (22 per cent). Dramatically, only one of twenty-three children trained both years remained aberrant throughout. With these small Ns, the difference in percentage is significant between the two-year and never-trained youngsters, but not between the two-year and nursery-trained groups. Implications for prevention also remained in evidence. Eleven of 14 (78 per cent) of two-year trained youngsters remained consistently adjusted at every measured time period from prenursery through first grade. Remarkably, such was also true of five of six (83 per cent) of those trained in nursery only. On the other hand, only one of six never-trained youngsters who began nursery adjusted was rated so consistently throughout.

In conclusion, one year of training was as beneficial as two with respect to the ultimate criterion goal—behavioral adjustment. Perhaps the ICPS skills obtained after one year of training, whether that year be nursery or kindergarten, were sufficient to guide adjusted overt behavior as demonstrated in the classroom (as measured through the first grade). Given the previously described findings on holding power, however, it is suggested that early nursery intervention is optimal in that youngsters trained at that time did begin kindergarten at a better behavioral vantage point. Nevertheless, the results suggest that if a child is not trained in nursery, it is not too late to affect his or her behavioral adjustment by altering his or her ICPS skills if trained a year later in kindergarten.

The question now becomes: Why is this training so effective? We believe (and the data support our belief) that individuals who develop the habit of problem-solving thinking can better evaluate and choose from a variety of possible solutions to a problem, turn to a different one in case of actual failure, and experience less frustration and fewer signs of maladaptive functioning. They are less likely to make impulsive mistakes, become frustrated and aggressive, or end up evading the problem entirely by withdrawing. We do know from another part of our research that a child's own mother is in a highly unique position to affect her child's thinking skills and behavioral adjustment. Though the mother may be in a paramount position for still longer-range impact, the results of these studies clearly show the teacher can play a predominant role in affecting a child's behavior when he or she teaches the child a problem-solving style of thinking.

## REFERENCES

Shure, M. B., and Spivack, G. "A Preventive Mental Health Program for Four-year-old Head Start Children." Paper Presented at Society for Research in Child Development, Philadelphia, 1973.

Shure, M. B., and Spivack, G. "A Mental Health Program for Kindergarten Children, Training Script." Philadelphia: Department of Mental Health Sciences, Hahnemann Medical College and Hospital, 1974a.

Shure, M. B., and Spivack, G. "Preschool Interpersonal Problem-Solving (PIPS) Test: Manual." Phildelphia: Department of Mental Health Sciences, Hahnemann Medical College and Hospital, 1974b.

Shure, M. B., and Spivack, G. "Training Mothers to Help Their Children Solve Real-Life Problems." Paper Presented at the Society for Research in Child Development, Denver, 1975.

Spivack, G. "A Conception of Healthy Human Functioning." *Research and Evaluation Report #15*, Philadelphia: Department of Mental Health Sciences, Hahnemann Medical College and Hospital, 1973.

Spivack, G., and Shure, M. B. *Social Adjustment of Young Children: A Cognitive Approach to Solving Real-Life Problems.* San Francisco, Jossey-Bass, 1974.

Spivack, G., and Shure, M. B., "Maternal Childrearing and the Interpersonal Cognitive Problem-Solving Ability of Four-Year Olds." Paper Presented at the Society for Research in Child Development, Denver, 1975.

# C. Middle and Later Childhood: Introduction

DURING THIS PERIOD of a child's life, the relatively simple social atom becomes increasingly complex. This complexity is not due simply to the fact that the child has entered school and is taking part in a wider array of social activities, but rather because of the sociocultural meanings that each of these activities carries. For example, children enter schools as boys and girls and thus carry with them the "myths" (unfounded beliefs) which are associated with their sex, apart from their unique fulfillment of being a particular boy or girl. Maccoby and Jacklin's summary of an enormous literature helps to clarify the unfounded beliefs as well as those for which there is established evidence. (Recent research by Sheila Tobias on "math anxiety" demonstrates the effects of such myths.) Children enter school as members of different races, and in a study by Rubovits and Maehr, we can observe the compounding effect of race with identification of students as being "gifted" or "nongifted." Birch points out that children starting school bear the further burdens of their parents' history of malnutrition when they were children, an intergenerational disadvantage of great force.

Sometimes children begin their formal education with the illusions of others, such as other persons' expectations that children of working mothers (Wallston) or adopted children (Levine) will be adversely affected by these situations, when the evidence does not, in general, support such a statement. Helping professionals as well as lay people hold stereotypes that influence choices. Only continual challenge to "conventional wisdom" can sort out myths from useful guides to action.

The paper by Klein, Alexander, and Parsons captures most clearly the complexity of human development. In a study dealing with families of delinquent youth and their nondelinquent siblings, the authors use a family systems intervention program, which seeks to modify this complex situation in three ways: first, at the rehabilitation level, aiming at the communication processes within the family; second, at a treatment level, involving efforts to prevent recidivism; and third, at the level of primary prevention, in seeking to prevent the nondelinquent siblings from coming into contact with the courts. Thus, they explicitly deal with individuals, groups, and institutions in a time perspective that encompasses the past, the present, and the future. I would suggest that all practitioners are involved with the same degree of complexities, but with varying degrees of explicit attention to these systemic events.

At the end of this section, readers should have some understanding of the basic tasks of children from about six years to puberty:

*Physical Tasks:* There are many challenges to the child as he or she moves into wider social orbits. Basic hygiene tasks must be mastered and maintained independently. Many physical activities become available to children of this age, helping muscle development, from gross movements to fine muscle control. Included in these activities are those that serve social ends, such as taking part in games with peers, handwriting, and the like.

*Psychological Tasks:* Language expansion increases rapidly during this period, as does the mastery of grammatical structures, which will serve the individual throughout life. Reading is a vital skill which begins and is refined during this time. With the growth of biological capacities for advanced thinking comes the use of symbols, in computation and in writing. Children of this age group develop in their sense of causal orientation regarding human as well as physical events, and this becomes vital as they use problem-solving skills in everyday life. A self-concept emerges to consolidate the many specific learnings that are rapidly occurring. With this sense of self comes a capacity for self-control, both in the domain of safety and with regard to social values, and in the taking on of the rules of society.

*Social Tasks:* A number of social roles are developed during this period as an individual becomes a member of special groups such as the school, clubs, a church. Each new membership outside the family adds to the independence of the child and to the range of interpersonal relationships he or she is forming with new people. The social atom grows larger and more complex. Increasingly there is clarification of one's sex role and the awareness of others of the same and the opposite sex. And with new relationships come the requirements of responsible behavior and moral values (cf. Havighurst, 1952).

# The Psychology of Sex Differences* [Summary and Commentary]

*Eleanor Emmons Maccoby and Carol Nagy Jacklin*

## Unfounded Beliefs About Sex Differences

1. *That girls are more "social" than boys.* The findings: First, the two sexes are equally interested in social (as compared with nonsocial) stimuli, and are equally proficient at learning through imitation of models. Second, in childhood, girls are no more dependent than boys on their caretakers, and boys are no more willing to remain alone. Furthermore, girls are not more motivated to achieve for social rewards. The two sexes are equally responsive to social reinforcement, and neither sex consistently learns better for this form of reward than for other forms. Third, girls do not spend more time interacting with playmates; in fact, the opposite is true, at least at certain ages. Fourth, the two sexes appear to be equally "empathic," in the sense of understanding the emotional reactions of others; however, the measures of this ability have so far been narrow.

Any differences that exist in the "sociability" of the two sexes are more of kind than of degree. Boys are highly oriented toward a peer group and congregate in larger groups; girls associate in pairs or small groups of age-mates, and may be somewhat more oriented toward adults, although the evidence for this is weak.

2. *That girls are more "suggestible" than boys.* The findings: First, boys and girls are equally likely to imitate others spontaneously. Second, the two sexes are equally susceptible to persuasive communications, and in face-to-face social-influence situations (Asch-type experiments), sex differences are usually not found. When they are, girls are somewhat more likely to adapt their own judgments to those of the group, although there are studies with reverse findings. Boys, on the other hand, appear to be more likely to accept peer-group values when these conflict with their own.

3. *That girls have lower self-esteem.* The findings: The sexes are highly similar in their overall self-satisfaction and self-confidence throughout childhood and adolescence; there is little information about adulthood, but what

* Reprinted from *The Psychology of Sex Differences* by Eleanor Emmons Maccoby and Carol Nagy Jacklin, with the permission of the publishers, Stanford University Press. © 1974 by the Board of Trustees of the Leland Stanford Junior University.

exists does not show a sex difference. However, there are some qualitative differences in the areas of functioning where the two sexes have greatest self-confidence: girls rate themselves higher in the area of social competence; boys more often see themselves as strong, powerful, dominant, "potent."

Through most of the school years, the two sexes are equally likely to believe they can influence their own fates, rather than being the victims of chance or fate. During the college years (but not earlier or later), men have a greater sense of control over their own fate, and greater confidence in their probable performance on a variety of school-related tasks that they undertake. However, this does not imply a generally lower level of self-esteem among women of this age.

4. *That girls are better at rote learning and simple repetitive tasks, boys at tasks that require higher-level cognitive processing and the inhibition of previously learned responses.* The findings: Neither sex is more susceptible to simple conditioning, or excels in simple paired-associates or other forms of "rote" learning. Boys and girls are equally proficient at discrimination learning, reversal shifts, and probability learning, all of which have been interpreted as calling for some inhibition of "available" responses. Boys are somewhat more impulsive (that is, lacking in inhibition) during the preschool years, but the sexes do not differ thereafter in the ability to wait for a delayed reward, to inhibit early (wrong) responses on the Matching Familiar Figures test (MFF) or on other measures of impulsivity.

5. *That boys are more "analytic."* The findings: The sexes do not differ on tests of analytic cognitive style. Boys do not excel at tasks that call for "decontextualization," or disembedding, except when the task is visual-spatial; boys' superiority on the latter tasks seems to be accounted for by spatial ability (see below), and no sex differences in analytic ability are implied. Boys and girls are equally likely to respond to task-irrelevant aspects of a situation, so that neither sex excels in analyzing and selecting only those elements needed for the task.

6. *That girls are more affected by heredity, boys by environment.* The findings: Male identical twins are more alike than female identical twins, but the two sexes show equivalent amount of resemblance to their parents.

Boys are more susceptible to damage by a variety of noxious environmental agents, both prenatally and postnatally, but this does not imply that they are generally more influenced by environmental factors. The correlations between parental socialization techniques and child behavior are higher for boys in some studies, higher for girls in others. Furthermore, the two sexes learn with equal facility in a wide variety of learning situations; if learning is the primary means whereby environmental effects come about, sex equivalence is indicated.

7. *That girls lack achievement motivation.* The findings: In the pioneering studies of achievement motivation, girls scored higher than boys in achievement imagery under "neutral" conditions. Boys need to be challenged by ap-

peals to ego or competitive motivation to bring their achievement imagery up to the level of girls'. Boys' achievement motivation does appear to be more responsive to competitive arousal than girls', but this does not imply a generally higher level. In fact, observational studies of achievement strivings either have found no sex difference or have found girls to be superior.

8. *That girls are auditory, boys visual.* The findings: The majority of studies report no differences in response to sounds by infants of the two sexes. At most ages boys and girls are equally adept at discriminating speech sounds. No sex difference is found in memory for sounds previously heard.

Among newborn infants, no study shows a sex difference in fixation to visual stimuli. During the first year of life, results are variable, but neither sex emerges as more responsive to visual stimuli. From infancy to adulthood, the sexes are highly similar in interest in visual stimuli, ability to discriminate among them, identification of shapes, distance perception, and a variety of other measures of visual perception.

# Sex Differences That Are Fairly Well Established

1. *That girls have greater verbal ability than boys.* It is probably true that girls' verbal abilities mature somewhat more rapidly in early life, although there are a number of recent studies in which no sex difference has been found. During the period from preschool to early adolescence, the sexes are very similar in their verbal abilities. At about age 11, the sexes begin to diverge, with female superiority increasing through high school and possibly beyond. Girls score higher on tasks involving both receptive and productive language, and on "high-level" verbal tasks (analogies, comprehension of difficult written material, creative writing) as well as upon the "lower-level" measures (fluency). The magnitude of the female advantage varies, being most commonly about one-quarter of a standard deviation.

2. *That boys excell in visual-spatial ability.* Male superiority on visual-spatial tasks is fairly consistently found in adolescence and adulthood, but not in childhood. The male advantage on spatial tests increases through the high school years up to a level of about .40 of a standard deviation. The sex difference is approximately equal on analytic and nonanalytic spatial measures.

3. *That boys excel in mathematical ability.* The two sexes are similar in their early acquisition of quantitative concepts, and their mastery of arithmetic during the grade-school years. Beginning at about age 12–13, boys' mathematical skills increase faster than girls'. The greater rate of improvement appears to be not entirely a function of the number of math courses taken, although the question has not been extensively studied. The magnitude of the sex differences varies greatly from one population to another, and is probably not so great as the difference in spatial ability. Both visual-spatial and verbal

processes are sometimes involved in the solution of mathematical problems; some math problems can probably be solved in either way, while others cannot, a fact that may help to explain the variation in degree of sex difference from one measure to another.

4. *That males are more aggressive.* The sex difference in aggression has been observed in all cultures in which the relevant behavior has been observed. Boys are more aggressive both physically and verbally. They show the attenuated forms of aggression (mock-fighting, aggressive fantasies) as well as the direct forms more frequently than girls. The sex difference is found as early as social play begins—at age 2 or 2½. Although the aggressiveness of both sexes declines with age, boys and men remain more aggressive through the college years. Little information is available for older adults. The primary victims of male aggression are other males—from early ages, girls are chosen less often as victims.

# Open Questions: Too Little Evidence, or Findings Ambiguous

1. *Tactile sensitivity.* Most studies of tactile sensitivity in infancy, and of the ability to perceive by touch at later ages, do not find sex differences. When differences are found, girls are more sensitive, but such findings are rare enough that we cannot have confidence that the difference is a meaningful one. Additional work is needed with some of the standard psychophysical measurements of tactile sensitivity, over a range of ages. Most of the existing studies in which the data are analyzed by sex have been done with newborns.

2. *Fear, timidity, and anxiety.* Observational studies of fearful behavior usually do not find sex differences. Teacher ratings and self-reports, however, usually find girls to be more timid or more anxious. In the case of self-reports, the problem is to know whether the results reflect "real" differences or only differences in the willingness to report anxious feelings. Of course, the very willingness to assert that one is afraid may lead to fearful behavior, so the distinction may not turn out to be important. However, it would be desirable to have measures other than self-report (which make up the great bulk of the data from early school age on) as a way of clarifying the meaning of the girls' greater self-attribution of fears and anxiety.

3. *Activity level.* Sex differences in activity level do not appear in infancy. They begin to be seen when children reach the age of social play. During the preschool years, when sex differences are found they are in the direction of boys' being more active. However, there are many instances in which sex differences have not been found. Some, but not all, of the variance among studies can be accounted for by whether the measurement situation was social. That is, boys appear to be especially stimulated to bursts of high activity by the presence of other boys. But the exact nature of the situational control

over activity level remains to be established. Activity level is responsive to a number of motivational states—fear, anger, curiosity—and is therefore not a promising variable for identifying stable individual or group differences. More detailed observations are needed on the vigor and qualitative nature of play.

4. *Competitiveness.* When sex differences are found, they usually show boys to be more competitive, but there are many studies finding sex similarity. Madsen and his colleagues find sex differences to be considerably weaker than differences between cultures and, in a number of studies, entirely absent. Almost all the research on competition has involved situations in which competition is maladaptive. In the Prisoner's Dilemma game, for example, the sexes are equally cooperative, but this is in a situation in which cooperation is to the long-run advantage of both players and the issue is one of developing mutual trust. It appears probable that in situations in which competitiveness produces increased individual rewards, males would be more competitive, but this is a guess based on commonsense considerations, such as the male interest in competitive sports, not upon research in controlled settings. The age of the subject and the identity of the opponent no doubt make a difference—there is evidence that young women hesitate to compete against their boyfriends.

5. *Dominance.* Dominance appears to be more of an issue within boys' groups than girls' groups. Boys make more dominance attempts (both successful and unsuccessful) toward one another than do girls. They also more often attempt to dominate adults. The dominance relations between the sexes are complex: in childhood, the sex segregation of play groups means that neither sex frequently attempts to dominate the other. In experimental situations in which the sexes are combined, the evidence is ambiguous on whether either sex is more successful in influencing the behavior of the other. Among adult mixed pairs or groups, formal leadership tends to go to males in the initial phases of interaction, but the direction of influence becomes more sex-equal the longer the relationship lasts, with "division of authority" occurring along lines of individual competencies and division of labor.

6. *Compliance.* In childhood, girls tend to be more compliant to the demands and directions of adults. This compliance does not extend, however, to willingness to accept directions from, or be influenced by, age-mates. Boys are especially concerned with maintaining their status in the peer group, and are probably therefore more vulnerable to pressures and challenges from this group, although this has not been well established. As we have seen in the discussion of dominance, it is not clear that in mixed-sex interactions either sex is consistently more willing to comply with the wishes of the other.

7. *Nurturance and "maternal" behavior.* There is very little evidence concerning the tendencies of boys and girls to be nurturant or helpful toward younger children or animals. Cross-cultural work does indicate that girls between the ages of 6 and 10 are more often seen behaving nurturantly. Within

our own society, the rare studies that report nurturant behavior are observational studies of free play among nursery school children; sex differences are not found in these studies, but the setting normally does not include children much younger than the subjects being observed, and it may be that the relevant elicitors are simply not present. Female hormones play a role in maternal behavior in lower animals, and the same may be true in human beings, but there is no direct evidence that this is the case. There is very little information on the responses of adult men to infants and children, so it is not possible to say whether adult women are more disposed to behave maternally than men are to behave paternally. If there is a sex difference in the tendency to behave nurturantly, it does not generalize to a greater female tendency to behave altruistically over varying situations. The studies of people's willingness to help others in distress have sometimes shown men more helpful, sometimes women, depending on the identity of the person needing help and the kind of help that is needed. The overall finding on altruism is one of sex similarity.

In Chapters 5 and 6, we raised the question of whether the female is more passive than the male. The answer is complex, but mainly negative. The two sexes are highly similar in their willingness to explore a novel environment, when they are both given freedom to do so. Both are highly responsive to social situations of all kinds, and although some individuals tend to withdraw from social interaction and simply watch from the sidelines, such persons are no more likely to be female than male. Girls' greater compliance with adult demands is just as likely to take an active as a passive form; running errands and performing services for others are active processes. Young boys seem more likely than girls to put out energy in the form of bursts of strenuous physical activity, but the girls are not sitting idly by while the boys act; they are simply playing more quietly. And their play is fully as organized and planful (possibly more so), and has as much the quality of actively imposing their own design upon their surroundings as does boys' play. It is true that boys and men are more aggressive, but this does not mean that females are the passive victims of aggression—they do not yield or withdraw when aggressed against any more frequently than males do, at least during the phases of childhood for which observations are available. With respect to dominance, we have noted the curious fact that while males are more dominant, females are not especially submissive, at least not to the dominance attempts of boys and girls their own age. In sum, the term "passive" does not accurately describe the most common female personality attributes.

Returning to one of the major conclusions of our survey of sex differences, there are many popular beliefs about the psychological characteristics of the two sexes that have proved to have little or no basis in fact. How is it possible that people continue to believe, for example, that girls are more "social" than boys, when careful observation and measurement in a variety of situations show no sex difference? Of course it is possible that we have not studied those particular situations that contribute most to the popular beliefs. But if this is the problem, it means that the alleged sex difference exists only in a limited range of situations, and the sweeping generalizations embodied in popular beliefs are not warranted.

However, a more likely explanation for the perpetuation of "myths," we believe, is the fact that stereotypes are such powerful things. An ancient truth is worth restating here: if a generalization about a group of people is believed, whenever a member of that group behaves in the expected way the observer notes it and his belief is confirmed and strengthened; when a member of the group behaves in a way that is not consistent with the observer's expectations, the instance is likely to pass unnoticed, and the observer's generalized belief is protected from disconfirmation. We believe that this well-documented process occurs continually in relation to the expected and perceived behavior of males and females, and results in the perpetuation of myths that would otherwise die out under the impact of negative evidence. However, not all unconfirmed beliefs about the two sexes are of this sort. It is necessary to reconsider the nature of the evidence that permits us to conclude what is myth and what is (at least potentially) reality. . . .

# Malnutrition, Learning, and Intelligence*
## *Herbert G. Birch*

RESEARCH ON THE relation of nutritional factors to intelligence has burgeoned over the past decade. . . .

[Before reviewing an extensive body of evidence, Dr. Birch defines some key terms:]

Intermittent and marginal incomes as well as a technology that is inadequate to support a population result less often in the symptoms characteristic of starvation than in subclinical malnutrition or what Brock (1961) has called "dietary subnutrition . . . defined as any impairment of functional efficiency of body systems which can be corrected by better feeding." Such subnutrition when present in populations is reflected in stunting, disproportions in growth, and a variety of anatomic, physiologic, and behavioral abnormalities

* From *American Journal of Public Health*, 62:6 (1972), 773–784. Reprinted by permission of the publisher and the author's estate.

(Birch and Gussow, 1970). Our principal concern in this country is with these chronic or intermittent aspects of nutritional inadequacy.

In less highly developed regions of the world, and indeed in the United States as well, chronic subnutrition is not infrequently accompanied by dramatic manifestations of acute, severe, and, if untreated, lethal malnutrition, particularly in infants and young children. . . . Hunger is a subjective state and should not be used as the equivalent of malnutrition, which is an objective condition of physical and physiologic suboptimum. . . .

[Dr. Birch next reviews a large number of specific studies conducted in various nations, dealing with the life experiences of women who become mothers, as well as with the birth and subsequent lives of their children. He summarizes this literature as follows, and draws some important implications:]

. . . On the basis of the evidence so far set forth it may be argued with considerable justification that one can reasonably construct a chain of consequences starting from the malnutrition of the mother when she was a child, to her stunting, to her reduced efficiency as a reproducer, to intrauterine and perinatal risk to the child, and to his subsequent reduction in functional adaptive capacity. Animal models have been constructed to test the hypotheses implied in this chain of associations, most particularly by Chow and his colleagues (1968). . . . The findings from these studies indicate that second and later generation animals who derive from mothers who were nutritionally disadvantaged when young, are themselves less well-grown and behaviorally less competent than animals of the same strain deriving from normal mothers. Moreover, the condition of the offspring is worsened if nutritional insult in its own life is superimposed on early maternal malnutrition.

A variety of factors would lead us to focus upon the last month of intrauterine life as one of the "critical" periods for the growth and development of the central nervous system. Both brain and body growth together with differentiation are occurring at a particular rapid rate at this time. It has been argued, therefore, that whereas marginal maternal nutritional resources may be sufficient, adequately to sustain life and growth, during the earlier periods of pregnancy the needs of the rapidly growing infant in the last trimester of intrauterine existence may outstrip maternal supplies. The work of Gruenwald et al. (1963) among others, would suggest that maternal conditions during this period of the infant's development are probably the ones which contribute most influentially to low birth weight and prematurity. Such concerns have led to inquiries into the relation of the mother's nutritional status in pregnancy to the growth and development of her child. In considering this question it is well to recognize that as yet we have no definitive answer to the question of the degree to which maternal nutrition during pregnancy contributes to pregnancy outcome. Clearly, whether or not nutritional lacks experienced by the mother during pregnancy will affect fetal growth is dependent upon the size and physical resources of the mother herself. Well-grown women are most likely to have tissue reserves which can be diverted to meet the nutritional needs of the fetus even when pregnancy is accompanied by significant degrees of contemporary undernutrition. Conversely, poorly grown women with minimal tissue reserves could not under the same set of circumstances be expected to be able to provide adequately for the growing infant.

Children coming from families in which the risks for exposure to malnutrition are high are unlikely to experience nutritional inadequacies only in early life. It is far more likely that earlier nutritional inadequacies are projected into the preschool and school years. Such a view receives support from numerous surveys as well as from recent testimony presented before the Senate Committee on Nutrition and Human Needs (1968–1970). Our knowledge of the degree to which children and families at risk continue to be exposed to nutritional inadequacies derive from a series of indirect and direct methods of inquiry. At an indirect level it can be argued that family diet in the main is very much dependent upon family income level. The report *Dietary Levels of Household in the United States* (1968) published by the United States Department of Agriculture underscores this proposition. According to a household survey conducted in the spring of 1965, only 9 per cent of families with incomes of $10,000 and over a year were judged as having "poor diets." However, the proportion of poor diets increased regularly with each reduction in income level, with 18 per cent of the families earning under $3,000 a year reporting poor diets, that is, diets containing less than two-thirds of the recommended allowance of one or more essential nutrients. Conversely, the proportion of "good" diets went from 63 per cent in the $10,000 and over category down to 37 per cent in the under $3,000 group. Of course, income alone is not an adequate indicator of socioeconomic status since in families with equal incomes more education appears to produce a better diet (Jeans, Smith & Stearns, 1952; Murphy & Wertz, 1954; Hendel, Burke & Lund, 1965). But, at the least such figures suggest that we must be seriously concerned with just how badly nourished are our poor in what we often claim is the "best-fed nation in the world."

The evidence we have surveyed indicates strongly that nutritional factors at a number of different levels contribute significantly to depressed intellectual level and learning failure. These effects may be produced directly as the consequences of irreparable alterations of the nervous system or indirectly as a result of ways in which the learning experiences of the developing organism may be significantly interfered with at critical points in the developmental course.

If one were to argue that a primary requirement for normal intellectual development and for formal learning is the ability to process sensory information and to integrate such information across sense systems the evidence indicates that both severe acute malnutrition in infancy as well as chronic subnutrition from birth into the school years results in defective information processing. Thus by inhibiting the development of a primary process essential for certain aspects of cognitive growth malnutrition may interfere with the orderly development of experience and contribute to a suboptimal level of intellectual functioning.

Moreover, an adequate state of nutrition is essential for good attention and for appropriate and sensitive responsiveness to the environment. One of the most obvious clinical manifestations of serious malnutrition in infancy is a dramatic combination of apathy and irritability. The infant is grossly unresponsive to his surroundings and obviously unable to profit from the objective opportunities for experience present in his surroundings. This unresponsiveness characterizes his relation to people, as well as to objects. Behavioral regression is profound; and the organization of his functions are markedly infantalized. As Dean (1960) has put it one of the first signs of recovery from the illness is an improvement in mood and in responsiveness to people—"the child who smiles is on the road to recovery."

In children who are subnourished one also notes a reduction in responsiveness and attentiveness. In addition the subnourished child is easily fatigued and unable to sustain either prolonged physical or mental effort. Improvement in nutritional status is accompanied by improvements in these behaviors as well as in physical state.

It should not be forgotten that nutritional inadequacy may influence the child's learning opportunities by yet another route, namely, illness. As we have demonstrated elsewhere (Birch & Cravioto, 1968; Birch & Gussow, 1970) nutritional inadequacy increases the risk of infection, interferes with immune mechanisms, and results in illness which is both more generalized and more severe. The combination of subnutrition and illness reduces time available for instruction and so by interfering with the opportunities for gaining experience disrupts the orderly acquisition of knowledge and the course of intellectual growth.

We have also pointed to intergenerational effects of nutrition upon mental development. The association between the mother's growth achievements and the risk to her infant is very strong. Poor nutrition and poor health in the mother when she was a girl result in a woman at maturity who has a significantly elevated level of reproductive risk. Her pregnancy is more frequently disturbed and her child more often of low birth weight. Such a child is at increased risk of neurointegrative abnormality and of deficient IQ and school achievement.

Despite the strength of the argument that we have developed, it would be tragic if one were now to seek to replace all the other variables—social, cultural, educational, and psychological—which exert an influence on intellectual growth with nutrition. Malnutrition never occurs alone, it occurs in conjunction with low income, poor housing, familial disorganization, a climate of apathy, ignorance and despair. The simple act of improving the nutritional status of children and their families will not and cannot of itself fully solve the problem of intellectual deficit and school failure. No single improvement in conditions will have this result. What must be recognized rather is that within our overall effort to improve the condition of disadvantaged children, nutritional considerations must occupy a prominent place, and together with improvements in all other facets of life including relevant and directed education, contribute to the improved intellectual growth and school achievement of disadvantaged children.

## REFERENCES

[only those reported in this excerpt]

BIRCH, H. G., and CRAVIOTO, J. Infection, nutrition and environment in mental development. In H. F. Eichenwald (Ed.) *The Prevention of Mental Retardation Through the Control of Infectious Disease*. Public Health Service Publication 1962. Washington, D.C.: U.S. Government Ptg. Office, 1968.

BIRCH, H. G., and GUSSOW, J. D. *Disadvantaged Children: Health, Nutrition and School Failure*. New York: Harcourt Brace and World, and Grune and Stratton, Inc., 1970, pp. 322.

BROCK, J. *Recent Advances in Human Nutrition*. London: J. & A. Churchill, 1961.

CHOW, B. F.; BLACKWELL, B.; HOU, T. Y.; ANILANE, J. K.; SHERWIN, R. W.; and CHIR, B. Maternal nutrition and metabolism of the offspring: Studies in rats and man." *A.J.P.H.* 58:668–677, 1968.

DEAN, R. F. A. The effects of malnutrition on the growth of young children. *Mod. Probl. Pediat.* 5:111–122, 1960.

GRUENWALD, P.; DAWKINS, M.; and HEPNER, R. Chronic deprivation of the fetus. *Sinai Hosp. J.*, 11:51–80, 1963.

HENDEL, G. M.; BURKE, M. C.; and LUND, L. A. Socioeconomic factors influence children's diets. *J. Home Econ.*, 57:205–208, 1965.

JEANS, P. C.; SMITH, M. B.; and STEARNS, G. Dietary habits of pregnant women of low income in a rural state. *J. Amer. Diet. Ass.*, 28:27–34, 1952.

MURPHY, G. H. and WERTZ, A. W. Diets of pregnant women: influence of socioeconomic factors. *J. Amer. Diet. Ass.*, 30:34–48, 1954.

Senate Committee on Nutrition and Human Needs. cf. parts 1 et seq. 1968–70.

# Pygmalion Black and White*
## *Pamela C. Rubovits and Martin L. Maehr*

IT IS NOT SURPRISING that research on experimenter expectancies (Rosenthal, 1966; Rosenthal & Fode, 1963; Rosenthal & Lawson, 1964) has been quickly applied to the classroom, with some studies finding that students perform in line with their teachers' expectations for them (Meichenbaum,

* Pamela C. Rubovits and Martin L. Maehr, "Pygmalion Black and White," *Journal of Personality and Social Psychology*, Vol. 25, No. 2 (1973): 210–218. Copyright 1973 by the American Psychological Association. Reprinted by permission.

Bowers, & Ross, 1969; Rosenthal & Jacobson, 1968). These findings, controversial though they may be (Claiborne, 1969; Elashoff & Snow, 1970; Rosenthal, 1969; Snow, 1969; Thorndike, 1968, 1969), provide a perspective on a problem of major concern: the teaching of black students by white teachers. Black students have been found to believe that their white teachers have low estimates of their ability and worth (Brown, 1968; Davidson & Lang, 1960). It has also been well documented that white teachers expect less of lower-class children than they do of middle-class children (Becker, 1952; Deutsch, 1963; Warner, Havighurst, & Loeb, 1944; Wilson, 1963). In line with Rosenthal and Jacobson's proposal (1968) that teacher expectations affect teacher behavior in such a way that it is highly likely that student performance is in turn affected, it would seem probable that differential teacher expectation for black students and white students is related to differential school achievement. Few, if any, studies have, however, directly observed and compared teacher-expectancy effects on black students and white students. The present study was designed to do just that, and it yielded surprising results—results that can be interpreted as a paradigmatic instance of "white racism."

The present study is replication and extension of a previous study (Rubovits & Maehr, 1971) that involved the systematic observation of teacher behavior following the experimental manipulation of expectations. The teachers, college undergraduates with limited classroom experience, each met with four students who had been randomly identified for the teacher as being "gifted" or "nongifted." The teachers did not differentiate in the amount of attention given to allegedly gifted and nongifted students; however, the pattern of attention did differ: Gifted students were called on and praised more than nongifted students. Thus, in this first study, teacher expectations were found to be related to teacher behavior in such a way that gifted students appeared to be encouraged and average students discouraged by their teachers.

The present study replicated the above procedure with one new dimension. Whereas the previous study looked at interaction of white teachers with white students, this study considered the interaction of white teachers with white students and black students; one of the students labeled gifted and one of the students labeled nongifted were black. This provided an opportunity to investigate whether or not white teachers interact differently with white students and black students, both bright and average, in ways that would differentially affect their school performance. In addition, the study attempted to identify what kind of teacher would most likely be affected by race and label. Each teacher's level of dogmatism was, therefore, assessed under the assumption that high- and low-dogmatism teachers would react differently to the stereotyping effects of race and label.

# Method

## Subjects

Two different groups of subjects participated in the study. The group referred to as teachers was composed of 66 white female undergraduates enrolled in a teacher training course. All teachers had expressed interest in teaching, but not all were enrolled in an education curriculum, and none had yet had teaching experience. All teachers were volunteers; however, they were given course credit for participating in this project. The teachers knew nothing of the experimental manipulations; they simply thought they were taking advantage of a microteaching experience provided for them.

The group referred to as students was comprised of 264 seventh and eighth graders attending three junior high schools in a small midwestern city. These students were randomly selected within ability groups and given no instruction as to how they were to behave.

## Measurement Procedures

In order to index the quality of teacher-student interaction, an instrument especially developed for this series of studies on teacher expectancy was employed. Although a more detailed description including reliability data may be found elsewhere (Rubovits, 1970; Rubovits & Maehr, 1971), the major features of this instrument should be noted. Briefly, the instrument is an observational schedule that requires a trained observer to record the incidence of six different teacher behaviors: (*a*) teacher *attention* to students' statements, subdivided into attention to requested statements and attention to spontaneous student statements; (*b*) teacher *encouragement* of students' statements; (*c*) teacher *ignoring* of students' statements; (*e*) teacher *praise* of students' statements; and (*f*) teacher *criticism* of students' statements.

The Rokeach Dogmatism Scale (Rokeach, 1960) was used to measure the teachers' authoritarianism. In addition, a questionnaire was given to each teacher in order to check the credibility of the experimental manipulations and to obtain some information on the teachers' perception of the students and the interpretations they gave to each student's behavior.

## Experimental Procedure

One week before teaching, each teacher was given a lesson plan which outlined the topic to be taught and specified major points to be covered. As in the previous study, a lesson plan on the topic of television was employed. This topic and plan prompted considerable involvement on the part of both teacher and student. All students were found to be quite interested in discussing television and actively participated. The teachers had little or no difficulty in starting and sustaining a discussion on the topic and generally seemed at ease, improving a great deal, adding and omitting points from the lesson plan, and using many original samples.

Attached to each teacher's lesson plan was a brief general description of the students she would be meeting. The teachers were told that an attempt would be made to have them teach as heterogeneous a group of students as possible. The teachers were also reminded that this was to be a learning experience for them, so they should be particularly alert to the differences between their students in terms of verbal ability, interest, quality of comments, etc.

The teachers were given no more information until just right before their teaching sessions, when each teacher was given a seating chart. This chart had on it each student's first name and also, under each name, an IQ score and a label indicating whether that student had been selected from the school's gifted program or from the regular track. The IQ score and a label had been *randomly* assigned to each student and did not necessarily bear any relation to the student's actual ability or track assignment.

For each teacher, a different group of four students was randomly selected from the same-ability-grouped class unit. Besides selecting from the same-ability units, one other restriction was placed on the selection of students; each session required two black students and two white students. One black student and one white student were randomly assigned a high IQ (between 130 and 135) and the label gifted. The other black student and the other white student were given lower IQs (between 98 and 102) and the label non-gifted.

Each teacher was given the seating chart before the students arrived and was told to familiarize herself with the names and to examine closely the IQ scores and labels under each name. When the students arrived, the teacher was instructed to ask each student to sit in the seat designated on the chart. The teacher was further instructed before beginning the lesson to look at each student and read again, to herself, the IQ score and label of each child. The necessity for doing this was emphasized to the teacher and justified by explaining that being aware of each student's ability level could help a teacher to deal with that student during the session.

The teacher then introduced herself and explained that she had come from the University of Illinois to try out some new teaching materials. In the meantime, an observer seated herself two rows behind the students. The observer began categorizing the teacher's behavior as soon as the teacher had introduced herself and continued tallying behavior for 40 minutes. It must be emphasized that the observer did not know what label had been assigned to each student.

After the teaching session, the observer and the teacher discussed what had transpired, with the observer attempting to start the teacher thinking about each student's performance in relation to his reported intelligence. The teacher then filled out a questionnaire and two personality inventories. After all of the teachers had participated, the experimenters went to the two classes from which teachers had been recruited and explained the study in detail, discussing with them the results and implications of the study.

# Results

## Interaction Analysis

Frequency counts were collected on each teacher for each of eight categories. Each teacher met with four different kinds of students: gifted black, nongifted black, gifted white, and nongifted white. For each category, therefore, every teacher received four scores, with each score indicating her interaction with one kind of student. These scores were treated as repeated measures on the same individual.

A multivariate analysis of variance was used to analyze the data from seven of the categories (see Tatsuoka, 1971). Category 1, it will be remembered, measures the total number of times the teacher attended to the statements of the student. Attention to two specific kinds of statements were included in Category 1—attention to spontaneous responses to the teacher's questions (Category 1a) and attention to statements specifically requested by the teacher (Category 1b). Although the frequency of counts for Category 1 was not simply a combination of those for the subcategories 1a and 1b, Category 1 is clearly related to Categories 1a and 1b. For this reason, data on Category 1 were not included in the multivariate analysis of variance but were analyzed in a separate univariate analysis of variance.

In both of these analyses, there was one between-subjects variable—dogmatism (level of teacher dogmatism based on a high-low median split). This is referred to as the *teacher* variable. The two within-teachers variables are based on student differences and, for purposes of discussion, are referred to as *student* variables: race (black–white) and label (gifted–nongifted).

## Student Variables: Race of Student

Each teacher met with two white students and two black students. Table 1 presents the mean number of teacher responses to black students and white students. . . .

# Discussion

As in a previous study (Rubovits & Maehr, 1971), teachers were found to treat students labeled gifted differently from students described as average.

Table 1

*Mean Teacher Interactions with Gifted and Nongifted Black Students and White Students*

| Category | Black | White | Combined |
|---|---|---|---|
| 1—Total attention | | | |
| Gifted | 29.59 | 36.08 | 32.83 |
| Nongifted | 30.32 | 32.33 | 31.32 |
| Combined | 29.95 | 34.20 | |
| 1a—Attention to unsolicited statements | | | |
| Gifted | 26.39 | 26.79 | 26.59 |
| Nongifted | 26.30 | 26.03 | 26.17 |
| Combined | 26.35 | 26.41 | |
| 1b—Attention to requested statements | | | |
| Gifted | 3.88 | 10.64 | 7.70 |
| Nongifted | 4.77 | 5.67 | 5.22 |
| Combined | 4.32 | 8.15 | |
| 2—Encouragement | | | |
| Gifted | 5.47 | 6.18 | 5.82 |
| Nongifted | 5.32 | 6.32 | 5.82 |
| Combined | 5.39 | 6.25 | |
| 3—Elaboration | | | |
| Gifted | 2.09 | 2.08 | 2.08 |
| Nongifted | 2.44 | 2.15 | 2.30 |
| Combined | 2.26 | 2.11 | |
| 4—Ignoring | | | |
| Gifted | 6.92 | 5.09 | 6.01 |
| Nongifted | 6.86 | 4.56 | 5.71 |
| Combined | 6.89 | 4.82 | |
| 5—Praise | | | |
| Gifted | .58 | 2.02 | 1.30 |
| Nongifted | 1.56 | 1.29 | 1.42 |
| Combined | 1.07 | 1.65 | |
| 6—Criticism | | | |
| Gifted | 1.86 | .77 | 1.32 |
| Nongifted | .86 | .68 | .77 |
| Combined | 1.36 | .73 | |

There was no difference in the *amount* of attention given to the supposedly different-ability groups, but there were differences in the *quality* of attention. Gifted students were called on more, thus replicating a previous finding (Rubovits & Maehr, 1971). Gifted students were also criticized more, but this difference may have been caused by the inclusion of black students in the gifted group as they were the recipients of almost all the criticism.

Considering the differences due to label for whites only, it can be seen that the gifted white student was given more attention than his nongifted counterpart, called on more, praised more, and also criticized a bit more. It is interesting, incidentally, that in the informal interviews with teachers the gifted white student was also chosen most frequently as the most liked student, the brightest student, and the certain leader of the class.

Of special interest, of course, are the comparisons of teacher interaction with black students and white students. In this regard, the present study provides what appears to be a disturbing instance of white racism. Black students were given less attention, ignored more, praised less and criticized more. More startling perhaps are the Race × Label interactions that suggest that it is the gifted black who is given the least attention, is the least praised, and the most criticized, even when comparing him to his nongifted black counterpart.

It is important to stress that these results are not easily attributable to an experimental artifact of some kind. There is no reason to suppose that the expectancy communication varied for race. Moreover, it cannot be argued that teachers were responding to any actual intellectual differences between black students and white students or to any incongruity between label and actual potential. Recall that students were specifically selected so as to be of equivalent intellectual ability regardless of race.

An obvious question, of course, is whether the expectancy resided in the observer or in the teacher. It is impossible to rule out observer expectancy effects completely. While the observer could not know which students were labeled gifted or average, it is obvious that she would know black from white. However, it is difficult to see how such knowledge might have determined the pattern of results that were obtained. First, the observational instrument is reasonably objective in nature, allowing for minimal judgment on the part of the observer (Rubovits, 1970). Second, the present authors in fact had no clear and obvious basis for postulating the results that did indeed occur. For example, it would have been equally logical to argue before the fact that young, idealistic teachers, most of whom expressed liberal beliefs, would make a special attempt to ingratiate themselves to blacks. Finally, the fact that high-dogmatic teachers were more inclined toward a prejudicial pattern than low-dogmatic teachers further suggests that the reported interactions were not just a figment of the observer's expectancy. If the observer were, in fact, the responsible agent, it would be difficult to see how, not knowing the dogmatism scores, she could have effected a generally predictable pattern for high and low dogmatists as well as the overall pattern. A bias leading toward differential observation of teacher–student interaction in the case of blacks and whites would presumably operate across all teachers regardless of dogmatism, thereby making it virtually impossible to obtain any meaningful Dogmatism × Race interaction. In brief, the most logical explanation of the results is that the teachers were indeed exhibiting the negative pattern toward blacks that the reported interactions indicate.

It is important to emphasize that this prejudicial pattern was not exhibited by all teachers. Teachers higher in dogmatism seemed to differentiate more in their treatment of blacks and whites. Moreover, one may wonder about the degree to which the patterns observed are unique to young, inexperienced teachers. After all, these teachers not only had little teaching experience but, as the questionnaire data would indicate, little experience of any kind with blacks. One might at least hope that the appropriate experience could be of benefit.

All in all, then, this study clearly suggests how teacher expectations may affect teacher behavior. Although the results must be interpreted within the limits of the study, with cautious generalization, the data do suggest answers to the question of why teachers are often able to do little to equalize the performance levels of blacks and whites.

## REFERENCES

BECKER, H. S. Social class variations in the teacher-pupil relationship. *Journal of Educational Sociology,* 1952, **25,** 451–465.

BROWN, B. The assessment of self-concept among four-year-old Negro and white children. (Cited by H. Proshansky & P. Newton: The nature and meaning of Negro self-identity) In M. Deutsch, I. Katz, & A. R. Jensen (Eds.), *Social class, race and psychological development.* New York: Holt, Rinehart & Winston, 1968.

CLAIBORNE, W. L. Expectancy effects in the classroom: A failure to replicate. *Journal of Educational Psychology,* 1969, **60,** 377–383.

DAVIDSON, H. H., & LANG, G. Children's perception of teachers' feelings toward them. *Journal of Experimental Education,* 1960, **29,** 107–118.

DEUTSCH, M. The disadvantaged child and the learning process. In A. H. Passow (Ed.), *Education in depressed areas.* New York: Bureau of Publications, Teachers College, Columbia University, 1963.

ELASHOFF, J. D., & SNOW, R. E. *A case study in statistical inference: Reconsideration of the Rosenthal-Jacobson data on teacher expectancy.* (Tech. Rep. No. 15) Stanford, Calif.: Stanford Center for Research and Development in Teaching, Stanford University, 1970.

MEICHENBAUM, D. H., BOWERS, K. S., & ROSS, R. R. A behavioral analysis of teacher expectancy effect. *Journal of Personality and Social Psychology,* 1969, **13,** 306–316.

ROKEACH, M. *The open and closed mind.* New York: Basic Books, 1960.

ROSENTHAL, R. *Experimenter effects in behavioral research.* New York: Appleton-Century-Crofts, 1966.

ROSENTHAL, R. Empirical vs. decreed validation of clocks and tests. *American Educational Research Journal,* 1969, **6,** 689–691.

ROSENTHAL, R., & FODE, K. L. The effect of experimenter bias on the performance of albino rats. *Behavioral Science,* 1963, **8,** 183–189.

ROSENTHAL, R., & JACOBSON, L. *Pygmalion in the classroom: Teacher expectation and pupils' intellectual development.* New York: Holt, Rinehart & Winston, 1968.

ROSENTHAL, R., & LAWSON, R. A longitudinal study of the effects of experimenter bias on the operant learning of laboratory rats. *Journal of Psychiatric Research,* 1964, **2,** 61–72.

RUBOVITS, P. C. Teacher interaction with students labeled gifted and nongifted in a microteaching situation. Unpublished master's thesis, University of Illinois, 1970.

RUBOVITS, P. C., & MAEHR, M. L. Pygmalion analyzed: Toward an explanation of the Rosenthal-Jacobson findings. *Journal of Personality and Social Psychology,* 1971, **19,** 197–203.

SNOW, R. E. Unfinished pygmalion. *Contemporary Psychology,* 1969, **14,** 197–199.

TATSUOKA, M. *Multivariate analysis.* New York: Wiley, 1971.

THORNDIKE, R. L. Review of *Pygmalion in the classroom*. *American Educational Research Journal*, 1968, 5, 708–711.

THORNDIKE, R. L. But do you have to know how to tell time? *American Educational Research Journal*, 1969, 6, 692.

WARNER, W. L., HAVIGHURST, R. J., & LOEB, M. B. *Who shall be educated?* New York: Harper & Row, 1944.

WILSON, A. B. Social stratification and academic achievement. In A. H. Passow (Ed.), *Education in depressed areas*. New York: Teachers College, Columbia University, 1963.

---

# The Effects of Maternal Employment on Children*
## *Barbara Wallston*

[The author of this paper reviews the research literature regarding the effects of maternal employment on children—preschoolers, school-age children, including adolescents—and then makes some general observations about this field of study.]

## Preschool Children

**Maternal Deprivation Framework.**    Much of the research on maternal employment began within the framework of the "maternal deprivation" literature. Yarrow (1964) in his review of this area, noted the difference between maternal separation and maternal deprivation, and pointed out that, *"maternal employment is considered in the context of separation because the fact of the mother's working has sometimes been equated with deprivation of maternal care"* (p. 116). Rossi (1965) noted the unwarranted extrapolation of the serious negative effects of prolonged parental separation to the conclusion that any separation of the mother and child is harmful. . . . Mead (1954) has condemned the over-emphasis on the importance of the tie between the child and its biological mother, and the unfounded insistence that any separation is damaging. *"On the contrary, cross-cultural studies suggest that adjustment is most facilitated if the child is cared for by many warm, friendly people"* (p. 477). Moreover, Yudkin and Holme (1963) pointed out that Bowlby, whose work on maternal deprivation is often extrapolated to the working mother's situation, actually distinguished between these. He cited evidence of

---

* Reprinted with permission from the *Journal of Child Psychology and Psychiatry*, 14 (1973): 81–95. © Copyright 1973. Pergamon Press, Ltd.

a normal development quotient (D.Q.) for children in the second, third, and fourth years of life cared for at day nurseries, while a comparable sample of institutionalized children was below the average D.Q.

Thus, it is clear that the maternal deprivation literature is not the proper source for conclusions regarding the effects of maternal employment on young children. . . .

**Studies of Young Children.** . . . Recent studies of day care centers suggest that a mother's working need not be detrimental but can actually be beneficial to a child's development. At Syracuse University, for example (Caldwell and Richmond, 1968; Caldwell and Smith, 1970), a comparison of lower and middle class children between 6 months and 4 years found that those attending a day care center designed to provide an enriching environment showed gains in developmental quotient while a non-intervention control group tested regularly showed a decline. Ratings of adjustment made by a psychiatrist who did not know when children had entered the program showed no differences in adjustment between those entering before or after the age of three (Caldwell and Smith, 1970). In addition, at 30 months of age, no differences in child-mother or mother-child attachment patterns were detected in interviews with the mothers or observations of mother-child interactions between children attending the center and the non-intervention control group (Caldwell *et al.,* 1970). The positive findings, thus far obtained, lend support to the notion that with adequate substitute care, a mother's working need not be detrimental, and can in fact, be beneficial to the child's development in terms of the positive D.Q. gains shown here. In conclusion, there is almost no direct evidence regarding the positive or negative effects of maternal employment on young children. . . .

**Preschool Literature Summary.** There seems to be no direct evidence of harmful effects of maternal employment on young children. What is crucial is the availability of proper substitute care. This is not readily available to many and serves as a major reason for mothers' not working in both England (Gavron, 1966) and the United States (Brooks, 1964). Mothers with very young children were least satisfied with child care arrangements and responded most positively to the question of possible use of a day care center (Ruderman, 1968).

# School Age Children (Pre-adolescents)

**Children's Characteristics.** Direct studies are available on school age children, to a greater extent than for infants. In a study of 6- to 11-year-olds, Nolan (1963) found no significant differences in academic achievement and peer acceptance, both rated by teachers, between children with either employed or homemaker mothers. . . .

**Further Distinctions Among Children of Working Mothers.** Several studies used the more sophisticated techniques suggested in the introduction, in that the independent variable was further subdivided. Woods (1968) administered a series of psychological tests to fifth grade children, who reported that their mothers were employed. The sample was largely lower class blacks. When the sample was divided into those reporting supervision (i.e. some sort of substitute care) and those without supervision, girls without supervision showed impoverished cognitive and personal development; they also perceived their mothers as less controlling and intrusive. Woods also noted that, *"in lower class American Negro families, maternal absence due to full-time employment was positively related to the social and intellectual development of their 10-year-old children"* (p. 4110-A). However, in this brief description, it was unclear whether this statement referred only to the supervised group, and if not, to whom full-time employed mothers were compared. Moreover, other differences between mothers who would leave children with or without supervision, might have been influential in mediating the poorer condition of unsupervised children. No indication as to whether these children came from intact families was made, and this is probably a relevant variable.

Hoffman (1963), using white intact families with children in the third to six grades, interviewed mothers, got teachers' ratings, a sociometric scale, and a questionnaire completed by the children. Working and non-working mothers were matched on father's occupation, sex of child, and birth order, and working mothers were classified as liking or disliking work.

> The overall pattern of findings suggests that the working mother who likes working is relatively high on positive affect toward the child, uses mild discipline, and tends to avoid inconveniencing the child with household tasks; the child is relatively nonassertive and ineffective. The working mother who dislikes working, on the other hand, seems less involved with the child altogether and obtains the child's help with tasks; the child is assertive and hostile [p. 102].

Hoffman also concluded that both groups of working mother children showed lower intellectual performance than the children of non-working mothers. . . .

**School-age Literature Summary.** In general, the literature on the school age child has avoided many of the pitfalls discussed in the introduction. However, the Siegel *et al.* (1963) and Woods (1968) studies indicate the potential importance of differential sex effects, and although the other studies controlled for sex, data were not analyzed separately within sex, so effects might have been masked. Also, the problem of how long the mother has worked and the type of substitute care provided has been ignored (except for the somewhat "crude" division into supervised and unsupervised children by Woods (1968)). Given these restrictions, it seems that the differences obtained between children divided on the global variable working and non-working mothers are not consistent. However, there seems to be a consistent difference depending on role satisfaction, with satisfied mothers, working or non-working, producing different and generally better effects than dissatisfied mothers. Further work using better dependent measures and designed to investigate how these effects are mediated is necessary.

## Adolescents

Adolescents have received more attention than other age groups, possibly because of the ease of getting a sample to complete a questionnaire (the most frequently used technique).

Achievement.    The results of studies of differential achievement for adolescents of working and non-working mothers are inconsistent. No differences on achievement or intelligence scores of secondary school students were found by George and Thomas (1967) in India or by Armstrong (1966) who studied Iowa high school students. Nye (1963a) similarly found no difference in high school students' grade point averages (GPAs); nor did Nelson in ninth graders' school achievement. However, Nolan (1963) found higher achievement among children of employed mothers, using teacher's ratings as a criterion. The latter study differs from the others in the more subjective criterion and in its use of a homogeneous lower class rural sample (the other samples were more heterogeneous). The latter is probably the more important difference, since Roy (1963) found that in his rural high school sample, children of employed mothers had higher academic performance, while in the urban sample, the reverse was true.

Banducci (1967) divided his sample on sex and SES (fathers who were laborers, skilled workers, and professionals). He found only three significant differences: for "skilled worker" boys, the GPA was higher with working than with non-working mothers; for "professional" boys the reverse was true; for "laborer" boys, those with working mothers had higher scores on the Iowa Tests of Educational Development; there were no differences in girls. Farley (1968) also found that college males whose mothers had worked when they were younger had higher GPAs than those who had had housewife mothers, while there was no difference in GPA for females. Again it is apparent that by not blocking on relevant variables, SES and sex in this case, differences in achievement in these studies may have been obscured.

Adolescent Studies Summary.    There is some evidence of differential attitudes and achievement of working and non-working mothers' children, with the effect different for males and females. Although some differential personality and activity patterns were also shown, there is no clear evidence for disturbance or maladjustment among children of working mothers.

## Conclusions and Implications

**General Results.**   The situation is even less clearcut with respect to maternal employment than the somewhat inconsistent findings summarized by Stolz (1960). She found no relation between maternal employment and delinquency, adolescent high school grades, and dependent-independent behavior. She did find more reported adolescent delinquency with maternal employment, but controlling for demographic variables eliminated this result. Elementary school children of working mothers were rated as lower in intellectual performance by teachers who knew the mother's work status. Finally, underlying characteristics of the mother may influence her attitude toward work and children with consequent effects on the children's behavior.

Because of the complexity of the studies reviewed, it no longer seems possible or realistic to conclude with a list of dependent variables related and unrelated to maternal employment as Stolz did. The most important steps forward in this area are the recognition of differential sex and social class behavior of the working mother and the nature of the substitute care, rather than dealing with the global independent variable, working versus nonworking mothers.

It is clear that the study of the effects of maternal employment must be separated from the research on maternal deprivation where institutionalized children have primarily been studied. Although more direct study of preschool children with working mothers is necessary, the literature thus far, including the indirect evidence from Israel and Russia, indicates no harmful effects where adequate substitute care is provided. Future studies, should, where possible, include long-term follow-up of children whose mothers worked before the children entered school. No consistent effects of maternal employment have been found with school age children, although both satisfied working and non-working mothers appear to be "better mothers" than their dissatisfied counterparts. Similarly, adolescent children of working mothers are not consistently disturbed or maladjusted. However, there is some evidence that lower class children, especially boys, of working mothers show higher school achievement than those of non-working mothers, while the reverse relationship holds for upper middle-class children. Differences in attitudes and activity of children with working and non-working mothers have not been consistent, but results thus far suggest that studying this relationship within a framework of sex-role typing effects might be useful. Such studies cannot determine cause and effect since the researchers cannot manipulate which mothers work. Therefore, care must be taken in using conclusions about positive or detrimental effects of maternal employment on children to encourage or discourage mothers interested in working. Until causation can be shown, there is danger in drawing implications for relevant social action from these studies.

**Future Research.**   . . . One final area mentioned by Stolz, and not really noted since then, is the effect of the cultural milieu on the process of family interaction. Stolz, in her final summary, eliminated research before World War II because of the changing environment. Today attitudes toward maternal employment are changing rapidly. Rapoport and Rapoport (1969), in their study of dual-career professional families noted that increasing emphasis on partnership of family life and the awareness on the part of such families of possible effects on their children. Rossi (1965) suggested that such knowledge causes guilt on the part of working mothers. DeRham (1965) noted that some guilt-ridden professional women overcompensate and become overprotective mothers. She further stated, *"this problem, of course, would never arise if the mothers were not made to feel guilty about their work in the first place through cultural pressures"* (p. 135). Thus, one reason for the lack of deficiency among kibbutz-reared children may be the acceptance of maternal employment. Rabin (1964) in interviews with kibbutz mothers found that most were fully satisfied with the collective education of their children. Thus, cultural acceptance can mitigate guilt, and possibly alleviate some of the negative effects of maternal employment. On the other hand, guilt may be one of the factors in bringing about increased mother-child interaction when the mother works. . . .

## REFERENCES

ARMSTRONG, R. F. (1966) Working mothers and teenage children in an Iowa community. *Diss. Abs.* 27, 3125A–3126A.

BANDUCCI, R. (1967) The effect of mother's employment on the achievement, aspirations, and expectations of the child. *Person. Guide. J.* 46, 263–267.

BETTELHEIM, B. (1969) *The Children of the Dream.* Macmillan, London.

BROOKS, JR., D. J. (1964) *A Study to Determine the Employment Potential of Mothers Receiving Aid to Dependent Children Assistance.* Cook County Department of Public Aid, Chicago.

BURCHINAL, L. G. (1963) Personality characteristics of children. In *The Employed Mother in America (Edited by Nye, F. I. and Hoffman, L. W.), pp.* 106–121, Rand McNally, Chicago.

CALDWELL, B. M. and RICHMOND, J. B. (1968) The Children's Center in Syracuse, New York. In *Early Child Care—The New Perspective* (Edited by Dittman, L. L.), Atherton Press, New York.

CALDWELL, B. M. and SMITH, L. E. (1970) Day care for the very young—prime opportunity for primary prevention. *Am. J. Public Hlth* 60, 690–697.

CALDWELL, B. M., WRIGHT, C. M., HONIC, A. S. and TANNENBAUM, J. (1970) Infant day care and attachment. *Am. F. Orthopsychiat.* 40, 397–412.

DERAHM, E. (1965) *The Love Fraud.* Clarkson N. Potter, New York.

DOUVAN, E. (1963) Employment and the adolescent. In *The Employed Mother in America* (Edited by Nye, F. I. and Hoffman, L. W.), pp. 142–164, Rand McNally, Chicago.

FARLEY, J. (1968) Maternal employment and child behavior. *Cornell J. Soc. Relat.* 3, (2), 58–71.

FRANKEL, E. (1964) Characteristics of working and non-working mothers among intellectually gifted high and low achievers, *Person. Guid. J.* **42**, 776–780.

GAVRON, H. (1966) *The Captive Wife: Conflicts of Housebound Mothers.* Routledge & Kegan Paul, London.

GEORGE, E. E. and THOMAS, M. (1967) A comparative study of children of employed mothers and unemployed mothers. *Psychol. Stud.* **12**, 32–38.

GEWIRTZ, H. B. and GEWIRTZ, J. L. (1969) Caretaking settings, background events and behavior differences in four Israeli child-rearing environments; some preliminary trends. In *Determinants of Infant Behaviour* (Edited by Foss, B. M.), Vol. IV, pp. 229–295, Methuen, London.

HOFFMAN, L. W. (1963) Mother's enjoyment of work and effects on the child. In *The Employed Mother in America* (Edited by Nye, F. I. and Hoffman, L. W.), pp. 95–105, Rand McNally, Chicago.

IRVINE, E. E. (1966) Children in kibbutzim: thirteen years after. *J. Child Psychol. Psychiat.* **7**, 167–178.

KING, K., MCINTYRE, J. and AXELSON, L. F. (1968) Adolescents' views of maternal employment as a threat to the marital relationship. *J. Marriage Fam.* **30**, 633–637.

KOHN-RAZ, R. (1968) Mental and motor development of kibbutz, institutionalized, and home-reared infants in Israel. *Child Developm.* **39**, 489–504.

MACE, D. R. (1961) The employed mother in the U.S.S.R. *Marriage Fam. Liv.* **23**, 330–333.

MEAD, M. (1954) Some theoretical considerations on the problem of mother-child separation. *Am. J. Orthopsychiat.* **24**, 471–483.

MOORE, T. (1969) Stress in normal childhood. *Hum. Relat.* **22**, 235–250.

NELSON, D. D. (1968) A study of school achievement and personality adjustment among adolescent children with working and non-working mothers. *Diss. Abs.* **29**, 153A.

NOLAN, F. L. (1963) Effects on rural children. In *The Employed Mother in America* (Edited by Nye, F. I. and Hoffman, L. W.), pp. 122–124, Rand McNally, Chicago.

NYE, F. I. (1963a) The adjustment of adolescent children. In *The Employed Mother in America* (Edited by Nye, F. I. and Hoffman, L. W.), pp. 133–141, Rand McNally, Chicago.

NYE, F. I. (1963b) Adjustment to children. In *The Employed Mother in America* (Edited by Nye, F. I. and Hoffman, L. W.), pp. 353–362, Rand McNally, Chicago.

NYE, F. I., PERRY, JR. J. B. and OGLES, R. (1963) Anxiety and antisocial behavior in preschool children. In *The Employed Mother in America* (Edited by Nye, F. I. and Hoffman, L. W.), pp. 82–94, Rand McNally, Chicago.

PETERSON, E. T. (1961) The impact of maternal employment on the mother-daughter relationship. *Marr. Fam. Liv.* **23**, 355–361.

POWELL, K. S. (1961) Maternal employment in relation to family life. *Marr. Fam. Liv.* **23**, 350–354.

POWELL, K. S. (1963) Personalities of children and child-rearing attitudes of mothers. In *The Employed Mother in America* (Edited by Nye, F. I. and Hoffman, L. W.), pp. 125–132, Rand McNally, Chicago.

RABIN, A. I. (1964) Kibbutz mothers view "collective education". *Am. J. Orthopsychiat.* **34**, 140–142.

RABIN, A. I. (1965) *Growing Up in the Kibbutz.* Springer, New York.

RABIN, A. I. (1969) Of dreams and reality: kibbutz children. *Children* **16**, 160–162.

RABKIN, L. Y. and RABKIN, K. (1969) Children of the kibbutz. *Psychol. Today* **3**, (4), 40.

RAPOPORT, R. and RAPOPORT, R. N. (1969) The dual career family. *Hum. Relat.* **22**, (1), 3–30.

ROSSI, A. S. (1965) Equality between the sexes: an immodest proposal. In *The Woman in America* (Edited by Lifton, R. J.), pp. 98–143, Beacon Press, Boston.

ROY, P. (1963) Adolescent roles: rural-urban differentials. In *The Employed Mother in America* (Edited by Nye, F. I. and Hoffman, L. W.), pp. 165–181, Rand McNally, Chicago.

RUDERMAN, E. A. (1968) *Child Care and Working Mothers: Study of Arrangements Made for Daytime Care of Children.* Child Welfare League of America, New York.

SHAPIRA, A. and MADSEN, M. C. (1969) Cooperative and competitive behavior of kibbutz and urban children in Israel. *Child Developm.* **40,** 609–617.

SIEGEL, A. E. and HAAS, M. B. (1963) The working mother: a review of research. *Child Developm.* **34,** 513–542.

SIEGEL, A. E., STOLZ, L. M., HITCHCOCK, E. A. and ADAMSON, J. (1963) Dependence and independence in children. In *The Employed Mother in America* (Edited by Nye, F. I. and Hoffman, L. W.), pp. 67–81, Rand McNally, Chicago.

SKARD, A. G. (1965) Maternal deprivation: the research and its implications. *J. Marr. Fam.* **27,** 333–343.

SMITH, H. C. (1969) An investigation of the attitudes of adolescent girls toward combining marriage, motherhood, and a career. *Diss. Abs.* **29,** 3883A.

SPARGO, C. J. (1968) Attitudes of mothers using day care centers toward their employment. Unpublished master's thesis, University of Wisconsin, Madison, Wisconsin.

SPIRO, M. E. (1965) *Children of the Kibbutz.* Schocken, New York.

STOLZ, L. M. (1960) Effects of maternal employment on children: evidence from research. *Child Developm.* **31,** 749–782.

SUSSMAN, M. B. (1961) Needed research on the employed mother. *Marr. Fam. Liv.* **23,** 368–373.

WAXLER, N. E. and MISHLER, E. G. (1971) Experimental studies of families. In *Advances in Experimental Social Psychology* (Edited by Berkowitz, L.), Vol. 5, Academic Press, New York.

WHITMARSH, R. E. (1965) Adjustment problems of adolescent daughters of employed mothers. *J. Home Econ.* **57,** 201–204.

WOODS, M. B. (1968) The unsupervised child of the working mother. *Diss. Abs.* 4110A.

YARROW, L. J. (1964) Separation from parents during early childhood. In *Review of Child Development Research* (Edited by Hoffman, M. L. and Hoffman, L. W.), Vol. 1, pp. 89–136, Russell Sage Foundation, New York.

YARROW, M. R. (1961) Maternal employment and child rearing. *Children* **8,** 223–228.

YARROW, M. R., SCOTT, P., DELEEUW, L. and HEINIG, C. (1962) Childrearing in families of working and non-working mothers. *Sociometry* **25,** 122–140.

YUDKIN, S. and HOLME, A. (1963) *Working Mothers and their Children.* Michael Joseph, London.

# Impact of Family Systems Intervention on Recidivism and Sibling Delinquency: A Model of Primary Prevention and Program Evaluation*

*Nanci C. Klein, James F. Alexander, and Bruce V. Parsons*

P REVENTION AS A BASIS for program design and development has begun to occupy a central place in the clinical goals of diverse disciplines (community and clinical psychology, public health nursing, community psychiatry, etc.) in the mental health field. Reasons for this trend are numerous, including recent epidemiological studies indicating the widespread occurrence of mental disorders requiring professional intervention (Garmezy, 1971; Srole, Langner, Michael, Opler, & Rennie, 1962). Other important factors, such as lack of availability of trained personnel, the current high and increasing costs of training, and the reduction in available funding and funding sources, have pointed to the inadequacies of present remediational programs and methods of evaluation, and have emphasized prevention as a persuasive concept (Sundberg, Tyler, & Taplin, 1973).

Concurrent with this acceptance of prevention as a major intervention strategy has been the identification of the family (the most potent socialization force) as a principal target for prevention programs (Caplan & Grunebaum, 1967). At the level of remediation (restoring functioning) or tertiary prevention, the family unit when identified as a dysfunctional system has received much therapeutic attention. However, evaluation of the effects of this treatment approach has been notoriously absent not only at the remediation level (Garmezy, 1971) but also at other levels of prevention as well (Broskowski & Baker, 1974; Flanagan, 1971; Ojemann, 1966).

One explanation for the paucity of systematic studies of the effectiveness of prevention programs lies in the frequent assumption that all varieties of intervention can adequately and appropriately be summarized within the simple dichotomy of prevention and remediation. Typically, programs for primary prevention are considered completely distinct from programs aimed at secondary prevention or remediation, and therefore they can only be separately evaluated.

* Copyright 1977 by the American Psychological Association. Reprinted by permission from *Journal of Consulting and Clinical Psychology*, 45:3 (1977): 469–474.

Representing a shift in focus from this assumption, the present investigation offers a multilevel evaluation model for determining the effectiveness of a family systems intervention program. This model involves evaluation of each level of preventive functioning of a single intervention program and is predicated on following four sequential steps: identification of process, modification of process (tertiary prevention), impact (secondary prevention), and long-range effect (primary prevention).

*Identification of process* involves specifying problem behavior (in this case, delinquency) and identifying potentially modifiable maladaptive processes assumed to influence those problem behaviors using either an empirical or a conceptual strategy. In an empirical approach, basic research studies are undertaken comparing deviant and "normal" samples. In a conceptual approach, a theory is used to generate variables that are hypothesized to be critical in modifying maladaptive behavior.

*Modification of process* includes the development, application, and evaluation of an intervention program with the purpose of modifying the maladaptive processes to match those of a "normal" or effective sample. This phase represents tertiary prevention, defined by Bower (1965) as that which is "done by way of treatment or rehabilitation" (p. 3). This first level of evaluation must include experimental controls for such confounds as maturation, attention, and pretest sensitivity in order to demonstrate that the intervention program has in fact produced the observable process changes.

*Impact* represents secondary prevention, which is defined by Caplan and Grunebaum (1967) as the reduction of existing cases of disability in the population. In this, the second level of evaluation, the program must empirically demonstrate a statistical reduction in the rate of reoccurrence of the disability following intervention. Again, appropriate methodological controls must be utilized.

*Long-range effect,* representing primary prevention, evaluates the intervention program in terms of its reduction of the incidence of new cases of disability in the population. Primary prevention, therefore, can focus either on modifications of the environment that reduce the overall probability of risk or on strengthening the potential recipients or hosts against harmful consequences (Caplan & Grunebaum, 1967).

The purpose of the present study is to describe the application of this model of program evaluation by demonstrating the primary prevention function of a family systems intervention program with families of delinquents. In the initial level of evaluation (remediation, tertiary prevention), Parsons and Alexander (1973) demonstrated that a behaviorally oriented short-term family systems approach, when compared to no-treatment controls and an alternative treatment, produced significant improvement in empirically derived process measures of family interaction. Subsequently, significant reduction in recidivism among the delinquents in the family systems intervention program 6–18 months following treatment was also reported (Alexander & Parsons, 1973). In demonstrating a reduction in problematic behavior with this nonreactive measure, these results reflect an effective process of secondary prevention, the intermediate level of evaluation.

The rationale for the third level of evaluation, or the primary prevention function, of the family systems intervention program follows from the philosophical basis of the intervention model. Based on systems theory (Haley, 1971; Watzlawick, Beavin, & Jackson, 1967), this intervention model explains deviant behavior as a function of the maladaptive and disintegrating system in which the identified delinquent individual is embedded (Alexander, 1973). The ultimate goal of the therapeutic process then becomes one of training the family in effective problem-solving techniques in order for the family unit to more adaptively meet the developmental changes inevitably occurring as children reach adolescence (Alexander, 1974; Malouf & Alexander, 1974; Coles, Alexander, & Schiavo, Note 1).

Therefore, to evaluate the primary prevention potential of this family system intervention approach, juvenile court records were examined 3 years following termination of the intervention program to obtain rates of court referrals for siblings of initially referred delinquents. If, as contended, the family systems approach modified the nature of family interactions to produce a more effective problem-solving unit, it would be expected that siblings of initially referred delinquents receiving the treatment would demonstrate fewer subsequent juvenile court contacts, supporting the primary prevention function of the treatment program.

# Method

## Subjects

During the treatment phase of the project (Parsons & Alexander, 1973), 99 families were referred by District 2 (Salt Lake County) of the Utah Juvenile Court to the Family Clinic at the University of Utah for referral problems representing primarily "soft" delinquency offenses. Upon detention, the families, with minor exceptions caused by program availability, were randomly assigned to either the treatment program, one of two comparison groups, or a no-treatment control group. Subsequent to the initial treatment program, follow-up records were available on 86 families of 38 male and 48 female delinquents, ranging in age from 13 to 16 years.

## Procedure

The first two levels of evaluation investigating remediation and secondary prevention functions of the behavioral family intervention program have been described in greater detail elsewhere (Alexander & Parsons, 1973; Parsons & Alexander, 1973) and are only briefly summarized here.

Process Study: Remediation or Tertiary Prevention. Based on prior research Parsons and Alexander (1973) generated an intervention program designed to modify family interaction process variables. A matching-to-sample philosophy was utilized, in which delinquent families were trained to interact in ways comparable to nonpathological (normal) families of adolescents. The treatment program involved a set of clearly defined therapist interventions focused on changing family interaction patterns in the direction of greater clarity and precision of communication, increased reciprocity of communication and social reinforcement, and contingency contracting emphasizing equivalence of rights and responsibilities for all family members. To control for the effects of maturation and professional attention, two comparison groups were used: (a) a client-centered family groups program and (b) a no-treatment control group. Representative of treatment programs in many juvenile court centers, the client-centered family groups program utilized a basically didactic group discussion focusing on feelings and attitudes about family relationships. Both comparison groups received testing on family interaction process measures under the same experimental and temporal conditions as did the primary treatment group. As can be seen in Table 1, the process (tertiary prevention) study also utilized controls for pretest sensitization, which was found to have no effect on posttest family process scores (Parsons & Alexander, 1973). However, the results did demonstrate that the intervention program, as compared to the client-centered and no-treatment comparison groups, significantly modified four interaction measures of family conflict resolution and interaction (see Table 1): (a) equality of speech; (b) silence; (c) frequency of positive interruptions; and (d) duration of positive interruptions.

Outcome Study: Secondary Prevention. At a 6- to 18-month interval following termination of treatment, a further study comparing the recidivism rates for identified delinquents in the behavioral family systems intervention program with those in the client-centered program and the no-treatment control group was then conducted. At this time, a third comparison group was added. This church-sponsored family counseling program was included in the original assignment of court families to treatment conditions, but it was unavailable for family process testing. This church counseling program was described as "eclectic-dynamic" in orientation, with an emphasis on insight and understanding as a vehicle for therapeutic change (Alexander & Parsons, 1973). As can be seen in Table 1, postproject court referrals for behavioral offenses, that is, recidivism, were found to be 50%–66% lower in the intervention program. Furthermore, reduction in recidivism rates was demonstrated to be statistically related to changes in family process (Alexander & Parsons, 1973).

Follow-up Study: Primary Prevention. By demonstrating positive impact on family process and recidivism, the previously cited studies support the

Table 1

*Three Levels of Evaluation*

| Group | n | Posttreatment measures of family interaction[a] | | | | % recidivism after 6–18 months[c] | % sibling referrals after 2½–3½ years[d] |
|---|---|---|---|---|---|---|---|
| | | Silence[b] | Equality | Frequency[b] | Duration[b] | | |
| No formal treatment | | | | | | | |
| No-treatment controls | 10 | 3 | 4 | 3 | 3 | 50 | 40 |
| Post hoc yoked controls | 46 | | | | | 48 | |
| Base rate for Salt Lake County | 2,800 | | | | | 51 | |
| Alternate treatments | | | | | | | |
| Client centered | 19 | 4 | 2 | 4 | 4[e] | 47 | 59 |
| Eclectic– dynamic | 11 | | | | | 73 | 63 |
| Short-term behavioral family systems treatment | | | | | | | |
| Pretest– treatment– posttest | 10 | 2 | 1[e] | 22 | | | |
| Treatment– posttest | 19 | 1[e] | 3 | 1 | 1[e] | | |
| Treatment only | 17 | | | | | | |
| M[f] | | | | | | 26 | 20 |

[a] Process study: Parsons and Alexander (1973).
[b] For the main effect of treatment, $p \leq .05$.
[c] Outcome study: Alexander and Parsons (1973); $x^2 = 10.5$, $p \leq .025$.
[d] Follow-up study: Klein, Alexander, and Parsons (Note 2); $x^2 = 13.83$, $p \leq .001$.
[e] For the interaction effect, $p \leq .05$.
[f] Based on a total of 46.

short-term behavioral family systems intervention program as an efficient and economical method of modifying maladaptive family interaction patterns and reducing the reoccurrence of delinquent behavior. In addition to predicting impact on subsequent delinquency, systems theory, as the theoretical basis for the intervention program, further implies a long-range effect. Specifically, the unit of treatment, and therefore the focus of change, is the family system, not a single identified member of the system. Since the goal of treatment is to modify the family system along communication and reciprocity variables to create a more efficient problem-solving unit, the program would be expected to assist the family in dealing more effectively with subsequent developmental changes in younger siblings.

Therefore, to evaluate the long-range effects of the program (primary prevention impact), juvenile court records were examined at a 2½–3½-year interval following completion of the intervention project to determine the incidence of sibling involvement with the court. Identification of siblings in families of 86 project delinquents involved a process of record retrieval, matching, and cross-checking for confirmation through the use of the court's computerized record system. The initial step, retrieval of the records of the 86 project delinquents, provided pertinent demographic information that formed the basis for sibling identification. This information included (a) full names and residences of responsible parents; (b) relationship of responsible parents to the identified delinquent, that is, mother and stepfather, adoptive parents, natural parents; (c) residence of the identified delinquent; (d) family income; (e) employment status of both parents; (f) religious affiliation of both parents; and (g) date of court disposition to the family intervention project.

Following this initial procedure, a search of all computerized records was conducted by matching names (of natural and stepparents), residences, and dates of court disposition (to determine the chronological sequence of project delinquent and sibling delinquent offenses). A cumulative file listing of all adolescents involved with the court since the Second District Juvenile Court was formed provided the cross-check resource.

In a limited number of cases, the computerized record of the project delinquent also identified a family code number. This number referred to a current family file in the court records office. Up-to-date summary sheets in the files included a listing of all family members (delinquent and nondelinquent) along with a cumulative record of court involvement of the delinquent family members.

## Results

The incidence of sibling involvement with the juvenile court in 86 project families is presented in Table 1. For purposes of comparison, Table 1 also contains previously described summary data from the tertiary prevention (process) study (Parsons & Alexander, 1973) and recidivism rates from the secondary prevention (outcome) study (Alexander & Parsons, 1973).

As can be seen, the randomly assigned no-treatment control group demonstrated a 50% recidivism rate and a 40% rate of sibling court involvement. The client-centered alternative treatment group demonstrated a 47% recidivism rate and a 59% rate of sibling involvement, whereas the eclectic-dynamic family program demonstrated a 73% recidivism rate and a 63% rate of sibling court referrals. Finally, the short-term behavioral family systems program demonstrated a significant ($p < .025$) reduction in recidivism rates to 26% and a significant ($p < .005$) reduction in sibling court involvement to 20%. Tests for significance used a 4 × 2 (Treatment Group × Subsequent Court Contact or Not) chi-square format. Thus, the intervention program produced an incidence of sibling delinquency one-third to one-half lower than the sibling delinquency rates in the other comparison groups.

Finally, comparable to the Alexander and Parsons (1973) study, an additional analysis was performed. Posttest family process measures were compared for families with sibling contact versus families with no sibling contact, independent of treatment condition. Although the findings in the earlier study were not replicated for sibling referrals on the two process measures of equality of talk time and silence, significant results were produced for the other two process measures. Families with no sibling contacts demonstrated significantly greater frequency of interruptions for clarification and feedback ($Ms = 26.7$ and 56.2, respectively), $t(25) = 2.096$, p<.025, and significantly greater duration of positive interruptions ($Ms = 9.4$ and 26.2, respectively), $t(27) = 4.32$, $p < .001$.

# Discussion

In conjunction with the two principal preceding studies (Alexander & Parsons, 1973; Parsons & Alexander, 1973), the present article suggests a viable program evaluation model using a three-level evaluative process focusing on the tertiary (remediation), secondary, and primary preventive functions of a single intervention program. Although applied here to a family systems intervention program with identified delinquents, this evaluation model is nevertheless far from being restricted in applicability to this specific area. Community interventions such as Head Start programs, alcoholism programs, and medical education programs, developed from a wide range of service delivery disciplines, can potentially be evaluated utilizing this program evaluation strategy.

Furthermore, in a time of diminishing resources, this model has particular relevance. Instead of dichotomizing remediation and primary prevention intervention approaches with subsequent economic competition for program implementation, this model suggests a more efficient utilization of resources. Remediation programs can be designed to include secondary and primary prevention goals at the time of their inception and implementation. Combining a clinical focus with an ultimate educative one at the outset of program development can provide a strong and compelling appeal to planning and policy decision makers.

A further conclusion can also be drawn from the two prior studies (Alexander & Parsons, 1973; Parsons & Alexander, 1973) and their culmination in the present article. To date, little substantive evidence has been generated to support juvenile delinquency prevention programs (Dixon & Wright, 1975). However, the present results closely demonstrate both the maintenance of long-term behavior change with identified delinquent adolescents and the prevention of sibling delinquency with a short-term specific behavioral family treatment program. These results, although contrary to the findings that positive change in an individual is only maintained for a short period following treatment termination (Bergin & Suinn, 1975; Liberman et al., 1972; Sloane, Staples, Cristol, Yorkston, & Whipple, 1975), can be explained by the fact that intervention occurs within the system. This maintenance of behavior change over time supports the assumption of systems philosophy that pathology does not occur in the identified patient, it occurs in the system in which the individual is embedded (Haley, 1971; Watzlawick et al., 1967). Intervention with the identified patient, if done individually, may produce positive change, but this change may also tend to be sabotaged over time by the system.

These results, as well as supporting a systems model, further emphasize that a focus on families per se is not sufficient to modify family interaction patterns or reduce recidivism and sibling referral rates. Although the treatment and two comparison groups involved some form of family intervention, it appears that the most efficacious focus in family intervention is on changing family interaction patterns in the direction of increased clarity and precision of communication and on increased reciprocity of communication and social reinforcement using reciprocal contingency contracting as a vehicle (Parsons & Alexander, 1973).

## REFERENCE NOTES

1. Coles, J., Alexander, J. F., & Schiavo, S. *A developmental model of family systems: A social-psychological approach.* Paper presented at the Theory Construction Workshop, National Council of Family Relations, St. Louis, October 1974.
2. Klein, N., Alexander, J., & Parsons, B. *Impact of family systems intervention on recidivism and sibling delinquency: A study of primary prevention.* Paper presented at the meeting of the Western Psychological Association, Sacramento, California, April 1975.

## REFERENCES

ALEXANDER, J. F. Defensive and supportive communications in normal and deviant families. *Journal of Consulting and Clinical Psychology*, 1973, 40, 223–231.

ALEXANDER, J. F. Behavior modification and delinquent youth. In J. C. Cull & R. E. Hardy (Eds.), *Behavior modification in rehabilitation settings.* Springfield, Ill.: Charles C. Thomas, 1974.

ALEXANDER, J. F., & PARSONS, B. V. Short-term behavioral intervention with delinquent families: Impact on family process and recidivism. *Journal of Abnormal Psychology*, 1973, 81, 219–225.

BERGIN, A., & SUINN, R. Individual psychotherapy and behavior therapy. *Annual Review of Psychology*, 1975, 26, 509–555.

BOWER, E. Primary prevention of mental and emotional disorders: A frame of reference. In N. Lambert (Ed.), *Protection and promotion of mental health in schools.* (Public Health Service Publication No. 1226.) Bethesda, Md.: U.S. Department of Health, Education, and Welfare, 1965.

BROSKOWSKI, A., & BAKER, F. Professional, organizational, and social barriers to primary prevention. *American Journal of Orthopsychiatry*, 1974, 44, 707–719.

Caplan, G., & Grunebaum, H. Perspectives on primary prevention. *Archives of General Psychiatry*, 1967, *17*, 331–346.

Dixon, M. C., & Wright, W. E. *Juvenile delinquency prevention programs: An evaluation of policy related research on the effectiveness of prevention programs.* Report on the findings of an evaluation of the literature (NSF Grant SSR73-07926 A01). Nashville: Peabody College for Teachers, 1975.

Flanagan, J. C. Evaluation and validation of research data on primary prevention. *American Journal of Orthopsychiatry*, 1971, *4*, 117–123.

Garmezy, N. Vulnerability research and the issue of primary prevention. *American Journal of Orthopsychiatry*, 1971, *4*, 101–115.

Haley, J. *Changing families: A family therapy reader.* New York: Grune & Stratton, 1971.

Leighton, A. H. *My name is legion: Foundations for a theory of man in relation to culture.* New York: Basic Books, 1959.

Liberman, B. L., Frank, J. D., Hoehn-Saric, R., Stone, A. R., Imber, S. D., & Pande, S. K. Patterns of change in treated psychoneurotic patients: A five-year follow-up investigation of the systematic preparation of patients for psychotherapy. *Journal of Consulting and Clinical Psychology*, 1972, *38*, 36–41.

Malouf, R., & Alexander, J. Family Crisis intervention: A model and technique of training. In R. E. Hardy & J. C. Cull (Eds.), *Therapeutic needs of the family.* Springfield, Ill.: Charles C. Thomas, 1974.

Ojemann, R. The purpose of the Fifth Institute of Preventive Psychiatry. In R. Ojemann (Ed.), *The school and the community treatment facility in preventive psychiatry.* Iowa City: University of Iowa, 1966.

Parsons, B. V., & Alexander, J. F. Short-term family intervention: A therapy outcome study. *Journal of Consulting and Clinical Psychology*, 1973, *41*, 195–201.

Sloane, R. B., & Staples, F. R., Cristol, A. H., Yorkston, N. J., & Whipple, K. *Short-term analytically oriented psychotherapy versus behavior therapy.* Cambridge, Mass.: Harvard University Press, 1975.

Srole, L., Langner, T. S., Michael, S. T., Opler, M. K., & Rennie, T. A. C. *Mental health in the metropolis: The midtown Manhattan study.* New York: McGraw-Hill, 1962.

Sundberg, N. D., Tyler, L. E., & Taplin, J. R. *Clinical psychology: Expanding horizons.* New York: Appleton-Century-Crofts, 1973.

Watzlawick, P., Beavin, J., & Jackson, D. *Pragmatics of human communication.* New York: Norton, 1967.

# Substitute Child Care*
# Recent Research and Its
# Implications
*Abraham S. Levine*

ADOPTION, FOSTER CARE, and institutionalization have long been regarded as central problems in child welfare research. In the last 5 years research centered on these subjects has turned up a number of important implications for practice. In this article I will summarize both research findings and their practical implications. The research on which my discussion is based is listed at the end, and the numbers in parentheses following the discussion of particular points flag specific references.

## Adoption

Most adopted children were born out-of-wedlock because more out-of-wedlock than in-wedlock children are available for adoption. Normal white children are easily placed, although the ratio of couples applying for children has gone down considerably in the past few years. For Negro children the story is different: most are not adopted. This is true although Negro couples adopt Negro children almost in proportion to the percentage of Negroes in the U.S. population. But the rate is inadequate because the number of Negro children needing adoption is proportionately greater than the number of white children in the same situation. Lack of interest in adoption, more than lack of knowledge about the need, accounts for the poor Negro adoption rate. And lack of interest stems, in no small part, from lack of income (1,2).

In about three-quarters of adoption cases, adoption is apparently sucessful. Agency placement has a higher rate of success than independent placement and is becoming the predominant means of placement.

Hard-to-place children (that is, children who have physical or mental handicaps, come from ethnic minority families, or are just "older") have as high success rates in adoption as normal children, although agency workers often place them with couples who do not fit the stereotype of the good adoptive couple (sound marital relationship, flexibility and outgoing personality, wholesome motivation for adoption, and acceptance of infertility). In placing handicapped children workers look for couples who do not have any appreciable bias toward such children and tend to be accepting of a child and

* From *Welfare-in-Review*, 10:1, (1972): 1–7.

his particular handicap. Also, it is quite possible that the stereotype couple only appears to have good adoptive qualities and the nonconforming couple only appears not to have them!

Children in good adoptive homes demonstrate capacity for overcoming the consequences of early deprivation. It appears that neither the child's family nor his background significantly affects adoption outcome (3). Nor do these attributes in the adoptive parents: age, income, education, socioeconomic status, and religion. Even similar physical characteristics in the adoptive parent(s) and child make little difference. And the assessment of motivation for adoption is a questionable predictor of successful adoptive parenthood—which fact brings the value of measuring devices into question (3).

What makes the difference is the adoptive parents' attitude toward children and child-rearing practices. The child grows and develops when he and other people are engaged in mutually fulfilling actions. Such actions entail the child's self-regulation and his initiative in dealing with others and reciprocal self-regulation and initiative in the people with whom he lives, studies, and plays. Disadvantaged children fail to grow and develop properly when such reciprocity is not the case (4).

Nevertheless, the adopted child has greater psychiatric disturbance than the child in an intact home. His disturbance often takes the form of aggressive acting-out rather than neurotic behavior. Why he has trouble we do not know, but there is much speculation. When speculation is dignified to the level of hypothesis, it takes the following form: the adopted child born out-of-wedlock is reacting to the poor prenatal care the unmarried expectant mother often receives. Actually, there is empirical evidence to support this speculation. Unmarried expectant mothers do receive poorer care than married expectant mothers. This finding offers additional support to arguments for expansion of services to unmarried mothers before and after they give birth.

The fact that criteria and measuring devices for valid assessment of adoptive parents and, in most cases, for adopted children are questionable argues for deemphasizing selection procedures and supporting the practice of some agencies of concentrating on preparing applicants for adoptive parenthood. In these agencies the worker tries to help the adoptive parents do a better job rather than spending much time in evaluating and assessing.

The most difficult duty adoptive parents have to perform is to tell the child that he is adopted, a duty made more difficult when the child is reticent to ask. Adoptive parents should be encouraged to volunteer information. The child can be told without too great a risk that he will seek his biological parents. As a matter of fact, child welfare workers often tell the adoptive parents who the natural parents are with the result that adoptive parents do very little "seeking out" of natural parents (5).

Couples seeking to adopt a child of another race are not neurotic but, rather, are often independent of community opinion. However, interracial adoptions are not likely to solve the problem of finding adoptive care for minority group children. What appears to be called for is some kind of sub-sidization of adoption, an idea that is beginning to take root. During 1968–69, three States—New York, California, and Minnesota—passed legislation subsidizing adoption (6). It is too soon to have good hard data on the results.

A significantly higher percentage of hard-to-place children achieve successful adoption in the home in which they were initially placed in long-term foster care than children placed in a home for short-term foster care. Perhaps the adoption method with the greatest potential is to choose foster parents with adoption in mind. Currently, legislation is being considered in some jurisidictions in support of such procedures. Under these proposals foster parents who have cared for a child for some specific period of time would be given preference if the child becomes legally available for adoption (4).

Foster parents may be as much employees of an agency as they are parents and as such are a giant step removed from being adoptive parents. In many cases the distance is shortened or eliminated by selecting foster parents who would be adoptive parents if their economic circumstances were different. Often the distinction between foster and adoptive care is, primarily, legal and, secondarily, economic. As a matter of fact, one aspect for study is the balancing of benefits and costs between foster family care and other arrangements such as day care or, in some cases, even institutional care.

# Foster Family Care

In 1967 there were about 230,000 children in foster family care, living, for the most part, in approved family homes, of which there were 132,000. The rate per 1,000 children in foster care increased slightly but steadily each year from 2.5 in 1933 to 3.2 in 1967. At the same time the rate of institutional care dropped from 3.4 to 1.1 (7).

Most children coming into foster care were from chronically deprived lower class families facing crises (8). Minority group children were over-represented, even though most children in foster care are white. Only 25 per cent of the children were living with both parents in an intact family (9).

The single most frequent cause of placement was the mother's illness—either physical or mental—which reason accounted for 40 per cent of the placements. About a third of the children were placed because of a host of family problems, including divorce and separation of the parents, abandonment of a child, and imprisonment of a parent. Most of the others were placed because they had emotional problems, and they were, therefore, in the group of children who usually remain in foster care the longest (10). Underlying all these causes was low socioeconomic status. Even so, foster care rates vary greatly among the States, and the data imply that they are more related to the affluence of the States than to actual need (11).

Foster home care is far from being a panacea. In the early 1960's a nationwide study supported by the Children's Bureau, Welfare Administration, U.S. Department of Health, Education, and Welfare (now in the Office of Child Development, Office of the Assistant Secretary for Administration and Management), found that 43 per cent of all children in foster home care under public auspices and 17 per cent of those in foster care under voluntary auspices were suffering from neglect or abuse. Public concern over such neglect or abuse has resulted in protective services, primarily under public auspices. Even so, there is a strong need for an expansion of knowledge about neglect and abuse to enable social workers to carry out the heavy responsibility for decisionmaking that is inherent in protective service (12) and to develop models of family behavior on which to assess family functioning in determining the extent of neglect and in considering the potential need for removal of the child from the family.

Neglect and abuse have been identified as the most important child welfare problem (12) and as a major cause for placement of children in foster care. To have neglect continue in foster care is to make a bad situation worse. What kinds of situations constitute neglect or abuse is to some extent a matter of community opinion and such opinion affects whether intervention will take place. Here are some illustrative cases, drawn from a research project on substitute child care and child neglect and abuse:

> Mrs. Pitts has two daughters, age 7 and 9. The children have lice and suffer from impetigo. . . . Mrs. Pitts has not kept clinic appointments or carried out the doctor's instructions.

More than 80 per cent of the respondents favored intervention as a necessary action in this case.

In contrast, we have a situation involving emotional disturbance:

> Jerry, a boy of 11, keeps to himself in school, does not play with other children, and seldom speaks to anyone. His teachers consider him tense and troubled. The parents have been asked to take Jerry to a guidance clinic, but have refused to keep the appointments because they do not feel the boy is having serious problems.

About 75 per cent of the respondents were opposed to protective intervention in this case. Apparently neglect of a physical condition was considered a good deal more serious than neglect of an emotional problem, although, actually, Jerry's problem was a good deal more serious than the Pitts children's and required long-term therapy.

In between there are cases in which sexual morality is involved:

> Mrs. Young is a divorced woman with three children under school age. She is fond of the children and gives them good, physical care. She is sexually promiscuous, however, and often has men staying overnight at her apartment.

How did the community vote? About 45 per cent of the respondents were for interventions, *but only if the mother received AFDC*. This result suggests a new kind of double moral standard!

Foster parents are not a homogenous group, even though they generally are members of the blue-collar or semiskilled working class and are beyond middle age. The biggest differences occur in temperament and in their reasons for choosing to be foster parents. Some prefer preschool age children, others teenagers; some prefer short-term contact, others close, long-term, quasi-adoptive relationships. If the temperaments of the child and the foster parents complement each other, the probability of the child's staying in the home increases. Failure is often associated with these influences: the child's having spent more than 2 years in an institution, the parents' lack of understanding of the meaning of foster care, the age of the child at placement, and the child's having been placed in a substantial number of different homes.

All these variables argue for substantial agency and worker efforts shortly after the child moves into placement. The strongest efforts have to be made at the point of placement. The most crucial of all placements is the first, and the most crucial time in the first placement is the early period.

But many variables besides those mentioned have to be considered in the light of current research. Some others associated with failure are the foster parents' lack of warmth toward and understanding of the child, autocratic family relationships, and natural children in the home of about the same age as the foster child. Some variables associated with success are economic well-being, the foster mother's being experienced in child care, and a cooperative relationship between foster father and mother.

In one study most of the 100 people interviewed considered foster parents as having healthy motives for boarding children. The simple love of children was the outstanding reason given, particularly in neighborhoods with a high concentration of boarding homes. The financial motive for foster care, though considered important, was stressed less often than expected. It was stressed most in neighborhoods in which agency recruitment efforts had met with the least success. Apparently this study indicates that people often attempt to clothe their behavior in idealistic reasons (13).

Despite the findings of a significant relationship between low socioeconomic status and poor foster care, the danger of overgeneralizing these findings was clearly pointed out in one study in New York City (14). This study found that a group of public assistance families, despite economic dependency and its associated problems, had a stable, wholesome family life and a capacity for serving needy children. To select families like these for foster homes and to set them up properly require creative effort by an agency's staff.

When they grow up foster children are usually indistinguishable from their neighbors as self-supporting persons—living in attractive homes; taking care of their children, worrying about them, and making parental mistakes; participating in neighborhood activities; and finding pleasure in associating with others. They do not, however, always regard themselves as being indistinguishable from other men and women because they remember that as foster children they *were* different from other children.

What the research does do is point out the need for greater flexibility in the provision of services. We should, for instance, consider and evaluate the extension of homemaker services for more hours a day and for more days when a family is in crisis. There is little question that better resources such as day care and homemaker services available at the point of crisis would reduce the necessity for placement of some children (12).

Nonprofessional workers in child welfare agencies are performing the same functions as professional workers, and—as far as can be ascertained—are performing these functions as satisfactorily.

The implication for practice is clear. Agencies can hire nonprofessional workers with assurance that they will do well. If the agency hesitates to give them autonomy, it can make them members of a team led by professional workers, knowing they will carry their weight.

# Institutional Care

Less empirical research has been done on institutional care of children than on either adoptive care or foster home care. Whatever research there is indicates that, generally, children in institutional care do not do so well in cognitive and speech development as children in natural homes. One question always arises on this point: Is it fair to match groups of children from institutions with groups of children from natural homes and poor institutions with good natural homes? There is considerable agreement, however, that young children in institutional care run the risk of emotional damage, though recent research does not support a case for the permanence of damage. But whether institutions might be better organized to contribute to the development of children under 3 years old is a question for further study.

Considerable conflict exists between nonprofessional and professional child care workers. The most serious consequence of their discord is high staff turnover, resulting, as it does, in discontinuity in the relationships children have established with institutional "parents."

Positive effects on children in institutional care derive from personal contact with auxiliary workers, as the results of the foster grandparent program sponsored by the Office of Economic Opportunity prove. Supplementary workers may be of special help to children in institutions because of the high turnover of full-time child care staff members (15).

Entrance into care at an early age and lack of contact with interested and concerned parents or other relatives are associated with a child's poor adjustment to an institution. Special individual stimulation in the institution is associated with more normal general development. Research suggests that we should not be too critical of institutions. For some children an institution is a satisfactory alternative to foster home care under certain conditions such as profound mental retardation. With a proper staff-child ratio, good programs, and a therapeutic environment, an institution can be satisfactory, given the alternatives, even for young children. The difficulty is in insuring the availability of conditions necessary to reduce the risk of emotional damage. The staff is the key, and workers must be supplied by a community willing to allocate resources—to pay good salaries to child care workers and to pay for their education. In turn social workers have to be willing to share with child care workers greater responsibility as coworkers on treatment teams. Also wider use of auxiliary workers such as foster grandparents is desirable.

One innovation likely to be fruitful would be the establishment of a substantial number of group homes in the neighborhood of a central institution (16). The institution would have such facilities as clinics and infirmaries; schools; and homemaker, babysitting, counseling, and casework services. The foster parents in charge of the group homes would be agency employees, paid at least a living wage. This idea is similar to a plan widely and successfully followed in Europe—the children's village—though not yet tried extensively in the United States. Such a child care complex is a natural setting for developing "new careers" for the poor.

The literature suggests that many children are not accessible to the kinds of treatment commonly used in children's villages. For them other methods such as behavior modification (which is little used in child care institutions) may be useful. Also, we need to provide the child in the institution with experience in community living as a transitional step from the institution to society.

## General Considerations

A good deal of the research I have described (as well as related research not included in the discussion) was supported by the Research and Demonstration Grant Program of the Children's Bureau, U.S. Department of Health, Education, and Welfare (HEW). Part of this program is now in the Social and Rehabilitation Service (SRS) of HEW. SRS-supported research will continue, with an even greater focus on the needs of the child welfare agency.

With Freud out of fashion, there is little broad theory that would serve as an appropriate conceptual umbrella in any of the fields that have been discussed.

Available research has certain shortcomings, chief of which is the absence of unambiguous findings. Replication of good research in various settings would be helpful in the development of useful generalizations and principles. Theories based solidly on research and practical findings would also be helpful. For example, how and why does the social worker take actions that help the child resolve conflicts and learn how to live in one home after coming from another that engendered hostile attitudes in him? Or on what basis should rational decisions be made to move a child from his own home or to work to maintain the home for the child? When should a child be removed from one foster home and placed in another? Child welfare research will have to give more effort to decisions affecting child welfare. A variety of ways useful in other contexts such as systems analysis and operations research do have application in such decisionmaking. Perhaps some of the unemployed engineers and related professional workers can find new applications for their kinds of skill not now being used by the aerospace industry.

Social policymaking is another field that has possible applications to child welfare research and, more specifically, to the three components of it I have discussed here. For example, what would be the effects of substitute care programs of family allowances, a guaranteed annual income, the President's welfare reform program, subsidized adoptions, and adequate wages for foster parents?

# Demonstrations or Experimental Research?

Most child welfare research on substitute family care has been demonstrative and evaluative. This is natural in a field where old ideas are tried and evaluated ad nauseum because it is easier to test them than more innovative methods. What happens if a degree of experimentation is introduced and something more spectacular is actually tried, with a control group available, and the seemingly diverse fields of child welfare and vocational rehabilitation are fused?

Recent research supported by SRS at the University of Wisconsin demonstrates that not only mental retardation in high-risk children but also the occupational and social failure of the mentally retarded mother can be reduced by a process called total or comprehensive family stimulation in slum families (17). All children, including infants, of the retarded mother are enrolled in a carefully prescribed program designed to make intellectual, academic, social, and occupational development easier. All preschool children are cared for 8 hours a day so that the mother can attend a rehabilitation program full time. She receives vocational training and instruction in homemaking, child-rearing, and basic education. Experience with groups of such mothers suggests that the experimental method may be a far more effective means of reaching and rehabilitating "cultural-familial" retarded adults than the traditional counseling-workshop method of vocational rehabilitation. Results with the children receiving treatment are outstanding compared to those with children in a control group. In many instances in the experimental families, children who entered as infants were, when about 2 years old, advanced developmentally beyond their 3- and 4-year-old brothers and sisters.

The results of this study provide us with the possibility of a real discovery in the reduction of some aspects of chronic dependency. The "total family stimulation" method should be pursued further and replicated in several different locales to better establish its range of possibilities.

# Where Do We Go from Here?

It would be difficult to "summarize" what is already largely a summary, in this instance of research on several aspects of child welfare. I could evaluate, from a cost-benefit or cost-effectiveness point of view, alternative services designed to achieve the same objective. But it is more difficult (if not impossible) to put a dollar value on many of the outcomes of social services than on rehabilitation services directed toward employment. SRS is developing a measuring methodology to indicate the relative effectiveness of different combinations of services designed to achieve the same outcomes. Cost analysis is well developed in the child welfare field so that at least we will be able to analyze for cost-effectivenesse alternative methods of delivering services designed to achive the same or similar outcomes.

Another broad and fruitful avenue to develop is preventive measures to keep as many children is possible out of long-term foster care or institutions. Here is where the benefits are not only in cost savings but also in more productive and happier members of society. Developing a science and technology of prevention is another aspect being emphasized in HEW's research program. Cost-effectiveness demonstrations should follow logically, and they are also being emphasized.

## REFERENCE NOTES

1. Elizabeth A. Lawder and others, *A Study of Negro Adoption Familes,* Division of Child Welfare Research and Demonstrations; Social and Rehabilitation Service; U.S. Department of Health, Education, and Welfare, Washington, 1971.
2. Social Planning Council of Metropolitan Toronto, *The Adoption of Negro Children— A Community Wide Approach,* The Council, Toronto, July 1966.
3. Benson Jaffee and David Fanchel, *A Follow-up Study in Adoption: Portrait of One Hundred Families,* Columbia University Press, New York, 1970.
4. Alfred Kadushin, "A Follow-up Study of Children Adopted When Older: Criteria of Success," *American Journal of Orthopsychiatry,* April 1967, pp. 530–37.
5. Clayton Hagen and others, *The Adopted Adult Discusses Adoption as a Life Experience,* Lutheran Social Service of Minnesota, Minneapolis, 1968.
6. Andrew Billingsley and Jeanne Giovannoni, "Research Perspectives on Interracial Adoptions," in Roger H. Miller, ed., *Race, Research, and Reason: Social Work Perspectives,* National Association of Social Workers, New York, 1969, pp. 47–77.
7. U.S. Department of Health, Education, and Welfare, *Children's Bureau Statistical Series No. 92,* U.S. Government Printing Office, Washington, 1968.
8. Child Welfare League of America, *The Need for Foster Care—An Incidence Study of*

*Requests for Foster Care and Agency Responses in Seven Metropolitan Areas,* The League, New York, 1969.

9. Shirley Jenkins and Mignon Sauber, *Paths of Child Placement—Family Situations Prior to Foster Care,* Community Council of Greater New York, New York, 1966.

10. Shirley Jenkins, "Duration of Foster Care—Some Relevant Antecedent Variables," *Child Welfare,* October 1967, pp. 334–41.

11. Seth Low, "Foster Care of Children—Major National Trends and Prospects," *Welfare in Review,* October 1966, pp. 12–21.

12. Alfred Kadushin, *Child Welfare Services,* The Macmillan Company, New York, 1967.

13. H. R. Schaffer and Evelyn R. Schaffer, *Child Care and the Family,* Occasional Papers on Social Administration, No. 25, G. Bell & Sons, London, 1968.

14. Patricia Garland, "Public Assistance Families: A Resource for Foster Care," in Alfred Kadushin, ed., *Child Welfare Services: A Source Book,* The Macmillan Company, New York, 1970, pp. 159–68.

15. Rosalyn Saltz, "Evaluation of a Foster-Grandparent Program," in Alfred Kadushin, ed., *Child Welfare Services: A Source Book,* The Macmillan Company, New York, 1970, pp. 518–26.

16. Helen L. Witmer and Charles P. Gershenson, eds., *On Rearing Infants and Young Children in Institutions,* Children's Bureau Research, Report No. 1, Children's Bureau, U.S. Department of Health, Education, and Welfare, Washington, 1967.

17. Rick Heber, *Rehabilitation of Families at Risk for Mental Retardation* (a progress report, October 1971), Rehabilitation Research and Training Center in Mental Retardation, University of Wisconsin, Madison (unpublished).

# D. Adolescence: Introduction

URING THE PERIOD of adolescence, the young person reaches nearly his or her full physical maturity (Tanner) although at different rates for girls and boys. In the sense of our metaphor of the social atom, the adolescent is nearly independent from the family of origin—at least in the physical sense—but may be at differential stages of social and psychological independence. This splitting off from one social group and attaching oneself to others is not without its problems, but unlike the overdrawn image of the adolescent in near-pathological turmoil, many young persons emerge reasonably well (Oldham). Certainly there is considerable evidence for social problems associated with the adolescent period, such as drugs (Johnston), unwanted teen-age pregnancy (Menken), school dropout (Howard and Anderson), but there is important information about the potentialities of this age, in creativity (Renzulli), in greater responsibility, and in mature handling of enormously stressful cultural situations.

Development is usually viewed as a progressive improvement where one social advance builds upon that of another. Indeed, most of the papers in this collection support this assumption, even with the recognition that not everyone travels along this path to perfection. Robins and Wish point out that it is equally possible to view deviance from a developmental perspective, to find early acts that predict later ones. This is vital information for the helping professional, making the understanding of developmental themes and variations all the more important as they now become logical points of intervention or prevention.

At the end of this section, readers should have some understanding of the basic tasks of adolescents:

> *Physical Tasks:* Puberty begins the second major growth spurt for an individual. With it are phenomena to be adjusted to, such as primary and secondary sexual characteristics. There is also the emergence of adult physical features as adolescents gain nearly their full adult height, weight, and physique. But there are wide variations in these biological developments, and adolescents must come to terms with too much or too little or uneven growth in every part of their bodies—and to the reactions others have to these phenomena.

209

*Psychological Task:* The meaning of these physical changes becomes part of the person's sense of self. There may be sexual attraction and sexual experimentation for some; indeed, after a period of sterility, adolescents are fully capable of bearing children whether or not they are able to care for them appropriately. This leads to challenges of values and social standards in a world that adolescents come to see in all its inconsistent glory and gore—that is, as it actually is, as contrasted to what some wish it to be. Abstract thinking and mature problem solving become possible, and these abilities are increasingly called upon with the development of independence (from family) and interdependence (on peers) in a rapidly changing society.

*Social Tasks:* At first, young persons are age-graded; that is, their privileges and responsibilities are assigned by their membership in a certain age group. But as they grow older, their unique personalities begin to develop at differential rates, and people begin to react to adolescents as individuals, first on one dimension, then on others. Social skills make up a major task at this time, conversations, athletic and social games, dancing, manners in general, and special tasks like driving. Dating—that complex set of social arrangements and activities by which young persons come to know persons of the opposite sex—is another task that faces most adolescents. These lead to another system of challenges—courtship, marriage, and family life skills, although many adolescents delay these tasks until early adulthood in favor of extended education and other activities. A small but increasing number of other older adolescents are exploring alternative forms of relating and companionship. This is the period for deep involvements with idealistic ventures and causes which, in some cases, set a lifelong orientation. (cf. Havighurst, 1952.)

# Sequence, Tempo, and Individual Variation in the Growth and Development of Boys and Girls Aged Twelve to Sixteen*

*J. M. Tanner*

F OR THE MAJORITY of young persons, the years from twelve to sixteen are the most eventful ones of their lives so far as their growth and development is concerned. Admittedly during fetal life and the first year or two after birth developments occurred still faster, and a sympathetic environment was probably even more crucial, but the subject himself was not the fascinated, charmed, or horrified spectator that watches the developments, or lack of developments, of adolescence. Growth is a very regular and highly regulated process, and from birth onward the growth rate of most bodily tissue decreases steadily, the fall being swift at first and slower from about three years. Body shape changes gradually since the rate of growth of some parts, such as the arms and legs, is greater than the rate of growth of others, such as the trunk. But the change is a steady one, a smoothly continuous development rather than any passage through a series of separate stages.

Then at puberty, a very considerable alteration in growth rate occurs. There is a swift increase in body size, a change in the shape and body composition, and a rapid development of the gonads, the reproductive organs, and the characters signaling sexual maturity. Some of these changes are common to both sexes, but most are sex-specific. Boys have a great increase in muscle size and strength, together with a series of physiological changes, making them more capable than girls of doing heavy physical work and running faster and longer. The changes specifically adapt the male to his primitive primate role of dominating, fighting, and foraging. Such adolescent changes occur generally in primates, but are more marked in some species than in others. . . .

Practically all skeletal and muscular dimensions take part in the spurt, though not to an equal degree. Most of the spurt in height is due to acceleration of trunk length rather than length of legs. There is a fairly regular order in which the dimensions accelerate; leg length as a rule reaches its peak first, followed by the body breadths, with shoulder width last. Thus a boy stops growing out of his trousers (at least in length) a year before he stops growing

* © Copyright 1971 The American Academy of Arts and Sciences. Reprinted by permission from *Daedalus*, 1971, 4:100, 907–930.

out of his jackets. The earliest structures to reach their adult status are the head, hands, and feet. At adolescence, children, particularly girls, sometimes complain of having large hands and feet. They can be reassured that by the time they are fully grown their hands and feet will be a little smaller in proportion to their arms and legs, and considerably smaller in proportion to their trunk.

The spurt in muscle, both of limbs and heart, coincides with the spurt in skeletal growth, for both are caused by the same hormones. Boys' muscle widths reach a peak velocity of growth considerably greater than those reached by girls. But since girls have their spurt earlier, there is actually a period, from about twelve and a half to thirteen and a half, when girls on the average have larger muscles than boys of the same age.

Simultaneously with the spurt in muscle there is a loss of fat in boys, particularly on the limbs. Girls have a velocity curve of fat identical in shape to that of boys; that is to say, their fat accumulation (going on in both sexes from about age six) decelerates. But the decrease in velocity in girls is not sufficiently great to carry the average velocity below zero, that is to give an absolute loss. Most girls have to content themselves with a temporary go-slow in fat accumulation. As the adolescent growth spurt draws to an end, fat tends to accumulate again in both sexes.

The marked increase in muscle size in boys at adolescence leads to an increase in strength. . . . Before adolescence, boys and girls are similar in strength for a given body size and shape; after, boys are much stronger, probably due to developing more force per gram of muscle as well as absolutely larger muscles. They also develop larger hearts and lungs relative to their size, a higher systolic blood pressure, a lower resting heart rate, a greater capacity for carrying oxygen in the blood, and a greater power for neutralizing the chemical products of muscular exercise such as lactic acid.[1] In short, the male becomes at adolescence more adapted for the tasks of hunting, fighting, and manipulating all sorts of heavy objects, as is necessary in some forms of food-gathering.

# Physical Maturation, Mental Ability, and Emotional Development

Clearly the occurrence of tempo differences in human growth has profound implications for educational theory and practice. This would especially be so if advancement in physical growth were linked to any significant degree with advancement in intellectual ability and in emotional maturity.

There is good evidence that in the European and North American school systems children who are physically advanced toward maturity score on the average slightly higher in most tests of mental ability than children of the same age who are physically less mature. The difference is not great, but it is consistent and it occurs at all ages that have been studied—that is, back as far as six and a half years. Similarly the intelligence test score of postmenarcheal girls is higher than the score of premenarcheal girls of the same age.[2] Thus in age-linked examinations physically fast-maturing children have a significantly better chance than slow-maturing.

It is also true that physically large children score higher than small ones, at all ages from six onward. In a random sample of all Scottish eleven-year-old children, for example, comprising 6,440 pupils, the correlation between height and score in the Moray House group test was $0.25 \pm 0.01$ which leads to an average increase of one and a half points Terman-Merrill I.Q. per inch of stature. A similar correlation was found in London children. The effects can be very significant for individual children. In ten-year-old girls there was nine points difference in I.Q. between those whose height was above the 75th percentile and those whose height was below the 15th. This is two-thirds of the standard deviation of the test score.

It was usually thought that both the relationships between test score and height and between test score and early maturing would disappear in adulthood. If the correlations represented only the effects of co-advancement both of mental ability and physical growth this might be expected to happen. There is no difference in height between early and late maturing boys when both have finished growing. But it is now clear that, curiously, at least part of the height-I.Q. correlation persists in adults.[3] It is not clear in what proportion genetic and environmental factors are responsible for this.

There is little doubt that being an early or a late maturer may have repercussions on behavior, and that in some children these repercussions may be considerable. There is little enough solid information on the relation between emotional and physiological development, but what there is supports the common sense notion that emotional attitudes are clearly related to physiological events.

The boy's world is one where physical powers bring prestige as well as success, where the body is very much an instrument of the person. Boys who are advanced in development, not only at puberty, but before as well, are more likely than others to be leaders. Indeed, this is reinforced by the fact that muscular, powerful boys on the average mature earlier than others and have an early adolescent growth spurt. The athletically-built boy not only tends to dominate his fellows before puberty, but also by getting an early start he is in a good position to continue that domination. The unathletic, lanky boy, unable, perhaps, to hold his own in the preadolescent rough and tumble, gets still further pushed to the wall at adolescence, as he sees others shoot up while he remains nearly stationary in growth. Even boys several years younger now suddenly surpass him in size, athletic skill, and perhaps, too, in social graces. . . .

It may seem as though the early maturers have things all their own way.

It is indeed true that most studies of the later personalities of children whose growth history is known do show early maturers as more stable, more sociable, less neurotic, and more successful in society, at least in the United States.[4] But early maturers have their difficulties also, particularly the girls in some societies. Though some glory in their new possessions, others are embarrassed by them. The early maturer, too, has a longer period of frustration of sex drive and of drive toward independence and the establishment of vocational orientation.

Little can be done to reduce the individual differences in children's tempo of growth, for they are biologically rooted and not significantly reducible by any social steps we may take. It, therefore, behooves all teachers, psychologists, and pediatricians to be fully aware of the facts and alert to the individual problems they raise.

# Trend Toward Large Size and Earlier Maturation

The rate of maturing and the age at onset of puberty are dependent, naturally, on a complex interaction of genetic and environmental factors. Where the environment is good, most of the variability in age at menarche in a population is due to genetic differences. In France in the 1950's the mean difference between identical twins was two months, while that between nonidentical twin sisters was eight months.[5] In many societies puberty occurs later in the poorly-off, and in most societies investigated children with many siblings grow less fast than children with few.

Recent investigations in Northeast England showed that social class differences are not only those associated with different sizes of family. The median age of menarche for only girls was 13.0 years, for girls with one sibling 13.2, two siblings 13.4, three siblings and over 13.7. For a given number of siblings the social class as indicated by father's occupation was unrelated to menarcheal age.[6] Environment is still clearly a factor in control of menarcheal age, but in England at least occupation is a less effective indication of poor housing, poor expenditure on food, and poor child care than is the number of children in the family.

During the last hundred years there has been a striking tendency for children to become progressively larger at all ages.[7] This is known as the "secular trend." The magnitude of the trend in Europe and America is such that it dwarfs the difference between socioeconomic classes.

The data from Europe and America agree well: from about 1900, or a little earlier, to the present, children in average economic circumstances have increased in height at age five to seven by about 1 to 2 cm each decade, and at ten to fourteen by 2 to 3 cm each decade. Preschool data show that the trend starts directly after birth and may, indeed, be relatively greater from age two to five then subsequently. The trend started, at least in Britain, a considerable time ago, because Roberts, a factory physician, writing in 1876 said that "a factory child of the present day at the age of nine years weighs as much as one of 10 years did in 1833 . . . each age has gained one year in forty years."[8] The trend in Europe is still continuing at the time of writing but there is some evidence to show that in the United States the best-off sections of the population are now growing up at something approaching the fastest possible speed.

During the same period there has been an upward trend in adult height, but to a considerably lower degree. In earlier times final height was not reached till twenty-five years or later, whereas now it is reached in man at eighteen or nineteen. Data exist, however, which enable us to compare fully grown men at different periods. They lead to the conclusion that in Western Europe men increased in adult height little if at all from 1760 to 1830, about 0.3 cm per decade from 1830 to 1880, and about 0.6 cm per decade from 1880 to 1960. The trend is apparently still continuing in Europe, though not in the best-off section of American society.

Most of the trend toward greater size in children reflects a more rapid maturation; only a minor part reflects a greater ultimate size. The trend toward earlier maturing is best shown in the statistics on age at menarche. . . . The trend is between three and four months per decade since 1850 in average sections of Western European populations. Well-off persons show a trend of about half this magnitude, having never been so retarded in menarche as the worse-off.[9]

Most, though not all, of the differences between populations are probably due to nutritional factors, operating during the whole of the growth period, from conception onward. . . .

## REFERENCE NOTES

1. J. M. Tanner, *Growth at Adolescence*, 2d ed. (Oxford: Blackwell Scientific Publications, 1962), p. 168.
2. See references in Tanner, *Growth at Adolescence*, and Tanner, "Galtonian Eugenics and the Study of Growth, *The Eugenics Review*, 58 (1966), 122–135.
3. Tanner, "Galtonian Eugenics."
4. P. H. Mussen and M. C. Jones, "Self-Concepting Motivations and Interpersonal Attitudes of Late- and Early-Maturing Boys," *Child Development*, 28 (1957), 243–256.
5. M. Tisserand-Perrier, "Etude comparative de certains processus de croissance chez les jeuneaux," *Journal de génétique humaine*, 2 (1953), 87–102, as cited in Tanner, *Growth at Adolescence*.
6. D. F. Roberts, L. M. Rozner, and A. V. Swan, "Age at Menarche, Physique and Environment in industrial North-East England," *Acta Paediatrica Scandinavica*, 60 (1971), 158–164.
7. J. M. Tanner, "Earlier Maturation in Man," *Scientific American*, 218 (1968), 21–27.
8. Tanner, *Growth at Adolescence*.
9. Details on average age of menarche of various populations and the methods for collecting these statistics will be found in Tanner, "Galtonian Eugenics."

# Talent Potential in Minority Group Students*

*Joseph S. Renzulli*

> It seems probable that our society discovers and develops no more than
> perhaps half its potential intellectual talent.
>
> *Robert J. Havighurst (1961)*

T HERE CAN BE little doubt that our nation's largest untapped source of human intelligence and creativity is to be found among the vast numbers of individuals in the lower socioeconomic levels, particularly among the approximately 20 million black Americans. It would be a monumental task to explore all of the causes that have contributed to our failure to discover, stimulate, and make the most efficient use of this neglected source of talent. Intensified efforts to overcome this failure are based in part on the simple realization that an invaluable natural resource is being wasted daily by a system of education that has shut its eyes and turned its back on the children of the poor. The by-products of this waste are evident in unprecedented urban turmoil, in unemployment and underemployment, in rising crime and delinquency rates, and most importantly, in the human despair that accompanies thwarted expression and creativity.

Although massive efforts have been directed toward overcoming the inadequacies of educational programming for the culturally disadvantaged, relatively little attention has been focused on those youngsters within the total population of disadvantaged youth who have unusually high potentials for learning and creativity. The numerous compensatory programs that deal mainly with remediation in the basic skill areas and preparation for entrance into the labor market generally have overlooked the talent potential that exists in lower socioeconomic and minority group youngsters. A number of persons have called attention to the dimensions of this untapped source of talent (Douglass, 1969; Torrance, 1968), and few would disagree that the time is long overdue for a systematic nationwide effort in talent retrieval. This article describes the dimensions of the talent potential among low socioeconomic and minority group members, and explores some of the issues and strategies involved in identifying talent potential and constructing educational

* Joseph S. Renzulli. "Talent Potential in Minority Group Students," *Exceptional Children,* 39 (1973): 437–444. Reprinted with permission of The Council for Exceptional Children and the author.

programs which will maximize the development of this unidentified and understimulated segment of our school population.

## The Nature and Scope of Talent Loss

What exactly are the dimensions of the talent potential among minority groups, and what will be the costs of further delay in providing opportunities for the expression of such potential? A large body of accumulated research clearly indicates that gifted and talented children can be found in all racial groups and at all of society's economic levels. With respect to family background, Terman's (1925–1959) study of gifted children showed that, in actual numbers, the nonprofessional segment of the general population contains more than twice as many gifted children as the professional group. Regarding racial and ethnic origin, Miles (1954) reported that many high IQ black children can be found in black communities. Studies by Jenkins (1948) and Witty and Jenkins (1934) indicated that race per se is not a limiting factor in intellectual development, that black children with high IQ's come from a variety of backgrounds, and that educational achievement of highly able black children resembles that of other gifted youngsters. In more recent years, the works of Hunt (1961), Bloom (1964), and others have called attention to the significant role that environment plays in intellectual development. The massive number of research studies summarized in these works have crucial implications for the role that education can and should play in developing the high potential of youngsters from all races and social classes.

In addition to those studies concerned mainly with the older or more traditional definitions of giftedness (i.e., giftedness in terms of IQ), a rapidly expanding body of literature dealing with a broader conception of talent development has recognized that children from depressed areas, low income groups, and racial minorities probably represent our largest unmined source of creative talent (Passow, 1966; Torrance, 1968). The importance of identifying and developing creative talents at all levels of society has caused leading philosophers and educators to focus their attention on this problem. In an article entitled, "Is America Neglecting Her Creative Minority?" Toynbee (1964) commented:

> To give a fair chance to potential creativity is a matter of life and death for any society. This is all-important, because the outstanding creative ability of a fairly small percentage of the population is mankind's ultimate asset, and the only one with which only man has been endowed [p. 4].

It cannot be denied that society stands to benefit from a systematic investment in the development of this vast source of untapped talent; yet, major inequalities of opportunity are still evident in our schools. The inferiority of

existing schools for low income and minority group children has been indicated clearly by studies which show that the longer children stay in these
schools, the further behind they become in achievement and the wider the
gap grows between what they should know and their actual level of performance (Coleman, Campbell, Hobson, McPartland, Mood, Weinfeld, &
York, 1966; Sexton, 1961). Average drops in measured intelligence of as
much as 20 points have been recorded as black children progress (or perhaps
it should be *re*gress) through grades (Passow, Goldberg, & Tannenbaum,
1967). Other studies dealing with delinquency, level of aspiration, self concept, aggressiveness, alienation, and a host of other variables reveal similarly
ominous findings about the current state of the school situation for disadvantaged youngsters (Coleman et al., 1966; Mathis, 1969; Williams & Byars,
1968). Under circumstances such as these, even the most highly able and
well-motivated students from minority groups surely must lose faith in a system where the probability of nonsuccess is so high.

In spite of these grim statistics, there is a growing realization that a wealth
of creative talent is lying unidentified and understimulated in schools that
serve urban ghetto and rural poor youngsters. The decade of the 1960's may
well be remembered as a period in our history when the education establishment began to pay serious attention to the detrimental effects which result
from the inferior opportunities that exist for a large segment of our population. Books such as *How Children Fail* (Holt, 1966), *Death at an Early Age*
(Kozol, 1967), *Pygmalion in the Classroom* (Rosenthal & Jacobson, 1968),
and *Crisis in the Classroom* (Silberman, 1970) have literally shocked us into
the reality of the situation. If we look upon the activities and pronouncements of the sixties as the first step in a direct frontal attack upon the problem of educational equality, then the heightened interest of that decade certainly can be regarded with optimism. But our view should not be blurred by
such optimism; for scattered attempts to "do something" for the culturally
disadvantaged thus far represent little more than the proverbial "drop in the
bucket" when compared to the great number of youngsters whose day to day
school experience is nothing short of an educational and psychological disas-
ter. If, on the other hand, the ground work laid during the sixties has not
been a false start, then action to correct this crucial problem in our schools
remains the challenge and the task before us. The remainder of this article
deals with some of the work that has been done in the area of identifying talent potential among low socioeconomic and minority group youngsters and
developing educational programs to help this talent potential be realized. . . .

## A Broadened Conception of Talent

In recent years a growing number of theorists and researchers have provided
us with a much broadened conception of the nature of human abilities. Fore-

most among the newer models is the well known structure of the intellect cube developed by Guilford (1967) and his associates. This model consists of a three dimensional classification system designed to encompass and organize 120 possible talents according to (a) the type of mental operation employed, (b) the content involved in the thinking process, and (c) the type of product which results from the act of thinking. Williams and Eberle (1967) developed a similar model which identified 23 classroom teaching strategies that can be used to develop seven productive thinking operations in various subject matter areas, while Taylor's (1968) multiple talent model isolated an additional set of distinguishable abilities in areas such as creativity, decision making, planning, forecasting, and communications.

Taylor suggested a grouping of talents based on the world-of-work needs and pointed out that if we limit ourselves solely to academic talent, only the top 10 percent will fall into the highly gifted class and only 50 percent of our students will have a chance to be above average (i.e., above the median). On the other hand, if we measure students across several different talents, the percent of highly gifted students will increase tremendously:

> When we arrange a group of students on each of several talent ladders, those at the bottom of the old academic talent ladder—those heretofore labeled "educationally deprived" will rise as a subgroup to be almost average as far as each of the other five types of talents are concerned. A third or more of them are likely to be above average on each new talent ladder. Since we have not been reaching these students, we should try eliciting as many different talents as possible. If we succeed, then those who had not been flourishing in the old talent area will discover some areas where they are promising individuals and perhaps even star performers [Taylor, 1968, p. 68].

Thus, the application of a multiple talent approach in our schools will result in greater numbers of students achieving higher degrees of success both in and out of school. According to Taylor, a natural by-product of this approach will be an increase in the student's individuality. Each student will experience and display his own unique profile across talents and will thus become more self-directed.

## Suggestions for Identification of Multiple Talents

The taxonomies developed by Bloom (1956) and Krathwohl, Bloom, and Masia (1964) provide another classification system for isolating cognitive and affective processes that clearly identify dimensions of man's repertoire of behaviors. These behaviors often are not measured by traditional tests of intelligence or are "buried" in the general scores which many of these tests yield. A good example is the limited range of abilities sampled by the *Scholastic Aptitude Tests* (SAT). According to a recent report by the Commission on Tests (1970), the SAT has been found to be mainly a measure of developed verbal, mathematical, and reasoning abilities, and thus, it fails to take account of the educational potential of college applicants who for one reason or another have been educationally disadvantaged. The Commission has recognized the need for a broader conception of college admission criteria and has suggested that the SAT be expanded to include measures of the following abilities:

1. Adaptation in new learning situations.
2. Problem solving in situations that require varied cognitive styles and skills.
3. Analysis, search, and synthesis behaviors.
4. Information management, processing, and utilization skills.
5. Nonstandard information pools.
6. Comprehension through experiencing, listening, and looking, as well as reading.
7. Expression through artistic, oral, nonverbal, and graphic, as well as written symbolization.
8. Characteristics of temperament.
9. Sources and status of motivation.
10. Habits of work and task involvement under varying conditions of demand [Commission on Tests, 1970, vol. 2, p. 44].

The Commission further suggested that test procedures should be redesigned (a) to broaden the varieties of subject matter, competencies, and skills assessed; (b) to examine achievement in a variety of contexts; (c) to make greater use of openended and unstructured indicators of achievement; and (d) to assess nonacademic achievement such as social competence, coping skills, avocational skills, and artistic, athletic, political, and mechanical skills.

With these and other models to assist in defining and classifying a variety of human abilities, the next step should consist of the selection or development of appropriate instruments to identify a broad range of talent potential. Bruch (1971) suggested using Guilford's model to diagnose different patterns of abilities reflected in existing test items and to specify factors and clusters of factors that represent the strengths and weaknesses of particular individuals or cultural groups. Tests then could be designed to fit cultural strengths, and such tests could be used to measure both conventional abilities and those talents which are valued most by an individual's own culture. Bruch further suggested a case study battery for the identification of gifted disadvantaged youngsters that would include a profile of their strengths and developmental needs, ratios of time in school to developmental levels and achievement levels, and an analysis of positive and negative factors (both sociocultural and personal) which either enhance or inhibit further development of talents.

## Torrance Tests of Creative Thinking

Additional strategies for identifying hidden talent among the disadvantaged have been developed by Torrance (1969). Through the use of instruments such as the *Torrance Tests of Creative Thinking* (Torrance, 1966), youngsters are given an opportunity to respond in terms unique to their own culture. Such an approach avoids the problem of evaluating the child through experiences that are common to the dominant culture, and at the same time helps to create a psychologically safe atmosphere which will motivate him to put forth his greatest effort. On the basis of research studies carried out with disadvantaged groups, Torrance (1964, 1967) has identified the following set of creative characteristics which he found to occur with relatively high frequency among disadvantaged children:

1. High nonverbal fluency and originality.
2. High creative productivity in small groups.
3. Adeptness in visual art activities.
4. High creativity in movement, dance, and other physical activities.
5. Ability to be highly motivated by games, music, sports, humor, and concrete objects.
6. Language rich in imagery.

Research conducted by Torrance and his associates over a period of 12 years has led to the conclusion that children of economically deprived and minority cultures seemed to perform as well as those from any other group. In a recent review of the literature dealing with the use of the *Torrance Tests of Creative Thinking,* Torrance (1971) summarized the results of 15 research studies which focused on the creative abilities of low socioeconomic and minority group children. Generally, these studies indicated that although whites surpassed blacks on verbal measures, there were no significant differences on scores of figural fluency, flexibility, and originality; and in some cases, the so-called disadvantaged groups surpassed the middle-class groups. Although measures of intelligence have been found consistently to correlate positively with socioeconomic status, the research summarized by Torrance seems to indicate that creativity bears little relationship to factors such as race, social class, and level of parental education. Thus, a convincing argument is presented for a relatively culture free method of identifying a bountiful supply of creative talent. Torrance expressed the belief that in many ways the life experiences of low socioeconomic youngsters may actually be more supportive of creative achievement than the experiences of more advantaged children.

> Their lack of expensive toys and play materials contributes to their skill in improvising with common materials. The large families and life styles of disadvantaged families develop skills in group activities and problem-solving. Positive values placed by their families on music, rhythm, dance, body expressiveness, and humor keep alive abilities and sensibilities that tend to perish in more advantaged families [p. 79]. . . .

[The author goes on to discuss two other indices for identifying creative talent: Alpha Biographical (Institute for Behavioral Research in Creativity, 1968) and the subcultural indices of academic potential (SCIAP, Grant & Renzulli, 1971).]

*Language and Developmental Considerations*

Two additional considerations should be pointed out in discussing the issue of identification. First, one of the major characteristics of the disadvantaged is their inability to master the linguistic and grammatical structures of the dominant culture. For this reason it is necessary to develop identification strategies which are not language dependent. Furthermore, because most youngsters have a greater facility with the spoken rather than the written word, it is especially important that the disadvantaged child not be required to "write down" all of his responses. Tape recorders or human recorders can serve in uncovering higher forms of thinking which might otherwise go undetected because of limited writing ability.

Finally, the identification of talent potential among the disadvantaged should be a continuous process that begins in the early years and that is carried out with unusual frequency. Until more and better predictive instruments are available, talent searches should take place in the classroom on a regular basis. Because of the dynamic nature of abilities such as creativity, efforts to make long range predictions should be replaced with frequent assessments of a variety of talents. These assessments should be followed by carefully designed classroom activities which are constructed specifically to enhance those talents which have been identified.

# Developing Talent Potential

Although strategies for identifying different types of human abilities are in varying stages of maturity, enough is known about developing talent potential to allow us to do some systematic programing in this area. Two major factors in the development of outstanding abilities are (a) the characteristics of the teacher and (b) the relevancy of the curriculum.

*Teacher Characteristics*

One major generalization about teacher characteristics stands out from the vast amount of recent literature dealing with programing for the disadvantaged: "Experienced teachers who feel personal satisfaction in working with disadvantaged students are the key to successful compensatory education in poverty area schools [*Phi Delta Kappan*, 1970, p. 338]." This was the finding of a study which investigated 32 programs reporting substantial improvements in the achievement of low income students. Thus, careful teacher selection appears to be a major consideration in programing for the disadvantaged. Furthermore, in situations where talent development is a primary goal, it is especially important to select teachers who are committed to the task of working with disadvantaged youngsters in the development of a variety of talents. Teachers without such knowledge are likely to approach talent development in a piecemeal and haphazard fashion. . . .

## Relevancy of the Curriculum

While remediation in the basic skill areas must be an important goal of compensatory education, it should not, of course, be the only objective of the programs which serve the disadvantaged youth. Activities for talent development can be built into areas of the curriculum, and because of the inherent fun and excitement of activities such as the type described above, added dividends are likely to accrue in the form of increased motivation and improved performance in the basic skills of learning.

High potential disadvantaged youngsters are vitally interested in the social changes taking place around them in their neighborhoods and in the society at large. . . .

A somewhat simplified and yet operational definition of a relevant curriculum is: a set of experiences which deal with topics and issues that youngsters would talk about if given a free choice. If we are really serious about a process centered rather than content centered curriculum (and experiences that attempt to promote specific talents certainly must be considered process oriented), then the issues that youngsters prefer to talk about, those that they discuss before and after the school bell rings, provide fertile ground for the development of a wide range of talents.

# Basic Elements of a Total Program of Talent Development

Although highly qualified teachers and relevant curricular experiences are considered to be major factors in programing for high potential youngsters, a total approach to talent development also should include a number of other characteristics. Douglass (1969) pointed out four essential elements of an ideal system for maximizing the talent potential of low socioeconomic and minority group members.

The first element is greater flexibility in the ways in which schools are operated and performance is evaluated. The classroom unit must be broken down into small learning modules where individuals and small groups become the main focus of instructional efforts. Although the school may continue to serve as a "home base" for the learning process, Douglass suggested that early in the elementary school years students should be provided with extended periods of learning time in institutions that usually are not considered schools:

> These would include places where knowledge is stored, such as art museums,
> science institutes, and libraries . . . places where knowledge is being put to work,

such as farms, hospitals, airports, machine shops, sheet metal works, and construction . . . places in which some kind of education or learning or on-the-job
training is under way . . . places where knowledge is being discovered such as
research institutes and laboratories [Douglass, 1969, pp. 10–11].

The second element would consist of an early start in the education and
socialization processes. Low socioeconomic group children often enter school
with the accumulated deficits that result from poor nutrition and limited
stimulation in infancy and early childhood. These deficits may lead to intellectual inhibition and an inability to take advantage of the educational opportunities that may be open to them in later life. Douglass advocated a program of nursing schools and day care centers where each child will be assured
of services of professionals and paraprofessionals who are knowledgeable
about early childhood experiences that are beneficial to later development.
These centers might be located throughout the community in schools, hospitals, or factories, and they should provide continuing education programs for
parents and substitute parents.

An early apprenticeship is the third element of a total program of talent development. Beginning at an early age, students should be given frequent exposure to different ways of making a living and of participating in leisure
time activities. Too often, children from low socioeconomic group families
have no real contact with a father figure or they see their parents employed
only in lower level occupations. They have little opportunity to observe the
variety of talents used in the broad spectrum of occupations, and thus, they
have a limited conception of the many kinds of talents that are valuable to
our society and available for their exploration. Early apprenticeship programs would help youngsters to see the real world's conception of talent
rather than the school's traditionally limited concern for only academic ability.

A final element which is necessary in the development of talent potential is
the creation of a more open system. The grade by grade progression has
failed to meet the needs of students who do not "fit in" at the start or who
are not willing to "play the game" by the existing rules. If we truly respect
the individual differences and preferences of all people in our society, then we
should not force them to follow a relatively prescribed system of learning.
Students should be free to alternate school and work experiences with other
experiences which they may wish to pursue. They should be free to drop out
of school for a given period of time and allowed to reenter the system without fear of punitive action or relegation to programs which are essentially
remedial in nature. Access to first rate educational programs should be readily available to every person at every stage of development regardless of his
previous success or lack of success in the system. A more open system will
allow adults as well as young people to have an opportunity to explore and
develop talents that may have been thwarted earlier in life.

# REFERENCES

Bloom, B. S. *Stability and change in human characteristics.* New York: John Wiley & Sons, 1964.

Bloom, B. S. (Ed.) *Taxonomy of educational objectives. Handbook I: Cognitive domain.* New York: David McKay, 1956.

Bloom, B. S. Davis, A., & Hess, R. *Compensatory education for cultural deprivation.* New York: Holt, Rinehart & Winston, 1965.

Bruch, C. R. Modification of procedures for identification of the disadvantaged gifted. *Gifted Child Quarterly,* 1971, **15**, 267–272.

Coleman, J. S., Campbell, E. Q., Hobson, C. J., McPartland, J., Mood, A. M., Weinfeld, F. D., & York, R. L., *Equality of educational opportunity.* Washington, D.C.: USGPO, 1966.

Commission on Tests. *I: Righting the balance, II: Briefs.* New York: College Entrance Examination Board, 1970.

Douglass, J. H. Strategies for maximizing the development of talent among the urban disadvantaged. Paper presented at the annual meeting of The Council for Exceptional Children, Denver, Colorado, April, 1969.

Grant, T. E., & Renzulli, J. S. *Sub-cultural indices of academic potential.* University of Connecticut, 1971.

Gregory, C. E. *The management of intelligence.* New York: McGraw-Hill, 1967.

Guilford, J. P. *The nature of human intelligence.* New York: McGraw-Hill, 1967.

Havighurst, R. J. Conditions productive of superior children. *Teachers College Record,* 1961, **62**, 524–531.

Holt, J. *How children fail.* New York: Dell, 1966.

Hunt, J. McV. *Intelligence and experience.* New York: Ronald Press, 1961.

Institute for Behavioral Research in Creativity. *Alpha Biographical Inventory.* Greensboro, N.C.: Prediction Press, 1968.

Jenkins. M. D. The upper limit of ability among American Negroes. *Scientific Monthly,* 1948, **66**, 339–401.

Key to compensatory education *Phi Delta Kappan,* 1970, **58**, 338.

Kozol, J. *Death at an early age.* Boston: Houghton-Mifflin, 1967.

Krathwohl, D. R., Bloom, B. S., & Masia, B. B. *Taxonomy of educational objectives. Handbook II: Affective domain.* New York: David McKay, 1964.

Mathis, H. I. The disadvantaged and the aptitude barrier. *Personnel and Guidance Jornal,* 1969, **47**, 467–472.

Niles, C. C. Gifted children. In L. Carmichael (Ed.), *Manual of child psychology.* New York: John Wiley & Sons, 1954.

Parnes, S. J. & Harding, H. F. (Eds.) *A source book for creative thinking.* New York: Charles Scribner's Sons, 1962.

Passow, A. H. The talented among the disadvantaged. *Accent on Talent,* 1966, **1**, 3–7.

Passow, A. H., Goldberg, M., & Tannenbaum, A. J. *Education of the disadvantaged.* New York: Holt, Rinehart, & Winston, 1967.

Rosenthal, R., & Jacobson, L. F. *Pygmalion in the classroom.* New York: Holt, Rinehart, & Winston, 1968.

Sexton, P. C. *Education and income.* New York: Viking Press, 1961.

Silberman, C. E. *Crisis in the classroom.* New York: Random House, 1970.

Taylor, C. W. Be talent developers . . . as well as knowledge dispensers. *Today's Education,* 1968, **57**, 67–69.

Terman, S. M. *Genetic studies of genius.* Stanford: Stanford University Press, 1925–1959. 5 Vols.

Torrance, E. P. *Education and the creative potential.* Minneapolis: University of Minnesota Press, 1964.

TORRANCE, E. P. *Torrance Tests of Creative Thinking: Norms-technical manual.* Princeton, N.J.: Personnel Press, 1966.

TORRANCE, E. P. *Understanding the fourth grade slump in creativity.* Athens: Georgia Studies of Creative Behavior, 1967.

TORRANCE, E. P. Finding hidden talents among disadvantaged children. *Gifted Child Quarterly,* 1968, 12, 131–137.

TORRANCE, E. P. How creativity development can awaken unrecognized potential. Paper presented at the conference on "Developing Unawakened and Unrecognized Potential" sponsored by the Minnesota State Department of Education, Minneapolis, April, 1969.

TORRANCE, E. P. Are the Torrance Tests of Creative Thinking biased against or in favor of "disadvantaged" groups? *Gifted Child Quarterly,* 1971, 15, 75–80.

TOYNBEE, A. Is America neglecting her creative minorities? In C. W. Taylor (Ed.), *Widening horizons of creativity.* New York: John Wiley & Sons, 1964.

WILLIAMS, F. E. & EBERLE, R. F. *Creative production in the classroom.* Edwardsville, Ill.: American of Edwardsville, 1967.

WILLIAMS, R. L. & BYARS, H. Negro self-esteem in a transitional society. *Personnel & Guidance Journal,* 1968, 47, 120–125.

WITTY, P., & JENKINS, M. D. The educational achievement of a group of gifted Negro children. *Journal of Educational Psychology,* 1934, 45, 585–597.

# The Health and Social Consequences of Teenage Childbearing*

## Jane Menken

TEENAGE CHILDBEARING is associated with a long list of adverse health and social consequences for young mothers and their infants. Yet, as of 1968 (the most recent year for which detailed data are available), one-fourth of 20-year-old girls had had at least one baby while in their teens. One-sixth of births in that year were to girls in their teens; a third of these—200,000 infants—were born to mothers 17 or younger,[1] and two-fifths of these 200,000 were born out of wedlock.[2] What is more, as birthrates and illegitimacy rates have declined, since the beginning of the 1960s, the proportion of all babies born to teenagers has risen appreciably,[3] and teenage illegitimacy rates have continued stubbornly to increase.[4]

Childbearing at any age is a momentous event for a woman. For the teenager, however, it is often accompanied by problems quite different from and far less benign than those experienced by older mothers.

* Reprinted with permission of the publisher and the author from *Family Planning Perspectives,* Volume 4, Number 3, July, 1972 (pages 545–53).

For the very young mother, the risks that her baby will be stillborn, or die soon after birth, or be born prematurely or with a serious physical or mental handicap are much higher than those for women in their twenties. Early childbearing is also associated with high parity and short birth intervals, compounding the already high risks to the life and health of the young mother and her infant. Moreover, bearing a first child while in her teens is likely to be a critical and highly adverse turning point in a young woman's life.[5] This is particularly true if the baby is conceived out of wedlock (as are nearly six in 10 of all first births to 15–19-year-olds[6]) or born out of wedlock (as are 27 per cent of births to this age group[7]). In Arthur Campbell's words:

> The girl who has an illegitimate child at the age of 16 suddenly has 90 percent of her life's script written for her. She will probably drop out of school, even if someone else in her family helps to take care of the baby; she will probably not be able to find a steady job that pays enough to provide for herself and her child; she may feel impelled to marry someone she might not otherwise have chosen. Her life choices are few, and most of them are bad. Had she been able to delay the first child, her prospects might have been quite different. . . .[8]

While the main focus of this article is on the medical aspects of teenage childbearing, some consideration will also be given to the social consequences to parent and child, and to what little is known about the social and economic conditions which may influence teenage childbearing.

## Teenage Births and Birthrates

As the U.S. birthrate declined in the the last decade, births to teenagers became a larger proportion of all births (see top deck of Table 1). In 1968, 17 per cent of all births were to teenagers, compared to 14 per cent in 1961. The increase was sharpest among nonwhites, among whom 29 per cent of births in 1968, compared to 20 per cent in 1961, were to teenagers. The concentration of out-of-wedlock births at young ages is even more striking (see bottom deck of Table 1): Nearly half of all out-of-wedlock births in 1968 were to teenagers, compared to 41 per cent in 1961. These changes were only partly due to increases in the numbers of teenagers in the population. An additional factor was the relative change in birthrates in the various age groups. Women 20 and older experienced greater declines in birthrates during the period 1961–1968 than did 15–19-year-olds.[9]

A slightly different perspective is obtained by examining the proportion of women bearing a child while in their teens, rather than the proportion of total births that occur to young mothers. The data presented in Table 2 show that, for women born in the United States between 1940 and 1951, the proportion who became mothers by the time they reached their eighteenth birthday declined by 25 per cent—from 12.5 per cent of girls born in 1939 to

Table 1

*Births, by Legitimacy Status and Color, for Total Population and for Teenagers, 1961 and 1968*

| | Births (in thousands) | | | | | Per cent of total births | | | |
|---|---|---|---|---|---|---|---|---|---|
| | Total | <15 | 15–17 | 18–19 | <20 | <15 | 15–17 | 18–19 | <20 |
| **All** | | | | | | | | | |
| 1968 | 3502 | 10 | 193 | 398 | 601 | 0.3 | 5.5 | 11.4 | 17.2 |
| 1961 | 4268 | 7 | 178 | 424 | 609 | 0.2 | 4.2 | 9.9 | 14.3 |
| Per cent change | −18.0 | 27.4 | 8.5 | −6.1 | −1.3 | | | | |
| **White** | | | | | | | | | |
| 1968 | 2912 | 3.1 | 121 | 306 | 430 | 0.1 | 4.2 | 10.4 | 14.7 |
| 1961 | 3601 | 2.8 | 125 | 347 | 475 | 0.1 | 3.5 | 9.6 | 13.2 |
| Per cent change | −19.1 | 10.9 | −3.2 | −12.9 | −9.4 | | | | |
| **Nonwhite** | | | | | | | | | |
| 1968 | 589 | 6.4 | 72 | 93 | 171 | 1.0 | 12.1 | 15.8 | 28.9 |
| 1961 | 667 | 4.7 | 53 | 77 | 135 | 0.7 | 7.9 | 11.6 | 20.2 |
| Per cent change | −11.7 | 37.3 | 36.3 | 20.8 | 27.2 | | | | |
| | Out-of-wedlock births (estimate, in thousands) | | | | | Per cent of total out-of-wedlock births | | | |
| **All** | | | | | | | | | |
| 1968 | 339 | 7.7 | 78 | 80 | 166 | 2.3 | 23.0 | 23.6 | 48.9 |
| 1961 | 240 | 5.2 | 45 | 48 | 98 | 2.2 | 18.8 | 20.0 | 41.2 |
| Per cent change | 41.2 | 48.1 | 72.7 | 66.7 | 68.7 | | | | |
| **White** | | | | | | | | | |
| 1968 | 155 | 1.9 | 28 | 39 | 69 | 1.2 | 18.3 | 25.1 | 44.6 |
| 1961 | 91 | 1.4 | 16 | 20 | 37 | 1.5 | 17.0 | 22.6 | 41.1 |
| Per cent change | 70.4 | 35.7 | 83.2 | 95.0 | 84.2 | | | | |
| **Nonwhite** | | | | | | | | | |
| 1968 | 184 | 5.8 | 49 | 42 | 97 | 3.2 | 26.9 | 22.4 | 52.5 |
| 1961 | 149 | 3.8 | 30 | 27 | 61 | 2.5 | 19.9 | 18.4 | 40.8 |
| Per cent change | 23.3 | 52.6 | 66.9 | 55.6 | 59.2 | | | | |

Sources: DHEW, *Vital Statistics of the United States, Vol. 1—Natality, 1968,* Tables 1–26, 1–41 and 1–51; 1961, Tables 2–9 and 2–12.

9.4 per cent of girls born 11 years later. A similar reduction occurred in the proportion starting their reproductive lives by age 20—from 33.8 per cent of girls born in 1939 to 25.9 per cent of girls born nine years later—a decline of 23 per cent. Despite this downward trend, the table shows that almost 26 per cent of the latest cohort for which data are available bore a child before age 20, and more than one-fourth of these mothers had at least two children.

Table 3 shows that between 1961 and 1968 illegitimacy rates (births per

Table 2

*Per cent of Birth Cohort Having at Least One Live Birth by Age 18 and Age 20: U.S. Birth Cohorts, 1939–1950*

| Cohort born during fiscal year | Per cent becoming mothers by age | | Per cent of mothers having at least two live births by age | |
|---|---|---|---|---|
| | 18 | 20 | 18 | 20 |
| 1940 | 12.5 | 33.8 | 18.5 | 34.6 |
| 1941 | 12.2 | 33.2 | 18.7 | 34.9 |
| 1942 | 11.5 | 31.9 | 19.0 | 34.5 |
| 1943 | 10.9 | 30.0 | 19.2 | 34.0 |
| 1944 | 11.0 | 30.0 | 19.3 | 33.6 |
| 1945 | 10.8 | 29.4 | 19.8 | 32.6 |
| 1946 | 10.8 | 29.4 | 19.3 | 31.0 |
| 1947 | 9.1 | 25.8 | 17.8 | 27.5 |
| 1948 | 9.5 | 26.4 | 17.8 | 27.0 |
| 1949 | 9.4 | 25.9 | 17.0 | 25.7 |
| 1950 | 9.4 | | 16.2 | |
| 1951 | 9.4 | | 14.8 | |
| Per cent decline | 24.8 | 23.4 | 20.0 | 25.7 |

Sources: Derived from cumulative birthrates by live-birth order and exact age of mother, *Vital Statistics of the United States, Vol. 1—Natality: 1968*, Table 1–17; *1967*, Table 1–17; *1966*, Table 1–18; *1965*, Table 1–18; *1964*, Table 1–19. Also, P. K. Whelpton and A. A. Campbell, "Fertility Tables for Birth Cohorts of American Women," *Vital Statistics—Special Reports*, Vol. 51, 1960, Part 1, Table 2, p. 78.

Table 3

*Estimated Illegitimacy Rates \* by Age of Mother: United States 1961–1968*

| Year | 15–44 | 15–19 | 20–24 | 25–29 | 30–34 | 35–39 | 40–44 |
|---|---|---|---|---|---|---|---|
| 1968 | 24.1 | 19.8 | 36.1 | 39.4 | 27.6 | 14.6 | 3.7 |
| 1967 | 24.0 | 18.7 | 38.6 | 41.4 | 29.8 | 15.3 | 4.0 |
| 1966 | 23.6 | 17.5 | 40.8 | 44.4 | 32.1 | 16.9 | 4.3 |
| 1965 | 23.4 | 16.7 | 38.8 | 50.4 | 37.1 | 17.0 | 4.4 |
| 1964 | 23.4 | 16.5 | 40.0 | 50.1 | 41.4 | 15.0 | 4.0 |
| 1963 | 22.5 | 15.3 | 39.9 | 49.4 | 33.7 | 16.1 | 4.3 |
| 1962 | 21.5 | 14.9 | 41.8 | 46.4 | 27.0 | 13.5 | 3.4 |
| 1961 | 22.6 | 16.0 | 41.2 | 44.8 | 28.9 | 15.1 | 3.8 |

Source: *Vital Statistics of the United States, 1968, Vol. 1—Natality*, Table 1–25.
\* Number of out-of-wedlock births per 1,000 single women in specified group.

Table 4

*Per cent of First Births Conceived Out of Wedlock for Women Aged 15–19 and 15–44, by Color: United States, 1964–1966 National Natality Survey*

| | Age of mother at first birth | | | | | |
| | 15–19 | | | 15–44 | | |
| | Total | White | Non-white | Total | White | Non-white |
|---|---|---|---|---|---|---|
| Number of first births (in thousands) | 442 | 348 | 94 | 1,180 | 1,008 | 171 |
| Per cent of first births which were: | | | | | | |
|   Illegitimate | 24.0 | 15.0 | 57.3 | 14.5 | 9.3 | 45.5 |
|   Born less than 8 months after marriage | 32.2 | 33.9 | 26.0 | 18.5 | 17.7 | 22.6 |
| Conceived out of wedlock | 56.2 | 48.9 | 83.3 | 33.0 | 27.0 | 68.1 |
| Per cent of legitimate first births which were conceived out of wedlock | 42.4 | 39.9 | 60.8 | 21.6 | 19.5 | 41.6 |
| Per cent of first births which were conceived out of wedlock and were later legitimized by marriage | 57.2 | 69.3 | 31.1 | 55.9 | 65.6 | 33.3 |

Source: Unpublished data, National Center for Health Statistics, 1964–1966 National Natality Survey.

1,000 single women) declined slightly for all age groups except for 15–19-year-olds. While teenagers did not have the highest rates of illegitimacy of all age groups (single women aged 20–34 had much higher rates), more of them—89 per cent in 1969—were unmarried than in any other age group.[10] Together, these factors result in a situation where close to half the mothers delivering infants out of wedlock are teenagers.

Illegitimate births represent a large proportion of total births to teenagers. In 1968, 40 per cent of births to mothers aged 15–17 and 20 per cent to 18–19-year-olds were illegitimate, compared to eight per cent of births to 20–24-year-olds, and about four per cent of births to women in the 25–34-year age group.[11] Standard vital statistics data do not indicate the number of out-of-wedlock conceptions that are legitimized by marriage. However, a National Natality Study conducted in 1964–1966 by the National Center for Health Statistics (NCHS) included date of marriage in the information obtained from a sample of over 2,500 mothers of legitimate first-born children.[12] Table 4 summarizes some of the findings. Fifty-six per cent of first-born children to girls aged 15–19 were conceived prior to marriage.* The lower proportion of out-of-wedlock conceived births among whites (49 per cent) than among nonwhites (83 per cent) may reflect differences in the availability of abortion. The data show a much greater probability for whites who deliver a premari-

* This assumes that births occurring within eight months of marriage were permaritally conceived.

tally conceived infant to marry before the birth occurs. Similar but more detailed results for Detroit in 1960 show that the proportion of births conceived out of wedlock which were legitimized increased from age 14 to age 17.[13]

# Medical Aspects

The medical literature generally discusses reproductive loss at specified stages on the continuum of development of the fetus and infant: fetal mortality, perinatal mortality (from 28 weeks of gestation through the first week of life), neonatal mortality (first 28 days of life) and postneonatal mortality (28 days through one year). The latter two are components of the standard measure of infant mortality, that is, deaths in the first year of life. These distinctions are important here in that fetal, perinatal and, to a lesser extent, neonatal mortality appear to be caused primarily by factors related to the *pregnancy* itself, while postneonatal mortality is attributed more often to environmental causes. The risks of reproductive loss vary with the age and parity of the mother. These two factors, while usually rising together, have quite different biologic interpretations: Age is a rough indicator of whether a young pregnant woman has reached full physical maturity or of whether the reproductive effectiveness of the older woman has begun to decline. Parity, on the other hand, reflects previous experience with the reproductive process.[14] The combination, parity at a certain age, is a result of the timing of births (the age at first birth and the rapidity with which subsequent ones occur).

Sociological interpretations of the age relationship are also plausible. The risk of childbearing at certain ages may be correlated with the risk of reproductive loss. Few data, however, are available to distinguish between the biological and sociological interpretations.

# Mortality and Maternal Age

To study the relationship of infant mortality to maternal age, it is necessary either to match a sample of infants' death certificates to infants' birth certificates or to request further information from the families. As a result, there have been only a handful of large-scale studies. Those in the United States and United Kingdom have shown consistently that the infant mortality rate is extremely high for mothers younger than 15, declines to a minimum in either the early or late twenties and increases fairly sharply thereafter.[15] Figure 1 illustrates this with data from a matched birth certificate/infant death certificate study.[16] This NCHS investigation succeeded in matching birth and death certificates for 94 per cent of the nearly 110,000 children born in 1960 who died

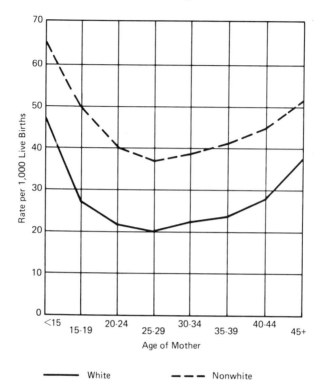

FIGURE 1. Infant mortality of white and nonwhite infants by age of mother: United States, 1960 Birth Cohort.

*Source:* Working Group, "Relation of Nutrition to Pregnancy in Adolescence," in *Maternal Nutrition and the Course of Pregnancy,* Committee on Maternal Nutrition, Food and Nutrition Board, National Research Council, National Academy of Sciences, Washington, D.C., 1970, Table 3, p. 144.

before reaching their first birthday.[17] The shapes of the curves are similar but, at all ages, the infant mortality rate is considerably higher among nonwhites than among whites.

When mortality among infants born to mothers younger than 20 is compared to the mortality of those whose mothers are aged 20–30, it can be seen that the differences are far greater in the first month of life than in the remainder of the first year (see Figure 2). In other words, just after birth, when biologic factors related to the pregnancy are the primary determinants of survival, risks to infants of young mothers are much higher than those to infants of older mothers in both color groups.

Postneonatal death rates are high and differences by color are least in mothers younger than 15, suggesting large and negative environmental influences for infants of the youngest mothers, regardless of color. It is well-documented that postneonatal mortality rates have declined over the past 30

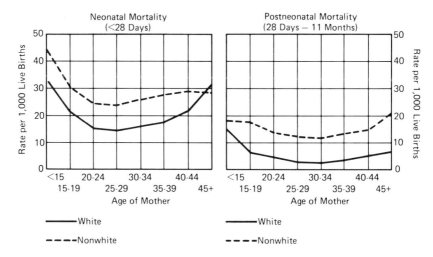

FIGURE 2. Neonatal and postneonatal mortality of white and nonwhite infants by age of mother: United States, 1960 Birth Cohort.
*Source:* Working Group, "Relation of Nutrition to Pregnancy in Adolescence," 1970, op. cit.

years more rapidly than have neonatal mortality rates, mainly the result of declining death rates from infectious disease.[18] However, for nonwhites the relative improvement in mortality conditions has occurred much more slowly. In 1960, at almost all ages, postneonatal mortality accounted for approximately one-fourth of the infant deaths in each maternal age group among whites, but closer to one-third of the deaths among nonwhites. Sam Shapiro and his colleagues examined infant mortality within the postneonatal period according to the age (in months) of the infant at death.[19] They found that the rates for whites and nonwhites increasingly diverged during the first four months. At that point, nonwhite infant mortality was three times that of whites.

Infant mortality by legitimacy status of the pregnancy was derived for the period 1964–1966, again by the NCHS, using data from the National Natality Survey and the National Infant Mortality Study.[20] Except for nonwhites aged 25–29, the rates shown in Figure 3 follow the age-pattern already described: The infant mortality rates for the out-of-wedlock births exceed those for legitimate births, and this differential increases with age. (The single exception is for nonwhites younger than 20 years, where the proportions of infants surviving the first year of life is greater for out-of-wedlock births.)

No U.S. data are available to reveal the mortality experience of infants conceived out of wedlock. However, it was found in England and Wales in 1949 that neonatal mortality among single live births was 16.4 per 1,000 for legitimate births, 22.4 per 1,000 for births ocurring in the first nine months

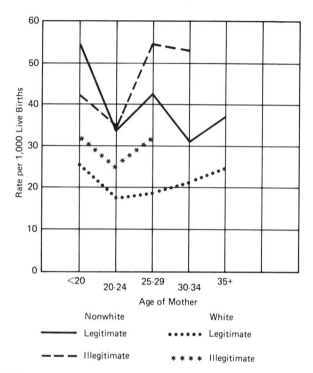

FIGURE 3. Infant mortality rates by color of child and legitimacy status by age of mother: United States, 1964–1966.

*Source:* "Infant Mortality Rates by Legitimacy Status: United States, 1964–1966," National Center for Health Statistics, Monthly Vital Statistics Report, Vol. 20, No. 5, 1971, Table 2, p. 3.

of marriage and 27.0 per 1,000 for out-of-wedlock births.[21] It is distinctly possible that these figures are at least partially the result of the age distribution of women conceiving premaritally, but they do suggest increased risks to infants whose conception precedes marriage.

Fetal death ratios (the number of reported fetal deaths of over 20 weeks' duration divided by total live births) for women younger than 20 are somewhat elevated when compared to women aged 20–29, but women over 30 are clearly subject to a far higher risk of not carrying their pregnancy to full term.[22] Again, nonwhites are exposed to higher risks at all ages. The fetal loss rate is greater for out-of-wedlock pregnancies in all age and color groups except for nonwhites under 15, for whom the ratio for pregnancies classed as legitimate is 45.6 per 1,000 live births compared with 29.0 for out-of-wedlock births. At all other ages, the differential in the ratio for legitimate vs. out-of-wedlock births is much greater for whites than nonwhites. What proportion of these reported fetal deaths is the result of induced abortion is unknown.

These preliminary results demonstrate that, at all stages of pregnancy and infancy examined, the very young mother is exposed to greater risks of losing her baby than for somewhat older counterparts.

# Influence of Parity

Risks of reproductive loss are highest for young women who have already had several live births and for older women. Data on fetal death rates for 1960–1961 show that the risks for young mothers at all parities are high, and increase rapidly with parity after the first birth (see Table 5).

Neonatal death certificates for infants born in the first three months of 1950, when matched to the infants' birth certificates, reveal a distinct pattern among white infants.[23] For parities beyond the first, the neonatal death rate for infants of 15–19-year-old mothers is quite high, declines for those in the twenties and then rises again after age 30. (see Table 6) There is no simple age pattern for nonwhites but neonatal mortality for both groups among young mothers rises rapidly with each parity after the first birth.

Similar U.S. data for the postneonatal period are not available. A series of studies following all children born in 1949 and 1950 in England and Wales[24] shows that, in the age period between four weeks and six months, the mortality rate for all parities follows the same pattern as for the neonatal rates displayed in Table 6.[25] At any maternal age, mortality increases with birth order after the first. In the last half of the first year, observed mortality is highest in infants of the youngest mothers. This pattern in postneonatal mortality holds for all socioeconomic groups, although the *level* of mortality rises

## Table 5
*Average Fetal Death Rates per 1,000 Live Births and Fetal Deaths, by Birth Order and Age of Mother: United States, 1960–1961*

| Birth order | All ages* | Age of mother | | | | | |
| --- | --- | --- | --- | --- | --- | --- | --- |
| | | 15–19 | 20–24 | 25–29 | 30–34 | 35–39 | 40–44 |
| First | 15.5 | 13.8 | 13.0 | 17.8 | 30.0 | 46.6 | 60.2 |
| Second | 11.2 | 12.2 | 9.4 | 10.7 | 14.6 | 21.0 | 32.2 |
| Third | 13.2 | 16.3 | 11.3 | 11.5 | 14.5 | 21.4 | 32.2 |
| Fourth | 16.0 | 23.1 | 14.4 | 13.9 | 15.8 | 21.9 | 31.0 |
| Fifth | 19.1 | 47.3 | 17.3 | 16.2 | 18.7 | 23.8 | 33.0 |
| Sixth and over | 28.8 | 72.7 | 23.3 | 22.4 | 25.2 | 31.6 | 43.4 |
| Total | 15.8 | 13.7 | 11.9 | 14.2 | 19.0 | 26.8 | 38.5 |

Source: S. Shapiro, E. Schlesinger and R. E. L. Nesbitt, Jr., *Infant, Perinatal, Maternal and Childhood Mortality in the United States,* Harvard University Press, Cambridge, Mass., 1968.
* Includes data for age groups under 15 years and 45 years and older.

Table 6

*Neonatal Mortality Rates per 1,000 Live Births, by Birth Order and Age of Mother: United States, January–March 1950*

| Birth order | Age of mother | | | | | | |
| --- | --- | --- | --- | --- | --- | --- | --- |
| | All ages | 15–19 | 20–24 | 25–29 | 30–34 | 35–39 | 40–44 |
| First | 19.1 | 21.2 | 16.6 | 17.3 | 24.1 | 28.7 | 30.9 |
| Second | 17.8 | 28.1 | 18.2 | 14.3 | 16.1 | 20.3 | 25.3 |
| Third | 19.7 | 35.3 | 22.0 | 17.7 | 16.9 | 19.8 | 26.4 |
| Fourth and over | 21.1 | 45.2 | 24.9 | 19.6 | 18.8 | 21.5 | 23.6 |
| Fifth | 26.9 | 68.8 | 35.8 | 25.5 | 25.5 | 26.1 | 28.0 |
| Total | 20.0 | 23.8 | 19.0 | 17.6 | 20.0 | 23.6 | 27.2 |

Source: S. Shapiro, E. Schlesinger and R. E. L. Nesbitt, Jr., *Infant, Perinatal, Maternal and Childhood Mortality in the United States,* Harvard University Press, Cambridge, Mass., 1968.

as the socioeconomic level declines.[26] Less detailed findings of an inverse relationship between mortality and occupation exist for fetal and neonatal mortality in areas of the United States.[27] The British Perinatal Mortality Survey, which studied all stillbirths and infants born alive in a single week in England and Wales in 1958, found similar inverse relationships between social class and the perinatal mortality rate (defined as stillbirths and deaths in the first week).[28]

In North Carolina, a study of perinatal mortality (defined as fetal deaths plus neonatal mortality) for mothers under 20 has indicated that mortality is highest when the mother is younger than 15, dips at age 16, and then declines slightly with each additional year to age 20.[29]

# Summary of Mortality Risks

Young women—particularly multiparous young women—and older women run an especially high risk that their babies will die at birth or soon after. Table 7 summarizes the evidence of the risk of mortality for infants of mothers in these given age groups compared to the risk to infants of mothers aged 20–24. Infant mortality for white mothers under 15 is over twice as high as for mothers in their early twenties. For younger mothers, the relative risk of fetal or neonatal death climbs as parity rises, so that neonatal mortality of the infants born to women younger than 20 who already have had three live births (last line) is 90 per cent higher than of infants of older mothers. The reverse situation holds for older mothers. Apparently, a mother who delivers a child after age 40 is more likely to have a liveborn child who survives the neonatal period if she has already had previous live births.

Table 7
Mortality Rate for Specified Age Groups Relative to the Rate for Infants of Mothers Aged
20–24, by Color

| | White | | | Nonwhite | | |
|---|---|---|---|---|---|---|
| Rate for women | (<15) | (15–19) | (40–44) | (<15) | (15–19) | (40–44) |
| Rate for women | (20–24) | (20–24) | (20–24) | (20–24) | (20–24) | (20–24) |
| **United States, 1960** | | | | | | |
| Infant mortality | 2.2 | 1.3 | 1.3 | 1.6 | 1.2 | 1.1 |
| Neonatal mortality | 2.2 | 1.3 | 1.4 | 1.8 | 1.2 | 1.2 |
| Postneonatal mortality | 2.8 | 1.4 | 1.1 | 1.3 | 1.3 | 1.0 |
| **United States, 1964–66** | | | | | | |
| **Infant mortality** | | | | | | |
| Legitimate births | na | 1.3 * | 1.3 † | na | 1.7 * | 1.1 † |
| Illegitimate births | na | 1.2 | ‡ | na | 1.2 | ‡ |
| **United States, 1967** | | | | | | |
| **Fetal death ratios** | | | | | | |
| **by parity** | | | | | | |
| First | na | 1.0 | 4.8 | na | 0.8 | 3.9 |
| Second | na | 1.2 | 3.5 | na | 1.2 | 3.9 |
| Third | na | 1.3 | 3.0 | na | 1.4 | 3.4 |
| Fourth | na | 1.4 | 2.3 | na | 1.5 | 2.6 |
| **United States, 1950** | | | | | | |
| **Neonatal mortality** | | | | | | |
| **Rates by parity** | | | | | | |
| First | na | 1.3 | 1.9 | na | 1.0 | |
| Second | na | 1.6 | 1.5 | na | 1.3 | |
| Third | na | 1.8 | 1.1 | na | 1.4 | |
| Fourth | na | 1.9 | 0.9 | na | 1.9 | |

Sources: "Infant Mortality Rates by Legitimacy Status: United States, 1964–1966," *Monthly Vital Statistics Report*, Vol. 20, No. 5, 1971, Table 2, p. 3; J. Loeb, *Weight at Birth and Survival of the Newborn, by Age of Mother and Total Birth Order, United States, Early 1950*, National Center for Health Statistics, Series 21, No. 5, 1965; S. Shapiro, E. Schlesinger and R. E. L. Nesbitt, Jr., *Infant, Perinatal, Maternal and Childhood Mortality in the United States*, Harvard University Press, Cambridge, Mass., 1968; Working Group, "Relation of Nutrition to Pregnancy in Adolescence," in *Maternal Nutrition and the Course of Pregnancy*, Committee on Maternal Nutrition, Food and Nutrition Board, National Research Council, National Academy of Sciences, Washington, D.C., 1970.
* Age group includes all mothers aged less than 20 years.
† Age group includes all mothers aged 35 or more years.
‡ Numerator does not meet standards of reliability or precision.
na = not available.

# Birth Intervals

Girls who have a first child at an early age tend also to bear their subsequent children in rapid succession.[30] There may be a selection process by which girls who are more fecund, or who have less access to abortion or contraception, or who are less effective users of contraception, may tend to marry and/or become pregnant early in their sexual experience. There is also some evidence that marriage at an early age is related to education and religion, two variables which have been associated with fertility in almost every study of the subject.[31] Short birth intervals have been linked to increased rates of stillbirth, prematurity, and neonatal and postneonatal deaths.[32]

# Prematurity

The increased risk of prematurity may be the most important medical aspect of teenage pregnancy.[33] The infant's maturity at birth is usually gauged by birth weight, although there are different developmental levels for the same weight in different populations.[34] It has been estimated that "the risk of death in the first year of life among infants who weigh 2500 grams or less at birth is 17 times the risk among infants weighing 2501 grams or more."[35] This has been verified in two national studies, one of neonatal mortality in 1950 and the other of mortality in the first year of life in 1960.[36] At all birth weights under 2500 grams, the neonatal mortality rate was lower in 1960 for nonwhites than for whites, implying that development maturity was not the same at a given birth weight for those two groups. Postneonatal mortality, however, was lower for whites than for nonwhites at all birth weights; the risk of postneonatal mortality for a white infant weighing more than 2500 grams at birth was little more than one-third that for a nonwhite infant.[37]

The percentage of infants weighing less than 2500 grams was greatest among very young mothers, and has been increasing for nonwhites since 1950 (see Table 8). In 1950, the percentage of infants of low birth weight increased greatly for young mothers of higher parity.[38] One hypothesis explaining the increasing frequency of low birth weight is that since 1950 there has been great effort to prolong "pregnancies which gave indication of terminating prematurely."[39] This could decrease fetal losses while increasing prematurity rates and tending to increase neonatal mortality.

Prematurity may be strongly associated with socioeconomic status. The 1963 National Natality Survey found that the relationship between the proportion of infants weighing less than 2500 grams and maternal age was similar to that shown in Table 8. When women were classified by family income, however, the differences in the proportion born prematurely varied little by age within any income group,[40] although a much larger proportion of women under 20 were in the lower income groups than were older women. In a study of infants liveborn in Baltimore between 1961 and 1965[41] birth weight was found to be related more, within each color group, to the trimester of pregnancy in which prenatal care began than to age, parity or socioeconomic status per se. However, the timing of prenatal care was highly correlated with socioeconomic status in this study. Those running the greatest risk of having

Table 8

*Percent of Low Birth Weight Infants, by Age of Mother and Color: United States, January–March 1950 and 1967*

| Age of mother | Total | | | White | | | Nonwhite | | |
|---|---|---|---|---|---|---|---|---|---|
| | Jan.–Mar. 1950* | 1967 | Difference | Jan.–Mar. 1950* | 1967 | Difference | Jan.–Mar. 1950* | 1967 | Difference |
| < 15 | 15.1 | 17.2 | +2.1 | 15.9 | 12.5 | −3.4 | 14.7 | 19.5 | +4.8 |
| 15–19 | 9.0 | 10.5 | +1.5 | 8.0 | 8.5 | +0.5 | 12.0 | 15.7 | +3.7 |
| 20–24 | 7.3 | 7.7 | +0.4 | 6.9 | 6.7 | −0.2 | 9.6 | 13.2 | +3.6 |
| 25–29 | 6.7 | 7.2 | +0.5 | 6.5 | 6.5 | 0.0 | 8.4 | 11.8 | +3.4 |
| 30–34 | 7.2 | 7.9 | +0.7 | 7.0 | 7.0 | 0.0 | 8.8 | 12.6 | +3.8 |
| 35–39 | 7.7 | 9.1 | +1.4 | 7.5 | 8.3 | +0.8 | 9.0 | 13.3 | +4.3 |
| 40–44 | 7.7 | 9.6 | +1.9 | 7.5 | 9.1 | +1.6 | 8.9 | 12.2 | +3.3 |
| ≥ 45 | 6.1 | 8.6 | +2.5 | 5.7 | 8.1 | +2.4 | 7.4 | 10.8 | +3.4 |
| Total | 7.4 | 8.2 | +0.8 | 7.0 | 7.1 | +0.1 | 9.7 | 13.6 | +3.9 |

Source: H. Chase, "Trends in 'Prematurity': United States, 1950–1967," *American Journal of Public Health*, 60:1978, 1970, Table 8.
* Excludes all live births recorded in Massachusetts.

an infant of low birth weight were unmarried black women who received no medical care, were younger than 15, were delivering their first child and were in the lowest socioeconomic category of the study. Just under 30 percent of infants born to mothers in this group are expected to weigh less than 2500 grams.

Increased mortality risk is only one of the dangers facing infants of low birth weight. Prematurity has also been linked to such conditions as epilepsy, cerebral palsy and mental retardation, and to higher risks of deafness and blindness.[42] In addition, studies of developing infants tested over a period of years for intelligence, motor development and similar traits showed improved scores as birth weight increased.[43]

# Other Problems

Various studies are not conclusive about the relationship of age of the mother to the intelligence of the child as well as to physical and mental handicaps. Benjamin Pasamanick and Abraham Lilienfeld found the risk of mental retardation was high for children of mothers younger than 20, and Raymond Illsley and others found that IQ increased with maternal age.[44] But, in another study, at each age the scores decreased with parity of the mother; this led one team of investigators to conclude that the difference in intelligence is due to the difference between families rather than within a family as the mother ages.[45] In considering the two high-risk groups of mothers—mothers younger than 20 and those older than 35—another study linked increased risks of congenital defects—such as intracranial or spinal injury, breathing difficulties and clubfoot—for first births to the young mothers. In addition, this study noted an increased risk of epilepsy for the first two parities among mothers younger than 20 years of age.[46]

Thus, whether because of biologic or environmental factors that affect the infant directly or indirectly through prematurity, the infant born to a teenage mother has a much higher risk than infants of somewhat older mothers of suffering specific severe handicaps.

## Maternal Mortality

Maternal mortality rates have undergone radical and rapid declines over the last 30 years. In 1940, the rate was 376 per 100,000 live births; in 1968 it was 25. For whites, the rate dropped from 320 to 17 and for nonwhites from 774 to 64.[47] Although a large and rapid decline has occurred, nonwhite maternal mortality is nearly four times that of whites. Rates are lowest for women younger than 30 but increase rather sharply thereafter. Color differences in mortality increase steadily with maternal age.[48] Mortality among nonwhites is lowest (40.9 per 100,000 births for women under 20 years of age, while for whites the rate for women aged 20–24 is slightly lower (11.0) than that of younger women (15.1). For women younger than 20 years, the color difference in maternal mortality is to a large extent due to differences in the death rates from three causes: toxemia (excluding abortion—12.6 for nonwhites vs. 3.4 for whites), abortion with sepsis (7.8 vs. 1.8) and ectopic pregnancy (2.4 vs. 0.7). The rates for toxemia and for abortion with sepsis are approximately 50 per cent higher for teenagers than for women 20–24 in each color group.

## Complications of Pregnancy

The complications of pregnancy most frequently mentioned for young mothers are toxemia, prolonged labor and iron-deficiency anemia. Poor diets, late or inadequate prenatal care, and emotional and physical immaturity may well be contributing factors. Biologic immaturity appears to be a problem while the mother is still growing.[49] However, the now voluminous literature on the pregnant teenager overwhelmingly points toward social rather than medical problems as the primary concern.[50]

This rather uniformly negative review ends with a single favorable relationship involving teenage pregnancies. A cooperative study carried out in the United States, Greece, Wales, Yugoslavia, Brazil, Taiwan and Japan estimated that "women having their first child when aged under 18 years have only about one-third the breast cancer risk of those whose first birth is delayed until the age of 35 years or more."[51]

## Social Aspects

An immediate consequence for pregnant adolescents is the often permanent disruption of schooling. One-third of 154 school systems with 12,000 or more students queried in 1968 by the Educational Research Service required girls to leave school as soon as it was known that they were pregnant.[52] An additional one-fifth forced them to leave well before the end of pregnancy. In 1970, a survey of 17,000 school systems found that scarcely one-third made any provisions for the education of pregnant school girls.[53] In Buffalo, of 123 girls excluded from school in 1963–1964 because of pregnancy, "101 wished to return to school and of these, 67 could not do so because of difficulties in making arrangements for care of their infants."[54]

Mothers who deliver babies out of wedlock represent a large segment of teenage mothers. Cutright estimated that, in 1966, 64 per cent of white infants and 6.4 per cent of nonwhite infants born out of wedlock were adopted. He also speculated that few, probably less than 10 per cent, were legitimized by later marriage.[55] The problems of illegitimacy are beyond the scope of this article. Clearly, however, many teenage mothers must encounter them.

Meanwhile, the outlook for the premaritally pregnant is not auspicious. They represent a large proportion of teenage brides; estimates range from at least 25 per cent of brides younger than 20 to more than half of 15–17-year-old brides.[56] A long-term study of a sample of white couples who had a first, second or fourth baby in Detroit in 1961 has described subsequent economic, social and demographic variables among the families.[57] The premaritally pregnant, who composed approximately one-fifth of the sample, were found in 1961, and still in 1965, to be economically disadvantaged in terms of occupation, income and assets when compared to other couples. This was not accounted for by shorter marital duration or younger age at marriage.[58] Neither was it accounted for by status of the parental families. In addition, the marital dissolution rate was higher for the premaritally pregnant (9.4 per cent) than for other couples in the study (3.3 per cent). This and other studies have shown that, in general, the divorce rates for teenage marriages are very high.[59] Furthermore, women who marry or have their first child very early in life tend to add children rapidly. For example, a 1965 study of child-spacing compares cumulative births by successive intervals since first marriage for women younger than 22 at marriage and for those who married at older ages.[60] Among women married between 1960 and 1964, the average number of children four years after marriage was 1.51 for the younger women as compared to 1.24 for women at least 22 years old at marriage. Similar findings come from the 1960 Census for narrower marital age categories.[61]

The only study found that examined the fertility experience of teenagers, irrespective of marital status, was carried out by J. Philip Keeve and his coworkers in a Middle Atlantic metropolitan county recently.[62] All birth certificates of infants born to mothers aged 12–19 and delivering between January 1, 1958, and December 31, 1967, were scrutinized. Successive births to the same mother were located and cohort fertility tables according to age at first birth constructed. For both color groups, the birthrates were higher in the inner city than in the surrounding county. Actual parity was underestimated since later births to girls who either married, left the area or delivered elsewhere could not be located by a study of this type. The data suggest that these girls were well on their way to having large and closely spaced families. Joe Wray examined exactly this situation, finding evidence that large family size is lined with decreased growth and intelligence as well as increased child mortality among the children, further evidence of problems linked to teenage childbearing.[63]

## The Individual and Society

Two interrelated problems are clearly delineated here. First, infants of young mothers, especially very young ones, are subject to higher risks of prematurity, mortality and serious physical or intellectual impairments than children of older mothers. For mothers younger than age 18—and especially for those younger than 15—biological as well as social influences appear to be important. For the teenager 18 and older the social aspects appear to affect pregnancy outcome most critically. Second, mothers and, perhaps, fathers and children are more likely to be disadvantaged in the socioeconomic sense and to find themselves in unstable family situations than those in families who postpone childbearing at least until the mother is in her early twenties. There is also an increased likelihood of high fertility. Demographic analyses indicate that, at any given time, the number of children a woman has borne is inversely related to her education and to other socioeconomic variables.[64] The evidence presented here supports the speculation that the clustering of highly fertile women in these groups may, at least partially, result from early childbearing.

The sequelae of early childbearing must concern anyone interested in the welfare of individuals. For society as a whole, the number of infants who have been born under circumstances deleterious to their development is a source of concern. These considerations of the welfare of individual human beings, and secondarily of society, surely overwhelm the question of population size. However, we should note that:

○ If, at the 1968 level of population and age-specific birth and death rates, no births occurred to teenagers younger than 18, and if this reduced the birthrate among 15–19-year-olds by 30 per cent, the population in 50 years would be five per cent smaller than it would be if the teenage birthrates remained constant.

○ If all births to teenage mothers were postponed, 75 per cent until ages 20–24, and the remainder until 25–29, the population would be 6.6 per cent smaller.

○ If all teenage births were eliminated, the result would be a population 15.1 per cent smaller than the size projected with unchanged rates. The net reproduction rate would be reduced from 1.16 to just over the stationary population value of 1.00.[65]

It seems reasonable to speculate that if postponing a first birth also reduces the rapidity with which successive ones occur, birthrates at older ages might also be reduced by postponing a large proportion of teenage births.

Any action with respect to preventing the sequelae of teenage childbearing must start from the belief that these are not inevitable consequences, totally dependent upon innate differences between women who have children while they are young, and the infants of these women, and women who postpone this activity, and their infants. The necessary assumption is that once a pregnancy occurs, the probabilities of prematurity, infant mortality and the social consequences can be altered, or that postponement of childbearing will itself alter these probabilities.

Age, in itself, may not be a direct causative factor in many of the problems associated with teenage pregnancy after a girl has reached full physical maturity at about age 18. Even if childbearing is postponed beyond age 20, unless social and economic conditions change for these young people they may encounter the same difficulties at a later age. However, postponement of parenthood may increase the chances that these changes will occur.

## REFERENCE NOTES

1. U.S. Department of Health, Education and Welfare (DHEW), *Vital Statistics of the United States, 1968, Vol. I–Natality*, U.S. Government Printing Office, Washington, D.C. (GPO), 1970, Tables 1–49 and 1–51

2. Ibid., Tables 1–26 and 1–51.

3. Ibid.; DHEW, *Vital Statistics of the United States, 1961, Vol. I–Natality*, GPO, 1963, Tables 2–9 and 2–12.

4. DHEW, 1970, op. cit., Table 1–25.

5. N. B. Ryder, "Nuptiality as a Variable in the Demographic Transition," paper presented at annual meeting of the American Sociological Association, 1960; H. B. Presser, "The Timing of the First Birth, Female Roles and Black Fertility," *Milbank Memorial Fund Quarterly*, 49:329, 1971; E. Pohlman, "The Timing of First Births: A Review of Effects," *Eugenics Quarterly*, 15:252, 1968.

6. Derived from unpublished data from the National Center for Health Statistics (NCHS), National Natality Survey, 1964–1966.

7. DEHEW, 1970, op. cit., Table 1–26.

8. A. Campbell, "The Role of Family Planning in the Reduction of Poverty," *Journal of Marriage and the Family*, 30:236, 1968.

9. DHEW, 1970, op. cit., Table 1–*136*.
10. U.S. Bureau of the Census, "Fertility Indicators: 1970," *Current Population Reports,* Series P-23, No. 36, GPO, 1971, Table 11, p. 23; For complete discussion of illegitimacy, see: P. Cutright and O. Galle, "Illegitimacy: Measurement and Analysis," Vanderbilt University, Nashville, Tenn., 1966 (mimeo).
11. DHEW, 1970, op. cit., Table 1–26.
12. NCHS, 1964–1966, op. cit.
13. W. Pratt, "A Study of Marriages Inolving Premarital Pregnancies," doctoral dissertation, University of Michigan, Ann Arbor, Mich., 1965.
14. E. Siegel and N. Morris, "The Epidemiology of Human Reproductive Casualties, with Emphasis on the Role of Nutrition," in Committee on Maternal Nutrition, Food and Nutrition Board, ed., *Maternal Nutrition and the Course of Pregnancy,* National Research Council of the National Academy of Sciences, Washington, D.C., 1970, p. 5.
15. Cf., e.g., Report of the Working Group, "Relation of Nutrition to Pregnancy in Adolescence," Committee on Maternal Nutrition, Food and Nutrition Board, 1970, op. cit., p. 163; J. A. Heady, C. Daley and J. N. Morris, "Social and Biological Factors in Infant Mortality, II. Variations of Mortality with Mother's Age and Parity," *Lancet,* 1:395, 1955.
16. Report of the Working Group, ibid.
17. H. Chase, "Infant Mortality and Weight at Birth: 1960 United States Birth Cohort," *American Journal of Public Health,* 59:59:1618, 1969.
18. S. Shapiro, E. Schlesinger and R. E. L. Nesbitt, Jr., *Infant, Perinatal, Maternal and Childhood Mortality in the United States,* Harvard University Press, Cambridge, Mass., 1968, p. 10.
19. Ibid., p. 23.
20. NCHS, "Infant Mortality Rates by Legitimacy Status: United States, 1964–1966," *Monthly Vital Statistics Report,* Vol. 20, No. 5, 1971.
21. J. A. Heady and J. N. Morris, "Social and Biological Factors in Infant Mortality. Variation of Mortality with Mother's Age and Parity," *Journal of Obstetrics and Gynaecology of the British Empire,* 66:577, 1959.
22. DHEW, *Vital Statistics of the United States, 1968, Vol. II—Mortality,* GPO, 1970, Part A, Table 3–4.
23. J. Loeb, *Weight at Birth and Survivial of the Newborn, by Age of Mother and Total Birth Order, United States, Early 1950,* NCHS, Series 21, No. 5, 1965.
24. J. A. Heady and J. N. Morris, 1959, op. cit.; S. L. Morrison, J. A. Heady and J. N. Morris, "Social and Biological Factors in Infant Mortality, VIII. Mortality in the Postneonatal Period," *Archives of the Diseases of Children,* 34:101, 1959.
25. S. L. Morrison, J. A. Heady and J. N. Morris, ibid.
26. Ibid.
27. S. Shapiro, E. Schlesinger and R. E. L. Nesbitt, Jr., 1968, op. cit., p. 66; H. Chase, "The Relationship of Certain Biologic and Socio-Economic Factors to Fetal, Infant and Early Childhood Mortality. II. Father's Occupation, Infant's Birth Weight and Mother's Age," New York State Department of Health, Albany, N.Y., 1962 (mimeo.).
28. D. Baird and A. M. Thompson, "General Factors Underlying Perinatal Mortality Rates," in N. Butler and E. Alberman, eds., *Perinatal Problems,* E. & S. Livingstone, London, 1969, Table 29, p. 27.
29. J. F. Donnelly, J. R. Abernathy, R. N. Creadick, C. E. Flowers, B. G. Greenberg and H. B. Wells, "Fetal, Parental, and Environmental Factors Associated with Perinatal Mortality in Mothers under 20 Years of Age," *American Journal of Obstetrics and Gynecology,* 80:663, 1960.
30. U.S. Bureau of the Census, "Childspacing," *U. S. Census of Population: 1960, Subject Reports,* Final Report PC(2)-3B, GPO, 1968, and "Marriage, Fertility and Childspacing, June, 1965," *Current Population Reports,* Series P–20 No. 186 GPO, 1969.

31. L. Bumpass, "Age at Marriage as a Variable in Socio-economic Differentials in Fertility," *Demography,* 6:45, 1969.
32. J. Wray, "Population Pressure on Families: Family Size and Childspacing," in Study Committee of the Office of the Foreign Secretary of the National Academy of Sciences, ed., *Rapid Population Growth,* Johns Hopkins Press, Baltimore, Md., 1971, p. 403.
33. S. Shapiro, E. Schlesinger and R. E. L. Nesbitt, Jr., 1968, op. cit., p. 47.
34. Ibid.
35. H. Chase, "Trends in 'Prematurity': United States, 1950–1967," *American Journal of Public Health,* 60:1967, 1970.
36. J. Loeb, 1965, op. cit.; H. Chase, "Infant Mortality and Weight at Birth . . . ," 1969, op. cit.
37. H. Chase, ibid., p. 1620.
38. J. Loeb, 1965, op. cit.
39. H. Chase, *International Comparisons of Perinatal and Infant Mortality. The United States and Six West European Countries,* NCHS, Series 3, No. 6, 1967, p. 28.
40. M. Kovar, *Variations in Birth Weight, Legitimate Live Births, United States, 1963.* NCHS, Series 22, No. 8, 1968.
41. G. Wiener and T. Milton, "Demographic Correlates of Low Birth Weight," *American Journal of Epidemiology,* 91:260, 1970.
42. A. Lilienfeld and B. Pasamanick, "Association of Maternal and Fetal Factors with the Development of Epilepsy. I. Abnormalities in the Prenatal and Paranatal Periods," *Journal of the American Medical Association,* 155:719, 1954; A. Lilienfeld and E. Parkhurst, "A Study of the Association of Factors of Pregnancy and Parturition with the Development of Cerebral Palsy: Preliminary Report," *American Journal of Hygiene,* 53:262, 1951; B. Pasamanick and A. Lilienfeld,"Association of Maternal and Fetal Factors with the Development of Mental Deficiency. I. Abnormalities in the Prenatal and Paranatal Periods," *Journal of the American Medical Association,* 159:155, 1955; M. Vernon, "Prematurity and Deafness: The Magnitude and Nature of the Problem among Deaf Children," *Exceptional Children,* 33:289, 1967; I. D. Goldberg, H. Goldstein, D. Quade and E. Rogot, "Association of Perinatal Factors with Blindness in Children," *Public Health Reports,* 82:519, 1967.
43. G. Wiener, "The Relationship of Birth Weight and Length of Gestation to Intellectual Development at Ages 8 to 10 Years, *Journal of Pediatrics,* 76:694, 1970; L. C. Eaves, J. C. Nuttall, H. Klonoff and H. G. Dunn, "Developmental and Psychological Test Scores in Children of Low Birth Weight," *Pediatrics,* 45:9, 1970; C. M. Drillien, "School Disposal and Performance for Children of Different Birthweight Born 1953–1960," *Archives of Diseases of Childhood,* 44:562, 1969; G. Wiener, R. Rider, W. Oppel, L. Fischer and P. Harper, "Correlates of Low Birth Weight: Psychological Status at Six to Seven Years of Age," *Pediatrics,* 35:434, 1965; S. H. Clifford, "High Risk Pregnancy I. Prevention of Prematurity the *Sine Qua Non* for Reduction of Mental Retardation and Other Neurological Disorders," *New England Journal of Medicine,* 271:243, 1964.
44. B. Pasamanick and L. Lilienfeld, "The Association of Maternal and Fetal Factors with the Development of Mental Deficiency: II. Relationship to Maternal Age, Birth Order, Previous Reproductive Loss and Degree of Deficiency," *American Journal of Mental Deficiency,* 60:557, 1956; R. Illsley, "The Sociological Study of Reproduction and Its Outcome," in S. A. Richardson and A. F. Guttmacher, eds., *Childbearing: Its Social and Psychological Factors,* Williams and Wilkins, Baltimore, Md., 1967.
45. R. G. Record, T. McKeown and J. H. Edwards, "The Relation of Measured Intelligence to Birth Order and Maternal Age," and "The Relation of Measured Intelligence to Birth Weight and Duration of Gestation," *Annals of Human Genetics,* 33:61 and 71, 1969.
46. H. B. Newcombe and O. G. Tarendale, "Maternal Age and Birth Order Correlations," *Mutation Research,* I:446, 1964.

47. U. S. Bureau of the Census, *Statistical Abstract of the United States, 1971*, GPO, 1971, Table 73, p. 55.
48. DHEW, *Vital Statistics of the United States, 1967, Vol. II—Mortality,* 1969, op. cit., Part A, Table 1–15.
49. Report of the Working Group, 1970, op. cit.; O. Stine and E. Kelley, "Evaluation of a School for Young Mothers: The Frequency of Prematurity among Infants Born to Mothers under 17 Years of Age, According to the Mother's Attendance of a Special School During Pregnancy," *Pediatrics,* 46:581, 1970.
50. For additional references see: National Library of Medicine Literature Search of Index Medicus, "The Pregnant Adolescent: Medical, Psychological and Social Care, January, 1967 through April, 1970."
51. B. MacMahon, P. Cole, T. N. Lin, C. R. Lowe, A. P. Mirra, B. Ravnihar, E. J. Salber, V. G. Valoaras and S. Yuasa, "Age at First Birth and Breast Cancer Risk," *Bulletin of the World Health Organization,* 43:209, 1970.
52. "Pregnant Teenagers," *Today's Education,* Vol. 59, 1970.
53. Ibid.
54. U. Anderson, R. Jenss, W. Mosher and V. Richter, "The Medical, Social and Educational Implications of the Increase in Out-of-Wedlock Births," *American Journal of Public Health,* 56:1866, 1966.
55. P. Cutright and O. Galle, 1966, op. cit.
56. U. S. Bureau of the Census, "Childspacing," 1968, op. cit., and "Marriage, Fertility and Childspacing, June, 1965," 1969, op. cit.; W. Pratt, 1965, op. cit.; P. Cutright and O. Galle, ibid.
57. R. Freedman and L. Coombs, "Childspacing and Family Economic Position," *American Sociological Review,* 31:631, 1966.
58. L. Coombs, R. Freedman, J. Friedman and W. Pratt, "Premarital Pregnancy and Status Before and After Marriage," *American Journal of Sociology,* 75:800, 1970; L. Coombs and R. Freedman, "Pre-marital Pregnancy, Childspacing, and Later Economic Achievement," *Population Studies,* 24:389, 1970.
59. L. Coombs and Z. Zumeta, "Correlates of Marital Dissolution in a Prospective Fertility Study: A Research Note," *Social Problems,* 18:92, 1970.
60. U. S. Bureau of the Census, "Marriage, Fertility and Childspacing . . . ," 1969, op. cit.
61. U. S. Bureau of the Census, "Childspacing," 1968, op. cit.
62. J. P. Keeve, E. Schlesinger, B. Wight and R. Adams, "Fertility Experience of Juvenile Girls: A Community-Wide Ten-Year Study," *American Journal of Public Health,* 59/2185, 1969.
63. J. Wray, 1971, op. cit.
64. U. S. Bureau of the Census, "Fertility Indicators: 1970," 1971, op. cit.
65. The projection program appears in E. van de Walle and J. Knodel, "Teaching Population Dynamics with a Simulation Exercise," *Demography,* 7:433, 1970.

# Drug Use During and After High School: Results of a National Longitudinal Study*

*Lloyd D. Johnston*

## Introduction

. . . THE PRESENT STUDY was focused on the incidence and distribution of drug use in a national sample of males in a particular age cohort—the high school class of 1969. Because it was drawn from that population when they were at the beginning of tenth grade (in the fall of 1966), it included both young men who completed high school and those who dropped out. Further, while it included young men who went on to college in the year after high school—a population in which drug use has frequently been studied—it also included a substantial number who went on to civilian employment, military service, and trade school. These latter groups generally have not been the subjects of systematic research. [Ed.: references 1–10.]

Two traditionally legal drugs (alcohol and cigarettes) were considered, along with five illicit drugs (marijuana, hallucinogens, amphetamines, barbiturates, and heroin). The frequency with which each of these drugs had been used during the high school years, as well as in the year following graduation, was one major focus of concern. A second was to determine the relationships between the use of each drug and use of any of the others. Still a third focus of the study was to explore the attitudes of contemporary youth toward drug use generally; and finally—and perhaps most importantly—to identify characteristics of young people or their major social environments which seemed to be associated with drug use, either as potential causes or consequences of use. . . .

## Sample

The initial sample was comprised of approximately 2,200 tenth-grade boys located in some 87 public high schools across the United States. They were sampled, using a stratified random sampling procedure, to be representative of all young men beginning public high school in the continental United States in the fall of 1966, a group which would eventually constitute the high

* From *American Journal of Public Health Supplement*, 1974, vol. 64, 29–37. Reprinted with permission of the American Public Health Association and the author.

school class of 1969 and many of whom would comprise the college class of 1973.

## Field Procedures

The initial data collection, which lasted nearly four hours, was conducted in the schools and included a personal interview, a group-administered paper and pencil questionnaire, and a series of ability tests. A very broad range of variables was covered, including background characteristics, affective states, behaviors, plans, and attitudes, values, and cognitive abilities.[11,13] Many of these variables were then remeasured on subsequent occasions to permit the assessment of change.

Nearly 97 per cent of the sampled subjects agreed to participate in the first data collection and provided a full set of completed instruments. This very high response rate provided a valuable set of initial data against which to calibrate the nature of eventual attrition from the longitudinal panel.

Since the initial survey, three follow-up studies have been conducted—all at locations outside, but in the vicinity of, the schools. Professional interviewers handled the administration on all occasions, and subjects were paid for participation in the three follow-up surveys: $2 for the first, $5 for the second, and $10 for the third.

## Retention Rates and Representativeness

By the time of the fourth data collection in 1970—a point three and one-half years beyond the initial data collection—73 per cent of the original sample (over 1,600 participants) had remained in the study continuously—a very high retention rate for such undertakings. . . .

## The Drug Instrument

Much of the data discussed here was derived from all four administrations; however, the questions specifically dealing with drugs—related attitudes, availability, etc.—were included only in the fourth and most recent survey. It took place in the spring of 1970—a point corresponding to one year after high school graduation for the great majority—after the investigators decided that the drug phenomenon merited some focused consideration in the study.

On that occasion, a small section of instrumentation on drugs was added to a "Confidential Information Questionnaire" which had been administered during the first three data collections and which had asked about the respondent's involvement in delinquent behavior. Each youth was handed the questionnaire by the interviewer and told to seal it in an attached envelope himself upon completion. He was also told that the interviewer would enclose the sealed envelope in a larger mailing envelope, containing the rest of his instruments, and mail the entire packet directly to Ann Arbor, Michigan shortly after completion of the session.

The key questions concerning drugs were grouped into four sets, each of which had a common stem. The initial set concerned friends' usage, and asked "How many of your friends would you estimate: 'smoke cigarettes'; 'smoke marijuana (pot, grass) or hashish'; 'take amphetamines (pep pills, bennies, speed, uppers)'; 'take barbituates (yellow jackets, red devils, downers)'; 'take heroin (smack, horse, H)'; 'take hallucinogens (LSD, Mescaline, Peyote, etc.)'; 'drink alcoholic beverages (liquor, beer, wine)'?" For each activity the respondent chose one of five answers, ranging from "all" to "none", to describe the proportion of his friends who used the drug.

The next two sets of questions asked about personal involvement in each of the same seven drug activities. The stem to the first set read "How often have you done this during part or all of the last year for other than medical reasons?" and the same seven drug activities were then listed. For each, the respondent chose from six answer alternatives: nearly every day, once or twice a week, once or twice a month, three to ten times a year, once or twice a year, and never. The time period covered by the question corresponded to the year after high school graduation, i.e. spring 1969 to spring 1970. The third set of questions was identical to the second except that it asked about the time period prior to graduation: "Previous to this past year (that is, before last summer) how often had you done this for other than medical reasons?" Although this is a retrospective question, which would normally make it suspect because of the questionable recall of respondents, accurate recall on these activities should have been enhanced immensely by the clear social and psychological significance of the activities being investigated as well as by the demarcation of the time period by a major event—high school graduation.

The fourth set of questions concerned attitudes toward drug use: "People differ on how they feel about individuals doing certain things. How do you feel about people your age doing each of the following things?" Again, the same seven drug activities were listed, but this time with different frequencies of use included in the question. For example, there were three marijuana activities which were rated separately: trying marijuana once or twice, smoking marijuana occasionally, and smoking marijuana regularly. Respondents could indicate that they strongly approved, approved, felt neutral, disapproved, or strongly disapproved of each activity. Those with no opinion because they lacked familiarity with the drug could check a sixth box. . . .

# Results

Quite a number of unexpected findings emerged from these explorations—particularly some having to do with the common assumptions about the causes and effects of drug use—but the first concerned the sheer prevalence of drug use in high schools during the period in question.

# Drug Use During High School

It was found that incidence of illicit drug use up to the point of normal high school graduation was considerably less than reports in the media and selected studies had led us to expect. Less than one-quarter of these males (22.5 per cent) reported having made *any* use of *any* of these illicit drugs before leaving high school in 1969; and nearly half of those used nothing more serious than marijuana (10.2 per cent of the sample). Of the 12.3 per cent of the sample using more serious illicit drugs one-third did so on an experimental basis only. Table 1 gives self-reported usage rates for the period prior to graduation and for the year following.

Marijuana was by far the most widely used such drug, with roughly one in five having smoked either it or its derivative, hashish. One out of every ten had tried amphetamines; one out of every fifteen hallucinogens; one out of sixteen barbiturates; and one out of sixty had at least *tried* heroin. However, roughly one-third of those using each drug could be classified as experimental users, since their usage was no higher than once or twice in a year.

If one considers weekly intake to constitute regular use of any of the illicit drugs, we can say that none of those drugs had been used on a regular basis by more than 2 per cent of the sample, with the single exception of marijuana. About 6 per cent reported smoking marijuana regularly at some time

Table 1
*Self-reported Usage Rates during the High School Years and the Year Following*

| Drug | During high school years | | Year after high school | |
|---|---|---|---|---|
| | Any use | Weekly use | Any use | Weekly use |
| Marijuana or Hashish | 21% | 6% | 34% | 10% |
| Hallucinogens | 7% | 1% | 11% | 1% |
| Amphetamines | 10% | 2% | 14% | 2% |
| Barbiturates | 6% | 1% | 9% | 1% |
| Heroin | 2% | 1% | 2% | 1% |
| Alcoholic Beverages | 81% | 33% | 89% | 44% |
| Cigarettes | 66% | 36% * | 68% | 41% * |

* The figures on cigarette use refer to daily rather than weekly use.

during high school, but less than 2 per cent had ever used it on a daily basis. . .

## Alcohol and Cigarettes

Turning to the two traditionally acceptable drugs, alcohol and cigarettes, our findings show that they clearly have remained the favorite of this younger generation. Roughly one-third had used alcoholic beverages on a weekly basis (or more often) during the high school years and a little over one-third had smoked cigarettes daily. The exceptional situation clearly was for a student not to have used cigarettes and alcoholic beverages at some time prior to leaving high school.

## Drug Use After High School

The number of users of all drugs jumped substantially in the year following graduation, though the increases did not represent very sizable proportions of the total population. Over one-third (36 per cent) reported using some illicit drug at least once during the year after high school. The largest increases in terms of a per cent of the sample reporting use of a drug were found for marijuana—up from 21 per cent during high school to 34 per cent afterward—and the regular use of alcohol—up from 22 per cent during high school to 33 per cent reporting regular use afterward. A more detailed exploration of changes in the rate of drug use in the year after high school revealed that most people who changed their rate of use did so in an upward direction, either starting or increasing use of a drug; but that the great majority of young men maintained the same rate of use or, for the most part, non-use.

## Higher Usage In Military Service

The greatest increase in the use of the more serious illicit drugs—specifically hallucinogens, amphetamines, and barbiturates—occurred in that sub-sample which went on to domestic military service in that year.* During the high school years, that group had a very similar profile of drug use to the one found for those who would enter civilian employment. However, the military group showed one of the highest rates of conversion while the civilian employed group showed one of the lowest, making their profiles on both legal and illegal drug use quite different by the year after high school. Had the military sample included those stationed overseas, a number of whom were in

---

* Drug use data were not gathered from the 48 respondents in military service who were stationed overseas.

Vietnam, the contrast almost certainly would have been more dramatic. A differential degree of drug availability may have had a lot to do with the high rate of increase observed in the military group. As will be discussed later, more servicemen perceived marijuana and heroin to be readily available than did the occupants of any other sector.

# Limited Use on Campus

Perhaps one of the more surprising findings concerned the prevalence of drug use on campus versus other sectors of the society. Certainly the popular conception has been that colleges and universities contain a disproportionate concentration of the illicit drug activity in the nation, particularly marijuana and hallucinogen use. However, our data tend to directly refute that conception, at least for individuals of freshman age. In the year after high school, the college sample showed 37 per cent using some illegal drug at least once during the year, a virtually identical rate to that for the entire sample, 36 per cent. About 35 per cent of those in college used marijuana and 10 per cent used some hallucinogen, versus 34 per cent and 11 per cent respectively for the whole sample—again, virtually identical rates. The college group used amphetamines, barbiturates, and heroin at somewhat lower rates than did their non-college peers (usage rates were 11 per cent, 7 per cent and 1 per cent respectively for college freshmen), indicating that at least for those of freshman age, overall illicit drug use was slightly less intense on the campuses than it was in the other sectors of the society taken together. Further, the regular use of alcohol and cigarettes was substantially lower on campus.

One must hasten to add, however, that this near parity in marijuana and hallucinogen use may not hold true in the later college years. We find that the group of young men who went into college in the year after high school showed a relatively high rate of increase in illegal drug use—particularly when compared to the group entering civilian employment. However, because the college-bound had substantially lower than average rates of drug use during high school, their high rate of increase only resulted in their "catching up" with their peers in the use of marijuana and hallucinogens in the year after. If the college group continues to show a higher than average rate of increase in succeeding years, they could attain a usage rate which would justify popularly held conceptions. We hope to resolve the question definitively by means of a follow-up study in the spring of 1974, a point corresponding to five years past high school graduation . . .

## *Attitudes About Drug Use: A Basic Conservatism*

The attitudes found among this broad sample from "the younger generation" in 1970 did, in fact, show that personal disapproval of illicit drug use was quite widespread. The great majority disapproved of using any of the illegal drugs other than marijuana, even on an experimental basis. In fact, over 55 per cent of the sample said they strongly disapproved of even experimental use of each. Only 1.5 per cent explicitly approved of experimenting with heroin. How much these attitudes may have shifted in the intervening period, either among this cohort, or from this cohort to the current cohort of 19-year-olds, is not clear. In the case of these respondents the question will be answered by the fourth follow-up survey, mentioned previously. . . .

## The Effects of Drug Use

Three commonly stated hypotheses about the effects of drug use were tested in the current study, i.e., that those young people who became involved with drugs tend to (1) become less involved in the social life of the school, (2) suffer in terms of their academic performance in school, and (3) become more involved in delinquent behavior.

# Drugs and the Marginally Involved

An analysis of levels of extra-curricular participation in the senior year of high school, as reported by the respondents, suggests that there is rather little relationship between illegal drug use and degree of participation in the non-academic life in the school. Those participating in less than three extra-curricular activities in their senior year used illegal drugs slightly more frequently than those participating in three or more, but the differences were not large. Further, they were explainable in terms of related background characteristics, leaving little evidence that non-addictive drug use is particularly associated with or caused by marginal involvement in the social life of the school.

# Effects on Grades

Since the respondents had reported their grade point averages at three different points in time, it was possible to explore the relationship between illegal drug use and academic performance to determine whether, as many contend, the use of drugs does seem to cause a lowering of grades. The answer seems to emerge rather clearly—drug use (short of addiction) does not seem to cause a deterioration in academic performance. What we find is that young people who use drugs during high school do have slightly lower self-reported grades on the average, but that these differences existed as far back as ninth grade, a time prior to the start of drug use for the vast majority. (Those who tried something more serious than marijuana had lower grades than those who went no further than marijuana, though none of the average differences are very large, since all groups had grade averages between C + and B −.) However, there does not seem to be any serious decrement over time in the grades of the "user groups." It seems either that their poorer academic performance had something to do with their becoming involved with drugs in the first place, or that some prior third factors were the cause of both the low grades and the drug use.

# Drugs and Delinquency

A comprehensive index of self-reported delinquency during twelfth grade showed a strong positive relationship to the use of all seven drugs during high school, both illicit and licit drugs. Three groups were defined for comparison purposes: (1) those who had used no illicit drugs during high school; (2) those who had used marijuana only; and (3) those who had used some other illicit drug. Users of marijuana only were found to be more delinquent than the non-user group by about six-tenths of a standard deviation. The group comprised of users of any of the more serious illicit drugs were more delinquent than the non-user group by about one full standard deviation in twelfth grade. These findings are certainly consistent with popularly held conceptions, and not really surprising since we have simply shown one class of illegal behavior (drug use) to be positively related to other classes of illegal behavior. (The relationship between delinquency and the use of the two legal drugs may have been less intuitively obvious.)

The more important finding, however, relates to likely cause and effect relationships involved. The basic question is, of course, whether drug use leads to crime, as many Americans believe.* Naturally, the present findings are relevant primarily to the non-addict population of drug users—the great majority. For that group we find that, although the user populations are substantially more delinquent than the non-user populations by the end of high school, the differences between them in delinquency were about as large as early as ninth grade, a point prior to the beginning of drug use for the vast majority. Thus, it appears that the more delinquent are substantially more likely to become users, but the users do not appear to increase their levels of delinquency. Whether delinquency plays an important role in getting certain young people involved with drugs in the first place, or whether delinquency and drug use are both the result of other factors remains to be determined. However, based on these data, we can state with fair confidence that becoming involved with marijuana—or the other illegal drugs, short of actual addic-

---

* Geiger, L. H. (1971) reported that 82 percent of the respondents polled in a nationwide telephone survey, conducted in August, 1970, agreed that "using marijuana leads people to commit crimes of violence." His report was delivered at the 26th Annual Conference of the American Association for Public Opinion Research.

tion—does not lead to noticeable increases in criminal behavior during the high school years. . . .

## Summary and Conclusion

Our findings indicate that the amount of non-addictive illegal drug use has been much less for American young people than reports in the media had suggested during the period in question, and that the relationships between non-addictive drug use and delinquency (as well as between drug use and academic performance) is far less serious than commonly has been assumed by the public. Clearly there has been an important generational change in this area, with an increasing proportion of American youth being interested in, and tolerant of, the use of psychoactive drugs. However, as of mid-1970 the vast majority of the age group studied were still cautious about illegal drugs and not deeply involved in them; and many of those who were involved made important distinctions between the different drugs and the different degrees of usage.* In fact, from the perspective of health and public safety one of the most important findings about levels of drug use may be the degree to which American young people are continuing to adhere to certain traditional practices—namely, the consumption of alcohol and cigarettes on a major scale.

Even though the best available evidence suggests that absolute levels of illicit drug use may be quite a big higher now than was observed for the high school class of 1969, we would expect that most of the relationships observed in this study could be extrapolated to more recent cohorts of high school and college students. Among those relationships are the two just cited; i.e. between drug use and delinquency, and between drug use and academic performance. Still a third is the relationship of certain drugs to membership in the counter-culture. A developmental trend, which we also would expect to hold up in the present, is the substantial increase in the use of both licit and illicit drugs which occurs in the year following high school graduation, particularly in the sectors which are most age-segregated—such as military service and college. Finally, note should be made again of the intriguing finding that there exists a general orientation toward psychoactive substances—both licit and illicit—which can explain some of the variance in all of the drug attitude and drug behavior variables included here, and which causes them all to be positively associated to some degree. Discovering the

* Early results from a follow-up study in 1974 suggest that, while the incidence of drug use had increased substantially in this cohort by the time they reached age 23, the ability of the majority to respond discriminately to the different drugs and to different level of usage remained essentially intact. Prevailing attitudes have changed rather little, with the exception that marijuana and alcohol use are now tolerated by a somewhat larger proportion of the cohort than was true four years earlier.

256 Readings in Human Growth and Development

causes of this general orientation, which has been replicated in a number of other studies, remains a serious challenge to researchers in the field.

REFERENCE NOTES [ED.: FROM THE ORIGINAL ARTICLE.]

1. Josephson, E., Haberman, P., Zanes, A., and Elinson, J. Adolescent Marijuana Use: Report on a National Survey. In S. Einstein and S. Allen, eds., *Proceedings of the First International Conference on Student Drug Surveys.* Farmingdale, N.Y.: Baywood Publishing Co., 1971.
2. National Commission on Marijuana and Drug Abuse. *Marijuana: A Signal of Misunderstanding.* New York: Signet, 1972.
3. National Commission on Marijuana and Drug Abuse. *Drug Use in America: Problem in Perspective, Second Report of the National Commission on Marijuana and Drug Abuse.* Washington, D.C.: U.S. Govt. Printing Office, 1973.
4. Gallup Opinion Index, Report No. 68 (Results of a Survey of College Students). Princeton, N.J.: Gallup International, February, 1971.
5. Gallup Opinion Index, Report No. 80 (Current Views of College Students on Politics and Drugs). Princeton, N.J.: Gallup International, February, 1972.
6. *Playboy,* September, 1970, pp. 182–184.
7. *Playboy,* September, 1971, pp. 208–216.
8. Gergen, M. K., Gergen, K. J., and Morse, S. J. Correlates of Marijuana Use Among College Students. *J. of Applied Social Psycholgoy,* 2:1, 1972, 1–16.
9. Groves, W. E. *Patterns of College Student Drug Use and Life Styles.* Paper prepared for the Columbia University Conference on the Epidemiology of Drug Use, San Juan, Puerto Rico, February, 1973.
10. Johnson, Bruce. American Way of Drugging, Sense and Nonsense in the Scientific Study of Drugs: An Anti-Commission Report. *Society.* 10:4, 1973, pp. 53–58.
11. Bachman, J. G., Green, S., and Wirtanen, I.D. *Youth in Transition, Volume III: Dropping Out—Problem or Symptom?* Ann Arbor: Institute for Social Research, 1971.
12. Johnston, Lloyd. *Drugs and American Youth.* Ann Arbor: Institute for Social Research, 1973.
13. Bachman, J. G., Kahn, R. L., Mednick, M. T., Davidson, T. N., and Johnston, L. D. *Youth in Transition, Volume I: Blueprint for a Longitudinal Study of Adolescent Boys.* Ann Arbor: Institute for Social Research, 1967.
14. Gold, Martin. *Delinquent Behavior in an American City.* Belmont, California: Brooks Cole, 1970.
15. Josephson, Eric. Adolescent Marijuana Use. 1971–1972: Findings from Two National Surveys *Addictive Diseases,* 1:1, 1974.
16. Gold, Martin and Reimer, David. *Report No. 1, National Survey of Youth '72: Research Design, Methods, and Changes in Delinquent Behavior of 13 through 16 year-old-American Youth from 1967 to 1972.* Ann Arbor: Intitute for Social Research, 1974.
17. Blum, Richard, and Associates. *Students and Drugs.* San Francisco: Jossey-Bass, 1970.
18. Andrews, F. M., Morgan, J. N., and Sonquist, J. A. *Multiple Classification Analysis, A Report on a Computer Program for Multiple Regression Using Categorical Predictors.* Ann Arbor: Institute for Social Research, 1969.
19. Suchman, Edward A. The "Hang-Loose" Ethic and the Spirit of Drug Use, in Michael Westheimer (Ed.) *Confrontation: Psychology and the Problems of Today.* Glenview, Ill.: Scott, Foresman, 1970, pp. 34–40.
20. Clarke, J. W. and Levine, E. L. Marijuana Use, Social Discontent and Political Alienation: A Study of High School Youth. *American Political Science Review.* 1971, 65, 120–130.

21. Robinson, John P. Rock Music Preference and Drug Abuse. Paper presented at the Annual Convention of the American Psychological Association. Honolulu, Hawaii, September, 1972.

# Early Identification of Potential School Dropouts: A Literature Review*

*Mary Ann Powell Howard and Richard J. Anderson*

M ANY CHILDREN who enter the public education system never stay to complete the typical 12 years of school. There are countless individual reasons that students do not graduate from high school. This article is a review of the literature on school dropouts.

Lichter et al. stated that "education is a basic requisite for responsible citizenship, for maintenance of our way of life, and for successful entry into today's complicated working world [28:159]." Warner emphasized that "our country's freedom and security are threatened when its youth are not educated to their maximum potential [55:21–22]." The Economic Opportunity Act of 1964 states that the "United States can achieve its full economic and social potential as a nation only if every individual has the opportunity to contribute to the full extent of his capabilities and to participate in the workings of our society [42:110]."

These statements do not reflect a new sentiment, but echo the 1852 concerns of the Massachusetts legislature that enacted a compulsory school attendance law to ensure that children of lower classes "become literate and moral," and thus be of benefit rather than danger to society [26:238]. By 1890, 27 states had compulsory attendance laws, and by 1918 every state had enacted such legislation [26]. Since that time, only South Carolina and Mississippi have repealed their laws, and South Carolina, after a trial period, reinstated the act [10].

The justification for these laws has broadened over the years, so that safeguarding society is not the only concern. With emerging industrialization, safeguarding the right of the child to at least some schooling to provide a chance for success and to protect him from being exploited by child labor be-

* Reprinted with the permission of the publisher and the authors from *Child Welfare*, LVII:4 (1978): 224–228.

came an equally important concern [26]. Today the right to a free public education has been extended to include all children, not just those who are mentally and physically able [56]. Thus the consideration of education as both right and a necessity has persisted.

Nonetheless, many of today's children are deciding not to complete their education. Thompson and Nelson predicted in 1963 that one of every three youths in the ninth grade would dropout during the 1960–70 decade [52:200]. Mary I. Crocker and M. Powell concur with this prediction [57:325]. Grant notes that although the percentage of dropouts has declined since the early 1960s, one-fourth of the young people in the United States today do not graduate from high school [19].

## Unemployment Factor

With one-fourth of the students dropping out and the number of jobs available for unskilled persons decreasing each year while the number of people to fill them increases, it is not surprising that the unemployment rate is of national concern [40:523–526; 22:29–32]. Thompson and Nelson found the unemployment rate of male dropouts is over twice the rate for male high school graduates not in college, and that employed high school graduates are more than three times as likely as employed dropouts to have white collar jobs [32:48–50]. Perrella and Waldman, in a study of students who had been out of school for 2 years, found that the males with more education made greater advances than those with less education over the period being studied [36:860]. The reasons for these advancements might be attributed to Goldberg's conviction: "When a young man or woman starts out in the world of work, he will have only three things to offer: his intellect, his education, his willingness. The better the education, the better the job and the better the chance of steady, uninterrupted employment." [18:9]

That a person drops out of school does not necessarily indicate a lack of ability. Nine surveys over three states indicated that the largest percentage of dropouts were in an average intellectual range, and that at least 11% had the ability to complete college [55:21]. According to these surveys about 121,000 of the pupils who dropped out before graduation in 1958 and 114,400 of those who dropped out before graduation in 1963 could have completed college. About 550,000 dropouts before 1958 and 520,000 before 1963 could have completed vocational-technical programs. About 220,000 dropouts before 1958 and 208,000 before 1963 left school with practically no vocational preparation or training. About 209,000 with an IQ below 80 dropped out before 1958, and 197,600 before 1963 [55:22].

Many studies have been conducted concerning programs to keep students in school. Major emphasis is being placed on individualized curriculum, work co-op programs and vocational courses. A more fundamental look at the problem reveals that high school programs are not always sufficient, since, as Bristow, Bachman, Hilton and others emphasize, dropping out is not an isolated event, but a culmination of conditions and actions experienced long before the decision [7:1,2:24]. Lloyd suggests that symptoms are indicated as early as sixth grade, and Zeaman states the seeds may be developing as early as first grade [30:166;59:12].

For the purpose of this study, a dropout is defined as "a pupil who leaves school, for any reason except death, before graduation or completion of a program of studies and without transferring to another school." [41:461].

## Literature Review

Hicks, in his study of dropouts, found that failure in school generally follows a well defined path, [23:9]. First, the student's interest sags. This results in the lowering of grades, which encourages skipping classes. The student, then in trouble with school authorities, becomes disruptive and is banished from class. After his parents are involved, he becomes increasingly negative and defensive, which eventually leads to his decision to flee. His reasons for leaving range from employment, marriage, health and friends, to inability to achieve, dislike of school, and rebellion against parents [52:201; 37:114;38:316;16:70;57].

These reasons, professed by students, may reflect deeper underlying factors. The review of the literature reveals two major sources—family history and academic difficulties. The most important factor in family history, according to Bachman and others, is socioeconomic status [1:27;29:276;9:117]. James B. Conant believes that the dropout rate tends to increase 70% in slum areas[52]. Schreiber reports that a study in Pennsylvania concluded that if a child, when he enters school at age 6, comes from a home where his father is not working and where there is no phone, the chances of his dropping out before graduation are 8 in 10 [47:7]. Williams found that more than half of the dropouts in his study were from families in which the occupation of the head of the household was relatively unstable and in the lowest income brackets [58:12]. Miller, Cohen, and Tseng concur with the correlation between income status and dropping out of school [34;11:118,53:462–466]. One reason for the correlation is suggested by Oscar Hoch.

> In all likelihood, his parents have also solved their school problems via the dropout circuit, and having to work long hours at a variety of odd jobs, they have neither the time, nor can they provide the model to encourage wayward youth to remain in school. Very often, the pupil's parents are actually indifferent to his decision to leave. This indifference is frequently expressed through their own doubts concerning the purpose and value of education, or their attitude

toward "getting ahead," which these parents do not relate to the potential advancement gained through education, but rather to the immediate financial return achieved by holding down a "respectable" job [25:100].

Williams agrees with the dropout correlation in families, noting that in a Maryland study 78.5% of the mothers and 80.3% of the fathers had also been dropouts [58]. Eargle and Miller report similar findings [13:162;34:5]. . . .

## Academic Predictors

Academic problems of the potential dropout provide important information. Studies have shown that two of the most important predictors are poor grades and being held back [54:74;12:529;27:420; 2:27]. Schreiber found that if a child is not achieving academically after first grade and has to repeat first or second grade, the chances of not graduating are 8 in 10 [45:7]. Swan, listing 11 recurring problems of dropouts, also mentions failure in one or more years of elementary or high school, especially first, second, eighth or ninth grade, as an indicator [31:42]. His list includes being a year or more below grade level in arithmetic and reading in seventh grade, attendance in several elementary schools, recent arrival in a city, low economic level, broken home, irregular attendance pattern, lack of participation in school affairs, difficulty in the community, girls going steady with older boys, and boy's ownership of a car [31:41–42].

Problems in reading and math are widely recognized characteristics of dropouts [48:330;51:95]. Berston found that three out of four dropouts admit having trouble with reading and spelling [6:208]. Penty found that three times as many poor readers as good readers dropped out before graduation [35:3]. Schuster and Schreiber report that the average dropout is 2 years behind in reading [48;47:52]. In math, Strom noted that dropouts had difficulty with abstract reasoning, generalizing, analyzing and inferring relationships [50:102]. Kelley also found that these students had difficulty dealing with abstract concepts [27].

A related problem mentioned by Brown and Peterson is that of being unable to memorize or retain information [8:438]. This inability affects all areas of a student's academic and personal life.

Another problem, perhaps not so readily recognized, is that of the student-teacher relationship. Hecht reports on studies that indicate that what a teacher expects of a child influences how the teacher behaves and how the child performs [21:172]. The more positive the relationship, the better the chances of success for the student.

Eargle also reports a positive correlation between academic success and teacher preference [13:162–169]. Teacher preference, according to his study, depends to a large degree on socioeconomic status. In the study, of the 40 children classified by the teacher, not one of the "most preferred" belonged to the lower class. One-half of the "least preferred" were from the lower middle class or below. Not a single child in this group was from the upper class, and only one was from the upper middle class. In this study only three children on the preferred list made a grade lower than a B, and 26 on the least preferred list made one or more grades below B.

Richter and Scandrette report another study in which teachers rated their students on motivation, industry, initiative, influence and leadership, concern for others, responsibility, integrity and emotional stability [39:127–131]. Results indicate that motivation, responsibility, emotional stability and concern for others are significant traits of successful students.

In a Midwestern community of 120,000, Frerichs asked teachers to fill out a form: "What I remember about ———." [17:532–534]. Classifying the responses as "favorable," "unfavorable," "no opinion," he found that the teacher's ratings were an accurate source for identifying primary school children who became dropouts. Thus, teachers, along with personal history and academic records, are resources in predicting dropouts.

## Summary

The review of the literature suggests that a student's decision to leave school before graduation is not an isolated decision, but one based on many interactive factors, both personal and academic, that may culminate in his becoming a "fugitive from failure," as Schreiber so poignantly phrases it [46:234]. These factors, often relatively easy to identify, include family status, socioeconomic status, parents' level of education, siblings' level of education, parents' value of education, parents' occupational status, student's motivation and aspiration, social contacts, mental and physical health, material possessions such as a car, participation in school and community activities, failure in one or more grades, reading and arithmetic progress, attendance in several schools, irregular school attendance and teacher's expectations and personality rating of students.

### REFERENCE NOTES [ED.: FROM THE ORIGINAL ARTICLE.]

1. Bachman, Jerald G. "Anti-dropout Campaign and Other Misanthropies," *Society*, IX (1972).
2. ———. "Dropouts Are Losers, Says Who?" *Today's Education*, (b) LXI (1972).
3. Bakal, Yitzhak, Madaus, William, and Winder, Alvin E. "A Motivational Approach to Compensatory Education," *Social Work*, XII, 2 (April 1968).
4. Bard, Bernard. "Why Dropout Campaigns Fail," *Saturday Review*, XLIX (1966).
5. Bell, James W. "A Comparison of Dropouts and Nondropouts on Participation in School Activities," *Journal of Educational Research*, LX6 (1967).
6. Berston, H. M. "The School Dropout Problem," *Clearing House*, XXXV (1960).

7. Bristow, William H. "Curriculum Problems Regarding Early School Leavers," XXIX (1964).

8. Brown, Stanley B., and Peterson, Ted T. "The Rebellious School Dropout," School and Society, XCIX (1969).

9. Cangemi, Joseph P., and Khan, Kanwar Habib. "The Psychology of Punishment and the Potential School Dropout," Education, XCIV (1973).

10. Children Out of School in America. A Report by the Children's Defense Fund of the Washington Research Project, Cambridge, Mass., October 1974.

11. Cohen, Stewart. "The Ghetto Dropout Analysis and Partial Solution," Clearing House, XLIV (1969).

12. Coplein, Leonard E. "Techniques for Study of Dropouts," Clearing House, XXXVI (1962).

13. Eargle, Zane E. "Social Class and Student Success," High School Journal, XLVI (1963).

14. Elliott, Delbert S.; Voss, Harwin L., and Wendling, Aubrey. "Capable Dropouts and the Social Milieu of the High School," Journal of Educational Research, LX (1966).

15. Faust, Helen F. "Books as an Aid in Preventing Dropouts," Elementary English, XLVI (1969).

16. French, Joseph L. "Characteristics of High Ability Dropouts," National Association of Secondary School Principals Bulletin, LIII (1969).

17. Frerichs, Allen H. "Identifying the Dropout-Prone in the Primary Grades," XLIII (1967).

18. Goldberg, Arthur J. "Keep Them in School," National Education Association Journal, L (1961).

19. Grant, W. Vance. "Estimates of School Dropouts," American Education, LI (1975), back cover.

20. Hackney, Ben H. Jr., and Reavis, Charles A. "Poor Instruction—the Real Cause of Dropouts," Education Digest, XXXIII (1968).

21. Hecht, Kathryn A. "Teacher Ratings of Potential Dropouts and Academically Gifted Children: Are They Related?", Journal of Teachers Education, XXVI, 2 (1975).

22. Heilbroner, Robert L. "No Room at the Bottom," Saturday Review, XL (1966).

23. Hicks, J. B. "All's Calm in the Crow's Nest," American Education, V (1969).

24. Hilton, Ernest. "When Does Dropping Out Begin?" Education Digest, 1973, XXXVIII (1973).

25. Hoch, Oscar. "The Dropout Syndrome," High School Journal, 1965, XLIX (1965).

26. Hunt, Thomas C., and Clawson, Elmer U. "Dropouts: Then and Now," High School Journal, LVIII (1975).

27. Kelley, Earl C. "Seeds of Dropouts," Childhood Education, XXXIX (1963).

28. Lichter, Solomon O., et al. "Prevention of School Dropouts," School and Society, XL (1962).

29. Liddle, Gordon P. "Psychological Factors Involved in Dropping Out of School," High School Journal, XLV (1962).

30. Lloyd, Dee Norman. "Antecedent Relationships to High School Dropout or Graduation," Education, LXXXIX (1968).

31. Matika, Francis W., and Sheerer, Rebecca. "Are the Causes of Dropouts Excuses?" National Association of Secondary School Principals Bulletin XLVI (1962).

32. Michelotti, Kopp. "Employment of High School Graduates and Dropouts, October 1973," Monthly Labor Review, XCVII (1974).

33. Millard, Thomas L. "Dropouts and the School," Educational Leadership, XXII (1965).

34. Miller, Leonard M. "The Dropout: Schools Search for Clues to His Problems," School Life, XLV (1963).

35. Penty, Ruth C. "Reading Ability and High School Dropouts," Educational Digest XXV (1960).
36. Perrella, Vera C., and Waldman, Elizabeth. "Out-of-School Youth—Two Years Later," Monthly Labor Review, LXXXIX (1966).
37. Pollack, Jack Harrison. "The Astonishing Truth About Girl Dropouts," Parents Magazine, XLI (1966).
38. Rich, Virginia N. "Dropouts and the Emotionally Disturbed," Journal of Secondary Education, XLI (1966).
39. Richter, James, and Scandrette, Onas. "Relationship Between Teacher Personality Ratings and Student Academic Success," Journal of Educational Research, LXV, 3 (1971).
40. Riendeau, Albert J. "Facing Up to the Dropout Problem," Clearing House, XXXVI (1962).
41. Ristow, Lester W. "Much Ado About Dropouts," Phi Delta Kappan, XLVI (1965).
42. Rowen, Robert B. "Impact of Federal Legislation on School Social Work," Social Work, XII 2 (April 1967).
43. Russell, Kenneth. "Stay in School," American Education, IV (1968).
44. "School Dropouts in Big Cities," School and Society, XLII (1964).
45. Schreiber, Daniel. "School Dropouts," National Education Association Journal, LI (1962).
46. ———. "The School Dropout—Fugitive From Failure," National Association of Secondary School Principals Bulletin, XLVI (1962).
47. ———. "700,000 Dropouts," American Education, IV (1968).
48. Schuster, Marjorie. "Lowering the Dropout Rate," Clearing House, XLV (1971).
49. Strom, Robert D. "The School Dropout and the Family," School and Society, XLII (1964).
50. ———. "A Realistic Curriculum for the Predictive Dropout," Clearing House, XXXIX (1964).
51. Theus, Robert. "Dropouts—Prevention and Cure," Clearing House, XLVI (1971).
52. Thompson, Michael L., and Nelson, Robert H. "Twelve Approaches to Remedy the Dropout Problem," Clearing House, XXXVIII (1963).
53. Tseng, M. S. "Comparisons of Selected Familial, Personality and Vocational Variables of High School Students and Dropouts," Journal of Educational Research, LXV, 10 (1972).
54. Vogel, Anita. "How to Check Dropouts," School Management, V (1961).
55. Warner, O. Ray. "The Scholastic Ability of School Dropouts," School Life, XLVII (1964).
56. Weintraub, Frederick J., and Abeson, Alan. "Appropriate Education for All Handicapped Children: A Growing Concern," in Nicholas J. Long, William C. Morse and Ruth G. Newman (eds.), Conflict in the Classroom: The Education of Emotionally Disturbed Children. Belmont, Calif: Wadsworth, 1976.
57. Whisenton, Joffre T., and Loree, M. Ray. "A Comparison of the Values, Needs and Aspirations of School Leavers With Those of Non-School Leavers," Journal of Negro Education, XXXIX (1970).
58. Williams, Percy V. "School Dropouts," National Education Association Journal, LII (1963).
59. Zeaman, Janeice. "Building Stay-in-School Power," American Education, X (1974).

# Childhood Deviance as a Developmental Process: A Study of 223 Urban Black Men from Birth to 18*

*Lee N. Robins and Eric Wish*

[Drs. Robins and Wish offer a view of deviance as a developmental process when one type of deviant act such as disobeying a teacher in the first grade can lead to other deviant acts later. This view would have important theoretical and practice implications. Theoretically, evidence in favor of such a perspective could link the fields of child development and deviance, whereas, as a practice matter, the developmental model could suggest points of preventive action by having knowledge about what more serious behaviors tend to follow which less serious ones.

To present evidence about this developmental view, Drs. Robins and Wish studied the patterns and sequencing of the ages at which 13 deviant behaviors were initiated during the childhood of 223 young black men who were born and raised in St. Louis between the years 1930 and 1934. These young men had attended public elementary schools for six years or more and had an intelligence score of at least 85.

The 13 deviant acts were (1) FAIL—elementary school academic problems; (2) ABSENCE—behavior problems in school as indicated by high rates of absences, notations of truancy, expulsion, or transfer to a reformatory; (3) DROPOUT—permanent withdrawal before graduation or temporary withdrawal for a semester or more; (4) ARREST—as indicated by court records; (5) DRINK—report of first drink before age fifteen; (6) SEX—report of first intercourse before age fifteen; (7) MARJ—use of marijuana before age eighteen; (8) BARB—use of barbiturates before age eighteen; (9)AMPH—use of amphetamines before age eighteen; (10) OPIATE—use of opiates before age eighteen; (11) LEFT HOME—leave parental home to live on his own before age eighteen; (12) MARRIAGE—before age eighteen; (13) ALC PROB—developed alcohol problems before age eighteen.]

## Results

*Frequency and Age of Initiation for Behaviors*

The 13 behaviors varied in frequency, age of first initiation, and whether they occurred predominantly early or late in the age span at risk. Table 1 shows

* Reprinted by permission of the authors and publisher, from *Social Forces*, 1977 (Dec.), 56:2,448–471. © *Social Forces*, 1977.

Table 1
*Deviant Behaviors in Childhood (223 Young Black men)*

| | Proportion doing this (%) | Age range of initiations | Median age at initiation |
|---|---|---|---|
| SEX | 56 | 4–14 | 13.1 |
| ABSENCE | 43 | 6–14 | 7.3 |
| DROPOUT | 39 | 6–17 | 16.2 |
| ARREST | 38 | 5–17 | 15.2 |
| FAIL | 34 | 6–13 | 7.7 |
| DRINK | 34 | 2–14 | 13.1 |
| LEFT HOME | 26 | 8–17 | 17.2 |
| MARIJUANA | 20 | 8–17 | 15.7 |
| MARRIAGE | 6 | 14–17 | 17.5 |
| BARBS | 6 | 11–17 | 16.5 |
| ALC PROB | 5 | 14–17 | 16.7 |
| AMPHS | 4 | 13–17 | 15.8 |
| OPIATES | 3 | 12–17 | 17.1 |

that the proportion of children committing these behaviors varied from 56 per cent who had sex experience before 15 to only 3 per cent who used opiates before 18.

Ages of first elementary school failure and absence could not precede age of school entry at 6, and marriage, which waited on puberty, did not occur before 14. Alcohol problems had to wait on some drinking experience. Otherwise, there were no absolute lower limits (as the not infrequent prepubertal sex experience shows). Sex, drinking, and arrests occurred in rare children even before school age, and first marijuana use and leaving home also occasionally occurred very early. Other drug use and alcohol problems occurred only in adolescence.

Elementary school problems were distinct from other behaviors in that they began early or not at all. Before their eighth birthday, more than half the children who would ever be seriously held back or truant had already been so. For all other behaviors, the majority of first occurrences were found in the last three years of the period at risk, defined as the period from the earliest age at which any child showed the behavior to the cutoff age of 15 or 18. The behaviors that occurred last of all were opiate use, leaving home, and marrying. . . .

## How Important Are These Specific Acts as "Causes"?

The fact that one act apparently increases the risk of another is not necessarily information of practical importance. Whether it is important depends in part on whether that first act is either a necessary or sufficient cause of the second. The first act approximates a necessary cause if the second act almost never occurs unless preceded by the first; it approximates a sufficient cause if the first act is almost invariably followed by the second. (Of course, from a purely practical point of view, necessary and sufficient causes which cannot be controlled are less important than less powerful causes that are subject to control. However, other things being equal, the potential for control is greatest when the cause is necessary or sufficient.)

Table 4 evaluates the degree to which each causal relationship found to be statistically significant or near statistical significance after our tests for spuriousness fulfills criteria for being necessary or sufficient. None of the "causal" behaviors in Table 4 appeared *sufficient* to produce further types of deviance. The closest approximations to sufficient causes were ABSENCE, which half the time was followed by DROPOUT, and ARREST, which was followed by early DRINKING in half the eligible cases. In only two other relationships, ABSENCE as a cause of LEAVING HOME and MARIJUANA as a cause of ARREST, did the "effect" actually occur in even one-third of the cases at risk following the "cause." Thus, if the occurrence of the precursor were used to select children for intervention to prevent their committing the second behavior, many children would be selected who probably were not going to commit the predicted deviance even if no intervention took place (or who would commit it only later, after they were adult).

While there are few sufficient causes in our list, there are a number of virtually necessary ones. OPIATES were used almost solely (92%) by children

Table 4
*Were Any Acts Necessary or Sufficient Causes of Others? (In Percent)?*

|  | Necessary? | Sufficient? |
|---|---|---|
|  | How often was the 2nd act preceded by the 1st? | How often was the 1st act followed by the 2nd? |
| *NEARLY NECESSARY* | | |
| MARJ → OPIATE | 92 | 15 |
| DRINK → AMPH | 85 | 10 |
| SEX → MARJ | 78 | 25 |
| DRINK → ALC PROB | 76 | 12 |
| DROPOUT → OPIATE | 75 | 8 |
| MARJ → BARB | 59 | 14 |
| *APPROACHING SUFFICIENT* | | |
| ARREST → DRINK | 21 | 51 |
| MARJ → ARREST | 16 | 36 |
| *BOTH (?)* | | |
| ABSENCE → DROPOUT | 60 | 54 |
| DRINK → LEAVE HOME | 58 | 44 |
| ABSENCE → LEAVE HOME | 55 | 33 |

who had already used MARIJUANA (even though very few marijuana users (15%) went on to use opiates before age 18). OPIATE users were also almost always (75%) previously high school DROPOUTS, although again only 8 percent of dropouts went on to use opiates before 18. The use of AMPHETAMINES was almost exclusively (85%) among children who had begun DRINKING before 15, as were ALCOHOL PROBLEMS (76%). MARIJUANA use was largely restricted (78%) to children who had already had sex experience.

One of these "necessary" causes seems obvious: a child who does not drink early hardly has time to develop alcohol problems before 18. Similarly, the role of marijuana as a necessary stepping-stone to opiates has been widely reported (Kandel). The other relationships are not self-evident. That amphetamine use rarely occurred in the absence of early drinking may reflect the fact that in the years when these men were adolescent, amphetamines were typically the last illicit drug to be initiated. Perhaps to already have reached this last outpost before 18 required a very early interest in mood-modifying drugs.

From the point of view of those who plan to intervene in the natural development of deviant behavior, the most useful discoveries are of early behaviors that are both necessary and sufficient causes of later behaviors. When these are used to flag "high risk" cases, the intervention is directed at almost all the children likely to show the behavior to be prevented and at almost no one else. Three of the causal links discovered between deviant behaviors approach, although they do not fulfill, both criteria: ABSENCE as a cause of both DROPOUT and LEFT HOME, and DRINK as a cause of LEFT HOME. If there is a practical message in our efforts, it is that centering efforts on preventing truancy in the first and second grade and drinking before 14 is likely to have the greatest payoff at least cost. . . .

## Discussion

Our excursion into the study of the development of deviance in the childhoods of young urban-born black men reviewed the frequency, ages at initiation, and temporal patterning of 13 forms of deviance. All 13 types of deviance were found to be statistically linked. Those behaviors beginning young were the most common and the most likely to occur alone. The patterning of deviance was not a random process. There were more highly deviant and more non-deviant children than would have been expected by chance. This set us looking to see whether there might be a developmental process at work.

Evidence supporting a developmental process included the facts that (1) the most frequently committed acts were those typically committed youngest, (2) strong positive correlations existed between behaviors, and (3) the strongest correlations were between pairs of behaviors initiated at about the same age and conceptually related. These findings suggested a developmental process made up of both quantitative and qualitative relationships.

Qualitative relationships were tested by an age-adjusted actuarial method followed by tests for spuriousness which required holding constant acts that were presumptive causes of both members of a pair of acts as well as the total number of prior acts. Eight relationships survived these tests. In addition, there were 9 relationships close to significance. While none of these early behaviors was *sufficient* to produce other behaviors, several were virtually *necessary*. Three relationships (ABSENCE→DROPOUT, DRINK→LEFT HOME, ABSENCE→LEFT HOME) came close enough to being both necessary *and* sufficient to make them attractive candidates for efforts at intervention.

The fact that most statistically significant relationships between specific pairs of behaviors were reduced by controlling on number of prior acts suggests that the development of deviance in childhood has an important quantitative aspect, as well as the qualitative aspect supported by relationships surviving these tests. If the developmental process *is* largely quantitative, it is possible to forecast which children will be the pioneers when new forms of deviance are introduced: they will be children who already have varied experience in "conventional" deviant behaviors. Evidence that this is the case has been supported by studies of the diffusion of drug experimentation among adolescents during the last decade. Drug experimentation began first among highly deviant children, then spread to a much more broadly based group.

Establishing the plausibility of a developmental process required special data and special analytic tools. In addition to the usual information about what behaviors had occurred, we needed to know at what age each behavior first occurred. These ages then had to be used in analysis both to establish the sequence of initiations and to cope with the problem of how much of the risk period for a potential second behavior had already elapsed before the first behavior occurred. Two sources of spuriousness had to be investigated—the common one, that some prior behavior may have caused both the presumed "cause" and "effect," and second, a source usually overlooked, that it may have been simply the fact that *some* deviant behavior occurred first, rather than a specific effect of the first behavior, which accounted for the increased risk. Our data were sometimes inadequate to handle all these requirements simultaneously. A larger and less homogeneous sample of children followed prospectively via a panel design would have quieted concerns about the validity and generalizability of our results.

The same results from even such a sample would not prove, however, that the relationships between number and types of behaviors are due to a developmental process. It remains possible, though perhaps improbable, that discovered relationships between temporally ordered behaviors, even when highly reliable, valid, and not explained by the number or type of other behaviors preceding them, could occur simply because common background factors produced both forms of deviance and thus accounted for the inter-correlations between them. To resolve this issue, background factors must be allowed to compete in the analysis with developmental processes—a difficult analytic problem indeed. Meanwhile, the present analysis has pinpointed some relationships between deviant behaviors which are prime candidates for further exploration in better samples and with more complex analyses.

We introduced this effort to explore the developmental patterns in deviance in the hopes that it would have theoretical as well as practical utility. How then does the postulation that deviance has its own developmental process fit into a general theory of deviance? A gap which the developmental approach can fill was pointed out by Cloward and Ohlin, who noted that "the pressures that lead to deviant patterns do not necessarily determine the particular pattern of deviance that results. . . . We must therefore explain each solution in its own right. . . ." The developmental view is not in conflict with the view that the social environment and the constitution of the actor play important roles in deviant behavior, but it adds an important element to the armamentarium of predictors: the behavioral history.

A developmental theory specifies which new deviant behavior is most likely to appear next. It postulates that if a new behavior is adopted, the odds are in favor of its being the behavior which is next in frequency and next in typical age of onset to the last deviant behavior adopted and which is in the same conceptual area as behaviors already in the repertoire. These are the implications of the developmental process's being both a quantitative and qualitative one. . . .

## REFERENCES

CLOWARD, R. A., and L. E. OHLIN. 1960. *Delinquency and Opportunity.* Glencoe: Free Press.
KANDEL, D. 1975. "Stages in Adolescent Involvement in Drug Use." Science 190 (November 28):912–14.

## [RELATED BIBLIOGRAPHIC MATERIALS]

ROBINS, LEE N. 1966. *Deviant Children Grown Up; A Sociological and Psychiatric Study of Sociopathic Personality.* Baltimore: Williams & Wilkins. Reprinted in 1974 in Huntington, New York: Krieger Publishing.
ROBINS, L. N., G. E. MURPHY, R. A. WOODRUFF, JR., and L. J. KING. 1971. "The Adult Psychiatric Status of Black School Boys." *Archives of General Psychiatry* 24 (April): 338–45.

# Adolescent Turmoil:
# A Myth Revisited *

*David G. Oldham*

THE DISTINCTION between normality and abnormality in the adolescent commonly poses a formidable challenge to the practicing mental health professional. Inherent in this challenge are issues concerning diagnosis, prognosis, and the decision to treat. The clinician who sees adolescent patients is frequently called upon to determine whether a teenager's difficulties fall within the spectrum of normative behavior, or whether there is psychopathology present which demands therapeutic intervention. Central to this clinical task is the conceptual issue of adolescent turmoil and its psychiatric significance. The clinician who views adolescence as a period of inevitable turbulence and disruption will approach the problem differently from his or her colleagues who regard normal adolescence as characterized by stability. It is the general thesis of this paper that the traditional "storm and stress" view of adolescence does not stand up to existing research data, and a review of the relevent literature leading to this thesis is presented. A revised concept of adolescent turmoil is outlined with emphasis placed on implications for diagnosis and treatment. Factors involved in the perpetuation of the mythical aspects of adolescent turmoil are considered, and the clinical assessment of adolescent symptomatology is discussed.

## The Traditional View of Adolescent Turmoil

> The young are in character prone to desire and ready to carry any desire they may have formed into action . . . They are changeful, too, and fickle in their desires, which are as transitory as they are vehement; for their wishes are keen without being permanent, like a sick man's fits of hunger and thirst. They are passionate, irascible, apt to be carried away by their impulses . . . If the young commit a fault, it is always on the side of excess and exaggeration . . . for they carry everything too far whether it be love or hatred or anything else.
>
> —*Aristotle*

> I would there were no age between ten and three-and-twenty, or that youth would sleep out the rest; for there is nothing in the between but getting wenches with child, wronging the ancientry, stealing, fighting.
>
> —*The Winter's Tale*, Act III, Scene iii

* Reprinted by permission of the publisher and the author from Journal of Continuing Education in Psychiatry, 39:3 (1978): 23–32.

The above passages from works of Aristotle and Shakespeare suggest the deep historical and philosophical roots of the view of adolescence as a period of inevitable turmoil, disruption, and maladaptive behavior. This view was first advanced in the modern professional literature by Hall who published a classic two-volume treatise on the psychology of adolescence.[1] Hall placed heavy emphasis on the biogenetic determinants of personality development, and he described normal adolescence as an era of "storm and stress" analogous to mankind's tumultuous progression from primitiveness to higher civilization. Hall writes that adolescent development "is suggestive . . . of some ancient period of storm and stress when old moorings were broken and a higher level attained." His theory was greatly influenced by Darwinian concepts of evolution and recapitulation, and it depicted adolescent turmoil as a biological necessity. The impact of Hall's storm and stress hypothesis was dampened somewhat by the findings of Mead who described the tranquility with which Samoan adolescents achieved adult status.[2] In further contributions by Mead, Benedict, and other cultural anthropologists, the marked intercultural variability of teenage behavior was documented, and the influence of environmental factors on adolescent development was emphasized.[3,4]

Although anthropological data challenged the inevitability of adolescent turmoil as described by Hall, subsequent psychoanalytic interpretations of adolescence advanced this concept, at least in regard to Western civilization. The first detailed psychoanalytic formulations of adolescence were written by Jones, Aichhorn, and Bernfeld.[5-7] These works reflect Sigmund Freud's ideas concerning biogenetic factors in the development of the personality, focusing on the disruptive effects of increased sexual and aggressive impulses confronting the adolescent ego. Later psychoanalytic literature has dealt more specifically with the concept of adolescent turmoil. Several important contributors postulate that major symptom formation is inevitable during normal adolescence, and that it is all but impossible to draw the line between normality and psychopathology. Anna Freud views adolescence as a normative interruption of peaceful growth and writes:[8,9]

> The adolescent manifestations of growth come close to the symptom formation of the neurotic, psychotic, or dissocial order and merge almost imperceptibly into borderline states, or fully fledged forms of almost all the illnesses. Consequently, the differential diagnosis between these adolescent upsets and true pathology becomes a difficult task.

Spiegel notes the resemblance of normative adolescent upheaval to psychotic episodes, and Fountain lists ineffective reality testing as a characteristic of normal teenagers which distinguishes them from normal adults.[10,11] Josselyn states that rapidly shifting behavior patterns resembling serious neurotic, psychotic, and character pathology in adults are typical of the teenage years.[12] She views symptom formation as a normative consequence of relative ego failure in adolescence but implies that such disturbance is likely to be transient and essentially benign. Erikson has made a substantial contribution to the understanding of adolescent identity formation which he outlines in terms of "normative crisis." [13] Erikson maintains that manifestations of adolescent turmoil (e.g., wide mood swings, acting-out behavior, and social alienation) result from the role diffusion that accompanies the normal identity crisis. He does state, however, that there are limits to normative adolescent disturbance, and he describes acute identity diffusion as a serious clinical entity which is neither transient nor benign. Blos reinforces the psychoanalytic position that adolescence is characterized by "well-recognized states of chaos," but he tends to emphasize the constructive nature of ego coping mechanisms during the teenage years. [14,15] Blos also comments on forms of adolescent turmoil which enter the realm of psychopathology:

> As clinicians we recognize in the adolescent's wholesale rejection of his family and his own past the frantic circumvention of the painful disengagement process. Such avoidances are usually transient and the delay self-liquidating. They might, however, assume extreme forms. We are familiar with the adolescent who runs away, drives off in a stolen car, leaves school, bums his way to nowhere, takes to promiscuity and drugs.

Several authors in the psychoanalytic literature have expressed concern for the adolescents who show no evidence of disruption and turmoil. Anna Freud contends that teenagers who remain "good children" and fail to show external signs of inner unrest are employing excessive defenses which impede normal maturation. Geleerd states, "Personally I would feel greater concern for the adolescent who causes no trouble and feels no disturbance," and Lindemann states that a tranquil adolescent period is not only indicative of a developmental disturbance, but that it can be an ominous prognostic sign. [16,17]

> We have learned to become equally concerned about those adolescents who show no evidence of disturbance and retain the patterns of allegiance, obedience to common family goals, and unmarred achievement throughout the puberty period. We know that such persons are likely to become profoundly disturbed at a later time.

The nature and significance of adolescent turmoil as described in the storm and stress tradition can be summarized as follows:

Adolescence is characterized by a lowering of ego strength coupled with an upsurge of aggressive and sexual impulses leading to disruption of the psychic equilibrium.

Adolescents normatively display varying degrees and kinds of symptomatology which resemble but do not constitute true psychiatric illness.

Psychiatric symptoms are common, transient, fluctuating, and essentially benign in most adolescents. Precise diagnosis, except in extreme cases, is difficult, if not impossible, to determine.

The prognosis of adolescent symptomatology is difficult, if not impossible, to determine.

Adolescents who do not display overt signs of turmoil are developmentally deviant and may be at high risk for serious psychopathology later.

## Research Studies of Adolescent Turmoil

Although Anna Freud has termed adolescence "the stepchild of psychoanalytic theory," there can be no doubt that psychoanalytic theory has had a profound impact on contemporary thinking about adolescent development.

Current diagnostic and treatment practices also reflect the influence of psychoanalytic thought concerning adolescent turmoil, but in recent years many of the postulates listed above have been challenged by a growing body of published data from a heterogenous group of investigators. This literature represents a general shift in the understanding and study of adolescents marked by less emphasis on data from small numbers of patients and more emphasis on normative data from large samples of teenagers. Longitudinal studies of both patient and nonpatient adolescents have been conducted in order to reexamine the storm and stress view of adolescence, and some general findings emerge which have important clinical implications for any who treat adolescents.

In the middle 1950's, Douvan and Adelson conducted an extensive interview and questionnaire study of over 3,000 teenage boys and girls chosen as a representative sample of the United States population of junior high school students.[18] This survey tapped a variety of attitudes and psychological dimensions, and Douvan and Adelson concluded that normative teenagers experience little of the inner turbulence or acting-out behavior ascribed to them in earlier literature. These teenagers were described as generally trusting their parents, participating in rule-making at home, and deriving much of their self-esteem from parental approval. Rebellion typically occurred in the form of minor disagreements with parents over matters of music and dress, but these adolescents shared with their parents a core of common values which remained stable. Douvan and Adelson state that normative adolescents do not show evidence of ego failure and disruption, but these authors describe their findings as "unexciting." They express concern over the typical adolescent's conservatism and relative freedom from inner and outer conflict.

Although the findings of this study contradict the inevitability of adolescent turmoil, the authors reinforce the venerable notion that the teenage years optimally are colored by passion, restlessness, and conflict.

The large-scale study by Douvan and Adelson supports the findings of Westley and Grinker, who studied late adolescents chosen for their good social adjustment and absence of psychiatric symptoms.[19,20] Both investigators found that their samples of college freshmen demonstrated impressive ego strengths, rewarding interpersonal relationships, and a well-developed sense of mortality. Grinker termed his college freshmen males "homoclites," meaning those who follow the common rule, and he stressed not only the absence of turmoil and identity crises in their lives, but also the adaptive coping skills they employed. Silber et al. came to similar conclusions about the high school seniors whom they selected for study on the basis of their academic and social success.[21] These adolescents are also described as eager to meet developmental challenges, and in this sense they seem to differ from those described by Douvan and Adelson. It may be argued that the adolescents studied by Westley, Grinker, and Silber et al. do not represent the middle majority of teenagers found in the Douvan and Adelson study, but the principal message in all of these reports seems to be that psychological turbulence during early and middle adolescence is not normative and is not associated with successful adjustment in late adolescence.

Offer and his colleagues at Michael Reese Hospital conducted an ambitious longitudinal study, The Modal Adolescent Project, which was designed in part to put the "turmoil hypothesis" to an empirical test.[22-25] In order to select a typical, or modal, group of adolescent boys for study over the four years of high school, an extensive Self-Image Questionnaire was administered to 326 freshmen attending two high schools. Using the concept of normality as statistical average, a group of 103 modal boys was selected with the intention of eliminating the extremes of psychopathology and superior adjustment. Repetitive interviews, psychological testing, and family studies revealed that these suburban middle-class boys experienced adolescence with a minimum of internal and external turmoil. Extensive followup study demonstrated that rebellious behavior normatively occurred only during early adolescence (ages 12 to 14) and was manifested by chronic disagreements with parents over matters of dress, household chores, and curfew hours. This rebellion did not involve delinquent acts or great emotional upheavals and was judged to initiate the emancipation process. This group of adolescents did report transient feelings of anxiety, depression, guilt, and shame, but the authors did not note marked fluctuation of affects or debilitating forms of anxiety and depression. With regard to the normative incidence of psychological disturbance, only seven per cent of the students evidenced significant emotional problems manifested by chronic delinquency and character pathology. This figure may be contrasted with the 23 per cent incidence of moderately severe emotional disorders found in adults in the Midtown Manhattan Project by Srole et al.[26] None of the adolescent subjects was hospitalized or became psychotic. Offer notes that these students tended to be "doers," with rather limited fantasy lives, who coped with aggression through competitive sports and occasional angry outbursts at family members. Sexuality was dealt with in early adolescence through denial and repression with a gradual increase in masturbation and heterosexual experimentation. By the end of the junior year of high school, 10 per cent of the subject group had sexual intercourse. No subject admitted to overt homosexual behavior. Prominent coping behaviors included cognitive planning, role rehearsal, humor, and limited self-observation. These adolescents maintained good relationships with adults and shared the basic values of their parents and cultural environment. Offer concludes that normative adolescents of today evidence comparatively little of the turmoil expected of them in the psychoanalytic literature. He also states that this lack of turmoil is associated with successful overall adjustment which continues into late adolescence and early adulthood.

The information gathered by Offer and his co-workers centers around the attitudes and coping skills of the middle majority of American teenagers, and it offers an impressive challenge to several aspects of traditional theory. Relatively unexplored in the studies mentioned thus far, however, are questions concerning the importance of symptom formation in adolescence. This gap in the literature has been attended to most extensively by Masterson and his associates at the Payne Whitney Clinic who conducted the Symptomatic Adolescent Research Project.[27-30] This study elucidated various symptom patterns found in 101 boys and girls, ages 12 to 18, seen consecutively as clinic patients, and in 101 nonpatient matched controls. Confirming one aspect of psychoanalytic theory was the finding that symptoms are indeed common in adolescence. Approximately 70 per cent of both patients and controls experienced symptomatic *anxiety* typically reported as familiar autonomic sensations, and about 40 per cent of both groups evidenced *depressive* phenomena often expressed as feelings of inadequacy. The patient group, however, had 50 per cent more total symptoms than controls, and the groups were strikingly distinguished when symptoms other than anxiety and depression were considered. Only five per cent of the controls manifested acting-out behavior while the corresponding figure was 17 per cent in the patients. Schizophrenia was the principal pattern in 10 per cent of the patients and in four per cent of the controls. Hysterical personality and hypochondriasis were absent in the controls and present in about 15 per cent of the patients.

Although Masterson's method for establishing experimental and control groups according to patient-nonpatient status results in some contamination of variables, the data do suggest that symptoms other than mild anxiety and/or depression are not common in healthy adolescents and may warrant professional attention. The adolescents judged to be "psychiatrically ill" on the basis of their symptom patterns also demonstrated impaired school and social functioning and disturbed family relationships. Adolescents judged "relatively healthy" displayed minimal symptoms, good social adjustment, and satisfying family interactions. The symptoms in the "relatively healthy" adolescents tended to be single, mild in intensity, and episodic in duration.

Masterson found that initial diagnosis in the disturbed adolescents was often difficult to make, but the difficulty lay not in distinguishing between adolescent turmoil and psychiatric illness, but in diagnosing the precise illness. This is a crucial finding which Masterson amplifies in the following statement.

> We found that adolescent turmoil was at most an incidental factor subordinate to that of psychiatric illness in the onset, course, and outcome of the various condi-

tions of our patients. . . . The decisive influence was psychiatric illness, not adolescent turmoil. . . . Without question, there is diagnostic difficulty which often is not resolved until time has passed, but it is not between turmoil and illness and in truth does not seem to be related as much to turmoil as to some of the problems inherent in the manifestations of psychiatric illness.

Masterson reexamined 72 of the 101 clinic patients five years after the initial evaluation and found not only that the symptom patterns persisted, but that there was a clearer differentiation of diagnosis rather than symptom fluctuation. Approximately two thirds of the patients retained moderate to severe impairment five years later, and although Masterson does not focus on relationships between treatment and improvement, he emphatically states that there is no basis for blandly assuming that adolescents will "grow out of" their symptomatic difficulties. In regard to the clinician who receives adolescent referrals, Masterson warns:

> . . . in his clinical evaluation the psychiatrist should substantially lower his index of concern as to what part of the clinical picture is related to turmoil. The burden of proof should be on the psychiatrist to establish that it is not illness if it has that clinical picture and, finally, that such diagnostic categories as adjustment reaction of adolescence, often used as a refuse or wastebasket, should be used with great care and with far more precise definition.

This study differs from those of Douvan and Adelson and Offer in its focus on disturbed adolescent patients, and it challenges aspects of established theory which were not addressed in the large-scale studies of normative teenagers. Masterson's findings do seem to have special relevance for the practicing psychiatrist, and they call into question common diagnostic practices involving the use of such categories as adjustment reaction of adolescence and transient situational disorder.

A recent study by Weiner and Del Gaudio examined adolescent psychopathology patterns and confirmed some of the previously mentioned findings regarding the traditional "turmoil hypothesis."[31] A cumulative psychiatric case register for Monroe County, New York, was used to study the diagnoses of 1,334 adolescent inpatients and outpatients between the ages of 12 and 18 during 1961 and 1962. Personality disorder was the most common primary diagnosis (31.4 per cent), and next in frequency was situational disorder (27.1 per cent). These diagnoses were followed by neurosis (13.3 per cent), schizophrenia (8.5 per cent), and "other" (14.8 per cent).

During a 10-year followup period of 723 members of the original cohort, there was a 54.1 per cent overall diagnostic stability, and 62.2 per cent complete subsequent agreement among patients originally diagnosed as schizophrenic. There was, however, a significant trend toward later diagnosis of schizophrenia including 14.4 per cent of those originally diagnosed as personality disorder, 11.2 per cent of situational disorders, and 21.5 per cent of the "other" category.

These data confirm Masterson's report that adolescent symptom patterns persist and tend to become more clearly differentiated over time. They also raise the possibility that clinicians hedge in diagnosing serious adolescent psychopathology with attendant delay in institution of appropriate treatment. Weiner and Del Gaudio note that adult and adolescent psychopathology shares many epidemiologic characteristics as well as persistence over time. They point out the continuance of myths alluding to normative adolescent turmoil and the benign effects of adolescent symptom formation. They also question the current use of situational disorder in diagnosis. It is noted that subsequent diagnostic agreement is less for situational disorders (14.9 per cent) than for any other major category, and that 11 per cent of the teenagers receiving this diagnosis were later found to be schizophrenic. Although this study and a survey of adolescents seen in outpatient clinics by Rosen et al. suggest that adolescents diagnosed as having situational disorders are treated as frequently as those with more serious diagnoses, it is apparent that overuse of such diagnoses as situational disorder and adjustment reaction could forestall intensive treatment needed by severely disturbed adolescents.[32]

Another very recent contribution to the literature which empirically tests several facets of the storm and stress view is an epidemiologic study by Rutter et al. from Great Britain.[33] Using interviews and questionnaires, the authors evaluated 2,303 rural boys and girls, ages 14 to 15, from the Isle of Wight. Inner turmoil manifested by feelings of misery and inadequacy occurred in 20 per cent of the sample, but the authors state that clinical depression occurred much less frequently. Outer turmoil defined as rebellious behavior was described as commonly occurring only in the children age 14, and it was characterized by verbal disagreements with parents over hairstyle, clothing, and other relatively trivial matters. This was the only normative alienation pattern noted.

Rutter and his colleagues seem to agree with Masterson that mild episodic depression is a common expression of turmoil and is easily distinguished from true psychiatric illness. They state that the prognosis for adolescent psychiatric disorder is much more dependent on diagnosis than age of onset, and that adolescent turmoil may be an intensifying factor in co-existing illness. This study is noteworthy for its confirmatory finding in a rural population of British youth and suggests the need for more study of normative behavior in teenage populations of various socioeconomic and cultural backgrounds.

From a synthesis of the studies reviewed, there emerges the following conceptualization of adolescent turmoil:

○ Adolescents normatively maintain psychic equilibrium as they struggle with developmental tasks.
○ Adolescent development is normatively associated with successful social and family adjustment which persists into early adulthood.
○ Adolescent "turmoil" is normatively manifested in mild forms of depression and anxiety and in minor disagreements with authority figures.

○ Symptoms other than mild depression and anxiety often are indicative of psychiatric illness and may warrant professional attention.

○ Adolescent symptom patterns tend to persist and become better differentiated over time.

○ Adolescent "turmoil" is distinguishable from psychiatric illness but may intensify concurrent disorders.

○ Difficulties in differential diagnosis during adolescence have more to do with obscurities inherent in the psychiatric diagnoses themselves than with the presence or absence of "turmoil."

# Reinforces of the Turmoil Mythology

Although evidence supporting the foregoing view of adolescent turmoil is compelling, there is good reason to believe that the time-honored myths refuted by such evidence are presently alive and well in clinical practice. At this point, it is in order to examine a few factors which may be perpetuating the storm and stress view of adolescence.

1. *Inappropriate Generalization from Samples of Deviant Adolescents.* The psychoanalytic literature has made a profound contribution to the understanding of adolescent development, and classical theory regarding adolescent turmoil continues to exert substantial influence in psychiatry. A major criticism directed toward psychoanalytic authors by certain investigators (e.g., Offer and Masterson) is that they have inappropriately used data from small numbers of adolescent patients to formulate theories of normative teenage behavior. This criticism seems valid in regard to the psychoanalytic view of adolescent turmoil, and it probably applies to mental health professionals in general who are prone to form attitudes and expectations concerning teenagers on the basis of their contact with the disturbed minority of the total adolescent population.

2. *The Generation Gap Myth.* The popular notion that adolescents and their parents are normally embroiled in conflict and hold values worlds apart has been promulgated in the mass media and given support by several influential sources in the professional literature, including Friedenberg, Coleman, Keniston, and Ackerman.[34-38] There can be no argument about the existence on a grand scale of teenage fads, tastes, and cultural heroes which hold little interest for the majority of adults, but there is substantial evidence challenging the existence of basic generational conflict. Elkin and Westley studied a population of children, ages 14 and 15, in a middle-class, suburban community and found that peer group investment was important but less influential in the lives of the teenagers than parental authority and guidance.[39] These adolescents and their parents tended to maintain effective communication and shared basic values.

Based on interviews with a sample of 100 public high school students in 1970, Gossett and co-workers also were much more impressed with the similarities of adolescent religious, political, and value orientations to current parental standards than with the occasional differences noted.[40]

Meissner conducted a questionnaire study of 1,278 high school boys, ages 13 to 18, and found that positive attitudes toward parents were maintained, although the older adolescents showed increasing resistance to parental control.[41] The father was consistently seen in the role of mediator of parental authority, while the mother was perceived as more understanding and receptive. About half of the boys termed their father "old-fashioned," but only 15 per cent reported that their parents were too strict. Internalization of parental norms was characteristic of the large majority of these teenagers.

Lewis and colleagues conducted an intensive study of 44 adolescent-containing families selected for their psychological health and social adaptiveness.[42] Although the generational boundaries in these healthy families were clear, parental power was not exercised in an authoritarian way, and negotiation was common. It was also noted that a core of "superego beliefs" remained unchallenged and shared by parents and children. Lewis et al. recognize the narrowness of their sample and do not speculate on the proportion of optimally functioning families in the general population, but this pioneering study, along with a similar project conducted with Canadian families by Westley and Epstein,[43] does confirm the extensive data of Douvan and Adelson, Offer, and others who found no significant generation gap in the families of normative adolescents.

3. *Popular Literature.* Our understanding of adolescent struggles has been tremendously enriched through sensitive portrayals written by authors such as James Joyce, J. D. Salinger, Sherwood Anderson, and Thomas Wolfe. Writers of this stature have elaborated profound descriptions of the inner lives of their adolescent characters, but it is quite apparent that it is not the normative teenager who captures the imagination of the artist or the fancy of the reading public. Several prototypic adolescents (e.g., Holden Caulfield and George Willard) have emerged from the popular literature, and the images they project are characterized by varying degrees of inner turbulence, painful introspection, exceptional sensitivity and vulnerability, and semidelinquent behavior. Atypical adolescence thus acquires an aura of mystique and glamor which serves to perpetuate the storm and stress myth. Inappropriate generalization occurs in this context as it does in other contexts previously mentioned. A corollary process involves the sensationalism so evident in television and motion picture portrayals of deviant teenagers.

4. *Attitudes of Mental Health Professionals.* There is considerable research and anecdotal data to suggest that many psychiatrists, as well as other professionals who work with teenagers, ascribe to and practice according to the storm and stress view of adolescence. In addition to the educational and training variables involved, there are personal factors which bear consideration. Our perceptions and expectations of teenage behavior are colored by our own adolescent experiences. Many professionals have difficulty dealing

with adolescent patients because of the feelings and memories that are stirred up about their own teenage years.

Burton et al.[44] and Henry et al.[45] have extensively studied the personal and social backgrounds of mental health clinicians, and their research suggests that, as a group, these professionals are likely to come from somewhat dysfunctional families. This finding increases the possibility that clinicians who have experienced a great deal of conflict during their teenage years and/or have parented "stormy" adolescent children, are biased toward seeing adolescent psychopathology as normal. An attitude of "anything goes during adolescence" may thus develop from very personal and idiosyncratic sources.

Such an attitude constitutes a position held, it is hoped, by only a few clinicians, but minimization and underdiagnosis of adolescent symptomatology is an apparently common practice. An opposite and equally extreme position would involve gross overinterpretation of superficial signs of nonconformity as evidence for serious pathology. Some clinicians are uncomfortable with and even threatened by adolescent fads in hairstyle, dress, and vernacular, and they may be inclined to regard as abnormal any deviation from their personal norms for adults and adolescents.

Although it is unlikely that many clinicians endorse either of these positions, it is highly probable that a variety of personal factors influence one's conceptualization of adolescent turmoil. Having some understanding of those personal factors is important for the professional who evaluates and treats adolescent patients.

# Clinical Assessment of the Adolescent Patient

It has been previously noted that the clinician faces a formidable challenge in determining whether or not an adolescent's symptoms signify psychological disturbance which requires therapeutic intervention. In contrast to the large body of literature addressing the theoretical aspects of this clinical problem, there is a paucity of literature providing practical guidelines for evaluation of the adolescent patient. The following section discusses an approach to diagnostic assessment and offers a framework for determining the meaning of symptoms in the adolescent patient.[46]

Many variables must be considered in the assessment process, and it is useful to organize these at three general levels: individual, family, and sociocultural.

1. *Individual Level.* The stage of development must be carefully considered in evaluating the adolescent patient. The physical and psychological differences between early and late adolescence are substantial, and the meaning of symptoms can be understood only if such differences are appreciated. The presenting symptoms of a junior high school student may have meaning entirely different from that of similar symptoms in a college freshman. Several developmental issues bear consideration:

Early adolescents use behavior much more than words to express and defend against conflicts. With maturation there is less reliance on behavioral expression, and the ability to verbalize feelings and conflicts is characteristic of late adolescents.

Normative worries change with age. Early adolescents commonly show intense preoccupation with body image and pubertal changes, while late adolescents achieve stable, positive feelings about body image and normal physiologic processes. Late adolescents tend to be much more concerned with issues involving identity, emancipation from the family, career choice, and heterosexual relationships.

Early adolescents normatively experience great flux in sense of identity, while late adolescents demonstrate relatively stable identity formation with emerging sense of life direction. The high school senior whose self-concept vacillates between omnipotence and worthlessness is of much greater concern than the eighth-grade student whose display of bravado one day is replaced by self-conscious withdrawal the next.

The nature of peer relationships changes with maturation. Early adolescents usually have one or two close friends of the same sex. As development progresses, the need for peer group support increases with a concomitant need to exclude adults from peer activities. Boys lag behind girls in development of heterosexual interests, but by middle adolescence there is active social contact between sexes accompanied by increasing sexual experimentation encompassing a wide range of normative behavior. In late adolescence the interpersonal relationships with both sexes become less narcissistic and more serious, and the need for group support diminishes. Greater clinical concern is warranted for the patient, age 18, who complains that his peers are "always letting me down" than for the patient, age 13, who presents with a similar complaint.

Relationships with parents and nonparental adults change as development proceeds. Early adolescents normatively defend against dependency on parents through minor rebellion over issues of dress, household chores, curfew hours, and the like. Delinquency and extreme alienation from parents, however, are not part of normative rebellion. Late adolescents tend to be concerned with realistic problems of emancipation and adopt a "live and let live" attitude toward parents. Early adolescents have few relationships with nonparental adults, while late adolescents show increasing investment in adult society and are able to maintain collaborative relationships with a number of nonparental adults.

In order to assess the meaning of symptoms at an individual level, it is necessary to clarify the number, duration, intensity, and form of the symptoms.

At one end of the clinical spectrum are youngsters who present with mild depression or anxiety of brief duration, clearly related to environmental stress and not associated with significant decline in functioning at home, in school, or with peers. Teenagers who present with this normative symptom pattern may experience considerable relief through the assessment process itself and through simple environmental manipulations. Clinical concern and the need for therapeutic intervention increase for youngsters who present with symptoms that are multiple, chronic, or intense. Compromised functioning in any area is also cause for concern. Nonspecific signs of ego weakness (e.g. impulsivity, low frustration tolerance, lack of observing ego) increase the likelihood that significant psychopathology is present.

At the most disturbed end of the spectrum are adolescents who present with severe symptoms of long duration which invade many areas of functioning. Profoundly disturbed adolescents may also present with bizarre symptoms of varying number and duration.

A thorough developmental history is essential for understanding symptoms at an individual level, and an attempt should be made to evaluate the process-reactive nature of the symptomatology. It is likewise important to identify current stress factors and to determine how the adolescent has coped with stress in the past.

Other individual variables which require careful exploration include school performance, peer relationships, and ego strengths.

A careful detailed school history is indispensable to the assessment process. A grade-by-grade account of school experience should be obtained from the adolescent and his or her parents, but this information is often conflicting and inaccurate. More objective data can be obtained by examining school records and report cards which reflect patterns of academic achievement, attendance, and peer interactions. Discrepancies among information provided by the adolescent, the parents, and the school may give clues to individual and family dynamics and should be noted. If the adolescent works, a similarly detailed job history is useful.

The quality of peer relationships is a potent measure of ego development and functioning, and this area should be carefully evaluated. As previously noted, peer relationship patterns change during adolescence, and the individual patient's stage of development must be kept in mind. Preference for significantly older or younger individuals is a frequent indication of disturbance, and sudden changes in peer preference may reflect significant psychopathology. Clinical concern is highest for adolescents who evidence sustained isolation from peers, a frequent role as peer scapegoat, or peer interactions based on antisocial behavior.

Adolescents are often referred for evaluation during times of crisis when their symptoms are most severe. At these times it is especially important to look for evidence of ego strengths and to assess coping skills. Ego strengths to evaluate include sublimatory capacity (e.g., hobbies, athletics, extracurricular activities), impulse control, sense of humor, capacity for self-observation, and likeability. Other positive characteristics to note include productivity in school and work, capacity to have fun, and the presence of at least one age-appropriate friendship.

2. *Family Level.* Some understanding of family system characteristics and

dynamics is essential to assessment of the adolescent patient. Clinical research has demonstrated relationships between individual and family levels of functioning, and it is impossible to understand the meaning of an adolescent's symptoms without insight into the family system. The previously noted work of Lewis et al. describes a useful approach to family evaluation and discusses how individual symptoms may express pathologic processes within the family. Suffice it to state here that it is important to determine the extent to which family system equilibrium is maintained by the symptoms of the identified adolescent patient. It is equally important to identify family processes which support the growth and autonomy of the adolescent.

3. *Sociocultural Level.* It is within the scope of this paper to make only a few general comments regarding the importance of social, economic, and cultural factors in the assessment of the adolescent.

Norms and expectations for academic achievement, impulse control, sexual behavior, and physical aggression vary significantly among subcultures, and markedly deviant behavior in one group may be considered highly adaptive in another.

Ego strengths and coping skills, as well as symptoms, must be evaluated in the context of sociocultural factors, and it is helpful to assess the adolescent's utilization of the sublimatory channels available in his or her environment. Sublimation, however, may not be a highly valued form of adaptation for adolescents in some subcultures, and open expression of sexual and aggressive impulses may be sanctioned. This observation underscores the necessity of viewing the adolescent's clinical picture from multiple perspectives.

# Summary

The theoretical issue of adolescent turmoil and its psychiatric significance is central to the clinical task of distinguishing between normality and abnormality in the adolescent. The traditional storm and stress view of adolescence postulates that serious turmoil and major symptom formation are characteristic of normal adolescent development. A number of clinical research studies report findings which strongly challenge the storm and stress view of adolescence and support the view that "turmoil" in the traditional sense is not the normative hallmark of the teenage years. Substantial data indicate that adolescent symptom formation is to be taken seriously, and that there is a need to lower the threshold of clinical concern for the symptomatic difficulties of adolescent patients.

It is likely that several factors are involved in perpetuation of the mythology surrounding the issue of adolescent turmoil. These factors seem to be professional, cultural, and personal in nature. It is important for the clinician who evaluates and treats adolescents to examine critically the sources of his or her own conceptualization of adolescent turmoil.

The clinical assessment of the adolescent patient involves consideration of a host of variables which may be approached from individual, family, and sociocultural perspectives. Individual characteristics which should be carefully evaluated include stage of adolescent development, nature of the symptoms, developmental history, school performance, peer relationships, and ego strengths. An estimate of the level of family system functioning should be made, and it is important to determine the role of the adolescent and his or her symptoms in family homeostasis. The sociocultural level of assessment is essential to the process of understanding the meaning of symptoms in the adolescent patient, and it should be integrated with the individual and family levels of assessment.

## REFERENCE NOTES

1. Hall, G. S., *Adolescence: Its Psychology and Its Relations to Physiology, Anthropology, Sociobiology, Sex, Crime, Religion, and Education*, Vols. I and II, Appleton, New York, 1904.
2. Mead, M., *Coming of Age in Samoa*, Morrow, New York, 1928.
3. Mead, M., "Adolescence in Primitive and Modern Society," in (F. V. Calverton & S. D. Schmalhausen, eds.), *The New Generation: A Symposium*, Macauley, New York, 1930.
4. Benedict, R., "Continuities and Discontinuities in Cultural Conditioning," *Psychiatry*, 1:161–167, 1938.
5. Jones, E., "Some Problems of Adolescence," *Br. J. Psychiatry*, 13:41–47, 1922.
6. Aichorn, A., *Wayward Youth*, Viking, New York, 1935.
7. Bernfield, S., "Types of Adolescence," *Psychoanal. Quart.*, 7:243–253, 1938.
8. Freud, A., *The Ego and the Mechanisms of Defense*, International Universities Press, New York, 1946.
9. Freud, A., "Adolescence," in *The Psychoanalytic Study of the Child*, Vol. 13, International Universities Press, New York, 1958. Pp. 255–278.
10. Spiegel, L., "Identify and Adolescence," in (S. Lorand & H. I. Schneer, eds.), *Adolescents: Psychoanalytic Approach to Problems and Therapy*, Hoeber, New York, 1961. Pp. 10–18.
11. Fountain, G., "Adolescent into Adult: An Inquiry," *J. Am. Psychoanal. Assoc.*, 9:417–433, 1961.
12. Josselyn, I., "The Ego in Adolescence," *Am. J. Psychiatry*, 24:223–237, 1954.
13. Erikson, E., "The Problem of Ego Identity," *J. Am. Psychoanal. Assoc.*, 4:56–121, 1956.
14. Blos, P., *On Adolescence*, Free Press, New York, 1962.
15. Blos, P., "The Second Individuation Process of Adolescence," in *The Psychoanalytic Study of the Child*, Vol. 22, International Universities Press, 1967. Pp. 162–186.
16. Geleerd, E., "Some Aspects of Psychoanalytic Technique in Adolescence," in *The Psychoanalytic Study of the Child*, Vol. 12, International Universities Press, New York, 1957. Pp. 263–283.
17. Lindemann, E., "Adolescent Behavior as a Community Concern," *Am. J. Psychother.*, 18:405–417, 1964.
18. Douvan, E., & Adelson, J., *The Adolescent Experience*, Wiley, New York, 1966.
19. Westley, W., "Emotionally Healthy Adolescents and Their Family Backgrounds," in (I. Goldstein, ed.), *The Family in Contemporary Society*, International Universities Press, New York, 1958.

20. Grinker, R. R., Sr., "Mentally Healthy Young Males (Homoclites)," *Arch. Gen. Psychiatry,* 6:405–453, 1962.
21. Silber, E., et al., "Competent Adolescents Coping with College Decisions," *Arch. Gen. Psychiatry,* 5:517–527, 1961.
22. Offer, D., & Sabshin, M., "The Psychiatrist and the Normal Adolescent," *Arch. Gen. Psychiatry,* 9:427–432, 1963.
23. Offer, D., Sabshin, M., & Marcus, D., "Clinical Evaluation of Normal Adolescents," *Am. J. Psychiatry,* 121:864–872, 1965.
24. Offer, D., "Normal Adolescents: Interview Strategy and Selected Results," *Arch. Gen. Psychiatry,* 17:285–290, 1967.
25. Offer, D., *The Psychological World of the Teenager,* Basic Books, Inc., New York, 1969.
26. Srole, L., et al., *Mental Health in the Metropolis: The Midtown Manhattan Study,* McGraw-Hill, New York, 1962.
27. Masterson, J., & Washburne, A., "The Symptomatic Adolescent: Psychiatric Illness or Adolescent Turmoil," *Am. J. Psychiatry,* 122:1240–1247, 1966.
28. Masterson, J., "The Symptomatic Adolescent Five Years Later: He Didn't Grow Out of It," *Am. J. Psychiatry,* 123:1338–1345, 1967.
29. Masterson, J., *The Psychiatric Dilemma of Adolescence,* Little Brown, Boston, 1967.
30. Masterson, J., "The Psychiatric Significance of Adolescent Turmoil," *Am. J. Psychiatry,* 124:1549, 1968.
31. Weiner, I., & Del Gaudio, A., "Psychopathology in Adolescence," *Arch. Gen. Psychiatry,* 33:187–193, 1976.
32. Rosen, B., et al., "Adolescent Patients Served in Outpatient Psychiatric Clinics," *Am. J. Pub. Health,* 55:1563–1577, 1965.
33. Rutter, M., et al., "Adolescent Turmoil: Fact or Fiction?", *J. Child Psychol., Psychiatry Allied Discipline,* 17:35–56, 1976.
34. Friedenberg, E., *The Vanishing Adolescent,* Beacon, Boston, 1959.
35. Coleman, J. S., *The Adolescent Society,* Free Press of Glencoe, New York, 1961.
36. Keniston, K., *The Uncommitted: Alienated Youth in American Society,* Harcourt, Brace, and World, New York, 1965.
37. Ackerman, N. W., *The Psychodynamics of Family Life,* Basic Books, New York, 1958.
38. Ackerman, N. W., "Adolescent Problems: A Symptom of Family Disorder," *Family Process,* 1:202–213, 1962.
39. Elkin, F., & Westley, W. A., "The Myth of Adolescent Culture," *Am. Soc. Rev.,* 20:680–684, 1955.
40. Gossett, J., Lewis, J., & Phillips, V., "Psychological Characteristics of Adolescent Drug Users and Abstainers," *Bull. Men. Clin.,* 36:425–435, 1972.
41. Meissner, W., "Parental Interaction of the Adolescent Boy," *J. Genetic Psychol.,* 107:225–233, 1965.
42. Lewis, J., et al., *No Single Thread: Psychological Health in Family Systems,* Brunner/Mazel, New York, 1976.
43. Westley, W., & Epstein, N., *The Silent Majority,* Jossey-Bass, Inc., San Francisco, 1969.
44. Burton, A., et al., *Twelve Therapists,* Jossey-Bass, Inc., San Francisco, 1972.
45. Henry, W., Sims, J., & Spray, S., *The Fifth Dimension,* Jossey-Bass, Inc., San Francisco, 1971.
46. Looney, J., Oldham, D., & Blotcky, M., "Teaching the Assessment of the Meaning of Symptoms in Adolescents," presented at the Annual Meeting of the American Academy of Child Psychiatry, Houston, Texas, 1977.

# E. Early and Middle Adulthood: Introduction

T HE YOUNG ADULT, with transition to social independence now complete, becomes the center of an autonomous social atom. This is not to say that ties to parents and family are severed; far from it. There is considerable evidence of a lifelong interchange between adult children and aging parents. Rather, the autonomy refers to taking on responsibilities as well as the privileges of adulthood. One of these responsibilities concerns the new family (Chilman) and how the couple attempts to regulate the production of offspring (Westoff and Jones; However, such private decisions become public social concerns as well as having implications for preservation of the species (Turner and Darity).

The day-to-day life of the young and middle age adult is filled with the routines required by society to maintain the social order. But various stages of this period are observable (Livson), with some being problematic (Shostak; Rohrlich et al.) or filled with potential (Bem; Wuthnow). These are but a few samples of events during this period of human growth and development. In each case, the social atom is growing as complex as the ones from which it developed, and it is producing new units that will, in turn, become autonomous.

By the end of this section, readers should have some understanding of the basic tasks of early and middle adulthood.

*Physical Tasks:* Nature produces the young; society produces the mature. In early adulthood, as the person is growing in social skills and resources, there is an imperceptible series of changes taking place within. In the thirties and forties these physical changes become increasingly evident, as the problems of overweight become visible and as sensory deterioration begins, as is evidenced in the need for bifocal glasses. However, the physical potentials of adolescence may come to maturity in the early and middle years as muscular strength is exercised.

*Psychological Tasks:* As the fruits of his or her labors emerge—children, results from employment, and the various forms of social activities—the young adult is faced with a series of tandem choices. Children require attention and resources that cannot be directed elsewhere; aging parents likewise make demands on time and energies that are no longer limitless. Employment may become a preoccupation that drowns out the other aspects of life, and yet it may also be a deeply satisfying activity. Pleasure-seeking, long forbidden to the immature, now becomes legally possible—sexual explorations, travel, other mind-expanding activities. But the conscience was formed in the young and continues to speak to the adult. And behind all of these activities and choices is the one event of which there is no choice: recognizing one's own mortality.

*Social Tasks:* Adulthood is synonymous with full-time work for most persons and evolving a standard of living commensurate with that work. But, in addition, adults must relate to various social institutions for their own sake, as well as for the sake of their children and their aging parents. The peak of social power and status is reached in these middle adult years, with privileges assigned accordingly. Civic contributions often peak at this time, as well as an involved social life. Yet middle age is unexplored territory compared to other phases of the life-span. Each adult is, to some extent, an explorer of his or her own life and circumstances, which give the results of the search a philosophical flavor as each individual seeks meaning from routine (cf. Havighurst, 1952).

---

# New Family Forms*
## *Catherine S. Chilman*

[In this excerpt, Dr. Chilman discusses some aspects of the social background that have influenced the family in the 1970s.]

## . . . Statistical Data

A quick look at the data will provide one level of understanding about what is going on.

**Marriage Rates.**   The marriage rate continues to be high, with over 90 per cent of the adult population having been married at least once.[1] However, today only 70 per cent of the young people between the ages of twenty-two and twenty-six have married. Some observers see this as evidence of a new trend in nonmarriage, or greatly deferred marriage, in a large segment of the

---

* Reprinted with permission of the publisher and the author from Catherine S. Chilman, "New Family Forms," *Social Welfare Forum,* 1973, New York: Columbia University Press, 1973.
[1] Bureau of the Census, *The Social and Economic Status of the Black Population in the United States, 1971* (Washington, D.C.: U.S. Government Printing Office, 1971), No. 42, p. 23.

youth population.[2] Although the monthly Vital Statistics Report (1973) shows that the marriage rate is higher than at any time in the past five years, this largely reflects remarriage among older people rather than the marriage of younger ones. The average age at first marriage is also somewhat higher than in the recent past, the peak of early marriages having been reached in 1955.

Since 1960 there has been a marked upsurge in the number of people living alone; households are being "uncoupled," as the experts say. This trend is particularly noticeable among the elderly and among young males.[3] Some claim that this trend may be equally strong among young females, but that the latter hesitated to report this to census takers.

**Divorce on the Increase.** The proportion of divorced people in this country has grown by about 80 per cent over the last ten years. The best estimate is that one fourth of all marriages end in divorce. Although it is frequently claimed that the United States has the highest divorce rate in the world, it is not entirely clear whether this is so, partly because of difficulties experienced by many countries in obtaining accurate statistics. Then too, high divorce rates do not necessarily mean higher rates of nonmarrieds in the population. For one thing, the United States has one of the highest marriage rates in the world; therefore, a larger proportion of the population is exposed to the possibility of divorce. Furthermore, with lengthened life expectancy, it is possible for marriages to last much longer than they once did (about fifty years), which creates a longer period of time in which divorce may be both tempting and possible. High divorce rates may be a sign of affluence. Today more people can *afford* divorces and their sequelae. At present, the total divorce rate is close to the all-time peak of 1946.[4] Nevertheless, only about 6 per cent of women and 4 per cent of men were in divorced status in 1971. However, twice as many black women (12.5 per cent) and one and one-half as many black men (5.5 per cent) were in divorced status at that time.

The great majority of divorces occur by the time people have reached age forty-five. The median age at first divorce is declining and probably is now at some point in the late twenties.[5] Although the largest number of divorces usually occur during the first five years of marriage, recent trends show another, smaller, peak when couples are in their early forties.

Contrary to popular impressions, the great majority of divorced people

[2] Paul C. Glick and Arthur J. Norton, "Perspectives on the Recent Upturn in Divorce and Remarriage," Population Association of America in Toronto, Canada (Washington, D.C.: Bureau of the Census, U.S. Department of Commerce, 1972).

[3] Bureau of the Census, *Current Population Reports; Population Characteristics: Marriage, Divorce, and Remarriages by Year of Birth,* June, 1971. Series P. 20, No. 239, September, 1972 (Washington, D.C.: U.S. Government Printing Office, 1972).

[4] U.S. Department of Health, Education, and Welfare National Center for Health Statistics, *Monthly Vital Statistics Report,* XXI (1973), 3.

[5] Bureau of the Census, *Current Population Reports.*

who remarry do not get divorced and remarried again. Only one per cent of those who had remarried by 1971 and were between ages forty-five and fifty-four had been divorced twice and married three times. Apparently, the belief that many people are engaging in "serial monogamy" is more titillating than true.

**Birth Rate Down.** The birth rate has been dropping sharply and is currently at the lowest point in our recorded history—down 10 per cent from 1971. About one fourth of young couples (with the husband under age thirty-five) are childless, compared to 18 per cent in 1960. According to the polls, the majority of young people today say that they desire one or two children, compared to the "ideal" family size of two to three children expressed ten years ago. (Today's young people had best keep the average family size to two children if there is not to be another serious population explosion.)

According to Conrad Taeuber, director of the 1970 Census, "it looks as if the years leading to 1985 will be the era of young marrieds," a result of the 1948–58 baby boom. Whether or not the great majority of these young people will marry is a moot point; whether or not most of them will have children is also moot; but it is clear there will continue to be a remarkably large youth population at least through 1984.

**Senior Families.** The decline in the birth rate, starting in the late 1950s, plus prolonged life expectancy means that the average age of the population will continue to rise during the next few decades. About 10 per cent of the population is over sixty-five, with over 25 per cent more females than males in this group. The majority of these men are married, and the majority of the women widowed, many of them living alone. The plight of our elderly is well-known; the major family-related fact is that the chances of remarriage for older women are slight, a situation leading to proposals that new marriage patterns, such as polygamy, be made acceptable for the elderly.

More demographic facts, with profound implications for the family, are the combination of early marriages, early childbearing, small family size, and long life expectancy. These trends have created a relatively new situation for married couples. On the average, they spend many more years of their marriage (twenty-five or more) without children in the home than with children present. Historically, child rearing was the central cultural reason for marriage throughout the life span; usually one parent died before the last child left home. Under modern conditions, long-lasting marriage needs a different rationale. Also, these new conditions offer an opportunity for a very long second honeymoon that can be extremely rewarding. In fact, various studies reveal that marital happiness tends to increase after the mid-forties and on into the sixties.[6]

[6] Catherine Chilman, "Families at Mid-Stage in the Family Life Cycle," *Family Life Coordinator*, XVII (1968), 297–312.

**More Women at Work.**   Urbanization and suburbanization often create new conditions that make a greater variety of family forms possible. Linked with this and related trends is the growth in female employment outside the home. Over 40 per cent of females of working age are in the labor force, a large number of whom are parents of young children. As greater numbers of women attain higher levels of education, and as better jobs become more available to them, fewer are likely to settle for traditional marriage and parenthood roles. In fact, some of the traditional patterns of homemaking and child care are on the way to becoming obsolete. They are largely based on nonpaid, small-unit, only partially mechanized hand labor, while the larger economy features wages and fringe benefits, mass production, and mechanization. As a result, home and family life have counterbalancing allures, but also maladaptive features—especially for wives and mothers.

# Major Developments

**Less Rationale for the Nuclear Family.**   All in all, current demographic and economic trends create a situation in which marriage and parenthood have little rationale as life patterns for virtually everyone. A variety of life styles would be more appropriate as an accepted social norm, both for the present and for the foreseeable future.

Such a variety would not constitute a major break with history. In fact, marriage and the family as known today were not the prevailing European pattern until the beginning of the last century. Earlier, it was something of a luxury.[7] And is it only recently that Western European countries have reached the affluence and industrialization that support marriage rates approximating those in the United States. Although all human groups that we know about have had some form of marriage and family organization from earliest times, this has not universally precluded coexisting life styles.

Again contrary to popular belief, the nuclear family does not reflect the highest form of family organization throughout history. According to some scholars,[8] the most primitive societies had small, nuclear families. Extended families were more characteristic of somewhat advanced agricultural societies. Industrialization tends to bring a return to the nuclear form.

Although earlier students saw the small nuclear family as the dominant form in the United States, later scholars found that there are actually a number of coexisting family structures: the strong kinship network system of various national groups such as the Jews, Italians, and Poles; the nuclear

[7] Jessie Bernard, *The Future of Marriage* (New York: World Publishing Co., 1972).

[8] Claude Levi-Strauss, "The Family" in Arlene Skolnick and Jerome Skolnick, eds., *Family in Transition* (Boston: Little, Brown and Co., 1971); Alan Lomax, "The Evolution of Culture and Expressive Style: A Comparative Approach to Social Change" in *Social Change and Human Behavior* (Washington, D.C.: N.I.M.H. U.S. Government Printing Office, 1972), pp. 41–68.

family of the WASPS (who, nevertheless, have many more kinship ties than is often supposed); and the one-parent family often (but not usually) found among blacks, especially at low-income levels in urban settings.[9]

Most family reformers do not actually call for an end to marriage and the family, and few actually challenge the importance of the family as a major form of social organization. Rather, some plead particularly for social norms that approve of a variety of life options;[10] others particularly decry the *nuclear* family as a major social form, pleading for extended families of people related by mutual interests. Such families, they say, would offer a greater breadth of human relationships and would help offset the depersonalizing forces of today's society.[11] A number of family reformers stress the need for social and legal acceptance of the various family forms that already exist in our society, and many emphasize the need for changed perceptions of female sex roles both within and outside family life. Others stress the need for less exclusivity in marriage and a calmer acceptance of extramarital affairs for both partners.[12]

**Rationale for Changes.** Among the other reasons for such proposals are:
1. Marriage tends to be worse for women than for men.

Although myth would have it otherwise, single women tend to be healthier and freer of neurotic symptoms than married ones. Further, since women usually seek to marry men who are somewhat more intelligent than themselves, the more brilliant females tend to not marry, while this tends to be true of the *least* capable males. On most indices, married men are likely to be the healthiest group in the population, and most secure in happiness, income, and over-all stability.[13] They are followed by single women, married women, and single men. If married women work, this seems to reduce their neurotic symptoms, as shown by a study comparing nonworking and working wives. Nevertheless, married women still have higher rates of emotional distress than single ones. Of course, it may not be that employment helps wives become less disturbed; comparatively better adjusted wives may seek employment.[14]

In terms of self-perception of happiness, a large number of wives rate their marriages as happy, and only about 3 per cent of both husbands and wives rate them as very unhappy. Furthermore, only about one fourth of single

[9] Skolnick and Skolnick, *op. cit.*

[10] Bernard, *op. cit.*

[11] Larry Constantine and Joan Constantine, "Dissolution of Marriage in a Nonconventional Context," *Family Life Coordinator*, XXI (1972), 457–62; Larry Constantine and Joan Constantine, "Where Is Marriage Going?" in Joann S. Delora and Jack R. Delora, eds., *Intimate Life Styles* (Pacific Palisades, CA: Goodyear Publishing Co., 1972).

[12] Morton Hunt, "The Future of Marriage," in Delora and Delora, *op. cit.*

[13] Bernard, *op. cit.*

[14] *Ibid.*

women (compared to nearly half of married ones) rate their lives as very happy. The single state brings about even higher rates of unhappiness for men than for women, however, with 20 per cent of single men seeing themselves as mostly unhappy, compared to about 12 per cent of single women.[15]

2. Marriage is particularly difficult for wives when there are children although parenthood appears to detract from the marital happiness of fathers as well.

Again, Bernard cites a number of studies to explode another myth: that childless marriages are less happy than those with children. The reverse appears to be true, on the average. In fact, one study[16] shows that children are considered particularly important to the marriage when the parents are not especially happy in their marital relationship.

3. The rates of sexual satisfaction for women have been lower than that for males.

Until fairly recently it was assumed that many females were naturally or untreatably nonorgasmic, that a large proportion of this group really did not object to this situation, and that the female sex drive was lower than that of the male. The double standard of sex morality was interwoven with these assumptions.

The research efforts of Kinsey in 1953 and of Masters and Johnson in 1966 and 1970, following the pioneering work of others reported by Brecher in a 1971 summary of research, have helped to shatter these illusions. We now find that the female sex drive is at least as strong as that of the male, perhaps stronger; that females may well have an orgasmic capacity superior to that of males; that sex interest and the capacity for sexual response continue far into old age for both males and females.

These findings, together with other social, economic, and political factors of contemporary life, combine to present a radically different view of human sexuality, especially female sexuality. With the addition of the "contraceptive revolution" that frequently includes legalized abortion, we certainly do have altered life situations, situations that lead to females having a new vision of possibilities for themselves. These visions may include more and better sex outside as well as within marriage; the choice of childlessness or only a few children; the choice of marriage or nonmarriage; in short, the choice of many kinds of life patterns. And if females seek wider freedoms and choices, this inevitably affects the options that are open to males. Of course, males not only react to female visions, they have plenty of their own, ranging from more liberated, nontraditional life styles for themselves to a reassertion of male power and dominance. Whatever position they take, both males and females are caught up in the sexual evolution.

4. I use the term "sexual evolution" advisedly because marked changes in sexual values and behaviors have been in progress for at least fifty years in

[15] *Ibid.*

[16] Eleanor Luckey and Janet Bain, "Children: A Factor in Marital Satisfaction," *Journal of Marriage and the Family,* XXXII, No. 1 (1970), 43–45.

this country. Higher rates of premarital and extramarital sex first occurred, especially for middle- and upper-class young women, in the 1920s, and of course, this female behavior affected male behavior. Primarily, it shifted nonmarital male sex behavior from relationships with prostitutes, call girls, and members of the "underclass" to relationships with their female peers. Changes in values in the more advantaged socioeconomic groups began to diffuse throughout the population somewhat later, although this diffusion is still far from complete.[17]

Until the late 1960s the chief features of the so-called "sex revolution" seemed to be attitudinal: more openness and honesty about sex behavior; lessened belief in the double standard; an increased acceptance of nonmarital sex if it were combined with affection and personal responsibility; recognition that sexual gratification of both husband and wife is an important and legitimate part of the marital relationship; and rising aspirations for self-actualization through sexual fulfillment.

Within the past few years, the rate of premarital sexual behavior has been rising somewhat.[18] For the most part, this higher rate is not synonymous with a higher rate of promiscuity; most of this behavior tends to occur within a semipermanent relationship. (This statement is most likely to apply to the more advantaged socioeconomic groups. The harshly adverse effects of poverty, especially when combined with racism and urban disorganization, tend to create more transitory and exploitative relationships between those males and females who are at the bottom of the socioeconomic ladder.[19])

Although we hear a great deal about more sexual promiscuity, as in the case of "group sex"[20] and as some people fantasy about communal arrangements, the incidence of such behavior is actually very low, probably involving less than one per cent of the population.

All in all, it is probably healthy that we are becoming more open and

[17] Catherine Chilman, *Growing Up Poor* (Washington, D.C.: U.S. Government Printing Office, 1966); Alfred C. Kinsey et al., *Sexual Behavior in the Human Male* (Philadelphia: W. B. Saunders Co., 1948); Alfred C. Kinsey and Paul H. Gebhard, *Sexual Behavior in the Human Female* (Philadelphia: W. B. Saunders Co., 1953); Mirra Komarovsky, *Blue Collar Marriage* (New York: Random House, 1964); Lee Rainwater and Karol Weinstein, *And the Poor Get Children* (Chicago: Quadrangle Books, 1960).

[18] Robert Sorensen, *Adolescent Sexuality in Contemporary America* (New York: World Publishing Co., 1973); John Zelnick and Melvin Kantor, "Adolescent Sex Behavior in the United States," *Family Planning Perspectives,* V. No. 1 (1973), 5–21.

[19] Boone Hammond and Joyce Ladner, "Growing Up in a Negro Slum Ghetto," in Carl Broderick and Jessie Bernard, eds., *The Individual, Sex and Society* (Baltimore: Johns Hopkins University Press, 1968), pp. 41–52; Oscar Lewis, *Children of Sanchez* (New York: Random House, 1961); Lee Rainwater, *Family Design* (Chicago: Aldine Publishing Co., 1965); Bernard Rosenberg and Joseph Bensman, "Sexual Patterns in Three Ethnic Sub-cultures of an American Under-class,' in J. Robbins and J. Robbins, eds., *An Analysis of Human Sexual Inadequacy* (New York: New American Library; 1971), pp. 361–72.

[20] Gilbert D. Bartell, *Group Sex* (New York: Wyden, 1971); James W. Ramey, "Emerging Patterns of Family Innovative Behavior in Marriage," *Family Life Coordinator,* XXI (1972), 435–56.

honest about our sex needs, interests, and behavior. For much too long, repression, secrecy, anxiety, and guilt about valid human drives have tortured males and females alike. It seems likely that if sexual attitudes and values become more tolerant, sexual behavior will also become freer. And this too is probably healthier for most people. Again, for much too long, many people, especially girls and women, have been badly thwarted in finding sexual fulfillment. Their resulting hostilities and depression have made lives hard for themselves and for their men. However, the current plea for *total* sexual freedom, so long as it is private and by mutual consent, may be unwise. Perhaps total freedom would place too much responsibility for decision-making on individuals; even in the animal world, as well as in the human world, there have always been formalized restraints on sexual behavior. We need to evolve new values that provide for more freedom, within well-defined limits, but not place the entire burden of decision-making on individuals. . . .

# Contraception and Sterilization in the United States, 1965–1975*

## Charles F. Westoff and Elise F. Jones

IN 1975, AN ESTIMATED three of every four married couples using contraception had been sterilized or were using the pill or an intrauterine device. A decade earlier, just a little more than one-third were using these highly effective methods.[1] The following account describes that extraordinary development during the decade since 1965.

## Sources of Data and Methodology

The 1975 National Fertility Study (NFS) is based on data collected from a national probability sample of continuously married (that is, once-married and currently married) women who were white, married fewer than 25 years and before the age of 25, and whose husbands also were once-married. For marriages of more than five years' duration, the sample consists of eligible women selected from the 1970 NFS sample who were reinterviewed after an

* Reprinted with the permission of the authors and publisher from *Family Planning Perspectives*, 1977, 9:4, 153–157.

interval of approximately five years.* A proportionate sample of 1,042 new respondents was added to represent marriages that occurred after 1970. These, together with the 2,361 women successfully reinterviewed, constitute a total sample of 3,403 respondents. The bulk of the analysis presented here relates only to women with these characteristics. We have prepared one table (Table 6), however, in which we estimate the distribution of contraceptive practice for the entire U.S. population of currently married women of reproductive age.

As might be anticipated, the 2,361 women successfully reinterviewed in 1975 were not entirely representative of the original target population of 2,825 women in a number of respects that could have some significance for estimates of contraceptive exposure. While difficult to evaluate, the extent of this bias does not appear to be sufficient to produce serious distortion in our estimates. Furthermore, the bias is partly corrected by standardizing the contraceptive exposure distributions for different study years on the 1970 distribution by duration of marriage (as in Table 1). This procedure also eliminates the effects of changes across the decade in the marriage duration composition of the sample, facilitating a description of time trends in contraceptive practice.

The primary comparisons of 1975 estimates are with data drawn from the 1965 and the 1970 NFS.[2] To supplement these bodies of data as well as to provide a picture of any more recent changes in contraceptive practice, we have included some tabulations from the 1973 National Survey of Family Growth,[3] which was also a national probability sample of women of reproductive age. For purposes of comparison with 1975 estimates, the samples from these other studies were reduced to continuously married white women married fewer than 25 years and before the age of 25, and living with once-married husbands. Correspondingly, women over age 44 have been eliminated from the 1975 sample, reducing the final sample size to 3,329 women.

## Trends in Aggregate Use

As may be seen in Table 1, there appears to have been a substantial increase in the total proportion of women currently using contraception—an absolute increase amounting to 11.4 percent since 1970 and 6.1 per cent since 1973. About one per cent of this relatively large increase can be attributed to the fact that some women who had been sterilized prior to 1970 reported in

---

* Blacks were reluctantly excluded from the reinterview because the original 1970 sample of blacks had serious biases and the numbers in each five-year marriage cohort would have been too small for many analyses. The decision to confine the analysis to intact first marriages was made in the light of our emphasis in the 1975 NFS on causal analysis rather than on parameter estimations for the total population. Moreover, women not currently married and women in second marriages would not be represented in sufficient numbers to permit separate analysis.

Table 1

Type of Exposure to the Risk of Conception Among Continuously Married White Women, by Whether Additional Births Were Intended, 1975, 1973, 1970 and 1965 (standardized on 1970 marriage duration distribution)

| Type of exposure | All women | | | | Intended more births | | | | Intended no more births | | | |
|---|---|---|---|---|---|---|---|---|---|---|---|---|
| | 1975 | 1973 | 1970 | 1965 | 1975 | 1973 | 1970 | 1965 | 1975 | 1973 | 1970 | 1965 |
| Total number | 3,329 | 3,906 | 3,784 | 2,826 | 1,209 | 1,448 | 1,310 | 982 | 2,120 | 2,458 | 2,474 | 1,844 |
| Percent total | 100.0 | 100.0 | 100.0 | 100.0 | 100.0 | 100.0 | 100.0 | 100.0 | 100.0 | 100.0 | 100.0 | 100.0 |
| Using contraception | 79.0 | 72.9 | 67.6 | 66.5 | 64.9 | 64.7 | 59.7 | 59.2 | 85.6 | 77.8 | 71.7 | 71.6 |
| Not using contraception | 21.0 | 27.1 | 32.4 | 33.5 | 35.1 | 35.3 | 40.3 | 40.8 | 14.4 | 22.2 | 28.3 | 28.4 |
| Pregnant, postpartum or trying to get pregnant | 12.0 | 13.1 | 15.0 | 16.4 | 27.9 | 28.1 | 30.5 | 31.1 | 4.5 | 4.5 | 6.8 | 7.5 |
| Sterile and other nonuse | 9.0 | 14.0 | 17.5 | 17.1 | 7.2 | 7.2 | 9.8 | 9.7 | 9.8 | 17.7 | 21.5 | 20.9 |
| Number of users | 2,617 | 2,853 | 2,558 | 1,901 | 806 | 930 | 783 | 581 | 1,811 | 1,923 | 1,775 | 1,320 |
| Percent total users | 100.0 | 100.0 | 100.0 | 100.0 | 100.0 | 100.0 | 100.0 | 100.0 | 100.0 | 100.0 | 100.0 | 100.0 |
| Wife sterilized | 16.3 | 10.8 | 6.8 | 4.7 | 0.0 | 0.0 | 0.0 | 0.0 | 22.6 | 15.6 | 9.7 | 7.4 |
| Husband sterilized | 15.0 | 11.2 | 7.2 | 4.1 | 0.0 | 0.0 | 0.0 | 0.0 | 20.9 | 16.3 | 10.3 | 6.3 |
| Pill | 34.3 | 35.5 | 35.4 | 28.4 | 59.5 | 58.2 | 51.2 | 43.2 | 24.1 | 25.5 | 28.5 | 22.0 |
| IUD | 8.7 | 9.5 | 7.5 | 1.1 | 11.6 | 12.1 | 7.9 | 1.3 | 7.7 | 8.4 | 7.3 | 1.1 |
| Diaphragm | 3.9 | 4.0 | 5.7 | 10.5 | 4.2 | 3.6 | 4.3 | 6.2 | 3.7 | 4.3 | 6.4 | 12.7 |
| Condom | 10.9 | 15.1 | 14.8 | 22.0 | 11.2 | 12.8 | 11.0 | 18.4 | 10.5 | 16.2 | 16.5 | 23.4 |
| Withdrawal | 2.0 | 2.3 | 2.3 | 4.0 | 2.0 | 1.7 | 1.8 | 3.0 | 2.0 | 2.6 | 2.6 | 4.3 |
| Foam | 3.6 | 5.3 | 6.6 | 3.1 | 4.7 | 6.9 | 10.2 | 4.6 | 3.4 | 4.4 | 5.0 | 2.1 |
| Rhythm | 2.8 | 4.0 | 7.1 | 11.5 | 4.4 | 2.9 | 7.0 | 12.9 | 2.6 | 4.5 | 7.2 | 10.0 |
| Douche | 0.4 | 0.5 | 2.3 | 3.4 | 0.3 | 0.2 | 2.3 | 2.9 | 0.4 | 0.7 | 2.3 | 3.6 |
| Other | 2.2 | 1.7 | 4.3 | 7.1 | 2.1 | 1.6 | 4.2 | 7.3 | 2.3 | 1.7 | 4.3 | 7.1 |

Note: In this and subsequent tables, percentage distributions may not add to 100.0 because of rounding.

1970 that the operation had been medically indicated, but five years later said that the procedure had been performed at least partly for contraceptive purposes. At least another one per cent can be attributed to the disproportionately greater refusal of women to be reinterviewed who were classified as "other nonusers" in 1970, which has the probable effect of underestimating the proportion of women so classified in 1975. Assuming that this proportion is one per cent, correction for this bias would place the proportion of continuously married white women currently using contraception at 78 rather than 79 per cent, but we recognize the vulnerability of our estimate.

As Table 2 shows, most of the increase in contraceptive use between 1973 and 1975 has occurred among couples married for 15–24 years, and it is concentrated entirely in the category of those who intend no more births (see Table 1). Combined with substantial increases in proportions using the most effective methods, this increase in contraceptive practice among couples in the later stages of their reproductive lives implies a significant reduction in unwanted births.

The estimates in Tables 1 and 2 are of *current* use of contraception. There has also been a considerable decline in the proportion of continuously married white women who have *never* used contraception. In Table 3, we present a historical cohort series of contraceptive use utilizing the 1955 and 1960 Growth of American Families (GAF) surveys* and the 1965, 1970 and 1975 NFS. In addition to the limitations already discussed, this tabulation is further limited to women 18–39 years of age because of the 1955 GAF study sample design.

The decline in the percentage who have never used contraception is clear and consistent across cohorts* and has reached a very low level indeed: Only 2.1 per cent of the 1966–1970 marriage cohort have pregnancy histories that reveal no use of contraception through 5–9 years of marriage, and among the most recent cohort, women married in 1971–1975, only 5.2 per cent are so classified over an average marriage duration of 2.5 years.

# The Pill

Among continuously married white women, the pill remains the most popular method of birth control in 1975, but its predominance is being threatened by sterilization. In 1975, as Table 2 shows, the pill continued to be the most widely used method only among women married fewer than 10 years. In fact, the data suggest a small decline in pill use between 1970 and 1973 among women married 5–14 years. The overall change is so slight—from 35.4 per cent in 1970 to 35.5 per cent in 1973 and to 34.3 per cent in 1975 (see Table 1)—that it seems more reasonable to infer stabilization rather than

---

* The only inconsistency is among women in the 1951–1955 cohort married for 15–19 years.

Table 2

*Type of Exposure to the Risk of Conception Among Continuously Married White Women, by Marriage Duration*

| Type of exposure | Years of marriage | | | | | | | |
|---|---|---|---|---|---|---|---|---|
| | <5 | | | | 5–9 | | | |
| | 1975 | 1973 | 1970 | 1965 | 1975 | 1973 | 1970 | 1965 |
| Total number | 1,041 | 1,090 | 1,010 | 600 | 703 | 882 | 853 | 614 |
| Percent total | 100.0 | 100.0 | 100.0 | 100.0 | 100.0 | 100.0 | 100.0 | 100.0 |
| Using contraception | 71.3 | 68.9 | 61.7 | 58.5 | 76.7 | 75.0 | 69.2 | 69.7 |
| Not using contraception | 28.7 | 31.1 | 38.3 | 41.5 | 23.3 | 25.0 | 30.8 | 30.3 |
| Pregnant, postpartum or trying to get pregnant | 23.2 | 25.0 | 29.6 | 34.5 | 17.4 | 18.5 | 19.7 | 19.4 |
| Sterile and other nonuse | 5.5 | 6.1 | 8.7 | 7.0 | 6.0 | 6.5 | 11.1 | 10.9 |
| Number of users | 742 | 748 | 623 | 351 | 539 | 661 | 590 | 428 |
| Percent total users | 100.0 | 100.0 | 100.0 | 100.0 | 100.0 | 100.0 | 100.0 | 100.0 |
| Wife sterilized | 0.8 | 1.9 | 0.3 | 0.0 | 11.7 | 9.4 | 3.9 | 2.1 |
| Husband sterilized | 0.7 | 0.6 | 1.0 | 0.3 | 10.0 | 9.0 | 4.2 | 3.0 |
| Pill | 64.8 | 64.1 | 57.1 | 53.3 | 38.6 | 39.4 | 42.9 | 34.6 |
| IUD | 8.1 | 9.7 | 8.5 | 1.4 | 14.5 | 14.5 | 11.4 | 1.9 |
| Diaphragm | 4.3 | 2.6 | 3.5 | 4.6 | 3.3 | 3.2 | 4.2 | 10.3 |
| Condom | 12.0 | 11.4 | 9.8 | 14.8 | 11.7 | 10.3 | 13.6 | 22.0 |
| Withdrawal | 1.8 | 1.6 | 1.4 | 2.8 | 1.7 | 2.1 | 1.4 | 2.6 |
| Foam | 3.4 | 4.3 | 8.2 | 4.8 | 4.6 | 8.2 | 8.8 | 3.5 |
| Rhythm | 1.8 | 2.0 | 5.0 | 8.5 | 2.2 | 2.2 | 4.7 | 10.7 |
| Douche | 0.4 | 0.2 | 1.8 | 3.7 | 0.2 | 0.4 | 1.0 | 1.2 |
| Other | 2.0 | 1.5 | 3.4 | 5.7 | 1.5 | 1.3 | 3.9 | 8.2 |

decline of pill use among most women. However, there is evidence of a substantial decline (about six percentage points) between 1973 and 1975 among women married 15 years or more.

Another perspective on the same question may be obtained from the tabulation of contraceptive methods by whether the woman intends to have additional children (see Table 1). Among women who intend *more* births, the proportion using the pill continues to increase (up eight percentage points since 1970) and completely dominates contraceptive practice; among women who intend *no more* births, there has been a decline (of about four percentage points) in pill use since 1970. Evidently, the pill has continued to strongly attract younger women in the early stages of family formation; but in recent years, their older counterparts, when faced with a long period of exposure to the risk of pregnancy after the birth of the last wanted child, have turned to other methods.

| | Years of marriage | | | | | | | | | | |
|---|---|---|---|---|---|---|---|---|---|---|---|
| | 10–14 | | | | 15–19 | | | | 20–24 | | |
| 1975 | 1973 | 1970 | 1965 | 1975 | 1973 | 1970 | 1965 | 1975 | 1973 | 1970 | 1965 |
| 632 | 731 | 731 | 571 | 553 | 710 | 626 | 636 | 400 | 493 | 564 | 405 |
| 100.0 | 100.0 | 100.0 | 100.0 | 100.0 | 100.0 | 100.0 | 100.0 | 100.0 | 100.0 | 100.0 | 100.0 |
| 85.9 | 80.8 | 75.4 | 73.7 | 85.9 | 71.6 | 67.9 | 70.6 | 79.5 | 67.8 | 65.4 | 62.2 |
| 14.1 | 19.2 | 24.6 | 26.3 | 14.1 | 28.4 | 32.1 | 29.4 | 20.5 | 32.2 | 34.6 | 37.8 |
| | | | | | | | | | | | |
| 6.2 | 8.0 | 8.5 | 7.4 | 2.9 | 3.0 | 4.5 | 5.5 | 1.5 | 1.8 | 1.6 | 3.0 |
| 7.9 | 11.2 | 16.1 | 18.9 | 11.2 | 25.4 | 27.6 | 23.9 | 19.1 | 30.4 | 33.0 | 34.8 |
| 543 | 594 | 551 | 421 | 475 | 513 | 425 | 449 | 318 | 337 | 369 | 252 |
| 100.0 | 100.0 | 100.0 | 100.0 | 100.0 | 100.0 | 100.0 | 100.0 | 100.0 | 100.0 | 100.0 | 100.0 |
| 20.6 | 15.3 | 7.4 | 7.1 | 27.8 | 13.3 | 13.4 | 9.1 | 30.2 | 18.8 | 13.6 | 8.3 |
| 22.7 | 15.1 | 7.8 | 5.2 | 23.8 | 18.7 | 12.2 | 5.8 | 25.5 | 18.2 | 15.4 | 8.7 |
| 25.2 | 22.4 | 28.1 | 20.7 | 15.8 | 22.0 | 20.7 | 10.5 | 10.4 | 16.0 | 14.6 | 8.7 |
| 9.0 | 11.2 | 8.2 | 0.7 | 5.1 | 6.4 | 4.0 | 1.1 | 3.8 | 2.2 | 2.7 | 0.0 |
| 1.7 | 3.9 | 6.4 | 10.5 | 4.0 | 5.7 | 8.2 | 13.8 | 7.5 | 6.1 | 8.1 | 17.1 |
| 8.8 | 17.1 | 16.0 | 25.9 | 9.5 | 19.2 | 19.1 | 25.8 | 12.6 | 21.6 | 18.4 | 23.8 |
| 1.1 | 1.5 | 3.3 | 4.5 | 3.4 | 3.9 | 2.8 | 5.1 | 2.5 | 3.3 | 3.5 | 6.3 |
| 4.4 | 6.6 | 6.7 | 3.6 | 2.9 | 2.2 | 4.2 | 1.3 | 1.9 | 3.7 | 3.0 | 0.8 |
| 3.5 | 4.6 | 8.2 | 13.5 | 4.0 | 6.2 | 9.2 | 12.9 | 3.1 | 6.6 | 10.6 | 13.5 |
| 0.4 | 0.5 | 1.6 | 3.3 | 0.6 | 1.0 | 3.1 | 4.7 | 0.6 | 0.8 | 5.1 | 5.2 |
| 2.6 | 1.9 | 6.4 | 5.0 | 3.2 | 1.5 | 3.1 | 9.8 | 1.9 | 2.5 | 4.9 | 7.5 |

# Sterilization

By 1975, the proportion of white couples using contraception who have been sterilized is only three percentage points below the proportion using the pill (see Table 1). The increase in reliance on contraceptive sterilization has been dramatic even over the short period (of about 27 months) between the 1973 and 1975 surveys. Among women married 20–24 years, use of sterilization increased from 37.0 per cent to 55.7 per cent; for those married 15–19 years, it grew from 32.0 per cent to 51.6 per cent; and for marriage durations of 10–14 years, the increase was from 30.4 per cent to 43.3 per cent (see Table 2). Sterilization is now the single most popular method for couples married 10 years or more.

Among couples who have had all the children they want, sterilization clearly dominates the field: 43.5 per cent compared with 24.1 per cent taking the pill (see Table 1). While relief from the necessity for continuous practice of contraception is surely one motive for sterilization, its increasing popular-

Table 3

*Percentage of Continuously Married White Women Aged 18–39 Who Have Never Used Contraception, by Marriage Duration, According to Marriage Cohort*

| Marriage cohort | Years of marriage | | | | |
|---|---|---|---|---|---|
| | <5 | 5–9 | 10–14 | 15–19 | 20–24 |
| 1931–1935 | | | | | 40.6 |
| 1936–1940 | | | | 32.8 | 19.4 |
| 1941–1945 | | | 23.2 | 19.9 | 19.4 |
| 1946–1950 | | 21.5 | 17.6 | 14.5 | 12.9 |
| 1951–1955 | 32.4 | 13.7 | 10.9 | 14.9 | 9.3 |
| 1956–1960 | 23.7 | 11.7 | 10.0 | 5.2 | |
| 1961–1965 | 15.4 | 8.3 | 5.1 | | |
| 1966–1970 | 9.6 | 2.1 | | | |
| 1971–1975 | 5.2 | | | | |

Note: The top two diagonals are from the 1955 and 1960 Growth of American Families (GAF) Studies; the bottom three are respectively from the 1965, 1970 and 1975 NFS.

ity also implies that couples are more willing to accept irreversibility of the decision to terminate childbearing. This appears to represent yet another step in the longterm trend toward rationalization of the childbearing process. Since 1973, female sterilization appears to be increasing somewhat more rapidly than male sterilization—perhaps because of the availability of new and relatively simple female surgical procedures. However, there is still little difference in the proportions of couples among whom the husband has been sterilized or the wife has been sterilized.

# The IUD

Use of the IUD, which increased sharply between 1965 and 1973, appears to have declined between 1973 and 1975 (see Table 1). This decline may be related to the widespread publicity about the dangers of the Dalkon Shield that appeared in 1974, and to subsequent withdrawal of this widely used device from the market. Only among women married as long as 20–24 years, who are least likely to intend further childbearing, is there some indication of a continued increase in the use of the IUD.

# Other Methods

The Diaphragm.    Drug company inventory reports suggest that the diaphragm is making a comeback and is appealing to younger women who are concerned about the risks of taking the pill for long periods of time. Our overall aggregate trend data provide no support for this hypothesis as of late 1975; they indicate a continued decline from 5.7 per cent of users in 1970 to 4.0 per cent in 1973 and 3.9 per cent in 1975 (see Table 1). However, a possibly emerging counter-trend is suggested among women who intend to to have more births. Among women intending no more births, the proportion using the diaphragm continued to decline. Thus, it is possible that the diaphragm is beginning to enjoy an increase in popularity among young women who are using contraception for spacing purposes; but the proportion using this method still remains very small—less than five per cent of virtually all intention and marital duration categories.

**The Condom.** Use of the condom continues to decline. Between 1965 and 1975, its use dropped by half (see Table 1). The only apparent exception to this generalization is among recently married couples; among couples married fewer than five years, condom use has increased slightly but steadily since 1970; and among those married 5–9 years, use appears to have increased since 1973. Whether these exceptions indicate the beginning of a reversal of long-term trends such as has been suggested of the diaphragm remains to be seen.

**Withdrawal, Foam, Rhythm and Douche.** The proportions relying on these remaining methods have all declined since 1973, with the possible exception of the residual category, "other methods" (which includes some multiple-method usage as well as other individual methods). Collectively, the four methods plus the "other methods" category now account for 11.0 per cent of total use (see Table 1).

# Trend in Use of Most Effective Methods

About three-quarters of those couples currently using contraception are using one of the most effective methods—sterilization, the pill or the IUD (see Table 4). A decade earlier, in 1965, this percentage was 38.3. It climbed to 56.9 per cent in 1970, to 67.0 per cent in 1973, and by 1975 reached 74.3 per cent. A similar pattern appears at each marriage duration, with the most dramatic increases evident at the longest durations. The striking pattern evident in previous years, when the highly effective methods were used more by recently married couples, has diminished over time; by 1975, there is little variation in use of highly effective contraception by marriage duration.

Table 4
*Percentage of Continuously Married White Couples Currently
Using Contraception Who Are Employing the Most Effective
Methods (sterilization, pill, IUD), by Marriage Duration
(standardized on 1970 marriage duration distribution)*

| Years of marriage | 1975 | 1973 | 1970 | 1965 |
|---|---|---|---|---|
| All durations | 74.3 | 67.0 | 56.9 | 38.3 |
| <5 | 74.4 | 76.3 | 66.9 | 55.0 |
| 5–9 | 74.8 | 72.3 | 62.4 | 41.6 |
| 10–14 | 77.5 | 64.0 | 51.5 | 33.7 |
| 15–19 | 72.5 | 60.4 | 50.3 | 26.5 |
| 20–24 | 69.9 | 55.2 | 46.3 | 25.7 |

# All Surgical Sterilizations

In any large population of couples of reproductive age, there is some incidence of sterility which results from surgery performed for reasons of pathology only. In view of the recent significant increases in the proportion of couples electing surgical sterilization at least partly for contraceptive reasons, the combined incidence by now should have reached a very high level. In Table 5, we have assembled estimates by marriage duration of the proportion of couples surgically sterilized for any reason. The most recent estimates for 1975 indicate that more than one-quarter of all white, continuously married couples at all durations of marriage, and 47 per cent of couples married 10–24 years, have been surgically sterilized (latter calculation not shown). These should be taken as low estimates of infecundity. They reflect only surgical sterilization, thereby excluding couples who cannot conceive or carry a pregnancy to term because of a variety of nonsurgical reason; in addition, they exclude categories other than white, continuously married couples, and we know from earlier studies that blacks have a higher incidence of sterility resulting from medical reasons and contraceptive sterilizations. The trends indicate major increases in surgical sterilization between 1970 and 1975 for all three operations specified. Increases in tubal ligations and vasectomies, but not in hysterectomies, are also evident at each duration after 1973.

If respondents reported sterilization as a method of family planning, it was classified as a contraceptive procedure. If they did not indicate use of any method, and subsequently reported that it was impossible for them to conceive because of an operation, they were then asked, "Was that operation done at least partly because you wanted no more children?" Virtually all tubal ligations and vasectomies were classified as at least partly contraceptive in intent. About half of women with hysterectomies reported that the purpose was exclusively medical. A total of 89.2 per cent of all sterilizing surgery was

Table 5
*Percentage of Continuously Married White Couples Surgically Sterilized, by Type of Procedure, According to Marriage Duration*

| Years of marriage | Total sterilized* | | | | Tubal ligation† | | | | Hysterectomy | | | | Vasectomy | | | |
|---|---|---|---|---|---|---|---|---|---|---|---|---|---|---|---|---|
| | 1975 | 1973 | 1970 | 1965 | 1975 | 1973 | 1970 | 1965 | 1975 | 1973 | 1970 | 1965 | 1975 | 1973 | 1970 | 1965 |
| All durations | 26.4 | 21.2 | 14.3 | 13.1 | 9.7 | 7.2 | 4.0 | 3.4 | 4.9 | 5.7 | 4.0 | 5.7 | 11.0 | 8.1 | 4.9 | 3.1 |
| Standardized‡ | 28.1 | 21.7 | 14.3 | 11.9 | 10.2 | 7.4 | 4.0 | 3.0 | 5.4 | 5.8 | 4.0 | 5.2 | 11.6 | 8.3 | 4.9 | 2.9 |
| <5 | 1.3 | 2.1 | 1.0 | 0.7 | 0.6 | 1.5 | 0.3 | 0.0 | 0.1 | 0.1 | 0.1 | 0.3 | 0.6 | 0.4 | 0.6 | 0.3 |
| 5–9 | 17.0 | 14.9 | 6.4 | 5.0 | 7.9 | 7.3 | 2.2 | 1.8 | 1.1 | 0.6 | 0.7 | 0.7 | 7.5 | 7.0 | 3.0 | 2.1 |
| 10–14 | 40.1 | 29.0 | 15.0 | 16.1 | 16.1 | 10.9 | 5.4 | 5.4 | 4.4 | 5.4 | 2.5 | 6.1 | 19.0 | 12.6 | 5.6 | 3.9 |
| 15–19 | 50.2 | 34.1 | 27.1 | 20.9 | 17.5 | 9.0 | 7.5 | 5.7 | 11.0 | 10.7 | 8.4 | 9.3 | 19.5 | 13.7 | 8.4 | 4.4 |
| 20–24 | 53.1 | 44.3 | 34.4 | 27.2 | 15.5 | 12.0 | 7.6 | 4.2 | 16.5 | 19.3 | 13.1 | 15.1 | 19.5 | 12.7 | 10.3 | 5.9 |

* Includes other types of operations, multiple operations and operations of unknown type.
† For 1975, includes laparoscopy.
‡ Standardized on 1970 marriage duration distribution.

therefore reported to be at least partly contraceptive in intent. It should be emphasized that such perceptions are subjective and not highly reliable. We know from our reinterview data that there was a distinct tendency for women in 1975 to report as partly contraceptive in intent those same procedures that in 1970 they had reported were performed exclusively for medical reasons. Moreover, there is obvious ambiguity in cases where pregnancy would be contraindicated on medical grounds. For these reasons, the estimates in Table 5 were prepared by type of surgery rather than by intent.

# 1975 Estimates for All Married Women

One objective of this article is to provide a set of estimates of types of exposure to the risk of conception for U.S. women in 1975. The preceding discussion and data have been limited to white women married before age 25 and in continuous first marriages. On the assumption that the differences in exposure between women with these characteristics and all currently married women were the same in 1975 as in 1973, simple ratio estimates for the

Table 6

*Estimated Types of Exposure to the Risk of Conception Among All Currently Married Women Under 45 Years of Age, 1975* *

| Type of exposure | No. of women † (in 000s) | % |
|---|---|---|
| Total | 27,170 | 100.0 |
| Pregnant, postpartum or trying to get pregnant | 3,478 | 12.8 |
| Other nonuse, including nonsurgically subfecund | 1,915 | 7.0 |
| Surgically sterilized (medical reasons only) | 1,063 | 3.9 |
| Surgically sterilized women (contraceptive reasons) | 3,791 | 14.0 |
| Surgically sterilized men (contraceptive reasons) | 3,017 | 11.1 |
| Pill | 7,140 | 26.3 |
| IUD | 1,742 | 6.4 |
| Diaphragm | 690 | 2.5 |
| Condom | 2,049 | 7.5 |
| Foam | 704 | 2.6 |
| Rhythm | 590 | 2.2 |
| Other | 1,016 | 3.7 |

* Estimated on the assumption that the ratio of the types of exposure among once-married, currently married white women to the types of exposure among all married women remained the same in 1975 as in 1973.

† Based on interpolated estimates of currently married women (excluding those "separated") in March 1975 and March 1976 as estimated in U.S. Bureau of the Census, "Marital Status and Living Arrangements: March 1975," *Current Population Reports* (CPR), Series P-20, No. 287, 1975, Table 1; and "Marital Status and Living Arrangements: March 1976," CPR, Series P-20, No. 306, 1977, Table 1.

larger population can be prepared. The result of this exercise is displayed in Table 6, where the classification of sterilization by intent is reintroduced.

The most dramatic result is that in 1975, the estimated total number (7.9 million) of surgically sterilized couples appears to exceed the number using the pill (7.1 million). In 1973, the total number of sterilized currently married couples was 6.1 million, and the number using the pill was 6.7 million (not shown). Even if we count only those operations which were reported as contraceptive in intent, the estimated total number (6.8 million) in 1975 is very close to the number of pill users.*

The main conclusion is that elective sterilization has been increasing rapidly in recent years and has nearly caught up with the pill, which experienced an earlier growth in popularity and has now plateaued, or is beginning to show signs of decline. Looking beyond the numbers themselves, we see that the meaning of these two methods is quite different: The pill predominates among the young and newly married, whereas sterilization is being increasingly chosen by couples who have had all the children they intend to have. In other words, the overall use of the two methods reflects in part their relative appeal among women who have had all the children they want, but is also influenced by the proportion who have reached this stage.

# Summary

On the basis of data collected in the 1975 NFS from interviews with continuously married white women, we have attempted to estimate aggregate changes in contraceptive practice that have occurred in the United States among currently married couples since 1973 and over the decade since 1965. The pill remains the most popular method of birth control among women married fewer than 10 years, but there is evidence of the possible beginning of a decline among most of the longer marriage duration categories.

The main challenge to the supremacy of the pill comes from the increasingly popular method of surgical sterilization, which clearly is now the most commonly used method of birth control among couples married 10 years or more, as well as among couples who have had all the children they intend. The rapid adoption of this method in the last few years—and especially of the female procedure, which has become technologically simpler—implies that contraceptive and medical sterilization operations probably now comprise the most frequent barrier to conception among all married couples of reproductive age. By 1975, nearly half of couples married 10–24 years were surgically

* We should reiterate that these estimates are wholly dependent on the assumption that the ratio of white to black and, especially, of continuously married to currently married women by type of exposure in 1973 also existed in 1975. In addition, to the extent that the 1975 sample lost some of its representativeness because of the failure to reinterview eligible respondents from the 1970 sample, there is potential for further error.

sterilized. Even excluding surgery for noncontraceptive reasons only, the incidence of contraceptive sterilization has probably almost reached the level of pill use.

Three-quarters of couples using contraception are now using the most effective methods available: contraceptive sterilization, the pill or the IUD. All of the trend data suggest a continuing increase in the reliance on such methods.

## REFERENCE NOTES

1. C. F. Westoff and N. B. Ryder, *The Contraceptive Revolution,* Princeton University Press, Princeton, N.J., 1977, Table II-3, p. 19.
2. 1965 NFS: N. B. Ryder and C. F. Westoff, *Reproduction in the United States: 1965,* Princeton University Press, N.J., 1971: 1970 NFS: C. F. Westoff and N. B. Ryder, 1977, op. cit.
3. K. Ford, National Center for Health Statistics, DHEW, "Contraceptive Utilization Among Currently Married Women 15–44 Years of Age: United States, 1973," *Monthly Vital Statistics Report,* Vol. 25, No. 7, Supplement, 1976.
4. 1955 GAF: R. Freedman, P. K. Whelpton and A. A. Campbell, *Family Planning, Sterility and Population Growth,* McGraw Hill, New York, 1959, 1960 GAF: P. K. Whelpton, A. A. Campbell and J. E. Patterson, *Fertility and Family Planning in the United States,* Princeton University Press, Princeton, N.J., 1966.

# Fears of Genocide Among Black Americans as Related to Age, Sex, and Region*

*Castellano Turner and William A. Darity*

THE UNITED NATIONS CONVENTION on Genocide has defined genocide as "acts committed with intent to destroy, in whole or in part, a national, ethnical, racial or religious group." [1] Using this general definition, it is evident that fears of genocide among black Americans are firmly based on historical and contemporary reality. Black Americans have been subjected to centuries of brutalization which needs no documentation here. But more importantly, the pervasiveness of white racism in the United States continues to create the circumstances for both direct and indirect forms of black genocide. [2] . . .

* Reprinted with the permission of the publisher and the authors from *American Journal of Public Health,* 63:12 (1973): 1029–1034.

# Family Planning as a Form of Genocide?

. . . The present study investigated the extent of genocide fears among a much larger and regionally varied group of black American. More specifically the relationship of such fears, age, sex, and region of the country was also examined. . . .

Summary of null hypotheses:

○ There is no difference in genocide fears between younger as compared to older black Americans.

○ There is no difference in genocide fears between males as compared to females.

○ There is no difference in genocide fears between northern blacks as compared to southern black.

# Method

[In 1900 Drs. Turner and Darity chose a sample of 1,890 black Americans living in the urban North (Philadelphia, Pennsylvania) or in the urban South (Charlotte, North Carolina) who were dwelling in either a low socioeconomic status (SES) area of the cities or a middle to high SES area. Households were randomly selected from street lists and a female between the ages of 15 and 44 was interviewed, along with her most significant male partner (usually her husband, but if she were single, divorced, or widowed, then her closest male friend, if any). A precoded and open-ended questionnaire was used by a male-female interviewing team at the person's home; interviewers were of the same sex and race as the respondents.]

# Results

Table 1 provides a general overview of the findings. The table presents the per cent agreement on the five genocide items by age, sex, and region. We are immediately struck by the extent of genocide fears in this sample. Item 3 ("As blacks become militant, there will be an attempt to reduce the black population.") receive the greatest over-all agreement and was affirmed by 62.6% of the sample. However, the statement (item 5) which most specifically implicates birth control programming as a genocidal plot received the smallest percentage of agreement (39.1%). . . .

# Conclusions and Implications

The findings of the present study indicate that genocidal fears are widely held in the black population and that the factors of age, sex, region and educa-

**Table 1**
*Per cent Agreement with Statements Related to Genocide by Region, Sex, and Age**

| Item | North Male Under 28 (N=325) | North Male 28+ (N=307) | North Female Under 28 (N=443) | North Female 28+ (N=369) | South Male Under 28 (N=62) | South Male 28+ (N=71) | South Female Under 28 (N=71) | South Female 28+ (N=112) | Total Sample (N=1877) |
|---|---|---|---|---|---|---|---|---|---|
| 1. Birth control clinics in black neighbor-hoods should be operated by blacks. | 66.5 | 59.3 | 55.5 | 56.6 | 66.1 | 53.5 | 45.1 | 51.8 | 58.2 |
| 2. As the need for cheap labor goes down, there will be an effort to reduce the number of blacks. | 56.5 | 45.2 | 61.1 | 53.4 | 42.6 | 47.9 | 40.8 | 37.8 | 51.1 |
| 3. As blacks become more militant, there will be an effort to decrease the black population. | 67.4 | 59.4 | 67.2 | 62.3 | 60.7 | 56.3 | 54.9 | 56.9 | 62.6 |
| 4. The survival of black people depends on increasing the number of black births. | 61.7 | 53.9 | 50.7 | 51.4 | 45.2 | 54.9 | 47.9 | 53.6 | 53.3 |
| 5. Birth control programs are a plot to eliminate blacks. | 55.9 | 36.2 | 42.0 | 39.9 | 22.6 | 33.8 | 19.7 | 22.3 | 39.1 |

* The age split was based on the closest approximation to the median of the sample as a whole.

tional level are related to the prevalence of these fears. On all items the younger group expressed more fear than the older group, and the northern group expressed more fear than the southern group. On all but item 2 the males expressed more fear than the females. And those with less education expressed greater fear than those who had received more education. It is of considerable significance that on 4 of the 5 items more than 50% of all people interviewed expressed agreement. Although the degree of expressed fear was lower when "birth control" as a genocidal technique was the specific issue, that 39% of the entire sample believed that "birth control programs are a plot to eliminate blacks" is ample basis for distress.

These results indicate that Black Americans have a great deal of fear and distrust of white Americans. However, it is not apparent that black Americans are against family planning in particular. On the contrary, there is considerable evidence that black women (if not black men) are even more positively inclined toward family planning than white women[3] and that fertility differentials by race are declining.[4] It has been suggested by Jaffe that the differences between the races are more a function of access to effective family planning instruction than to differences in ideal family size.[5]

The lower status respondents were more likely to express genocide fears than were those of higher status. Those who have been victimized in the past are likely to be the most sensitive to perpetration of new crimes. The young, lower status, northern black male (the most expressive of genocide fears) has every reason to wonder why white America is pushing family planning in the black community at the same time that it fails to push for equity in education and in occupational opportunity.

What then are the implication of the findings reported here? We suggest that black Americans over time have been forced into a stance of suspicion with regard to white Americans and family planning programs are simply a new context of that suspicion. It is noteworthy that the greatest degree of agreement is found where the issue of black control of family planning (as against white control) is at issue. The potential ambivalence created by the fear of genocide and the desire to use family planning methods is clear. It is thus evident, that genocide fears of black Americans are continuing to create barriers to the effective use of family planning methods. We conclude that this dilemma will remain unresolved until the life circumstances of black Americans improve.

## REFERENCE NOTES

1. Drost, P. N. Genocide: United Nations Legislation on International Criminal Law. Leyden: A. W. Sythoff, 1959.
2. National Advisory Commission on Civil Disorders. Report of the National Advisory Commission on Civil Disorder. New York: Bantam Books, Inc., 1968.
3. Bogue, Donald J. Family planning in the Negro ghettos of Chicago. Paper presented at the Milbank conference on Negro Population, New York, October 1969.

4. Campbell, Arthur A. White-non white differences in family planning in the United States. Health, Education, and Welfare Indicators, February 1966, pp. 13–21.

5. Jaffe, Frderick S. Family planning and poverty. Journal of Marriage and the Family, Vol. 26, No. 4, November 1964, pp. 467–470.

# Beyond Androgyny: Some Presumptuous Prescriptions for a Liberated Sexual Identity*

*Sandra Lipstiz Bem*

I CONSIDER MYSELF an empirical scientist, and yet my interest in sex roles is and has always been frankly political. My hypotheses have derived from no formal theory, but rather from a set of strong intuitions about the debilitating effects of sex-role stereotyping, and my major purpose has always been a feminist one: to help free the human personality from the restricting prison of sex-role stereotyping and to develop a conception of mental health which is free from culturally imposed definitions of masculinity and feminity. . . . What I should like to do in this paper is to summarize the data on psychological androgyny that we have collected over the last four years. . . .

The ideal or healthy personality has traditionally included a concept of sexual identity with three basic components: (1) a sexual preference for members of the opposite sex; (2) a sex-role identity as either masculine or feminine, depending upon one's gender; and (3) a gender identity, i.e., a secure sense of one's maleness or femaleness (c.f., Green, 1974). I should like to comment in this paper on each of these three components in turn.

## Sexual Preference

With respect to the first component, that of sexual preference, my remarks can be brief. Let me simply assert, along with the proponents of gay liberation and the recently enlightened American Psychiatric Association, that one's sexual preferences ought ultimately to be considered orthogonal to any con-

* Keynote Address for APA/NIMH Conference on The Research Needs of Women, Madison, Wisconsin, May 31, 1975. To be published in J. Sherman & F. Denmark (Eds.), *Psychology of Women: Future Directions of Research.* Psychological Dimensions, in press. Reprinted by permission of the author.

cept of mental health or ideal personality. Let us begin to use the terms "homosexual" and "heterosexual" to describe acts rather than persons and to entertain the possibility that compulsive exclusivity in one's sexual responsiveness, whether homosexual or heterosexual, may be the product of a repressive society which forces us to label ourselves as one or the other.

## Sex-Role Identity

I turn now to the concept of sex-role identity, a concept which has traditionally been conceptualized in terms of masculinity and femininity. Both historically and cross-culturally, masculinity and femininity have represented complementary domains of positive traits and behaviors. Different theorists have different labels for these domains. According to Parsons (Parsons & Bales, 1955), masculinity has been associated with an instrumental orientation, a cognitive focus on getting the job done or the problem solved, whereas femininity has been associated with an expressive orientation, an affective concern for the welfare of others and the harmony of the group. Similarly, Bakan (1966) has suggested that masculinity is associated with an "agentic" orientation, a concern for oneself as an individual, whereas femininity is associated with a "communal" orientation, a concern for the relationship between oneself and others. Finally, Erikson's (1964) anatomical distinction between "inner" (female) and "outer" (male) space represents an analogue to a quite similar psychological distinction between a masculine "fondness for what works and for what man can make, whether it helps to build or to destroy" and a more "ethical" feminine commitment to "resourcefulness in peacekeeping and devotion in healing."

My own research has focused on the concept of psychological androgyny. As such, it has been predicated on the assumption that it is possible, in principle, for an individual to be both masculine and feminine, both instrumental and expressive, both agentic and communal, depending upon the situational appropriateness of these various modalities; and even for an individual to blend these complementary modalities in a single act, being able, for example, to fire an employee if the circumstances warrant it, but to do so with sensitivity for the human emotion that such an act inevitably produces.

The possibility that a single individual can embody both masculinity and femininity has, of course, been expressed by others as well. Jung (1953) described the anima and animus which he believed to be present in us all, and more recently, Bakan (1966) has argued that viability—both for the individual and for society—depends on the successful integration of both agency and communion. Moreover, the concept of androgyny itself can now be found not only in the psychological literature (e.g., Berzins & Welling, in press; Block, 1973; Pleck, 1975; Spence, Helmreich, & Stapp, 1975), but in the literature of other disciplines as well (e.g., Bazin & Freeman, 1974; Gelpi,

1974; Harris, 1974; Heilbrun, 1973; Secor, 1974; Stimpson, 1974). . . .

Although there is no previous research which bears [directly on the hypothesis that traditional sex roles do restrict behavior in important human ways], a review of the relevant literature nevertheless corroborates our underlying assumption that a high level of sex-typing may not be desirable. For example, high femininity in females has consistently been correlated with high anxiety, low self-esteem, and low social acceptance (e.g., Cosentino & Heilbrun, 1964; Gall, 1969; Gray, 1957; Sears, 1970; Webb, 1963); and, although high masculinity in males has been correlated during adolescence with better psychological adjustment (Mussen, 1961), it has been correlated during adulthood with high anxiety, high neuroticism, and low self-acceptance (Harford *et al.*, 1967; Mussen, 1962). In addition, greater intellectual development has been correlated quite consistently with cross sex-typing, i.e., with masculinity in girls and with femininity in boys. Boys and girls who are more sex-typed have been found to have lower overall intelligence, lower spatial ability, and lower creativity (Maccoby, 1966).

The point, of course, is that the two domains of masculinity and femininity are both fundamental. In a modern complex society like ours, an adult clearly has to be able to look out for himself and to get things done. But an adult also has to be able to relate to other human beings as people, to be sensitive to their needs and to be concerned about their welfare, as well as to be able to depend on them for emotional support. Limiting a person's ability to respond in one or the other of these two complementary domains thus seems tragically and unnecessarily destructive of human potential.

In addition, it would also seem to be the case that masculinity and femininity may each become negative and even destructive when they are represented in extreme and unadulterated form. Thus, extreme femininity, untempered by a sufficient concern for one's own needs as an individual, may produce dependency and self-denial, just as extreme masculinity, untempered by a sufficient concern for the needs of others, may produce arrogance and exploitation. As Bakan (1966) has put it, the fundamental task of every organism is to "try to mitigate agency with communion." Thus, for fully effective and healthy human functioning, both masculinity and femininity must each be tempered by the other, and the two must be integrated into a more balanced, a more fully human, a truly androgynous personality. An androgynous personality would thus represent the very best of what masculinity and femininity have each come to represent, and the more negative exaggerations of masculinity and femininity would tend to be cancelled out.

## The Bem Sex-Role Inventory

With this model of perfection in mind, I then moved to the more mundane task of trying to bring the concept of androgyny down to empirical reality. I began by constructing the Bem Sex-Role Inventory (or BSRI), a paper-and-

Table 1
*The Masculine, Feminine, and Neutral Items on the BSRI*

| Masculine items | Feminine items | Neutral items |
|---|---|---|
| 49. Acts as a leader | 11. Affectionate | 51. Adaptable |
| 46. Aggressive | 5. Cheerful | 36. Conceited |
| 58. Ambitious | 50. Childlike | 9. Conscientious |
| 22. Analytical | 32. Compassionate | 60. Conventional |
| 13. Assertive | 53. Does not use harsh language | 45. Friendly |
| 10. Athletic | 35. Eager to soothe hurt feelings | 15. Happy |
| 55. Competitive | 20. Feminine | 3. Helpful |
| 4. Defends own beliefs | 14. Flatterable | 48. Inefficient |
| 37. Dominant | 59. Gentle | 24. Jealous |
| 19. Forceful | 47. Gullible | 39. Likable |
| 25. Has leadership abilities | 56. Loves children | 6. Moody |
| 7. Independent | 17. Loyal | 21. Reliable |
| 52. Individualistic | 26. Sensitive to the needs of others | 30. Secretive |
| 31. Makes decisions easily | 8. Shy | 33. Sincere |
| 40. Masculine | 38. Soft-spoken | 42. Solemn |
| 1. Self-reliant | 23. Sympathetic | 57. Tactful |
| 34. Self-sufficient | 44. Tender | 12. Theatrical |
| 16. Strong personality | 29. Understanding | 27. Truthful |
| 43. Willing to take a stand | 41. Warm | 18. Unpredictable |
| 28. Willing to take risks | 2. Yielding | 54. Unsystematic |

Note: The number preceding each item reflects the position of each adjective as it actually appears on the Inventory. A subject indicates how well each item describes himself or herself on the following scale: (1) Never or almost never true; (2) Usually not true; (3) Sometimes but infrequently true; (4) Occasionally true; (5) Often true; (6) Usually true; (7) Always or almost always true.

pencil instrument which permits us to distinguish androgynous individuals from those with more sex-typed self-concepts.

Unlike most previous masculinity-femininity scales, the BSRI treats masculinity and femininity as two orthogonal dimensions rather than as two ends of a single dimension (see Constantinople, 1974, for a critique of previous sex-role inventories).[1] Moreover, masculinity and femininity each represent *positive* domains of behavior. Too often femininity has been defined simply as the absence of masculinity rather than as a positive dimension in its own right, a practice which may itself be partially responsible for the negative picture of the feminine woman which emerges in the psychological literature. For one, I wanted to give the feminine woman an equal chance to be no "sicker" than anyone else. . . .

Psychometric analyses on the BSRI indicate that it is quite satisfactory as a measuring instrument (Bem, 1974). As anticipated, the Masculinity and Femininity scores turned out to be empirically as well as conceptually independent (average $r = -.03$), thereby vindicating our decision to design an inventory that would not treat masculinity and femininity as two ends of a single

dimension. Moreover, the *t*-ratio itself is internally consistent (average
$\alpha = .86$), reliable over a four-week interval (average $r = .93$), and uncorrelated
with the tendency to describe oneself in a socially desirable direction (average
$r = -.06$). . . .

[Dr. Bem and her colleagues conducted a series of ingenious experiments designed to ask whether traditional sex roles actually do lead some people to restrict
their behavior in accordance with sex-role stereotypes. These experiments involved removing obvious barriers to cross-sex behavior and then observing what a
subject did. For example, subjects were left alone for ten minutes in a room with a
tiny kitten, although they were observed through a one-way mirror. Would a
masculine or feminine or androgynous man or woman play with the kitten in such
circumstances? These and other stimulus conditions have been reported in a
series of papers by Bem and colleagues (Bem, 1975; Bem and Lenney, 1976;
Bem, 1977; Bem, Martyna, and Watson, 1976) and are summarized in the following
section of the paper.]

## Summing Up

I believe that we are now in a position to state some of the things we have
learned about androgyny and sex-typing. I shall begin with the men because
they're easy. Consider, first, the androgynous male. He performs spectacu-
larly. He shuns no behavior just because our culture happens to label it as
female, and his competence crosses both the instrumental and the expressive
domains. Thus, he stands firm in his opinions, he cuddles kittens and bounces
babies, and he has a sympathetic ear for someone in distress. Clearly he is a
liberated companion for the most feminist among us.

In contrast, the feminine male is low in the instrumental domain, and the
masculine male is low in the expressive domain. Because at least one-third of
college-age males would be classified as masculine under our definition, it is
particularly distressing that the masculine males were less responsive in all of
the diverse situations that we designed to evoke their more tender emotions,
to tug, if only a little, on their heartstrings. I do not know, of course, whether
the masculine men were simply unwilling to act out any tender emotions that
they might have been experiencing, or whether their emotionality is sufficiently inhibited that they did not readily experience the emotions we sought
to tap. But in either case, their partners in the interaction received less emotional sustenance than they would have otherwise.

We cannot conclude, of course, that masculinity inhibits all tender emotionality in the masculine male. Obviously, none of the laboratory situations
that we devised was as powerful as, say, having a child who becomes ill or a
friend who seems about to have a nervous breakdown. We can conclude,
however, that their thresholds for tender emotionality are higher than all the

other men and women we have observed. And that, I believe, is sufficient cause for concern.

Let us turn now to the somewhat more complex pattern of results shown by the women. Like their male counterparts, androgynous women also fare well in our studies. They, too, willingly perform behaviors which our culture has labeled as unsuitable for their sex and they, too, function effectively in both the instrumental and the expressive domains.

In contrast, the masculine woman is low in the expressive domain, and the feminine woman is low in the instrumental domain. Thus, for both men and women, sex-typing does function to restrict behavior. Masculine individuals of both sexes are high in independence but low in nurturance, and feminine individuals of both sexes are high in nurturance but low in independence.

In addition, however, it will be recalled that feminine women were not consistently high even in nurturance. That is to say, they were more nurturant toward the lonely student and the baby than they were toward the kitten, and there was even some evidence that they were more nurturant toward the lonely student than toward the baby (Bem, Martyna, & Watson, 1976).

What is the source of this variability? Although there is some evidence that the lonely student may have been especially able to arouse the nurturant sympathies of the feminine women (Bem, Martyna, & Watson, 1976), it seems noteworthy that feminine women were the most nurturant in that one situation where the subject was required, as a listener, to play a relatively passive or responsive role with no need to take any responsibility whatever for initiating or even sustaining the interaction. In contrast, it seems noteworthy that feminine women were the least nurturant in that one situation where the subject was actually required to remove a kitten from its cage personally and spontaneously in order to be nurturant toward it. This leads me to speculate that femininity may be what produces nurturant feelings in women, but that at least a threshold level of masculinity is required to provide the initiative and perhaps even the daring to translate those nurturant feelings into action.

These speculations about the feminine woman conclude what I think I have learned up to this point about the evils of sex-typing and the potential promise of androgyny. As I started earlier, however, the major purpose of my research has always been a political one: to help free the human personality from the restricting prison of sex-role stereotyping and to develop a conception of mental health which is free from culturally imposed definitions of masculinity and femininity.

Certainly androgyny seems to represent the fulfillment of this goal. For if there is a moral to the concept of psychological androgyny, it is that *behavior* should have no gender. But there is an irony here, for the concept of androgyny contains an inner contradiction and hence the seeds of its own destruction. Thus, as the etymology of the word implies, the concept of androgyny necessarily presupposes that the concepts of masculinity and femininity themselves have distinct and substantive content. But to the extent that the androgynous message is absorbed by the culture, the concepts of masculinity and femininity will cease to have such content and the distinctions to which they refer will blur into invisibility. Thus, when androgyny becomes a reality, the *concept* of androgyny will have been transcended. (See Rebecca, Hefner, & Oleshansky, 1976, and Hefner, Rebecca, & Oleshansky, 1975, for a discussion of the concept of sex-role transcendence.)

## Gender Identity

. . . Even if people were all to become psychologically androgynous, the world would continue to consist of two sexes, male and female would continue to be one of the first and most basic dichotomies that young children would learn, and no one would grow up ignorant of or even indifferent to his or her gender. After all, even if one is psychologically androgynous, one's gender continues to have certain profound physical implications.

Thus, being a female typically means that you have a female body build; that you have female genitalia; that you have breasts; that you menstruate; that you can become pregnant and give birth; and that you can nurse a child. Similarly, being a male typically means that you have a male body build; that you have male genitalia; that you have beard growth; that you have erections; that you ejaculate; and that you can impregnate a woman and thereby father a child. No matter how psychologically androgynous you may be, you typically "inherit" one or the other of these two sets of biological givens, and you do not get to choose which of the two sets you would prefer.

Precisely because these are biological givens which cannot be avoided or escaped, except perhaps by means of a very radical and mutilating surgery, it seems to me that psychological health must necessarily include having a healthy sense of one's maleness or femaleness, a "gender identity" if you like. But I would argue that a healthy sense of maleness or femaleness involves little more than being able to look into the mirror and to be perfectly comfortable with the body that one sees there. One's gender does dictate the nature of one's body, after all, and hence one ought to be able to take one's body very much for granted, to feel comfortable with it, and perhaps even to like it.

But beyond being comfortable with one's body, one's gender need have no other influence on one's behavior or on one's life-style. Thus, although I would suggest that a woman ought to feel comfortable about the fact that she can bear children if she wants to, this does not imply that she ought to want to bear children, nor that she ought to stay home with any children that she does bear. Similarly, although I would suggest that a man ought to feel perfectly comfortable about the fact that he has a penis which can become erect, this in no way implies that a man ought to take the more active role during sexual intercourse, nor even that his sexual partners ought all to be female.

Finally, I would argue that a healthy sense of one's maleness or femaleness becomes all the more possible precisely when the artificial constraints of gender are eliminated and when one is finally free to be one's own unique blend of temperament and behavior. When gender no longer functions as a prison, then and only then will we be able to accept as given the fact that we are male or female in exactly the same sense that we accept as given the fact that we are human. Then and only then will we be able to consider the fact of our maleness or femaleness to be so self-evident and nonproblematic that it rarely ever occurs to us to think about it, to assert that it is true, to fear that it might be in jeopardy, or to wish that it were otherwise.

## REFERENCE NOTES

1. As Spence, Helmreich, and Stapp (1975) and Strahan (1975) have pointed out, this definition of androgyny serves to obscure what could be a potentially important distinction between those individuals who score high in both masculinity and femininity, and those individuals who score low in both. Accordingly, Spence, Helmreich, and Stapp (1975) recommend dividing subjects at the median on both the masculinity and the femininity scales and then deriving a *fourfold* classification of subjects as either masculine (high masculine-low feminine), feminine (high feminine-low masculine), androgynous (high masculine-high feminine), or undifferentiated (low masculine-low feminine). In an attempt to clarify whether one or the other of these two definitions of psychological androgyny was likely to have greater utility for future research, we administered the BSRI along with a variety of other paper-and-pencil questionnaires, and we also reanalyzed the results of our laboratory studies with the low-low scorers separated out. On the basis of the available evidence, I now believe that a distinction between high-high and low-low scorers does seem to be warranted, that the term "androgynous" ought to be reserved only for those individuals who score high in both masculinity and femininity, and that the BSRI ought henceforth to be scored so as to yield four distinct groups of masculine, feminine, androgynous, and undifferentiated subjects. See the articles by Bem (1977) and Bem, Martyna, and Watson (1976) for a full discussion of this issue. It should be noted, however, that this change in scoring only serves to strengthen the findings reported in this article.

## REFERENCES

BAKAN, D. *The duality of human experience.* Chicago: Rand McNally, 1966.

BAZIN, N. T., & FREEMAN, A. The androgynous vision. *Women's Studies,* 1974, 2, 185–215.

BEM, S. L. The measurement of psychological androgyny. *Journal of Consulting and Clinical Psychology,* 1974, 42, 155–162.

BEM, S. L. Sex-role adaptability: One consequence of psychological androgyny. *Journal of Personality and Social Psychology,* 1975, 31, 634–643.

BEM, S. L., & LENNEY, E. Sex-typing and the avoidance of cross-sex behavior. *Journal of Personality and Social Psychology,* 1976, 33, 48–54.

BEM, S. L. On the utility of alternative procedures for assessing psychological androgyny. *Journal of Consulting and Clinical Psychology,* 1977, 45, 196–205.

BEM, S. L., MARTYNA, W., & WATSON, C. Sex-typing and androgyny: Further explorations of the expressive domain. *Journal of Personality and Social Psychology,* 1976, 34, 1016–1023.

BERZINS, J. I., & WELLING, M. A. The PRF ANDRO Scale: A measure of psychological androgyny derived from the Personality Research Form. *Journal of Consulting and Clinical Psychology,* in press.

BLOCK, J. H. Conceptions of sex role: Some cross-cultural and longitudinal perspectives. *American Psychologist,* 1973, *28,* 512–526.

CONSTANTINOPLE, A. Masculinity-femininity: An exception to a famous dictum. *Psychological Bulletin,* 1974, *80,* 389–407.

COSENTINO, F., & HEILBRUN, A. B. Anxiety correlates of sex-role identity in college students. *Psychological Reports,* 1964, *14,* 729–730.

ERIKSON, E. Inner and outer space: Reflections on womanhood. In R. J. Lifton (Ed.), *The woman in America.* New York: Houghton Mifflin, 1964.

GALL, M. D. The relationship between masculinity-femininity and manifest anxiety. *Journal of Clinical Psychology,* 1969, *25,* 294–295.

GELPI, B. C. The politics of androgyny. *Women's Studies,* 1974, *2,* 151–160.

GRAY, S. W. Masculinity-femininity in relation to anxiety and social acceptance. *Child Development,* 1957, *28,* 203–214.

GREEN, R. *Sexual identity conflict in children and adults.* New York: Basic Books, 1974.

HARFORD, T. C., WILLIS, C. H., & DEABLER, H. L. Personality correlates of masculinity-femininity. *Psychological Reports,* 1967, *21,* 881–884.

HARRIS, D. A. Androgyny: The sexiest myth in disguise. *Women's Studies,* 1974, *2,* 171–184.

HEFNER, REBECCA, M., & OLESHANSKY, B. Development of sex role transcendence. *Human Development,* 1975, *18,* 143–158.

HEILBRUN, C. G. *Toward a recognition of androgyny.* New York: Alfred A. Knopf, 1973.

JUNG, C. G. Anima and animus. In *Two essays on analytical psychology: Collected works of C. G. Jung.* (Vol. 7.) Bollinger Foundation, 1953. Pp. 186–209.

MACCOBY, E. E. Sex differences in intellectual functioning. In E. E. Maccoby (Ed.), *The development of sex differences.* Stanford, Ca.: Stanford University Press, 1966. Pp. 25–55.

MUSSEN, P. H. Some antecedents and consequents of masculine sex-typing in adolescent boys. *Psychological Monographs,* 1961, *75,* No. 506.

MUSSEN, P. H. Long-term consequents of masculinity of interests in adolescence. *Journal of Consulting Psychology,* 1962, *26,* 435–440.

PARSONS, T., & BALES, R. F. *Family, socialization and interaction process.* New York: Free Press, 1955.

PLECK, J. H. Masculinity-femininity: Current and alternative paradigms. *Sex Roles,* 1975, *1,* 161–178.

REBECCA, M., HEFNER, R., & OLESHANSKY, B. A model of sex-role transcendence. *Journal of Social Issues,* 1976, *32,* 197–206.

SEARS, R. R. Relation of early socialization experiences to self-concepts and gender role in middle childhood. *Child Development,* 1970, *41,* 267–289.

SECOR, C. Androgyny: An early reappraisal. *Women's Studies,* 1974, *2,* 161–169.

SPENCE, J. T., HELMREICH, R., & STAPP, J. Ratings of self and peers on sex-role attributes and their relation to self-esteem and conceptions of masculinity and femininity. *Journal of Personality and Social Psychology,* 1975, *32,* 29–39.

STIMPSON, C. R. The androgyne and the homosexual. *Women's Studies,* 1974, *2,* 237–248.

STRAHAN, F. Remarks on Bem's measurement of psychological androgyny: Alternatives, methods and a supplementary analysis. *Journal of Consulting and Clinical Psychology,* 1975, *43,* 568–571.

WEBB, A. P. Sex-role preferences and adjustment in early adolescents. *Child Development,* 1963, *34,* 609–618.

# Middle-aged Blue-Collarites at Home: Changing Expectations of the Roles of Men and Women*

*Arthur B. Shostak*

W ITH OUR ATTENTION directed by the media to modish manhood models that are presently "good copy," such as the *Esquire* man, we overlook the contemporary plight of a far more numerous, but far less exotic bloc of middle-aged males, the manual worker contingent of over 30 million American men. As husbands, lovers, and fathers, they are challenged today as never before—and they are hurting.

Data and evidence here are uneven and frustrating in being far more suggestive than compelling[1]—but they do point consistently in one direction: Blue-collar marriages appear to fail far more often than do those in other social classes, marital unhappiness appears greater in these than in other families, and blue-collar wives impress researchers as the least content of all married women.[2]

The bedroom, in particular, is a winnerless battleground:

> working-class and middle-class couples engage in essentially the same kinds of sexual behaviors in roughly the same proportions. But working-class wives express considerably more discomfort about what they do in the marriage bed than their middle-class sisters . . . he asks; she gives. And neither is satisfied with the resolution.[3]

Blue-collar males remain ambivalent about female sexuality and often retain a lingering covert distinction between the girls they marry and the girls they use. Their women remain sensitive to this, unconvinced by contrary reassurances and wary about engaging in sexual behaviors that seem to threaten their traditional "good girl" status. As the men now claim to want sex lives freer and more enriched with mutual enjoyment, their women are under increasing pressure to "understand." "Yet, given the widely divergent socialization practices around male and female sexuality, the wish is but another impossible fantasy."[4]

The picture is comparably strained where the relations of 40-year-old blue-collarites to their young adult sons are concerned. Typical of the numerous deep-set rifts between the generations is a basic argument over the linkage be-

---

* Paper prepared for this volume, March 1978. An earlier and substantially different version appeared in *Occupational Mental Health*, 2:3 (1972): 2–7. See also the author's new book, *Blue Collar Stress*, Reading, Mass.: Addison-Wesley, 1979.

tween a day's work and a worker's manhood. In the words of a concerned 29-year-old UAW local union president—

> Fathers used to show their manliness by being able to work hard and have big, strong muscles and that kind of bullshitting story. The young guy now . . . his kick would be just the opposite . . . It isn't more manly to do more than you should. That's the difference between the son and his dad.[5]

Similarly, many younger men reject traditional factory supervision of the "blame-and-bellow" variety, whatever the more passive attitudes of middle-aged workers: The UAW leader notes—

> There's a substantial number of people that are Vietnam War vets. They didn't come back home wanting to take bullshit from foremen who haven't seen as much of the world as he had, who hasn't seen the hardships. [*sic*][6]

The generations may also differ significantly in their race and life-style attitudes:

> The young black and white workers dig each other. There's an understanding. The guy with the Afro, the guy with the beads, the guy with the goatee, he doesn't care if he's black, white, green, or yellow. The older guys still call each other niggers and honkies. But that doesn't happen with the younger set here.[7]

Overall, as younger blue-collarites rapidly adopt a value framework researchers call "the New Morality"—more liberal sexual mores; a lessening of automatic obedience to, and respect for, established authority; the transformation of "wants" in life to presumed "social rights" or entitlements; and so on—the generation gap appears to deepen, widen, and harden.[8]

### Changing Role Expectations: Missing the Mark.

Why the considerable discontent in the private lives of middle-aged male blue-collarites? Apparently because many of their blue-collar wives and children are asking new things of them, things they are presently ill-equipped to provide.

To understand this is first to understand the repressive childhood and adolescent lives of many middle-aged blue-collarites. Nearly half in a major 1976 study proved to be veterans of troubled family histories (alcoholism, 40 per cent; divorce or desertion, 36 per cent). Most singled out material deprivation as *the* dominant experience of their childhood. Most remembered growing up in a chaotic world filled with anger, fear, and loneliness.[9] Persuaded early that neither they nor their parents had much control over life, these men have struggled self-consciously to shape lives very opposite from those they begrudge and suppress in their own biographies. They have sought family stability where they knew uncertainty, material well-being where they knew poverty, and situational control where they knew only unpredictability. And they have done so even when the quest has resulted in outmoded rigidities as the price of homelife stability, futile materialism as the price of (mortgaged) affluence, and fragile rituals as the price of (transparent) control.

Table 1
*Historic Role Analysis: Middle-Age Male Blue-Collarite*

| Roles | Content | Rule | Expectation | Consequence |
|---|---|---|---|---|
| Husband | Rugged containment | "Keep 'em in their place" | Little friendship and sharing | Stranger and loner |
| Lover | Virile braggadocio | "Get all you can" | Little ecstasy and experimentation | Inadequate lover; self-deceived |
| Father | Authoritarian rule | "Teach 'em their place" | Little intimacy and adventure | Unresponsive father; readily abandoned by grown children |

Decisive in their manhood has been the struggle both to bury—and yet also to honor—their own past. Loyalty is paid to a *machismo* model of rugged containment, virile braggadocio, and authoritarian rule. As husbands, they followed the old man's lead in "Keeping the little lady in her place."[10] As lovers, they followed streetcorner counsel in "getting all they could."[11] And as fathers, they sought to replicate those harsher aspects of their own childhood that they now romantically credit with keeping them on "the straight and narrow." Accordingly, even if it meant using the blustered threat to "break heads," these fathers intended to "teach the kids to stay in *their* place"!

From one generation to another, throughout the late 1800s and on until the mid-1900s, role expectations changed very little. Traditional role prescriptions felt only the slightest impact from the Americanization process, the Suffragette Movement, the Mass Society's influence, the Gay Twenties' bohemianism, and the exotic like. Instead, generation after generation of blue-collar males expected little friendship in marriage, little experimentation and growth in sex relations (within marriage, that is), and little camaraderie and intimacy from parenthood. They were encouraged instead to settle for the ego-inflating myth of themselves as "real" men, the *only* real men, and certainly males more manly than their white-collar lessers (betters?). As such they came to have a responsibility to the role itself, a duty to appear hard, stoic, unconcerned, and persevering . . . convinced as they were that the best ways were the old ways. (See Table 1.)

**Changing Role Expectations: Setting New Goals.** Since the end of the Second World War, the *machismo*-based, time-honored prescription for blue-collar male adulthood has come under unrelenting attack: Wives and children alike increasingly rail against a formula that has historically resulted only in a stranger-as-husband, a stranger-as-lover, and a stranger-as-parent.

The sources of new pressure for reform are many and different, ranging from the unanticipated by-products of effective contraception by blue-collar women to the unanticipated by-products of TV viewing by blue-collar children and parents alike. Regardless of variation, however, the pressure steadily builds, as does the bewilderment and tension-level of the target group.

Large numbers of blue-collar women, for example, have been newly freed by their use of effective contraceptives from their historic bondage to unwanted pregnancies (or induced miscarriages and abortions, legal or otherwise). As they have gained, for the first time in history, the power to conceive at will, many are drawing their husbands into earnest family planning discussions and family well-being reviews. Choosing to have fewer children than ever before, these blue-collar mothers are advising their husbands to invest more heavily than ever in parenting—for there will be less of it in their lifespan than true of all previous blue-collar generations. More companionship, more emotional support, and more personal attention are sought by these women from their men than ever before.

Another source of change originating with the distaff side concerns the social revolution some commentators judge *the* most weighty of modern times—or the massive recent switch of women from cloistered home to relatively more cosmopolitan factory, office, or store.[12] Blue-collar women who work, as do nearly half (a larger proportion than in any other social class), appear to put two related expectations to their men: First, many urge the adoption of mannerisms, attitudes, values, or behaviors modeled for the women by nonblue-collarites encountered at work (or that the young woman at the next machine never stops boasting and fantasizing about). Second, many urge their husbands to experiment with a host of homelife reforms, aimed at creating a warmer, more loving family than either spouse knew in his or her own childhood. In this way, working women can relieve anxieties about the human cost to their own family possibly entailed in their work-related absence from home.[13]

Blue-collar women, in short, are far more worldly—and far more out in the world—than ever before. They explore life-styles that their mothers and grandmothers feared, despised, and shunned—and they appear to thrive instead on the adventure. They parlay their new worldliness into expansive expectations of their men and thereby set both sexes a dizzying agenda of unprecedented personal growth . . . with all the attendant transitional strain and uncertainty.

The situation is much the same where the middle-aged worker's children are involved. The kids go to more cosmopolitan schools than he did and seem to grow up faster. They join a more homogenized teen culture than any he knew and may learn more from the most powerful cultural equalizer of all, TV programs, than he ever did from the radio. Popular TV shows like "Family" and "Happy Times" help blue-collar youngsters scrutinize synthetic models of middle-aged parenthood that are more sensitive, more communicative, and more constructively emotional than is possibly true of their own households. Captivated by silver-screen shadows, many may ask the "old man" for new attitudes and behaviors—and, commonly a fan of the very same TV shows, the "old man" may often be uneasily aware of these new expectations.[14]

Finally, the middle-aged worker himself provides a hesitating source of change with his own inherent restlessness and curiosity. Many, for example, find themselves intrigued by light-humored TV treatment (a la "Johnny Carson") of the nascent men's movement, with its encouragement of the American male's search for richer expressiveness. If directly asked, workers, of course, will feign indifference or hostility:

> Yet if one listens carefully to what lies beneath the surface of their words, the same stirrings for more connection with other parts of themselves, for more intimate relations with their wives are heard from working-class men as well. Often inchoate and inarticulately expressed, sometimes barely acknowledged, these yearnings, nevertheless, exist.[15]

Armed with numerous rationalizations for not redesigning their role, middle-aged male blue-collarites must ultimately respond to what appears to be the "bottom-line" in the entire matter: ". . . in the working class, the process of building a family, of making a living for it, of nurturing and maintaining the individuals in it 'costs worlds of pain'."[16]

Summary.    A small number of powerful and relatively recent social developments are shaking the very foundations of a century-old prescription for the role (husband, lover, father) of the middle-aged blue-collar male. Where the worker once gave no thought to following in the old man's footsteps as a moody, enigmatic, macho-sensitive type, he is now set a very different formula of expectations: He is to strive instead for deep-coursing intimacy with this wife, erotic artfulness with his lover (wife and/or mistress), and open and genial affability with his children. (See Table 2.)

Much combines to slow progress in meeting these new role expectations and to stir doubts about the ultimate outcome of this contest between the traditional and the reform models . . . at least for the contemporary cohort of middle-aged workers.

For one thing, the worker is being asked to change role models at a midstream point in his life, as it were, and this is an intrinsically threatening and habit-defying task few middle-aged Americans will undertake. Second, many workers take much solace from the myth of a man's home as his castle and of the man as boss of his household (at least that, if nothing else!). Ego-boosting myths like these have helped such men live with the "hidden injuries of class," or the low self-esteem that can accompany a sense of insignificance and powerlessness in a class-conscious nation like our own.[17] Some, therefore, fear a serious loss of personal power if the spouse and children gain parity and if the blue-collar home and family, a worker's last bastion of per-

Table 2
*Explanatory Model*

| Role | I. A<br>Public role<br>linkage | I. B<br>Private role<br>discontents | II. A<br>Role<br>expectations:<br>traditional | II. B<br>Role<br>expectations:<br>transitional | III<br>Sources of<br>new role<br>definitions |
|---|---|---|---|---|---|
| *Husband* | Sex role<br>stereotyping | Unhappy<br>marriages | Impersonal<br>stolidness | Warm com-<br>panionship;<br>intimate | Blue-collar<br>women as<br>change-agents |
| *Lover* | Envy of seem-<br>ingly happier<br>others | Disappointing<br>sexual<br>relationships | "Marlboro<br>Country"<br>sexist | Sensitive<br>coexplorer;<br>reassurer | Changing cultural<br>ethos; "New<br>Morality" |
| *Father* | Escape-seeking,<br>rather than<br>authentic<br>growth effort | Dissolution of<br>paternal<br>self-esteem | Parents as<br>unquestioned<br>authoritarians | Pal and<br>modernist | Family planning;<br>impact; erosion<br>of excessive pa-<br>ternal authority |

sonal authority, move toward an uncertain egalitarianism. Third, many earnestly believe that basic job and economic insecurities, the kind that never completely disappear and that sap a man's energy and sense of self-reliance all his life, overshadow all else. These insecurities draw attention away from new role expectations—almost regardless of the emotional risks entailed. Finally, many will agree that "the terrible thing about class in our society is that it sets up a context for dignity."[18] As such, middle-aged workers may opt to find an immediately familiar, if ultimately self-defeating, source of enhanced dignity in the option to stonewall it rather than to risk change in traditional roles.

On the other side is a new declaration of intent from blue-collar women, children, and the more progressive of the middle-aged workers themselves—the intention to live as other than muffled beings, disappointed in life and one another. They gain strength from their innate grasp of a precious convergence that can enrich middle-age:

> Love and sexuality become more important to men once they have lost the sexual urgency of adolescence; sexual expression becomes more important to women once they have lost the diffuse romanticism of adolescence and learned about their bodies. The two sexes meet in mid-life.[19]

They also gain from the camaraderie and role models offered them by younger blue-collarites, their sons and daughters, who search alongside of them for class-sensitive aids to lives of less pain, more pleasure, and finer-than-ever-adulthood.

Whereas the resolution of this contest in old versus new role prescription remains unclear, at least this much is certain: The challenges the middle-aged blue-collar worker faces in redefining his manhood are clearly those of *all* American males as well, and the outcome here is hardly a matter only of academic concern.[20] Employing the very best we have, taking up our uneven professional skills and our still fuzzy humanistic vision, we have a prime obligation to assist in the turbulent emergence in the 1980s of a new blue-collar man.

## REFERENCE NOTES

1. "It is clear that traditional sociological descriptions of blue-collar people are not very accurate. Although it cannot be shown definitely, this low level of theoretical acuity may result from a lack of contact or simple dislike of working class people." Leonard Beeghley, "Embourgeoisement, Authoritarianism, and Blue-Collar Workers: A Review." Presented to the Section on Poverty and Human Resources, Annual Meeting, Society for the Study of Social Problems, Chicago, September 1977. P. 25 (used with permission).

2. The data are footnoted in Chapter 8, "Blue-Collar Families," in A. Shostak, *Blue-Collar Life* (New York: Random House, 1969), pp. 139–140. Especially helpful here is Nathan Hurvitz, "Marital Strain in the Blue-Collar Family," in Shostak and Gomberg, eds., *Blue-Collar World* (Englewood Cliffs, NJ: Prentice-Hall, 1965), pp. 92–109. See also Mirra Komarovsky, *Blue-Collar Marriage* (New York: Random House, 1964), pp. 199, *passim.;* Jesse Bernard, *Women, Wives, Mothers: Values & Options* (Chicago: Aldine, 1975); Pamela Roby's essay in *Economic Independence for Women,* ed. Jane R. Chapman (Beverly Hills, CA: Sage, 1976).

3. Lillian B. Rubin, *Worlds of Pain: Life in the Working-Class Family* (New York: Basic Books, 1976), p. 138. See also Lee Rainwater, *Family Design: Marital Sexuality, Family Size, and Contraception* (Chicago: Aldine, 1965), pp. 68, 100–101; Lee Rainwater et. al., *Working Class Wife* (Chicago, ILL: Oceana, 1959). On the relatively bolder attitudes and behavior of better-off males, see Carol Tavris, "The Sex Lives of Happier Men," *Redbook* (March 1978), pp. 193–199.

4. Rubin, *op. cit.,* p. 139.

5. "Gary Bryner," as quoted in Studs Terkel, ed., *Working: People Talk About What They Do All Day and How They Feel About What They Do* (New York: Pantheon, 1976), p. 189. See also Mike Cherry, *On High Steel* (New York: Ballantine, 1974), one of the best first-person accounts of blue-collar (ironworker) life ever published.

6. Terkel, Working, *op. cit.,* p. 192. See also Stanley Aronowitz, *False Promises* (New York: McGraw-Hill, 1973); Anon., "Labor's Big Swing from Surplus to Shortage," *Business Week,* February 20, 1978, p. 75.

7. Terkel, *op. cit.,* p. 193. On the bigotry of older blue-collarites, forty to sixty years of age, see "Race" in E. E. LeMasters, Blue-Collar Aristocrats: Life-Styles at a Working-Class Tavern (Madison, WIS: University of Wisconsin Press, 1975), pp. 187–189, *passim.*

8. Especially helpful is the analysis in "The New Generation of Hard Hats, in LeMasters, *op. cit.,* pp. 193–197. Indispensable here is Daniel Yankelovich, *The New Morality: A Profile of American Youth in the 70's* (New York: McGraw-Hill, 1974). See also Arthur Shostak, "Politics, Conflict, and Young Blue-Collarites: Old Dssensus and New Consciousness," in Lewis Coser and Otto N. Larsen, eds., *The Uses of Controversy in Sociology* (New York: Basic Books, 1976), pp. 74–94.

9. See in this connection, Rubin, *op. cit.,* pp. 3–48, *passim:* ". . . the dominant theme is struggle and trouble. These realities not only reflect the past, but dominate the present—consciously or unconsciously underpinning . . . the way they play out their roles in the new families they form as adults" (p. 48).

10. See, for example, Robert O. Blood, Jr., and Donald M. Wolfe, *Husbands and Wives: The Dynamics of Married Living* (New York: Free Press, 1960).

11. Invaluable is a searing short story, "Audrey," in Leonard Kriegel, *Notes for the Two-Dollar Window: Portraits from an American Neighborhood* (New York: Saturday Review Press, 1976), pp. 95–133.

12. "The entry of women into the workforce is perhaps the demographic trend that most profoundly influences curriculum, services, the child's environment and the whole family structure." Joseph F. Coates, "Population and Education: How Demographic Trends Will Shape the U.S.," *The Futurist,* February 1978. See also Eli Ginzberg, Alice M. Yohalem, eds., *Corporate Lib: Women's Challenge to Management* (Baltimore: John Hopkins, 1973); Eli Ginzberg, *The Human Economy* (New York: McGraw-Hill, 1976).

13. See, for example, Louise Kapp Howe, *The Future of the Family* (New York: Simon and Schuster, 1972); Lois W. Hoffman and F. Ivan Nye, *Working Mothers* (San Francisco: Jossey-Bass, 1974).

14. Thirty per cent of all households, including 31 per cent of "Manual Workers," 30 per cent of "Clerical & Sales," and 21 per cent of "Professional & Business" types, identified watching TV as the favorite way to spend an evening in a March '77 Gallup Poll; the next highest choice was reading (20 per cent) for "Professional and Business," "Dining Out" (12 per cent) for "Clerical & Sales," and "Home with Family" (15 per cent) for "Manual Workers." *The Gallup Opinion Index,* September 1977, Report No. 146, p. 14.

15. Rubin, op. cit., pp. 128–129. Though Gallup Poll results cannot be adjusted to "breakout" data for blue-collar households headed by middle-aged men, the data from a 1977 poll (Gallup Opinion Index, November, 1977, Report No. 148, p. 7) suggest that about one third of manual workers are dissatisfied with the future facing them and their family whereas only about a fifth of professional and business workers are dissatisfied. However, the same poll showed changes in satisfaction since 1973 to be in the positive direction, especially for manual workers.

16. Rubin, op. cit., p. 215. See also Arthur B. Shostak, "Blue-Collar Mental Health: Changes Since 1968," *Journal of Occupational Medicine* (November 1974), pp. 741–743.

17. Invaluable here is Richard Sennett and Jonathan Cobb, *The Hidden Injuries of Class* (New York: Knopf, 1972).

18. Ibid., p. 147. Cf. Richard Balzer, *Clockwork: Life in and Outside An American Factory (Garden City, NY: Doubleday & Co., 1976).*

19. Carol Tarvis and Susan Sadd, *The Redbook Report on Female Sexuality: 100,000 Married Women Disclose the Good News About Sex* (New York: Delacorte Press, 1977), p. 158. See also Anthony Pietropinto and Jacqueline Simenauer, *Beyond the Male Myth: A National Survey* (New York: Times, 1978); Bernie Zilbergeld, *Male Sexuality: A Guide to Sexual Fulfillment* (Boston: Little, Brown, 1978).

20. Invaluable in this connection is Peter Chew, *The Inner World of the Middle-Aged Man* (Boston: Houghton Mifflin, 1977). See also George E. Vaillant, *Adaptation to Life* (Boston: Little, Brown, & Co., 1977); James O'Toole, *Work, Learning, and the American Future,* (San Francisco: Jossey-Bass, 1977).

# Peak Experiences: Some Empirical Tests *

## Robert Wuthnow

. . . THIS ARTICLE presents some exploratory findings regarding peak experiences † from a systematic random sample of 1,000 persons in the San Francisco–Oakland area. Evidence is presented on the incidence of peak experiences of several different kinds, on the kinds of life styles which tend to be associated with these experiences, and on some of the social implications which these experiences have.

The sample was a three-stage stratified random sample drawn to be representative of all persons age 16 and over living in the five counties making up the San Francisco–Oakland Standard Metropolitan Statistical Area according to 1970 census figures. The sample was drawn in such a way as to overrepresent youth age 16 through 30. For our purposes, however, a weighting factor has been assigned to make the sample representative of the actual age distribution of the Bay Area population. The data was collected in hour-long interviews conducted by a team of forty professional interviewers during the spring and summer of 1973. An overall response rate of 78 per cent was obtained. This data was collected as part of the Berkeley Religious Consciousness Project under a grant from the Ford Foundation to the Institute for Religion and Social Change in Honolulu (see Glock and Bellah, 1976; Wuthnow, 1976, for further details on the survey).

## The Incidence of Peak Experiences

. . . To obtain a general sense of how common or uncommon peak experiences are, respondents were asked questions about three kinds of peak experiences. These questions attempted to encompass the major kinds of peak experiences that people might have had and were phrased in terms which were as general as possible. The first, designed to elicit peak experiences bearing religious interpretations, asked if people had "ever had the feeling that you were in close contact with something *holy or sacred.*" The second asked about having "experienced the *beauty of nature* in a deeply moving way."

* Reprinted by permission of the author and the publisher from the *Journal of Humanistic Psychology*, 18:3 (1978): 59–75.

† ["Peak experiences" are described by Abraham Maslow as "the most wonderful experience or experiences of your life, happiest moments, ecstatic moments, moments of rapture" (Maslow, 1962).]

And the third, asked about "feeling that you were in *harmony with the universe.*" Respondents were asked to state whether or not they had had each kind of experience. In addition, those who had such an experience were asked whether or not it had had a deep and lasting influence on their life. Those who had not were asked whether or not they would like to have an experience of this kind.

Table 1 shows the responses to these questions. It indicates clearly that these kinds of peak experiences are common to a wide cross-section of people. One person in two has experienced contact with the holy or sacred, more than eight in ten have been moved deeply by the beauty of nature, and close to four in ten have experienced being in harmony with the universe. Of these, more than half in each case have had peak experiences which have had deep and lasting effects on their lives.

It is also of interest to note that people who have not had these peak experiences tend more often than not to be desirous of having them. More than three-fourths of those not having had a peak experience in nature would like to, as would about half of those not having had a mystical or a religious peak experience. . . .

[The author then analyzes his data to discover whether peakers (i.e., people who have intense peak experiences and who are oriented toward valuing these experiences) tend to exhibit a distinctive way of life, and, if so, whether such a style of life has any consequences for the way in which a person lives and relates to others. Dr. Wuthnow cites Maslow (1962) who suggested that self-actualizing people are likely to be more at peace with themselves than the average person; they should be able to rise above the petty concerns of everyday life, such as status consciousness; and they should tend to be more interested in helping to eradicate social problems. Dr. Wuthnow presents a discussion of his research in which these statements were put to an empirical test.]

Table 1

*Frequency of Peak Experiences*

| Response | Percentage and kind of experience | | |
| --- | --- | --- | --- |
| | Contact with the sacred | Beauty of nature | Harmony with the universe |
| Yes, and it has had a lasting influence on my life. | 27 | 49 | 22 |
| Yes, but it hasn't had a lasting influence on my life. | 23 | 33 | 17 |
| No, but I'd like to. | 25 | 14 | 34 |
| No, I don't care whether I ever do. | 25 | 4 | 27 |
| Total percentage | 100 | 100 | 100 |

Note.—$N = 1000$.

# Discussion

Given the present data, we have been able to engage in little more than an exploratory investigation of peak experiences. The fact that these data, unlike virtually all previous data regarding peak experiences, are from a systematic sample of people in the general community has, nevertheless, led to some important results. We have learned that peak experiences are widely spread. Virtually everyone appears to have them of one kind or another. The data have also shown that they are about equally common among the young and the old and among men and women. They do appear to be somewhat more common among the educated than the uneducated. This may be a function of the way in which the present questions were worded, however. We have also seen that peak experiences do not appear to be mere chance occurrences that have little to do with the rest of a person's life. Instead they appear to be but one, although a significant, aspect of a self-actualizing style of life. The data give no hint that peak experiences are, as some have suggested, more common among pathological types of personalities. Rather, they appear to be associated with introspective, self-aware, self-assured personalities. Finally, we have learned that peak experiencers do, as Maslow (1970) suspected, exhibit some important differences in values from nonpeakers. In particular, they appear to be less materialistic, less status conscious, and more socially concerned than nonpeakers.

This last finding appears to be especially worthy of further attention. Although a great deal of interest has been shown in peak experiences in recent years, practically all of this interest has been devoted to describing the purely psychological (and physiological) characteristics of these experiences. Scarcely any attention has been given to their social significance. Certainly, it is important to understand the psychological and physiological processes that take place during the course of these experiences. Their significance is likely to be enhanced if it can be shown that they have therapeutic effects for individuals (e.g., that they can be used to cure states of depression, that they can make people happier, that they can enable people to better cope with anxiety and frustration, or that they can simply make people more aware of their own human potential). But, at the same time, the social potential of peak experiences should not be neglected. If they have none, this fact should be documented. However, if these experiences do, as the present data suggests, encourage people to be less concerned about status and about material possessions and more concerned with helping others, this possibility needs to be explored. It needs to be understood so that its potential for relieving such problems as social disintegration, prejudice, or poverty can be made known. This is especially the case at the present time when much of the energy which was spent during the 1960s in pursuit of social and political reforms appears to have been turned toward the pursuit of inward experiences.

REFERENCES

ADLER, N. *The underground stream: New life styles and the antinomian personality.* New York: Harper & Row, 1972.

FINGARETTE, H. *The self in transformation: Psychoanalysis, philosophy and the life of the spirit.* New York: Harper & Row, 1963.

GLOCK, C. Y., & BELLAH, R. (Eds.), *The new religious consciousness.* Berkeley & Los Angeles: University of California Press, 1976.

LASKI, M. *Ecstasy: A study of some secular and religious experiences.* London: The Cresset Press, 1961.

MASLOW, A. *Toward a psychology of being.* Princeton, N. J.: D. Van Nostrand Company, 1962.

MASLOW, A. *Religions, values, and peak-experiences.* New York: The Viking Press, 1970.

MOGAR, R. Current status and future trends in psychedelic (LSD) research. *Journal of Humanistic Psychology,* 1965, 2, 147–166. Reprinted in Charles T. Tart, (Ed.), *Altered States of Consciousness.* Garden City, N.Y.: Doubleday & Company, 1972, pp. 391–408.

OWENS, C. The mystical experience: Facts and values. *Main Currents in Modern Thought,* 1967, 23(2). Reprinted in John White (Ed.), *The highest state of consciousness.* Garden City, N.Y.: Doubleday & Company, 1972, pp. 135–152.

PRINCE, R. Mystical states and the concept of regression. *Psychedelic Review,* 1966, 8. Reprinted in John White (Ed.), *The highest state of consciousness.* Garden City, N.Y.: Doubleday & Company, 1972, pp. 114–134.

ROSZAK, T. *The making of a counter culture.* Garden City, N.Y.: Doubleday & Company, 1969.

SAVAGE, C., FADIMAN, J., MOGAR, R. & ALLEN, M. The effects of psychedelic therapy on values, personality, and behavior. *International Journal of Neuropsychiatry,* 1966, 2, 241–254.

WUTHNOW, R. *The consciousness reformation.* Berkeley & Los Angeles: University of California Press, 1976.

WUTHNOW, R., & GLOCK, C. Religious loyalty, defection, and experimentation among college youth. *Journal for the Scientific Study of Religion,* 1973, 12(2), 157–180.

# The Effects of Divorce: A Research Review with a Developmental Perspective*

*John A. Rohrlich, Ruth Ranier,
Linda Berg-Cross, and Gary Berg-Cross*

ACCORDING TO THE 1970 U.S. Census about one out of four marriages end in divorce; this figure has now risen to one in three and continues to rise. Seventy per cent of divorcing couples have children under the age of 18. Thus about one out of every seven children is affected by divorce. However, these

* Reprinted with the permission of the authors and the *Journal of Clinical Child Psychology,* 6:2(1977):15–20.

figures do not include the permanent separations and desertions, which are estimated to equal the number of legal divorces. In total it is probable that two of every seven children in the U.S. experience some form of parent separation. In light of these statistics it is not surprising that researchers are becoming very involved in assessing the effect parent separation has on children.

Whether or not divorce increases a child's chance of needing the services of a mental health professional has not been thoroughly established, but there is a general feeling, running through the available literature, that separation or divorce increases a child's risk. To fully understand the effect of divorce one needs to realize that many factors are involved and that divorce is not a short-lived event but rather a series of stages, with each stage having its own consequences. The environmental stress caused by separation or divorce is only one factor that is likely to precipitate behavioral and emotional problems in children. Other factors which may be important are parental fighting after the divorce (Anthony, 1974; Westman, Cline, Swift & Kramer, 1970), the personalities and pathology of persons who divorce (Blumenthal, 1967; Brun, 1964; Loeb, 1966; Loeb & Price, 1966), societal expectations (Brandwein, Brown & Fox, 1974), lack of emotional support for divorced parents (Brandwein, et al., 1974) and father absence (Herzog & Sudia, 1969, an extensive review). The purpose of this paper is to review the available literature on divorce with particular emphasis on how children at different stages are differentially affected by divorce. The therapeutic implications of these findings will then be discussed.

# The Consequences of Divorce for the Child at Different Developmental Stages

## Infancy

With the median duration of marriages that end in divorce being 6.7 years, many children experience divorce while they are quite young. It may seem that divorce during pregnancy or within the first six months spares the child possible separation anxiety and therefore severe trauma, but Klatskin (1972) has pointed out that the child may still be in danger. The greatest potential danger for the child in this period is that the primary caretaker, usually the mother, may be so overwhelmed by the experience that she may suffer severe depression and be unable to adequately care for the child. If the care given the infant is inappropriate or insufficient, disturbances are likely to occur in feeding, sleeping, and elimination patterns. The child may become irritable and difficult to comfort. When the mother is unable to respond appropriately the use of a mother substitute can be helpful until the mother is well enough to again supply the emotional "give and take" necessary.

Even in cases where there is no depression it is likely that the mother, the usual custodial parent of young children, will begin working and spending many hours away from her child. Psychoanalytic theory (Goldstein, Freud & Solnit, 1973) places emphasis on the continuity of both relationships and environment for a child's normal development. The stability of the external world is believed to be necessary for the child to successfully deal with the changes inherent in the normal developmental process. Disruptions in the continuity of the parent-child relationship during the first 18 months, whether from mother to babysitter or from mother to day care center, may lead to feeding problems, sleep disturbance, or crying.

The literature cited here on the effects divorce can have on infants is entirely theoretical in nature and quite conservative (i.e., it is primarily based on analytic concepts). Indeed, empirical research may show that infants from divorced families prosper as much as other infants do in good day care facilities (see Yudkin & Holme, 1969) and that day care services may even provide a healthy mother substitute during the crisis period.

In later infancy when children are developing autonomy (1–2 years old) they require firm but reassuring outer controls. The infant must not feel that their need for choice or their need to demand appropriately will mean the end of their existence. Consequently the parents' reaction to the child is more important than the separation of the parents per se. Divorce may cause a parent to be unable to supply the encouragement and love the child needs to become independent or may cause the parent to be over-involved and too restricting toward the child.

Klatskin (1972) suggests that the most likely detrimental consequence in later infancy is for the parent who assumes custody to transfer the love for the lost partner to the child. This can lead to overprotectiveness and inhibition of the child's age appropriate level of independence both then and in later years.

## Preschool Years (3–5)

When the child moves into the preschool years the consequences of divorce shift because the child of this age is more aware of the loss of a parent. While previously the effect on the child depended largely on the parents' reaction, now the child's own personality and coping mechanisms begin to play a part as well. Though the child may have been aware previously that something was wrong in the parent's relationship, they must now struggle to comprehend the cause of the separation.

During the earliest part of the preschool period the manifestations of the child's anxiety are likely to result in loss of the most recently acquired skills. The child may begin to soil or wet its pants, change eating habits, show sleep disturbance, or have tantrums. These changes are usually temporary and when a new routine is established in the household, control is regained (Klatskin, 1972).

Later in the preschool period the manifestations of the crisis change from regressive behavior to more inner directed conflict. This is the period when children are developing strong ties to parents of the opposite sex and may be experiencing Oedipal conflicts. If the child is fantasizing the death or elimination of the same sex parent and divorce or separation occurs the child may develop very powerful guilt feelings. That is, the child may actually see themself as the cause of the separation. This can of course be felt at later stages as well, for example if the child has been the scapegoat of many arguments.

A study by McDermott (1968) looked at the effect of divorce on 16 children between the ages of three and five who were attending a preschool. These children were not from a clinic population. The study is unique because it included observations (descriptive reports) of the children prior to the divorce as well as during and after the divorce. These data allowed the authors to learn about the most immediate effects of divorce as well as more long term effects of 1–2 years. The immediate effects were strikingly apparent to the teachers of these children. In several instances the teachers noticed great changes in a child's behavior only to later learn of the divorce or separation when discussing the child's behavior with one of the parents. McDermott found that the reactions of the 16 children fell into four groups. Three of the children fell into what was called the "unchanged" group. These children did not show changes in the quality of their behavior. Yet the label is not intended to imply that these children were unaffected by the divorce process. Rather, their adaptive mechanisms seemed better able to cope with the stress. Possibly they had also been better prepared by parents who anticipated the child's guilt, anger, or blame, and helped them work through these feelings. Each of these three children seemed to have distinct relationships with each parent and the parents were on good terms following the divorce. Prior to the divorce the children in this group were described as well-adjusted, well-liked, spontaneous, and imaginative.

The largest group of children, labeled the "sad-angry" group, included seven boys and one girl. These children showed clear signs of shock, anger, and depression. They made frequent use of denial and regression to deal with their problem. In actual behavior they became possessive, noisy, restless, and aggressive. Other children who seemed to be enjoying themselves were disrupted, especially if they were playing house. In addition to the aggressive unfriendly behavior there was a pronounced sadness. Some children cried or sat alone and several said they weren't happy any more. For some children the depression caused them to give up activities and to be unable to play creatively. A few children discontinued their art for a couple of months and those who continued often drew pictures of children looking for their house, some other object, or even their parents. The play that was initiated regressed from the human and family sphere to the animal world. Readjustment for these children typically began in six to eight weeks.

A third group, two children, seemed more "lost and detached" than the others. It was felt that both of these children had long-standing disturbances in their ego development. One of these children after the divorce began to lose all of his personal belongings, couldn't find his locker, was unwilling or unable to dress, provoked rejection, and made insatiable demands for affection. This child was seen at a clinic but little change was observed. The other child, a girl, was totally self-absorbed, tearful, tense, uninterested in any imaginative play, soiled and wet occasionally, began to suck her thumb, and started to masturbate openly. This child was also seen at a clinic and returned to her prior level of adjustment in about three months.

The three girls who composed the last group took on a pseudo-adult role and were considered to have "hidden problems." These girls scolded and lectured other children, became concerned with health and manners, began dressing inappropriately for preschool, and became very concerned with neatness. Overall there seemed to be a sudden constriction of personality. It may be that they were identifying with a real or fantasized part of the mother which developed increased meaning because of the divorce. Unfortunately these children were not observed long enough to know whether the immediate constriction of personality had a long-lasting effect. While these girls seemed to consolidate their identification with their mother, an overview of boys' responses suggested they were withdrawing from identification with their fathers. The boys were all within the stage when they would normally be changing their primary love object from the mother to the father. Several factors were hypothesized to account for the decreased identification. These children may have felt guilt over the satisfaction of winning the battle for the mother or possibly lost their aggressive tendencies because there was no longer an antagonist upon which to safely aggress. A third possibility is that these boys were afraid of being punished for displaying masculine aggressiveness like their fathers. In summary, this study shows that most preschoolers will be affected in some manner but also that most will return to their predivorce adjustment in about two to three months. Long term effects, however, are not known. Those children most vulnerable seem to be those who are the least well-adjusted prior to the divorce.

## School Age (6–12)

When children enter school the influence of the parents lessens and the influence of teachers and peers becomes increasingly important. Intellectual demands from teachers and social norms established by peers are typically the major stresses. Part of the interaction with peers includes comparisons of oneself and one's family. This can present an additional burden for the child whose parents are divorced. During this time of moving out into the world and establishing relationships it is important that the child's energy be kept free for these purposes. The danger of divorce is that it can focus all of the child's energy into the family and restrict the growth of newly acquired but unstable autonomy.

Though many, if not most, children referred to mental health clinics are be tween six and twelve years old, few studies have focused specifically on the effects of divorce on children of this age range. Most studies take a cross section of "divorced" children with no regard for how old they were when the parents were divorced. Since the child's age at divorce and the elapsed time since the divorce are not accounted for, it is impossible to know which effects are immediate consequences and which are long-term. Worse, it may be that important effects are missed entirely. For example, divorce when a child is seven may have no profound effect on latency development but characteristic difficulties may arise in adolescence.

One recent study (Kelly & Wallerstein, 1976; Wallerstein & Kelly, 1974, 1976) has taken account of some of the difficulties in earlier studies and should eventually provide information on both long-term and immediate effects. The project, begun in 1970, observed families shortly after the initial separation, 12–18 months later, and planned for future interviews. The subject population is well educated, racially nearly homogeneous (white), and young. The study was not undertaken in an urban area because it was believed that the environmental stresses of crime, poverty, and crowding might make the effects specifically due to divorce less discernible. Persons within Marin County, California who sought legal divorce were advised of the availability of free counseling for themselves and their children. Help was given to parents in interpreting the crisis for their children, in planning postdivorce arrangements, and in discussing ways of easing the effect on the children. Each child and his parents were seen by a member of an interdisciplinary clinical staff for four to six individual sessions spaced over a period of approximately six weeks. In total 60 families with 131 children decided to participate.

In this study the 57 children between 7 and 10 years old were clearly distinguishable from the 5 and 6-year-old children (although their data was not sufficiently analyzed to be reported in detail) but those between 7 and 10 also broke into two groups; 7 and 8 years old (the early latency group) and 9 and 10 years old (the late latency group). Most striking was the pervasive sadness of the early latency group. Unlike the preschool children, these youngsters were unable to employ denial and fantasy. They were aware of their suffering but without a means to relieve it. Unable to sublimate their feelings as could older children, they appeared immobilized. Most of these younger latency children were worried about their futures and even whether there would be a place for them to grow up. Crying was not uncommon, especially in boys. The feelings of insecurity were accompanied by feelings of deprivation, shown in play and also manifested by demands for new toys or clothes. The seven and eight-year-old boys missed their fathers and felt rejected more than those of other ages, but they were generally unable to express anger at their parents as do late latency children. The bitter fighting that was common in this sample of 26 couples aggravated the loyalty conflicts. One-fourth of the younger latency age children felt a specific pressure to align with one parent but found this difficult to do. While the preschool children often felt responsible for the divorce, this was uncommon among both early and late latency age children. Also, both younger and older latency age children wished their parents were together despite the fighting.

Children in late latency (N = 31) at the time of the divorce took a sober attitude to the separation and worked hard to master conflicting feelings. While the younger children were sad and seemingly without defenses against their feelings, the 9 and 10-year-old children used denial, avoidance, courage, and activity to master their feelings, as well as seeking support from others. Unlike the younger group, they felt shame over the divorce and, as previously mentioned, expressed anger at one or both parents. Demanding and aggressive behavior in both older and younger children was increased due to the lack of disciplinary experience of most of the mothers. Some children, however, became more compliant and others showed a realistic concern for the parents' emotional health. The older children, more than any other age group, felt lonely and as if the custodial parent was emotionally moving away because it seemed these parents were occupied with their own lives and futures. As with early latency children one-fourth were pressured by a parent to align against the other parent, but unlike the younger group, they did generally form a coalition. One-half of the 9 and 10-year-olds showed a noticeable decline in both school performance and the ability to relate to peers. At the follow-up one year later all but 4 of the 15 children who had shown an academic decline had returned to their prior levels of performance.

In total, of the 26 early latency age children, 13 improved or maintained earlier developmental achievements, four maintained the negative postdivorce reaction, six were considered significantly worse, and three were unavailable at follow-up. The 31 later latency age children showed more of a bimodal distribution with 15 not only having lost the immediate reaction of fear, shame, and worry, but also feeling content with their new family, friends, and in a few cases stepparents. For these 15 children anger was the most noticeable remaining effect. The other 14 children available for observation showed more distress, sometimes with depression and lowered self-esteem. Very few of the total group of children found that they could maintain a good relationship with both parents.

Other studies which have examined the effect of divorce on latency age children have not employed intensive clinical observation nor have they controlled for the age of the children at the time of the divorce. Nevertheless, the studies are important. Some compare the effect of divorce with other types of parent loss and many use behavior checklists. One study (Felner, Stolberg, & Cohen, 1975) lends support to the growing realization that not all types of broken homes affect children in the same manner. The study, part of a primary prevention project, compared children with a history of parent death, and children from intact homes. Two behavior checklists were completed by each child's teacher. All of the children compared were referred to the program because of either behavioral or educational problems. Both the separation/divorce group and the death group showed statistically significant differences from their control groups regarding overall adjustment. Additionally, the separation/divorce group was different from its control group for each of the 12 acting-out items. The death group was different from its control group on 15 of the 16 moody/withdrawn items. The separation/divorce group was more often described as restless, obstinate, disrupting, impulsive, and so forth, while the death group was more often described as unhappy and moody. Hetherington (1972) and Felner et al. (1975) have found very similar results. An additional interesting fact which emerged was that while the children of disrupted homes were rated as more maladjusted, only 20% of referred children came from disrupted homes, a figure very close to that found in the overall population. It is difficult to know why this should be. It may be that more deviant behavior is tolerated from children from disrupted homes or possibly that less is expected of these children.

A partially conflicting study (McDermott, 1970) compared a large number of clinic cases including 116 cases where the parents were divorced and 22 where the parents were separated. Children up to the age of 14 were included but most were of latency age when seen at the clinic. It was found that running away from home, poor home behavior, and poor school behavior were all more frequent in the divorce group than in the intact group. Two findings not previously reported were that in the divorce group presenting problems were more specific and that the duration of the presenting problem was shorter, on the average. The authors interpret this to mean that children of divorced parents are reacting to an acute stress, the parent separation. It seems, however, that the nature of the presenting problem, anti-social behavior, was more likely to require immediate attention and to be more easily specifiable than the anxiety of neurotic symptomatology. Contrary to the results of the study by Felner, et al. (1975) and others, the divorce group showed more depression as well as aggressive behavior when compared with the intact group. Moderate or severe depression was considered to exist in 34.3% of the cases.

## Adolescence

Achieving independence from parents is the major goal of adolescents. Most adolescents become inconsistent in behavior, sometimes acting much younger, seeking the protection and nurturance they once knew, and at other times acting quite mature, seeking acceptance as adults from their parents.

Attitudes, like behavior, are inconsistent and ambivalent. Parents are almost certainly to be faced with negative outbursts. The effect of divorce on the adolescent can be to either overburden them as they struggle to break away from the primary love objects, or to accelerate their growth toward adulthood. This acceleration, however, also can be detrimental if it occurs prematurely; that is, before the normal detachment has begun.

In the large study by Wallerstein and Kelly (1974) there were only 21 children over the age of 13, reinforcing the established fact that children are usually much younger when divorce occurs. While this represents only a small number of children from the total study, the lack of systematic research on adolescence and divorce makes even this small sample valuable.

The adolescents' reactions were similar in several ways. For each the experience was a painful event that produced a sense of betrayal, a feeling of loss, and anger. Consistent with the reactions of latency age children, adolescents do not feel responsible for the divorce. Feeling responsibility seems to be a reaction restricted to preschool children. Loyalty conflicts, however, are not the sole property of any one age group. In defending themselves against the pain of family dissolution, all of the adolescents tried, with varying degrees of success, to use distancing and withdrawal as a means of protection. The distancing was accomplished by increased social activity and avoidance of the home. It seems that emotional detachment is necessary, at first, to keep the adolescent development intact. Yet at a later date almost all of the children were able to be supportive and empathic to their parents. Common among adolescents who made a healthy adjustment was the adoption of a more realistic and futuristic orientation. This group of adolescents were able to form independent judgments of each parent and relinquish viewing them as a unit. This differentiation of the parents can help these youngsters to become more accepting of personality differences in general and thereby make their own identity formation easier.

Unfortunately, not all of the adolescents fared well after the divorce. Several subgroups of adolescents considered in need of therapeutic help were identified. One group, the most severely affected, showed an indefinite delay in the mastery of the normative tasks of adolescence. These delays seemed to be the result of the particular parent-child relationships. In one case the mother of a 13-year-boy suffered with a severe hysterical illness. She had psychosomatic symptoms, was depressed, and had a history of suicide attempts. Prior to the divorce the boy and his mother were very close and she was openly seductive toward him. After the divorce he became overly protective of her, very jealous of her dates, sleepless when she was out, and preoccupied with her illnesses, fearing she would die of cancer. A year after the divorce the boy's reactions had intensified and he was further away from autonomy and independence than ever.

In another case the delay into adolescence lasted almost two years. An adolescent girl of 13 had an intense relationship with her father, though her father was abusive to the other two children and the wife. For the last 1½ years of the marriage the parents only communicated by written notes. Finally the wife filed for divorce and the husband was never heard from again, although he sent child support. The girl became very depressed and continually worried about her father. She lost contact with friends, played dolls with younger children, and slept with her mother. After two years she seemed to be gradually returning to her predivorce adjustment although she was still quite subdued. Her resumption of age appropriate behavior coincided with her mother's remarriage.

A third type of pathological adjustment found by Wallerstein and Kelly was manifested not as a blocking or delay of adolescence but as a pseudoadolescent response, premature heterosexual activity. The difference between true adolescent heterosexual activty and this type lies in the reason for the sexual activity. For example, Wallerstein and Kelly report a case of a 14-year-old girl who began her sexual adventures when she discovered that her father was having an affair with a neighbor. She described her fantasies of her father's sexual activity and threw rocks at his mistress' window. The girl's mother slowly began to lose judgment, became depressed, and soon took young lovers into the house. The girl continued her sexual activity, drinking, and drug use, and after one year the family situation was unchanged.

In addition to these three severely pathological adjustments there were those adolescents who displayed aggressive and anti-social behavior due to the loss of necessary behavioral constraints and positive models. These were adolescents who had not fully established their own inner controls. The absence of the parental constraints in regard to sexual and aggressive behaviors caused added stress in the two areas already presenting conflict in most adolescents.

Finally there were those children for whom the divorce was only one more episode in a long-standing history of emotional deprivation and inadequate parenting. These adolescents were likely to continue developing as they had unless they received therapeutic help and important environmental supports.

As was found in the research on preschool children (McDermott, 1968), adolescent adjustment to divorce is highly correlated with the predivorce adjustment of the child and the emotional health of the parents. When parents' own needs cause them to revert to adolescent modes of behavior the child's ability for mastering nomal adolescent tasks is profoundly disturbed. Those adolescents who either benefited or were not hurt by the divorce were able at the beginning to maintain distance from the parental crisis. Healthy parents were able to allow their children to do so.

## Summary and Criticism

Clearly it can be seen that there is a paucity of research on the effects of divorce on children. Moreover, the existing research is not without flaws. One significant problem is the disregard for the child's age at the time of the divorce. Failure to take this factor into account confuses the immediate and long term effect of divorce. A second major difficulty is the lack of research using a random sample of children. The large project by Wallerstein and Kelly (1974, 1976; Kelly & Wallerstein, 1976) is one of the best efforts in the area of divorce because it attacks the problem from a developmental perspective. Still, it is flawed by a non-random sample and the lack of objective measures.

Even without a large or flawless body of research some generalizations can be made. It is clear that the effect of divorce does vary with the developmental level of the child, at least during the first year following divorce. The work by McDermott (1968) suggests that most preschool children will return to predivorce adjustment in about three months but that those children who were disturbed prior to the divorce will become worse or take longer to overcome the crisis. Note, this does not mean that these children will not continue to want their parents to reunite or that there will not be a lingering tension on the parent-child relationship because of the divorce. Children of latency age seem more resigned to the outcome but if they are older latency children there will probably be a residue of anger toward one or both parents. For adolescents the divorce may be constructive by helping the child move toward complete autonomy and away from parents. Yet, as for younger children, there is a chance that the divorce will harm the child. Usually the harm appears to be a result of the particular parent-child relationship or parent-parent relationship which develops after the divorce. The mental health of the parents and the predivorce adjustment of the child are two important factors in all age groups.

## Help for the Children of Divorced Parents

The manner in which parents deal with the question of divorce before they separate is directly relevant to the effect divorce has on children. Explaining divorce to children is the first step in keeping the crisis from damaging the child. Parents, anxious and guilty about divorce, often delay telling their children of an impending divorce. This delay forces the child to observe the continued conflict within the family and allows the child's fantasy to aggravate the problem causing fear and insecurity. Bringing the problem into the open takes away the mystery and may lessen the child's fear. Kapit (1972) suggests that when possible both parents should tell the children of the divorce. This helps assure the child that although there is conflict the parents are willing to work together for the child's good. The parent or parents should explain to the child calmly and with a feeling of confidence about the future. Expressions of depression, pessimism, and anxiety by the parent should be avoided. The actual words the parent uses need to be suited to the child's level of understanding; therefore, where there is more than one child each should be told individually. Young children will not be able to understand the abstract word "divorce" and should be told that their parents have decided not to live in the same house any more. Pitcher (1969) suggests, however, that the words "marriage" and "divorce" be used in addition because of the likelihood that the child will frequently hear these words from others. Pitcher also suggests avoiding telling the child that his parents do not love each other any more; this wording may cause the child to fear that the love for them may sometime end as well. Further, parents should avoid telling the intimate details of why they are separating and keep to the facts which pertain to the child's future. Most important is that the parents tell the truth. If they are unsure about who the child will live with, this should be acknowledged.

Preparing children for divorce is an important step in keeping the detrimental effects of this experience at a minimum. The job of the mental health professional at this time is to give the parents confidence so they are able to tell their children of the separation and to do so in an optimistic and sensitive manner. Whether the parents have been in therapy and decided to divorce or whether they simply come for advice at the time, they need to understand that their child will certainly feel hurt and may very well feel anger, guilt, or fear. The child should be allowed, even encouraged, to express these feelings. Concerned and understanding parents can help the child tremendously. Parent counseling of this sort is a first preventative step. At the time of the actual divorce the mental health professional's role is quite different. (In fact the use of mental health professionals as advisors of the court is relatively new.)

The rights and welfare of children are now being considered more seriously in regard to custody and visitation. It is no longer the case as in feudal times that a child automatically goes to the father (personal property) or as in recent industrial times that the child automatically goes to the mother. The book, *Beyond the Best Interests of the Child,* (Goldstein, et al., 1973) has been very influential in this area and several courts are now using behavioral scientists in some or all custody decisions (Benedek & Benedek, 1972; Brun, 1964; Sheffner & Suarez, 1975; Westman, 1971; Westman, Cline, Swift, & Kramer, 1970). The purpose of including behavioral scientists in these decisions is twofold. First, the child in question can be placed with that person most likely to become their psychological parent and second, those children in need of therapeutic help can be identified early. Goldstein et al. (1973) place great emphasis on the finality of custodial decisions because of the possible damage caused by discontinuity of parent-child relationships. By involving mental health professionals in the custody decision families may come for help much sooner than is typical and if later court battles arise the mental health worker is a necessary part of it. The current legal structure regrettably allows for frequent custody battles. At both the time of the divorce and later if such battles occur, the mental health worker's role is to help the court decide in the child's best interest.

Still there are those cases in which manipulation of custody or visitation is not the solution. In some cases the court advisor might support discontinuing visitation or advise placement with neither parent, while in other cases the need is for parent, child, or family-oriented psychotherapy. Due to the large number of possible problems it is impossible to outline a strategy for each case, but some examples are useful.

Some cases require a primarily didactic approach while others a primarily therapeutic approach. For example, a single parent may be faced for the first time with the responsibility of disciplining their child, as might occur when previously the other parent took this responsibility. In such cases a didactic approach may be all that is required. However, the parent may be either too disturbed to cope with the child's difficulties or possibly a diffusion of generational boundaries may exist, as when a mother attempts to replace her husband with her adolescent son. When these circumstances exist, a primarily therapeutic rather than a didactic approach is needed. Minuchin (1974) reports that a diffusion of generational boundaries is not uncommon after divorce. While the mother may want to involve the ex-husband it is the therapist's task to treat the "new" system and establish the mother as the sole parent. The therapist may choose to have a few sessions with the children and the father, but without the mother, to help these persons negotiate a relationship. But it is not always the entire family or single parent that needs to be treated.

One might be faced with a child, probably poorly adjusted prior to divorce, who shows severe disturbance. The child may be feeling guilty about causing the divorce, feel rejection from one or both parents, or feel anger, all of which the child may be hesitant or afraid to express. Sometimes in such cases education or ventilation can prove useful. However, more often one is dealing with the problem of how to substitute for the loss felt by younger children or how to mourn the loss felt by older children. Anthony (1974) has found that in working with children who have reacted adversely to divorce, the child's fantasy of the family can be a valuable tool in helping the child. The utopian fantasy which the child creates often signals its needs, dissatisfactions, conflicts, and the way in which these problems can be solved. Using the child's fantasy it is possible to help the child face the reality of the situation.

Thus, by examining the effects of divorce with a developmental orientation the work of the mental health professional can be directed toward the specific needs within each area of crisis, thus maximizing help for parents and children.

## REFERENCES

ANTHONY, E. J. Children at risk from divorce: A review. In E. J. Anthony & C. Koupernik (Eds.) *The child in his family: Children at psychiatric risk* (Vol. 3). New York: John Wiley, 1974.
BENEDEK, E. P., & BENEDEK, R. S. New child custody laws: Making them do what they say. *American Journal of Orthopsychiatry*, 1972, 42, 825–34.

BLUMENTHAL, M. D. Mental health among the divorced. *Archives of General Psychiatry*, 1967, **16**, 603–08.

BRANDWEIN, R. A., BROWN, C. A., & FOX, E. M. The social situation of divorced mothers and their families. *Journal of Marriage and the Family*, 1974, **36**, 498–514.

BRUN, G. The child of divorce in Denmark. *Bulletin of the Menninger Clinic*, 1964, **28**, 3–10.

FELNER, R. D., STOLBERG, A., & COWEN, E. L. Crisis events and school mental health referral patterns of young children. *Journal of Consulting and Clinical Psychology*, 1975, **43**, 305–10.

GOLDSTEIN, J., FREUD, A., & SOLNIT, A. J. *Beyond the best interests of the child.* New York: Free Press, 1973.

HERZOG, E., & SUDIA, C. E. Family structure and composition. In R. R. Miller. (Ed.) *Race, research and reason: Social work perspectives.* New York: National Association of Social Workers, 1969.

HETHERINGTON, E. M. Effects of father absence on personality development in adolescent daughters. *Developmental Psychology*, 1972, **7**, 313–26.

KAPIT, H. E. Help for children of separation and divorce. In I. R. Staurt & L. E. At (eds.), *Children of separation and divorce.* New York: Grossman, 1972.

KELLY, J. B., & WALLERSTEIN, J. S. The effects of parental divorce: Experiences of the child in early latency. *American Journal of Orthopsychiatry*, 1976, **46**, 20–32.

KLATSKIN, E. H. Developmental factors. In I. R. Staurt & L. E. Abt (Eds.), *Children of separation and divorce.* New York: Grossman, 1972.

LOEB, J. The personality factor in divorce. *Journal of Consulting Psychology*, 1966, **30**, 562.

McDERMOTT, J. F., JR. Parental divorce in early childhood. *American Journal of Psychiatry*, 1968, **124**, 1424–32.

McDERMOTT, J. F., JR. Divorce and psychiatric sequelae in children. *Archives of General Psychiatry*, 1970, **23**, 421–27.

MINUCHIN, S. *Families and family therapy.* Cambridge, Massachusetts: Harvard University Press, 1974.

PITCHER, E. G. Explaining divorce to young children. In E. A. Grollman (Ed.), *Explaining divorce to children.* Boston: Beacon Press, 1969.

SHEFFNER, D. J., & SUAREZ, J. M. The postdivorce clinic. *American Journal of Psychiatry*, 1975, **132**, 442–44.

WALLERSTEIN, J. S. & KELLY, J. B.. The effects of parental divorce: The adolescent experience. In E. J. Anthony, & C. Koupernik (Eds.) *The child in his family: Children at psychiatric risk* (Vol. 3) New York: John Wiley, 1974.

WALLERSTEIN, J. S., & KELLY, J. B. The effects of parental divorce: Experiences of the child in later latency. *American Journal of Orthopsychiatry*, 1976, **46**, 256–69.

WESTMAN, J. C. The psychiatrist and child custody contests. *American Journal of Psychiatry*, 1971, **126**, 1687–88.

WESTMAN, J. C., CLINE, D. W., SWIFT, W. J. & KRAMER, D. A. The role of child psychiatry in divorce. *Archives of General Psychiatry*, 1970, **23**, 416–20.

YUDKIN, S., & HOLME, A. *Working mothers and their children.* London: Sphere Books, 1969.

# Patterns of Personality Development in Middle-aged Women: A Longitudinal Study*

*Florine B. Livson*

LIFE EXPANDS AT FIFTY—for non-traditional women who live traditional lives. More traditional women move smoothly into middle age with little change in life-style. I will take a longitudinal look at personality development from adolescence to middle age in twenty-four women who had achieved a relatively high level of psychological health by age fifty—with special attention to changes in the middle adult years (ages 40 to 50).

The decade between ages forty and fifty, most investigators agree, brackets a critical transition in the life span, often punctuated by stress [1, 2, 3]. At forty most individuals are still engaged in tasks begun as young adults; at fifty a person is middle-aged. The decade of the forties brings a change in time perspective linked to a growing awareness of death as a personal reality [4]. As time perspective narrows, there is a tendency to turn inward, to reappraise one's self and one's goals. By the late forties and early fifties, however, this process tends to stabilize with a redefinition of goals and coming to terms with oneself [2, 3].

For women who are housewives and mothers, the transition into middle age is usually linked to the departure of children and the biological changes of menopause. The post-parental years as a significant phase in a woman's life is a relatively new social phenomenon. With increased longevity—today a woman of forty-five will live on the average thirty-three more years—and with smaller families and the earlier departure of children, a woman can expect a longer period without her children than in earlier generations. The average woman today retires from mothering at forty-seven as compared with fifty-five at the end of the last century [5]. These writers point out that this is also the average age at menopause and the age when the number of women in the labor force rises most sharply.

How do the challenges of change at mid-life—social and biological—affect psychological well-being in women? Investigators do not agree. Medical and psychiatric literature abounds with accounts of the stresses of the climacteric and the so-called involutional disorders. Recent studies of healthy women in the community, however, question the generality of these observations. The departure of children—once the process of separation is completed—often

* Reprinted from the *International Journal of Aging and Human Development*, 1976, 7:2, 107–115, by permission of the publisher and the author.

leads to improved life satisfaction in the post-parental years [4, 6]. Menopause for many women is less stressful than commonly believed and post-menopausal women may even view this biological change as a positive event [6, 7]. Bart reports that in cultures in which women's social status rises in the middle years, menopause is not seen as stressful [8]. Neugarten observes that when major role losses in middle life are predictable and occur "on schedule" in the normal life course, they can be anticipated and worked through without disrupting the woman's sense of self [4].

Do role changes in the middle years allow some women not only to adapt but to expand their psychological horizons? Parts of the personality that were suppressed because they were not congruent with the roles of mother and young adult may surface to add new dimensions to the person. Does moving out of the mothering role, for example, allow a woman more flexibility in whether or not she conforms to traditional feminine sex roles? Chiriboga and Thurnher [6] report that sixty-year-old women view themselves as more assertive and effective than do women at fifty and Neugarten and Gutmann [9] find that women become more accepting of their aggressive impulses in the later years of life.

The present study describes two patterns of personality development leading to psychological health by age fifty in women who have been observed since adolescence. It explores differences between women whose personalities expand in the decade between forty and fifty and those who continue on more or less the same course throughout the middle years.

The twenty-four women in this study are drawn from a larger group of forty-two women who remained in the longitudinal Oakland Growth Study (Institute of Human Development, Univeristy of California, Berkeley) throughout adolescence (ages 11 to 18) and at *both* adult follow-ups (roughly ages 40 and 50).[1] They were selected on the basis of relatively high scores on an index of psychological health at age fifty (see below).

The California Q sort developed by Block was used to obtain personality profiles of participants at each of the four age periods studied: early and late adolescence, approximately ages forty and fifty [10, 11].[2] Q sorts at these

[1] Participants in the Oakland Growth Study, which began in 1931–32 with over 200 boys and girls entering junior high school, were observed continuously throughout their junior and senior high school years and were interviewed again intensively in the late 1950s and 1960s. All were white. The forty-two women who remained in the study at all four age periods are (at age 50) predominantly middle-class housewives. Their average educational level is slightly beyond high school. They tend to be of slightly higher socioeconomic status than those who dropped out, better educated, and more effective socially. All but one married and have children. Average family size is between two and three children. The group, on the whole, is family-centered, though about half have part-time jobs and a few work full time. One-third have been divorced, but most are remarried. They are predominantly Protestant, urban, and financially comfortable.

[2] Each respondent was Q-sorted independently by at least two judges (clinically trained psychologists and psychiatric social workers) at each age period; judges had no access to data from other age periods. Mean interjudge reliabilities (computed by the Spearman-Brown prophecy formula) for Oakland Growth Study women ranged from .73 to .75.

four ages made it possible to assess personality changes over time and to estimate overall level of functioning, or "psychological health." The index of psychological health, developed by Livson and Peskin [12], was the correlation between each woman's $Q$ sort and an "ideal" sort of a psychologically healthy person, representing a composite of sorts by four clinical psychologists.[3] The psychological health sort stresses qualities such as warm, giving, responsible, productive, insightful—and relatively free of neurotic signs. Psychological health scores are not related to intelligence or socioeconomic status and do not favor either sex.

Using this measure, I selected the healthiest members of the larger sample at age fifty for study: twenty-four women who scored above the mean on the index of psychological health. Two groups of healthy women were identified: seventeen whose health had *improved* from ages forty to fifty; and seven whose health had remained high and *stable* since forty.

Are these two groups, both psychologically healthy by age fifty, made up of women with different personality styles? Does each follow a different path of development toward this "end product" over the four age periods? I will contrast the two groups on the basis of significant personality (Q-sort) differences between them at each age level.[4] Though, for ease of exposition, each group will be described as a separate personality type, it should be kept in mind that these descriptions are relative one to the other.

# Traditionals and Independents

## Age Fifty Differences

The stable group at fifty are gregarious, nurturant women, pleased with their appearance, and conventional in their outlook. They place high value on closeness with others. They are seen as "feminine." I have called this group *traditionals*. Interviewers describe them as charming, cordial, generous, good hostesses. Their sociability is expressed in trusting, protective relations with others. Their defenses are of a hysterical type—anxiety is handled by repression and somatization—but their defenses work well. Overall, these are well-functioning, conforming women who are extroverted in that they turn outward for satisfaction. They rely on ego functions that further interpersonal skills. These qualities are well-suited to traditional roles of wife and mother—which may account for their high psychological health score at forty when their children were still dependent. These are women with minimal conflict between their personalities and social role.

---

[3] The reliability of the composite sort is .95, reflecting an average first-order interjudge agreement of .82.

[4] Differences reported at each age level are significant at least at the .10 level.

Improvers present a different picture. These women at fifty are ambitious, skeptical, and unconventional in their way of looking at things. They rely on their intellect to cope with the world. I have labelled this group *independents.* Being verbal and expressive, they impress others as interesting people with high intellectual ability. (They do not in fact differ from traditionals in IQ as measured by the WAIS at age 50.) In brief, they are more autonomous than traditionals and more in touch with their inner life. They cope with conflicting feelings by insight and direct expression, rather than by conformity and repression. They are "doers," with interests in activities that are skill-oriented, rather than primarily social. Their main satisfactions come from developing their "selves," rather than attachment to others.

The two groups do not differ significantly in their demographic characteristics at fifty. Both are predominantly upper-middle class, financially comfortable, and Protestant. Their educational levels are similar—slightly beyond high school. Average family size of both groups is between two and three children, and average ages of children are comparable, ranging from nineteen to twenty-five. At least half of both groups still have some children living at home.

In their life-styles at fifty, however, traditionals are more home-oriented. All are currently married and primarily housewives. One-third of independents are divorced or widowed and have full-time jobs.

## Patterns of Development

How do traditionals and independents differ earlier in life? What path does each follow over the life span leading to psychological health by age fifty? I will trace the development of each group by describing personality differences between them at each age period. Both groups by early adolescence reveal a ground plan—a core characterological style—that evolves over the life span, roughly following Erikson's stages of adult development [13].

**Traditionals.** From early adolescence, traditionals are gregarious, feminine, conventional, and rely on repressive defenses. However, these key strategies in dealing with life are less fully formed than at later periods. Traditionals' gregariousness has not yet differentiated into the more subtle social skills observed later. There are signs of insecurity.

By late adolescence, they develop a more integrated, articulated style. These are popular, sociable young women in high school, successful in their femininity and perfecting their social skills. Signs of anxiety have dropped away. They are establishing, in Erikson's terms, ego identity.

By age forty, gregariousness remains their most prominent characteristic, but has now matured beyond the popularity of adolescence. They are close, trusting, and giving in their relationships with others. Poised and aware of the impression they create, they arouse liking. They have evolved a repertoire of skills that serve their core needs for sociability—and these needs themselves have matured, in the sense of becoming less narcissistic or self-oriented. They seem well into the stage of intimacy described by Erikson. The aging crisis of the forties described by many investigators does not seem to affect them.

By age fifty, traditionals have developed a protective attitude toward others. Their gregariousness, while remaining at a high level, has evolved beyond intimacy and trust into nurturance. Traditionals, by fifty, have moved into Erikson's middle adult stage of generativity. Their femininity is now clearly colored by this quality of protectiveness.

**Independents.**   Like traditionals, independents reveal key personality traits in early adolescence that hold up to age fifty and organize their adult development. From early adolescence, independents value intellectual matters and are achievement-oriented, introspective, and unconventional. Like traditionals, however, they reveal signs of insecurity in this earlier period.

By late adolescence, independents achieve a more integrated level of functioning. Their intellectuality is now enriched by an interesting, arresting style. They now appear brighter than traditionals. (Again, there are no differences between groups in tests of actual ability.) The anxiety apparent earlier has eased off. They are developing a consistent, adaptive personality style.

By age forty the picture changes. Independents are depressed, irritable, conflicted. They no longer use their intellectuality in an adaptive way. Their originality and introspectiveness have turned to fantasy and daydreams. They seem out of touch with their intellectual interests and creative potential. Their overall psychological health score is relatively low. These women who seemed to be progressing toward a firm identity in adolescence appear to have regressed. They do not move into the stage of intimacy observed in traditionals by this age. Whether this regression is a brief transitional crisis around forty, or whether it was continuous throughout the adult years, I cannot say since Q sorts were not available for early adulthood. There is some retrospective evidence, however, that these women had higher morale in the early years of mothering when they could exercise their achievement skills in child-care.

This crisis is resolved by age fifty with a dramatic rebound in their intellectuality and a general freeing of emotional life. Intellectual skills that declined by forty again rise to prominence. By fifty, independents seem to revive the identities they were developing in adolescence. At the same time, closeness to others and trust increase. Independents are now giving, warm, sympathetic, and open in their feelings. Having settled the earlier issue of ego identity, these women by fifty move into the stage of intimacy achieved by forty in the traditional group.

# Discussion

Both groups by fifty have evolved a "self" consistent with earlier characterological positions, but more differentiated and complex. Each, however, follows a different course with different timing. . . . I suggest that the key factor is the fit between a woman's life-style and personality. Traditional personalities fit conventional feminine roles. . . . (They continue to find satisfaction in these roles, even as their children grew older and leave home.) . . .

Independents do not so easily fit conventional definitions of femininity. By age forty, when children are moving into adolescence, they seem to be confronted with an identity crisis. . . . I would suggest that it is disengagement from the mothering role by fifty that stimulates these women to revive their more assertive goal-oriented skills. . . .

For women with a conventionally feminine orientation, traditional roles do not seem particularly restricting. For women who are less conventionally feminine—who prefer to deal with life in modes usually defined as masculine—traditional roles can be restricting. . . . But role expectations change at different life periods and in different social contexts. In many cultures, and to an extent in our own, recent evidence suggests that sex roles become less distinct and even converge in the second half of life. [14] Middle age can loosen the boundaries of one's life-style and call forth suppressed parts of the self.

## REFERENCE NOTES

1. E. Frenkel-Brunswik, Adjustments and Reorientation in the Course of the Life Span, In B. L. Neugarten (ed.), *Middle Age and Aging: A Reader in Social Psychology,* University of Chicago Press, Chicago, pp. 74–84, 1968.
2. R. L. Gould, The Phases of Adult Life: A Study in Developmental Psychology, *American Journal of Psychiatry, 129*:5, pp. 33–43, 1972.
3. D. J. Levinson, C. M. Darrow, E. B. Klein, M. Levinson and B. McKee, The Psychosocial Development of Men in Early Adulthood and the Mid-life Transition, In D. F. Ricks, A. Thomas and M. Ruff (eds.), *Life History Research in Psychopathology, 3,* University of Minneosta Press, Minneapolis, 1974.
4. B. L. Neugarten, Adaptation and the Life Cycle, *Journal of Geriatric Psychiatry, 4,* pp. 71–87, 1970.
5. B. L. Neugarten and J. W. Moore, The Changing Age-Status System, In B. L. Neugarten (ed.), *Middle Age and Aging: A Reader in Social Psychology,* University of Chicago Press, Chicago, pp. 22–28, 1968.
6. D. Chiriboga and M. Thurnher, Concept of Self, In M. Lowenthal, M. Thurnher, and D. Chiriboga, *Four Stages of Life,* Jossey-Bass, San Francisco, pp. 62–83, 1975.
7. B. L. Neugarten, V. Wood, R. J. Kraines and B. Loomis, Women's Attitudes Toward the Menopause, In B. L. Neugarten (ed.), *Middle Age and Aging: A Reader in Social Psychology,* University of Chicago Press, Chicago, pp. 195–200, 1968.
8. P. Bart, Depression in Middle-Aged Women, In V. Gornick and B. K. Moran (eds.), *Women in Sexist Society,* Basic Books, New York, pp. 163–186, 1971.
9. B. L. Neugarten and D. Gutmann, Age-Sex Roles and Personality in Middle Age: A Thematic Apperception Study, In B. L. Neugarten (ed.), *Middle Age and Aging: A Reader in Social Psychology,* University of Chicago Press, Chicago, pp. 77–84, 1968.

10. J. Block, *The Q-sort Method in Personality Assessment and Psychiatric Research,* Charles C. Thomas, Springfield, Ill., 1961.
11. J. Block, in collaboration with N. Haan, *Lives Through Time,* Bancroft Books, Berkeley, Calif., 1971.
12. N. Livson and H. Peskin, Prediction of Psychological Health in a Longitudinal Study, *Journal of Abnormal Psychology, 72,* pp. 509–518, 1967.
13. E. H. Erikson, *Childhood and Society,* W. W. Norton & Co., New York, 1950.
14. D. Gutmann, The Cross-Cultural Perspective: Notes Towards a Comparative Psychology of Aging, In J. Birren and K. W. Schaie (eds.), *Handbook of Aging Psychology,* Van Nostrand Reinhold, New York, 1977.

# F. Later Adulthood: Introduction

WHAT DOES IT MEAN to have aged successfully (Butler) or to have lived successfully (Elwood)? The finality of this stage makes these questions imperative, but do not forget that later adulthood encompasses a very long period of time for many individuals. Increasing numbers of persons are living into advanced years and, with various forms of social or medical supports—or in spite of them—are dealing with the challenges of aging quite well (Glenwick and Whitbourne).

This is not to say that growing old in America is easy, for it is not. The social atom begins to disintegrate long before the individual dies. The same forces that presented barriers to life development continue to impose burdens for persons in later adulthood (Hechinger). The meaning of frustration, discrimination, and degradation may be exacerbated because of the frailties and vulnerabilities of old age.

Illness is not the same thing as aging, but with age come increasing infirmities and longer bouts with sickness. It is a difficult thing to come to terms with the process of dying, whether of a stranger or a relative or oneself. But it is a task for society: different cultures are more or less willing to face death and to prepare their members for it (Gilfix). And when it comes to one spouse, there is a new social role for the other, widowhood (Silverman). The social atom is broken, but life does not stop, for the widow(er) is bound within a network of relationships that may help to sustain her (him), and to offer the potentiality of forming new connections as a partial substitute for the old. Life goes on; the larger society demands it.

By the end of this section, readers should have some understanding of the basic tasks of later adulthood.

> *Physical Tasks:* The physical changes hinted at during middle age now emerge full force in the old. There are various forms of decrements in functioning, strength, agility, and endurance that leave their mark in untoward changes in physical health and possibly in mental functioning. The older person must adjust to these changes. But old age is not all physical deterioration; many older persons retain or maintain a vigorous body and a sound mind by planned efforts. Sexual capabilities continue into late adulthood.

*Psychological Tasks:* Psychologically, older persons must be adapters. They make adaptations to physical changes, as to changes in social states. The task is to make these adaptations as satisfying as possible and to take the long view, of life, now and overall. Awareness of death makes older persons more aware of the meaning of life and perhaps better observers of it.

*Social Tasks:* Many of the social tasks of later adulthood are negative. Retirement marks leaving income-producing activities, as well as the network of colleagues. Older persons have to sustain the inevitable social losses that befell them through death, separation, and geographical mobility of their adult children and grandchildren. Conserving personal energy and money becomes necessary to many; spending both at the right time and place may become all-engrossing, and not spending these resources when they are needed becomes problematic. It is through vicarious enjoyments in the new social atoms they have been part of, grandchildren, or grand ideas they have endowed that some older persons find contentment. Others maintain their ordinary personal pursuits and are sustained by these. There is no one way of being old nor of finding meaning in one's life and in one's death (cf. Havighurst, 1952).

# Successful Aging*
*Robert N. Butler*

ONE OF JAMES THURBER'S fables tells of a man who reported to his wife that he saw a unicorn in his garden. Thinking her husband had lost his mind, she surreptitiously called the police and a psychiatrist. However, it was a setup, and they took her away instead. The husband tricked the police and the psychiatrist into thinking his wife had made it all up. The American humorist always offered morals at the conclusion of his fables, and in this case, it was: *Don't count your boobies before they are hatched.* Those who think of older people as boobies, crones, witches, old biddies, old fogies, as out-to-pasture, boring, garrulous, pains-in-the-neck, as unproductive, worthless people, have another think coming. They had better not count their boobies before they are hatched. Great numbers of old people need not be and are not in institutions and, given a fighting chance in a society that has devalued them, can maintain a viable place in society. Indeed, at any one moment of

* From *Mental Hygiene,* 58:3 (1974):6–12. Permission to reprint is by the courtesy of the Mental Health Association, 1800 N. Kent Street, Arlington, Virginia 22209.

time, 95 per cent of the persons over 65 live in the community. In our social policies and in our therapeutic programs we need, of course, to have in mind a basic standard of health and not have our thinking dominated by stereotypes of frailty, psychopathology, senility, confusion, decline, and institutionalization. However, there is, of course, no point to developing illusions concerning healthy, successful old age. Like all periods, it has its difficulties. There are problems to be dealt with. There are needs to be fulfilled. But old age can be an emotionally healthy and satisfying time of life, with a minimum of physical and mental impairments. Many older people have adapted well to their old age with a minimum of stress and a high level of morale.

Study of *normal* development has seldom gone beyond early adult years, and the greatest emphasis has been on childhood. There have been relatively few centers for the study of adult human development. These centers have studied small population samples, usually of white, affluent middle-class people, composed about equally of men and women. This work at the University of Chicago, Duke University, the University of California and, for a brief period, at the National Institute of Mental Health has helped provide us with some understanding of successful mental health in aging.

In our culture few people think of old age as a time of potential health and growth. This is partly realistic, considering the lot of so many older people who have been cast aside, become lonely, bitter, poor, and emotionally or physically ill. American society has not been generous or supportive of the *unproductive*—in this case, old people who have reached what is arbitrarily defined as the retirement period. But in a larger sense, the negative view of old age is a problem of Western civilization.

The Western concept of the life cycle is decidedly different from that of the Orient, since it derives from an opposite view about what *self* means and what life is all about. Oriental philosophy places the individual self, his life span, and his death *within* the process of human experience. Life and death are familiar and equally acceptable parts of what self means. In the West, on the other hand, death is considered outside of the self. To be a self or person one must be alive, in control, and aware of what is happening.

The greater and more self-centered or narcissistic Western emphasis on individuality and control makes death an outrage—a tremendous affront to man rather than the logical and necessary process of old life making way for new. The opposite cultural views of East and West evolve to support two very different ways of life, each with its own merits. But the Western predilection for *progress,* conquest over nature, and personal self-realization has produced difficult problems for the elderly and for those preparing for old age.

This is particularly so when the national spirit of a nation and of an historical period have emphasized and expanded the notion of measuring human worth in terms of individual productivity and power. Thus, old people are led to see themselves as *failing with age*—a phrase that refers as much to self-worth as it does to physical strength.

Religion has been the traditional solace by promising another world wherein the self again springs to life, never to be further threatened by loss of its own integrity. Even though Western man's consummate dream of immortality is fulfilled by it, the integration of the aging experience to his life process still remains incomplete. Increasing secularization produces a frightening void that frequently is met by avoiding and denying the thought of one's own decline and death, and by forming self-protective prejudices against old people.

In some respects, we have come now to deal somewhat more openly with death itself. But aging—that long prelude to death—has become a kind of obscenity, something to avoid.

Medicine and the behavioral sciences have mirrored social attitudes by presenting old age as a grim litany of physical and emotional ills. Decline of the individual has been the key concept; neglect, a major treatment technique. Until about 1960 most of the medical, psychological, psychiatric, and social work literature on the aging was based on experience with the sick and the institutionalized, even though only 5 per cent of the elderly were confined to institutions.*

The few research studies that have concentrated on the healthy aged give indication of positive potential. But the general, almost phobic, dislike of aging remains the norm, with healthy old people being ignored and the chronically ill receiving half-hearted custodial care. Only those elderly who happen to have exotic or *interesting* diseases or emotional problems, or substantial financial resources ordinarily receive the research and treatment attention of the medical and psychotherapeutic professions.

Health care is approaching a $100 billion-a-year business—second only to the food industry. However, the health care industry does not reflect the various human ills in due proportion. Although chronic disease accounts for two-thirds of our nation's health costs, certainly two-thirds of our medical school curriculum, medical manpower, intellectual emphasis, research, health delivery system are not devoted to this important group of diseases. With the advent of a national health insurance plan and the struggle that is now beginning to ensue in Congress and in the Administration with respect to the character of that insurance plan, it has to be recognized that none of the plans under consideration face realistically the facts of life, disease, and aging.

What is healthy old age? To begin with, one must remember that science and medicine have historically been more concerned with treating what goes wrong than with clarifying the complex interwoven elements necessary to

---

* This 5 per cent is a most significant minority, of course, with major needs. And, ultimately, some 20 per cent of older people require institutional care, at least under the current health care system that does not provide comprehensive home care.

produce and support health. Typical of this is the treatment of coronary attacks after the fact rather than prescribing a preventive program involving diet, exercise, protection from stress, and the absence of smoking. Most of the elderly's major diseases could be cited as examples of this same phenomenon. The tedious and less dramatic process of prevention requires an understanding of what supports or what interferes with healthy development throughout the course of life. We spend only 4 cents of every health dollar on prevention.

In 1946 the World Health Organization defined health as *a state of complete physical, mental, and social well-being and not merely the absence of disease or infirmity*. This definition represents, of course, an ideal with many possible interpretations. But the three components of health—physical, emotional and social—compose the framework in which one can begin to analyze what is going well in addition to what is going wrong. The attempt must be made to locate those conditions that enable humans to thrive and not merely survive.

We cannot look at health simply as statistical or typical. If that were the case, dental caries, which affects about 90 per cent of the population might be considered healthy. Moreover, health cannot be looked at simply as a state. It is a *process* of continuing change and growth. What may be apparent health at one moment in time may already contain the beginnings of illness to develop fully in still another moment.

Old age is a period where there is unique developmental work to be accomplished. Childhood might be broadly defined as a period of gathering and enlarging strength and experience; whereas, the major developmental task in old age is to clarify, deepen, and find use for what one has already obtained in a lifetime of learning and adapting. The elderly must teach themselves to conserve their strength and resources where this is necessary, and to adjust in the best sense to those changes and losses that occur as part of the aging experience.

The ability of the elderly person to do this is contingent upon his physical health, personality, earlier life experiences, and the societal supports (adequate finances, shelter, medical care, social roles, recreation) he receives. It is imperative that old people continue to develop and change in a flexible manner if health is to be promoted and maintained. Failure to adapt at any age, under any circumstances, can result in a physical or emotional illness. Optimum growth and adaptation may occur all along the course of life, when the individual's strengths and potentials are recognized, reinforced, and encouraged by the environment in which he lives.

To develop, then, a clear depiction of what old age can be like, we must contrast the mythological with a realistic appraisal of old age. Let me present a sketch that I first gave in 1959 to a group of nursing home owners in Maryland. This is the stereotype of old age, and it hasn't changed much in the last 15 years.

An older person thinks and moves slowly. He does not think as he used to, nor as creatively. He is bound to himself and to his past and can no longer change or grow. He can neither learn well nor swiftly, and even if he could, he would not wish to. Tied to his personal traditions and growing conservatism, he dislikes innovations and is not disposed to new ideas. Not only can he not move forward, he often moves backwards. He enters a second childhood, caught often in increasing egocentricity and demanding more from his environment than he is willing to give to it. Sometimes he becomes more like himself, a caricature of a lifelong personality. He becomes irritable and cantankerous, yet shallow and enfeebled. He lives in his past. He is behind the times. He is aimless and wandering of mind, reminiscing and garrulous. Indeed, he is a study in decline. He is the picture of mental and physical failure. He has lost and cannot replace friends, spouse, jobs, status, power, influence, income. He is often stricken by diseases which in turn restrict his movement, his enjoyment of food, the pleasures of well-being. His sexual interest and activity decline. His body shrinks; so, too, does the flow of blood to his brain. His mind does not utilize oxygen and sugar at the same rate as formerly. Feeble, uninteresting, he awaits his death, a burden to society, to his family, and to himself.

There are certain major associated myths. There is *the myth of aging itself*—the idea of chronological aging, measuring one's age by the number of years one has lived. It is clear that there are great differences in the rates of physiological, chronological, psychological, and social aging from person to person and also within each individual.

Then there is *the myth of unproductivity*. But in the absence of diseases and social adversities, old people tend to remain productive and actively involved in life. There are dazzling examples like the 82-year-old Arturo Rubenstein working his hectic concert schedule; or of the 72-year-old Benjamin Dugger discovering the antibiotic aureomycin. Numbers of people become unusually creative for the first time in old age, when exceptional and inborn talents may be discovered and expressed. In fact, many old people continue to contribute usefully to their families and community in a variety of ways, including active employment.

Third, there is *the myth of disengagement* that older people prefer to be disengaged from life, to withdraw into themselves, choosing to live alone or perhaps only with their own peers. Ironically, a few gerontologists hold these views. One study, *Growing Old, the Process of Disengagement*, presented a theory that mutual separation between the aged person and society is a natural part of the aging experience. There is no evidence to support this as a generalization. Disengagement is only one of the many patterns of reaction to old age.

Fourth is *the myth of inflexibility*. The ability to change and adapt has little to do with one's age and more to do with one's lifelong character. But even this statement has to be qualified. One is not necessarily destined to one's character in earlier life. The endurance, strength, and stability in character structure are remarkable and protective, but most, if not all, people change and remain open to change throughout the course of life right up to its termination unless, of course, they are affected by major, massive destruction of brain tissue, illiteracy, or poverty.

Fifth is *the myth of senility*—the notion that old people are or inevitably become senile, showing forgetfulness, confusional episodes, and reduced attention. This is widely accepted. Senility, in fact, is a layman's term—unfortunately used by doctors to categorize the behavior of the old. Some of what is called senile is the result of brain damage. But anxiety and depression are also frequently lumped in the same category of senility, even though they are treatable and reversible. Old people, like the young, experience a full range of emotions, including anxiety, grief, depression and paranoid states. It is all too easy to blame age and brain damage when accounting for the mental problems and emotional concerns of later life.

Drug tranquilization—much overused in the United States—is another frequently misdiagnosed, but potentially reversible, cause of so-called senility. Malnutrition and unrecognized physical illnesses such as congestive heart failure and pneumonia may produce *senile behavior* by reducing the supply of blood, oxygen, and food to the brain. Alcoholism, often associated with bereavement, is another cause. Late-life alcoholism is a serious and common problem.

Now, of course, irreversible brain damage is no myth, and cerebral arteriosclerosis or hardening of the arteries of the brain and so-called senile brain disease marked by the mysterious dissolution of brain cells are major and serious conditions that do impair human development in old age.

Sixth is *the myth of serenity*. In contrast to the previous myths that view the elderly in a negative light, this myth portrays old age as a kind of adult fairyland. Old age is presented as a time of relative peace and serenity, when people can relax and enjoy the fruits of their labors after the storms of life are over. Visions of carefree, cooky-baking grandmothers and rocking-chair grandfathers are cherished by younger generations.

However, older persons experience more stresses than any other age group, and these stresses are often devastating. Depression, anxiety, psychosomatic illnesses, paranoid states, garrulousness, and irritability are some of the internal reactions to them.

Depressive reactions are particularly widespread in late life. In fact, *25 per cent of all suicides in the United States occur in people over 65.*

Another frequent companion of old age is grief, either for one's own losses or for the ultimate loss of oneself. Apathy and emptiness are common sequels to the initial shock and sadness that follow the loss of close friends and relatives. Physical disease and social isolation can follow bereavement.

Anxiety is another common feature. There is much to be anxious about, with poverty, loneliness and illness heading the list. Anxiety may manifest itself in many forms—rigid patterns of thinking and behavior, helplessness, manipulativeness, restlessness and suspiciousness, sometimes to the point of paranoid states.

The stereotyping and myths surrounding old age can partly be explained by lack of knowledge and by insufficient daily and/or professional contact with varieties of older people. But there is another powerful factor operating—a deep and profound prejudice against the elderly, which is found to some degree in all of us.

In thinking about how to describe this, I coined the word *ageism* in 1968:

> Ageism can be seen as a process of systematic stereotyping of and discrimination against people, because they are old—just as racism and sexism can accomplish this with skin color and gender. Old people are categorized as senile, rigid in thought and manner, old fashioned in morality and skills. Ageism allows the younger generations to see older people as different from themselves. Thus, they subtly cease to identify with their elders as human beings.*

Over the years I have tried to enumerate certain characteristics that help define tendencies to be observed in older people. They are not inevitable nor are they found to the same degree in each person who manifests them. They do show themselves regularly enough to be considered typical of people who have lived a long time and are viewing the world from the special vantage point of old age.

Old age is the only period of life with no future. Therefore a major task in late life is learning not to think in terms of the future. Children are extremely future-oriented and look forward to each birthday as a sign of growing up. The middle aged, as Schopenhauer said, begin to count the number of years they have left before death rather than the number of years since birth. In old age, one's time perspective is shortened even further as the end of life approaches. Some avoid confronting this fact by retreating to the past. Others deny their age and continue to be future-oriented. The latter are the people who fail to make wills, leave important relationships unresolved, put off enjoyments, and experience boredom.

A more satisfying resolution is found among those elderly who begin to emphasize the quality of the present, of the time remaining, rather than the quantity. When death becomes imminent, there tends to be a sense of immediacy, of the here and now, of living in the moment.

Only in old age can one experience a personal sense of the entire life cycle. This comes to its fullness with the awareness of death in the forefront. There is the unfolding process of change, the experiencing of a sense of time, the seasoning or sense of life experience with a broadening perspective and the accumulation of factual knowledge of what is to be expected at the different points of the life cycle.

Old age inaugurates the process of the *life review,* promoted by the realization of approaching dissolution and death. It is characterized by the progressive return to consciousness of past experience, in particular the resurgence of

---

* Butler, R.N. "Ageism: Another Form of Bigotry." *The Gerontologist* 9:243–46, 1969. Butler, R. N. and Lewis, Myrna I. *Aging and Mental Health,* St. Louis, Missouri: The C. V. Mosby Company, 1973.

unresolved conflicts that can now be surveyed and integrated. The old are not only taking stock of themselves as they review their lives; they are trying to think and feel through what they will do with the time that is left and with whatever material and emotional legacies they may have to give to others.

They frequently experience grief. The death of others, often more than their own death, concerns them. Perplexed, frightened at being alone and increasingly depressed, they at times become wary or cautious to the point of suspicion about the motivations of others. If unresolved conflicts and fears are successfully reintegrated, they can give new significance and meaning to an individual's life, in preparing for death and mitigating fears.

What can we do to help move society to a more balanced view of older people, and how can we help older people to prevent problems in later life and to favor successful aging? How can we treat already troubled older people to help them successfully age? We cannot review all of the relevant factors, of course. They vary from preventive measures like a major attack on the known antecedents of arteriosclerosis that requires change in dietary habits and physical activity. We must certainly face the enormous problem of alcoholism in the United States. Many people with lifelong excessive alcoholic intake are now surviving into old age, and many older people are taking up alcohol following grief and loneliness.

There is the need for a major reformation of our culture's sensibility toward old people through use of the media, which can help transform our views of what older people are really like and how to help them enhance their sense of themselves. There is also the political approach. Older people are learning to assert themselves for what they need, thereby winning self respect.

There are two forms of psychotherapy that can be helpful to older people, from both the preventive and therapeutic perspectives. These two treatment forms I call *life review therapy* and *life cycle group therapy.*

Life review therapy includes the taking of an extensive autobiography from the older person and from other family members. Such memoirs can also be preserved by means of tape recordings, of value to children in the family. In instances of persons of note, memoirs have considerable historical importance and should be placed in archives for many reasons, including furthering our understanding of creativity and improving the image of our elders. The use of the family album, the scrapbook and other memorabilia, searching out of geneologies and pilgrimages back to places of emotional import evoke crucial memories, responses and understanding in patients.

The consequences of these steps include expiation of guilt, exorcism of problematic childhood identifications, resolution of intrapsychic conflicts, reconciliation of family relationships, transmission of knowledge and values to those who follow, and renewal of the ideals of citizenship.

Such life review therapy can be conducted in a variety of settings from outpatient, individual psychotherapy to counseling in senior centers to skilled listening in nursing homes. Even non-professionals can function as therapists by becoming trained listeners as older persons recount their lives. Many older people can be helped to conduct their own life reviews. The process need not be expensive.

Reminiscence of the old has all too often been devalued—regarded as a symptom, usually of organic dysfunction and felt to bespeak aimless wandering of the mind or living in the past. We recognize, of course, the value of reminiscence as seen in the great memoirs composed in old age, which may give fascinating accounts of unusual and gifted people.

We see the role of the life review in film and fiction. Ingmar Bergman's beautiful 1957 motion picture, *Wild Strawberries,* shows an elderly physician whose dreams and visions concerned his past as he changed from remoteness and selfishness to closeness and love. Literature is replete with examples of the life review. Ernest Hemingway's *The Snows of Kilimanjaro,* Samuel Beckett's *Krapp's Last Tape,* Leo Tolstoy's *The Death of Ivan Ilych.*

Since 1970 Myrna I. Lewis, a social worker colleague of mine, and myself have conducted four age-integrated psychotherapy groups of about 8 to 10 members each with one contrasting middle-aged group. We have integrated persons ranging from age 15 to over age 80 in each of the four groups, based on the belief that age segregation as practiced in our society leaves very little opportunity for the rich exchange of feeling, experience, and support possible between the generations.

The groups are oriented toward persons experiencing a crisis in their life ranging from near normal to pathological reactions to adolescence, education, marriage or single life, divorce, parenthood, work and retirement, widowhood, illness and impending death. Thus, such groups are concerned not only with intrinsic psychiatric disorders but with preventive and remedial treatment of people as they pass through the usual vicissitudes of the life cycle.

Criteria for membership include absence of active psychosis and presence of life crisis, acute, subacute or chronic. Of course, reaction to life crises follow traditional diagnostic categories, including depression, anxiety states, hypochondriasis, alcoholism, drug misuse. Our groups are balanced for age, sex, and personality dynamics. We meet once a week for one-half hour. Individual membership in a group averages about 2 years. New group members are asked to participate for a minimum of 3 months.

The life cycle crises approach to group therapy is neither strictly encounter nor strictly psychoanalytic. Rather, it can be equally concerned with the interaction among group members as determined by reality and the past histories and problems of each member. The goal is the amelioration of suffering, the overcoming of disability, and the opportunity for new experiences of intimacy and self fulfillment.

We believe that both forms of therapy can be very useful in the nursing home, mental hospital and other institutions. Age integration helps to recapitulate the family—something woefully missing for many older people. The garrulousness of older people reflects a social symptom and an intense desire in the face of death to deal with one's individual life.

These are but two examples of how we can approach the older patient in and out of institutions. Indeed, older persons' families—when they exist (and we must remember that one-fourth of older people have no family at all)— can themselves participate in therapeutic processes.

When older people look back on their lives, they regret more often what they did not do rather than what they have done. Medicine should regret its failures to act responsibly in the health care—including mental health care— of older people. Physicians and psychotherapists should not assume that nothing can be done for older people. Nor should the public. No one should count older people as boobies before they are hatched.

# Old Age and the Quality of Life*
## *Thomas W. Elwood*

QUALITY OF LIFE is an expression which is difficult to convert into mean-ingful operational terms. While there may be a degree of consensus regarding some of the particular elements which comprise this entity, it is doubtful that there is unanimity with respect to the quantity of each element required. Economic means, a measure of self-respect, and good health would probably be included in any list of items deemed necessary for a satisfactory quality of life, but there remains some confusion as to which are the indepen-dent and which the dependent variables among these elements. Each is not found in uniform quantities at the various junctures along the age continuum. My proposition is that, with the advent of old age in the United States, most elements considered essential for a suitable quality of life decrease substan-tially.

## Profile of the Aged

The elderly in this country represent about 10 per cent of the total popula-tion, or roughly 20 million persons. Kalish suggests that the typical older per-son is a widowed white woman; she probably has about 9 years of formal ed-ucation, is not presently employed in any fashion, lives in the central city, receives most of her income from social security, has at least one chronic

* Reprinted from *Health Services Reports*, 87:10 (1972): 919–931.

health condition that does not limit her mobility, and will live into her eighties.[1]

The aged resemble minority groups when measured by socioeconomic criteria. Having used U.S. census data and other sources of data to construct similarity indexes, Palmore and Whittington contend that gaps between the aged and the nonaged in the crucial areas of income, employment, and education are steadily and substantially increasing.[2] Viewed in the context of a report issued in March 1972 by the U.S. Commission on Population Growth, which estimated that there will be 40 million elderly Americans 50 years from now,[3]. these disparities assume even greater significance.

The expressed concerns of the elderly usually revolve around the pivotal issues of income and health. A documentary on the aged televised in the Philadelphia area provided an opportunity for old people to telephone the station and state their concerns while the program was still in progress. The station received 334 calls. The major categories according to content were income maintenance and health and health entitlements.[4]

Another study, which dealt with the hopes that the aged have for their future, showed that good health far outweighed any other consideration.[5]

Health care is expensive for the old person on a small income. A report of the Senate's Special Committee on Aging indicated that per capita health expenditures in fiscal year 1971 were $861 for persons 65 and older, but only $250 for those under 65. Medicare in fiscal year 1971 covered only 42 per cent of the total health payments of the elderly. Health care costs keep going up for all Americans, but for the older person the problem is compounded. He has only about half the income of those under age 65 but even with Medicare, he pays more than twice as much for health services. He is twice as likely as a young person to have one or more chronic diseases, and much of the care he needs is of the most expensive kind. And while costs go up, services available under Medicare and Medicaid go down—a process which was accelerated considerably in 1971.[6,7]

# Perception of the Elderly by Others

Inadequate financial resources account for only one set of problems which beset the elderly. Growing old in America is something which many people view with extreme displeasure. This phenomenon is accompanied by the great emphasis on youthfulness. The nation as a whole spends a good deal more on cosmetics which preserve or contribute to a youthful appearance than it does on its elderly citizens. In a review of 264 jokes about aging, more than half reflected a negative view; those dealing with physical disability or appearance, age concealment, old maids, and mental abilities were most negative.[8]

When people meet for the first time, physical appearance provides a cue upon which inferences can be made about personal characteristics. Old age is difficult to hide. A slowness in gross motor ability and skin imperfections distinguish the old from others. Many older persons increase their visibility through reliance on crutches, canes, and hearing aids.

Children learn that there are differences between handicapped and nonhandicapped peers and attach varying degrees of social stigma to various handicaps.[9] It is likely that these negative attitudes are carried into adulthood, since the U.S. culture places a high value on physical beauty and the ability to perform vigorous activities. Assessed in such framework of values, old age is viewed with repugnance because of its association with a variety of handicaps.

## Shifts in Taboo Subjects

Anything pertaining to sex was a taboo subject during earlier periods in American history. Today, sex is a topic for more open discussion and display. The reverse is true for the subject of death. Several decades ago most people experienced the death of an infant or an older relative in the home. Now, many young adults have no idea what it is like to experience the death of someone intimate. An analysis of euphemisms used in this country to describe death suggests that whenever it emerges as a topic of everyday parlance, it is dealt with rather gingerly. The necrology section of many professional journals exemplifies this by referring to a colleague as one who passed on instead of one who died. "Died" denotes an undesirable finality whereas "passed on" can be interpreted as wishful thinking about some new state of being into which the deceased has moved.

Death has replaced sex as a forbidden topic in modern day culture. Yet, there is an exception with respect to sex in connection with the elderly. The thought that old people participate in as well as enjoy sexual activity often brings nervous smiles to the faces of younger people. Many professionals would probably find it disquieting and possibly even distasteful to deal with elderly clients who have sexual problems.

The idea that old people might remarry or cohabit outside the conventional bonds of marriage seems ludicrous to some people. Proposals to allow elderly men and women to live in communal arrangements or to permit single persons of the opposite sex to share rooms in nursing homes would probably be reacted to with disgust by many.

Social policy serves to enforce such negative attitudes by not allowing old persons to marry or live together without suffering the consequences of losing a portion of their social security benefits. Sexual maladjustment is acceptable in the young, but not the old. One must ask how these attitudes on death and sex affect the health of the elderly and the care which they receive.

# Attitudes of Health Professionals

Health professionals probably differ little from the rest of the population in their fears and concerns about growing old. A recent study of medical interns showed that the acutely ill patient was most highly esteemed because he allowed the physician an opportunity to exercise his curative powers. The low rankings of these categories of patients with long-term illnesses may reflect the frustration and anxiety that often result when highly trained and cure-oriented young physicians encounter patients whose pathologies are difficult to manage and treat successfully.[10] This issue is critical since the old are often among the majority of those labeled as long-term patients.

Another survey of medical students had results which prognosticate little encouragement for the future of geriatrics. Attitudes of first-year medical students toward the aged were compared to those of fourth-year students. The two groups had about the same attitudes insofar as they perceived older people as more emotionally disturbed than young people, as dull, apathetic, socially unpleasant and withdrawn, disagreeable, dissatisfied, and disruptive of social and family welfare. Not only should these observations lead to questions on the value of current teaching in medical sociology, but one must also ask if the usual values in medical practice apply to the aged.[11] The relation between the negative attitudes just cited and the care given by other health professionals was the subject of a recent paper.[12]

Schools and training centers have devoted little attention to programs aimed at preparing health professionals for work and the elderly. For example, the 1969–70 catalogues of medical schools in the United States were reviewed for their content of geriatrics and gerontology. At 51 of the 99 schools existing in January 1970, there was no mention of the subject of aging in the school history, the curriculum deliberations, outlines of courses, staff structure, research, or other content.[13]

It would be profitable to conduct a similar study of schools of public health to ascertain the extent to which graduates have an understanding of and a sensitivity toward an age group which consumes a substantial portion of the nation's health resources. It appears that those in public health must share an indictment of negligence as reflected in the lack of doctoral dissertations related to problems of aging, according to the results of a study.[14]

During the period 1934–69, the number of dissertations on aging numbered 667 or 0.25 per cent of the total number listed for all scholarly fields. Of the dissertations in the biological, medical, psychological, and social sciences, the 667 on aging were only 0.5 per cent of the total in those relevant fields. The health sciences were credited with 29 dissertations during the 35 years. In the discipline of psychology it is likely that more dissertations on child development are produced in a single year than have been produced on aging for the entire period.

## Preventive Health Measures

A certain amount of fatalism is often associated with growing old. Those who anticipate decrements in hearing and acuity of vision or experiencing a general deterioration of health are not surprised if these losses occur. Nor is it likely that they will act promptly to correct these problems. This is lamentable since many elderly persons could become more functional if treated. Recently, hundreds of older people took advantage of a free multiphasic health screening program which was offered as part of a cooperative effort between a county health department and a California National Guard unit. The professional and paraprofessional personnel of the 143d Evacuation Hospital donated their services and the use of their equipment to screen elderly persons from the San Antonio Health District in southeast Los Angeles.

For many who attended, this was the first complete physical examination in 25 or 30 years because, they said, they cannot afford an annual routine physical examination, and they do not believe that government insurance provides funds for preventive health checkups. The medical problems uncovered shocked even the professionals, making them more aware of the need for immediate action to provide preventive health services for the often overlooked elderly.[15]

One aspect of preventive health intervention worthy of increased attention is the strength of the association between illness and the occurrence of critical life incidents such as the loss of a spouse through death or divorce and the subsequent effect this event has on surviving family members. Chester noted that marriage breakdown is attended by a considerable volume of stress for women which manifests itself in medical or quasi-medical terms and that symptoms tend to be concentrated on the periods when separation is imminent or immediate.[16]

The transition in status resulting from the death of a marriage partner may be even more traumatic in its consequences. The departure of grownup children from the home often increases the bonds of interdependency between older parents. The loss of a spouse may create great social and psychological upheaval for the remaining partner. Krant and Sheldon suggest that this loss may be expressed in physical and mental illness.[17]

More studies are needed in order to carefully document the relationship between critical life events such as mandatory retirement and death of a spouse and the onset of physical or mental illness. If the association proves to be a strong one, additional efforts will have to be expended in the development of programs designed to modulate the harmful effects of these life incidents. Silverman's report of a widow-to-widow program in which one widow helps another widow to make the necessary adjustments during the transition to this new state is an example of the type of intervention which may be fruitful in reducing illness.[18]

# Health Problems of the Aged

Other health problems facing old people are more directly related to the observation that the human body is analogous to a machine that wears out and breaks down. Dental health is a case in point. Gordon mentions that tooth loss with its resultant loss of masticatory function can reduce digestive efficiency. The predigestive reduction of food particles is necessary to the proper digestion of food. General health can be more easily maintained with a healthy oral condition. The advantages of oral health in the prevention, early detection, and cure of malignancies and other oral pathoses are beyond measure.[19]

Unfortunately, too many elderly persons see no utility in having extensive dental work done late in life, and they are thus denied the pleasures of eating particular foods which are nutritious as well as satisfying. Missing teeth may also detract from the quality of speech.

Speech problems pose another handicap which characterized the elderly, although this problem is amenable to proper intervention. Cooper maintains that geriatric patients are seldom referred for vocal rehabilitation. Those who complain of vocal fatigue or tired voice turn to the use of lozenges as a remedy, but the relief provided in these cases is only temporary. Tired voice can be corrected by vocal rehabilitation within 3 to 6 months, yet physicians seldom refer patients for such treatment.[20]

Many older persons are confined to a relatively inactive existence because of foot ailments. This loss of mobility also serves to reduce a person's sense of independence. Hsu states that in elderly patients, in contrast to young ones, disabling foot lesions can easily have disastrous results, especially when infection intervenes. The early application of simple therapeutic measures can provide striking relief and stop the rapid downhill course.[21]

Advancement into the late age brackets is also associated with an increase in accidents. Rodstein proposes that accidents among the aged may be the first manifestation of acute disease or the result of chronic illness. This proposal assumes significance if one considers that, after the onset of acute illness, the decreased sensitivity to pain in the elderly and their lessened febrile response to infection may lead them to continued ambulation, increasing the risk of an accident.[22]

Many of the aged are subsisting on nutritionally inadequate diets. A recent publication of the Public Health Service mentions indirect factors also pointing to nutritional deficiency among the elderly. As a rule, they have a reduced water intake. They develop a preference for sugars. The decreased appeal of food may be related to a loss of taste buds and reduced sense of smell. Loss of teeth may also be a factor. Absorption may be impaired by the reduction in the quantity of digestive enzymes and gastric acidity.[23]

The likelihood that older persons do not eat properly is greater for those who live alone. Even when the dollar can be stretched far enough to purchase wholesome foods, many of the aged lack transportation to the store or they are physically unable to get there. Eating meals at regular intervals is often replaced by a daily regimen of frequent snacks.

Certain social problems which receive national attention also affect the elderly rather severely. Bock writes that people 65 and older continue to commit more than their proportionate share of suicides. Although only 10 per cent of the population, they contribute about 25 per cent of the reported suicides.[24]

Drug addiction receives widespread coverage by the news media, but mainly in relation to young people. It has been assumed in the past that the disappearance of persons over the age of 45 from narcotic registers and police records was due either to their having died or abandoned the habit. Yet a study of opiate use among older inhabitants of a major American city shows that the problem is greater than expected, but it differs in pattern from abuse by younger age groups and does not appear amenable to any presently conceived treatment modality.[25]

Anyone who had ever had to take medicine is aware of the confusion that may arise. The uncertainty can increase if one has to take two medicaments with differing doses and schedules. It is not uncommon to be muddled over whether one should arbitrarily double the next dose because of omitting to take medicine at an originally recommended time. Such problems would seem to be more prevalent among the elderly than in other age groups. Usually, having one or more chronic illnesses necessitates taking various kinds of pills. Inadequate vision and loss of memory could easily lead to improper dosage.

Schwartz and co-workers found that a significant factor in error-making appears to be whether or not the patient lives alone. Potentially serious errors in dosage were made by 42 per cent of patients living alone in contrast to 18 per cent of those who lived with one or more people. Although some groups of patients were less error prone than others, errors occurred among all categories of patients in the study sample with sufficient frequency to require that the entire elderly, chronically ill population of the clinic be considered at least potentially at risk.[26]

Over-the-counter sales represent a large volume of the drug business in this country. Worthless products offer the buyer relief from pain, insomnia, that run-down feeling, and other ailments. Medical and other types of mail frauds which bilk aged persons out of millions of dollars are common. The Arthritis Foundation estimates that more than $300 million are spent annually on useless and misrepresented drugs and treatment by the victims of this one disease alone. By their nature, medical frauds probably affect the elderly more than any other segment of our populace.[27]

## Suggested New Approaches

Several problems which affect the elderly have been highlighted in this paper. Obviously, not all of them can be remedied solely through the efforts of health professionals. Deficiencies in housing and income maintenance, for example, must be approached from a much wider perspective. Denial of old age and the glorification of youth are prevalent in American society, thereby making it most unlikely that health workers will do much to change the situation until they first change their own appraisal of these matters.

Many of the problems, however, can be encountered using an educational approach. Just as recent attempts have been made to make social services more responsive to the needs of minority groups, similar efforts must be made on behalf of the aged. While it is unlikely that old people will be recruited into schools and professional health training programs to be prepared for careers working among their brethren, as has been the case with various ethnic or racial groups, those now at these training centers should be brought to realize that important differences may exist between them and those whom they will serve.

Senior citizen centers have been built around the country. Their existence provides soothing assurance to those who might feel troubled about the neglect of the elderly by other members of society. However, Tissue discovered that the wide array of activities at such a center has a central theme which, by and large, represents a continuation of middle-aged, middle-class recreational styles. Not only do the activities of the center seem ill suited for the working class, but the whole concept of a nonlocal, broad-based, regional social facility appears inappropriate for persons accustomned to local rather than cosmopolitan social patterns.[28]

Indeed, Londoner's analysis challenges the notion that older adults need only recreational and leisure programs. The challenge of old age is the challenge of learning new ways of living. Educational programs must be developed to help older adults acquire new competencies, enabling them to meet the new demands that emerge with the narrowing of their physical and social environments.[29]

Middle-class, well-educated, young and middle-age professionals should recognize that their perceptions and values may be quite different from those of the elderly. If staffs of programs fail to take these differences into account, it is unlikely that their goals will be fully achieved. The notion that old bodies are beyond repair needs to be dispelled at both the level of the provider of health care and at the level of the elderly themselves. Health departments must be more imaginative in seeing to it that their services reach those most in need of them. The example mentioned previously, teaming up with the National Guard, is an inventive way in which a health department can conduct multiphasic screening.

Since many old people are not healthy enough to go to clinics or cannot do so because of an inadequate public transit system, health departments should ponder the feasibility of sending mobile units around the city with staff to conduct dental, hearing, vision, and foot examinations as well as to perform simple corrective procedures.

It is somewhat ironic that older homeowners pay a large share of their limited incomes for property taxes, a great part of which has traditionally gone toward the support of local school systems. Regrettably, many older couples spend most of a lifetime meeting mortgage payments in order to own their homes but are later compelled to relinquish them because their retirement income is not sufficient to pay taxes. School resources, which they have paid for all their adult lives, could be used to aid the elderly. School buses, which are unused many hours a day, could transport them to health facilities for care and bring them to school cafeterias for at least one nutritious meal a day.

At schools and other municipal sites, instruction on health insurance benefits, home care programs, and other health related matters could be offered to the elderly. To bring about such programs of instruction, public health workers need to forsake their traditional avoidance of the political arena and communicate with politicians. Voters who are shown how tax dollars can thus aid the elderly could be rallied to apply additional pressure. Elected officials are usually receptive to ideas which add to the public image that they are satisfactorily performing their obligations.

School health educators and local health officials could investigate the possibility of capitalizing upon the tremendous energy and social concerns of today's youth. Young people who have access to cars could drive old people to treatment facilities. Invoking the compassion of youth might also lead them to offer rides to old people as some measure of relief from their drab existence of being confined to a small dwelling. Youngsters without cars could help by shopping for old persons who are not ambulatory, and they could also deliver prescriptions.

Paradoxically, the young are enchanted with the artifacts of previous generations, but not with the people who represent these generations. It is intriguing to observe the young paying generous sums of money to buy outdated clothing and flocking to old movies, but avoiding the very people who patented these nostalgic life styles. Old persons could provide first-hand accounts of their impressions of what it was like to emigrate to a new land and live through two World Wars and the Great Depression, yet seldom are they asked to do so. The schools could play a dynamic role in establishing linkages between generations as well as endeavor to prepare the young for their inevitable passage to old age. School health instruction may also act as a focal point for dealing with negative stereotypes which apply to the old and the infirm of all ages.

The elderly themselves need to be educated about the necessity of taking adequate preventive action to preserve their health. Suchman found that one problem in educating the public to behave rationally in the face of symptoms relates to the individual person's natural tendency to under-emphasize symptoms which are neither severe nor incapacitating. Since many chronic diseases do not have serious and incapacitating initial symptoms, it is difficult to induce the public to seek early medical care.[30] Another study of related interest showed that among a group of the aged was in terms of activity. Health was important only as it became poor health and interfered with daily activity and maintenance of independence. This perception makes for difficulty in motivating people to seek medical care for the many ailments that are not severely handicapping and makes even more difficult attempts to make preventive services meaningful.[31]

Merely reaching the old person can pose a difficulty because many of them live such isolated lives. Despite the great achievements often credited to the use of the mass media, Booth and Babchuk discovered that mass media appeared to be wholly inconsequential in selecting health services. When the counsel of others was sought for the selection of health services and personnel, the middle-aged and elderly usually consulted only one other person. Only under emergency conditions was the advisor likely to be a physician or someone associated with the field of medicine. The most isolated in our society, the aged and the poor, have the greatest need for nurturance and information in connection with health care decisions, but are the least likely to have the advantages of such counsel.[32]

One way of making certain that preventive health messages reach the elderly is by issuing them face to face in a medical care setting like the hospital. Health educators could do this directly or in conjunction with hospital staff. It might well be a function of health educators and would, of course, depend on the willingness of other health personnel to engage in such tasks. Social workers in a health care setting might fit appropriately into such a cooperative venture. Another alternative would be to have old persons brought together in some arrangement similar to the suggestion made previously of using school facilities. Advancement to old age is invariably accompanied by an increase in hospitalization. Health education efforts could be expended along several avenues in such a setting.

Patients with dental and voice problems could be informed of the possibility that their conditions are treatable. Those who might feel self-conscious or embarrassed about applying for this sort of treatment may need strong support. The same feeling would pertain to the perceived reduction in personal attractiveness which results from the use of prosthetic devices. Inquiries could be made about knowledge of foot hygiene and instruction subsequently given, since failure to take proper care of the feet might lead to premature immobilization.

Older patients, especially those who live alone, could be asked to describe their eating habits, the types of food they eat, and over-the-counter pharmaceuticals they purchase. They could be assisted in formulating a diet appropriate to their income and warned against spending precious money on products backed by false advertising.

The older person could be instructed concerning susceptibility to accidents and advised of actions they can take to reduce the probability that these misfortunes will occur. Something as insignificant as securely fastening a loose rug to the floor can reduce the hazard of a serious fall, to cite one example.

The proliferation of services and the various qualifications for receiving them can be confusing to persons of all ages. The elderly need to know what services are available and, more importantly, how to use them properly. They need information about Medicare, Medicaid, and other public entitlements such as homemaker and visiting nursing services. Health educators can demonstrate their resourcefulness in getting this important information across to the aged in a clear and concise manner.

# Conclusion

This paper has posited that good health is integral to any definition of the quality of life. The elderly can experience a higher quality of life if they are financially solvent, are shown more respect by other age groups, and are in better health. The quality of life of old people would be enhanced immeasurably if their needs received increased attention by those in the health professions.

## REFERENCE NOTES

1. Kalish, R. A.: Of social values and the dying: A defense of disengagement. Fam Coordinator 21: 81–94, January 1972.
2. Palmore, E., and Whittington, F.: Trends in the relative status of the aged. Social Forces 50: 84–91, September 1971.
3. Population and the American future. The report of the Commission on Population Growth and the American Future. U.S. Government Printing Office, Washington, D.C., March 1972.
4. Brody, E. M., and Brody, S. J.: A ninety-minute inquiry: The expressed needs of the elderly. Gerontologist 10: 99–106, summer 1970.
5. Gubrium, J. F.: Self-conceptions of mental health among the aged. Mental Hyg 55:398–403, July 1971.
6. U.S. Senate: Developments in aging: 1971 and January–March 1972. A report of the Special Committee on Aging. Report No. 92-784. U.S. Government Printing Office, Washington, D.C., May 5, 1972, pp. 23, 24.
7. Hey, R. P.: The challenge of age. Christian Science Monitor 63: 12, Nov. 15, 1971.
8. Palmore, E.: Attitudes toward aging as shown by humor. Gerontologist 11: 181–186, pt. I, autumn 1971.
9. Richardson, S. A.: Handicap, appearance, and stigma. Soc Sci Med 5: 621–628, December 1971.
10. Reynolds, R. E., and Bice, T. W.: Attitudes of medical interns toward patients and health professionals. J. Health Soc Behave 12: 307–311, December 1971.

11. Leake, C. D.: Editorials. Geriatrics 24: 57–60, July 1969.
12. Elwood, T. W.: The relationship of health education to gerontology. Int J Health Educ 15: 177–193, July–September 1972.
13. Freeman, J. T.: A survey of geriatric education: catalogues of United States medical schools. J Am Geriatr Soc 19: 746–762, September 1971.
14. Moore, J. L., and Birren, J. E.: Doctoral training in gerontology: an analysis of dissertations on problems of aging in institutions of higher learning in the United States, 1934–1969. J Gerontol 26: 249–257, April 1971.
15. Pacino, F. G.: For low income citizens—the first health exam in 25 years. Calif Health 29: 12, 13, May 1972.
16. Chester, R.: Health and marriage breakdown: experience of a sample of divorced women. Br J Prev Soc Med 25: 231–235, November 1971.
17. Krant, M. J., and Sheldon, A.: The dying patient—medicine's responsiblity. J. Thanatology 1: 1–24, January–February 1971.
18. Silverman, P. R.: Widowhood and preventive intervention. Fam Coordinator 21: 95–102, January 1972.
19. Gordon, R. H.: Meeting dental health needs of the aged. Am J. Public Health 62: 385–388, March 1972.
20. Cooper, M.: Voice problems of the geriatric patient. Geriatrics 25: 107 –110, June 1970.
21. Hsu, J. D.: Foot problems in the elderly patient. J Am Geriatr Soc 19: 880–886, October 1971.
22. Geriscope. Geriatrics 24: 34–38, September 1969.
23. Working with older people: the practitioner and the elderly. PHS Publication No. 1459. U.S. Government Printing Office, Washington, D.C., March 1969, vol. 1, p. 20.
24. Bock, E. W.: Aging and suicide: the significance of marital, kinship, and alternative relations. Fam Coordinator 21: 71–79, January 1972.
25. Capel, W. C., Goldsmith, B. M., Waddell, K. J., and Stewart, G. T.: The aging narcotic addict: an increasing problem for the next decades. J. Gerontol 27: 102–106, January 1972.
26. Schwartz, D., Wang, M., Zeitz, L., and Goss, M. E. W.: Medication errors made by elderly, chronically ill patients. Am J Public Health 52: 2018–2029, December 1962.
27. Spectrum. Geriatrics 24: 56, 61, June 1969.
28. Tissue, T.: Social class and the senior citizen center. Gerontologist 11: 196–200, pt. I, autumn 1971.
29. Londoner, C. A.: Survival needs of the aged: implications for program planning. Aging Hum Develop 2: 113–117, May 1971.
30. Suchman, E. A.: Stages of illness and medical care. J Health Hum Behav 6: 114–128, fall 1965.
31. DiCicco, L., and Apple, D.: Health needs and opinions of older adults. Public Health Rep 73: 479–487, June 1958.
32. Booth, A., and Babchuk, N.: Seeking health care from new resources. J Health Soc Behav 13: 90–99, March 1972.

# Beyond Despair and Disengagement: A Transactional Model of Personality Development in Later Life*

*David S. Glenwick and Susan K. Whitbourne*

A PERVASIVE THEME in gerontological research of the past two decades is the attempt to explain and predict personality changes in later adulthood. However, the numerous studies which have accumulated in this field have represented little in the way of substantive knowledge of psychological adaptation as affected by the aging process. Three of the dominant theoretical approaches—ego analytic, disengagement, and symbolic-interaction—though seemingly disparate, possess one common shortcoming. They all devote insufficient attention to the dynamics of the interaction between developmental and social forces during the period of old age.

The ego analytic viewpoint is represented by Erikson, whose widely known theory deals with psychosocial stages of ego development throughout the life cycle [1]. Each of these stages revolves around a crisis facing the individual which may be thought of as a period of heightened vulnerability to specific maturational, psychological, and social forces. Whether or not a favorable outcome is achieved depends in part upon the resolution of earlier stages, but more importantly, upon the dynamic interplay between the factors within and external to the individual. Although Erikson presupposes the similarity of the eight crises, it may be seen that the eighth differs qualitatively from the first seven. All of the earlier seven are basically rooted in the context of current activities and experiences such as the infant's feelings of trust or mistrust toward the caretaker. As a second example, the adolescent's identity crisis regarding ideology and occupation is strongly related to college experiences [2, 3]. Furthermore, the outcomes of each of the first seven stages will influence the resolution of future crises.

In contrast, the eighth crisis stage of ego integrity versus despair centers around both considerations of the future (the inevitability of death) as well as the re-evaluation of one's past. The formulation of a philosophical outlook on one's personal history seems like a necessary step to face impending death with some measure of equanimity and appears to have therapeutic effects on present adjustment [4]. However, preoccupation with the past entails a cer-

* Reprinted by permission of the publisher and the authors from the *International Journal of Aging and Human Development*, Vol. 8(3), 1977–78. © 1977, Baywood Publishing Co., Inc.

tain denial of present experiences. Erikson's theory does not allow for an explanation of how the individual deals constructively and positively with physical, psychological, and social losses that are occurring at the present time.

The disengagement theory, advanced initially by Cumming and Henry, further reinforces the conception of the aged person as one who avoids contact with the present social environment [5]. In its early formulations, the theory emphasized the adaptive results of mutual withdrawal of the older person from society. The original theory was criticized for its assertion of the inevitability and desirability of disengagement, as well as its failure to adequately consider the social structure and cultural trends operating in any society [6, 7]. Maddox [8] observed quite different patterns of adaptation than those found in the Kansas City Study, and criticized the sample and methods employed by Cumming and Henry. Lowenthal, Thurnher, and Chiriboga [9] more recently found that a disengaged pattern was adaptive for individuals who were "self-protective and emotionally bland." Even for these individuals, disengagement was less of an intrinsic process than a "deliberate sorting out and sloughing off of unwanted responsibilities."

Neugarten has since refined the disengagement theory by combining developmental and social-psychological factors in explaining the process of aging [10]. According to this view, while psychological disengagement or withdrawal developmentally precedes social disengagement, there are individual variations. As Neugarten puts it [10], "In short, disengagement proceeds at different rates and different patterns in different people in different places and has different outcomes with regard to psychological well-being." Moreover, she claims, these changes are developmental rather than responsive since research has indicated that intrapsychic changes occur earlier in middle age than do the actual social losses which begin in the sixties. The findings reported by Neugarten and associates upon which much of this theory and the revision are based seem open to question, however, as they were cross-sectional [11]. In addition, while some of the results reach statistical significance, they are rather small in an absolute sense. Finally, many of those analyses were based upon data derived from ratings and as such are subjective and of questionable reliability.

If, for the purpose of discussion, we accept those results and Neugarten's interpretation in terms of disengagement theory, we still must consider what is meant by equating social factors with social losses. This line of reasoning represents an overly narrow definition of social influences and ignores the social learning which occurs during the period of old age. Some of this learning involves being able to adapt to the changing role demands of, for example, retiree, widow or widower, grandparents, and "senior citizen" within the community at large. In limiting the definition of social influences to losses, disengagement theory cannot legitimately characterize social influences as developmental in nature. In summary, the revised version of the disengagement theory would appear to be at best an *interactional* theory, in which the individual and the environment both contribute to changes with aging. Furthermore, the disengagement theory and its variants seem guilty of maintaining rather definite boundaries between (overemphasized) developmental and social forces.

Symbolic interaction theorists, by stressing the importance of cultural history and interpersonal interactions in shaping adult behavior, have attempted to correct what they perceive as an excessive attention to developmental factors [7, 12]. For the interactionists, it is the effects of societal trends and social structures (rather than personality traits) that are crucial in determining the results of the interactions among the aging and between the aging and others. Such concepts are valuable in highlighting the impact of our institutions and systems on situational adjustment and human experience. However, they seem to excessively downplay the contribution of developmental forces, as well as the two-way nature of the relationship between society and the individual.

Searching for a more inclusive paradigm of personality than the ones just discussed, we can find some suggestive thoughts in a model designed to account for the development of psychological deficits in high-risk children. Developmental psychologists Sameroff and Chandler, reviewing research in the area, criticize most studies for their failure to consider both the reproductive and caretaking histories of such children [13]. They observe that long-range predictions of the intellectual and psychological outcome of such prenatal and perinatal defects as prematurity and anoxia have been successful only when such environment factors as family situation and socioeconomic status have been included. Similarly, in explaining why certain youngsters are physically abused or neglected by parents, Sameroff and Chandler advocate taking into account not only the child-rearing environment (e.g., a disturbed parent) but also those qualities of the child (e.g., temperament) that single it out for special treatment. At first glance, an interactional model of development, combining both (1) the child's physical and psychological make-up and (2) environmental variables, to predict outcome would appear to follow from this stance. However, Sameroff and Chandler argue that only a *transactional* model can provide understanding of etiology as well as prediction, since both the child and the environment are in a constant process of change, change which is partially determined by the influence of each upon the other. As they note, "the child alters his environment and in turn is altered by the changed world he has created." A dynamic transactional model is better able to capture this "continual and progressive interplay" than is a static interactional one. The two components of the transactional model are therefore "the plastic character of the environment and the organism as an active participant in its own growth."

Extending this transactional model to apply to personality changes in later life implies that the physiological, sensory, and behavioral changes within the individual that are associated with the aging process are occuring *simulta-*

*neously* with social and environmental ones. Rather than search for cause and effect, one must see the combination of these variables as co-determining the person's behavior at any one point in time. Moreover, the effect of these interactions is cumulative, so that those occurring at an earlier point in development jointly affect those which evolve subsequently. This model can be conceptualized according to the following diagram:

$$T_1 \qquad T_2 \qquad T_3 \qquad \qquad T_n$$
$$\begin{Bmatrix} I \\ E \end{Bmatrix} \rightarrow \begin{Bmatrix} I \\ E \end{Bmatrix} \rightarrow \begin{Bmatrix} I \\ E \end{Bmatrix} \rightarrow \quad \cdots \quad \rightarrow \begin{Bmatrix} I \\ E \end{Bmatrix},$$

where T = Time of observation, I = Individual factors, and E = Environmental factors. To illustrate how this process operates, consider the case of an elderly man living in the community whose health has declined to the point at which institutionalization becomes necessary. Observing this person at Time 1, we may view his declining health as a function of internal changes as well as a possible lack of support services in his surroundings. Placement in an institution may result in an observation at Time 2 of poorer health. While one might conclude that his deterioration is a result of physiological processes, it is also possible that institutionalization itself has created his worsened condition. It has been found that passivity during the first year of institutionalization may be a predictor of morbidity [14]. Such passivity may itself be reinforced by the institutional environment, which fosters dependency [15], and creates "learned helplessness" in the elderly resident [16]. Thus, the passivity shown by the older person, which may lead to poorer psychological adaptation and/or physical health, has been at least partially acquired through the selective reinforcement of such behaviors in the institution.

The transactional model would suggest that it would not be particularly meaningful to separate the relative contributions of internal and external variables in predicting developmental change. Rather, it must be accepted that both operate jointly and cumulatively over time. Baltes and Schaie have postulated a model that takes into account stimulus, organismic, and response variables both concurrently and historically in order to explain developmental processes [17]. However, implicit in this model is the assumption that the three categories of variables may potentially be separated from each other, and that by the isolation of their effects, both explanation and prediction will be possible. The actual differentiation of these highly interrelated variables is, however, a difficult task. Some support for the extent of such a problem is evidenced in the literature on developmental changes in adult intelligence. The distinction between environmental factors (cohort and time of measurement effects) and maturational factors (age effects) has been demonstrated to be a theoretical and methodological conundrum [18, 19]. Moreover, to attempt to arrive at a "true" age function independent of cultural, historical, and social influences on individual ontogeny is not essential if one accepts a transactional model.

The present model has certain similarities to other approaches to the treatment of environmental and individual processes as contributing to behavior. Aspects of Riegel's dialectical model of adult development relate to this issue [20]. In considering the relative merits of trait *vs.* situational approaches to personality, Argyle and Little have also concluded that studying the interaction of stable individual characteristics with variations due to the environment leads to a better understanding of behavior than attempting to distinguish between the two [21].

Though approaching the aging process from an ecological perspective, Lawton and Nahemow arrive at much the same conclusion as that of the transactional model [22]. Drawing upon Helson's adaptation level theory, they present a theory in which adaptive and maladaptive behaviors are regarded as the product of transactions between individual competence and environmental press. Lawton and Nahemow further demonstrate how the ecological viewpoint is valuable in understanding such real-world phenomena as the effects on the elderly of planned housing, relocation, institutionalization, and transportation. Illustrative of the potential of this approach is a study of housing adjustment which found that in housing for higher socioeconomic groups, residents' personal qualities accounted for a greater proportion of the variance of adjustment, while for lower economic groups, environmental factors accounted for more of the variance [23].

In summary, the transactional model postulates the following: In approaching later adulthood, the individual possesses a constellation of personality attributes influenced by both biological and psychosocial factors. In the beginning of the aging period, the individual is subject to the effects of the environment in terms of both persons and settings. The modifications produced by these social factors will be the product of the people and settings themselves and the manner in which the individual (with a unique personality and cognitive make-up) acts upon and is acted upon by these persons and settings. This dynamic process continues in such a fashion throughout the years of later life. Furthermore, whether the person remains more or less stable or undergoes considerable change during this period will depend upon the degree of diversity of social factors within the environment. Contributing to this ongoing course are the cognitive, neurological, and physical alterations within the individual, which themselves are nonuniform across adults.

Research into this process will undoubtedly be difficult and challenging. Present behavioral and environmental events will by necessity assume as much importance as past ones. Such contemporary social influences are as specific as an elderly women's closest relative and as general as the political, cultural, and economic forces at work in the society at large—forces which themselves are continually in a state of flux over the course of time. A focus upon individual differences, rather than group, will also be required, with greater attention to multivariate analyses.

Thus, while the transactional model offered here certainly does nothing to lessen the already complicated models of life-span research, it may aid us in arriving at a more veridical conception and truer appreciation of the diversity and complexity involved in the development of human behavior [24].

## REFERENCE NOTES

1. E. H. Erikson, *Childhood and Society,* 2nd ed., Norton, New York, 1963.

2. J. E. Marcia, Development and Validation of Ego-Identity Status, *Journal of Personality and Social Psychology, 13,* pp. 551–558, 1966.

3. A. S. Waterman and C. K. Waterman, A Longitudinal Study of Changes in Ego-Identity Status During the Freshman Year at College, *Developmental Psychology, 5,* pp. 167–173, 1971.

4. R. N. Butler, The Life Review: An Interpretation of Reminiscence in the Aged, in B. L. Neugarten (ed.), *Middle Age and Aging,* University of Chicago, Chicago, 1968.

5. E. Cumming and W. H. Henry, *Growing Old: The Process of Disengagement,* Basic Books, New York, 1961.

6. R. J. Havighurst, B. L. Neugarten, and S. S. Tobin, Disengagement and Patterns of Aging, in B. L. Neugarten (ed.), *Middle Age and Aging,* University of Chicago, Chicago, 1968.

7. A. M. Rose, A Current Theoretical Issue in Social Gerontology, *The Gerontologist, 4,* pp. 46–50, 1964.

8. G. L. Maddox, Persistence of Life Style Among the Elderly: A Longitudinal Study of Patterns of Social Activity in Relation to Life Satisfaction, *Proceedings of the Seventh International Congress of Gerontology, 6,* pp. 309–311, 1966.

9. M. F. Lowenthal, M. Thurnher, and D. Chiriboga, *Four Stages of Life,* Jossey-Bass, San Francisco, p. 237, 1975.

10. B. L. Neugarten, Personality Change in Late Life: A Developmental Perspective, in C. Eisdorfer and M. P. Lawton (eds.), *The Psychology of Adult Development and Aging,* American Psychological Association, Washington, D. C., p. 330, 1973.

11. B. L. Neugarten & associates, *Personality in Middle and Late Life,* Atherton Press, New York, 1964.

12. H. Becker, Personal Change in Adult Life, *Sociometry, 27,* pp. 40–53, 1964.

13. A. J. Sameroff and M. J. Chandler, Reproductive Risk and the Continuum of Caretaking Casualty, in F. D. Horowitz, M. Hetherington, S. Scarr-Salapatek, and G. Siegel (eds.), *Review of Child Development Research, 4,* University of Chicago, Chicago, p. 234, 1974.

14. S. Tobin and M. Lieberman, *Last Home for the Aged,* Jossey-Bass, San Francisco, 1976.

15. S. K. Gordon and W. E. Vinacke, Self- and Ideal Self-Concepts and Dependency in Aged Persons Residing in Institutions, *Journal of Gerontology, 26,* pp. 337–343, 1971.

16. M. E. P. Seligman, *Helplessness: On Depression, Development, and Death,* W. H. Freeman & Co., San Francisco, 1975.

17. P. B. Baltes and K. W. Schaie, On Life-Span Developmental Research Paradigms: Retrospects and Prospects, in P. B. Baltes and K. W. Schaie (eds.), *Life-Span Developmental Psychology: Personality and Socialization,* Academic Press, New York, 1973.

18. P. B. Baltes and K. W. Schaie, On the Plasticity of Intelligence in Adulthood and Old Age: Where Horn and Donaldson Fail, *American Psychologist, 31,* pp. 720–725, 1976.

19. J. L. Horn and G. Donaldson, On the Myth of Intellectual Decline in Adulthood, *American Psychologist, 31,* pp. 701–719, 1976.

20. K. F. Riegel, Adult Life Crises: A Dialectic Interpretation of Development, in N. Datan and L. H. Ginsberg (eds.), *Life-Span Developmental Psychology: Normative Life Crises,* Academic Press, New York, 1975.

21. M. Argyle and B. R. Little, Do Personality Traits Apply to Social Behavior? *Journal for the Theory of Social Behavior, 2,* pp. 1–35, 1972.

22. M. P. Lawton and L. Nahemow, Ecology and the Aging Process, in C. Eisdorfer and M. P. Lawton (eds.), *The Psychology of Adult Development and Aging,* American Psychological Association, Washington, D. C., 1973.

23. W. P. Mangum, *Adjustment in Special Residential Settings for the Aged: An Inquiry Based on the Kleemeier Conceptualization,* Unpublished Doctoral Dissertation, University of Southern California, 1971.

24. J. R. Nesselroade and H. W. Reese, *Life-Span Developmental Psychology: Methodological Issues,* Academic Press, New York, 1973.

# Widowhood and Preventive Intervention*

*Phyllis R. Silverman*

WIDOWHOOD CAN BE VIEWED as that social category which every married person will enter when one of the couple dies first. Most people put aside any thought that this change of status will happen to them. Most contemporary traditions and patterns of behavior support people in their reluctance to face death and its consequences for family life. In fact few people understand what it means to be widowed.[1] While it is common to rehearse for marriage during courtship no similar rituals prepare the individual for the inevitable termination of this marriage when one of the partners will die. Any verbal discussion of what widowhood involves rarely occurs even when the spouse is seriously ill and death is anticipated. On the other hand *silent* consideration of what is involved may be taking place in an older population as people observe their friends who are becoming widowed.

Berardo (1968) pointed out that the examination of widowhood is a neglected aspect of study in the family life cycle. He noted that the widowed are a growing population and that they have a high risk of developing social and emotional difficulties. (Berardo, 1968)

In 1968 there were approximately 11,000,000 widowed individuals in the

* From The Family Coordinator, 21:1(1972): 95–102. Copyright © 1972 by the National Council on Family Relations. Reprinted by permission of the author and the publisher.

[1] The very word "widow" has very negative connotations. Many widows feel as if it implies they are damaged, a second class citizen. The same associations are not true for the word "widower."

United States, while in 1960 there were only 9,000,000. For all age groups: men were becoming widowers at the rate of 5.9/1000 or 251,000 a year while women were becoming widows at the rate of 13.9/1000 or 592,000 per year. The widowed are increasingly a female population. Widowhood is not solely a problem of the elderly as one-fourth of those widowed are under 65. However, many people grow to old age as widows and widowers. For example, of those who die of old age, on the average women have been widows for 18.5 years and men have been widowers for 13.5 years. (Carter and Glick, 1970).

Berardo (1968) raised questions about what life is like for these men and women who no longer have a husband or wife with whom to share their life. Other researchers have approached the question of widowhood from other viewpoints. For example, the sociologists, Marris (1958) and Lopata (1969, 1970), have looked at the content of the widow's social life; Maddison (1968) and Parkes (1964, 1967, 1970) as psychiatrists have been concerned with the mental health implications of widowhood; and the insurance companies (LIAMA, 1970) have examined the adequacy of their programs for meeting the needs of the surviving widow. This growing interest is beginning to influence caregiving practices. (Gerber, 1969) The Widow-to-Widow program is one effort to develop appropriate modes of helping the widowed. (Silverman, 1969)

# The Widow-to-Widow Program

This paper will discuss several aspects of what it means to be widowed based on experiences of the Widow-to-Widow program. The program developed in response to the finding that most caregivers who might normally be available to the widowed were fearful of a bereaved individual, attempting to shut off his or her mourning prematurely and then withdraw while there was still great need. (Silverman, 1966) Most people hope that the widow's grief will be short lived and time bound. They find it difficult to tolerate the prolonged anguish of acute grief. The recital of a few platitudes by the clergy or the offering of a prescription by the physician may give these caregivers a sense of doing something but in fact the widow reported that this helped very little.

Most widowed people did not seek out mental health professionals since they were not seen as appropriate to their need. They did not see themselves, and correctly so, as having psychiatric problems. Instead, as Silverman (1966) reported, they found another widowed person to be most helpful. The Widow-to-Widow program was an experiment to test the feasibility of another widow becoming a caregiver to the newly widowed. It was hypothesized that she would be able to use her own experience to help others, that her special empathy would enable her to understand the support needed, that she could accept the new widow's distress over an extended period of time, and that she would be accepted if she offered her assistance to the new widow. (Silverman, 1967)

In this program the new widow did not solicit help. In part this was because a newly bereaved person is usually too disorganized and too unsure of his or her needs to reach out and ask for assistance. Since the widowed are at a high risk of developing psychiatric problems (Volkart and Michael, 1957), the question was asked: could intervention such as the Widow-to-Widow program prevent such disabilities from occuring? A public health model of prevention was followed, i.e., attempting to reach every member of the target population even those who might be "immune" and not need any assistance. Therefore, the Widow-to-Widow program tried to reach all the widowed women under the age of 60 in a given community. For another widow this contact was easier since she seemed to have a legitimate interest in helping and could act in the context of a neighbor or friend who had similar personal experience. (Silverman, 1971) The goal of such intervention is not simple, since it is difficult to say what is being prevented. What is poor mental health? The findings of the Widow-to-Widow program indicate that widows and widowers often develop emotional disturbance when they cannot give up their role of wife or husband, i.e., when they try to continue to live as they had when their spouse was alive. A good part of the intervention seems to involve helping them make this transition from wife to widow.

Widowhood does not just happen when a spouse dies. A woman may legally become a widow at this point; however, the legal fact does not always coincide with her social and emotional acceptance of the role. Goffman (1961) wrote of a moral career in a role. This is a useful concept here. In his terms the widow becomes a member of a social category after undergoing a dramatic status transition. There is a regular "sequence of change that this career entails in the person's self, and in his framework of imagery for judging himself and others." (Goffman, 1961, 127–128) A "change over time, as is basic and common to the members of this social category takes place and the individual becomes socialized to the role." (Goffman, 1961)

To assume the role of widow, one needs to know how to play this part. In some cultures the role is clearly defined. (Mathison, 1970) The widow is expected to be in mourning the remainder of her natural life. Mourning, and the public behavior which is viewed as an expression of it, is the dominant force in her life. It may not be pleasant but at least she knows who she is and what is expected of her and she never has to give up what attachment she has to her deceased husband. In sharp contrast in the United States a person's mourning is supposed to be of short duration and to end before the new widow or widower understands what the new role means or how it will affect his life. This pressure to not express one's bereavement can in fact only intensify the grief. (Gorer, 1967). It seems safe to say that the period after the death of a spouse is an "anomic" situation; an individual at the threshold of a career as a widow or widower does not know what to do, what it means, and what to expect of himself and for himself.

The remainder of this paper is devoted to examining this dilemma created by widowhood and describes one way of helping to cope with it. The experience on which this paper is based is primarily with widows under 60. From other experience it would seem that the critical transition involving a role change is no different for widowers (with necessary modifications specific to the role of husband) or for people over 60.

## Giving Up the Role of Wife

Initially the new widow is numb.[2] Very often at the time of the funeral she appears calm and able to cope with her various social responsibilities and all the many chores connected with the funeral and the ongoing care of her family. At this time it is normal and appropriate for her to act as if she is still her husband's wife. She plans the funeral according to his wishes or as she thinks he would have wanted it. In her initial reactions, in how she expresses her feelings, and in what she tells the children she behaves in ways that are true to his style and their life together. She does not think of herself as a widow.

It is safe to say the real anguish and distress of grief has not yet begun. As the numbness lifts, something changes and the widow falls apart. The pain seems to emanate from the growing awareness of the finality of the loss, as the widow is forced to confront the terrible fact: her husband is gone permanently. It can take up to two years to accept this fact. Mourning, however, is not something that ends and then the widow is able to return to her life as before.

Evidence from the Widow-to-Widow program indicated that one does not recover from grief. It is not a disease from which one is cured. It is a necessary process which if avoided creates its own problems.[3] A woman's sense of self is changed, and the very nature of her outer world is different. She has to recognize that it can never be the same.[4] There is no *restitution ad integrum.*[5]

---

[2] Mourning has been characterized as a process. Bowlby (1961) described three stages: impact, recoil, and recovery or adjustment. These phases have been helpful in understanding and describing the widows' behavior during the first year of bereavement.

[3] Lindemann (1944) and Parkes (1967) describe some of the negative consequences for people who cannot or do not grieve, noting that this can lead to serious mental illness. Parkes (1970) noted that the individual who still pines for her husband, feels his presence in the house, and cannot accept the fact that he is gone one year after his death is most likely to have a poor outcome from the mental health point of view.

[4] Lindemann (1944) wrote "the bereaved is surprised to find how large a part of his customary activity was done in some meaningful relationship to the deceased and has lost its significance. Especially the habit of social interaction—meeting friends, making conversation, sharing enterprises seems to have been lost."

[5] Von Witzleben (1958), found a reference in the work of Freud that is not often quoted: ". . . there was no restitution ad integrum after a serious affective loss. The structure of one's inner world . . . will never be the same. Not only is the identity of self changed but also that of the outer world is different" . . . Freud wrote to a friend who lost his son. "We know that the most poignant grief is blunted after such a loss; but we remain inconsolable and never can we find a substitute. Whoever takes his place, even if he were to fill it completely will always remain totally different, and actually that is as it should be. It is the only way to preserve a love that in reality one does not wish to relinquish."

It is more accurate to talk of making an accommodation or an adjustment or of making the past history, and therefore a prologue to the future.

Before reaching this accommodation several widows served by the Widow-to-Widow program, talked of experiencing a low point, where in fact they felt they could as easily die as live. . . . What helped [one widow] make the choice was her ability to see another role for herself, other than wife. Widowhood involved a different way of life, but nonetheless it could be meaningful as well.

The direction the change took in part was related to how much the role of wife permeated the lives of these women; did they have a total commitment to this role or did it occupy only a part of their life?

The woman who works has a good part of her identity invested in her role as a secretary, a physician, a salesgirl, and so forth. Her marital status can be irrelevant to this situation. Even if she still maintains her image of herself as wife, this does not create a conflict for her at work and she still can function well there. This may be why many women return to work as soon as possible. However, the fact that a woman can still identify herself with an intact role may postpone a confrontation with her new reality at home. Some of these women, to their surprise, found that six months or a year later they began to feel lonely and to mourn in a way they had not done before. . . .

A woman whose entire sense of self was invested in being a wife and mother, will begin her career as a widow with less delay. . . . Her life is suddenly barren and she has no meaningful role available to her. These women have to find a way of accepting an altered reality in which they have no one to share their daily lives. They have lost the opportunity for an intimate social and emotional relationship that for most people comes only in marriage. (Lopata, 1969) Unlike the working woman who has at least one viable role available to her, these women have to develop new roles for themselves sometimes from whole cloth. (Lopata, 1970)

Even socially a new widow may do well until she tries to socialize with other couples. She is the fifth wheel and it is unclear to whom she relates. What is expected of another woman's husband in seeing that she is comfortable, in paying her check, and the like? . . . There are other roles available to the new widow. In some instances the woman's role as mother, sister, or daughter was more important than that of wife. When her husband dies these roles do not change and her life can continue as before. In an older population a woman is seldom the first to be widowed in her group and her widowed friends provide her with a ready reference group. This may not be acceptable to her since she may not be able "to accept herself as one of them yet."

In summary, the drama of the status transition the individual undergoes to become a widow can be described as starting when the new widow realizes that this word applies to her. At this point she knows there is no returning from the grave, and the loneliness, the pining, the pain really burst out. She has passed what can be called an initiation stage, but she is not necessarily able to act on her recognition of this reality. Grief can be seen as an inner struggle not to assume the widow role, to deny at some level the reality of the loss, to recapture and to live in the past. When this fails for her then a woman can recover, and her career as a widow begins, and it is with this definition of herself that she must live until she either remarries or dies. It is here that an educational process must begin for she is finding her way in a social category always known to mankind, but yet ignored in the present day so that she is essentially a pioneer since neither religious nor social tradition can really guide her.

## REFERENCES

BERARDO, FELIX M. Widowhood Status in the United States: Perspective on a Neglected Aspect of the Family Life-Cycle. *The Family Coordinator,* 1968, 17, 191–203.

BOWLBY, JOHN. Processes of Mourning. *The International Journal of Psychoanalysis,* 1961, 13, 317–340.

CARTER, HUGH AND PAUL C. GLICK. *Marriage and Divorce: A Social and Economic Study.* Cambridge: Harvard University Press, 1970.

GERBER, IRWIN. Bereavement and Acceptance of Professional Service. *Community Mental Health Journal,* 1969, 5, 487–496.

GOFFMAN, ERVING. The Moral Career of a Mental Patient. *Asylums.* New York: Doubleday and Co., 1961.

GORER, GEOFFREY. *Death, Grief, and Mourning.* Garden City: Doubleday Co., and Anchor Book, 1967.

LIFE INSURANCE AGENCY MANAGEMENT ASSOCIATION. *The Onset of Widowhood,* 1970, 1.

LINDEMANN, ERICH. Symptomatology and Management of Acute Grief. *American Journal of Psychiatry,* 1944, 51, 141–148.

LOPATA, HELENA Z. Loneliness: Forms and Components, *Social Problems,* 1969, 17, 248–261.

LOPATA, HELENA Z. The Social Involvement of American Widows, *American Behavioral Scientist,* 1970, 14, 41–57.

MADDISON, DAVID. The Relevance of Conjugal Bereavement for Preventive Psychiatry, *British Journal of Medical Psychology,* 1968, 41, 223.

MARRIS, PETER. *Widows and Their Families.* London: Routledge and Kegan Paul, 1958.

MATHISON, JEAN A. Cross-Cultural View of Widowhood. *Omega,* 1970, 1, 201–218.

PARKES, C. MURRAY. Recent Bereavement as a Cause of Mental Illness. *British Journal of Psychiatry,* 1964, 110, 198–204.

PARKES, C. MURRAY. Nature of Grief, *International Journal of Psychiatry,* 1967, 3, 5–8.

PARKES, C. MURRAY. The First Year of Bereavement, *Psychiatry,* 1970, 33, 444.

SILVERMAN, PHYLLIS R. Services for the Widowed During the Period of Bereavement. *Social Work Practice.* New York: Columbia University Press, 1966.

SILVERMAN, PHYLLIS R. Services to the Widowed: First Steps in a Program of Preventive Intervention. *Community Mental Health Journal,* 1967, 3, 37–44.

SILVERMAN, PHYLLIS R. The Widow-to-Widow Program. *Mental Hygiene,* 1969, 53, 333–337.

SILVERMAN, PHYLLIS R. The Widow as Caregiver. *Mental Hygiene,* 1970, 54, 540–547.

SILVERMAN, PHYLLIS R. Factors Involved in Accepting an Offer of Help. *Archives of The Foundation of Thanatology,* 1971.

VOLKART, E. H. AND S. T. MICHAEL. Bereavement and Mental Health. In A. H. Leighton, J. H. Clauser, and R. N. Wilson (Eds.) *Explorations in Social Psychiatry.* New York: Basic Books, 1957, 281–307.

VON WITZLEBEN, HENRY D. On Loneliness. *Psychiatry,* 1958, 21, 37–43.

# California Natural ~~Death~~
# Nation's First*
*Michael Gilfix*

T HE RECENTLY ENACTED (January 1, 1977) California Natural Death Act is
the first of its kind in the entire nation. It is, therefore, of particular interest to everyone who is concerned about a person's right to a natural death.

In essence, the act provides that in certain circumstances "life-sustaining
procedures" may be withheld or withdrawn if a person is terminally ill. Such
procedures may include artificial respirators or the use of electric shock to
restart a heart that has ceased beating.

The major features of the act are discussed in detail below and in subsequent sections.

The only way a person can take advantage of the act is by executing or filling out a "directive," which is a document instructing a physician about the
termination of life-sustaining treatment. The new law sets forth the exact
form of the document.

To execute a directive, a person must be at least 18 years of age, mentally
competent, and signatures of two witnesses must be obtained.

Because of concerns about improper influences and coercion, neither
witness can be related to the person signing the directive, have any claim to
that person's estate or play any role in that person's medical care. The difficulties encountered by nursing home residents in finding appropriate witnesses will be discussed below.

A directive must be signed by the person who will be affected by it. A
parent may not sign on behalf of a child, nor a guardian on behalf of his
ward.

Significantly, a person has a right to refuse medical treatment even if he
does not sign a directive. This right is firmly established in the law. It is entirely likely that an informed, mentally sound patient will arrive at an understanding with his doctor about when, for example, chemotherapy will be discontinued as a treatment for cancer. However, if that same person loses the
ability to communicate with his physician because of a medical crisis, a directive may represent the only expression of his medical care desires. As such, it
serves a useful and possibly vital function.

It is important to note that the effective life of a Natural Death Act directive is five years, when it expires. A new directive must be executed at that
time.

* Reprinted by permission from *Perspective on Aging*, Vol. VI, No. 4 Issue of July/August
1977, published by The National Council on the Aging, Inc., Washington, D.C. 20036.

The execution of a directive has no bearing on a person's life insurance policy or on his ability to obtain life insurance. If a policy contains language to the contrary, it is invalid.

## Not to Hasten Death

It is also important to realize that a directive cannot be used to hasten death. It is designed only to allow the natural process of dying, and then only in narrowly circumscribed situations. Fears that the act implicitly or explicitly sanctions euthanasia are simply without basis.

For the same reasons, the carrying out of a directive is not considered a suicide. Further, it does not—in any way—interfere with the use of medication to relieve pain.

The caution with which the California legislature proceeded in passing the Natural Death Act is reflected in the ease with which a person can revoke the directive. Revocation can be achieved by physically defacing, destroying or canceling a directive. If a person is physically unable to do any of these things, the law specifically provides that any of them may be done by someone else, in the presence of the person and at his direction. Though the possibility of abuse in this procedure is obvious, no reasonable alternative exists if a physically disabled person is to be given the same revocation rights that belong to able-bodied persons.

One controversial provision is that a person need not be mentally competent to revoke a directive. As pointed out above, mental competence is required to sign one. This concerns many persons who want to be bound by a carefully considered and rational decision made before a life-threatening situation arises.

## Act's Concern Legitimate

Yet the concern of the act is also legitimate: It is difficult to determine the competency of a person in such a situation. Moreover, not requiring "competency" at the time of revocation avoids a possible mistake (*i.e.,* invalidating a revocation because the person is "incompetent") that may result in an earlier death.

A new directive may, of course, be executed at any time after a revocation. All the original formalities must be followed in any reexecution.

Criminal penalties do exist if a person forges the directive of another and thereby causes the early termination of life-sustaining procedures. In certain circumstances, that person may be found guilty of unlawful homicide. The same criminal charges may be brought against a person who conceals a valid revocation and, as a result, causes a directive to be followed.

---

### DIRECTIVE TO PHYSICIANS

Directive made this _____ day of _____ (month, year).

I _____, being of sound mind, willfully and voluntarily make known my desire that my life shall not be artificially prolonged under the circumstances set forth below, do hereby declare:

1. If at any time I should have an incurable injury, disease, or illness certified to be a terminal condition by two physicians, and where the application of life-sustaining procedures would serve only to artificially prolong the moment of my death and where my physician determines that my death is imminent whether or not life-sustaining procedures are utilized, I direct that such procedures be withheld or withdrawn, and that I be permitted to die naturally.

2. In the absence of my ability to give directions regarding the use of such life-sustaining procedures, it is my intention that this directive shall be honored by my family and physician(s) as the final expression of my legal right to refuse medical or surgical treatment and accept the consequences from such refusal.

3. If I have been diagnosed as pregnant and that diagnosis is known to my physician, this directive shall have no force or effect during the course of my pregnancy.

4. I have been diagnosed and notified at least 14 days ago as having a terminal condition by _____, M. D., whose address is _____ _____, and whose telephone number is _____. I understand that if I have not filled in the physician's name and address, it shall be presumed that I did not have a terminal condition when I made out this directive.

5. This directive shall have no force or effect five years from the date filled in above.

6. I understand the full import of this directive and I am emotionally and mentally competent to make this directive.

Signed _____

City, County and State of Residence _____

_____

The declarant has been personally known to me and I believe him or her to be of sound mind.

Witness _____

Witness _____

This directive complies in form with the "Natural Death Act" California Health and Safety Code, Section 7188, Assembly Bill 3060 (Keene).

---

If a person willfully damages, destroys or conceals another's valid directive without consent, he may be found guilty of a misdemeanor.

A directive will be carried out only if certain conditions are satisfied. Perhaps most importantly, a directive is *legally binding* only if signed and witnessed at least 14 days after a person is found, by two doctors, to have a terminal condition.

If a person becomes terminally ill after signing a directive, the doctor is given discretion to decide whether or not to honor that directive. The doctor may then consider such things as the opinions of other family members and personal knowledge of the patient's desires. Clearly, the importance of discussing death and dying with one's physician and family is paramount. Such discussions may be the crucial factor in the doctor's decision about respecting or rejecting the patient's final wish about his own death.

Life-sustaining procedures may be terminated or withdrawn only when death is imminent and will finally result whether or not such procedures are used. Because the term "imminent" is not defined in the act, the attending physician is given discretion to decide when a patient's condition has reached the "terminal" stage.

Perhaps because of this latitude given the physician, the judgment of two doctors is required, rather than just one.

One critical exception is that life-sustaining procedures will not be withheld or terminated if a woman is pregnant, regardless of her other physical condition.

## Many Conditions to Be Met

Because so many conditions must be satisfied before a directive will be followed, it is useful to list them.

○ All requirements (*i.e.,* age, mental state, witnesses) must have been satisfied when the directive was executed.
○ The directive must have been executed at least 14 days after the declarant was certified in writing by the attending and another physician as "terminal," as that term is defined in the act.
○ The directive must have been entered into the patient's medical file, thus making the attending physician aware of its existence.
○ The directive must not have been revoked.
○ If competent, the patient must have affirmed his/her desire to have the directive carried out.
○ Any "life-sustaining procedures" involved must be included in the statutory definition.
○ The attending physician must be convinced that those procedures would, if continued, do no more than postpone the moment of death *and* that death is in any event imminent.

Assuming that all these conditions are met, the attending physician is legally required to honor a directive. If the physician refuses to do so, he must transfer the patient to a physician who will honor it.

If the physician willfully refuses to honor a valid directive, he can be found guilty of "unprofessional conduct" by the California Board of Medical Quality Assurance. Such a finding can result in penalties ranging from probation to the revocation of the physician's license to practice medicine.

The act specifically provides that a physician cannot be charged with any criminal offense for a refusal. It also provides that the physician may not be sued by anyone, such as a family member, for not carrying out a directive. For example, the failure of a doctor to follow a directive may result in the continued use of expensive medical equipment. Notwithstanding this economic burden, the doctor cannot be sued to recover the expenses. Nor may the physician be sued to recover for harm to the patient's dignity or for suffering unnecessarily prolonged. Yet, both of these concerns are at the very heart of the act.

Many persons are concerned that the act simply does not go far enough. Consider first the fact that a physician is *required* to follow a directive only if it is executed 14 days after the person is found to be in a terminal condition. Because "terminal" here means that death must be imminent, only a tiny minority of persons will survive the two-week period and then be able to sign the directive. For example, it is not until the condition of many cancer victims has deteriorated to the point where communication is impossible that death will be "imminent." Consider also the person who is in a coma and who cannot, therefore, execute a directive. Persons in such conditions cannot benefit from the full force of the act. They can only hope that a previously executed directive will be followed.

Interestingly, one can envision a situation where the absence of a directive could result in an earlier termination of life-sustaining procedures than if a directive were in existence. Indicative is the patient who has lost all cognitive abilities but may, nevertheless, live for years. In the absence of a directive, such a patient may be allowed to die when his life is threatened by an illness such as pneumonia. A physician may choose this course because of personal philosophy, the desires of family members or an agreement made with the patient prior to his illness.

If, on the other hand, a directive is in effect, life-sustaining procedures cannot be withheld until the patient's condition satisfies definitions contained in the act. Because the definition of "terminal illness" is so narrow, the physician may not feel legally able to withhold medical assistance.

# Difficulty Hinders Effort

One difficulty uniquely confronts residents of nursing homes. In an effort to guarantee them the right to make free and voluntary choices, it is required that one of two witnesses to their directives be a patient advocate or an ombudsman, as may be designated by the California Department of Aging.

The problem lies with the fact that, to date, no mechanism for the designation of patient advocates or ombudsmen has been in existence. Because no qualified witnesses exist, nursing home residents have been effectively denied use of the California Natural Death Act.

The California Natural Death Act satisfies few proponents of an individual's right to a natural death because of its limited application. Yet, it stands as a laudable beginning—a necessary first step in the movement to grant greater autonomy to the individual.

It is the hope of Californians who support this movement that the act will be amended so as to address the limitations pointed out above. It is also hoped that the California Natural Death Act will prove to be a harbinger of greater national responsiveness to an issue too long submerged in a sea of ignorance and emotionalism.

# Growing Old in America*
# An Interview with Margaret Mead
*Grace Hechinger*

M ARGARET MEAD celebrates her 75th birthday this year [ed.: 1977]. We went to see her in her office, tucked away in a Victorian turret of New York City's Museum of Natural History. It is the same place she began her work 50 years ago—cozy, comfortable and cluttered with books and memorabilia.

To get there, we had to take a large museum elevator, walk down long, dimly lit corridors lined with fossil specimens and finally climb a tiny winding staircase. Few with her fame could resist the temptation to move to grander and more accessible quarters. But one secret of Margaret Mead's long and productive life is her ability to know instinctively what is right for her.

She has been acclaimed "one of the greatest women alive" and is known throughout the world as a pioneer in her chosen field of anthropology. She is the author of nearly two dozen books and countless articles on primitive peoples and all aspects of family life.

A petite and lively woman, she's seated behind her large desk, which overflows with papers and other evidence of work in progress, and beams her famous smile as she talks. Dr. Mead's energy and unflagging interest in life pervade her own unique and inspiring perspective on old age in America.

* Reprinted from July 26, 1977 issue of *Family Circle Magazine*. © 1977 The Family Circle, Inc.

**Family Circle**: America has a bad reputation for our treatment of the elderly. Do you think it is warranted?

**Dr. Mead**: America is pretty negligent in this respect. As a nation of imigrants, we have always put a tremendous premium on youth. The young people, the first generation born here, understood American life better than their parents, who had come from other countries. In the more uprooted families, grandparents became a source of embarrassment. Though children whose grandparents were not English-speaking might learn to understand their grandparents' language, they would refuse to speak it.

But at least older people used to stay in the family. Homes were big, and there was room for extra aunts and grandparents. Families lived close together in communities. Today we have many more old people than in the past. And we have changed our whole life-style. The flight to the suburbs in the last 25 years has done a great deal of harm. In these age-segregated, class-segregated communities, there is no place for old people to live near the young people they care about. So the poor ones are stacked away in nursing homes, which are sometimes called "warehouses for the old." The more affluent ones move into golden ghettos or go to Florida, but they too are segregated and lonely.

**FC**: How were the elderly treated in some of the primitive cultures you have studied?

**Dr. Mead**: You don't find many early or primitive societies that treat old people as badly as the civilized societies do. The very earliest civilizations, of course, had to let their older people die, very often because they weren't strong enough to walk the necessary distance to find food. But as soon as there were ways of storing food, older people were looked after.

**FC**: Do you see any parallel in the way America treats its older people and the way we treat our children?

**Dr. Mead**: Our treatment of both reflects the value we place on independence and autonomy. We do our best to make children independent from birth. We leave them all alone in rooms with the lights out and tell them, "Go to sleep by yourselves." And the old people we respect most are the ones who will fight for their independence, who would sooner starve to death than ask for help.

We in America have very little sense of interdependence. The real issue is whether a society keeps its older people close to children and young people. If old people are separated from family life, there is real tragedy both for them *and* the young.

**FC**: How could we structure our society to help bring older people back into the lives of their families?

**Dr. Mead**: It is primarily a question of replanning, of building communities where older people were welcome—not necessarily your own grandmother but somebody's grandmother. Older people need to live within walking distance of shops and friends and family. They need younger people to help with the heavy chores, to shovel the snow and cut the grass so they can continue to live on their own.

FC: What do you think about the way we approach retirement?

Dr. Mead: The practice of early retirement is terribly wasteful. We are wasting millions of good years of good people by forcing them into retirement. The men especially suffer. Whether or not women work, they've always had to do the housekeeping and the shopping and the planning. So when they retire, they still have some continuity in their lives. But the men are admirals without a fleet. They don't know what else to do but die.

FC: What can we do to keep older people active in community life?

Dr. Mead: We can do many things. Some universitites are building alumnae housing on campuses so that graduates will be able to move back near the universities. Some can teach, and all can enjoy the lectures, the intellectual stimulation and being near young people.

We shouldn't drop people from the PTA when their last child leaves school. We should have a grandparents' association that works for the local schools. At present, older people vote against school bond issues for schools their children once attended. They get selfish because they're no longer involved.

FC: It has been a fond American myth that in the good old days— whenever those were—we treated old people much better. Did the elderly really have fewer problems?

Dr. Mead: For one thing, there weren't a great many older people, and the ones that lived long lives were very, very tough.

Older people are more frail today. Many are the kind who would have died during infancy in earlier times and have had uncertain health all their lives. I had never seen an older person lying around like a vegetable, taking up the energy of doctors and nurses, until I was 28 years old. Every old person I knew as a child was somebody I could admire and listen to and enjoy.

When we're involved with old people whose hearing and eyesight go and who have to be cared for, we don't treat them like people, and that is frightening to old and young alike.

FC: When you were a child, grandparents had a much more active role in child-rearing than they do today. Do you believe that grandparents can educate their grandchildren?

Dr. Mead: If only today's grandparents would realize that they have seen more social change than any other generation in the history of the world! There is so much they could pass on!

In the small towns of earlier times, one good grandmother went a long way with her stories, her store of old-fashioned songs and her skills in the vanishing arts. From her, children absorbed a sense of the past and learned to measure time in meaningful biological terms—when grandmother was young, when mother was young, when I was young. Dates became real instead of mere numbers in a history book.

When my grandmother died in 1928 at the age of 82, she had seen the entire development of the horseless carriage, the flying machine, the telephone, the telegraph and Atlantic cables, radio and silent films.

Today, telephoning has largely replaced the family correspondence of two generations ago. I still treasure a letter that ends: "You are always in the thoughts of your grandmother by the sea. P.S. 'Apartment' is spelled with one 'P.' "

FC: Was your grandmother very important to you when you were growing up?

Dr. Mead: One of my grandmothers, who always lived with us, was the most decisive influence on my life. She sat at the center of our household. Her room was the place we immediately went to when we came home from school. We did our lessons on the cherry-wood table with which she had started housekeeping. Later it was my dining room table for 25 years.

I think my grandmother was the one who gave me my ease in being a woman. I had my father's mind, which he had inherited from her. Without my grandmother's presence—small, dainty and pretty—I might have thought having my father's mind would make me masculine. Though she was wholly without feminist leanings, she taught me that the mind is not sex-typed.

You know, one reason grandparents and grandchildren get along so well is that they can help each other out. First-person accounts of the parents when *they* were children reduces parental fury over disorders and fads of "the younger generation" and does away with such pronouncements as: "My father would never have permitted me to. . . ."

In small-town schools, there used to be teachers who taught two generations of children and mellowed in the process. They were there to remind the children that their parents had once been young, played hookey and passed forbidden notes in school. They were also able to moderate the zeal and balance the inexperience of young teachers.

FC: It is a popular belief that the way people were treated as children influences the way they treat older people. Do you agree?

Dr. Mead: There is a story that I like about a father bird who was carrying a little bird in its beak over the river. The little bird was completely in the power of the father bird. The older bird said, "My son, when I am old, will you care for me?"

The little bird said, "No, father, but I will care for my children the way you have cared for me."

The story shows something of the way affection is passed down through the generations. But it also reveals a fear of aging. In this country, some people start being miserable about growing old while they are still young, not even middle-aged. They buy cosmetics and clothes that promise them a young look.

A concomitance to the fear of aging is a fear of the aged. There are far too many children in America who are badly afraid of older people because they never see any. Old people are not a regular part of their everyday lives. Also, children are aware that their middle-aged parents cling to youth.

FC: It's true. We Americans are obsessed with staying young. There are not enough models like you, Dr. Mead, to show younger people goals to grow toward.

Dr. Mead: We have always had a good number of lively old people—it is just the proportions that are changing. We had Bernie Baruch sitting on his park bench, advising one president after another. We have many physicians who go on practicing late in life. Writers, too, and justices of the Supreme Court.

FC: How can middle-aged and young people lessen the fear of growing old?

Dr. Mead: It's very important to prepare yourself. One useful thing is to change all your doctors, opticians and dentists when you reach 50. You start out when you are young with everybody who looks after you older than you are. When you get to be 50, most of these people are 65 or older. Change them all and get young ones. Then, as you grow older, you'll have people who are still alive and active taking care of you. You won't be desolate because every one of your doctors is dead.

Another thing is to consider what you want to do later in life while you are still young. If you think of your whole life-span and what you are going to do at one stage and then at another, and incorporate these plans in your life picture, you can look forward confidently to old age. If you associate enough with older people who do enjoy their lives, who are not stored away in any golden ghettos, you will gain a sense of continuity and the possibilities for a full life.

FC: How did you plan for your life when you were young?

Dr. Mead: I went to work at the Museum of Natural History as a young girl, and of course I had no idea how long I'd stay. You don't when you are 24. Then I saw a doddering old man walking around the corridors, and I asked, "What is he doing here?" I was told, "He is working on a book. He retired 20 years ago." I discovered that at the Museum they keep you until you die. And so I decided to stay right there.

FC: How do you think people can learn to appreciate the past?

Dr. Mead: I frequently have my students interview older people. For the Bicentennial, we developed a model book called *How to Interview Your Grandfather*. It is the reverse of a baby book. The students made up the questions simply by thinking of what they wanted to know about the past. The older people adore being asked. They stop complaining that nobody is interested in them or that "nobody listens to me anymore. . . ." And the young people find that what they have to say is fascinating.

FC: It's so important for children to sense the treasure of memory, both personal and national.

Dr. Mead: Another thing we are doing with students is to tell them to write an autobiography for their as-yet-unborn grandchildren. What would you like your grandson or granddaughter to know about you? Thinking like this gives young people a new perspective about the future. They begin to realize that someday they themselves will be old.

My mother was very fond of Robert Browning. She used to quote these lines from *Rabbi Ben Ezra.* They are favorites of mine:

> Grow old along with me!
> The best is yet to be,
> The last of life,
>     for which the first was made:
> Our times are in His hand
> Who saith 'A whole I planned,
> Youth shows but half; trust God:
>     see all, nor be afraid!'

PART III

SPECIAL
POPULATIONS
AND ISSUES
IN HUMAN
GROWTH AND
DEVELOPMENT

AS PART OF the social environment, the helping professional moves into the orbit of the client—but to what effect? The worker's background characteristics affect the help to be given. Articles in this section have been selected to stress the importance of these questions: the issues of race (Siegel) or sex (Wesley) of the worker and the client; the question of the social class (Lorion) of each; the problems in communicating with people with whom the worker may share few life experiences (Reul; Lewis; Ho; Gibson). These differences are often held up as barriers to helping, and indeed they may be. But the evidence suggests that, with planned and conscious effort, these barriers may be partially overcome to the end of more nearly effective understanding and service.

The metaphor of the social atom suggests that no one is so different that someone cannot communicate with him or her. Moreover, the metaphor of shells of the social atom suggests that communication may be directed toward basic biological conditions that all people share, as well as toward special cultural and social matters that particular groups hold in common. Then it may become possible to deal with the unique combinations of experiences that distinguish this person with whom you are speaking from every other individual you have ever met. Problems and potentialities may be thought about in the abstract, but they must be acted upon in the particular.

# A Brief Review of the Effects of Race in Clinical Service Interactions*

*Jerome M. Siegel*

## Counseling and Psychotherapy

DURING THE PAST fifteen years there has been an increased interest in the factor of race in psychotherapy due largely to the growing awareness of the special life experiences that black people bring to therapy. These experiences, as well as the attitudes and responses of both white and black therapists to black patients, have been the subject of a number of recent papers.

Clinical speculation about the factor of race in psychotherapy and coun-

* From *American Journal of Orthopsychiatry*, 44:4 (1974): 555–562. Copyright © 1974. The American Orthopsychiatric Association, Inc. Reproduced by permission.

seling has been largely concerned with possible barriers between the black patient and the white therapist. Perhaps the most frequently mentioned barrier is that of the black patient's distrust of the white therapist as part of his pervasive distrust of the entire white world.[24,25,26,30] This distrust purportedly results in what Vontress[30] has called the "Negro Self-Disclosure Reserve," or the black patient's unwillingness to reveal himself to a representative of the white world. Also seen as a barrier to successful interracial therapy is the white therapist's unconscious (or conscious) racism, which Adams[1] saw as possibly causing strong negative countertransference reactions that interfere with successful outcome in psychotherapy. Among remedies for this racist-based countertransference, Adams recommended that the therapist, himself, undergo personal treatment.

The differing cultural backgrounds of the white therapist and the black patient has been another barrier mentioned in the literature,[30] with the black patient not only suffering from the communication gap presumably encountered by an lower-class patient dealing with a middle-class therapist, but from a special gap caused by the white therapist's inability to comprehend the idiom of the ghetto, and his total ignorance of black everyday life.

Finally, Grier and Cobbs[19] note the distortion caused by the sympathetic, aware white therapist, who focuses so closely on the stressful and pathogenic background of ghetto life that he cannot bring the individual psychopathology into clear focus against this background.

There has also been some speculation about the possible unique problems created when both the patient and therapist are black. Vontress[30] has suggested that if the white therapist is seen by the black patient as the enemy, the black therapist may be seen as something worse, the enemy's collaborator. Vontress also made the point that the black therapist will be accepted by the black patient only as long as he proves to the patient that he is competent to help him.

Calnek[10] has also dealt with some of the difficulties that may arise when both therapist and patient are black. Among these, he has mentioned over-identification with the patient as perhaps the chief problem of blacks working with blacks, and has seen this over-identification as an invitation for the patient to gripe about racial problems without giving the patient help with his non-racial problems. Calnek also mentioned the black therapist's possible tendency to deny racial identification with the black patient as a defense against the therapist's own strong emotional responses to being black. Also mentioned by Calnek is the possible tendency of the black therapist to imitate the white middle class, and to put as much psychological distance as possible between himself and the lower-class black patient.

There is some speculation that therapeutic difficulties between black therapists and black patients may possibly derive from the therapist's training. Two recent papers[20,21] have pointed to the tendency of psychiatric residency programs to psychologically "whiten" the racial identity of their black residents by ignoring the factor of race. This factor, plus the absence of black supervisors as role models in these programs, presumably fosters a training climate that may not promote in the young black psychiatrist a strong identification with the problems of poor black people.

It is worthy of mention at this point that some attention has been paid to problems arising when the therapist is black and the patient is white.[18,27]

A small but growing number of empirical studies have explored such issues as the preference of black clients for black or white service givers, attitudes of psychiatric residents toward black and white patients, inpatient treatment of blacks and whites, and depth of self-exploration in the initial interview by black patients treated by black and white therapists. Like the research on the effects of race of the examiner in psychological testing, this research has provided contradictory results.

Dubey[14] did a survey in a black Cleveland neighborhood and found that the black respondents did not prefer to patronize blacks over whites as occupants of various social roles—*e.g.,* "would you rather talk with a Negro social worker or with a white social worker?" (p. 113). However, a study in Chicago by Brieland[6] indicated that blacks interviewed by black interviewers did prefer to be served by black service givers (doctor, teacher, lawyer, etc.) when the question was worded so that the hypothetical black or white service givers were equally competent. Blacks' preference for black service givers was strongest for doctors and weakest for lawyers. Another question asked which race the respondents preferred if the white service giver was described as more competent. Here competence proved to be more important than race and the majority of blacks who had preferred blacks when the race choice was an equal competence race, altered their preference in favor of the white service givers. This survey also found that only a small proportion of the total respondents would not accept service from a white service giver.

Brieland also explored the question of what blacks prefer to be called (*i.e.,* Black, Afro-American, Negro, Colored, etc.). Brieland found that if the labels were limited to three, Black, Negro, and Colored, 53% of his respondents preferred "Negro," 24% preferred "Black," and 19% preferred "Colored." Lessing and Zagorin[22] reported the results of a readership poll on preferred ethnic label by Ebony magazine in 1968 that indicated different results. Of 2,000 respondents, 48% preferred "Afro-American," 23.3% preferred "Black," 12% preferred "African American," 8.1% chose "Negro," and only three per cent preferred "Colored." This disparity between the Ebony poll and Brieland's Chicago neighborhood poll on the differing place of "Negro" (most preferred out of three choices in the Chicago poll, second least preferred out of five in Ebony poll) may be a function of class differences. It would seem that Ebony readers who respond to a poll by mail are more middle class than Brieland's Chicago respondents, who were described as low income. . . .

Like the research on the factor of race in psychological testing, the above research paints a rather hazy and blurred canvas from which no clear trends are discernible. The client-centered studies discussed above seem to have been conducted with a passable degree of experimental rigor, and the finding of the greater self-exploration of black patients paired with black therapists is, at this time, possibly the only indication of the greater effectiveness of black therapists with black patients. The client-centered studies were also the only ones to explore the issue of race in psychotherapy by looking at psycho-therapeutic process (taped interview rated for client self-exploration). The client-centered studies, however, were only concerned with an initial inter-view or single interview, and the question that arises now is whether or not the greater self-exploration of black patients with black therapists would have still been evident during the middle of therapy. Barrett and Perlmutter[5] have made the distinction between the intake interview and following ses-sions with the recommendation that the black client might benefit more from an intake with a fellow black although once into the system, a competent white counselor might serve equally as well. The client-centered studies have only looked at process in the single interview situation, and rather than providing information about therapeutic process in general as regards race, may have only underscored the importance of providing the black client with a black interviewer when he is possibly most apprehensive, namely during initiation into a strange, new program. There is also some evidence that black inpatients do better when they can interact with black ward personnel.

It is evident that current research into the role of race in counseling and psychotherapy and into blacks' racial preference in helpers is too scanty to permit any definite conclusions. There is some evidence[2,5,12,31] that blacks do respond well to competent whites filling helper roles. This is confirmed by the studies by Brieland[6] and Dubey,[14] which indicated that competence is more important than race of helper when blacks were asked to indicate hypotheti-cal preferences. There is then no firm research evidence at this point to in-dicate that blacks would do appreciably better with black rather than white therapists. To invoke the old cliché, more research is needed in this area, and the most likely avenues are therapeutic process (*i.e.,* an examination of what does go on in therapy when the patient is black and the therapist is black or white), and therapeutic outcome (*i.e.,* a follow-up comparison of blacks treated by blacks and blacks treated by whites).

## Conclusions

1. In psychological testing with blacks, the factor of the race of the examiner is probably no more salient than any other aspect of the tester, such as age, sex, and individual personality characteristics.
2. Black psychiatric inpatients seem to improve more when they have black ward personnel with whom to interact.

3. There is some evidence that white psychiatric residents see white psychiatric outpatients as more acceptable for treatment than black outpatients.

4. Competence is more important than race when blacks are either asked for hypothetical preferences for professional service givers, or when they have passed through a counseling program.

5. There is some evidence that, for optimal results, black patients should be paired with black staff for the intake interview.

6. Despite much clinical speculation about the possible inability of white clinicians to help black patients, there is little evidence to suggest that this is the case. In fact there is no research on therapeutic outcome comparing black and white therapists with black patients.

7. More research needs to be done on the possible effects of clinician's race on the black patient. Such research should focus especially on therapeutic process and therapeutic outcome.

8. There is some evidence that the label "Negro" was preferred to the label "Black" by lower class blacks five years ago.

## REFERENCE NOTES

1. Adams, P. 1970. Dealing with racism in biracial psychiatry. J. Amer. Acad. Child Psychiat. 9:33–43.
2. Backner, B. 1970. Counselling black students: any place for Whitey? J. Higher Ed. 41:630–637.
3. Banks, G., Berenson, B. and Carkhuff, R. 1967. The effects of counsellor race and training upon counselling process with Negro clients in the initial interviews. J. Clin. Psychol. 23:70–72.
4. Banks, W. 1972. The differential effects of race and social class in helping. J. Clin. Psychol. 28:90–92.
5. Barrett, F. and Perlmutter, F. 1972. Black clients and white workers: a report from the field. Child Welfare 51:19–24.
6. Brieland, D. 1969. Black identity and the helping person. Children 16:170–176.
7. Bucky, S. and Banta, T. 1972. Racial factors in test performance. Develpm. Psychol. 6:7–13.
8. Burrell, L. and Rayder, N. 1971. Black and white students' attitudes toward white counsellors. J. Negro Ed. 40:48–52.
9. Caldwell, M. and Knight, D. 1970. Section B: the effect of Negro and White Examiners on Negro intelligence test performance. J. Negro Ed. 39:177–179.
10. Calnek, M. 1970. Racial factors in countertransference: the black therapist and the black client. Amer. J. Orthopsychiat. 40:39–46.
11. Carkhuff, R. and Pierce, R. 1967. Differential effects of therapist race and social class upon patient depth of self-exploration in the initial clinical interview. J. Cons. Psychol. 31:632–634.
12. Cimbolic, P. 1972. Counsellor race and experience effects on black clients. J. Cons. Clin. Psychol. 39:328.
13. Davis, W. and Gillette, A. 1969. Relationship between patients' responses to objective tests and examiners' characteristics. Psychol. Reports 25:487–491.
14. Dubey, S. 1970. Blacks' preference for black professionals, businessmen, and religious leaders. Public Opinion Quart. 34:113–116.
15. France, K. 1973. Effects of "white" and "black" examiner voices on IQ scores of children. Develpm. Psychol. 8:144.
16. Gardner, W. 1972. The differential effects of race, education, and experience in helping. J. Clin. Psychol. 28:87–89.

17. Gould, L. and Klein, E. 1971. Performance of black and white adolescents on intellectual and attitudinal measures as a function of race of tester. J. Cons. Clin. Psychol. 37:195–200.

18. Grier, W. 1967. When the therapist is Negro: Some effects on the treatment process. Amer. J. Psychiat. 123:1587–1591.

19. Grier, W. and Cobbs, P. 1968. Black Rage. Basic Books, New York.

20. Jones, B. et al. 1970. Problems of black psychiatric residents in white training institutes. Amer. J. Psychiat. 127:798–803.

21. Lawrence, L. 1970. On the role of the black mental health professional. Presented to American Public Health Association combined session with American Orthopsychiatric Association regional meeting, Houston.

22. Lessing, E. and Zagorin, S. 1972. Black power ideology and college students' attitudes toward their own and other racial groups. J. Pers. Soc. Psychol. 21:61–73.

23. Lowinger, P. and Dobie, S. 1968. The attitudes of the psychiatrist about his patient. Comprehensive Psychiat. 9:627–632.

24. Rosen, H. and Frank, J. 1964. Negroes in psychotherapy. In Mental Health of the Poor, F. Riessman, J. Cohen and A. Pearl, eds. Free Press, New York.

25. Sager, C., Brayboy, T. and Waxenberg, B. 1972. Black patient-white therapist. Amer. J. Orthopsychiat. 42:415–423.

26. Sattler, J. 1970. Racial "experimenter effects" in experimentation, testing, interviewing, and psychotherapy. Psychol. Bull. 73:137–160.

27. Schacter, J. and Butts, H. 1968. Transference and countertransference in interracial analyses. J. Amer. Psychoanal. Assoc. 16:792–808.

28. Solkoff, N. 1972. Race of the experimenter as a variable in research with children. Develpm. Psychol. 7:70–75.

29. Turner, C. and Spivack, G. 1971. Staff-patient interaction, race and patient behavior on a psychiatric ward. Ment. Hyg. 55:499–503.

30. Vontress, C. 1969. Cultural barriers in the counselling relationship. Pers. Guid. J. 48:11–17.

31. Winston, A., Pardes, H., and Papernik, D. 1972. Inpatient treatment of blacks and whites. Arch. Gen. Psychiat. 26:405–409.

# Socioeconomic Status and Traditional Treatment Approaches Reconsidered*

*Raymond P. Lorion*

A WARNING SOUNDED by Hollingshead and Redlich (1958) more than a decade ago remains equally pertinent today:

The suggestion that different social classes receive different treatment for mental illness may come as a shock, but to repress facts because they are distasteful and

* From *Psychological Bulletin*, 1973, Vol. 79, No. 4, 263–270. © Copyright 1973 by the American Psychological Association. Reprinted by permission.

incongruent with cherished values may lead to consequences even more serious than those we are trying to escape by substituting fantasy for reality [p. 4].

Given the critical discrepancy between the demand for mental health services (Zax & Cowen, 1972) and their current or projected availability (Albee, 1969), it is becoming increasingly important to identify patient populations for whom given therapeutic interventions are effective. Accordingly, Strupp and Bergin (1969) identify as the principal empirical question for future research in therapy: "What specific therapeutic interventions produce specific changes in specific patients under specific conditions [p. 20]?" While this is an extremely complex question, it must be resolved if services are to be allocated realistically.

To plan optimal mental health services for low-income individuals, research findings dealing with their experiences in applying for outpatient treatment at mental health facilities must be critically assessed. Notwithstanding the availability of relevant data, programs continue to be designed and operated, based on strongly held views without empirical grounding. Given the recent proliferation of innovative treatment approaches for the poor (e.g., Guerney, 1969; Minuchin, Montavo, Guerney, Rosman, & Schumer, 1967; Small, 1971; Sobey, 1970), therapists' treatment options have increased dramatically. Economic factors decrease the likelihood that such patients will be assigned to classical therapy approaches. Lerner (1972) raises several important issues relative to such decisions and emphasizes the need for careful considerations of therapeutic effectiveness lest two separate yet unequal treatment systems evolve—one for the poor and another for the well-to-do. In this context, the present paper reviews findings dealing with low-income patients applying for mental health services at clinics emphasizing traditional treatment approaches.

# Class IV Versus Class V

Defining a group's characteristics is an essential precondition to considering its experiences! The most widely used instrument for determining socioeconomic status in psychotherapy research has been the Hollingshead Index of Social Position, developed for use in the New Haven community study (Hollingshead & Redlich, 1958). Initially, the Index defined class status in terms of three variables: area of residence, occupation, and educational background. Later, it was revised to exclude residence (Hollingshead, 1957) and a correlation of .97 between these two forms has been reported (Myers & Bean, 1968). The Index identifies five socioeconomic status levels, the highest being Class I; the lowest, Class V. Table 1 summarizes the major characteristics of the classes. Although the Index was developed specifically for the New Haven community in the 1950s, it is assumed to have some continuing

Table 1

*Occupational, Educational, and Familial Characteristics of Five Socioeconomic Status Levels*

| Class | Occupational level | Educational level | Family structure |
|---|---|---|---|
| I | Salaried positions in policy-making executive level; private-practice professionals | Professional degrees; A.B. level and beyond | Modal nuclear family of parents and children, with stability encouraged |
| II | Salaried positions in business and professions; minor professionals included | A.B. level or partial college | Modal nuclear family of parents and children with stability encouraged |
| III | "Middle-class" administrative, clerical, sales, technical, and semiprofessional positions | High school diploma | Modal nuclear family of parents and children with stability encouraged |
| IV | "Working-class" skilled and semiskilled manual occupations in unionized trades and industries | High school or technical school diploma with some below tenth grade | Modal nuclear family often three generations, instability more common than I–III |
| V | "Poor" semiskilled and unskilled manual occupations nonunionized with irregular employment | High school diploma infrequent with many not completing eighth grade | Modal nuclear family extended to 3–4 generations; divorce, separation, and instability common |

*Note.* The socioeconomic status levels are referenced in Hollingshead and Redlich, 1958.

generality. Future revision of this and related indices, however, should reflect the profound educational, economic, and social changes of the last two decades—changes felt mostly by low-income groups. Recent studies of low-socioeconomic-status groups continue to rely on the Index as the critical socioeconomic status measure, without correction for ongoing social change. Findings to be reviewed must be evaluated with this limitation in mind.

The two low-income groups (Classes IV and V) have generally been perceived as similar on the basis of certain commonly shared characteristics. Both are typically involved in manual occupations, are removed from the middle- and upper-class "prestige race," are "down-to-earth," are pragmatically oriented (Miller & Riessman, 1969), tend to live in informal, comfortable relationships with others, and appreciate the affectionate bite of humor (Gans, 1962). These communalities notwithstanding, it is misleading to ignore significant differences between these two groups and thus to consider them as a homogeneous segment of the population.

Miller and Riessman (1969) suggest that the unskilled, irregular, Class V worker lacks the disciplined, structured, working-class approach. He is less able to cope with life's demands because of its seeming hopelessness. Although higher socioeconomic status groups neither admire nor understand the Class IV working man, they can appreciate the products of his skill and efforts. The poor, however, are objects of the prejudice and lack of concern of all other classes, including Class IV. Class V members are far less likely to attain middle-class goals and possessions than are working-class members. Labor unions, a prime means of organization and political power for the working class, are often inaccessible to the Class V worker. The combination of economic insecurity and familial instability limits the poor to a crisis reactive existence (Miller, 1964) not generally experienced by Class IV members. Class V existence is further characterized by a lack of control over the forces governing an individual's existence (Alinsky, 1967; Haggstrom, 1964).

Differentiations among Class V members are themselves extensive (Riessman, Cohen, & Pearl, 1964). The poor include unskilled and irregularly employed whites and nonwhites, migrant farm workers, numerous minority group members, ghetto dwellers, and tenant farmers. Sarbin (1970) notes that Class V consists of both the respectable and the degraded poor, the latter being continual participants in a culture of poverty. Inclusion in such a culture identifies one as "disinherited" and thereby as "not included in the collectivity that makes up the 'real' society of 'real' people [Rainwater, 1970, p 9]."

While the preceding account is descriptive and anecdotal, it suggests the need to avoid generalized references to the "lower classes." Classes IV and V include different groups with differing life styles—a distinction typically ignored in the findings reviewed.

Fishman (1969) and Thomas and Sillen (1972) are strongly critical of the relative absence of empirical data about the feelings, motivations, and behavior of the poor, both white and nonwhite. A similar lack is also true for the working class. While Gans (1962) and Minuchin et al. (1967) provide some insights into the life-styles of the poor, more rigorous, integrated evaluations of ego strengths, problem-solving capacities, and cognitive organizations are needed for these groups. Allen (1970) identifies needed areas of research with the poor and emphasizes the contribution that such studies would make. At present, there is little scientific data about such matters.

While many innovative treatment approaches are ahistorical (Small, 1971; Sobey, 1970; Yamamoto & Goin, 1965), traditional therapies tend more to consider knowledge of the cultural background of patients in trying to understand the evolution of a patient's disorder (Savitz, 1952). Lerner (1972) questions whether in the absence of such knowledge it is possible for the therapist to empathize optimally with a patient and hence establish therapeutic relationships comparable to those observed with middle- and upper-class patients. This caution must be seriously considered in an assessment of previous research findings with low-income groups.

Furthermore, therapeutic contracts and goals must recognize and operate within the realistic limits of the patient's environment (Chess, Clark, & Thomas, 1953; Green, 1946). To ignore the social reality of a patient's existence while attempting to implement change in therapy may be self-defeating. Failure may often follow when the environment into which a patient must return will not accept such change (Thomas & Sillen, 1972); at such time it may be a sign of health for a patient to refuse change and to withdraw from treatment.

Schneiderman (1965) suggests that it might be helpful to the low-income patient if the profesional assesses his adaptive and problem-solving capacities in relation to the situations in which they occur. Without such knowlege, the professional may be subject to ethnocentric prejudgments about the patient's behavior. Healthy middle-class solutions may not be healthy for the problems of low-income people. Cohen (1964) and Fishman (1969) have both suggested that some forms of behavior, deviant by middle-class standards, are the *only* available mastery outlets for low-income individuals and *must* be used to avoid loss of self-esteem or a sense of degradation. Grier and Cobbs (1968) perceive few other alternatives as typically available to ghetto dwellers. For the poor, aggression and acting out against authority figures are important coping devices in dealing with certain ego threats (Grey, 1969). Such behaviors may be necessary substitutes for the low-income person's impulses to cry, plead, or talk things over—each socially unacceptable (Fishman & McCormack, 1969; Silberman, 1964).

## Socioeconomic Status and Treatment

Although Classes IV and V have been described as the most psychiatrically "impaired" segment of society (Srole, Langer, Michael, Opler, & Rennie, 1962), they have the least chance of obtaining professional help in outpatient facilities (Hollingshead & Redlich, 1958; Srole et al., 1962). Kadushin (1969) reports that less than 5% of all patients seen at Manhattan Mental Health Clinics were members of minority groups—a proportion far below general population rates for that area. In the studies reviewed below, socioeconomic status correlates significantly and negatively with acceptance for and duration of individul psychotherapy, with experience level of assigned therapist, but not with a patient's diagnostic category or source of referral. These findings take on greater significance in that the data were drawn from records of clinics in which ability to pay was *not* a condition for treatment.

A number of reports from the New Haven studies indicate that low socioeconomic status is negatively related to acceptance for individual psychotherapy (Hollingshead & Redlich, 1958; Redlich, Hollingshead, Roberts, Robinson, Friedman, & Myers, 1953; Robinson, Redlich, & Myers, 1954). Similarly, the case records reviewed by Schaffer and Myers (1954), Myers and Auld (1955), Redlich (1958), and Myers and Schaffer (1967) confirm the importance of socioeconomic status in treatment decisions. At the New York Veterans Regional Office, being assigned to psychotherapy, rather than to a somatic treatment, was significantly correlated with a patient's socioeconomic status level (Bailey, Warshaw, & Eichler, 1960). Theapist's ratings of patient motivation and acceptability for treatment related significantly and negatively to socioeconomic status for the 22 Veterans Administration clinics surveyed (Bookbinder & Gusman, 1964; Raskin, 1961). Rosenthal and Frank (1958) found through an analysis of case records of 384 applicants for outpatient treatment that psychiatrists refer to therapy persons most like themselves, that is, whites rather than nonwhites and those in the upper rather than in the lower income range. Class V applicants were least likely to be accepted for psychotherapy at the University of Utah Medical School Clinic (Codes, Branch, & Allison, 1962). Shader (1970) noted that low-socioeconomic-status applicants to a walk-in clinic were significantly more likely to receive drugs than individual psychotherapy.

Attrition rates among low-income patients assigned to individual psychotherapy were significantly higher than for their middle- and upper-class controls. Myers and Roberts (1959) observed that low-income applicants accepted for therapy either quit in disgust or were dropped as failures. Low-socioeconomic-status patients seen in Veterans Administration settings terminated prematurely significantly more often than did patients from other socioeconomic status levels (Dengrove & Kutash, 1950); Sullivan, Miller, & Smelser, 1958; Winder & Hersho, 1955).

At the Phipps Psychiatric Clinic, social class and attrition were significantly and negatively related (Imber, Nash, & Stone, 1955; Frank, Gliedman, Imber, Nash, & Stone, 1957; Rosenthal & Frank, 1958; Imber, Frank, Gliedman, Nash, & Stone, 1956). Neither residents nor patients could be "pressured" by clinic administrators to maintain a relationship that was mutually unsatisfying. Nash, Hoehn-Saric, Battle, Stone, Imber, and Frank (1965) report that socioeconomic status related positively to therapist's ratings of patient attractiveness, ease of establishing rapport, and good prognosis, each of which related significantly to treatment duration. A review of 300 case records further confirms the negative relation between socioeconomic status and attrition rates (Katz, Lorr, & Rubenstein, 1958; Lorr, Katz, & Rubenstein, 1958). In addition, Schneiderman (1965), working in a Family Service Clinic, found that with declining socioeconomic status level, there was a greater likihood that the social worker, rather than the patient, would initiate termination.

Social class has thus been shown to be an important determinant of acceptance for, and duration of, individual psychotherapy (Sanua, 1966). Low-socioeconomic-status applicants are significantly less likely to be assigned to individual treatment, and if assigned, are more likely to terminate prematurely. These relations have been observed across a variety of settings in different parts of the country. Generally speaking, low-socioeconomic-status contraindicates individual therapy.

The prepotency of socioeconomic status in treatment decisions is reflected in reports that assignment to therapy is more a function of social class than of diagnosis (Myers & Auld, 1955; Myers & Schaffer, 1967; Robinson, Redlich, & Meyers, 1954). The absence of a relation between treatment disposition and diagnosis has been observed in the records of Veterans Administration clinics (Bailey, Warshaw, & Eichler, 1960), of the Phipps Clinic (Imber et al., 1955, 1956), of the New York State Psychiatric Institute (Budner, Escover, & Malitz, 1964), and of the University of Chicago Medical School (Heine & Trosman, 1960). Among diagnostically comparable low-socioeconomic-status applicants for therapy at the Los Angeles General Hospital, unemployment (Yamamoto & Goin, 1965) or minority group membership (Yamamoto, James, Bloombaum, & Hatter, 1967) caused them to be seen as even less appropriate for therapy.

There has been no systematic verification of Schaffer and Myers' (1954) finding that low-income patients are disproportionately assigned to inexperienced therapists. Studies of low-socioeconomic-status patients in individual therapy have almost exclusively used residents, medical students, or psychology interns as therapists; senior staff members apparently did not treat Class IV or V patients in these studies. This datum indirectly supports the view that socioeconomic status is a determinant of who will treat a patient. While it has not yet been established that experienced therapists produce more positive outcomes (Bergin & Garfield, 1971; Lerner, 1972; Meltzoff & Kornreich, 1970) Sanua's (1966), argument that lower income patients may not appreciate inexperienced therapists deserves consideration.

The tendency to see Class IV and V individuals as part of a blurred, homogeneous, "lower-class" obscures essential empirical questions. It is valid to ask whether treatment outcomes are the same for these two groups. All too often comparative analysis between Classes IV and V has been impossible because samples studied were not even coded with this distinction in mind. That Class IV applicants differed significantly from Class V applicants in acceptance rates for therapy (Coles, Branch, & Allison, 1962) suggests that Class IV and V treatment experiences are not identical. Furthermore, unemployment and minority group membership, characteristics of Class V, significantly differentiated low-income applicants accepted for therapy (Yamamoto & Goin, 1965; Yamamoto et al., 1967). Although far from conclusive, such data underscore the need to identify more systematically, specific socioeconomic-status-related factors involved in treatment decisions.

Conclusions about entering or remaining in therapy drawn from the studies reported, do not establish a relation between socioeconomic status and treatment outcome (Truax & Carkhuff, 1967). Katz, Lorr, and Rubenstein (1958) did not find social class differences among patients designated as "successes" by their therapists; all socioeconomic status levels were represented approximately equally among successful patients. Similar observations have been reported by Rosenthal and Frank (1958), Brill and Storrow (1960), and Coles, Branch, and Allison (1962). Albronda, Dean, and Starkweather (1964) provide suggestive evidence supporting Frank's (1961) view that overcoming reality factors associated with continuation in therapy for low-socio-economic-status patients may reflect an extremely strong motivation for change. After the eleventh interview, low-income patients responded slightly better to treatment than did higher socioeconomic status controls. The potential for positive outcome in traditional treatment approaches with low-income patients has been documented in an important study reported by Lerner (1972). In addition, the economic feasibility of providing such treatment was also supported by Lerner's (1972) findings.

The studies reviewed also ignore the fate of those rejected for, or rejecting, treatment. Brandt (1964) and Riess and Brandt (1965) provide data suggesting that significant numbers of "rejectees" enter treatment elsewhere. Does the low-income "rejectee" apply and meet a similar fate at another mental health facility? Is he accepted for treatment elsewhere? Conceivably, the initially rejected low-income applicant may become part of a pool of repeatedly rejected applicants, accepted low-socioeconomic-status applicants, or successful therapy cases. Data bearing on such questions do not exist!

The observed discrepancy between acceptance and outcome data for low-income therapy patients has generated a number of explanations—few empirically tested. Truax and Carkhuff (1967) suggest that the acceptance data typically reflect prejudices common to the field. Gundlach and Geller (1958), Miller and Mishler (1959), and Koegler and Brill (1967) conclude that selection factors related to socioeconomic status more often meet therapist needs than treatment requirements. Fierman (1965) dismisses all socioeconomic status limitations to treatment as myths with no basis whatsoever in reality. In his view, the very factors used to rationalize exclusion of low-income individuals from treatment justify their need for therapy.

In a satirical essay, Adams and McDonald (1968) point up an analogy between the reception of low-income applicants at clinics and the "cooling-out" practices that con men use on their victims. They suggest that the "real purpose" of the intake interview is to amass evidence that the poor are neither treatable nor motivated. Similarly, McMahon (1964) argues that the fact that therapists "permit" so many of the poor to refuse treatment, without allowing them to understand what they are rejecting, is tantamount to a *"de facto* practice of disengagement from the poor [p. 287]."" Chessick (1971) states that treatment decisions based merely on a patient's economic qualifications violate a basic human right "to be able to receive the best possible medical care regardless of socioeconomic status [p. 37]."

Although the current social climate favors the practice of indicting policymakers for apparent prejudicial distribution of services (Thomas & Sillen, 1972), the soundness of explaining the findings on this basis alone can be challenged. In fact, the data reviewed indicate that Class IV and V applicants simply do not receive, or continue in, individual psychotherapy. The defensibility of the view that rejected or prematurely terminating patients would have profited from therapy as much as "successful" low-socioeconomic-status patients do, is questionable. Furthermore, there is no evidence indicating that terminators did not, in fact, profit to some degree. There are far too many individual difference variables to justify such conclusions without solid objective data. Clearly, it is inequitable for socioeconomic status factors alone to determine who should receive treatment and in what form. The discrepancy between acceptance and outcome data underscores this fact. Equally, it is unreasonable to assume that alternative forms of treatment do disservice to those not receiving individual therapy.

## REFERENCES

ADAMS, P. L., & McDONALD, N. F. Clinical cooling out of poor people. *American Journal of Orthopsychiatry,* 1968, 38, 457–463.

ALBEE, G. W. The relation of conceptual models of disturbed behavior to institutional and manpower requirements. In F. N. Arnhoff, E. A. Rubenstein, & J. C. Speisman (Eds.), *Manpower for mental health.* Chicago: Aldine, 1969.

ALBRONDA, H. F., DEAN, R. L., & STARKWEATHER, J. A. Social class and psychotherapy. *Archives of General Psychiatry,* 1964, 10, 276–283.

ALINSKY, S. D. The poor and the powerful. *Psychiatric Research Reports,* 1967, 21, 22–28.

ALLEN, V. L. (Ed.) *Psychological factors in poverty.* Chicago: Markham, 1970.

BAILEY, M. A., WARSHAW, L., & EICHLER, R. M. Patients screened and criteria used for selecting psychotherapy cases in a mental hygiene clinic. *Journal of Nervous and Mental Disease,* 1960, 130, 72–77.

BERGIN, A. E., & GARFIELD, S. L. *Handbook of psychotherapy and behavior change.* New York: Wiley, 1971.

BOOKBINDER, L. J., & GUSSMAN, L. J. Social attainment, premorbid adjustment, and participation in inpatient psychiatric treatment. *Journal of Clinical Psychology,* 1964, 20, 513–515.

BRANDT, L. W. Rejection of psychotherapy: The discovery of unexpected numbers of pseudo-rejectors. *Archives of General Psychiatry,* 1964, 10, 310–312.

BRILL, N. Q., & STORROW, H. A. Social class and psychiatric treatment. *Archives of General Psychiatry,* 1960, 3, 340–344.

BUDNER, S. S., ESCOVER, H., & MALITZ, S. The relationship of social personality, and psychiatric factors to choice of psychiatric therapy. *Comparative Psychiatry,* 1964, 5, 327–333.

CHESS, S., CLARK, K. B., & THOMAS, A. Importance of cultural patterns in psychotherapy. *Psychiatric Quarterly,* 1953, 27, 102–114.

CHESSICK, R. D. *Why psychotherapists fail.* New York: Science House, 1971.

COHEN, J. Social work and the culture of poverty. In F. Riessman, J. Cohen, & A. Pearl (Eds.), *Mental health of the poor.* New York: Free Press, 1964.

COLES, N. J., BRANCH, C. H. H., & ALLISON, R. B. Some relationships between social class and the practice of dynamic psychotherapy. *American Journal of Psychiatry,* 1962, 118, 1004–1012.

DENGROVE, E., & KUTASH, S. B. Why patients discontinue treatment in a mental hygiene clinic. *American Journal of Psychotherapy,* 1950, 4, 457–472.

FIERMAN, L. B. Myths in the practice of psychotherapy. *Archives of General Psychiatry,* 1965, 12, 408–414.

FISHMAN, J. R. Poverty, race, and violence. *American Journal of Psychotherapy,* 1969, 23, 599–607.

FISHMAN, J. R., & McCORMACK, J. Mental health without walls: Programs for the ghettos. In J. H. Masserman (Ed.), *Current psychiatric therapies,* Vol. 9. New York: Grune & Stratton, 1969.

FRANK, J. D. *Persuasion and healing: A comparative study of psychotherapy.* New York: Schocken Books, 1961.

FRANK, J. D., GLIEDMAN, L. H., IMBER, S. D., NASH, E. H., & STONE, A. R. Why patients leave psychotherapy. *Archives of Neurology and Psychiatry,* 1957, 17, 283–299.

GANS, H. J. *The urban villagers.* New York: Free Press, 1962.

GREEN, A. W. Social values and psychotherapy. *Journal of Personality,* 1946, 14, 199–228.

GREY, A. L. Social class and the psychiatric patient: A study in composite character. In A. L. Grey, (Ed.), *Class and personality in society.* New York: Atherton, 1969.

GRIER, W. H., & COBBS, P. M. *Black rage.* New York: Bantam, 1968.

GUERNEY, B. *Psychotherapeutic agents: New roles for nonprofessionals, parents, and teachers.* New York: Holt, Rinehart & Winston, 1969.

GUNDLACH, R. H., & GELLER, M. The problem of early termination: Is it really the terminee? *Journal of Consulting Psychology,* 1958, 22, 410.

HAGGSTROM, W. C. The power of the poor. In F. Riessman, J. Cohen, & A. Pearl (Eds.), *Mental health of the poor.* New York: Free Press, 1964.

HEINE, R. W., & TROSMAN, H. Initial expectations of the doctor-patient interaction as a factor in continuance in psychotherapy. *Psychiatry,* 1960, 23, 275–278.

HOLLINGSHEAD, A. B. *Two-factor index of social position.* New Haven: Author, 1957.

HOLLINGSHEAD, A. B., & REDLICH, F. C. *Social-class and mental illness.* New York: Wiley, 1958.

IMBER, S. D., NASH, E. H., & STONE, A. R. Social class and duration of psychotherapy. *Journal of Clinical Psychology,* 1955, 11, 281–294.

IMBER, S. D., FRANK, J. D., GLIEDMAN, L. H., NASH, E. H., & STONE, A. R. Suggestibility, social class, and the acceptance of psychotherapy. *Journal of Clinical Psychology,* 1956, 12, 341–344.

KADUSHIN, C. *Why people go to psychiatrists.* New York: Atherton, 1969.

KATZ, M. M., LORR, M., & RUBENSTEIN, E. A. Remainer patient attributes and their relation to subsequent improvement in psychotherapy. *Journal of Consulting Psychology,* 1958, 22, 411–413.

KOEGLER, R. R., & BRILL, N. Q. *Treatment of psychiatric outpatients.* New York: Appleton-Century-Crofts, 1967.

LERNER, B. *Therapy in the ghetto.* Baltimore: John Hopkins University Press, 1972.

LORR, M., KATZ, M. M., & RUBENSTEIN, E. A. The prediction of length of stay in psychotherapy. *Journal of Consulting Psychology,* 1958, 22, 320–327.

McMAHON, J. T. The working class psychiatric patient: A clinical view. In F. Riessman, J. Cohen, & A. Pearl (Eds.), *Mental health of the poor.* New York: Free Press, 1964.

MELTZOFF, J., & KORNREICH, M. *Research in psychotherapy.* New York: Atherton, 1970.

MILLER, S. M. The American lower-classes: A typological approach. In F. Riessman, J. Cohen, & A. Pearl (Eds.), *Mental health of the poor.* New York: Free Press, 1964.

MILLER, S. M., & MISHLER, E. G. Social class, mental illness, and American psychiatry: An expository review. *Millbank Memorial Fund Quarterly,* 1959, 37, 174–199.

MILLER, S. M., & RIESSMAN, F. The working-class subculture: A new view. In A. L. Grey (Ed.), *Class and personality in society.* New York: Atherton, 1969.

MINUCHIN, S., MONTALVO, B., GUERNEY, B. G., ROSMAN, B. L., & SCHUMER, F. *Families of the slums: An exploration of their structure and treatment.* New York: Basic Books, 1967.

MYERS, J. K., & AULD, F. Some variables related to outcome of psychotherapy. *Journal of Clinical Psychology,* 1955, 11, 51–54.

MYERS, J. K., & BEAN, L. L. *A decade later: A follow-up of social class and mental illness.* New York: Wiley, 1968.

MYERS, J. K., & ROBERTS, B. H. *Family and class dynamics in mental illness.* New York: Wiley, 1959.

MYERS, J. K., & SCHAFFER, L. Social stratification and psychiatric practice: A study of an outpatient clinic. In S. K. Weinberg (Eds.), *The sociology of mental disorders: Analysis and readings in psychiatric sociology.* Chicago: Aldine, 1967.

Nash, E. H., Hoehn-Saric, R., Battle, C. C., Stone, A. R., Imber, S. D., & Frank, J. D. Systematic preparation of patients for short-term psychotherapy II: Relation to characteristics of patient, therapist and the psychotherapeutic process. *Journal of Nervous and Mental Disease,* 1956, **140,** 374–383.

Rainwater, L. Neutralizing the disinherited: Some psychological aspects of understanding the poor. In V. L. Allen, *Psychological factors in poverty.* Chicago: Markham, 1970.

Raskin, A. Factors therapists associate with motivation to enter psychotherapy. *Journal of Clinical Psychology,* 1961, **17,** 62–65.

Redlich, F. C. Social aspects of psychotherapy. *American Journal of Psychiatry,* 1958, **114,** 800–805.

Redlich, F. C., Hollingshead, A. B., Roberts, B. H., Robinson, H. A., Friedman, L. Z., & Myers, J. K. Social structure and psychiatric disorders. *American Journal of Psychiatry,* 1953, **109,** 729–734.

Riess, B. F., & Brandt, L. W. What happens to applicants for psychotherapy? *Community Mental Health Journal,* 1965, **1,** 175–180.

Riessman, F., Cohen, J., & Pearl, A. *Mental health of the poor.* New York: Free Press, 1964.

Robinson, H. A., Redlich, F. C., & Myers, J. K. Social structure and psychiatric treatment. *American Journal of Orthopsychiatry,* 1954, **24,** 307–316.

Rosenthal, D., & Frank, J. D. The fate of psychiatric clinic outpatients assigned to psychotherapy. *Journal of Nervous and Mental Disorders,* 1958, **127,** 330–343.

Sanua, V. D. Sociocultural aspects of psychotherapy and treatment: A review of the literature. In L. E. Abt & B. F. Riess (Eds.), *Progress in clinical psychology.* New York: Grune & Stratton, 1966.

Sarbin, T. R. The culture of poverty, social identity, and cognitive outcomes. In V. L. Allen (Ed.), *Psychological factors in poverty.* Chicago: Markham, 1970.

Savitz, H. A. The cultural background of the patient as part of the physician's armamentarium. *Journal of Abnormal and Social Psychology,* 1952, **47,** 245–254.

Schaffer, L., & Myers, J. K. Psychotherapy, and social stratification. *Psychiatry,* 1954, **17,** 83–93.

Schneiderman, L. Social class, diagnosis, and treatment. *American Journal of Orthopsychiatry,* 1965, **35,** 99–105.

Shader, R. I. The walk-in service: An experience in community care. In T. Rothman (Ed.), *Changing patterns in psychiatric care.* New York: Crown, 1970.

Silberman, C. E. *Crisis in black and white.* New York: Vintage, 1964.

Small, L. *The briefer psychotherapies.* New York: Brunner & Mazel, 1971.

Sobey, F. *The non-professional revolution in mental health.* New York: Columbia University Press, 1970.

Srole, L., Langer, T. S., Michael, S. T., Opler, M. K., & Rennie, T. A. C. *Mental health in the metropolis: The midtown Manhattan study.* New York: McGraw-Hill, 1962.

Strupp, H. H., & Bergin, A. E. Some empirical and conceptual bases for coordinated research in psychotherapy. *International Journal of Psychiatry,* 1969, **7,** 17–90.

Sullivan, P. L., Miller, C., & Smelser, W. Factors in length of stay and progress in psychotherapy. *Journal of Consulting Psychology,* 1958, **22,** 1–9.

Thomas, A., & Sillen, S. *Racism and psychiatry.* New York: Brunner & Mazel, 1972.

Truax, C. B., & Carkhuff, R. R. *Toward effective counseling and psychotherapy.* Chicago: Aldine, 1967.

Winder, A. E., & Hersho, M. The effect of social class in the length and type of psychotherapy in a Veterans' Administration Mental Hygiene Clinic. *Journal of Clinical Psychology,* 1955, **11,** 77–79.

Yamamoto, J., & Goin, M. K. Social class factors relevant for psychiatric treatment. *Journal of Nervous and Mental Disease,* 1965, **142,** 332–339.

Yamamoto, J., James, Q. C., Bloombaum, M., & Hatter, J. Racial factors in patient selection. *American Journal of Psychiatry,* 1967, **124,** 630–636.

ZAX, M., & COWEN, E. L. *Abnormal psychology: Changing conceptions.* New York: Holt, Rinehart & Winston, 1972.

---

# The Women's Movement and Psychotherapy*

*Carol Wesley*

FEMINISTS HAVE ATTACKED orthodox approaches to counseling on the grounds that they have promoted a sexist and male supremacist ideology using the stereotypes of sex roles as criteria for a double standard of normalcy. This paper sets forth the theories of feminine psychology as found in the paradigms of Freudianism, neo-Freudianism, and learning theory and discusses the implications of such ideology for the client-therapist relationship. It also suggests suitable alternatives to the traditional models of therapeutic intervention that can be used by social workers to help their clients, male or female, realize their full potential as human beings.

Marmor interprets the salient features of the classical psychoanalytic view of femininity as follows:

○ Anatomy is destiny: Women's nature is determined solely by her anatomy, specifically by the fact that she does not possess a penis. Thus the formation of the female's personality is influenced by her ability to reproduce. The psychologically normal woman is concerned chiefly with the roles of wife and mother.

○ Penis envy: Because she does not have a penis, the female child considers herself defective and is therefore naturally envious of the male. The woman's clitoris is inadequate to provide libidinal gratification and this loss is only partially compensated for by the possibility of giving birth to a male child.

○ Faulty development of the superego: Just as the feminine castration complex pushes the girl away from her mother into an Oedipal attachment with her father, the male castration complex pushes the boy away from his father and to his mother. Because the girl has more difficulty resolving the Oedipal conflict, she has a lesser capacity for sublimation.

○ Masochism and passivity: As a result of the woman's general feelings of inferiority and inadequacy, aggressiveness is focused inward, which results in a masochistic personality. Furthermore, because of her sexual role as receptor, the woman naturally develops passive tendencies in all social roles.[1]

* © 1975 National Association of Social Workers, Inc. Reprinted from *Social Work*, Vol. 20, No. 2 (March 1975), pp. 120–124 with permission of the publishers and the author.

# Neo-Freudian View

There is currently a call for a reevaluation of the Freudian representation of woman's condition in a male-dominated society and of the Freudian stereotype that women are passive, submissive, dependent, and nonassertive—all innate character traits that are considered desirable and normal.[2] Thus classical psychoanalytic theory is male oriented and emphasizes the male as the model for normalcy. Rice and Rice point out:

> What is more significant, however, is how anatomical differences have been built by psychoanalytic theorists into a powerful system of psychological, moral, intellectual, and societal values that transcend mere physiology.[3]

Lidz and Erikson, two neo-Freudians whose works are widely read in courses in human growth, betray similar biases of feminine inferiority. Lidz suggests that two crises face the adolescent female. She must learn to resolve the dilemma of wanting to show that "her intellect is a good as a boy's," while realizing that she is inadequate because of her anatomy. And she must resolve these inadequacies by limiting her self-expression and seeking a man who will vicariously grant her some status through his achievements.[4]

In *Childhood and Society,* Erikson furthers the stereotyped concept of woman as wife and mother by devoting seventeen pages to the development of the male adolescent and a single paragraph to that of the female. He writes:

> . . . the sister's crisis will come when she becomes a mother and when the vicissitudes of child training will perforce bring to the fore the infantile identification with her mother.[5]

Erikson's negligence implies that, in contrast to the male, the female is of little importance.

Lidz stresses rigid sex-linked roles within the family as a determining factor of personality and sexuality as well as a reinforcement of the general integrative development of the offspring. He writes:

> . . . the spouses must form a coalition as parents, maintain the boundaries between the generations, and adhere to their respective sex-linked roles. . . . Either a cold and unyielding mother or a weak and ineffectual father is apt to distort the family structure and a child's development. . . . Perhaps it is pertinent to note that a cold and aloof mother can be particularly detrimental to a daughter who requires childhood experiences with a nurturing mother to attain the maternal characteristics she will need as a woman. . . .[6]

In another work, Lidz again suggests the inferiority of the female in relation to marital schism and skew. The mother in the skewed family is characterized by feelings of inferiority. Because she is unable to accept her passive role in life, she seeks to live vicariously through her son. The mother in the schismatic family is again seen to be lacking self-esteem, as a result of her childhood trauma of "being a girl." She therefore inhibits her daughter's growth by failing to model appropriate role behavior.[7]

Erikson attempts to characterize some of woman's psychological traits as the direct derivation of her anatomical structure. He found that psychosexual determinants were present in children's play and advanced the thesis that women are prone to be more concerned with "inner space," as opposed to men's preoccupation with "outer space." In a series of experiments, Erikson found boys' conception of space to resemble the phallic-intrusive organization of the male anatomy whereas girls' spatial configurations suggest the inwardly based procreative system. Erikson then suggests that the spatial configurations in children's play symbolize an innate sexual identity that is independent of pressure or reward.[8]

In a later effort to clarify his earlier statements in response to the feminists Kate Millet and Elizabeth Janeway, Erikson emphasizes that "the modalities of a woman's existence reflect the ground plan of her body *among other things*—as men's modalities reflect that of the male body" and, further, that the combination of personality, history, and anatomy influence human fate.[9] Thus Erikson suggests that the differentiation of spatial configurations observed in his experiment may reflect the manner in which each sex experiences existence in space, but it is the totality of the person that influences spatial differences. Erikson goes on to qualify his views in light of feminist ideology by suggesting that the development of these findings should be explored further. However, he concludes the article by once more stereotyping women. He notes that as birth control has liberated women to choose roles other than those of mother or spinster, so arms control should liberate men to choose roles other than those of the warrior or the conqueror. Thus Erikson again correlates feminine identity with biological function.

## Effect on Behavior

In contrast to the psychoanalytic paradigm, modeling theory suggests that all behavior is learned. Thus the child learns male-female stereotypes from his parents and others around him.[10] Karlen observes that by the age of 3 children have established their sex role. Boys, for example, show far more aggression than girls; they tend to vent it on other boys and to respond to it with counteraggression. Girls show less aggression and, when they do show it, it is usually prosocial.[11] In America, aggressiveness is a traditionally male sex-typed behavior in contrast to the feminine trait of passivity. Girls are taught that such traits as dependence, passivity, and conformity are desirable; boys are taught to inhibit such characteristics. Kagan writes:

> Sex-role standards dictate that the female must feel needed and desired by a man. She must believe that she can arouse a male sexually, experience deep emotion,

and heal the psychological wounds of those she loves. . . . The American male traditionally has been driven to prove that he was strong and powerful; the female to prove that she was capable of forming a deeply emotional relationship that brought satisfaction and growth to the partner—sweetheart or child.[12]

According to Kagan, sex-role differences among children arise from three sources: (1) A child reared at home is inclined to behave like the other members of his sex. Thus the young male child identifies with the father or surrogate father and emulates his attributes; these "masculine" characteristics are thus passed on to another generation. (2) The child is vulnerable to peer-group pressure. The boy who is clumsy on the football field is less likely to question his sexual identity if he lives in a community that idealizes intellectual pursuits as opposed to athletic prowess. (3) Sex-role identity relies heavily on social interaction in adolescence. The ability to maintain sex-role-linked relationships is a prime factor in the adult sex-role standard.[13]

Although hormonal influence has been suggested as an argument to explain premenstrual anxiety, religious and cultural attitudes may also affect the way a woman reacts to menstruation.[14] Just as children learn that women are passive and unassertive, they also learn that women reaction emotionally to reproduction.

Paige cites a distinct correlation between menstrual distress and social factors in members of particular religious groups. Among Jews, for example, traditional taboos and rituals are connected with menstruation, and the menstruating woman is looked on as sexually unclean and an outcast until she is purified. Thus those women who observe the social and hygienic rituals and who think that sex during menstruation is unclean and embarrassing are most likely to have menstrual distress. Following the dictates of her religion concerning motherhood and original sin, the Catholic woman may view menstrual distress as an integral part of being a woman. Paige goes on to say that those women who believe the woman's place is in the home, who are virgins, and who have no career plans are likely to have severe menstrual symptoms.[15]

Menstrual symptoms can also be explained by social rigidity—the degree of separateness between the sexes, generations, or ethnic groups that exists in society. Highly rigid societies have the strongest menstrual restrictions and the highest degree of male solidarity, which would influence the menstrual attitudes and practices of women.[16]

Thus the girl is taught not only how to think about her reproductive role, but how to think about herself in intellectual terms. Little girls are taught at an early age to have certain aspirations and standards of achievement. Data even suggest that independent, bright, and creative girls receive less affection and less attention from their teachers than do boys.[17] For the adult woman, the ramifications of such a childhood lead to only one source of gratification—the family. Levine, Kamin, and Levine warn:

> Too often, going to a psychiatrist because of intense frustration in this type of situation is merely asking for trouble. A woman may be confronted for being "bad" or "sick," for not fulfilling the role of a "normal" woman. . . . She can "cope" or adapt to the scene, modify her aspirations, suffer in silence, get herself hospitalized, or walk out. . . .[18]

Chesler suggests that women enter therapy with the same sense of urgency and desperation with which they enter marriage. They are encouraged to take part in therapy just as they are to take part in marriage. Both are socially approved institutions; both maintain social control. Chesler concludes: (1) Women "go crazy" more often than men for a number of reasons and that this craziness tends to be self-destructive rather than destructive of others. (2) Most females diagnosed as neurotic are really victims of societal demands and discrimination and are neither "sick" nor "mentally ill." (3) The therapist-client relationship reinforces a value system that is psychologically damaging to the client and emotionally rewarding to the therapist.[19] In this society, it is the female prerogative rather than a male privilege to seek help with emotional problems. The male mystique requires stoicism.

> Society seems to be proclaiming that, if a woman has problems, it is all right for her to get sick as long as she is only "a little sick." She may have any set of feelings she wishes . . . as long as her house, husband and children are at least minimally cared for. However, she *must not* act-out her anger, pain or frustration or society will exact a price through its institutions . . . in the mental hospital her label will probably lead to treatment that reinforces the socially approved behavior patterns, e.g., passivity and compliance, the resistance to which may have been a factor leading to her institutionalization. In both instances, she receives treatment oriented toward producing the desired degree of social conformity.[20]

Furthermore, Chesler notes that the myth of motherhood exists within the client-therapist relationship—maternity is exclusively a female property; women need to be mothers and to be responsible for the development of the children.[21] Rheingold states:

> St. Augustine said: "Give me other mothers and I will give you another world." I believe that obviation of disturbed mother-child relationships on a large scale would result in signal improvement of psychiatric and social problems.[22]

Women, thus, are responsible for their children to the extent that they are blamed for their offspring's mental problems or praised for their achievements.

## Standards of Normalcy

Gove and Tudor argue that woman's roles in modern industrial society have given her a negative self-image, and a higher incidence of depression—characteristics that promote mental illness.[23] Broverman et al. concur and describe a double standard in the therapeutic framework that contributes to stereotypic labeling and a higher incidence of feminine "neurosis." [24] They hypothesize that clinicians have different concepts of health for men and women and that these attitudes reflect the stereotyped sex-roles that are prevalent in society. Although the clinicians' view of a healthy man does not differ significantly from the conceptions of a healthy adult, the views of a healthy, mature woman do differ substantially. According to clinicians, healthy, mature women are supposed to be more submissive, less independent, less adventurous, less competitive, more excitable in minicrises, more easily hurt, more emotional, more conceited about their appearance, less objective, and less interested in mathematics and science.

It is clear that to be "normal," woman must meet the norms specified by male clinicians. Behavior that is acceptable in one sex is not at all acceptable in the other—in most communities, for instance, the aggressive girl who joins the Little League ball team is considered nonconformist while her brother on the same team is accepted without question.

In studies designed to show sexual bias in the patient-therapist system, Fabrikant has found evidence that supports the Broverman studies. Again the results show that male characteristics are considered positive and female traits are seen as strongly negative. Furthermore, patients and therapists alike still retain many stereotypes, and women who accept the feminine stereotypes of themselves find themselves behaving in norms considered substandard for the mature adult. However, Fabrikant's studies show that this may be changing—evidence points to new attitudes being transmitted to both male and female patients, which suggests that the therapist does not always perpetuate the ideology of male supremacy. Perhaps, Fabrikant suggests, this is a result of the influx of young, less traditional therapists. [25]

Because the testing of hypotheses is never totally objective, the therapist's preconceived notions may influence labeling and promote the higher incidence of mental illness among women. [26] In an experiment at Harvard, Robert Rosenthal showed that if a group of experimenters has one hypothesis about what they expect to find and another group has the opposite one, each group will find evidence to support his own hypothesis. When told that rats had been bred for dullness, the experimenters found that the rats learned to run mazes poorly; when told the rats were bred for brightness, the experimenters found that the rats learned to run the mazes quickly. [27] Thus a therapist who believes women to be passive, conceited, and unassertive will find women to have these qualities, and the therapist who believes women to be strong, assertive, and independent will find evidence to support that hypothesis.

Stevens suggests that the therapist's underlying attitude toward female patients is communicated in subtle and uncontrollable ways. No matter how hard the therapist tries to remain neutral, the client receives the message by the whole stance of the relationship—tone of voice, areas focused on, facial expressions, posture, and demeanor. When the therapist accepts society's prescribed role for women,

> . . . the therapist's unconscious attitude toward his patient is to some extent antitherapeutic. Because his contempt for her is usually ego syntonic for her, it may do no more than perpetuate her own self-contempt; it certainly will not help her overcome that self-contempt.[28]

# Consciousness-Raising

An alternative solution to traditional therapy for women is the consciousness-raising group. In contrast to the psychoanalytic paradigm that fosters stereotyping or the client-centered phenomenological approach that may fail the woman who enters therapy without goals or a clear sense of identity, the consciousness-raising group focuses on changing the social structure and culture through the individual.[29] If the psychoanalyst focuses on personal inner dynamics and the phenomenologist on individual perception, the consciousness-raising group focuses on an explanation for individual conflict, tension, or discomfort in the sociocultural context. Central to the ideology behind consciousness-raising is the belief that the individual, the social structure, and the culture are interrelated. Change generally occurs both within the group and within the individual. Kirsh describes four group processes or stages that build on previous development:

1. *Opening up:* Each member relates experiences leading to understanding, knowledge, and confidence. This results in an intimacy that frees the women to share their opinions, views, and problems. All expressions of feelings are accepted.
2. *Sharing:* The expression of personal problems leads to a realization that an individual's problems are not hers alone, but are common to all. Deep friendships develop as well as a sense of comradeship and community. A final function of this stage is a resolution of personal frustration and self-doubt that can lead to communal action for social change.
3. *Analyzing:* The group goes beyond personal problems and those of a small group and focuses on problems of women and society.
4. *Abstracting:* The group begins to examine social institutions to see how they fulfill human needs and potentials. The group looks at itself as a mass of ideologies that may be used for massive social change.[30]

Change in individuals who attend a consciousness-raising group generally consists of an improved self-image, increased self-acceptance, a greater sense of self-worth, and an improved image of women in general. Women also report more independence, confidence, and higher ambitions. As Allen writes:

> Working together strengthens the group to become a place that provides direction for the individual to discover both the ability to meet her own individual needs

and her role in meeting needs in the women's movement. The group can become a place for us to get encouragement, help, and support to learn, grow, and act, and a place to come back to for criticism for we want to learn from our mistakes.
. Our group then is hopefully becoming a place where women whose lives are meaningless can begin to find meaningful activity.[31]

According to Lazarus, behavior therapists were teaching women to be more assertive and self-sufficient long before Women's Liberation. Such terms as "penis envy" or "castration anxiety" do not exist in the behavioral framework. He quotes Brodsky as follows:

> The C-R [consciousness-raising] group starts with the assumption that the environment, rather than intrapsychic dynamics, plays the major role in the difficulties of the individuals.[32].

Furthermore, behaviorists work on the principle that men and women have been conditioned to the concepts of masculine and feminine. Lazarus writes:

> Behavior therapy is primarily a goal-oriented, problem solving enterprise in which the therapist's didactic role as trainer or teacher-clinician deflects attention from "transference" or the patient-therapist relationship onto significant issues in the client's life outside of the treatment dyad.[33]

Thus behavior modification, which uses such techniques as modeling, reinforcement, and feedback, may help a woman become more assertive, and conflicts over sex roles may be alleviated.[34]

## Implications

The effects of the women's movement on therapy suggest two implications for social work practice and education—the need to train therapists to be effective in helping women achieve their individual potential and the need for individual therapists to be aware of their own social conditioning and biases. Rice and Rice make three suggestions for training therapists: (1) Courses dealing with the psychology of women should be established in the core curriculum of psychotherapy training, thus teaching individuals to be experts on the differences and the individual roles of the two sexes and the cultural and societal myths that may cause discrimination. (2) Therapists should be trained to be "open proponents for alternative life-styles and sex roles." This would insure their active support of change in patients even at the risk of initiating discussion of nontraditional roles. (3) Therapists should be stimulated to see beyond the individual patient and work for social change, thus realizing their potential as agents of change.[35]

This recognition of the therapist's responsibility to the community generates a political view of the client-therapist relationship. The therapist must realize not only that every encounter with the client somehow alters the social system, but also that she (he) bears a two-fold responsibility of supporting the client in the environment as well as supporting the larger system in accepting and coping with new behaviors.[36] Thus the woman may need support in asserting herself within an oppressive status quo, but so may the larger system (the family or organization) need support and guidance in learning to accept the woman's new awareness and life-style.

As Stevens suggested, personal awareness and consciousness are prerequisites for effective psychotherapy.[37] Rice and Rice concur, adding that the therapist

> . . . must be carefully and honestly attuned to his own social conditioning, which influences his attitudes and beliefs, but he must also become cognizant of the inherent social or personal gains he may accrue in resisting change.[38]

Sensitivity training is suggested for both novice and experienced therapists to help them evaluate and remedy personal sex-role bias. Personal consciousness begins with the desire to alleviate existing social injustices, thereby contributing to the liberation of all. As men must learn that it is woman's right to seek self-actualization and personal achievement, so must women learn that men suffer from reciprocal sex-role stereotypes and that male liberation, like female liberation, requires the same self-awareness and honesty.[39] Human liberation is the goal.

## REFERENCE NOTES

1. Judd Marmor, "Changing Patterns of Femininity: Psychoanalytic Implications," in Jean Baker Miller, ed., *Psychoanalysis and Women* (New York: Brunner/Mazel, 1973), pp. 196–203.
2. See Juliet Mitchell, *Psychoanalysis and Feminism* (New York: Pantheon Books, 1974); and Shulamith Firestone, *The Dialectic of Sex* (New York: Bantam Books, 1972).
3. Joy K. Rice and David G. Rice "Implications of the Women's Liberation Movement for Psychotherapy" *American Journal of Psychiatry,* 130 (February 1973) p. 191.
4. Theodore Lidz, *The Person* (New York: Basic Books, 1968). *See* also Mary C. Schwartz, "Sexism in the Social Work Curriculum,' *Journal of Education for Social Work,* 9 (Fall 1973), pp. 65–70.
5. Erik Erikson, *Childhood and Society* (New York: W. W. Norton & Co., 1963), p. 321.
6. Lidz, op. cit., pp. 58–60.
7. Theodore Lidz, *The Origin and Treatment of Schizophrenic Disorders* (New York: Basic Books, 1973), pp. 32–33, 43–44.
8. Erik Erikson, "Womanhood and the Inner Space (1968)," in Jean Strouse, ed., *Women and Analysis* (New York: Grossman, 1974), pp. 291–319.
9. Erik Erikson, "Once More the Inner Space: Letter to a Former Student," ibid., p. 323.
10. Albert Bandura, *Psychological Modeling* (Chicago: Aldine Publishing Co., 1971), p. 17.
11. Arno Karlen, *Sexually and Homosexually* (New York: W. W. Norton & Co., 1971), p. 502.
12. Jerome Kagan, "Check One: Male, Female," *Psychology Today,* 3 ( July 1969), p. 40.
13. Ibid., pp. 52–53.
14. Judith Bardwick, *Psychology of Women* (New York: Harper & Row, 1971), p. 38.

15. Karen E. Paige, "Women Learn to Sing the Menstrual Blues," *Psychology Today,* 7 (September 1973), pp. 41–46.
16. Ibid.
17. Saul Levine et al., "Sexism and Psychiatry," *American Journal of Orthopsychiatry,* 44 (April 1974), p. 331.
18. Ibid., p. 332.
19. Phyllis Chesler, "Men Drive Women Crazy," *Psychology Today,* 5 ( July 1971), p. 18.
20. Ephraim M. Howard and Joyce L. Howard, "Women in Institutions: Treatment in Prisons and Mental Hospitals," in Violet Franks and Vasanti Burtle, eds., *Women and Therapy* (New York: Brunner/Mazel, 1974), p. 378.
21. Phyllis Chesler, *Women and Madness* (New York: Doubleday, 1972), pp. 73–74.
22. Joseph Rheingold, *The Fear of Being a Woman* (New York: Grune and Stratton, 1964), p. 689.
23. *See* Gove and Tudor, "Adult Sex Roles and Mental Illness," *American Journal of Sociology,* 78 ( January 1973), p. 831.
24. Broverman et al., "Sex Role Stereotypes and Clinical Judgments in Mental Health," in Judith Bardwick, ed., *Readings on the Psychology of Women* (New York: Harper & Row, 1972), pp. 320–324.
25. Benjamin Fabrikant, "The Psychotherapist and the Female Patient: Perceptions, Misperceptions and Change," in Franks and Burtle, eds., *Women in Therapy,* pp. 89–109.
26. *See* Naomi Weisstein, "Psychology Constructs the Female, or The Fantasy Life of the Male Psychologist," in Phil Brown, ed., *Radical Psychology* (New York: Harper & Row, 1973), p. 403.
27. Ibid.
28. Barbara Stevens, "The Psychotherapist and Women's Liberation," *Social Work,* 16 ( July 1971), pp. 14–15.
29. Rice and Rice, op. cit., p. 194.
30. Barbara Kirsh, "Consciousness-Raising Groups as Therapy for Women," in Franks and Burtle, eds., *Women and Therapy,* pp. 326–354.
31. Pamela Allen, *Free Space: A Perspective on the Small Group in Women's Liberation* (Washington, N.J.: Times Change Press, 1970), p. 62.
32. Arnold A. Lazarus, "Women in Behavior Therapy," in Franks and Burtle, eds., *Women in Therapy,* p. 228.
33. Ibid., p. 221.
34. Robert E. Alberti and Michael L. Emmons, *Your Perfect Right* (San Luis Obispo, Calif.: Impact, 1974), pp. 69–71; and Fabrikant, op. cit., p. 85.
35. Rice and Rice, op. cit., pp. 194–195.
36. Seymour L. Halleck, *The Politics of Therapy* (New York: Harper & Row, 1972).
37. Stevens, op. cit., p. 12.
38. Rice and Rice, op. cit., p. 195.
39. *See* Abraham Maslow, *Toward a Psychology of Being* (New York: Van Nostrand Reinhold Co., 1968), p. 25.

# Communicating with the Migrant*
*Myrtle R. Reul*

S OCIAL WORKERS all over the country report that as many as half of the low-income families who apply to their agencies for service fail to follow through in a continuing relationship. An examination of this seeming lack of interest pinpoints some of the obstacles to communication with low-income clients, especially migrant farm workers. A major part of the problem is disparity between what the client thinks he will get from the agency and what the agency sees as its function.

The migrant knows he has a problem. He does not come to a social work agency expecting to be told this; he comes seeking a solution. He expects the worker to take over his problem, to solve it by telling him what to do, or by doing it for him. There is usually nothing in the migrant's experience that prepares him for a relationship with a worker who asks how he feels about his problems, or how he feels about his mother. He can see no connection between his problem and this approach to help. He is frustrated in what may be his first attempt to get assistance.

The therapeutic relationship is based on the belief that the condition that brings a client to an agency can be ameliorated by "talking it through." Insight can be gained, and the "talking through" of feelings can provide a catharsis. This is the frame of reference for the therapist or for the agency. It is not the frame of reference for migrants, most of whom have difficulty expressing themselves verbally.

For a worker to communicate with migrants, it is necessary to know something of their life style, how they travel, how they live and work, how they view their world, and how their world is viewed by nonmigrants. This knowledge is essential before a worker can assess whether a migrant is in touch with reality. What is the reality of his experience against the background of his racial or ethnic culture? What is the pattern of his learned communication, both verbal and nonverbal, within his own culture, as well as with those in positions of authority, such as social workers?

My husband and I spent 54 weeks as migrant farm workers, traveling about the country. We worked in the fields, orchards, and packing sheds. We saw many things that adversely affect communication between migrants and nonmigrants. We found the migrant to be part of a distinct subculture whose most obvious feature is poverty—but a poverty more extreme, more secret, more insidious than that found in any ghetto. As early as 1951 the President's

* From Myrtle R. Reul, "Communicating with the Migrant," *Child Welfare*, XLIX:3 (1970):137–145. © Copyright 1970 Child Welfare League of America. Reprinted by permission.

Commission on Migrant Labor reported, "Migrant farm laborers move restlessly over the face of the land, but they neither belong to the land nor does the land belong to them." [1]

Not only are migrants rejected because of their occupation, but there are unique aspects of the migrant subculture that cause isolation. "There is an aloneness for the seasonal worker created by the temporary status of his employment. The two greatest factors which motivate his becoming a migrant worker are: (1) limited work near his own home, and (2) the promise of work or better opportunities somewhere else. Yet his stay in any community can be determined by a whimsical change in the weather—a freeze, a windstorm, hail, an entire crop is wiped out and he and his family are forced to move on, searching for another job." [2]

# Who Are the Migrants?

Within the migrant streams can be found a cross section of all races and of most ethnic groups. There are migrants whose ancestors were among the early colonists and migrants who were born in Mexico or the West Indies. There are migrants who are aged and newborn, those who are physically handicapped, and those who are well.

Migrants have a common fate and a shared experience, but they do not have a common culture. They are bound together by the tasks they do, by the crops they harvest, and it is through this bond that they communicate with each other and the outer world. "Their lives, no matter where they work, are measured by the crops. They talk of personal events and relate them to the harvest. The baby was born in the tomatoes of Ohio. They do not mean these things happened in the fields. They are saying these are the crops that control their lives and became a calendar to record all significant events." [3]

The principal migration of agricultural workers is along five main streams, from the South toward the North and back South. There are also those, mainly freewheelers, who follow a whisper of work, looking always for the gold at the end of the rainbow.

The East Coast Stream, of approximately 50,000 migrants, leads from the Everglades of Florida up the Atlantic seacoast. This stream is made up mainly of Southern-born Negroes, Puerto Ricans, and over 10,000 white and black day-haul workers from Northern cities. The Central River, largest of all with about 150,000 workers, originates in south Texas and moves north on both

---

[1] President's Committe on Migratory Labor, "Migratory Labor in American Agriculture," in *Children in Migrant Families* (Washington, D.C.: Government Printing Office, Children's Bureau, 1960), 2.

[2] Myrtle R. Reul, "Isolation of Farm Workers," *Michigan State Economic Record* ( June 1967), 3.

[3] Myrtle R. Reul, *Where Hannibal Led Us* (New York: Vantage Press, 1967), 102.

sides of the Mississippi. They are mainly Mexican-American, with some Southern Negroes and whites.

About 100,000 workers make up the third stream, which moves up and down the West Coast, staying mainly in California. They are Mexican-Americans, Caucasians, Indians, Negroes, and Orientals. The fourth stream of migrants is found in the Southwest, working in Arizona, New Mexico, and southern California. The predominant culture is Mexican-American, with some Mexicans, Indians, and a few Negroes and whites. The fifth stream is concerned only with the grain harvest and includes about 50,000 workers, mainly white, who originate in Texas and Oklahoma.

## The Art of Communication

Webster defines communication as a two-way process, transmitting and receiving. This implies there must be a sender and a receiver and that each must understand the language of the message to be conveyed, whether verbal or nonverbal. Even more important is the unspoken intent in back of the message; this, too, must be understood. Spiegel identifies the process: "When communication is consummated between persons, the experience is of an almost incommunicable, buoyant sense of openness. . . . There is a sense of 'being on the same wave length,' 'in tune with each other,' 'in touch'."[4]

One reason communication becomes so complicated is that even though an individual defines a relationship, he can invalidate this definition by qualifications that deny his communication. " 'I think you should do that, but it's not my place to tell you so'; in this way he defines the relationship as one in which he tells the other person what to do, but simultaneously denies that he is defining the relationship in this way."[5]

There are four levels on which communication is affected: feeling, thinking, speaking, and behavior. These four levels at times are in conflict with each other. An individual may behave or speak in a way that belies his thinking or his feelings. This is an experience that the migrant often encounters; he senses the prejudice, the distrust, or dislike toward him which may not be expressed in words, but is betrayed in action and in intonation, or is conveyed at the feeling level.

"There is an unspoken contempt for pickers. It is there in making them wait for wages until convenient for the grower to pay. It is there in the way they are addressed . . . The contempt is like an invisible wall. It is an aloofness which gives one the sensation of being unwanted . . . We sensed others were on guard because they did not trust having a migrant farm

---

[4] Rose Spiegel, "Specific Problems of Communication in Psychiatric Conditions," *American Handbook of Psychiatry, Vol. I* (New York: Basic Books, 1959), 914–915.

[5] Jay Haley, *Strategies of Psychotherapy* (New York: Grune and Stratton, 1963), 88.

worker so near. There were some who were afraid. That emotion, too, was transmitted. . . ."[6]

If human communication took place only on the verbal level, the defining of the relationship would be relatively simple. However, human beings not only communicate, but they communicate about the communications. They qualify what they say.

Messages are qualified by (1) facial expression, (2) body movement, (3) intonation. An upward inflection, a slight smile, a hesitation, or silence when an answer is expected can change the entire meaning of a statement. Also, there is appraisal of whether the communication is sincere or deceitful, whether the speaker is serious or joking. In addition, the migrant must understand communication within his own culture, and how it differs from the expectation of the dominant society.

# Conditions Affecting Migrant Communication

## Distrust of Words

The migrants' acceptance of conditions, either working or living, with what has been described as "fatalism" may be a conservation of psychic energy for more immediate things—worry over the baby's cough, having money to get to the next crop, or to buy food, or pay a bill. We noted an intuitive sensitivity migrants have developed to the feeling level of others. This is a sort of "tuning in" to what another is thinking, rather than to what he is saying. Too often for the migrant, the spoken word does not ring true.

They are promised jobs that may not materialize because growers advertise for 100 workers when they need 50. In communities where the tourist season coincides with the harvest, migrants find food at increased prices when they arrive. They are victimized by loan sharks, high-pressure salesmen, and sometimes their own crew leaders or fellow migrant workers.

The attitude of an individual under these circumstances is one of basic mistrust. The migrant is conditioned to expect deceit in words.

## Leisurely Tempo of Speaking

Some of the ethnic cultures represented by migrants employ a leisurely tempo in their conversation or carry out a prescribed dialogue before the main points of a question are answered. They feel it is "rude" to discuss serious topics without a sort of "warmup" period in which individuals evaluate each other. This is in some ways related to the establishing of a relationship with a schizophrenic client. The migrant, like the schizophrenic, may fear close rela-

---

[6] Reul, *op. cit.,* 268–269.

tionships. In this situation he must come to regard the worker as a less-threatening force than other people; therefore, any relationship must be established slowly, at a pace the migrant determines.

## Impoverishment of Vocabulary

The improverishment of the migrant's vocabulary is, of course, a barrier to communication. The migrant child hears little speech in complete sentences or about topics outside the personal experiences of his family. He is exposed to incorrect grammar and inaccurate pronunciation. There may be a good deal of dialogue between the mother and the infant. This may represent not so much an effort by her to teach the child words as a need to view the infant as a love object. The baby or young child is the chief source of entertainment for the migrant family. Parents and older siblings spend hours playing with the baby. This ends abruptly with the advent of the next child, who becomes the center of attention while the older child is expected to assume responsibility for himself and those younger.

Abrupt shifts in attention and accompanying feelings of desertion can account for underdeveloped ability to comprehend language. Bernstein discusses another aspect of development that applies to migrant children, namely, the tendency for adults to exercise arbitrary authority, reflected in such phrases as "Do it 'cause I told you to." The migrant child hears such talk not only from his parents, but from the adult world. His parents are told what to do in the same way. The child hears arbitrary statements that carry implied authority values along with the threat of punishment, including loss of job. Frequent exposure to such categorical statements limits the range of learning. It makes it difficult for a child to question and to express curiosity about things he sees or tasks in which he is involved.[7]

## Isolation

There has been a number of recent studies on the effect of isolation. Ruff describes the effects of physical and psychological distance on communication. In experiments conducted at McGill University, isolation produced "generalized impairment of perception." This appeared to result from loss of an internal frame of reference used in structuring perceptual experience.[8]

"Although it is difficult to generalize about the effect of isolation on cogni-

[7] Basil Bernstein, "Social Class and Linguistic Development: A Theory of Social Learning," in A. H. Halsey, Jean Floud, and Charles Arnold Anderson, eds., *Education, Economy, and Society* (New York: Free Press, 1961).

[8] George R. Ruff, "Isolation and Sensory Deprivation," in Silvane Arieti, ed., *American Handbook of Psychiatry, Vol. III* (New York: Basic Books, 1966), 362–376.

tive skills, subjects consistently refer to the inability to maintain goal-directed thought." [9]

A major question is: Does the migrant's type of isolation affect his perceptive ability? Does a client, migrant or nonmigrant, who is cut off from meaningful contacts with others, perceive his world as it really is?

## Delimited Environment

The migrant's conceptualization of his surroundings is neither instrumental in affording consistent understanding and mastery of events or feelings, nor in line with what he sees happening to nonmigrants. On one hand, the migrant hears that if he works hard, does not become a public charge, is ambitious, honest, and self-reliant, he will be able to rise to any height; on the other hand he knows from experience that other people are contemptuous of his work. The acceptance of such "mutually contradictory experiences requires paralogical thinking." [10] Such an environment can afford training only in irrationality. The world that the migrant perceives for others needs to be denied for himself.

## Sleep Deprivation

Luby and Gottlieb, in an article on sleep deprivation, describe experiences that are known to migrants and affect their communication. With loss of sleep "cognitive disorganization begins with a general slowing of thought processes, accompanied by word searching. Subjects . . . stray from topic to topic. . . . New learning is interfered with because the attentional or set impairment will not allow for the acquisition of new memories." [11]

It is the exception rather than the rule for a migrant to have a comfortable, undisturbed night of sleep. He may doze in a bus, car, or truck in transit. He may curl up on a narrow cot, in a bed already crowded with other family members, or on two chairs pulled together. He may stretch out on the ground on a pile of straw, or on the floor. His room may be infested with bedbugs, mosquitoes, or "kant sees." The wall above his head may drip with humidity, or may be white with frost. He may share a room with strangers, or sleep in a barn surrounded by the sounds of cows and horses. His rest may be disturbed by the quarrels of his neighbors, the cries of his children, or his own hunger, or his anxiety. He may be so physically exhausted he cannot relax into sleep.

[9] R. B. Voas, "A Description of the Astronauts' Task in Project Mercury," *Human Factors,* III (1961), 149–165.

[10] Theodore Lidz, Stephen Flick, Alice R. Cornelison, *Schizophrenia and the Family* (New York: International Universities Press, 1965), 180.

[11] Elliot D. Luby and Jacques S. Gottlieb, "Sleep Deprivation," in *American Handbook of Psychiatry,* Vol. III, 406–418.

## Repeated Loss of Job

Ginsburg, in a study of employment, came to the conclusion that the emotional implication of losing one's job was so great that the only counterpart he could cite was the "loss of love the child suffers from a rejecting parent, especially a child who has not done anything to deserve it." There are some whose first reaction to loss of work is "fear and bewilderment, combined with optimism, born of wishful thinking," [12] but with repeated experiences of loss of work, even these individuals become traumatized until they are afraid to tackle a new job.

This is what one would expect of anyone in the migrant's position, because he has known repeated situations of job loss. He will continue to know such experiences. He must not think too much about it or he will be traumatized by his anxiety and fear that someday he will find no work.

## Depersonalization

There is much in the experience of the migrant that can result in the "depersonalization phenomena," which Cattell describes as "feelings of unreality in reference to the self, the body, the external world, or the passage of time; feelings of unreality or detachment associated with states of elation; an 'as if' quality; and loss of affective response." [13]

The migrant's total experience is one of constant change from one job to the next. A sense of orientation is difficult to maintain. Migrants frequently travel in a truck roofed by a canvas tarpaulin that shuts out any view of passing countryside.

"Because the truck box is enclosed, there is no sensation of distance nor of nearness. There is only the sensation of sameness. It is a sameness with a rolling, jerking, bumping motion . . . The only reality in all that world of open highways, of small grocery stores and service stations, the only reality in all that world is the familiar outlines of the trucks. The trucks become an island of security. The trucks become a refuge that is familiar in a world of strangeness and indifference." [14]

## Masking Denial

Denial in various ways confuses communication. Some of this denial takes the form of "masking," which is both a conscious and an unconscious form of deception. It is behaving as if a situation did not exist. Lidz, Fleck, and Cornelison describe "masking" as containing "a large degree of self-decep-

---

[12] Sol W. Ginsburg, *A Psychiatrist's Views on Social Issues* (New York: Columbia University Press, 1963), 146–161.

[13] James P. Cattell, "Depersonalization Phenomena," in *American Handbook of Psychiatry,* Vol. III, 88–100.

[14] Reul, *op. cit.,* 217–218.

tion, as well as an effort to conceal from others; but it involves a conscious negation, as well as an effort to unconsciously deny." The migrant, unable to accept or alter his situation, ignores it and proceeds as if it does not exist.[15] It is only by reinforcing such a defense that he is able to function. He has to conserve his psychic and physical energy for the task at hand, and let tomorrow take care of itself.

One Spanish-American migrant told us about his fears and how he handled them. "He shrugged his shoulders and smiled wanly. . . . Sometimes he wondered what would happen to his family if he admitted to himself that he had a dull ache low in one side and a hard lump there that would not go away. Some day he would go to a doctor but that took money, which today he did not have. . . ."[16]

## Communicating with the Migrant

Much of the communication with the migrant must be on the feeling, or nonverbal, level. Basic to communication is the necessity to "listen," whether the client speaks or not. When the migrant does not speak, the worker has to tune in with every sense of empathy to receive the message the migrant may make every effort to conceal. The migrant's effort to shut himself away lessens as he senses the quiet acceptance of his worker.

It may be difficult for a migrant to take part in a conventional interview, to describe a situation, and to say how he feels. On the other hand, he can roleplay and show the worker what transpired, as well as what he did about it. Insight in these cases should not be seen as the major goal, but rather assistance to the migrant to reorganize old cognitive patterns so that new and more adequate responses are facilitated, as well as help to the worker to understand better the migrant's position.

The migrant may feel ill at ease in an office. Accustomed to action, to using his hands for tasks as well as for gestures, he may be better able to talk about his concerns in his own home, or in the field—in a setting where there will be distractions. A factor here is that the migrant knows little, if any, privacy.

The experiences of four researchers interviewing Mexican-Americans on details of their marriages illustrate what a social worker conducting an interview in a migrant camp may expect. "Often there were small children in and out. On at least six occasions, there were other females 'sitting in' on either part or all of the interview. In some of these cases, the respondent insisted that 'she had no secrets' from that person and responses were not inhibited by their presence."[17]

[15] Lidz, Fleck, and Cornelison, *op. cit.*, 181.
[16] Reul, *op. cit.*, 219.
[17] Roland G. Tharp, Arnold Meadow, Susan G. Lennhoff, and Donna Satterfield, "Changes in Marriage Roles Accompanying the Acculturation of the Mexican-American Wife," *Journal of Marriage and the Family* (August 1968), 408.

The purpose of the initial interview must be understood not only by the migrant, but by the worker. What does the social worker hope to accomplish? Is the interview to involve the migrant in an educational program such as Head Start, or job training? Is this contact to acquaint the migrant with community resources? Is it to establish an ongoing relationship for migrants who will "settle out" and need help establishing themselves in the community? Is this a situation where the migrant himself is faced with a crisis? Is this to be long-range treatment with the hope of changing the migrant's life style, or his personality structure?

## Migrants' Fears

Fear of being changed and losing self-identity is a crucial factor. This is in back of much of the migrants' reluctance to become involved with social workers. Migrants have been so exposed to pressure salesmen and confidence men that they are quick to wonder what the social worker really wants. They are likely to make the social worker prove he is different. Strangers in a migrant camp create other fears. There are migrants who have reasons for keeping their identity or whereabouts unknown. They may fear that a stranger is a policeman or a bill collector.

Some growers in recent years have felt threatened by the attempts to involve migrants in educational programs, or to recruit them for other types of work. There have been many cases of pirating workers at the peak of the harvest, or encouraging worker discontent, and growers are afraid of such actions. Their attitude toward "do-gooders" has been transmitted to the migrants and in some cases has in turn been projected by the migrants to social agencies. There is also a confusing number of new programs for migrants under the direction of education, public health, social work, or religious organizations, each with a slightly different approach.

I have heard migrants complain that so many well-meaning individuals are in the fields doing research or trying to involve them in educational programs that they (the migrants) have trouble finishing the harvest.

We found our greatest success in relating to migrants came when they first saw us around the camps, riding in their trucks, or working with them in the fields. We had no pressure of time. We sat quietly entering into their isolation, conveying by our presence that we were willing to talk but we were not forcing ourselves into their private world. The struggle to maintain privacy is a vital part of migrant existence, and anyone who respects privacy will have less difficulty establishing a relationship. We were also careful not to begin with a personal question. Even, "How many children do you have?" can appear as criticism to a woman who feels someone may think she should not have had eight or 12.

We also were careful not to ask questions one after another. The migrant often experiences rapid-fire questions which can traumatize him to the point where he feels as if he is being "peeled like an onion, layer by layer until nothing is left." We found it was easier for migrants to talk if they were busy with their hands and were not seated in a face-to-face position. Riding in a bus, hanging up clothes, picking strawberries, or sorting apples on a conveyor belt—these were the times when the migrants talked of their fears, hopes, and dreams.

## Nonverbal Communication

The migrant, in an interview, situation, needs to know that verbal communication is unnecessary. Insistence upon verbal communication only forces him into ways of denial. This may be evidenced by a near muteness, lack of spontaneity, a reduction of answers to a minimum. He may tell the social worker, whom he considers naive, an obvious untruth in an attempt to shock her. The migrant may show impatience with questions, be bitter and sarcastic, or make accusations. He may show his need for power over a hostile world by being shrewd and deceptive. There is much bragging about drinking, sexual experiences, gambling success, and even money earned in other crops.

This sort of behavior is certainly not unique to migrants. "When communication becomes too frustrating, man finds ways to protect himself by withdrawing, screening, or otherwise controlling the exchange. But through this control the feedback characteristics frequently are lost, so that the purpose of communication—correction of information and performance—is defeated." [18]

In an attempt to shield his identity from a threatening world, the migrant may pretend he has forgotten names and facts. He may hesitate to speak. He may mask his concern about the interview with a flurry of unrelated activities, approaching them as if they were the most important tasks in the world. He may attempt to show that he, too, has such middle-class values as cleanliness, or that he owns a transistor radio, or television. A mother may search frantically for a comb and begin to smooth a toddler's hair or grab a broom and put an older daughter to sweeping the floor or the yard. There is often loud laughter or wrestling among teenagers, or they may suddenly turn on a radio, full blast. Conversation at any point may be interrupted with much to-do about something else. This may be rivalry for the worker's attention or an indication that certain members of the group feel neglected and left out.

Even those who are silent are communicating by watching. They watch the social worker for his reaction. They watch their member who is the most

---

[18] Jurgen Ruesch, "General Theory of Communication in Psychiatry," in *American Handbook of Psychiatry, Vol. I,* 903.

vocal to see that he does not betray too much, too fast. If this seems to be happening, someone breaks in with a contradiction, or changes the subject to a less-threatening issue.

Whenever a stranger is present there is a good deal of spontaneous interaction among family or group members. Although a middle-class family might be more discreet in front of a stranger, the migrant family may use this interaction as a means of relieving anxiety. With Spanish-Americans, Indians, or other bilingual migrants there are frequent lapses into the home language. Those who are bilingual may pretend they do not understand English. This is a form of control, but more importantly, it is a way of maintaining identity.

Most adult migrants were forced as young children into a pseudomaturity through the need to help support their family by working in the fields or by taking over the responsibility of the home so their parents could work. The result of early pseudomaturity is an immature, infantile personality.

The social work approach seemingly most successful in working with immature personalities involves (1) reaching out, going to where the client is, with sustaining procedures of reassurance and suggestions; (2) exerting direct influence through educational programs, of which group procedures and role-playing have been the most effective; and (3) providing opportunities for emotional catharsis through ventilation of fears, hopes, ambitions, and anger.

Problems of communication are especially complex for the migrant because of his experiences and his culture and because of his own awareness of non-verbal interaction. If listened to carefully, however, he will communicate. He will express his needs and his feelings, but not always in words.

# Cultural Perspective on Treatment Modalities with Native Americans*
*Ronald Lewis*

## Introduction

. . . I WOULD LIKE to invite you to look at mental illness through the eyes of the Native Americans. Although outwardly, there have been numerous changes among the Native Americans' traditions, their basic orientation toward mental health and physical health (which are not seen as separate enti-

* From a paper presented at the NASW Professional Symposium, San Diego, California, November 1977. Reprinted by permission of the author.

ties) is the reflection of an unseen harmony between an individual and his environment. It includes three areas: the natural living world, relationships with fellow human beings, and the mystical. Mental illness indicates an imbalance between man and any of the three above areas or all the above areas (Native Americans approach this matter in an holistic manner). The illness is attributed to the breaking of societal norms, to a contact with mystical powers, or to malevolence on the part of others. If one adheres to this perspective of mental illness, one can view the Native Americans as a community of people, struggling valiantly, but caught between two life-styles, two cultures, and all the ensuing complexities.

To work with Native Americans, one must effect a blending of the Western philosophy and the Native American philosophy. Native Americans are often willing to accept new ideas if they fit into their culture. This paper represents one attempt at syncretizing the Western and Native American philosophies in order to develop styles of working with the Native Americans. Treatment modalities with Native Americans must include cultural understandings.

## Healing Powers

In working with Native Americans, one must first recognize the cultural concept of healing power. To the Native American, healing power is evident in all of nature. Nature, the life process itself, offers people numerous opportunities for healing power if they are willing to open themselves up to such awareness. For the Native American, the healing process is not compartmentalized, but is evident in all he does. This is an holistic approach and is done to validate an inwardness as a means to achieving insights as well as an experiential connection with the world of nature. For example, Native American religious celebrations are often a community effort to promote and share this very mode of healing. Here is a merging of social interdependency and inwardness in order to connect human beings with nature.

A creative mental health worker can blend Western philosophy with Native American healing events. In addition, the worker can time some of his or her efforts at insightful awareness with important positive experiences that emerge for the client or groups as a result of ceremonial happenings. For example, therapy was held after a ceremonial dance and at the patient's home [disguised cases]:

> Ben Dancewell is a thirty-four-year-old full-blooded Cheyenne-Arapahoe who was medically diagnosed as an alcoholic. He is married and has four children. He is an excellent dancer and has won several contests. The timing of the therapy was unique in that it was held after the ceremonial dances.
>
> The ceremonial dances served Ben in many therapeutic ways such as (1) helping him to ventilate his feelings; (2) helping him possess a unique sense of identity

and pride in his culture; (3) giving him a great sense of belonging through being with other Native Americans. (4) As he dannced, one could see other Indians giving him support; therefore, he gained a unique support system. (5) This experience enhanced his altruistic feelings and made him uniquely ready for therapy.

In attendance was his entire primary family, as well as his parents. Each week, he began to ventilate, for example, about his pride at being an Indian but how he felt inferior when he was in the majority culture. After several sessions of ventilating and using the extended family as support, drinking diminished and he was able to hold a job.

A variation on this technique can occur when a client reports an individual experience with some power-revealing event in his life. If the social worker is able to appreciate the Native American's attunement with nature, he or she can make use of both positive and negative forces reported by the client in his or her personal dialogue with the vast and varied world of nature. This will help clarify directions and conflict that emerge in the client's awareness. Sometimes the social worker can help the client assess both meaning and potential actions to such events.

Joe Nighthawk, a twenty-one-year-old full-blooded Cherokee, severely depressed, came to the therapist very excited because a nighthawk (sacred bird to the Cherokee) had been found injured in his backyard and he had nursed it back to health. To him this was indeed a good omen. Instead of passing it off as pure superstition, the therapist stated that he was pleased because, with the appearance of the omen, improvement in all areas of life might occur and that maybe this sign meant he should use the positive forces and strength in his life to cope. The patient appeared very encouraged and elated as he left the office.

At other times the worker will encourage the client to make use of a sorcerer or medicine man who can deal with such phenomena in ways available to the helping professional. The worker may ask the aid of the medicine man (or religious leaders).

Ben Brown, a thirty-five-year-old full-blooded Creek Indian, came to the P.H.S. Clinic complaining, in Creek, of many psychosomatic complaints such as nausea, vomiting, and trembling. He was checked medically, and the doctors suggested that it was psychosomatic. The wife led the therapist aside and suggested a "curse has been put on him, and only the religious leader could cure him; could she use him." The therapist concurred. Once a week the medicine man met with the man. No information concerning the man's curse was discussed with the therapist or any members of the family. Sessions were dealt with secretly, but the psychosomatic manifestations began to diminish and the Indian returned to his job and family.

An important form of revealing power forces is that of dreams and visions. The worker needs to appreciate the Native American's way of perceiving such occurrences. Dreams and visions are commonly prophetic rather than revealing of historical conflicts. "Psychotic" phenomena will often have a similar positive meaning to the Native American.

> One Indian woman who was very depressed over her husband's death reported a dream in which her husband came back to her as a bird. In her husband's voice, the bird said that he was in a better place now and was waiting for her to join him. He said that she must be strong for the grandchildren. After talking about the dream the woman seemed happier and relieved about her future. The therapist expressed confidence in the message of the dream, but did not attempt to interpret it. This type of situation needs no interpretation to an Indian person—its meaning is quite clear.

What is of critical importance is the worker's attitude toward use of dreams, visions, and power forces. If he or she takes an unaccepting paternalistic stance toward such "superstitions," he or she will quickly lose whatever power of influence the Native American client may have given him or her. That is why the "Don Juan" experience of Carlos Castaneda has been so immensely important. One cannot look at the world through rational, pragmatic eyes. Daniel Noel's book, *Seeing Castaneda,* is an effort to understand Castaneda's writings as a valid although vastly different way of understanding reality.[1]

## Natural Helping Systems

When dealing with Native Americans, mental health work must take on a systems perspective. The worker must be able to analyze problem-solving networks that Native Americans follow. When the Native American has a problem, he or she first goes to the immediate family. If the problem is not resolved there, the social network is then contacted. This includes friends, neighbors, relatives, a bar, or anywhere else where one will listen. Next the person will go to the spiritual or religious leader. If the problem still is not resolved, the person may go to the tribal council. The last place the person will go for help after all else has failed or if he or she is dying or has done something drastic is a formal agency.

One reason for the failure of mental health work with Native Americans offered by mainstream society is that it has not established linkages with the natural helping system. Too often social workers have set up medical model mental health offices and have expected the Native Americans to come there for help.

Not only have mental health workers not established linkages with the natural helping systems, but they have also proved unknowledgeable in the traditional medicine and healings that are practiced in their area. In addition, the attitudes of the mental health workers have driven these practices underground.

Because it is so important to be able to use the natural helping system for the good of the Native American people, it is essential that the mental health worker understands the system with which he or she must work. Minuchin states:

> Like the anthropologist, the mental health worker joins the culture with which he is dealing. In the same oscillating rhythm, he engages and disengages. He experiences the pressures of the cultural system. At the same time he observes the system, making deductions that enable him to transform his experience into a community map from which he derives therapeutic goals. To understand and know a system in this intimate, experiential way is a vital component of community therapy [p. 124].[2]

The community map approach was used by this psychiatric social worker and a paraprofessional in developing the first comprehensive mental health program for Native Americans in Oklahoma. Rather than hanging out a shingle and waiting for clients, the mental health workers used the first six months in a friendly professional outreach program. The workers began this outreach program by going to the families of known mentally ill patients whose names were obtained from the Indian Health Service. In informal discussions, it was discovered where the family went for help in crisis situations. After obtaining permission from the family, the mental health workers visited the social network, which contains significant others, such as cousins, aunts, uncles, and so on. It was found from the social network that the religious leaders were a very important aid in the care and treatment of the mentally ill. Finally, the mental health workers very quietly visited the tribal community meetings, explaining to the tribe that they worked with those people who had personal problems. Within six months, through the use of this community map, the workers found more clients coming to the office than they could handle. They did not destroy the broader community health care delivery system but became a part of the natural helping system of the community. (See Figure 1.).

Too often in our services to the Native American people, inadvertently we bypass the natural helping system. We must learn to work with the community as it is, not as we would like for it to be.

The community helping system for the Native American represents a refuge in a highly hostile environment. It is a trusted source of aid rather than a suspected source of surveillance, which is the way most Native Americans view the health care delivery systems provided by the whites. Health care delivery systems must blend in with the community they are to serve.

## Self-help Groups

A third concept of treatment modality is that of peer or self-help groups. Self-help groups can be defined as voluntary associations among individuals who

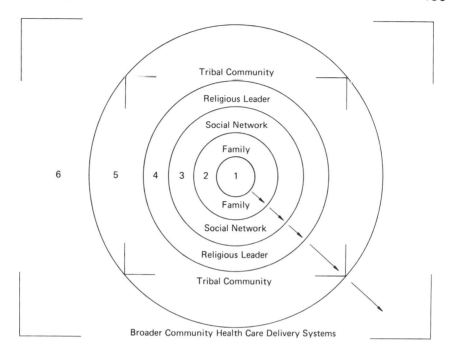

1. Individual
2. Goes to family first
3. Then to extended family (cousins, aunts, uncles, etc.) — social network
4. Religious leader
5. Tribal council
6. Finally formalized health care delivery system

FIGURE 1. Helping methodology must take on a system perspective.
   *Schema:* Individual seeking aid. Numbered in order of significance for Native American and path followed for seeking help.

share a common need or problem and who seek to use the group as a means of dealing with that need or problem.[3] Although self-help groups have existed for a long time, mental health professionals are now beginning to look seriously at the self-help model.[4] Self-help groups have taken a variety of forms: Alcoholics Anonymous, Synanon, Seven Steppers, Take Off Pounds Sensibly, Recover, Inc., and cultural identity groups such as the Black Muslims. Self-help groups have traditionally avoided leadership from helping professionals.

The Native Americans have had a long history of attempting mutual self-help. They have tried to cope with life, however ineffectively, by the use of peer self-help groups, while relating very little to organizations that are imposed upon them—to be of aid, the mental health worker must become part of that self-help organization.

The self-help groups could be developed along these lines:

1. Assessment and counseling (group therapy, family planning).
2. Environmental arrangements (halfway houses, nursing homes, homemaker services).
3. Training, education, and equipment (work training, nutrition, home management).
4. Protective and legal (protective services for adults and children, legal aid).
5. Liaison (information and referral, resource mobilization-social change).
6. Transportation (escort service).
7. Social advocacy.

My experience has taught me that regardless of where you start in a self-help group, you will come back to one major topic: the Native Americans' realistic rage at dehumanizing forces that have oppressed them for so long. This is a theme that will inevitably reoccur—that of dissatisfaction with the impersonal order of a contemporary society that does not adequately provide for the needs of its members. "Native Americans will not be helped by anybody or any policy which assumes that they are the problem that needs to be changed. It is the environment, the system, the bureaucracy that is the problem."[5]

Every self-help group, regardless of its stated goals, must give the Indian pride and dignity in who and what he or she is. Wilfred Pelletier, a full-blooded Indian, described his life as an Indian and the importance of this self-realization:

> The first step towards surviving in an alien environment is to feel proud of who you are. Being surrounded by an aggressive and confident majority has made me somewhat defensive; I have spent a lot of years trying to convince myself, after being told all my life that I was no good because I was an Indian, that I am really all right. That I am a human being like everyone else and that maybe we Indians did have something to contribute to society, something that was sadly missing in the dominant culture.[6]

The journey of the Indian people is not an outward journey to find good housing, plumbing, and so on, but the first journey is an inward one to regain pride and dignity in themselves. The mental health workers are in a unique position to help the Native Americans regain this pride and dignity in themselves.

## Conclusion

Mental health and mental illness must be redefined so that this definition applies to all cultures. As long as we look at the individual as the cause of mental illness then we will continue to "blame the victim."

It was succinctly stated when Mary Richmond said that "the good social worker . . . does not go on helping people out of a ditch. Pretty soon she begins to find out what ought to be done to get rid of the ditch." [7]

Three types of treatment modalities have been discussed that have proved effective in the treatment of mental illness in Native Americans: healing powers, natural helping systems, and self-help groups. Each of these concepts is an integral part of the Native Americans' culture dealing with their basic belief in the unseen harmony that should exist between an individual and the individual's environment. These concepts then must become a part of the mental health worker's methodology in the treatment of mental illness.

We don't know how effective our therapeutic modalities are with Native Americans. Is it possible that some of our treatment modalities run counter to the community concept of mental health and mental illness? Do we really know from data available what constitutes a Native American community and its constituents? Is it necessary that the values of the therapeutic community take on the values of the community being served? These questions need to be asked and some attempt made to seek answers to them. Thus, I hope that this paper will encourage others to look in a different way at the psychopathological aspects of Native Americans and, in addition, to question basic therapeutic methods.

## REFERENCE NOTES

1. Daniel Noel, *Seeing Castaneda* (New York: G. P. Putnam's Sons, Capricorn Books, 1976), p. 5.
2. Salvador Minuchin, *Family and Family Therapy* (Harvard University Press, 1974), pp. 2 and 3.
3. *Journal of Applied Behavioral Science,* Vol. 12, No. 3, 1976, p. 433.
4. *The Journal of Applied Behavioral Science,* Special issue/Self-Help Groups, Volume 12, No. 3, July-August-September, 1976.
5. *Journal of Applied Behavioral Science,* Vol. 12, No. 3, 1976, p. 454.
6. Wilfred Pelletier, "For Every North American Indian Who Begins to Disappear, I Also Begin to Disappear," unpublished personal paper, p. 5.
7. Mary F. Richmond, *Social Diagnosis* (New York: Russell Sage Foundation, 1917) p. 13.

## REFERENCES

ATTNEAVE, CAROLYN. *Psychiatric Annals,* Volume 4, No. 1, November 1974.
CAFFERTY, PASTORA SAN JUAN, and LEON CHESTANG. *The Diverse Society: Implications for Social Policy,* National Association of Social Workers publication No.: CBC-072-C Washington, D.C., 1976.
CAPPS, WALTER HOLDEN. *Seeing With A Native Eye.* New York: Harper and Row, 1976.
*The Journal of Applied Behavioral Science.* "Self-help Groups." Volume 12, No. 3, 1976.
MINUCHIN, SALVADOR. *Families and Family Therapy.* Cambridge, Massachusetts: Harvard University Press, 1974.
RICHMOND, MARY F. *Social Diagnosis* New York: Russel Sage Foundation) 1917.
THOMAS, ALEXANDER, and SAMUEL SILLEN. *Racism and Psychiatry.* Secaucus, New Jersey: Citadel Press, 1974.

# Social Work With Asian Americans*
*Man Keung Ho*

ASIAN AMERICANS are one of the most neglected minorities in America.[1] Unlike the blacks, Chicanos, and recently the American Indians, Asian Americans have tried to maintain their social structure with a minumum of visible conflict with the host society. Historically, they have accepted much prejudice and discrimination without voicing strong protests.[2] Their cultural heritage as Asians, historical experiences in a discriminatory society, and their unique problems and concerns are relatively unknown to other Americans.

In fact, Asian Americans frequently have been described as "the most silent minority," "the quiet Americans," or "the model minority." Pei-Ngor Chen attributes such a misconception to two significant factors: the general public's tendency to stereotype ethnic groups and Asian tendencies to hide the "darker side" of their culture, as well as other cultural values militating against self-assertion and open expression of thoughts and feelings to outsiders.[3] It is unfortunate that the prevalent belief that Asian Americans are somehow immune to the effects of white discrimination has served to mask a multitude of problems, such as poverty, unemployment, physical and mental illness, educational deficiences, and social service inadequacy and unavailability. Problems of Asian Americans and their experiences resulting from white American discrimination have been discussed elsewhere.[4] This article focuses on the indigenous cultural influences operating among Asian Americans and social work intervention with this unique ethnic group.

---

\* Reprinted with permission of the publisher, Family Service Association of America, from *Social Casework*, 57:3 (March 1976): 195–201.

[1] The definition of an Asian American remains necessarily broad and flexible—it has traditionally included the Chinese and Japanese, and more recently the Filipino, Korean, and South Sea Islanders, especially from Guam and Samoa.

[2] Roger Daniels and Harry H. L. Kitano, *American Racism: Exploration of the Nature of Prejudice* (Englewood Cliffs, N.J.: Prentice-Hall, 1970); Gail DeVals and Karen Abbott, The Chinese Family in San Francisco, unpublished master's thesis, University of California, Berkeley, 1966; Samuel M. Lyman, *The Asian in the West* (Reno, Nev.: University of Nevada, 1970).

[3] See Pei-Ngor Chen, The Chinese Community in Los Angeles, *Social Casework*, 51:10 (December 1970).

[4] See Ford H. Kuramoto, What Do Asians Want? An Examination of Issues in Social Work Education, *Journal of Education for Social Work*, 7:3 (Fall 1971): Harry L. Kitano, ed., *Asians in America* (New York: Council on Social Work Education, 1971): Ronald A. Kimmigh, Ethnic Aspects of Schizophrenia in Hawaii, *Psychiatry*, 23:4 (1960): Pei-Ngor Chen, Samoans in California, *Social Work*, 18:2 (March 1972).

# Salient Cultural Values

## Filial Piety

At the beginning of the mid-nineteenth century, the lure of the Mountain of Gold, intensified by social upheavals and natural disasters in many of the Asian countries, began drawing the excess populations of Asia to the Americas. These Asian immigrants brought with them the cultural trappings of a rigid social order in which they generally occupied the lowest position. Among the fundamental beliefs of Asian society were the doctrines of filial piety and an unquestioning respect for and deference to authority. Thus, the individual was expected to comply with familial and social authority, to the point of sacrificing his own desires and ambitions.

## Parent-Child Interaction

Clearly defined roles of dominance and deference based on paternalism virtually preclude any discussion and debate in a traditional Asian family. The role of the parent is to define the law; the duty of the child is to listen and obey. Communication flows one way, from parent to child. Directive messages predominate, and exchanges are generally brief and perfunctory. Constantly battered by prohibitions and orders, the Asian child begins to see himself as an obeyer rather than a director. The second generation of Asian American families no doubt has altered considerably this traditional family structure, but the configuration of the traditional parent-child interaction is basically unchanged.[5]

## Self-control

Asians generally are taught to respect all elders and to enhance the family name by outstanding achievement in some aspect of life, such as academic or occupational success. Conversely, an individual learns quickly that dysfunctional behavior such as juvenile delinquency, unemployment, or mental illness, reflects upon the entire family. If he feels his behavior might disrupt family harmony, he is expected to restrain himself. Indeed, Asian culture values highly self-control and the inhibition of strong feelings.[6]

## Shame as a Behavioral Influence

Seen from an Asian American point of view, individualism, with its emphasis on aggressive competition with those of any status, conflicts totally with

[5] Edwin O. Reischauer and John K. Fairbank, *East Asia: The Great Tradition* (Boston: Houghton Mifflin, 1960), p. 33.

[6] See Karen A. Abbott, *Harmony and Individualism* (Taipei: Oriental Cultural Service, 1970).

traditional Asian respect for authority and filial piety toward parents and ancestors. Violation of that tradition almost inevitably leads to family tension and possible disruption. It is understandable, therefore, that if the Asian American is unable to acquiesce to the teachings and commands of family elders, he will suffer a sense of guilt and shame which colors his behavior, not only in his home but in his total society as well.

## Middle Position Virtue

In the training of children, Asian parents emphasize a social norm that cultivates the virtues of the middle position, in which an individual should feel neither haughty nor unworthy. In pursuing this norm, both the child and his peer group are held responsible for his actions. For example, a teacher, in talking to the misbehaving child about a given incident, will at the same time involve the entire class, making the child's destructive behavior a class problem that needs correcting for the sake of the group.

## Awareness of Social Milieu

An Asian's consciousness of the welfare of the group also is related to his acute awareness of his social milieu, characterized by social and economic limitations and immobility. Thus, he becomes highly sensitive to the opinions of his peers and allows the social nexus to define his thoughts, feelings, and actions. In the interest of social solidarity, he subordinates himself to the group, suppressing and restraining any disruptive emotions and opinions. Moreover, an Asian American's compliance with social norms, which provides him with social esteem and self-respect, is so fundamental that even differences in wealth and social status are considered no excuse for deviation.

## Fatalism

Fatalism, a calm acceptance of one's situation, also pervades the Asian American culture. Constantly buffeted by nature and by political upheaval over which he clearly had no control, the original Asian immigrant adopted a philosophical detachment and resignation that allowed him to accept what he perceived to be his fate with equanimity. Instead of trying to ascertain underlying meanings in events, the Asian met life pragmatically. He became adept at making the most of existing situations rather than attempting to understand and control his environment to create his own opportunities. It is unfortunate that this adaptabiltiy, the very factor that contributed to his original success in America, would later become a serious handicap; his continuing silence could only let him fall further behind the alien American culture that encouraged, and indeed demanded, aggressiveness and outspoken individualism.

*Inconspicuousness*

Experiences with segments of American society which were racist further convinced the Asian immigrant of the need and value of silence and inconspicuousness. Fear of attracting attention was particularly acute among the thousands of immigrants who had come to America illegally to circumvent genocidal immigration laws designed to decimate the Asian American colonies by preventing formation of new ones and denying replacement members to established ones. If caught, these immigrants had little hope of justice; the California Supreme Court ruled in 1855 that their testimony was inadmissible as evidence.[7] Fear and distrust still linger today among the descendants of these immigrants. It is understandable why Asians are extremely reluctant to turn to governmental agencies for aid, even in cases of dire need.

# Implications for Social Work Practice

In view of the potential suspicion and feelings of guilt and shame of the Asian American client who needs social services, initial social worker contacts with him require unique skills and a high level of sensitivity. Considering the Asian American client as an individual who may react differently to conflicts, and considering intra- and intercultural group differences, the worker should never let stereotypes cause him to assume knowledge of the client's needs and reactions without first consulting with him.[8] Instead, an open-minded attitude usually will be a key to opening up the client to reveal and discuss his problems. . . .

# Conclusions and Implications

The term "Asian American" encompasses many ethnic groups, each with intragroup differences; different individuals within each subgroup may react differently to certain conflict or crisis situations. Therefore, it is impossible for a social worker always to know exactly how to react to an Asian American client. As a result, it is necessary that the worker be willing to plead ignorance when necessary, to listen more carefully, to be less ready to come to conclusions, and to be more open to having his presuppositions corrected by the client. That is, he must want to know what the situation is and must be receptive to being taught.[9] Such an unassuming humanistic attitude is the key to working with Asian Americans.

Additionally, working effectively with the Asian American requires more

[7] Lyman, *The Asian in the West.*

[8] *See* Man K. Ho, *Cross-Cultural Counseling, Vocational Guidance Quarterly,* 21:3 (March 1973).

[9] Alfred Kadushin, The Racial Factor in the Interview, *Social Work,* 7:92 (May 1972).

than merely understanding his cultural background, his American experience, and his present problems. Most importantly, the worker needs to respect him as an individual first, and as an Asian American second. A worker who assumes that traditional Asian society is "primitive" and Western self-directed society is "modern" will be less likely to respect the Asian American as an individual. Respecting an Asian American as a worthy person with cultural differences simply means recognition of the fact that "yellow is not white and white is not right." [10]

Finally, recognizing the fact that yellow is not white has many other important implications, the most obvious being that social work practice knowledge based on white culture is inadequate when applied to Asian Americans. It also implies that there is a need for social work education to incorporate Asiatic culture content in its current curriculum. For Asian American social problems to be effectively ameliorated, there is a need to educate more Asian American social workers and to provide inservice training to agency staff who are currently working with Asian Americans.

[10] Kuramoto, What Do Asians Want? p. 12.

---

# Chicanos and Their Support Systems in Interaction with Social Institutions*
*Guadalupe Gibson*

## The Chicanos †

> . . . as a people, Mexican-Americans are the creation of the imperial conquest of one nation by another through military force.[1]

MEXICAN-AMERICANS constitute the second largest minority in the United States.[2] Of the estimated 7.2 million Chicanos,[3] approximately 85 per cent of

* This paper was specially prepared for this book. Some of the ideas expressed in this paper are based on other articles by the author, particularly "An Approach to Identification and Prevention of Developmental Difficulties Among Mexican-American Children," *American Journal of Orthopsychiatry* 48(1978): 96–113, and "Child Welfare and the Welfare of Mexican-American Children," in *Human Services for Mexican-American Children,* edited by Andres A. Tijerina, Center for Social Work Research, School of Social Work, The University of Texas at Austin, 1978.

† The terms *Chicano* and *Mexican-American* are used interchangeably. Spanish-speaking and Spanish-surnamed people of Mexican descent, a very heterogenous group, have not agreed on nomenclature. Some prefer to be called Hispanic; others, Latin American, Latinos, Spanish-American, Mexicanos, Raza, and so on.

them reside in the Southwest—Arizona, California, Colorado, New Mexico, and Texas.[4] The others are scattered throughout the other forty-five states.

It is beyond the scope of this paper to make a historical presentation, but it is important to note that their unique historical experiences, their cultural and linguistic characteristics, have set Chicanos apart and that, because of their *mestizaje,* their mixed Spanish and Indian background, they have been subjected to stresses of racial discrimination in countless ways, but most significantly in education and employment.[5] They have been oppressed, deprived, and disadvantaged.

Social scientists have long presented Chicanos in a damaging and stereotypic manner, as an ahistorical, backward, unassimilable, tradition-bound group caught between two cultures.[6,7,8] They were also contrasted with the Anglos* as lazy, unmotivated, happy-go-lucky people, creators of their own problems. Social institutions using these studies to understand Chicanos and operating from an ethnocentric, assimilative perspective, failed to provide adequate or relevant services for them. In spite of this, some Chicanos succeeded, but many, because of their oppressed, impoverished condition, not only did not succeed or even protest, but often accepted the Anglo view of them as part of their own self-concept.[9] It is important to emphasize here that Chicanos, like members of other ethnic groups, reflect intracultural diversity. As Gomez and Cerda have pointed out:

> Mexican-Americans are the well-to-do and the very poor, the well-educated and the illiterate, the migrants from Mexico and the American born. Then there are the professionals and the agricultural laborers; the successful and those who struggle for survival. . . . there are the sober, settled conservatives, the loud vociferous activists, and the liberals; the monolinguals in English; and the monolinguals in Spanish; and the bilinguals. There are those who use strictly Spanish names (Juan Jose de la Garza y Menchaca) and those who prefer the American way (Joe Williams Menchaca or Mary Lou Jimenez).[10]

It was not until the Chicano Movement of the sixties that Chicanos were able to say *ya basta,* enough. They condemned the blatant disrespect for differences in a society that persisted in adhering to the philosophy of the "melting pot" despite its pluralistic makeup. They demanded their rights to human dignity, to self-respect, to the maintenance of their cultural bonds. They demanded that their rights as bilingual and bicultural be recognized and that relevant educational, health, and welfare programs be provided for them.

This paper will attempt to describe the strengths within the Chicano culture, the support systems available to Chicanos, and the cultural affronts they have suffered in interaction with social institutions—the church, the schools, the "work place," and social services. It will also describe the implications for social work practice and strategies that may be helpful in providing relevant services to Mexican-Americans.

---

* *Anglo* is a general term referring to white people of the dominant society. It is recognized that some white ethnics resent being labeled Anglos.

# Dignidad, Carnalismo y la Familia

Chicanos, in their struggle to survive in what has often been a hostile environment, have made maximum use of the support systems that their culture and their reality have provided. The family has been pivotal for them, and their language and behaviors attest to it. Two basic values that reflect the Chicanos' philosophy of life and their concepts of interpersonal relationships are (1) the importance of the dignity of each individual, *su dignidad-personalismo,* and the respect for all human life and (2) the responsibility of human beings for each other, or mutualism, sometimes referred to as *carnalismo.* These two values are intrinsically related, one supporting the other. *Dignidad,* dignity, in Spanish has a broader conceptual meaning than "worth." It also means *self-respect. Personalismo,* personalism, is the philosophy that emphasizes the person or personality as the supreme value and the ultimate reality. It focuses on the inner importance of the person and centers attention on the inner qualities of the individual that constitute his or her uniqueness, goodness, and worth. This form of individualism contrasts with Anglo individualism, which values the person in terms of his or her ability to compete for higher social and economic status. *Carnalismo* means "blood relationship," as for example, *primo carnal,* first cousin; but as used by Mexican Americans, it means *hermandad,* brotherhood. Ideally, the concept embraces the whole ethnic group and is intended to extend to the whole human race. It is characterized by depth of feeling one might experience toward the closest blood relatives and subsumes loyalty and allegiance.[11] Through the interrelationship of these two values, Chicanos make certain commitments to each other and have certain expectations from each other. Each person is expected to assume some responsibility and obligation for assisting others, not only relatives but also friends. This help is extended not only to maintain their and the others' *dignidad,* their self-respect, but also to enhance it and, through mutualism, to help others become self-actualized. Respect for elders stems from this same value base.

This humanistic approach to interpersonal relationships constitutes the essence of family life. The actual operationalization of these values, however, is highly individualistic, and the *how* may depend on time, place, and circumstance within which the person finds himself or herself. According to Gilbert, for instance, actual personal service exchange is more prevalent among siblings,[12] undoubtedly because of their proximity. For relatives who live in other *barrios* or even in other communities, there is a lower level of exchange. Also it appears that a stable ongoing exchange relationship with close kin increases as economic stability increases.[13]

This value system is the foundation for the ascribed importance of the family to the individual. The interdependence of, and attachment to, family members is referred to as *familism.*[14] Familism requires that the needs of the family collectively supersede individual needs. From the Anglo perspective, which frequently ignores the complexity of forces impinging on Mexican-Americans, this is considered a dysfunctional characteristic.

The extended family, that network of relatives that radiates from the nuclear family, continues to be very significant to Chicanos. The extended family is more prevalent in rural areas. It includes more than two generations, with grandparents, aunts, and uncles or other relatives, living, if not in the same household, at least contiguously or relatively nearby. Kinship ties provide avenues of exchange for communication, finances, counseling, and moral support.[15] They provide security for its members through the sharing of available goods by all. Members of the family at least find comfort in knowing that this would happen if they were to need support. When members of a family live in different neighborhoods or even in different towns, the assumed psychological support of relatives prevails. The idea of helping or being helped becomes an attitude even if help is not given or received. Social workers attempting to help are often bewildered by this and seem unable to understand how a family that is barely making ends meet will share what little they have with others outside the immediate family. Further, social workers often view this reliance on the family for advice, counseling, and support as pathological and label clients as "passive," "immature," and "dependent."

Chicanos are person-oriented rather than goal-oriented. This orientation has been a source of consternation to employers, teachers, business people, and particularly to social workers, who become annoyed when Mexican-Americans fail to keep appointments, miss work, or do not follow through. Often Chicanos "drop everything" in response to a call for help, articulated or implied, by relatives, even distant ones, *compadres,** and even friends. This is most often interpreted by Anglos as the Chicanos' desire to avoid work and responsibility, when in reality they are behaving as responsible people within their value system. Conflicts and dilemmas and concomitant stress experienced by Chicanos when they fail to respond to the needs of others are often contemptuously disregarded by social workers.

But the most important factor about *la familia,* as it is with all families, is the nurturance and socialization role that it assumes. It is the institution that is responsible for the identity-formation of the children. The humanistic approach to interpersonal relationships among Chicanos constitutes the essence of family life. Parents value children, who are the *raison d'être* for the family. Fertility among Mexican-Americans is higher than in the average American family, and this is related to the fact that the majority of them are Catholics.[16] Ideally, children learn from infancy that the family is the single most important unit in life. It becomes the core of their thinking and behavior and

---

* This system of *compadrazgo,* which reflects the influence of Spain, includes sponsors at baptism and other sacramental rituals. These sponsors become *padrinos* or *madrinas* to the child and *compadres* to the parents. They assume responsibility not only for the spiritual and corporal well-being of the children, but, if necessary, may offer support in many ways to the entire family.

the center from which their views of the world extend.[17] Children are taught to respect and value others as they are respected and valued. They learn about male and female roles, as well as sibling roles. They are expected to do chores according to their age and sex. They learn the patterns of expected behavior.[18] Obviously, there are some disorganized families, for whatever reason, who are unable to provide a positive socialization experience for their youngsters; but the majority of children, even those who come from very poor families, are adequately prepared, have a positive self-concept, and learn to trust. According to Goodman and Beman, who made a comparative study of children, "The strength of intra-family affection declared by *barrio* children is conspicuous by contrasting with responses of the Negro and Anglo children we interviewed."[19]

# El Barrio

According to Ruiz, *el barrio* is a basic unit of the social system, a concept that transcends geographic, political, and class boundaries.[20] However, the term is usually applied to poor communities where Chicanos live and is often used interchangeably with the term *ghetto*. Valdez presents a broader view of it:

> *El Barrio* is many things to many people—a dictionary definition to some, a "state of mind" or a "state of being"; to some it is "home"; to others a place where they used to live and which they occasionally visit to revive old memories . . . *el barrio* is a physical entity, possessing buildings, streets, and people which exist—or have existed—in time and space. *Los barrios* are both territorial and class-ethnic realities.[21]

The *barrio* is a social institution.[22] Sotomayor pointed out that for a "group of people who have been consistently rejected by the environment and who value the group and tend to cluster in familial and neighborhood arrangements, the *barrio* has offered a feeling of belonging and cohesion."[23] It is that world within which the Chicano children first become socialized outside the home. What they learned at home is usually reinforced in the *barrio*, that life is human-life-centered, as opposed to activity-centered. Their ascribed status and role are recognized. It can very well be for most Mexican-American children that they spend the first five years of their lives with practically no contact with the community beyond the *barrio*.[24] Their self-identity as Chicanos is strengthened through the *barrio*. The *barrio* provides an informal system of service through child care help, some health care by providing home remedies when indicated, and crisis help among relatives and friends. Sanchez reported that in a *barrio* in San Antonio, women related that they supervised each other's children. Without being asked, they assumed this mutual responsibility.[25] For many children what lies beyond the *barrio* "is likely to be fuzzy and vague."[26] The child's understanding of the culture and the ways of the groups are reinforced, not in the abstract, but in interaction with the people in the *barrio*—his or her sense of respect for elders; authority mostly resting with the father but shared by mother and, at times, older siblings and neighbors; and affectionate warmth.[27]

## The Church, Religion, and Spirituality

Just as the culture of Mexican-Americans includes a range of life-styles, not surprisingly so does it include a range of religious beliefs and values.[28] For Chicanos, religion is part of culture. These concepts are so closely interwoven that they are almost one and the same. Religious beliefs and values buttress family values.[29] An estimated 90 per cent of Chicanos are declared Roman Catholics[30] even though an increasing number are nonpracticing.[31] Some have seen the church as oppressive and even racist. Some have historically been anticlerical.[32]

Bishop Patricio Flores, the first Chicano bishop, reminisced at a National Encuentro, "Not too long ago, it was common for churches to have signs saying, 'Mexicans not allowed' or 'The last four benches reserved for Mexicans.'"[33] These conditions have improved as the "Latinization" of the church, a slow process, is progressing, even though 120 years after the Mexican-American people of the Southwest came under the jurisdiction of the Catholic Church of the United States.[34] *Mariachi* masses are not uncommon as there are now nine Hispanic bishops and the number of Chicano priests is slowly increasing.[35] These priests have established a nationwide association, *Padres Asociados para Derochos Religiosos, Educativos y Sociales* (PADRES), Priests Associated for Religious, Educational, and Social Rights. The members have been devoting much of their time and effort toward helping Mexican-Americans improve their economic and social conditions through education. As ethnocentrism within the church is eliminated, more Chicanos, particularly among the middle-class youth, seem to become more active in the church.[36] As evangelizing efforts by a number of Protestant sects have increased, primarily the Pentecostal groups, more Chicanos have become Protestants.

Although the church has at times been one of the "insensitive social institutions" with which Chicanos have interacted, it has also often been a source of socialization and support. Their religious beliefs, particularly the cult of the Virgin Mary, have sustained them through innumerable crises.

## Educational Systems

Probably no other factor has contributed more heavily to the low socioeconomic, oppressive state of Chicanos than educational deprivation. Lack of educational opportunities and the "push-out" system result in Chicanos having the highest dropout rate in the United States.[37] Contrary to widespread belief among Anglos, Mexican-American parents want their children to be well educated and well prepared to hold employment compatible with their interest and ability.[38] They have a deep belief in the maxim, *Saber es poder,* knowledge is power. But historically, the educational system has not been sensitive to the needs of Chicanos. Quality education has not always been available in the rural areas or the poor urban *barrios.* Schools have been poorly staffed and poorly equipped. Children finishing from these schools have been ill-prepared to enter college or the labor market. The most persistent and pernicious problems that Chicano children encounter result from the fact that the majority of them speak only Spanish or a smattering of English. Yet upon first entry into the schools they have been expected to speak only English. Many youngsters have been severely traumatized because of the penalty attached to the speaking of Spanish in school. What has been even worse is that these same children very early, before they acquired the necessary language skills, were administered tests in English that were based on Anglo middle-class norms. As a consequence of their failure, many were relegated to classes for the mentally retarded.[39] Many retained the label for the rest of their lives.

Even though the importance of language to Mexican-American children was finally recognized by Congress in 1965, bilingual classes are not always available, and if they are, they are often snared in old attitudes and prejudices.[40] "The suppression of the Spanish language is the most overt act of cultural exclusion"[41] in the schools.

For Chicano children and youth, attendance at school often puts them in a cultural bind. Their culture and language are denigrated. Their parents are made to appear inadequate and helpless. The cultural beliefs and values of white society appear to be superior and certainly are favored by the teachers. They are frequently pushed to make value choices that at times alienate them from their families. Their struggle for ethnic identity—for personal identity— is painful and difficult indeed.

These conditions appear to be improving as more Chicanos have had better opportunities for higher education, even for attaining advanced degrees. Many of them are choosing the field of education. Also the number of Anglo educators who are growing in sensitivity to Chicano issues continues to increase.

## Employment and the "Work Place"

Problems of unemployment, underemployment, and general economic exploitation have long plagued Mexican-American people.

> The U.S. Commission on Civil Rights has pointed out that women—*and men from minority groups*—are farther from equality than they were in 1960 . . . . For

many minority groups the unemployment rate is two to three times the rate of majority males . . . For minority and teenage females, the unemployment situation is even worse ranging from *four to nine times the rate of teenage majority rates.* [emphasis added][42]

A recent report from Washington made specific the rate of unemployment among Chicanos. The rate of unemployment for the total population was 7.0 per cent but for Chicanos it was 10.1 per cent. Chicanas fared about equally with Chicanos, but for teenagers it was 17.7 per cent.[43]

Economic exploitation of Mexican-Americans has taken many forms over the years: Depriving people from contributing to Social Security; hiring people by the day and paying below minimum wage levels; threatening people with the *migra,* immigration officers, if they complain, a threat that is taken seriously even by the native-born Chicanos and legal aliens because it takes time to prove their status, if they can prove it at all. Women, particularly, are not only underpaid but often are sexually harassed. There is also the fact of being hired last but fired first. The most devastating outcome of unemployment is, of course, poverty, which, in turn, generates problems of poor health, including malnutrition, family dependency, family disorganization or disintegration, and crime.

Underemployment is another serious problem caused by racism and sexism also. In Texas, for instance, statistics indicated that a disproportionate number of Chicanos who completed four years of college suffered higher rates of poverty as compared with Anglos who had only high school diplomas.[44] The consequences of underemployment may appear less dramatic than those of chronic unemployment, but they are just as pernicious—low self-esteem, apathy, depression, and poor mental health generally. Some Chicanos have had to face problems of overemployment, especially immediately following the enactment of the Civil Rights Act. They were promoted or hired to fill positions for which they were ill-prepared. This move on the part of some employers appeared as if they were deliberately setting Chicanos up for failure or were trying to prove their point, that Chicanos "just could not cut it."

## Health, Mental Health, and Welfare Systems

The issues of health care delivery that impinge on Chicanos have been critical for a long time. The problems are all too apparent, though not fully documented.[45] Morbidity rates are high, and life expectancy for Latinos is an estimated 57 years, compared to 72 for the general population; for Chicano farm workers, it is 49 years. Infant mortality among Latinos is believed to be the highest in the nation.[46] Malnutrition bordering on starvation for some children has been documented.[47]

Over the past ten or twelve years, considerable attention has been given by

Chicanos to the problems of service delivery utilization in health, especially mental health. Prior to the civil-rights movements, the onus of responsibility for underutilization of services was placed squarely on Chicanos. Their fatalism, their present-orientation, their so-called lack of ambition and drive, their distinct culture values, and their approach to life were used to explain the problem. They were stereotypically labeled unmotivated; disinterested; non-verbal, even alingual, not speaking either Spanish or English adequately; superstitious. In other words, the victims were constantly blamed.[48] Chicanos, however, primarily attribute their underrepresentation in such services to the insensitivity of the professionals to their cultural and linguistic needs. They see the system as unmotivated to, and uninterested in, providing the services they need. Arias stated that Chicano patients in large urban hospitals regularly suffer from "overdoses of inattention and insensitivity," that they are at times "considered as criminal intruders," and that "their inability to speak English is viewed as pathological."[49] In rural areas "often they get no medical attention at all."[50] Chicanos, particularly those who are poor, receive less health care than the rest of the population.[51]

Chicanos use home remedies and other cures recommended by relatives, friends, and neighbors when illnesses do not appear serious. They consult *curanderos* * when folk illnesses are suspected or when medical resources are not available to them. But Chicanos are concerned about the health and mental health of their children and will use facilities that are responsive to their needs. This has been demonstrated by their participation in programs such as those available in Tucson, East Los Angeles, Oakland, and San Antonio. Services should take into consideration the client's social, economic, and political circumstance and should be provided by bilingual-bicultural staffs who are aware of cultural nuances and thus who use treatment approaches that are compatible with the clients' level of acculturation.[52]

The situation should continue to improve as the recommendations recently made by the President's Commission on Mental Health are being implemented, particularly the recommendation accepted by the commission to use culturally relevant treatment for mentally ill or emotionally disturbed Hispanics.[53]

The Social Welfare System and other social services have been insensitive to Chicano needs in comparable ways. For over a decade now, since the civil-rights movements, the Chicano community—including Chicano social work educators, practitioners, students, and particularly *la gente del barrio,* the people of the *barrio*—has expressed much concern over the irrelevance of social work services.[54] It has viewed the social work profession as a perpetra-

* *Curandero (curandera* for females) literally means "healer" or "curer." It applies to people who have special knowledge and skills to treat folk diseases, using herbs and other remedies. The knowledge is based on old Spanish and Indian medical practice and on empirical experiences. It is believed that *curanderos/as* are endowed by God with the gift of healing. *Curanderismo* has religious overtones.

tor of society's outright negligence and institutional insensitivity. Chicanos maintain that schools of social work continue to graduate "pacification agents" whose primary therapeutic approach stems from a personal deficiency theoretical frame of reference, which often, if not always, fails to recognize the impact that dysfunctional social structure has had on them.[55] Morales sees a growing gulf between what social work states its mission is and what it is actually doing. He asserts that poor communities need social workers with knowledge and skills to do both clinical work and who are able to intervene via social action on community systems.[56]

## Implications for Practice

In spite of great diversity[57] among them, social workers are fairly close in agreement in recognizing the mission of social work to be "to ameliorate suffering, alleviate distress, ameliorate poverty and injustice, take care of people and alleviate social problems."[58] NASW has given the elimination of poverty and racism a high priority during the past few years. Yet because society which sanctions the profession, has continued to adhere tenaciously to the mythic philosophy of the melting pot, it has been difficult for social workers in practice to recognize, accept, and, most importantly, value differences. Therefore, the profession, in spite of its values, mainly functions ethnocentrically, under the misconception that social work practice is universal in its application.[59]

To accomplish the mission of the profession and address its priorities in a pluralistic society, composed of different racial, ethnic, and socioeconomic groups, social workers need to develop a dual perspective.[60] This perspective is an attitudinal and cognitive approach that requires a "conscious and systematic process of perceiving, understanding and comparing simultaneously the values, attitudes and behaviors of the larger societal system with those of the client's* immediate family and community system."[61]

In terms of services to the Mexican-American people, social workers using the dual perspective need to view them in interaction with many systems some of which are supportive—the family, the *barrio,* and the church—even though at times ambivalently, and some of which are not only nonsupportive, but which may even be hostile—educational, place of employment, the police, and the judicial. Often Chicanos find themselves hopelessly, and even dangerously, victimized by these unsupportive, insensitive systems, which impose society's rules and practices that reflect institutional racism.

Traditionally, social workers have relied heavily on "talking therapies" anchored in middle-class, white value-based theoretical frames of reference,

---

* The term *client* refers to all client systems, whether individual, family, group, community, or larger macro units in planning.

probing into the clients' psyche searching for the root of the problem. The primary focus has been to help the clients develop self-understanding. But as Fischer stated, attempts to change the clients' situation by increasing their understanding of the internal causes of their maladaptive behavior results in little impact, if any, on a basically disruptive environment, which creates and/or supports the behavior. Neither will this approach enable them to cope with the immediate everyday problems.[62]

Providers of services to Chicanos, to be effective, need to

1. Use an eclectic model of social work practice. According to Fischer, this model

   (1) rationally and systematically incorporates the best known knowledge currently available, i.e., that which has the greatest potential for being translated into effective services for our clients; and (2) allows, indeed demands, objective demonstration of that effectiveness . . . An eclectic approach . . . to practice . . . would consist of a variety of interventive principles and procedures, derived from different systems of individual change.[63]

   This requires that social workers avoid being rigidly loyal to any one practice approach; instead of directing conceptual and treatment attention to the person exclusively, they need to analyze the client's behavior in its connection with the various systems of which he or she is part.[64]

2. Acquire new and/or additional knowledge about the Mexican-American people that will help them (a) expand their understanding of the heterogeneity among them, (b) understand the concepts of bilingualism and biculturalism, and (c) learn appropriate techniques.

3. Develop certain interpersonal skills essential for practice with Mexican-Americans, principally bilingual and bicultural skills.

# Conclusions

This paper has attempted to describe Mexican-American people and their supportive systems in interaction with social institutions, a monumental task for such a brief paper. The implications for service delivery are certainly not exhaustive. It is hoped that social workers who are serious about providing culturally relevant and linguistically syntonic services to Chicanos will continue to search the literature on Chicanos by Chicanos, which is now increasing. It is also anticipated that agencies serving the Mexican-American community will (1) recruit bilingual-bicultural social workers, (2) provide an *ambiente,* ambience or atmosphere, conducive to bilingual-bicultural practice, (3) provide in-service training for their staffs to prepare them better for practice with Chicanos, and (4) provide at least some exposure to the needs of Chicanos for the board members and others participating in the development and implementation of policy. The information that needs to be conveyed is that social work practice with Chicanos needs to go beyond the dimension for work with individuals to that which includes working with groups, with the *barrio,* with caregivers, and with authoritarian systems and also with practitioners from other disciplines to develop social resources, to effect change, and to encourage community development.[65]

Preventive services must be available to Chicanos, too. From a preventive standpoint, services to Chicanos should go from the ameliorative approach to one aimed at the positive goal of enhancing normal development. The need for preventive services in the *barrio* by making the environment more sensitive and supportive needs to be underscored. The well-being of Mexican-American children needs to be safeguarded by providing the resources necessary to prevent malnutrition and developmental difficulties, to promote their mental health, to identify their strengths, and to enhance the quality of their lives. This should be given high priority. Adequate, culturally relevant, and linguistically syntonic services, which are accessible geographically as well as psychologically, need to be established.

And most importantly, it is imperative that all Chicanos have an opportunity to develop a positive self-concept through the integration of "the persisting, selective, cultural patterns with new behavioral strategies" developed through the process of inner change and sociocultural adjustment,[66] with a minimum of conflict, which will enable them to maintain their *dignidad.*

## REFERENCE NOTES

1. Alvarez, Rodolfo, "The Psychohistorical and Socioeconomic Development of the Chicano Community in the United States," *Social Science Quarterly,* 53(1973): 920–942.
2. Grebler, Leo; Moore, Joan W.; and Guzman, Ralph, *The Mexican-American People.* New York: The Free Press Publishers, 1970.
3. "It's Your Turn in the Sun," Cover Story, *Time,* October 16, 1978.
4. Alvirez, David, and Bean, Frank D., "The Mexican-American Family," in *Ethnic Families in America,* edited by Charles H. Mindel and Robert W. Habenstein. New York: Elsevier, 1976.
5. Aragon, M., "Their Heritage-Poverty," in *The Chicanos: Mexican-American Voices,* edited by E. Ludwig and J. Santistivan. Baltimore: Penguin Books, 1971.
6. Romano, Octavio, "The Anthropology and Sociology of the Mexican-Americans' History," in *Voices,* edited by Octavio Romano. Berkeley: Quinto Sol Publications, 1973.
7. Vaca, N., "The Mexican-Americans in the Social Sciences," *El Grito,* 4(1970): 17–51.
8. Montiel, Miguel, "The Social Science Myth of the Mexican-American Family, in *Voices,* edited by Octavio Romano. Berkeley: Quinto Sol Publications, 1973.
9. Dworkin, A., "Stereotypes and Self-Images Held by Native-Born and Foreign-Born Mexican-Americans," in *Chicanos: Social and Psychological Perspectives,* edited by N. Wagner and M. Haug. Saint Louis: C. V. Mosby, 1971.
10. Gomez, Ernesto, and Cerda, Gilberto, "Chicano Dialectal Language," *The Social Significance and Value Dimension of Current Mexican-American Spanish: Implications for Practice,* edited by Ernesto Gomez and Roy Becker. San Antonio: Our Lady of the Lake University of San Antonio, 1977.
11. Aguirre, Lydia R., "The Meaning of the Chicano Movement," in *La Causa Chicana, The Movement for Justice,* edited by Margaret M. Mangold. New York: Family Service Association of America, 1972.
12. Gilbert, M. Jean, "Extended Family Integration Among Second-Generation Mexican-Americans," in *Family and Mental Health in the Mexican-American Community,*

edited by J. Manuel Casas and Susan E. Keefe. Los Angeles: The Spanish-Speaking Mental Health Research Center, 1978.

13. Ibid.
14. Grebler, et al., op. cit.
15. Garcia-Bahne, Betty, "La Chicana and the Chicano Family," in *Essays on La Mujer,* edited by Rosaura Sanchez and Rosa Martinez Cruz. Los Angeles: Chicano Studies Center Publications, 1977.
16. Alvirez and Bean, op. cit.
17. Ibid.
18. Ibid.
19. Goodman, Mary Ellen, and Beman, Alma, "Child's-Eye-Views of Life in an Urban Barrio," in *Chicanos: Social and Psychosocial Perspectives,* edited by N. Wagner and M. Haug. St. Louis: The C. V. Mosby Company, 1971.
20. Ruiz, Juliette, ed., *Chicano Task Force Report.* New York: Council on Social Work Education, 1973.
21. Valdez, Daniel T., "The Barrios Come Alive," *La Luz* (August 1972).
22. Sotomayor, Marta. "Mexican-American Interaction with Social Systems," in *La Causa Chicana: The Movement for Justice,* edited by Margaret M. Mangold. New York: Family Service Association of America, 1972.
23. Ibid.
24. Goodman, Mary Allen, and Beman, Alma, op. cit.
25. Sanchez, Delfino, "Research on La Familia." Edgewood School District. San Antonio, Texas, 1975. Mimeographed.
26. Goodman, Mary Ellen, and Beman, Alma, op. cit.
27. Ibid.
28. Mendes, Helen, *Some Religious Values Held by Blacks, Chicanos and Japanese Americans and Their Implications for Casework Practice.* Monograph #4. Boulder, Colorado: Western Interstate Commission for Higher Education, 1974.
29. Ibid.
30. Ibid.
31. Lara-Braud, Jorge, "The Status of Religion Among Mexican-Americans," in *La Causa Chicana: The Movement for Justice,* edited by Margaret M. Mangold. New York: Family Service Association of America, 1972.
32. Ibid.
33. Sandoval, Moises, "The Latinization of the Catholic Church," *Agenda* 8(6): 4–7 (November 1978).
34. Ibid.
35. Ibid.
36. Ibid.
37. Nava, Julian, "Educational Challenges in Elementary and Secondary Schools," in *Mexican Americans Tomorrow: Educational and Economic Perspectives,* edited by Gus Tyler. Albuquerque: University of New Mexico Press, 1975.
38. Padilla, Amado M., "Psychological Research and the Mexican American," in *La Causa Chicana: The Movement for Justice,* edited by Margaret M. Mangold. New York: Family Service Association of America, 1972.
39. *The Six-Hour Retarded Child.* A report on a conference on problems of education of children in the inner city. August 10–12, 1969. Washington, D.C.: U.S. Printing Office.
40. Steiner, Stan, *La Raza: The Mexican American.* New York: Harper & Row, 1969.
41. *The Excluded Student-Educational Practices Affecting Mexican Americans in the Southwest.* Report III, U.S. Commission on Civil Rights. Washington, D.C.: U.S. Government Printing Office, May 1972.
42. "Women are Still Lagging in Equality," *The San Antonio Star,* October 15, 1978.

43. Langley, Roger, Washington Correspondent, "Study Shows Employment Lowest among Hispanics," *San Antonio Express/News,* December 14, 1978.

44. Souflee, Federico J., and Valdez, George, *Proceedings of the Texas-New Mexico Symposium on the Delivery of Mental Health Services to Mexican Americans,* Austin, Texas, April 1978.

45. Arias, Ron, "Sick to Death of the Health Mess," *Nuestro* (October 1978).

46. Ibid.

47. Steiner, op. cit.

48. Ryan, W., *Blaming the Victim.* New York: Pantheon Books, 1971.

49. Arias, op. cit.

50. Ibid.

51. Ibid.

52. Arias, Ron, "A Better Approach to Mental Health," *Nuestro* (October 1978).

53. *Report to The President's Commission on Mental Health* from the Special Population Sub-Task Panel on Mental Health of Hispanic Americans. Esteban L. Olmedo, Ph.D. and Pedro Lecca, Ph.D., Coordinators. Reprinted by the Spanish-Speaking Mental Health Research Center, May 1978.

54. Gibson, Guadalupe; Gomez, Ernesto; and Santos, Yolanda, "Bilingual-Bicultural Service for the Barrio," *The Social Welfare Forum, 1973.* New York: National Conference on Social Welfare, Columbia University Press, 1974.

55. Ibid.

56. Morales, Armando, "Beyond Traditional Conceptual Frameworks," *Social Work.* Special Issue on Conceptual Frameworks. 22(5): 387–393 (September 1977).

57. Simon, Bernece K., "Diversity and Unity in the Social Work Profession," *Social Work.* Special Issue on Conceptual Frameworks. 22(5): 394–400 (September 1977).

58. Morales, op. cit.

59. Souflee, Federico, Jr., "Social Work: Acquiescing Profession," *Social Work.* Special Issue on Conceptual Frameworks. 22 (5): 419–421 (September 1977).

60. Norton, Dolores G., *The Dual Perspective; Inclusion of Minority Content in the Social Work Curriculum.* New York: Council on Social Work Education, 1978.

61. Ibid.

62. Fischer, Joel, *Effective Casework Practice: An Eclectic Approach.* New York: McGraw-Hill Book Company, 1978.

63. Ibid.

64. Ibid.

65. Frey, Louise A., and Edinburg, Golda M., "Helping, Manipulation and Magic," *Social Work.* 23(2): 88–93 (March 1978).

66. Mostwin, Danuta, D.S.W., "Family Mental Health in a Pluralistic Society," *Social Thought.* 4(2): 21–31 (Spring 1978).

PART

STATISTICAL
TABLES

# Tables as Tools for Planning and Accountability: "Why?" and "How?" to Read Statistical Tables

TO TURN A PHRASE, if a picture is worth a thousand words, then a statistical table is worth a thousand pictures. At least, a specific behavior or life experience of thousands, perhaps millions, of persons may be succinctly, if abstractly, described by a set of numbers arranged in columns and rows. By disentangling this specific event from the web of human life, we are enabled to examine it with greater insight and attention in order to obtain its full measure of social meaning. For example, we may know from our personal experience the feelings and thoughts involved in sexual behavior, including those that result in the birth of a child. But Table 1 ("Estimates of World Population, 1650–2000") magnifies just one aspect of this fundamental event in estimating how many people were born at certain times during the past three hundred years and how many are likely to be alive by the end of this century.

No matter what our personal experiences have been in conceiving or not conceiving children, these summary facts give us a perspective on an enormous social event—the total population—of which we are just one minute instance. Yet the table informs us, if we choose to listen, that though you and I may be just one person each, we are a multitude endangering our own species with overpopulation and the attendant dangers, not simply reducing quality of life but influencing whether millions of persons will survive beyond birth. Thus, we may approach an abstract table ready to read about the collective behaviors of the many so as to predict the nature of social life and its risks for specific individuals—including our clients and ourselves. You and I are among those counted in these tables.

Any one table is but a choice among many possible tables, each reflecting one facet or another in the complexity of human life and behavior. Each table is a story told from one point of view when there are many others. Therefore, read each table with care for what it says, what it doesn't say, and what is said only incompletely or elliptically.

# How to Read a Table

Tables are constructed according to a general system of rules. The title of a table indicates what facet or facets of human life and behavior are being examined, and, most importantly, the title may indicate the relationship of one event to others. For example, Table 2 is entitled "Population of the United States, by Age, Sex, and Race, 1975." Approach each table as if the title were a question, and expect to find information answering the question. From Table 2, the implicit questions are these: How many Americans are there by various age groupings? How many male and female Americans are there? How many white and black Americans are there? Depending on how the table is organized, one might also expect to find how many black females there are who are over 65 years of age or other combinations of facets. Obviously, these are complex questions, and they make even greater demands on readers by grouping different persons under one heading. For instance, the category of *aged 65 and over* many contain persons who may differ in age as much as thirty or forty years. However, the first task in reading a table is to identify the implicit question(s) it is posing.

The second task in understanding a table is to figure out how the question is going to be answered; that is, what the terms and categories mean and how they are arranged. Some terms are assumed to be commonly understood, like white and black as labels for racial groups. Be careful. Words mean different things to different people. In Table 2, black refers exclusively to Negro, as contrasted with other nonwhites. And so Table 2 adds information about Native Americans, various oriental and Polynesian Americans, and others. Likewise, it is often important to recognize special subgroups within the broader categories, like persons of Hispanic origin; this is added to Table 2 to give a more nearly well-rounded picture of the population of the United States. By the simplification of events into broad categories, information may be lost from sight unless the reader is attentive to definitions that are usually provided in the tables themselves or elsewhere in the paper.

Tables are arranged to be brief summaries of information. They may provide partial information of such a nature as to enable the reader to calculate further data as desired. For example, Table 3 ("Population of the United States by Marital Status and Sex, 1975") doesn't state directly the total number of widowed persons as being about 11,921,000—the sum of widowers and widows—because it is more significant to point out in the table the enormous differences in widowhood by the sexes. This leads to another point about tables—they should stimulate readers to ask questions about differences or trends that emerge in the data. With regard to widowhood, a reference to a research study is given in Table 3 that may help explain this large discrepancy and may also lead to preventive and interventive responses by helping professionals. Unfortunately, not many tables provide this. Thus, for the applied social scientists, tables have served their full purpose when they raise questions, provoke consideration of significant differences in life experiences reported by the data, and perhaps lead to considerations of what helping professionals might do to resolve the population problems or potentials that emerge. Obviously, tables do not tell us what to do, but what needs doing.

Tables should be self-contained; that is, the figures should add up to (nearly) 100 per cent of the events accounted for (given minor discrepancies due to rounding, and so on). For example, Table 5 ("Households by Type of Head, 1975") contains one set of numbers—68.2, 10.0, and 21.8—which logically should add up to another number—100.0—because they bear a parts-to-whole relationship. Data in other tables, such as Table 7 ("Median Income of Families and Individuals by Race, 1950–1975") are not to be added. They represent discrete events in time and answer the question, What has been the median income of specified types of persons on four different occasions (1950, 1960, 1970, and 1975)? Trends that emerge are useful as feedback to collective action. Are we distributing wealth more equitably in recent years than in the past? Answers to this complex question are facilitated by including a category of the ratio of white and black median incomes. It is clear that no amount of individual experiences could as easily summarize these events; tables are absolutely necessary. Indeed, tables may be powerful tools in illuminating human relationships and the impact of social programs. This type of information becomes vital in helping professionals' attempts to document the need for change and to show their accountability in having generated change in desired directions. But, again, be careful, for it is possible to *lie with statistics* (cf. Darrell Huff, 1954).

Because each table tells its own story from its particular perspective, it often becomes necessary to look at several tables simultaneously. For example, consider the question whether women have achieved practical economic security. One might look at Table 9 ("Married women [Husbands Present] in the Labor Force, by Age, and Presence of Children, 1950–1975"), which reveals an increasing proportion of women with paid jobs. And yet, if viewed in connection with Table 8 ("Median Income of Families and Individuals, by Sex, 1950–1975"), one might observe the inconsistent changes in relative income of males and females over this period of time. One hopes that additional questions not answered by these tables will be raised that will motivate readers to search further. Does having any sort of job mean economic security? What types of jobs do women and men hold? . . . No one table is sufficient to document any complex aspect of human life. But when they are viewed in combination, we begin to see at large what our personal experiences reveal only imperfectly.

Tables are no better than the information from which they are originally derived. Usually, a citation at the bottom of the table will provide this information. I have tried to use commonly available sources so that readers could continue their explorations of additional tables. On occasion, I have tried to provide links to additional readings that grapple with particular questions raised in a table, including some articles in this book.

# Why the Choice of the Particular Tables Found in This Book?

My rationale for choice of tables in Part IV of this book reflects the lifespan itself. The tables begin with issues of birth and population data—what numbers and types of persons are born and how they survive to later ages. Within the vast amount of available data, I have selected and modified tabular information to what I think is most useful for applied social scientists who seek to get a grasp of social events and trends. In effect, I have tried to provoke basic questions and to supply the broad statistical perspectives against which answers could be posed. These are the beginnings of answers, not the end.

A next group of tables considers how people organize themselves for living—by forming households and families, by working and earning income, by obtaining formal education, and perhaps by receiving assistance from society in times of need. Human need, as reflected in these tables, may be long-term—such as those aided by many of the social welfare, educational, and crime programs—or specific to a given population at a certain time. Each becomes a type of problem or challenge to helping professionals. As one specialized in a career, it is likely that the information one accumulates and the tables that are pertinent will likewise become more focused: from federal censuses to specific national surveys to particular studies of a given community. Our need to know grows more focused, but we never lose our need to have a general perspective in which to place the particular.

A final group of tables reflects the end of life; the facts of homicide and suicide; the major causes of mortality for persons of different ages, sexes, and races. The differences among persons continues to the end of life as they had been expressed at the beginning, reflecting the unequal distribution of opportunities and resources, as well as personal strengths and weaknesses.

The reader should know that there are many other sources of tabular information that could be useful in planning and understanding social change. The following sources suggested may be a point of departure: publications from the National Center for Health Statistics (United States Department of Health, Education, and Welfare; Public Health Service; Health Resources Administration; National Center for Health Statistics; Center Building, 3700 East-West Highway, Hyattsville, Maryland 20782).

There are various encyclopedias, almanacs, and yearbooks that compile tabular data. For example, *Facts on File* (1940 to date) contains detailed information on special social and political issues. *Statistical Abstracts,* published by the United States Government annually, contains a wealth of information on every facet of life in this country. The *Encyclopedia of Social Work* (1975 or latest edition) includes selected tables of interest to members of that profession. Some journals present continuing sets of data on various issues, such as the *Social Security Bulletin.* The time devoted to locating information resources is well spent.

Table 1

*Estimates of World Population, 1650–2000 (millions of persons)*

|  | 1650 | 1750 | 1850 | 1950 | 1975 | (2000) |
|---|---|---|---|---|---|---|
| Total World | 470 | 694 | 1,094 | 2,543 | 3,967 | 6,253 |
| Africa | 100 | 100 | 100 | 219 | 399 | 813 |
| North America (USA, Canada) | 1 | 1 | 26 | 166 | 237 | 296 |
| South America (Mexico, Central, South America) | 7 | 10 | 33 | 164 | 323 | 619 |
| Asia | 257 | 437 | 656 | 1,409 | 2,288 | 3,636 |
| Europe (includes all USSR) | 103 | 144 | 274 | 572 | 728 | 855 |
| Oceania | 2 | 2 | 2 | 12 | 21 | 33 |

Sources: For 1650 to 1850, United Nations, *Proceedings of the World Population Conference, 1954*, vol. 3 (New York, 1955): "The past and future population of the world and its continents," Table 1, p. 266.

For 1950 to 2000, *Statistical Abstracts*, 1976, Tables 1442, 1443, and 1446. Note that the projections of the year 2000 are made according to three sets of assumptions that generate low, middle, and high population figures. The figures used here are the middle ones. The high estimate is over 8 billion. Nicholas J. Demerath (*Birth Control and Foreign Policy*, 1976) puts these figures into perspective; "If the world population were to be compressed into a village of 1,000 with the continents comprising the neighborhoods, there would be roughly: 575 Asians, 200 Europeans, 85 Africans, 85 North Americans (55 U.S. Citizens), 55 South Americans/ 1000 total. In the village there would be about 300 whites and 300 professed Christians. Of the total income generated, half would go to the U.S. citizens." (pp. 5–6).

467

**Table 2**

*Population of the United States by Age, Sex, and Race,\* 1975 (in thousands)*

| Age groups | Total population | % of total | White Male | White Female | Black Male | Black Female |
|---|---|---|---|---|---|---|
| Total | 213,137 | | 90,423 | 94,775 | 11,646 | 12,811 |
| Under 5 | 15,896 | 7.5 | 6,729 | 6,413 | 1,209 | 1,186 |
| 5–13 | 33,456 | 15.7 | 14,333 | 13,702 | 2,420 | 2,401 |
| 14–17 | 16,941 | 7.9 | 7,314 | 7,018 | 1,176 | 1,163 |
| 18–21 | 16,330 | 7.7 | 7,032 | 6,929 | 1,016 | 1,072 |
| 22–24 | 11,028 | 5.2 | 4,764 | 4,750 | 612 | 692 |
| 25–34 | 30,783 | 14.4 | 13,417 | 13,472 | 1,501 | 1,764 |
| 35–44 | 22,759 | 10.7 | 9,798 | 10,109 | 1,110 | 1,343 |
| 45–54 | 23,764 | 11.1 | 10,276 | 10,890 | 1,054 | 1,212 |
| 55–64 | 19,780 | 9.3 | 8,461 | 9,408 | 787 | 760 |
| 65 and over | 22,400 | 10.5 | 8,299 | 12,082 | 934 | 1,043 |
| | | 100.0 | | | | |

Source: *Statistical Abstracts,* 1976, Table 28.

\* In addition to white and black Americans, there were also the following numbers of persons (in 1970):

| | |
|---|---|
| Native American | 793,000 |
| Japanese | 591,000 |
| Chinese | 435,000 |
| Filipino | 343,000 |
| Other | 721,000 (Includes Aleuts, Asian Indians, Eskimos, Hawaiians, Indonesians, Koreans, Polynesians, and others.) |

Source: *Statistical Abstracts,* 1976, Table 24.

In 1975, there were 11,202,000 persons of Spanish origin. Of these, 6,690,000 were Mexican, 1,671,000 were Puerto Rican, and the remainder were of other Spanish origin. (Source: *Statistical Abstracts,* 1976, Table 42.)

See also C. S. Chilman, "Public social policy and population problems in the United States," *Social Service Review,* 1973, 47:4, 511–530.

**Table 3**

*Population of the United States \* by Marital Status and Sex, 1975*
*(in thousands, for persons 18 years and over)*

| Marital status | Males | | Females | |
|---|---|---|---|---|
| | Number | Per cent | Number | Per cent |
| Single | 14,098 | 20.8 | 11,007 | 14.6 |
| Married | 49,409 | 72.8 | 50,257 | 66.7 |
| Widowed | 1,817† | 2.7 | 10,104† | 13.4 |
| Divorced | 2,545 | 3.7 | 3,978 | 5.3 |
| Total | 67,869 | 100.0 | 75,345 | 100.0 |

Source: *Statistical Abstract,* 1976, Table 45.

\* These figures exclude the armed forces, except those living off post or with families on post.

† For a statistical analysis of the large differences between widowed males and females, see G. F. Grannis. "Demographic perturbations secondary to cigarette smoking," *Journal of Gerontology,* 1970, 25:1, 55–63. He concludes that "the ratio of elderly females to males and the ratio of widows to widowers have changed during the past 75 years to the extent expected on the basis of national cigarette consumption by males and the known relation of the degree of cigarette smoking to premature mortality of males" (p. 62).

Table 4

*Expectations of Life\* by Race and Sex, United States, 1975*

| Age | White | | Nonwhite | | All persons of this age combined |
|---|---|---|---|---|---|
| | Male | Female | Male | Female | |
| 0 | 69.4 | 77.2 | 63.6 | 72.3 | 72.5 |
| 1 | 69.6 | 77.1 | 64.4 | 73.0 | 72.7 |
| 2 | 68.6 | 76.2 | 63.4 | 72.1 | 71.8 |
| 3 | 67.7 | 75.2 | 62.5 | 71.1 | 70.8 |
| 4 | 66.7 | 74.3 | 61.6 | 70.2 | 69.9 |
| 5 | 65.7 | 73.3 | 60.6 | 69.2 | 68.9 |
| 6 | 64.8 | 72.3 | 59.7 | 68.3 | 67.9 |
| 7 | 63.8 | 71.3 | 58.7 | 67.3 | 67.0 |
| 8 | 62.8 | 70.4 | 57.7 | 66.3 | 66.0 |
| 9 | 61.9 | 69.4 | 56.8 | 65.3 | 65.0 |
| 10 | 60.9 | 68.4 | 55.8 | 64.4 | 64.0 |
| 15 | 56.0 | 63.5 | 50.9 | 59.5 | 59.1 |
| 20 | 51.4 | 58.6 | 46.3 | 54.7 | 54.4 |
| 25 | 46.9 | 53.8 | 42.1 | 49.9 | 49.8 |
| 30 | 42.2 | 49.0 | 38.0 | 45.3 | 45.1 |
| 35 | 37.6 | 44.2 | 33.8 | 40.7 | 40.4 |
| 40 | 33.0 | 39.4 | 29.8 | 36.2 | 35.8 |
| 45 | 28.5 | 34.8 | 26.0 | 32.0 | 31.4 |
| 50 | 24.3 | 30.3 | 22.4 | 27.9 | 27.1 |
| 55 | 20.4 | 26.0 | 19.2 | 24.1 | 23.1 |
| 60 | 16.8 | 21.9 | 16.3 | 20.7 | 19.4 |
| 65 | 13.7 | 18.1 | 13.7 | 17.5 | 16.0 |
| 70 | 10.9 | 14.4 | 11.3 | 14.4 | 12.8 |
| 75 | 8.5 | 11.2 | 9.7 | 12.5 | 10.2 |
| 80 | 6.7 | 8.6 | 8.5 | 11.0 | 8.0 |
| 85 | 5.2 | 6.5 | 7.1 | 9.1 | 6.2 |

Source: National Center for Health Statistics, via Metropolitan Life, *Statistical Bulletin,* May 1977.

\* A person of a given age, sex, and race in 1975 was expected to live the number of years indicated.

Table 5
Height and Weight, by Age and Sex
Part I: Heights (in centimeters)* and Weight (in Kilograms)* by sex and age†

| Age | Males: height percentile | | | Males: weight percentile | | | Females: height percentile | | | Females: weight percentile | | |
|---|---|---|---|---|---|---|---|---|---|---|---|---|
| | 10% | 50% | 90% | 10% | 50% | 90% | 10% | 50% | 90% | 10% | 50% | 90% |
| Birth | 48.1 | 50.6 | 53.3 | 2.9 | 3.4 | 4.1 | 47.8 | 50.2 | 51.0 | 2.8 | 3.4 | 3.9 |
| 1 | 72.4 | 75.2 | 78.1 | 8.9 | 10.7 | 11.5 | 70.6 | 74.2 | 77.1 | 8.4 | 9.8 | 11.3 |
| 2 | 84.2 | 87.5 | 91.1 | 11.2 | 12.6 | 14.5 | 82.0 | 86.6 | 91.0 | 10.7 | 12.3 | 14.4 |
| 3 | 92.3 | 96.2 | 100.5 | 13.0 | 14.6 | 16.7 | 90.5 | 95.7 | 101.1 | 12.5 | 14.4 | 17.0 |
| 4 | 99.3 | 103.4 | 108.5 | 14.6 | 16.5 | 18.8 | 97.6 | 103.2 | 109.6 | 14.2 | 16.4 | 19.7 |
| 5 | 103.7 | 108.7 | 114.7 | 16.1 | 18.4 | 21.2 | 103.0 | 109.1 | 115.4 | 15.8 | 18.4 | 22.3 |
| 6 | 111.2 | 117.5 | 123.5 | 18.6 | 21.9 | 25.6 | 110.6 | 115.9 | 122.3 | 18.0 | 21.1 | 24.6 |
| 7 | 116.9 | 124.1 | 130.5 | 20.8 | 24.5 | 29.2 | 116.8 | 122.3 | 128.9 | 20.2 | 23.7 | 27.8 |
| 8 | 123.1 | 130.0 | 137.3 | 23.2 | 27.3 | 33.1 | 122.1 | 128.0 | 134.6 | 22.0 | 26.4 | 31.7 |
| 9 | 128.3 | 135.5 | 142.6 | 25.5 | 29.9 | 36.7 | 127.0 | 132.9 | 140.4 | 23.9 | 28.9 | 35.9 |
| 10 | 132.8 | 140.3 | 147.5 | 27.7 | 32.6 | 40.8 | 131.7 | 138.6 | 146.0 | 25.9 | 31.9 | 40.7 |
| 11 | 137.3 | 144.2 | 151.8 | 30.1 | 35.2 | 45.0 | 137.0 | 144.7 | 153.4 | 28.4 | 35.7 | 45.5 |
| 12 | 142.4 | 149.6 | 157.9 | 32.7 | 38.3 | 49.7 | 142.6 | 151.9 | 160.6 | 31.5 | 39.7 | 50.6 |
| 13 | 146.6 | 155.0 | 165.3 | 35.0 | 42.2 | 55.9 | 149.1 | 157.1 | 164.8 | 36.2 | 45.0 | 56.5 |
| 14 | 152.1 | 162.7 | 172.4 | 39.6 | 48.8 | 62.1 | 153.0 | 159.6 | 167.0 | 41.3 | 49.2 | 60.5 |
| 15 | 157.8 | 167.8 | 176.7 | 45.1 | 54.5 | 67.0 | 155.2 | 161.1 | 168.1 | 44.2 | 51.5 | 62.6 |
| 16 | 162.8 | 171.6 | 179.7 | 50.4 | 58.8 | 71.4 | 156.1 | 162.2 | 169.0 | 45.8 | 53.1 | 64.0 |
| 17 | 165.5 | 173.7 | 181.6 | 53.3 | 61.8 | 74.7 | 156.3 | 162.5 | 169.4 | 46.6 | 54.0 | 65.0 |
| 18 | 166.3 | 174.5 | 182.4 | 54.4 | 63.1 | 76.7 | 156.3 | 162.5 | 169.4 | 47.0 | 54.4 | 65.5 |

* Adapted from Lowrey, G. H.: *Growth and Development of Children*, 6th edition. Copyright © 1973 by Year Book Medical Publishers, Inc., Chicago. Used by permission.
† To convert centimeters into inches, divide centimeters by 2.54. To convert kilograms into pounds, multiply kilograms by 2.2. "Height (or weight) Percentile" refers to the heights (or weights) achieved by certain specified portions of the population measured.

471

**Table 5**

*Part II: Desirable Weight by Height for Persons 25 years or older* *

| Height in centimeters | Males (by bone type) (in kilograms) | | | Height in centimeters | Females | | |
|---|---|---|---|---|---|---|---|
| | Small frame | Medium frame | Large frame | | Small frame | Medium frame | Large frame |
| 157.5 (5'2") | 50.8—54.4 | 53.5—58.5 | 57.2—64.0 | 147.3 (4'10") | 41.7—44.4 | 43.5—48.5 | 47.2—54.0 |
| 160.0 | 52.2—55.8 | 54.9—60.3 | 58.5—65.3 | 149.8 | 42.6—45.8 | 44.4—49.9 | 48.1—55.3 |
| 162.6 | 53.5—57.2 | 56.2—61.7 | 59.9—67.1 | 152.4 | 45.3—47.2 | 45.8—51.3 | 49.4—56.7 |
| 165.1 | 54.9—58.5 | 57.6—63.1 | 61.2—69.0 | 154.9 | 44.9—48.5 | 47.2—52.6 | 50.8—58.1 |
| 167.6 | 56.2—60.3 | 59.0—64.9 | 62.6—70.8 | 157.5 | 46.3—49.9 | 48.5—54.0 | 52.2—59.4 |
| 170.2 | 58.1—62.1 | 60.8—66.7 | 64.4—73.0 | 160.0 | 47.6—51.3 | 49.9—55.3 | 53.5—60.8 |
| 172.7 | 59.9—64.0 | 62.6—69.0 | 66.7—75.3 | 162.6 | 49.0—52.6 | 51.3—57.2 | 54.9—62.6 |
| 175.3 | 61.7—65.8 | 64.4—70.3 | 68.5—77.1 | 165.1 | 50.3—54.0 | 52.6—59.0 | 56.7—64.4 |
| 177.8 | 63.5—68.1 | 66.2—72.6 | 70.3—78.9 | 167.6 | 51.7—55.8 | 54.4—61.2 | 58.5—66.2 |
| 180.3 | 65.3—69.9 | 68.1—74.9 | 72.1—81.2 | 170.2 | 53.5—57.6 | 56.2—63.1 | 60.3—68.1 |
| 182.9 | 67.1—71.7 | 69.9—77.1 | 74.4—83.5 | 172.7 | 54.9—59.4 | 58.1—64.9 | 62.1—69.9 |
| 185.4 | 69.0—73.5 | 71.7—79.4 | 76.2—85.8 | 175.3 | 57.2—61.2 | 59.9—66.7 | 64.0—71.7 |
| 188.0 | 70.8—75.8 | 73.5—81.7 | 78.5—88.0 | 177.8 | 59.0—63.5 | 61.7—68.5 | 65.8—74.0 |
| 190.5 | 72.6—77.6 | 75.3—83.9 | 80.8—90.3 | 180.3 | 60.8—65.3 | 63.5—70.3 | 67.6—76.2 |
| 193.0 (6'4") | 74.4—79.4 | 78.0—86.2 | 82.6—92.6 | 182.9 (6'0") | 62.6—67.1 | 65.3—72.1 | 69.4—78.5 |

* Adapted from the desirable weight table of the Metropolitan Life Insurance Company, by permission. Height is with shoes on and weight with indoor clothing.

## Table 6
### Households,* by Type of Head, 1975 (in thousands)

("Households" are defined as comprising all persons who occupy a housing unit—house, apartment, or rooms that constitute a separate living quarter.)

| Type of head | Number | Per cent |
|---|---|---|
| White | 62,945 | 100.0 |
|   Husband-Wife | 42,951 | 68.2 |
|   Other Male Head | 6,295 | 10.0 |
|   Female Head | 13,700 | 21.8 |
| Negro and Other | 8,175 | 100.0 |
|   Husband-Wife | 4,000 | 48.9 |
|   Other Male Head | 1,103 | 13.5 |
|   Female Head | 3,073 | 37.6 |

Source: *Statistical Abstracts*, 1976, Table 53.

\* Of the total number of households, approximately 19.6% consisted of one person, 30.6% of two persons, 17.4% of three persons, 15.6% of four persons, 9.0% of five persons, 4.3% of 6 persons, and 3.5% of seven or more persons. Source: *Statistical Abstracts*, 1976, Table 51.

Also see I. F. Davidoff, "Living together" as a developmental phase: A holistic view, *Journal of Marriage and Family Counseling*, 1977, 67–76; B. E. Cogswell, Variant family forms and life styles: Rejection of the traditonal nuclear family, *The Family Coordinator*, 1975, 391–406, as well as the Eiduson chapter in this book.

Table 7
*Median Income of Families and Individuals, by Race,† 1950–1975*

| Year | White Families | White Unrelated individuals* | Black and other races Families | Black and other races Unrelated individuals | Ratio of black and others to white Families | Ratio of black and others to white Unrelated individuals |
|------|------|------|------|------|------|------|
| 1950 | $ 7,608 | $2,495 | $3,888 | $1,798 | 0.51 | 0.72 |
| 1960 | 10,604 | 3,380 | 5,871 | 1,940 | 0.55 | 0.57 |
| 1970 | 14,188 | 4,551 | 9,032 | 3,109 | 0.64 | 0.68 |
| 1975 | 14,268 | 5,099 | 9,321 | 3,392 | 0.65 | 0.67 |

Source: *Statistical Abstracts*, 1976, Table 650.

* "Unrelated individual" refers to a person who is not living with any relative and who is not an inmate in an institution.

† See also E. B. Palmore and K. Manton, "Ageism compared to racism and sexism," *Journal of Gerontology*, 1973, 28:3, 363–369. T. Sowell, in "Ethnicity in a Changing America," *Daedalus*, 1978 (Winter) 107:1, 213–237, notes that the mean family income of the total U.S. population of employed workers in 1969 was $10,678. There were two ethnic groups that exceeded this mean income, Japanese Americans ($13,377) and Chinese Americans ($12,176). On the other hand, Black Americans ($6,821), Native Americans ($6,621) and Puerto Ricans ($6,728) were far below the average, whereas West Indians ($9,821) and Filipino Americans ($10,395) were only somewhat below. (p. 214) Sowell seeks to explain some of these variations in income in terms of such factors as median age—Puerto Rican Americans have a median age one-half that Russian Americans, and older persons have reached higher income levels than younger ones, whatever ethnic background. Another factor is fertility. For example, native Black Americans average more than one child per woman than Black Americans born in the West Indies. Thus many factors are involved in income data.

Table 8
*Median Income of Families and Individuals, by Sex,* 1950–1975*

| Year | Male Male head of family | Male Unrelated individual | Female Female head of family | Female Unrelated individual | Ratio of female to male Family | Ratio of female to male Unrelated individual |
|------|------|------|------|------|------|------|
| 1950 | $ 3,435 | $1,539 | $1,922 | $ 846 | 0.56 | 0.55 |
| 1960 | 5,857 | 2,480 | 2,968 | 1,377 | 0.51 | 0.56 |
| 1970 | 10,480 | 4,540 | 5,093 | 2,483 | 0.49 | 0.55 |
| 1975 | 14,816 | 6,612 | 6,844 | 3,978 | 0.46 | 0.60 |

Source: *Statistical Abstracts*, 1976, Table 657.

* See also E. B. Palmore and K. Manton, "Ageism compared to racism and sexism," *Journal of Gerontology*, 1973, 28:3, 363–369.

Table 9

*Married Women (Husbands Present) in the Labor Force, by Age, and Presence of Children,* * 1950–1975*

| Married women in the labor force, as a percentage of married women in the population: | 1950 | 1960 | 1970 | 1975 |
|---|---|---|---|---|
| Married women, husband present | 23.8 | 30.5 | 40.8 | 44.4 |
| With no children under 18 years old | 30.3 | 34.7 | 42.2 | 43.9 |
| With children 6–17 years old only | 28.3 | 39.0 | 49.2 | 52.4 |
| With children under 6 years old | 11.9 | 18.6 | 30.3 | 36.6 |
| Also with children 6–17 | 12.6 | 18.9 | 30.5 | 34.3 |
| Total number (in 1000s) | 8,550 | 12,253 | 18,377 | 21,111 |

Source: *Statistical Abstracts,* 1976, Table 576.

* For an analysis of the effects of working mothers on children, see C. Etauch, "Effects of maternal employment on children: A review of recent research," *Merrill-Palmer Quarterly,* 1974, 20:2, 71–98, as well as the Wallston chapter in this book.

Table 10

*Marriage and Divorce Rates in the United States,* * 1950–1970*

| Year | Marriage rates (per 1000 population) | Divorce rates (per 1000 population) |
|---|---|---|
| 1950 | 11.1 | 2.6 |
| 1960 | 8.5 | 2.2 |
| 1970 | 10.6 | 3.5 |
| 1975 | 10.0 | 4.8 |

Source: *Statistical Abstracts,* 1976, Table 97.

* See the discussion by Rohrlich, Ranier, Berg-Cross, and Berg-Cross in this book on the effects of divorce.

## Table 11

*Employment and Unemployment, by Age, Sex, and Race, 1975 (persons 16 years and over)*

| | Total noninstitutionalized population | Civilian labor force | | | Not in labor force |
|---|---|---|---|---|---|
| | | Total | Per cent employed | Per cent unemployed | Per cent of total noninstitutionalized population |
| Total | 153,516,000 | 92,613,000 | 91.5 | 8.5 | 38.2 |
| Male | | | | | |
| total | 73,494,000 | 55,615,000 | 92.1 | 7.9 | 21.5 |
| Negro and other than white | 8,360,000 | 5,734,000 | 86.2 | 13.7 | 27.3 |
| Female | | | | | |
| total | 79,954,000 | 36,998,000 | 90.7 | 9.3 | 53.6 |
| Negro and other than white | 9,766,000 | 4,795,000 | 86.0 | 14.0 | 50.7 |

Source: *Statistical Abstracts,* 1976, Table 571.

B. Burdetsky ("Troubled transition: From school to work," *Worklife,* 1976, 1:11,2–8) provides another perspective on the unemployment picture.

*Comparison of selected unemployment rates, 1967–1976 \**

| Year | U.S. rate | Adult male 20+ | Adult female 20+ | Youth 16–24 | White teen-ager 16–19 | Black teen-ager 16–19 |
|---|---|---|---|---|---|---|
| 1967 | 3.8 | 2.3 | 4.2 | 8.7 | 11.0 | 26.5 |
| 1968 | 3.6 | 2.2 | 3.8 | 8.7 | 11.0 | 25.0 |
| 1969 | 3.5 | 2.1 | 3.7 | 8.4 | 10.7 | 24.0 |
| 1970 | 4.9 | 3.5 | 4.8 | 11.0 | 13.5 | 29.1 |
| 1971 | 5.9 | 4.4 | 5.7 | 12.7 | 15.1 | 31.7 |
| 1972 | 5.6 | 4.0 | 5.4 | 12.1 | 14.2 | 33.5 |
| 1973 | 4.9 | 3.2 | 4.8 | 10.5 | 12.6 | 30.2 |
| 1974 | 5.6 | 3.8 | 5.5 | 11.8 | 14.0 | 32.9 |
| 1975 | 8.5 | 6.7 | 8.0 | 16.1 | 17.9 | 36.9 |
| 1976 | 7.6 | 5.7 | 7.3 | 14.6 | 16.8 | 36.8 |

Source: Bureau of Labor Statistics.

\* First seven months.

Table 12
*Trends in Social Welfare Expenditures Under Public Programs, 1950–1975*

| Year and source of funding | Total social welfare (TSW) | TSW as % of total gov't. outlay | Per cent allocated to specific programs | | | | | | |
|---|---|---|---|---|---|---|---|---|---|
| | | | Social insurance | Public aid | Health & medical programs | Veterans programs | Education | Housing | Other |
| Total | | | | | | | | | |
| 1950 | $ 23,508,000. | 37.6 | 21.0 | 10.6 | 8.8 | 29.2 | 28.4 | .1 | 2.0 |
| 1960 | 52,293,000. | 38.0 | 36.9 | 7.8 | 8.5 | 10.5 | 33.7 | .3 | 2.2 |
| 1970 | 145,761,000. | 47.8 | 37.5 | 11.3 | 6.7 | 6.2 | 34.9 | .5 | 2.8 |
| 1975 (prelim.) | 286,547,000. | 58.4 | 43.1 | 14.1 | 5.8 | 5.8 | 27.4 | 1.0 | 2.7 |
| Federal | | | | | | | | | |
| 1950 | $ 10,541,000. | 26.2 | 20.0 | 10.5 | 5.7 | 60.6 | 1.5 | .1 | 1.7 |
| 1960 | 24,957,000. | 28.1 | 57.3 | 8.5 | 7.0 | 21.5 | 3.5 | .6 | 1.7 |
| 1970 | 77,334,000. | 40.1 | 58.5 | 12.5 | 6.2 | 11.6 | 7.6 | .8 | 2.9 |
| 1975 (prelim.) | 165,944,000. | 54.9 | 59.8 | 16.0 | 5.1 | 9.9 | 5.2 | 1.4 | 2.5 |
| State and Local | | | | | | | | | |
| 1950 | $ 12,967,000. | 60.1 | 21.9 | 10.7 | 11.3 | 3.7 | 50.3 | NA | 2.1 |
| 1960 | 27,337,000. | 58.3 | 18.3 | 7.3 | 10.0 | .4 | 61.3 | .1 | 2.6 |
| 1970 | 68,427,000. | 62.3 | 13.8 | 10.0 | 7.3 | .2 | 65.8 | .2 | 2.8 |
| 1975 (prelim.) | 120,604,000. | 64.3 | 20.1 | 11.5 | 6.8 | .1 | 57.8 | .5 | 3.1 |

Source: Adapted from *Statistical Abstracts*, 1976, Table 459.
Readers might be interested in several recent books dealing with related topics to those mentioned in this table.
Sheila B. Kamerman and Alfred J. Kahn have written a very useful overview of *Social Services in the United States: Policies and Programs* (1976). It emphasizes areas of child care, child abuse and neglect, children's institutions and alternatives, family planning, and community services to the aged.
Jerry L. Weaver's book, *National Health Policy and the Underserved: Ethnic Minorities, Women, and the Elderly* (1976) is most useful in understanding power struggles involved in providing and receiving social services.

Table 13

*Education: Highest Level of School Completed by Sex, Race, and Age, 1975*

| Race, sex, and age (two selected age groups) | Per cent of population completing | | | Median school years completed |
|---|---|---|---|---|
| | Elementary school (0–8 years) | High school (9–12 years) | College (1 to 4 or more years) | |
| All Races | 21.9 | 51.8 | 26.3 | 12.3 |
| Male | 22.4 | 46.8 | 30.8 | 12.4 |
| Female | 21.4 | 56.3 | 22.3 | 12.3 |
| age group | | | | |
| 25–29 years | 5.7 | 52.7 | 41.6 | 12.8 |
| 55 years and over | 40.2 | 43.2 | 16.6 | 10.6 |
| Negro, total | 35.1 | 49.4 | 15.4 | 10.9 |
| age group | | | | |
| 25–29 years | 7.5 | 64.9 | 27.7 | 12.5 |
| 55 years and over | 67.0 | 26.6 | 6.5 | 7.5 |

Source: *Statistical Abstracts*, 1976, Table 200.
See also the paper by Mary Ann Powell Howard and Richard J. Anderson on "Early identification of potential school dropouts: A literature review," which is a chapter of this book.

Table 14

*Crime and Crime Rates, by Type, 1960–1975*

| Year & number of offenses (in 1,000s) | Violent crimes | | | | | | Property crimes | | | |
|---|---|---|---|---|---|---|---|---|---|---|
| | Total | Total | Murder | Forcible rape | Robbery | Aggravated assault | Total | Burglary | Larceny & theft | Motor veh. theft |
| 1960 | 3,384 | 288 | 9.1 | 17.2 | 108 | 154 | 3,096 | 912 | 1,855 | 328 |
| 1965 | 4,739 | 387 | 10.0 | 23.4 | 139 | 215 | 4,352 | 1,283 | 2,573 | 497 |
| 1970 | 8,098 | 739 | 16.0 | 38.0 | 350 | 335 | 7,359 | 2,205 | 4,226 | 928 |
| 1975 | 11,257 | 1,026 | 20.5 | 56.1 | 465 | 485 | 10,230 | 3,252 | 5,978 | 1,001 |

Source: *Statistical Abstracts*, 1976, Table 252.
In a provocative book, *Crowding and Behavior* (New York: Viking Press, 1975), Jonathan L. Freedman explores the relationship between various types of crimes and the density of living areas. Many people believe, based on their own experiences as well as from animal studies, that increased densities lead to aggressive behavior. In one study of 117 large metropolitan areas in the United States, Freedman and his colleagues correlated degree of density with rates of crime and found a small but appreciable tendency for higher density to be associated with higher crime rates. But density is also associated with other possible causal factors, such as poverty, educational level, and ethnicity. So Freedman went a step further and discovered that when density was "controlled" statistically for its independent influence, "the level of density under which [people] live plays no role in the amount of crime they commit" (p. 57). He also distinguished between crimes against person (violent crimes in the table above) and against property. The assumption is that the higher the density, the more likely there are to be crimes against persons. But again his results are just the opposite. There may be many reasons why people commit crimes, but, according to Freedman, "there is no evidence that crowding is one of them" (p. 69).

Table 15

*Homicide and Suicide Rates, by Sex, Selected Countries, 1973 (crude rate per 100,000 population)*

| Country | Homicides | | Suicides | |
|---|---|---|---|---|
| | Males | Females | Males | Females |
| USA | 15.5 | 4.3 | 17.5 | 6.8 |
| Canada | 3.2 | 1.7 | 17.4 | 6.9 |
| France | 1.1 | 0.5 | 23.3 | 9.3 |
| Germany (Fed. Rep. of) | 1.5 | 0.9 | 26.3 | 14.1 |
| Israel | 0.6 | 0.6 | 8.4 | 6.5 |
| Japan | 1.6 | 1.0 | 19.4 | 14.2 |
| Poland | 1.4 | 0.6 | 20.3 | 4.1 |
| Puerto Rico | 25.3 | 4.1 | 17.0 | 3.7 |
| Sweden | 1.2 | 0.9 | 29.4 | 11.2 |
| Switzerland | 0.9 | 0.5 | 28.2 | 11.2 |
| United Kingdom (England & Wales) | 1.0 | 0.8 | 9.2 | 6.2 |

Source: *Statistical Abstracts,* 1976, Table 262. (Data taken from UN World Health Organization, *World Health Statistics,* Annual.)

Suicide, even though it appears to be an ultimate individual act, has been shown to be influenced by social forces since the classic studies by Emile Durkheim.* More recent work, such as by Andrew Henry and James Short (*Suicide and Homicide: Some Economic, Sociological, and Psychological Aspects of Aggression,* 1954) has demonstrated the interconnectedness of individual acts and the major dimensions of the social environment.

In response to these high levels of suicide, suicide prevention centers and crisis (telephone) centers have been established in the United States (see the work of Faberow, Shneidman, among others), but in Britain a different approach has been taken by means of Samaritan centers using the technique of befriending. (See, for example, R. Fox in Shneidman, ed., *Suicidology: Contemporary Developments* [1976].)

* *Suicide* (1897; rpt. 1951).

Table 16

*Suicide Mortality Rates (per 100,000 population), by Sex, Race, and Age Groups, 1974 (United States)*

| Age | Male | | Female | |
|---|---|---|---|---|
| | White | Negro and other | White | Negro and other |
| 5–14 yrs | 0.8 | 0.4 | 0.2 | 0.2 |
| 15–24 | 17.8 | 12.9 | 4.8 | 3.9 |
| 25–34 | 23.3 | 22.9 * | 8.7 | 6.3 * |
| 35–44 | 23.8 | 15.6 | 12.1 | 4.5 |
| 45–54 | 28.3 | 11.9 | 14.1 | 4.0 |
| 55–64 | 32.1 | 12.5 | 11.0 | 3.4 |
| 65 years and over | 38.9 | 15.3 | 7.7 | 2.3 |

Source: *Statistical Abstracts,* 1976, Table 263.

* For an analysis of this pattern, see R. H. Seiden. "Why are suicides of young blacks increasing?" *HSMHA Health Reports,* 87:1,3–8.

Table 17
*Top Ranked Cause of Death, By Age, Sex, and Race (1972)* \*

| Sex and race | Ages: 5–9 | 10–14 | 15–19 | 20–24 | 25–29 | 30–34 | 35–39 | 40–44 | 45–49 | 50–54 | 55–59 | 60–64 | 65–69 | 70–74 |
|---|---|---|---|---|---|---|---|---|---|---|---|---|---|---|
| White Male | MVA 128 | MVA 399 | MVA 815 | MVA 762 | MVA 526 | MVA 376 | AHD 851 | AHD 1861 | AHD 3539 | AHD 5874 | AHD 9331 | AHD 13759 | AHD 20100 | AHD 27684 |
| White Female | MVA 70 | MVA 157 | MVA 229 | MVA 170 | MVA 127 | MVA 119 | MNB 203 | AHD 355 | AHD 726 | AHD 1483 | AHD 2871 | AHD 5448 | AHD 10035 | AHD 17094 |
| Black Male | MVA 153 | MVA 306 | H 858 | H 1287 | H 1395 | AHD 1321 | AHD 1301 | AHD 2359 | AHD 3860 | AHD 6074 | AHD 7616 | AHD 11040 | AHD 17006 | AHD 19146 |
| Black Female | MVA 77 | MVA 92 | H 174 | H 256 | H 267 | AHD 301 | AHD 689 | AHD 1278 | AHD 2155 | AHD 3545 | AHD 6005 | AHD 9857 | AHD 13512 | AHD 15437 |

Source: Adapted from *Probability Tables of Deaths in the Next Ten Years from Specific Causes*, compiled by the Health Hazard Appraisal group by Harvey Geller, chief statistician for the U.S. Public Health Service Cancer Control Program, Methodist Hospital of Indiana, Indianapolis, Indiana, 1972.
\* The numbers in each cell represent the chance in 100,000 of the individual's dying from the stated cause. The symbols represent the following:
MVA = Motor Vehicle Accident
AHD = Arteriosclerotic Heart Disease
MNB = Malignant Neoplasms of the Breast
H  = Homicide

# Name Index

# Subject Index